Henry Abarbanel

English School and Family Reader, for the Use of Israelites

Containing Selections in Prose and Verse, Historical Accounts...

Henry Abarbanel

English School and Family Reader, for the Use of Israelites
Containing Selections in Prose and Verse, Historical Accounts...

ISBN/EAN: 9783337098742

Printed in Europe, USA, Canada, Australia, Japan

Cover: Foto ©Thomas Meinert / pixelio.de

More available books at **www.hansebooks.com**

ENGLISH
SCHOOL AND FAMILY
READER,

FOR THE USE OF ISRAELITES,

CONTAINING

SELECTIONS IN PROSE AND VERSE, HISTORICAL ACCOUNTS,
BIOGRAPHIES, NARRATIVES, NOTICES, AND
CHARACTERISTICS ON

JUDAISM,

PAST, PRESENT AND FUTURE.

BY H. ABARBANEL.

"If a regular gradation of sufferings exists, then Israel has reached the highest step;
if the duration of sorrows, and the patience with which they are endured, ennoble, then
the Jews may challenge the nobility of all countries ; if a literature is called rich, which
possesses but a few classical tragedies, what place then is due to a tragedy which lasts
fifteen centuries being composed and represented by the heroes themselves."—ZUNZ.—
Synagogal Poesy of the Middle Ages.

NEW YORK :
ROGERS & SHERWOOD,
21 & 23 BARCLAY STREET.
1883.

IN THREE PARTS.

PART I.

Narrative and Descriptive.

PART II.

Historical and Biographical.

PART III.

Scientific and Instructive.

PREFACE.

It has been my purpose in the preparation of this work to furnish the facilities necessary for the cultivation and improvement of Jewish youth, who, in the course of my experience, I have observed with regret lack much of that religious education which, at an early age, should be inculcated, in order to qualify him to become a useful member of the Jewish community in after life.

A nation unacquainted with her Past, has no mind for her Present, and no eye for her Future.

Mindful, then, that it is of the greatest importance for the Israelitish youth to know what happened to his ancestors, during the last 1800 years, and what they have accomplished in a spiritual direction, I have prepared the following pages for that purpose—a collection strictly graded from first to last, and commencing with lessons more simple than those at the close of the book.

As for the numberless Readers made use of in Public Schools, I have no desire to detract one iota either from their merits or their usefulness, but they are nevertheless unfitted for the instruction of Jewish youth, on account of the sectarianism which one meets with in almost all of them; and whilst other confessions are furnished in a manifold manner, the scanty supply in this branch of Hebrew Literature has left a vacancy for an English Reader adapted for Israelitish Schools and Families.

Is it likely that a Jewish child can reap any benefit from hearing the New Testament read almost every morning on entering the school-room? Will the Jewish mind improve while being trained to sing hymns in praise of a strange religion? Does it enhance Jewish learning by making use of Readers full of sectarianism? Or is it possible that the Jewish child should know anything of Judaism, when all the public schools, both high and low, fail to teach a single word of Hebrew, nor is there even a Professorship for Oriental Literature anywhere to be met with?

The Author therefore believes that he renders the Israelitish school some service, by submitting from the works and periodicals of Drs. Jost, Zunz, Graetz, Philippson, Geiger, Fraenkel, Sachs and others the most important and interesting parts suitable for schools, being so elaborated and arranged, that the teacher will be able, considering the beautiful literary character of the works they were selected from, to make the book at once the means of a pleasing and instructive study.

There is a variety of subjects and of styles adapted to the age and progress of the student: there is also a copiousness of information, and an anxiety on the part of the Author to inculcate sound morals and good manners: so as to aid in forming a literary taste for Hebrew lore, and to impress upon the student the usefulness of the Hebrew language, which has become of late almost indispensable.

The Reader now submitted to the public contains no sectarianism, and although intended for Hebrew institutions, it is nevertheless adapted for all classes and creeds, merely conveying to the reader some interesting and useful information in regard to Judaism, and will, no doubt, prove of great value to the Christian student in a religious, moral and historical point of view.

The principles of elocution I have omitted, inasmuch as every teacher is not willing to use them; besides, they are not a necessary part of a reading book, and, in case their use should appear indispensable, the want can easily be supplied by consulting any of the public school readers, which generally contain all the needful information.

In the preparation of the work the Author gratefully remembers the kindness shown to him by various gentlemen and teachers from whom he obtained permission to translate and copy some of their productions; and to the Jewish press, also, he is much indebted for the assistance he received in being allowed to chronicle a large amount of useful and valuable information.

Brief explanatory notices have been affixed to most of the selections, and the definitions of the most difficult words have been given. In fine, the Author persuades himself, as he has spared no pains to embody in his book every excellence of a good Reader according to the object in view, it will be acceptable to teachers and all others who take an interest in forwarding the sacred cause of education.

H. A.

CONTENTS.

PART I.

NARRATIVE AND DESCRIPTIVE,

from page 7 to 87.

*Those marked with asterisk were written or translated by the author, and many of the remaining pieces were so altered as to be adapted for the object in view.

PART II.

HISTORICAL AND BIOGRAPHICAL.

From page 88 to 286.

PART III.
SCIENTIFIC AND INSTRUCTIVE.
From page 286 to 432.

POETRY.
PART I.

CONTAINS ALSO A

BIBLICAL AND HISTORICAL MEMORIAL TABLE,

TOGETHER WITH A

CHRONOLOGY.

From the creation unto the present time.

————o————

INDEX TO AUTHORS.

PART FIRST.

——o——

NARRATIVE AND DESCRIPTIVE.

——o——

" 'Tis education forms the common mind;
Just as the twig is bent the tree's inclined."

QUINTILIAN.

THE VALUE OF BOOKS.

THERE are so many wise and good things written in books that every one should easily endeavor to cultivate a taste for reading. There are many thousands of books, and all that is written in them is either about the world which God has made, or about the thoughts and sayings of His creatures on whom He has bestowed the power to think and to speak.

Some books describe the earth itself, with its land and water; or the air and clouds; or the sun, the moon, and the stars, which shine so beautifully in the sky. Some tell us about the things that grow out of the ground—the many millions of plants, from little mosses and slender blades of grass, up to great trees and forests. Some also contain accounts of living things, such as worms, flies, fishes, birds and four-footed beasts; and some, which are the most numerous, are about men and their doings.

These books about men are the most important to us, for men are the most wonderful of God's creatures in this world, since they alone are able to know and to love Him, and to try of their own accord to do His will. Besides, we ourselves are human beings, and may learn from such books what we ought to think, and do, and try to be. Some of them describe what sort of people have lived in olden times, and in other countries. By reading these we know what is the difference between our own nation and the famous nations which lived and flourished in the early periods of the world's history. Such were the Egyptians, who built the Pyramids—the most stupendous buildings of stone ever constructed by men; and the Babylonians, who had a city of huge walls, built of bricks, and furnished with a hundred brazen gates.

They tell us also of the Jews, to whom the commands of God were given; of the Greeks, who knew best how to make fine statues and buildings, and to write books; of the old Romans, that wonderful people who lived in the ancient city of Rome, how skillful they were in war, and how they could govern the nations they subdued.

It is from books, also, that we may learn what kind of men lived in our own country before it was peopled with emigrants from Europe, or even with wild Indians whom they found here ; of the Aztecs, who lived in Mexico and Peru, and their curious customs and wonderful civilization ; and something also of the singular mounds in various parts of our country, built by a people the memory of whom has passed away.

We may also learn what kind of men lived in olden times in the northern parts of Europe and Asia, and how they passed to the south and west, overturning civilized nations in their course, and founding the present nations of Europe ; how some of these people came to live in England, and planted there a mighty kingdom lasting to our own time, and spreading its power and influence through every part of the world.

And we shall see, too, how religion has spread to nearly every part of the earth, to make the people wiser and more peaceful, and more noble in their minds. Besides learning all these things, we should try to learn from books what are the best and wisest thoughts, and the most beautiful words, and how men are able to lead right lives, and to do a great deal to make the world better. If we try to be better for all we read, as well as wiser, we shall find books a great help toward goodness as well as knowledge·

ADAPTED.

PYRAMID.—Plain triangles; their several points meeting in one.
THE BABYLONIANS—Inhabitants of Babylo- nia, a country in Western Asia, now a part of Asiatic Turkey. It was situated on the Eu- phrates River.

USE THE PEN.

USE the pen! there is magic in it,
  Never let it lag behind;
Write thy thought—the pen can win it
  From the chaos of the mind.
Many a gem is lost forever
  By the careless passer by,
But the gems of thought should never
  On the mental pathway lie.

Use the pen! reck not that others
  Take a higher flight than thine;
Many an ocean cave still smothers
  Pearls of price beneath the brine;
But the diver finds the treasure,
  And the gem to light is brought;
Thus thy mind's unbounded measure
  May give up some pearl of thought.

Use the pen! the day's departed
  When the sword alone held sway,
Wielded by the lion-hearted,
  Strong in battle, where are they?
All unknown the deeds of glory
  Done of old by mighty men,
Save the few who live in story,
  Chronicled by sage's pen.

Use the pen! but let it never
  Slander write with dead-black ink
Let it be thy best endeavor
  But to pen what good men think.
Thus thy words and thoughts securing
  Honest praise from wisdom's tongue,
May in time be as enduring
  As the strains which David sung.

ADAPTED.

CHAOS—Confusion.
BRINE - Water impregnated with salt—the sea.
SAGE--Wise, grave, prudent.

WISDOM.

Surely there is a vein for the silver, and a place for gold *where* they fine it. Iron is taken out of the earth, and brass is molten *out* of the stone. He setteth an end to darkness, and searcheth out all perfection; the stones of darkness and the shadow of death. The *flood* breaketh out from the inhabitant; *even the waters* forgotten of the foot; they are dried up, they are gone away from men. As for the earth, out of it cometh bread: and under it is turned up as it were fire. The stones of it are the place of sapphires; and it hath dust of gold. There is a path which no fowl knoweth, and which the vulture's eye hath not seen. The lion's whelps have not trodden it, nor the fierce lion passed by it. He putteth forth his hand upon the rock, he overturneth the mountains by the roots. He cutteth our rivers among the rocks; and his eye seeth every precious thing. He bindeth the floods from overflowing; and the thing that is hid bringeth he forth to light. But where shall wisdom be found, and where is the place of understanding? Man knoweth not the price thereof; neither is it found in the land of the living. The depth saith: It is not in me; and the sea saith: It is not with me. It cannot be gotten for gold, neither shall silver be weighed for the price thereof. It cannot be valued with the gold of Ophir, with the precious onyx, or the sapphire. The gold and the crystal cannot equal it; and the exchange of it shall not be for jewels of fine gold. No mention shall be made of coral or of pearls; for the price of Wisdom is above rubies. The topaz of Ethiopia shall not equal it, neither shall it be valued with pure gold. Whence, then, cometh Wisdom, and where is the place of understanding? Seeing it is hid from the eyes of all living, and kept close from the fowls of the air. Destruction and Death say: We have heard the fame thereof with our ears. God understandeth the way thereof, and he knoweth the place thereof. For He looketh to the ends of the earth, and seeth under the whole heaven. To make the weight for the winds, and He weigheth the waters by measure. When He made a decree for the rain, and a way for the lightning of the thunder. Then did He see it, and declare it. He prepared it, yea, and searched it out, and unto man He said: Behold the fear of the Lord, that is Wisdom; and to depart from evil, that is understanding.—Job xxviii.

Onyx—Is a half-clear gem, of which there are several species.
Sapphire—A precious stone of a blue color.

Ruby—A precious stone, of a red color, next in hardness to the diamond.
Topaz—A yellow gem.

ONE BY ONE.

One by one the sands are flowing—
One by one the moments fall;
Some are coming, some are going;
Do not strive to catch them all.

One by one thy duties wait thee;
Let thy whole strength go to each;
Let no future dreams elate thee:
Learn thou first what these can teach.

One by one (bright gifts from heaven)
Joys are sent thee here below;
Take them readily when given—
Ready, too, to let them go.

One by one thy griefs shall meet thee;
Do not fear an arm'd band;
One will fade as others greet thee—
Shadows passing through the land.

Do not look at life's long sorrow—
See how small each moment's pain;

God will help thee for to-morrow,
Every day begin again.

Every hour that fleets so slowly,
Has its task to do or bear;
Luminous the crown and holy
If thou set each gem with care.

Hours are golden links—God's token—
Reaching heaven; but, one by one.
Take them lest the chain be broken
Ere thy pilgrimage be done.

MISS PROCTOR.

LUMINOUS—Shining.

| PILGRIMAGE—A long journey.

THE BIBLE.

A BOOK which has been handed down to us from ancient times, hallowed by the veneration of ages, as the repository of God's revelation; a book which contains the truths most interesting to man, which lays down the code of his duties, and rules for his conduct through life; which defines those principles on which human happiness depends, and without which civil society would be impossible; such a book must necessarily form, at all times, a subject of anxious study and earnest investigation.

That book is the Bible; and it is not surprising that, in a long course of centuries, it has given rise to thousands of commentaries and disquisitions, and that the human mind should still continue to exercise its ingenuity in attempts to ascertain the meaning and intention of every part of its contents. We, to whom the Bible was addressed and intrusted, and who have had to adapt our life to its prescriptions, have naturally, more than any other people, applied ourselves to study, understand and elucidate the sacred volume. For its language was our own language, its history was bound up with our history, its spirit and life with our national spirit and life.

From the time when Moses enjoined on every Israelite the duty of making himself conversant with the law, and of teaching it to his children (Deut. xi: 7, vi. 19), and commanded that even every king should make for himself a copy of it, and should constantly consult it (xvii: 18), down to the later epochs of our national history, when thousands of scholars were flocking to the academies in spite of the prohibitions and obstacles set up by the Romans, its study has always been considered and accepted by the Israelite as a duty. After the dispersion, the Jew attached himself more passionately than ever to this sacred Book; it became his only solace amid adversities and persecutions, and his rallying•point amid the dissolving influences by which he was surrounded; and when, in the middle ages, the darkness of ignorance covered Europe, the Book was the bright star which enlightened its mental faculties.

These circumstances, aided by uninterrupted traditional information, which may be traced back to the earliest times, led to Israel's possession of the most intimate knowledge of the Bible that can possibly exist among ordinary men. Where interpretation was needed, that interpretation was settled by authority, learning and argument usually combined; and, consequently, to the enlightened Jews, few difficulties occur in the proper understanding of both the letter and spirit of the sacred Book

Thus it happens that the Jewish mind and conscience are entirely satisfied with the Bible, and that all attempts that have been made for ages to detach us from it have proved unavailing. When professors of other creeds—having but a superficial acquaintance with the language of the Bible and its idiom, and without the advantage of the traditional lore and the local and historical knowledge accumulated by our forefathers—when such men, who read the Bible through the medium of their preconceived notions, and whose only interest in it is dictated by the necessity of finding therein some pegs on which to hang new-fangled doctrines, foreign and abhorrent to it—when such men gravely tell us that we do not understand our Bible, and they alone have the key to its true meaning, they succeed only in raising a smile of pity on our lips. When, in times gone by, men of the same class sought to enforce their propositions with the sword, the fagot and the rack, our forefathers wavered not, but they readily laid down their lives and all that was dearest to them, rather than yield up their faith in the One God, and in their Bible.

L. J. A.

COMMENTARY—To write notes or remarks upon.
DISQUISITIONS—Examinations, inquiry.
ELUCIDATE—To explain.
LORE—Lesson, instruction, doctrine.
To ENJOIN—To order.

INTERPRETATION—Explaining.
SUPERFICIAL—Slight knowledge.
PRECONCEIVED—To be of opinion beforehand.
NEW-FANGLED—A foolish form of novelty.
RACK—An engine of torture.

BE FIRM.

Be Firm! whatever tempts thy soul
To loiter ere it reach its goal,
Whatever siren voice would draw
Thy heart from duty and its law;
Oh, that distrust! go bravely on,
And till the victor crown be won,
Be Firm!

Firm when thy conscience is assailed,
Firm when the star of hope is veiled,
Firm in defying wrong and sin,
Firm in life's conflict, toil and din,
Firm in the path by martyrs trod—
And, oh, in love to man and God
Be Firm!

ADAPTED.

SIREN—Bewitching, enticing.

MARTYR—One who by his death bears witness to the truth.

DEVOTION IN PRAYER.

A PIOUS man was engaged in prayer whilst traveling on the high-road One of the nobles of the land, who knew him, was passing by and saluted him, but the pious man did not mind the salutation and continued his prayer. The nobleman became vexed, and with a great effort he waited till the man had finished his prayers; where-upon he, in an excited manner, said to him: "Thou art a stupid fellow, for thou hast sinned against thine own law, which commands man to take care of his life. But thou hast just risked thy life unnecessarily Why did you not respond to my salutation? If I had split your head open with my sword, who could have called me to account?"

"Sir! I pray, suppress your wrath; I hope to quiet you, if you will allow me only a few words in reply. Think, for instance, that while you were standing in conversation with your king, a friend in passing by saluted you. Should you like to be interrupted in your conversation with the king in order to answer that salutation?"

"Woe unto me if I were to do so."

"Now, I pray, dear sir! consider only the respect you thus pay to man! a mortal man, who is here to-day and to-morrow in the grave; whilst myself, who stood facing the King of kings, the immortal King, what should I have done?"

The nobleman assuaged his wrath, and the pious man continued his journey in peace.

TALMUD (see Part Third of the Reader.)

To ASSUAGE—To pacify.

ON PRAYER.

PRAYER is the soaring of the soul toward God, an appeal to His mercy, in homage to his greatness; how seriously it behooves us to perform this duty in a proper manner! In this life, while man is assailed by so much suffering, so many anxieties, and endures so much misery and sorrow, whence can he seek aid and consolation? Can his fellow-man, his companion in weakness and impotence, be his comforter? As a child in his grief appeals instinctively to his parents, so man in his distress appeals to his heavenly Father, who alone can aid him. Anxieties and misery attack us in vain, when we resist them by seeking consolation from Him who knows our sorrow. "Toward the mountains I raise my eyes," says the Psalmist; "thence will come my aid."

What cannot fervent prayer obtain? When the sentence of con-demnation is borne to the heavenly tribunal, let us pray, and God may revoke it. Moses, prostrate at the summit of Sinai, stayed by prayer the arm of the Eternal already raised to exterminate guilty, idolatrous Israel! We will not fear, then, loaded though we be with sin, we will not fear to offer our repentance to the Lord; we

ROR THE USE OF ISRAELITES.

ll pray for ourselves and others, and hope, though we fear; for a
day or a night not begun or ended with prayer might be a fatal one
to us or to one dear to us—the last day or the last night. Prayer
would indeed be imperfect, did it lead us toward God only when
in trouble or in fear, or had it no other motive than that our wants
should be supplied. Besides supplication, is it not just and proper
that we should offer our thanks and gratitude to our merciful Father
for the daily blessings He bestows and the miracles He renews for
our preservation, our sustenance and our existence?

But prayer does more than this. When the mind is imbued with
the idea of God, we contemplate His greatness and wonders, and
then a sentiment is awakened within us of veneration and delight
at His glory, His omnipotence, His wondrous works; this divine
joy, this soaring of the soul, find vent in words of blessing and
praise, as expressed in the divine harmony of the Psalms: "How
wondrous are Thy works, O Lord! How profound are Thy
thoughts!"

But how should we pray?

To move the lips mechanically, without feeling prayer in the
heart, is an offence to God. To pray mentally without a devout
attitude, is to fail in respect toward the Great Being with whom
we desire to hold communion.

Above all, we should take heed lest prayer become an act of
routine, a duty fulfilled hastily, amid noise, irreverence, and disturb-
ance; we should attune our hearts to devotion; retire to some
silent spot, assume an humble, a contemplative posture, and resign
our souls to God; then only can we hope to be in communion with
Him.

But to present ourselves humbly before God is not all; we must
bring faith—faith that gives life to prayer and warms the heart;
and, above all, prayer must proceed from purity of intention, the
desire to do that which is pleasing in the sight of God, and also
from filial submission to His will.

Oh! that our minds could be fully impressed with the glory of
God, or that we could duly reflect on His holiness! Faith teaches
us that our God, of whose majesty even Moses could not bear the
glorious presence, is near us when we pray. He sees and hears us;
He knows every thought of the soul, every secret of the heart. Yes,
He, the holy God, is near; and should we, who bow with respect
and humility before a mortal somewhat above us in rank and power,
not watch over our words and deeds in the presence of the King of
kings, before whom terrestrial monarchs are as a grain of dust?
How dare we, in His presence, give ourselves up to levity of any
kind? Let us, then, strictly observe the duty of prayer, for it is
the life of the soul; early in the morning let us appear before the
Lord, offer Him the first fruits of the day; the purity of our actions

may depend on the fidelity with which we fulfill this first duty.
But, before praying, let us examine ourselves, remember what we
are, and reflect on the nature of God before whom we appear; then
will our hearts be filled with sentiments of humility, respect and
devotion, and thus we shall become worthy of addressing the
Creator of the Universe. A day should not pass without returning
thanks for the favors God has granted; before retiring to rest we
should recall to mind every event of the day, and repent of any unworthy act we may have committed; and thus reconciled to God,
we may be able to invoke His protection, for ourselves and others,
from the dangers of the night. Not alone during the stated times
of prayer, but in every circumstance of life—in joy as in sorrow—
should we have God in our hearts and in our thoughts.

Yes, Lord! it is to Thee I turn to pour out my grief and
anguish; it is to Thee I render homage for the happy days it pleases
Thee to bestow. If affliction assail me, oh! teach me to bear it
according to Thy will; if joy be my portion, I will say, it is God
who giveth it.   HESTER ROTHSCHILD.

HESTER ROTHSCHILD—A lady of the Hebrew persuasion residing in England, of great
literary attainments, and authoress of several works on religious and instructive topics.

To SOAR—To mount intellectually.   IMPOTENCE—Want of power.
To IMBUE—To pour into the mind.   ROUTINE—Regular habit.
TERRESTRIAL—Earthly.

HE OF PRAYER.

HIDDEN in the ancient Talmud,
Slumbereth this legend old,
By the stately Jewish Rabbis
To the listening people told:
Jacob's ladder still is standing,
And the angels o'er it go,
Up and down from earth to heaven,
Ever passing to and fro;
Messengers from great Jehovah,
Bringing mortals, good or ill,
Just as we from laws unchanging,
Good or evil shall distill.
He of Death, with brow majestic,
Cometh wreathed with asphodel;
He of Life, with smile seraphic,
Softly saying, "All is well."
He of Pain, with purple pinions,
He of Joy, all shining bright;
He of Hope, with wings cerulean;
He of innocence, all white.
And the rustling of their pinions,
With the falling of their feet,
Turneth into notes of music,
Grand and solemn, soft and sweet.

One—and only one—stands ever
On the ladder's topmost round.
Just outside the gate celestial,
List'ning as to catch some sound;
But it is not angel music
Unto which he bends his ear.
'Tis the passing prayer of mortals
That he patient waits to hear.
By him messengers are flitting,
But He ever standeth there,
For He is the Great Sandalphon
Who is gathering every prayer.
In his hands they turn to garlands,
From whose flowers a fragrance floats
Through the open gates celestial,
Mingled with the angels' notes.
For outside the golden portal
Of that city of the skies
All the earthly dross and passion
Of the prayer of mortal dies.
'Tis the heavenly essence only
That can find an entrance there,
Turned into the scent of flowers
By Sandalphon—Him of Prayer.
                                   J. T.

ASPHODEL.—Day lily.   SERAPHIC - Angelic.
CERULEAN—Blue, sky-colored.   CELESTIAL.—Heavenly.

THE MYSTERIES OF PROVIDENCE.

THE appointed path is often a dark path, and the way in which the Lord leads us enshrouded in shade and mystery.   What then? We are to march boldly on in the course of duty, and trust the Lord to care for consequences, and bring all things right at last.   And we are under no obligation to understand the drift and bearing of things that surround us.   It is enough to know that all things are working together for our good.   Even Abraham "went out, not knowing whither he went," yet guided by the counsel of his God. We cannot tell why our present lot is so portioned out to us, nor what God means by all the providences which He appoints.   It belongs not to us to know the hidden purpose of Him who made us. Will you ask the soldier, thrown into the heat of battle, to explain the plan of the general?   How could he?   If he has done his duty —if he has thrown himself into the struggle—he has only seen the disorder of the charge, the flashing of the arms, the cloud of smoke and dust, he has only heard human cries, mixed with the deafening sound of artillery.   To him all was disorder and chaos; but upon the neighboring heights one eye followed the combat; one hand directed the least movement of the troops.   So there is a battle which is pursued through the ages.   It is that of truth, of love and justice, against error, egotism, and inquity.   It belongs not to obscure soldiers, thrown into the fight, to direct the contest; it ought to suffice us that God conducts it; it is for us to remain at the post He assigns to us, and to struggle there firmly, "even unto the end."

And when we look back from the very heights of triumph—to which we now turn our eyes with longing and with hope -- when we trace the well-remembered path along which God hath led our feet from warfare to victory, and from weariness to rest, all will be plain, and clear, and blessed, in the presence of Him who has said: "What I do thou knowest not now, but thou shalt know hereafter."

H. O.

EGOTISM—Too frequent mention of a man's self.

TRUTH.

TRUTH is the basis of all practical goodness; without it all virtues are mere representations wanting reality; and having no foundation they quickly prove their evanescent nature, and disappear as "the morning dew."

Whatever brilliant abilities we may possess, if the dark spot of falsehood exists in our hearts it defaces their splendor and destroys their efficacy.   If truth be not our guiding spirit we shall stumble upon the dark mountains, the clouds of error will surround us, and we shall wander in a labyrinth, the intricacy of which will increase as we proceed in it.   No art can unravel the web that

falsehood weaves, which is more tangled than the knot of the
Phrygian king.

Falsehood is ever fearful, and shrinks beneath the steadfast,
piercing eye of truth. It is ever restless in racking the invention,
to form some fresh subterfuge to escape detection. Its atmosphere
is darkness and misery; it lures but to destroy, and leads its followers into the depths of misery.

Truth is the spirit of light and beauty, and seeks no disguise; its
noble features are always unveiled and shed a radiance upon every
object within their influence. It is robed in spotless white, and,
conscious of its purity, is fearless and undaunted; it never fails its
votaries, and conducts them through evil report and good report,
without spot or blemish; it breathes of heaven and happiness, and
is ever in harmony with the Great First Cause.

The consciousness of truth nerves the timid and imparts dignity
and firmness to their actions. It is an internal principle of honor
which renders the possessor superior to fear; it is always consistent
with itself, and needs no ally. Its influence will remain when the
lustre of all that once sparkled and dazzled has passed away.

II. O.

EVANESCENT—Vanishing.
LABYRINTH—A place formed with inextric-
able windings.
PHRYGIA—In Asia Minor.
SUBTERFUGE—An evasion, a trick.

VOTARY—One devoted to any particular person or cause.
UNDAUNTED—Bold.
GORDIAN KNOT—An intricate knot made by
the Phrygian king

THE TRUTH SEEKER.

GOES searching for the light of truth,
To light his way, adorn his youth,
Till sparkling truths his mind unfold,
With pearls of beauty, gems of gold.

The light of truth then makes him shine
In robes of splendor, most divine;
It opes a fount of life within,
And frees the mind from erring sin.

It lifts the soul in waves of light,
To learn the truth in shades of night;
It purifies the stream of life
Of all the hells of hate and strife.

From every source of life below
It seeks the truth of God to know,
And opens wide the way of life,
To quiet realms above the strife.

Of errors dark and dismal hells,
Where vice and sorrow ever dwells,

It constitutes within the man
A saving grace, a godly plan.

That only truth can make us free,
And lift above all misery;
That God in man must be enshrined,
A *power* of the human mind—

Of light and life, and joy and peace.
That constant seeking must increase,
To founts of truth that ever glow,
A saving grace from earthly woe.

The more you use them on your way,
The brighter shines your living day;
Truth is the coin of every clime,
The golden gem for all of time;
It passes current everywhere,
The richest boon that we can heir.

ADAPTED.

THE MORAL DIGNITY OF LABOR.

One of the highest distinctions which God has conferred upon man is that love of labor with which He has bound him to the world. The more industrious man shows himself, the more happily he enjoys the fruits of his exertions. The less, however, man seeks to work for his own maintenance, the more he lowers within him that mighty spirit of *self-dependence* which is the prime mover of so many noble actions in life. There is a great recreative power in labor, and although it often makes our body tired and our spirit weary and faint, still, after hours of rest, it inspires us with new love for the work we have to perform. We fully believe, therefore, that labor is one of the greatest *civilizers* of the world; and that the more active and industrious a nation is, the happier and more contented it is. On the other hand, however, it must be admitted, that the more indolent and idle people are, the more corrupt become their tastes, the coarser their manners, and the harder their feelings.

There is a moral dignity in labor which raises and elevates every human being. But as our Scripture dwells so often with great emphasis upon the importance of labor, let us, in this instance, speak on the moral dignity of labor.

Nearly all the ancient people of the world hated and despised labor, when it was not of a political or spiritual kind. From Greece down to Egypt, physical labor was laid upon the shoulders of a working class, who were exposed to the utmost contempt, and subjected to the most brutal treatment at the hands of those who were their masters and rulers. Even the great philosophers amongst the Greeks and Romans, from Plato and Aristotle to Seneca and Cicero, could not raise themselves above such degrading views. When we therefore read to-day that our brethren in Egypt did not hearken unto Moses for anguish of spirit and *hard labor*, we can really feel with them, and understand their wretched condition. Man likes to work ; but if no redeeming points result from his work, if not the slightest appreciation is shown to him by those for whom he toils, his labor is that of the animals of the field which work by dint of bridle and command. We are, for this reason, not astonished that our forefathers could not listen to Moses, for their mental strength was entirely exhausted by the physical burdens which were laid upon them. In opposition to these degrading notions of the ancients, who looked at labor as an occupation fit merely for slaves, the Jewish religion raised labor for the first time to a moral height, saying: "Six days shalt thou labor and do all thy work. But the seventh is the Sabbath in honor of the Lord thy God. On it thou shalt not do any work ; neither thou, nor thy son, nor thy daughter, nor thy man-servant, nor thy maid-servant, nor thy cattle, nor the stranger that is within thy gates."

PART I.—2

In order to guard man from being entirely absorbed by labor, the Sabbath was appointed a moral and religious institution, whose purpose it is to strengthen the physical life of man, to raise him above the more materialistic aims, and to fill his soul with thoughts and ideas that reach beyond this earthly realm. If, therefore, labor in its ultimate purpose has such a spiritual tendency in elevating and refining the soul of man, it is greatly to be wished that we give our Sabbath day a more sanctified expression and a more dignified celebration. " Labor, without the rest on Sabbath day, demoralizes man, fosters the love of self, places us on a level with irrational creation, and gives the soul a mere menial position in the great household of God." But there is still another point in labor which demands our attention for a few minutes. If we do not mistake, labor is nothing else than a social contract between man and man, by which the one desires that a certain duty, task, or obligation shall be performed by the other. Now, as a compensation for these duties to be performed, society has adopted to give us an *equivalent*—MONEY. And still society is wrong, if it merely measures the value of labor—as is too often done in mercantile countries—from a monetary point of view.

By doing so, it reduces labor to a dry mechanism, and deprives it of its high, moral character. There are various kinds of labor which you never can pay with money— say, even with heaps of money. Let us take, for instance, the profession of a physician. There is not a vocation in life which more deserves the esteem and good-will of society than that pursued by the class of men we call physicians. They are, in the true and real meaning of the word, the most faithful servants of humanity. They heal the sick ; they comfort the suffering ; they often clothe the naked ; and, by the help of God and their own skill, they not only drag many invalids from the gates of death, but also bring strength and hope into those dark and dreary rooms, where anxiety and fear held watch over the life of a beloved person. And do you think that you can adequately remunerate by money the labors of a physician, who is at your disposal day and night? We do not think so. A physician is more often recompensed by that moral dignity, or fervent love, which he finds in his ennobling occupation. Another instance : Society is not always just and noble in its treatment of that class of fellow-laborers whom we call teachers and governesses. Neither teachers nor governesses are compensated for the work in which they are engaged by the amount of payment they receive or by the position they occupy in society. They preside over the intellectual and moral training of youthful minds, and such presidency should be honored with marks of approbation. Many young men are indebted to their teachers for the manly and healthy tone of their souls ; and many women owe their gentle sentiments and refined feelings chiefly to governesses. And in what way are these real benefactors of society treated? They get a small, scanty salary ; and, although their minds and feelings are highly cultured, and their intellect is expanded, still, in the social scale of estimation, they have to give way to the aristocracy of birth, to the aristocracy of wealth, and to the spurious aristocracy of success ful adventurers. What would become of the moral and intellectual state of society if teachers and instructors acted in accordance with the small degree of appreciation with which their services are acknowledged ? I am sure the world would soon become a wilderness, and the human mind an unweeded garden, producing distasteful fruits. But, Heaven be praised ! the true leader of education is actuated in the performance of his duties by a higher motive than that of money. The moral dignity of labor leads him on in spite of many drawbacks ; and, although his merits are ignored, and his labor slighted, still, to speak with Lord Brougham, "If he rests from his work, he bequeaths his memory to the generation whom his teachings have blessed, and sleeps under the humble but not inglorious epitaph, commemorating *one in whom mankind lost a friend*, and no man got rid of an enemy."

If we look into our Bible we find that "labor" is greatly appreciated throughout the whole book. Abraham, Isaac and Jacob were watchful shepherds ; Moses received his divine message when feeding the flock ; David exchanged the shepherd's staff for the royal sceptre, and King Saul and the Prophet Elisha were taken from the plow to enter upon higher spheres of activity. Physical labor was so highly valued amongst our brethren that, at the time when Nebuchadnezzar conquered Jerusalem he took a thousand Jewish smiths and blacksmiths with him from Palestine to Babylon. After they returned from Babylon it was the custom in Israel that every learned man combined with his learned pursuit a trade or handicraft. Thus we are told that the great Hillel was a woodcutter ; Rabbi Joshua, a pinmaker ; Rabbi Nehemia Hakador, a potter ; Rabbi Judah, a tailor ; Rabbi Joshua Hasandler, a shoemaker ; and Rabbi Judah Hanechtan, a baker. In Jerusalem there were at one time so many coppersmiths that they had their own synagogue.

In fine, we recommend the moral dignity of labor most warmly and emphatically to all classes, but especially to our poor people. If anything can release them from their wretched position, it is the zeal and perseverance with which they should devote themselves to labor, for it is one of the highest sentiments of honor to know that we ourselves are the procurers of our own support and maintenance.

Let then each and every one of us remain steady and faithful to the occupation of his choice, and I am sure that the love of labor must ultimately redeem us from the heavy pressure of tiresome hours ; it must protect us from want and indigence, and make us

contented with ourselves, contented with the world, and thankful
towards God. H. BAAR.

REV. DR. H. BAAR—Superintendent of the New York Hebrew Orphan Asylum, formerly
minister of the Seel St. Congregation, Liverpool, England, and noted for his great pedagogical
knowledge.

MATERIALITY—Material existence not spirit-
uality.
ARISTOCRACY—Which places the supreme
power in the nobles.

SAVANT—A man of learning.
EPITAPH—An inscription of a tombstone.
SPHERE—Compass of action.

THE BEACON.

When sailing on a stormy sea,
Encompassed by the night,
How anxiously the sailors watch
For but one gleam of light.

And when upon the distant shore
They see the beacons flame,
Oh! then a hundred voices rise
In grateful, glad acclaim.

What though the storm-winds fiercely
blow,
And lowery is the sky;
What though the waves in fury dash
O'er reefs and breakers nigh?

That beacon light will lead them safe
The stormy waters o'er,
Like some bright messenger of God,
To friends and native shore.

Thus burns within the human heart,
A glorious beacon light,

Which doth the sea of life illume
In tempest, gloom and night.

When compassed by the waves of sin,
The shoals and reefs of shame,
Oh! then that beacon is, in truth,
A spark of heavenly flame.

What though temptation's power is great,
And gilded vice is strong,
What though around the storm-tossed
bark
Is heard the siren's song?

That guiding star will lead man on
In triumph to that shore,
Where sin and pain can never come,
And joy reigns evermore.

Oh! wouldst thou see the beacon light,
Whose rays will never wane,
Then ever keep within thy heart
A conscience free from stain.

MAX MEYERHARDT.

MAX MEYERHARDT—An eminent lawyer residing at Rome, Ga., possessing great literary
attainments, and a constant contributor to the Jewish press.
SIREN—A goddess who enticed men by singing; bewitching, fascinating.

RICHES AND WISDOM.

RICHES and ease, it is perfectly clear, are not necessary for man's
highest culture, else the world would not have been so largely indebted to those who have sprung from the humble ranks.

Indeed, so far from poverty being a misfortune, it may, by vigorous self-help, be converted even into a blessing, rousing a man to
that struggle with the world through which, though some purchase
ease by degradation, the right-minded and true-hearted will find
strength, confidence, and triumph.

The knowledge and experience which produce wisdom can only
become a man's individual possession and property by his own
action; and it is as futile to expect these without laborious, pains-
taking effort as it is to hope to gather a harvest where the seed has
not been sown.

It is said of a Bishop, who possessed great power, that he was asked by his stupid and idle brother to make a great man of him. "Brother," replied the Bishop, "if your plow is broken, I'll pay for the mending of it; or, if your ox should die, I'll buy you another; but I cannot make a great man of you—a plowman I found you, and, I fear, a plowman I must leave you."

But the same characteristic feature of energetic industry happily has its counterpart among the other ranks of the community. The middle and well-to-do classes are constantly throwing out vigorous offshoots in all directions—in Science, Commerce, and Art—thus adding effectively to the working power of the country. Indeed, the empire of England and India was won and held chiefly by men of the middle classes, men, for the most part, bred in factories, and trained to habits of practical business. It is the diligent hand and head that acquires self-culture, wisdom, and riches.

Even when men are born to wealth and high social position, any solid reputation which they may achieve is only attained by energetic application; for, though an inheritance of acres may be bequeathed, an inheritance of knowledge cannot.

The wealthy man may pay others for doing his work for him, but it is impossible to get his thinking done for him by another, or to purchase any kind of self-culture. Fortune has often been blamed for its blindness, but fortune is not so blind as men are. Fortune is usually on the side of the industrious, as the wind and waves are on the side of the best navigators.

The difference between riches and wisdom is the close observation of little things, which is the secret of success in business, in art, in science, and in every pursuit in life. The difference between men consists, in a great measure, in the intelligence of these observations. Solomon said: "The wise man's eyes are in his head, but the fool walketh in darkness; the non-observant man goes through the forest, and sees no firewood."

ADAPTED.

CHARACTERISTIC – Pointing out the true character.

COUNTERPART—The corresponding part.
SELF-CULTURE—The art of self-improvement.

WORK.

THERE are times when a heaviness comes over the heart, and we feel as if there was no hope. Who has not felt it? For this there is no cure but work. Plunge into it, put all your energies into motion, rouse up the inner man, act, and this heaviness shall disappear as the mist before the morning sun.

There arise doubts in the human mind which sink us into lethargy, wrap us in gloom, and make us think that it were bootless to attempt anything. Who has not experienced them? Work! That is the cure. Task your intellect; stir up your feelings, rouse the soul, do, and these doubts, hanging like a heavy cloud upon the mountain, will scatter and disappear, and leave you in sunshine and open day.

There comes suspicion to the best of men, and fears about the holiest efforts, and we stand like one chained. Who has not felt this? Work! Therein is freedom. By night, by day, in season and out of season, work, and liberty will be yours. Put in requisition mind and body, war with inertness, snap the chain-link of selfishness, stand up as a defender of the right, be yourself, and this suspicion and these fears will be lulled ; and, like the ocean storm, you will be purified by the contest, and able to bear and breast any burden of human ill.

Gladden life with its sunniest features, and gloss it over with its richest hues, and it becomes a poor and painted thing, if there be in it no toil, no hearty, hard work. The laborer sighs for repose. Where is it? What is it? Friend, whoever thou art, know it is to be found alone in work. No good, no greatness, no progress is gained without this. Work, then, and faint not; for therein is the well-spring of human hope and human happiness.

CASSIUS M. CLAY.

CASSIUS M. CLAY—An eminent American statesman and orator, born in the County of Hanover, Virginia, April 12, 1777, and died June 20, 1852. He was a lawyer, and in 1806 chosen to the Senate of the United States, and afterward became Secretary of State under the Presidency of John Quincy Adams.

LETHARGY—A morbid drowsiness.	INERTNESS—The state or quality of being
BOOTLESS—Useless.	inert—dull.

HELP THY BROTHER.

If thou canst speak one little word
  To cheer thy brother on his way,
Then fearless let thy voice be heard,
  Perchance 'twill change his night to
    day.

If thou canst cast one ray of hope,
  To him, when sinking in despair,
Perchance 'twill prove a saving rope,
  Fail not to do thy duty there.

If thou canst do a kindly deed,
  Fail not to act the helper's part,
No matter what thy brother's creed,
  He'll feel thy kindness in his heart.

If thou canst lift a fallen one,
  Who journeys on in paths of sin,
Be sure in this thy duty's done,
  Though thou no earthly crown may
    win.   ADAPTED.

EFFECTS OF OUR DEEDS.

THE common and popular notion is that death is the end of man, as far as this world is concerned; that the grave which covers his form covers and keeps within its chambers all his influence; and that the instant he has ceased to breathe, that instant the man has ceased to act.

It is not so; it is a popular mistake. We die, but leave an influence behind us that survives ; the echoes of our words are still repeated and reflected along the ages.

A man has two immortalities: one he leaves behind him, and it walks the earth, and still represents him; another he carries with him to that lofty sphere, the presence and glory of God. "Every man is a missionary, now and forever, for good or evil, whether he intends it or not. He may be a blot, radiating his dark influence outward to the very circumference of society; or he may be a blessing, spreading benedictions over the length and breadth of the world; but a *blank* he cannot be. The seed sown in life springs up in harvests of blessings, or harvests of sorrow." ADAPTED.

IMMORTALITY - Exempt from death.   BENEDICTION—Blessing
MISSIONARY - One sent to propagate religion.

SAVING FOR OLD AGE.

No one denies that it is wise to make a provision for old age; but we are not at all agreed as to the *kind* of provision it is best to lay up. Certainly, we *shall* want money; for a destitute old man is, indeed, a pitiful sight. Therefore, *save money* by all means. But an old man needs just that particular kind of *strength* which young men are most apt to waste. Many a foolish young man will throw away, on a holiday, a certain amount of nervous energy, which he will never feel the want of till he is seventy; and *then* how much he will need it! It is curious, but true, that a bottle of champagne at twenty may intensify the rheumatism of three-score. It is a fact that, overtasking the eyes at fourteen, may necessitate the aid of spectacles at forty, instead of eighty.

We advise our young readers to be *saving of health* for their old age; for the maxim holds good with regard to health as to money, "Waste not, want not." It is the greatest mistake to suppose that any violation of the laws of health can escape its penalty. Nature forgives no sin, no error. She lets off the offender for fifty years sometimes, but she catches him at last, and inflicts the punishment just *when, where*, and *how* he feels it most. Save up for old age, but save knowledge; save the recollection of good deeds and innocent pleasure; save pure thoughts; save friends; save rich stores of that kind of wealth which time cannot diminish, nor death take away. ADAPTED.

CHAMPAGNE—A kind of wine.   INTENSIFY —To render more intense.

A PSALM OF LIFE.

TELL me not, in mournful numbers,
  Life is but an empty dream!
For the soul is dead that slumbers,
  And things are not what they seem.

Life is real! life is earnest!
  And the grave is not its goal;
Dust thou art, to dust returnest,
  Was not spoken of the soul.

Not enjoyment, and not sorrow,
Is our destined end or way;
But to act, that each to-morrow
Find us further than to-day.

Art is long, and time is fleeting,
And our hearts, though stout and
   brave,
Still, like muffled drums, are beating
Funeral marches to the grave.

In the world's broad field of battle,
In the bivouac of life,
Be not like dumb, driven cattle!
Be a hero in the strife!

Trust no future, however pleasant!
Let the dead Past bury its dead!

Act—act in the living Present !
Heart within, and God o'erhead.

Lives of great men all remind us
We can make our lives sublime,
And departing, leave behind us
Footprints on the sands of time.

Footprints, that perhaps another,
Sailing o'er life's solemn main,
A forlorn and shipwrecked brother,
Seeing, shall take heart again.

Let us, then, be up and doing,
With a heart for any fate;
Still achieving, still pursuing,
Learn to labor and to wait.
             H. LONGFELLOW.

HENRY W. LONGFELLOW, a native of Portland, Maine, was graduated at Bowdoin College in 1825, where he was professor of modern languages for several years, and afterward held a similar professorship in the University of Cambridge from 1836 to 1854. He held a very high rank among the authors of America, and was one of the most popular poets.

ELIJAH AT MOUNT HOREB.

"Go forth," it had been said to Elijah, "and stand upon the mount before the Lord." The prophet hears it, and leaves his cave; and no sooner is he gone forth than signs occur which announce to him the approach of the Almighty. The sacred historian here, indeed, depicts, in simple language, a most sublime scene.

The first sign was a tremendous wind. Just before, probably, the deepest silence had prevailed throughout this dreary wilderness. The mountain tempest breaks forth, and the bursting rocks thunder, as if the four winds, having been confined there, had, in an instant, broken from their prisons to fight together. The clouds are driven about in the sky, like squadrons of combatants rushing to the conflict. The sandy desert is like a raging sea, tossing its curling billows to the sky. Sinai is agitated, as if the terrors of the law-giving were renewed around it. The prophet feels the majesty of Jehovah; it is awful and appalling. It is not a feeling of peace, and of the Lord's blissful nearness, which possesses Elijah's soul in this tremendous scene; it is rather a feeling of distressing distance. "A strong wind went before the Lord, but the Lord was not in the wind."

The terrors of an earthquake next ensue. The very foundations of the hills shake and are removed. The mountains and the rocks, which were rent by the mighty wind, threaten now to fall upon one another. Hills sink down, and valleys rise; chasms yawn, and horrible depths unfold, as if the earth were removed out of its place. The prophet, surrounded by the ruins of nature, feels still more of that divine majesty which "looketh upon earth, and it trembleth." But he still remains without any gracious communication of Jehovah in the inner man. The earthquake was only the second herald of the Deity. It went before the Lord, " but the Lord was not in the earthquake."

When this had ceased, an awful fire passed by. As the winds had done before, so now the flames came upon him from every side, and the deepest shades of night are turned into the light of day. Elijah, lost in adoring astonishment, beholds the awfully sublime spectacle. and the inmost sensation of his heart must have been that of surprise and dread, but he enjoys. as yet, no delightful sensation of the divine presence; " the Lord was not in the fire."

The fire disappears and tranquillity, like the stillness of the sanctuary, spreads gradually over all nature, and it seems as if every hill and dale—yea, the whole earth and skies—lay in silent homage at the footstool of Eternal Majesty. The very mountains seemed to worship, the whole scene is hushed to profound peace; and now he hears a "still, small voice." "And it was so when Elijah heard it, he wrapt his face in his mantle," in token of reverential awe and adoring wonder, and went forth, " and stood at the entrance of the cave."

H. A.

SQUADRON—A part of an army or part of a fleet.

CHASM—A cleft, a gap, an opening.

SANCTUARY—A holy place.

HOMAGE—To pay respect by external action.

ELIJAH, THE PROPHET.

He dwelt in a lonely spot
  By the side of a flowing brook;
His soul held commune alone with God
  In nature's open book;
No easy home at eve,
  No household gods are there,
No prattling voices to cheer the heart.
  And blend in the evening prayer.

When the god of day sank down
  To his couch in the golden west,
No silken coverlet—bed of down—
  Wooed his tired limbs to rest;
The soft sky, with its twinkling stars,
  Was his canopy overhead,
The dry leaves pillowed his weary brow,
  The cold, damp earth was his bed.

No chalice of burnished gold
  With rich wine sparkling high
Was held to his lips, but he quenched
  his thirst,
When his throat was parched and dry,
At the rippling brook that wound
  Like a ribbon among the trees,
And his heated face was fanned at eve
  By the gentle murmuring breeze.

No slave obeyed his will,
  Or spread on the festal board
Costly viands, all rich and rare,
  Or tempting nectar poured;
But the ravens brought bread and flesh,
  When the flowers were kissed with
    the dew
In the morning dawn, and when twi-
    light came
  The heaven-sent birds came too.

What a glorious scene was there !
  The grand old man of God
In that lonely spot, far from the haunts
    of man,
  With his couch the humble sod;
Yet, not forsaken—Jehovah still,
  From the great white throne above,
Remembered and cared for his humble
    wants
  With a father's tender love.

Ahab, the wicked king,
  In a lordly palace dwelt,
While Elijah, the lowly son of God.
  On the damp turf humbly knelt;
The wild birds brought him food,

And he drank from the flowing stream,
But, oh! through the mist of the dim
    earth life
He saw heaven's glorious gleam.

Ahab's guilty career was run,
And he died as the wicked die;

And the prophet without even tasting
    death,
Was caught up to God on high
In a chariot of glowing fire;
  When his great earth work was done
He rose up to grace Jehovah's court,
  And his heavenly crown was won.

R. A. LEVY.

CHALICE—A cup, a bowl.
NECTAR—The supposed drink of the heathen
gods

CHARIOT—A carriage of state or pleasure.

THE VALUE OF GOD'S LOVE.

ARTABAN sent a Rabbi a jewel of great value, requesting him to send an article in return which would be of equal worth. The Rabbi sent him a *mesusa* (a small capsule which contains a portion of the holy law, according to the Mosaic Code, and is generally attached to the door-post to keep God always in mind). "What!" said Artaban, "I have sent you an object which is worth so much gold, and you return me a present of hardly any value." "Friend!" answered the Rabbi, "all your riches and mine also are not equal to the object I sent you. Besides, consider that your present requires my care and attention in preserving it; whilst mine keeps watch over you, and with it you may rest in safety. For the holy law accompanies you in this world, attends you while you sleep in death, and, at the awakening, you will find it again."—Proverbs vi: 22.

TALMUD.

THE LIFE OF MAN COMPRISED IN RELIGION.

THE law seizes upon man at every step, at every period of his life, and in each corner of his dwelling; it thus imposes upon him a commandment, in order to give him an opportunity to acquire a reward. By laboring in the fields, yoke not the ox and the ass together. In sowing seed, do not sow, in the same place, seeds of various kinds. At reaping time, leave a share for the poor. In preparing food, set apart a portion for the priest. When going to hunt birds, take not the mother with the young ones. In establishing a new plantation, enjoy its fruit only after three years. At a funeral procession, do not inflict pain by making incisions in your own flesh. In attending to the beard, do not clip it according to heathen custom. In building, make a railing around your roof to prevent accidents. Each small portion of man wishes to be consecrated by some meritorious act; therefore the law contains 248 commandments, as many parts as those into which the human body is capable of being dissected. Each day of the year wishes to be dedicated to some noble work; and thus the law comprises 365 prohibitions, the number of days belonging to the solar year.

The law is like a sheet-anchor to him who suffers shipwreck ; as long as he clings to it, he remains safe ; and, so long as man connects himself with the law, he is also saved.

TALMUD.

INCISION—A cut or wound made with a sharp instrument.
MERITORIOUS—Deserving of reward.

THE KING AND THE LABORERS.

A CERTAIN king had in his garden an immense ditch, which was so deep that the eye could scarcely reach the bottom.

One day he hired some laborers, and ordered them to collect earth and other materials to fill the ditch with.

A few went to look at the ditch, and, perceiving its immense depth, said in their silly way: "How is it possible to fill this ditch ?" And they showed no desire to undertake the task. But others, more sensible again than they, said : "What does it matter that the ditch is so very deep? We are paid by the day, and, as we feel happy in having found work, we ought to do our duty in filling the same, as far as we possibly can accomplish." Thus also with man, who ought not to say: "Oh! how immeasurable is God's law! It is deeper than the sea—how many precepts! How are they all to be fulfilled ?"

But God says to man : " You are paid by the day ; do your work as far as lies in your power, and don't think of others."

TALMUD.

THE TONGUE.

"Go and fetch me a piece of meat from the shambles, even the best of its kind," said Rabbi Simeon to his servant Tobia. The man went and brought him a tongue. "Bring me," said he at another time, " a piece of meat of the worst quality you can get at the shambles," and again the servant brought him a tongue. " What is the meaning of this?" inquired the astonished Rabbi. And the intelligent servant answered : "The tongue is the best, and also the worst in the world. If it is a good one, there is nothing better ; if it is a slanderous one, then there is nothing worse." " Life and death is dependent on the tongue," said the wise king.—Prov. xviii: 21.

TALMUD.

WHAT WE SHOULD HAVE.

HAVE a tear for the wretched ; a smile for the glad ;
For the worthy applause ; an excuse for the bad.
Some help for the needy ; some pity for those
Who stray from the path where true happiness flows.

Have a laugh for the child in her play at your feet ;
Have respect for the aged, and pleasantly greet
The stranger that seeketh for shelter from thee ;
Have a covering to spare if he naked should be.

Have a hope in thy sorrow, a calm in thy joy ; ·
Have a work that is worthy thy life to employ ;
And, oh! above all things on this side the sod,
Have peace with thy conscience and peace with thy God.

ADAPTED.

A HEBREW PARABLE.

An old Hebrew story tells us how a poor creature one day came to the Temple from a sick bed on tottering limbs. He was ashamed to come, for he was very poor, and had no sacrifice to offer. As he drew near, he heard the loud choir chanting : " Thou desirest not sacrifice, else would I give it ; the sacrifices of God are a broken spirit ; a broken and contrite heart, O God, thou wilt not despise." Other worshipers came, passed before him, and offered their sacrifice ; but he had none. But at length he prostrated himself before the priest, who said: " What wilt thou, my son ; hast thou an offering?" And he replied: "No, my father, for last night a poor widow and her children came to me, and I had nothing to offer them but the two pigeons which were ready for the sacrifice." " Bring, then," said the priest, "an ephah of fine flour." " Nay, but, my father," said the old man, "this day my sickness and poverty have left only enough for my own starving children. I have not even an ephah of flour." " Why, then, art thou come to me?" said the priest. " Because I heard them singing, 'The sacrifices of God are a broken spirit.' Will he not accept my sacrifice if I say, 'Lord, be merciful to me, a sinner?'" And the priest lifted the old man from the ground, and he said : " Yes, thou art blessed, my son ; it is thy offering which is better than thousands of rivers of oil."

S. F. P.

EPHAH—A Hebrew measure of three pecks and three pints; or, according to some, of seven gallons and four pints.

UNHAPPY MEN.

In this life, men, while they are perpetually achieving success, are far from being happy. There are men whose vineyards bear abundant clusters ; but who do not know how to make their wine out of them ; or, to drop the figure, men live in this world, and attain success in a great variety of directions, but do not know how to manufacture happiness out of it. How is it? What is the matter? Why are not men happy? What is it that distresses them? How large an element of care enters into common life? How large an element of fear? How large an element of greediness? How dissatisfied men are because their success is not so large as they desire! How much envy and jealousy there are among them! One looks out of his palace, and sees other palaces going up that are finer than his, and that are owned by men who own more than he does; and, though he has more than heart could wish, he loses the flavor of his own affairs, because somebody has more property than he. And so with unsatisfied ambition, with over-greediness, with complaining discontent, and with narrow selfishness, men are perpetually cutting themselves, as the old heathen did in their worship. So men, by care, by envy, by the malign passions, are taking away the flavor of true contentment from themselves. Men seldom have peace in this great discordant world. In the din and rush of human life, you can seldom find peace.

H. W. BEECHER.

REV. HENRY WARD BEECHER is an eloquent clergyman and public lecturer, living in Brooklyn, New York.
MALIGN—Unfavorable, malicious.

SONG OF REBECCA.

When Israel, of the Lord beloved,
Out of the land of bondage came,
Her Father's God before her moved,
An awful guide in smoke and flame.
By day, along the astonished lands,
The clouded pillar glided slow;
By night, Arabia's crimsoned sands
Returned the fiery column's glow.

There rose the choral hymn of praise,
And trump and timbrel answered keen;
And Zion's daughters poured their lays
With priest's and warrior's voice between.
No portents now our foes amaze,
Forsaken Israel wanders lone,
Our fathers would not know Thy ways,
And Thou hast left them to their own.

But present still, though now unseen,
When brightly shines the prosperous day,
Be thoughts of Thee a cloudy screen,
To temper the deceitful ray.
And, oh! where stoops on Judah's path
In shade and storm, the frequent night,
Be Thou, long suffering, slow to wrath,
A burning and a shining light!

Our harps we left by Babel's stream;
The tyrant's jest, the Gentile's scorn;
No censer round our altar beams,
And mute are timbrel, trump, and horn;
But Thou hast said, the blood of goat,
The flesh of rams, I will not prize,
A contrite heart, an humble thought,
Are mine accepted sacrifice.

WALTER SCOTT.

SIR WALTER SCOTT, one of the most eminent names in English literature was born in Edinburgh, April 15, 1771, and died on September 21, 1832 He is the author of a great many works.
ISRAEL and JUDAH are terms used to desig- | PORTENTS—Omens of coming ill.
nate the Jewish people. | CENSER—A vessel in which incense is burned.
TIMBREL—An ancient Hebrew drum. | BABEL'S STREAM—The river Euphrates, on
ZION—A hill in Jerusalem; a figurative | which Babylon was situated.
term for Jerusalem.

DISINTERESTEDNESS.

ABOUT the middle of the last century, there lived in Prague the celebrated Rabbi, Serach Eidlitz, a man of profound learning and great capacity, renowned not only on account of his vast knowledge of Hebrew lore, but also owing to his mathematical talent, of which his work on arithmetic gives ample proof. According to the custom then prevailing, he divided his time in study and teaching, whilst his wife, by means of a few wares, tried to procure the necessaries of life for their modest household. Eidlitz knew well the many resources which, by his talents, were placed at his disposal; but he always declined every recompense, because he thought it incompatible with the words of our sages: "Who thus misuses what he has found, shall be rejected." However, in course of time, the circumstances of this learned man became more and more distressing, so that he was often obliged to deny himself even the common necessaries of life. Nevertheless, he persevered, and sought to hide his poverty, being afraid, in case it became known, it might appear as if he were asking for assistance. About this time, he received one day a visit from an old friend, the Rabbi Israel Fraenkel, President of the congregation, to whom, in course of conversation, Eidlitz, in confidence, disclosed the true state of his affairs. At their next interview, Fraenkel, in the most tender manner, made Eidlitz an offer in money, which he, however, refused at once. "Well," replied Fraenkel, "you know that God has blessed me with riches, and that, on account of my temporal occupations, I cannot find sufficient time, which, necessarily, the study of the law requires. If you then absolutely refuse this trifle, I shall certainly say that you do it merely to deprive me in respect to my deed of my share of salvation in the world to come." This remark had the desired effect, and out of respect for his friend Eidlitz took the gift. Thus time passed on, the two friends often met, but, as may easily be supposed, the matter was never broached. After a few years Eidlitz took ill, and soon died. Fraenkel, in virtue of his official capacity, then went to the house of the deceased, in order to take an inventory of his possessions. This was certainly a mere formal proceeding, for he well knew how poor Eidlitz died. In his study he found a large chest filled with MSS. and other things of some value to the late owner, for he would never intrust the key to anybody during lifetime. But what was Fraenkel's astonishment, when he found also among the contents of the chest, a small, round, hard parcel, carefully wrapped up and sealed, and which, on opening, contained a bag of money having a ticket attached, on which stood the words: "Deposited by my friend. the Rabbi Israel Fraenkel!"

A similar case is related of the well-known Rabbi Herz Scheier, of Mainz, who died in 1824, and, according as set forth in the Talmud, adhered strictly and conscientiously to the precept that Jewish Ministers and men of learning should always act disinterestedly toward their congregations, whose welfare they ought to seek on all occasions. He was placed in affluent circumstances and therefore declined to take the usual salary, which the congregation offered him; but in course of time his wealth dwindled away, and he became reduced to that extent that he was compelled to accept a yearly salary of 1,000 florins. During eight years he continued to do so, but

after that time an outstanding debt, which he had already given up for lost, was unexpectedly paid him, and the first thing the good and pious Rabbi did with the 10,000 florins thus received was the repayment of the 8,000 florins which he had drawn from the congregation the last eight years.
H. A.

INCOMPATIBLE—Inconsistent with something else.
SALVATION—Preservation from eternal death.

CONSCIENTIOUSLY — Scrupulous, exactly just.
DISINTERESTEDLY—Indifference to profit.

MODESTY OF OUR SAGES.

ONCE upon a time R. Gamliel and R. Joshua went to sea; the former providing himself with biscuits, whilst the latter took also in addition a large quantity of flour with him. Being questioned as to the reason of providing himself with such a quantity of provisions, R. Joshua answered: "There is a star which appears on the horizon only once in seventy years; he misleads the sailor, and the time of his appearance is just now due." Astonished at the astronomical knowledge of R. Joshua, R. Gamliel inquired: "How is it that being possessed of such vast learning, you are nevertheless compelled to seek for a livelihood upon these dangerous paths?" "You feel surprised at my circumstances," replied R. Joshua; "you had better express your astonishment at the two learned men on the Continent, R. Elieser, son of Chasma, and R. Jochanan, son of Godgada, who are capable of calculating every drop the ocean contains, and yet they have hardly sufficient of the common necessaries of life." When afterwards the Nassi R. Gamliel sent for these two learned men, in order to put an end to their temporal wants by investing them with office, both of them declined the kind offer. R. Gamliel had to send a message a second time accompanied by these words: "Do not believe that I bestow upon you dominion; no such thing, for I merely impose upon you a task." Whether they complied with the second call the Talmud does not state.
TALMUD.

KING SANHERIB BEFORE JERUSALEM.

THE general stood quietly viewing his men,
In great numbers encamped around him then.
"To-morrow, to-morrow we penetrate
Like a raging sea ev'ry city gate.
Like hungry wolves and tigers resembling,
Destroy the people already trembling.
Yes, to-morrow, to-morrow is the day,
When gladness will meet me every way."

There he stood, and whilst he thus was speaking,
His army round was sleeping and dreaming.
They were sleeping and dreaming that same night,
Of victory and booty in bloody fight.
But as soon as morn began to appear,
The angel had destroy'd his army clear.
Sanherib alone stood amidst the death,
And in dread from the holy land he fled.
KOSARSKI.

MEDITATIONS ON THE BIBLE.

After the light, *i. e.*, the life of the universal soul, God created the firmament with its constellations, determined the limits of the sea, covered the earth with vegetation, with plants, trees, flowers, fruits, and all the treasures, and all that is magnificent; peopled plain and mountain, forest, air, and ocean, with innumerable and various creatures destined to nourish, to serve, to charm a being that was to come at the end and who was to be the masterpiece of the Creator and the king of creation—man.

Like a mother full of affection and tenderness, who uses all her solicitude and all her heart to trim up the cradle, to prepare with angel's kisses the nourishment, the garments, and all the necessaries of the body and soul, of the child that is to be born, so did the Deity make touching and splendid preparations to receive the son of His love, and offer Him at His birth all earthly good, all happiness, all felicity. The sun and the stars should shine in all their celestial brilliancy, the birds chant their sublime canticles, the flowers exhale their divine fragrances, the ocean vibrate its waves and expand its grandeur; the valley and the hills cover themselves with crops, with flocks, and untold blessings; all nature should sing and smile, put on its holiday raiment, and prepare its feasts; all should be harmony, light and charm. Paradise should be ornamented with all the splendors of heaven, when the child of the Eternal—Adam—should make his entry into the world.

The manner in which the creation of the world is narrated by the Bible—with a simplicity so full of grandeur—shows the prodigious, all-powerfulness of the Most High, and at the same time the divinesource of that Book.

"Why," says a Midrash, "has the Lord on the third day created the plants, the trees, the fruits, and the luminaries on the fourth day?" It was in order to manifest His supreme power in fertilizing the earth without the heat of the sun. If creation were the result of natural phenomena and the Scriptures the work of man, the author would apparently have created the sun before the products of the soil.

Legend says: "That two great luminaries shall reign in the firmament" had been decided by the Almighty. Then appeared the sun in all his magnificent beauty, his light an ocean of fire; his heat sending forth life and happiness; all his being imposing and majestic.

At his side was the moon, his equal in beauty. She became angry at the splendor of the sun—she wanted to be the greatest of the luminaries; the greatness of others ravished her of her happiness and made her pine with grief. The Deity was wroth, because of the culpable jealousy of the moon. His voice of thunder was heard in the vast space of the universe.

"The one who is not contented with what is great, and looks with envy on that which is still greater, must return to what is common. Let the greatness of the moon disappear, her size diminish; her light shall henceforth be pale and weak, like an eternal stigma of envy. The one who would not share her brilliancy and magnificence with another shall henceforth be subordinated to others, condemned to feel forever her decrease and punishment," God said: and it was so.

"Oh! pardon, forgiveness," sighed the moon, trembling. "The jealous only can obtain forgiveness." said the Lord with graciousness, "in doing good." The moon accepted the advice. Since then she travels during night over the universe, consoling the unfortunate, a sweet companion to the lonely wanderer, a guide to the one who goes astray, a faithful friend to all those who are afflicted or in despair—a ray of hope and mercy, penetrating into prisons, or shining upon the couch of suffering.

When everything was ready, achieved, accomplished, God said to the angels*: "Let us make a being that resembles us." Then before the Divine Majesty appeared respectfully, JUSTICE, who implored: "Sovereign Judge of the World, create not man, for injustice marks out his footsteps. Without pity for his fellows, he drives the widow out of her house, the orphan from his hereditary asylum; he robs his brother with barbarous hand of his own; even the most fortunate and noble kings and princes do not spare the property of their subjects, which they have acquired through hard toil and saving." "No; create him not," prays the amiable and sweet PEACE. "The one whom thou wilt cause to be born rejects concord and love; hatred and quarrel walk at his side; I can see nations and empires drowned in blood; father and son differ in their belief; husband and wife mar the harmony of their house, forgetting in vain frivolities the most precious gifts of life—love and union."

"And falsehood," added TRUTH, "is his character; falsehood in the house of God, falsehood in the domestic hearth, falsehood in the temple of justice, falsehood in the life of the individual, falsehood in the life of the masses."

And so on they spoke. Then appeared the most gracious angel of the Creator, MERCY, with his sweet and affable features, and kneeling down, he said: "Pray, Father, create him. I will be his guide, his companion, his organ. If passion and error draw him on to evil, I shall bear him back into the right way, refresh his downcast heart, revive his courage, bring him back to his God, help him to struggle against his downfall, elevate and ennoble him."

The good Lord listened to the tender supplications of his dear angel. Man was called into existence—a being full of sinfulness,

*We have no knowledge of the angels. The plural is used, because both the divine and physical natures were united in man.

needing forever his guardian angel, who shall always, from the hour of his birth to that of his death, accompany him, guide him, sustain him. Angel of Mercy, our dearest companion from the cradle to the grave, infallible and indispensable friend at all hours of our existence, we greet thee! Mayest thou never forsake us! Man was not created like the rest of creation by a simple word of God, or the sole manifestation of His will, but with *the dust of the earth* (*Oafermin Hoadomoh*).

This humble origin, forever recalled in the name of *Adam*, was to banish from society all pride, all inequality, all pretension to a superiority of birth or caste, all unjust domineering of the one over the other. "Consider from whence thou comest, and whither thou goest, and in whose presence thou must in futurity render an account in JUDGMENT, *and thou wilt not sin.*"—*Aboth iii : 1.*

B. J. C. i.

CANTICLE—A song of Solomon.
OAFER MIN HOADOMOH (Hebrew)—Dust from the earth.
CONSTELLATION—A cluster of stars.
SOLICITUDE—Anxiety.
FELICITY—Happiness.

PHENOMENON—Anything striking by a new appearance.
LUMINARY—Any body that gives light.
STIGMA—A mark of infamy.
HEREDITARY—Descending by inheritance.
INFALLIBLE—Incapable of mistake.

PSALM XXVII.

The Lord is my light : my salvation is He,
Of whom shall my soul be afraid ?
The Lord is the fortress and shield of my life,
Of whom shall I entertain dread ?

When workers of evil draw near to my side,
When my foes form 'round me a wall,
The hand of my God doeth battle for me,
The wicked ones stumble and fall.

If an army itself should array 'gainst me,
My heart would acknowledge no fear;
If bloodshed should threaten my peaceful pursuits,
God's presence would always be near.

One thing that I've asked of the Lord, will I seek,
It is, that I ever may dwell
In His house, whose loveliness far exceeds all
That the voice of mortal can tell.

His pavilion is e'er my refuge from sin,

His temple the shrine of my heart;
Oh ! how can I pour out my praises to Him
Whose mercy will never depart.

Hear, Lord, when my voice calleth loudly to Thee,
Be gracious and answer my prayer;
Thou, who art the source of all help and support,
Wilt not give me up to despair.

My father and mother no more lavish love
On the child once guarded with care;
But solitude bringeth no sorrow to me,
For the Lord is my portion and share.

Lord, show me the path on which I must go,
Let my way be even and straight;
Oh ! do not resign me to doers of wrong,
Who are ruled by malice and hate.

Ye people of Israel, wait on the Lord,
Be strong and courageous in right;
Pray fervently in His ineffable name,
And your souls shall be bathed in light.   J. M.

SHRINE—A case in which something sacred is deposited.

INEFFABLE—Unspeakable.

AMBITION.

ALEXANDER THE GREAT, in his travels amidst deserts and barren lands, came at last to a river, which flowed between two verdant shores. The surface of the water was quite smooth, and not the slightest breeze was perceptible. It was the picture of content- ment, and silently seemed to say: Behold here the seat of peace and quietness. Thousands of happy thoughts this beautiful scenery might have produced in a contemplating mind; but how could it have soothed Alexander, who was full of ambitious plans, whose ear had become accustomed to the clashing of arms, and the groans of the dying warrior? Alexander continued his journey, but he soon felt exhausted, and was obliged to seek for rest. He fixed his tent on the shores of a river, drank some water thereof, which seemed to him very refreshing, being of a sweet and agreeable taste, and even spread a sweet fragrance all over the place. "Surely," he said, "this river, enjoying such peculiar advantages, must take its source in a country rich in blessings. Let us find out where it springs from." Following thus for some time the shores of the river, he at length arrived at the gates of Paradise. These were closed, and he knocked, demanding in his usual peremptory man- ner to be admitted at once.

"Thou canst not have admission here," a voice from within called unto him; "this is the gate of the Master." "I am the Master, Lord of the whole earth," replied the impatient monarch. "I am Alex- ander, the Conqueror; what! do you hesitate to admit me?" "No," he was answered, "here no conqueror is known but he who con- quers his passions; the just only are allowed to enter here." (Ps. cxviii: 20.)

Alexander tried hard to gain admittance, but neither threats nor entreaties had any effect. He then said to the keeper who held watch at the gates of Paradise, "You know that I am a great king, who has received the homage of many nations; if you really refuse to admit me, give me at least some kind of a keepsake, in order that I may surprise the world in showing that I have been as far as this, the place which no mere mortal ever reaches."

"Here, silly man," replied the keeper, "here I give you some- thing which can heal all sorrows. Moreover, one glance at it will teach you wisdom, such as you have never thought to be master of! Now, go your way."

Alexander took hastily what was given him and then returned to his tent. But how astonished did he feel, when he perceived that his present was nothing but part of a human skull. "This, then, is that nice keepsake," he said, "which they offer to a king and a hero like me! This, then, is the fruit of all my labor, all the dangers and troubles I have hitherto undergone?" Enraged and disappointed in his hopes, he threw away the miserable portion of the mortal integument. "Great king," said a wise man, who noticed the act, "do not despise this present, however insignificant it may appear in your eyes; it possesses, nevertheless, extraordinary qualities, of which you may soon convince yourself by weighing it with gold or .silver." Alexander said he should like to try, and, ordering a pair of scales, placed the skull in one and the gold in the other. He was immediately surprised to find the one containing the skull going down. More gold was fetched, and the more they put on the scale, the more it went up. "It is extraordinary," said Alexander, "that such a small portion of matter should vanquish so much gold. Is there no counterbalance to be had, in order to produce an equilibrium?"

"Certainly," said the wise man, "very little will suffice." Whereupon he took a small portion of earth and covered the bone with it, which caused the scale in which it lay to rise immediately. "This is certainly very singular!" Alexander now exclaimed; "could you not explain to me this remarkable phenomenon?" "Great king!" replied the wise man, "this fragment of a bone is the part in which the human eye is inclosed, and, although in its extent limited, it is nevertheless unlimited in its desires; the more it has, the more it wants; neither gold nor silver, nor any earthly possession, is able to satiate its wishes. But being once placed in the grave and covered with earth, there it finds a limit for all its eager desires."

TALMUD.

ALEXANDER THE GREAT was King of Macedonia, 3656 A. M.

INTEGUMENT—Anything that covers or envelops another.

COUNTERBALANCE—To act against with an opposite weight.

EQUILIBRIUM—Equally of weight.

THE SON OF SORROW.

NEAR the wild waves' lonely strand
Sate Sorrow once, from heaven bann'd,
And with her hands, in thoughtless play,
A human figure formed of clay.

Zeus came and asked, "What's this, I pray?"
"'Tis but a lifeless shape of clay;
Oh! grant my wish—with power divine
Breathe life into this image mine."

"So let it be; but then he's mine
By virtue of my craft divine."
"No, no," responded Sorrow, sad,
"He is my own, my chosen lad.

"'Twas I who formed him of this earth."
"But 'twas my breath that gave him birth."

Then outspake Earth, "I have a claim
Upon this being of sin and shame.

"From out my bosom torn he came,
And I my rights must back reclaim."
"Saturn," said Zeus, "shall judge the case.
We'll plead before him face to face."

The judgment was, "Let none complain,
All three shall property retain.
Zeus gave him life! so, when he dies,
His soul shall mount beyond the skies.

"When soul's forever hushed in sleep,
His frame, O Earth, is thine to keep.
But thine, O Sorrow, all his days
Of life to walk within thy ways.

"And while his feet on earth delay

Thou shalt be with him every day;
Thy saddening sighs his breath shall be,
His face a counterpart of thee."

So spake the Almighty's dread command,

That while runs out Time's fleeting
sand,
In *life* man is to sorrow given,
In *death* to earth—*his soul to heaven!*

H. Phillips, Jr.

ZEUS, SATURN—Planets worshiped by the Romans and Greeks.

RESIGNATION.

It was toward evening on a Sabbath day, and Rabbi Meir had
been occupied for some hours in the academy, where he expounded
the holy law to his numerous pupils, rejoicing in the study of the law
and the religious attention with which his words were received.

In the meantime his house had, in a very short period, become a
house of grief, for his two hopeful sons had suddenly died. Only
the mother was at home and left to herself with the two corpses.
Unhappy woman! Overcome with grief, she looked motionless upon
the two beloved faces, whether she could yet discover a spark of life
in them, and, bent from sorrow, she also thought of her poor husband,
who, in a few moments, would behold this awful spectacle.

But in deference to an all-wise Providence, and out of love to her
husband, she seemed to feel wonderfully strong in her unfortunate
position. With maternal hands she spread a pall over the bed
where her beloved sons were lying, and then went in the ante-room
to await her husband.

It was already night when her learned husband returned home,
and after he had put his foot into the room, he said, "And the sons?"
"They may have remained at the academy," answered the mother, in
a weak and trembling voice, and turning her eyes toward Heaven,
to avoid the looks of her husband.

"It seemed to me I did not behold them among the pupils." The
wife did not answer, while she handed to him the wine and the wax
taper, in order to implore the Divine blessing for the week to come.

The Rabbi finished the religious act, and with increasing anxiety
he inquired: "But the children, dear wife?"

"They are perhaps taking a walk," answered his wife, and in the
meantime she placed some bread before her husband, who had been
without food for some time.

The Rabbi ate a small piece, and after thanking the Almighty for
all earthly gifts, he called out: "How long do our sons stay away
this evening! But don't you know anything more particular concerning them, dear wife? And why do you appear so down-hearted?"

"Because, my dear husband, I have to ask your kind advice. Listen,
dear; the day before yesterday came a friend, and gave me some
costly jewels to keep for him, and now he has returned and demands
them of me back again. Alas! (she said, weeping) I did not expect

to see him so soon.   Should I return him his property?"   "My dear
wife, this doubt is sinful."   "But I liked these jewels so well!"
"They don't belong to you."   "They were so dear to me! perhaps
even to you, sir."   "My wife!" cried the Rabbi, perplexed, who now
began to suspect something extraordinary and fearful ; "what doubt,
what thoughts! to keep back goods intrusted to you—a holy cause!"
"It is true," answered the wife, with tears, "but it is necessary that
you should assist me in returning them.   Come and look at the
intrusted jewels."

And with hands benumbed she took the hands of the confused
husband, led him into the room, and lifted the pall.   "Behold here the
jewels ; God has demanded them."   At this sight, the poor father
began to shed tears of sorrow, and exclaimed : "Oh, my children!
my children !   Sweetness of my existence ! Light of my eyes! Oh,
my children !"   "My husband, have you not told me that we are
obliged to return what has been given in trust to us, if the owner
demands it back?"

With eyes dim from tears she looked, motionless, into the Rabbi's
countenance, who was overcome with astonishment at her unspeakable tenderness.   "Oh, my God !" said he, "dare I murmur against
Thy will ?   Thou hast given me a religious and blessed woman for a
wife."

And the unhappy couple threw themselves down upon their faces
and began to pray and lament by repeating the sacred words of Job:
"God has given it and God has taken it again : the name of God be
praised forever."   TALMUD.

DEFERENCE—Submission, regard.

OUR PROMISES.

RABBI AKIBA BEN JOSEPH and some of his disciples were passing
the ruins of the holy Temple, when a jackal came out from the place
where the Holy of Holies formerly stood, and where the glory of the
Lord had throned over the Cherubim.   His companions began bitterly to weep at the sight, while the Rabbi burst out into joyful ex-
clamations.   His astonished disciples exclaimed, "Rabbi, why dost
thou laugh?"   "Why do you weep?" was his reply.   "How can we
refrain from weeping?" answered they, "when we see the glorious
and holy Temple of the Lord in ashes, the idolatrous heathen lording
over the ruins, and that most sacred spot where the Lord of the universe deigned visibly to dwell—that spot is now the abode of unclean
animals ?   How is it possible that the eyes which see this destruction
and desecration—caused by our sins and those of our ancestors—
should abstain from shedding abundant tears, or the oppressed bosom
from giving vent to its poignant grief?"   "Aye,' said the Rabbi,
"the prophet said: 'The mountain of Zion is desolate ; jackals

dwell upon it ;' and ye weep ye have seen this fearful denunciation fulfilled ; but the same prophet has likewise said : 'Thus saith the Lord, behold, I will bring again the captivity of Israel's tents, and have mercy on his dwelling-places ; and the city shall be rebuilt upon her ruins, and the Temple shall be restored to its former appearance ; and therefrom shall proceed thanksgivings and the voice of rejoicing ; and I will multiply them, and they shall not be diminished; I will glorify them, and they shall not be humbled.' "   TALMUD.

LORDING—Lord, spoken in contempt or ridicule.
GIVING VENT—To utter.

POIGNANT—Severe.
DENUNCIATION—A public menace.

AT PASSOVER.

Lead me, O Lord! loud cries the 'pris-
    oned soul,
Out of this aimless strife;
In which unseen, unsought the heavenly
    goal,
I breathe imperfect life,
In sordid atmosphere of worldly care,
    That bars the pathway to the gates
    of prayer.

Lead me, O Hand Divine! safe 'mid the
    shadows
Of superstition wrought;
And let me find the summer's dew-
    gemmed meadows
That skirt the heights of thought;
The pure, unclouded vision give to me,
Blest with the gleam of immortality.

Lead me afar from whisperings of
    temptation,
Born of grim poverty!
Thine only be the contrite heart's ova-
    tion;
To worship only Thee,
The joyful choice of aspirations blest
With recognition of Thy law's behest.

Lead me, O Hand Divine! that through
    the ages
Hast wandering Israel led;
With light illumined souls of prophets,
    sages,
Sweet Freedom's guidance shed
Over the darkened ways, where 'neath
    the rod
Thy captive children raised the soul
    of God !

Lead me, long weeping in the exile
    dreary,
By the tempestuous sea,
Burdened with soul-tasks, disenchanted,
    weary,
To find my rest in Thee !
Their names are written proud and high
    In music and in art,
And Fame so wide arena boasts
    Where they bear not a part.

Through forums and through senate halls
    Their silvery accents roll,
And with Isaiah's burning fire
    Enchant the human soul.
And Judah seems to bear aloft
    Aladdin's wondrous lamp,
While earth, responsive, yields her gems
    Where Judah's exiles tramp.

Although they roam without a land—
    From Salem darkly hurled—
Her princes rule, with magic hand,
    The destinies of the world.
They are a power the nations feel
    In every throbbing core,
The strange influence of that tribe
    Which roams creation o'er.

Imperial race ! thy splendors gilt
    The glimmering dawn of Time,
When Earth lay blushing in the arms
    Of Eden's golden prime.
And brighter yet the flames shall rise
    Where Salem's altar stood—
Time's last great act shall charm the
    world
In our Messiah's word.

                                J. T.

THE FOLLY OF DISCONTENT.

THERE was a man by the name of Baruch, who possessed the treasures of India and Arabia, to whose riches there was no end; whose magnificent surroundings ministered to every temporal delight, whose amiable wife and lovely children left nothing to be desired; yet, in the midst of all, he was most miserable. His complaints grieved all about him. He was ready to destroy his own life to be rid of his troubles. Then he heard that there was in Memphis, in the land of Mizraim, a great prophet, and taking two camels and a trusty servant, with much treasure, he started to see the prophet

In the desert through which they had to pass, they lost their way; and both men and beasts were ready to perish with thirst. Then Baruch began to appreciate the water that flowed in his fountain in Damascus, and would have given a camel's load of jewels for a single draught. In their search for water the servant was struck blind; yet he faltered not in his devotion to his master.

Baruch now felt himself to be the cause of the misery in his own house, and the misery of his servant, and bewailed greatly. Then he cried to God, saying, "Destroy me, for I am not worthy of the mercy Thou hast shown me; and the burden of my sins oppresses my soul grievously!" Then there was a noise like the rushing of a brook from the rocks. The camel stretched out his neck, and Baruch hastened to the place and found a clear and abundant fountain, at which they all, both men and beasts, slaked their raging thirst. Then Baruch praised the Lord for His wonderful mercy and goodness.

When all were refreshed by the fountain, the servant proposed to make ready to pursue the journey. But Baruch said he had found in the desert the wisdom he sought from the prophet of Mizraim, and was now ready to return home. Baruch's wife and children wondered at his quick return, and wept for joy. Then Baruch told them how, in the desert, he had learned humility, and had been enabled to see the grace of the All-Merciful; and that he now returned to them a new man, with peace in his heart more precious than silver or gold. Henceforth, he walked meekly and cheerfully, helping the poor, and doing good in all the country. H. A.

LAND OF MIZRAIM—Egypt. | DAMASCUS—A large city in the western part of Asiatic Turkey.

NAHUM ALL'S WELL.

A TALMUDIC LEGEND.

There lived a holy man of yore, | Stone-blind he was—he had no feet—
Whose praise I will endeavor; | His skin and flesh were wasted—
The Lord laid on him plagues full sore, | And nothing he did drink or eat
Yet murmur breathed he never. | To him with relish tasted.

He said, " All's well, O Lord, my God !
Thy work is naught but kindness;
A blessing blossoms from Thy rod, ·
Thou sav'st me from soul-blindness.

" The body full of base designs,
Thy mercy all hath wasted;—
Eyes that had darted envious fires—
Feet that to mischief hasted."

He thanked his God, however he fared,
No mishaps ever galled him;
In wonder people at him stared,
And Nahum All's Well called him.

Once over the land he had to pass,
To help a sickly neighbor;
He sat himself on his she ass,
His crutches rest from labor.

A cock he also had along,
To give him timely warning;
That he might praise his God in song
At earliest gleam of morning.

He reached an inn at close of day,
But shelter was denied him;
He lit a torch and jogged away,
Within a wood to hide him.

A puff of wind his torch out blew,
But this no wise discouraged him;
Good Nahum said: " All's well—this
too !"
And on the ground he laid him.

A fox crept slowly up and stole
The cock and quick retreated;

" All for the best !" thus in his soul
The pious man repeated.

A lion came, to pieces tore
The ass that much he needed.
" All's well !" said Nahum, as before,
And on his way proceeded.

At morn a tale of woe he learned;
Last night armed men descending
Had sacked the inn, and killed and
burned,
Like beasts their victims rending.

" Now see," said Nahum, " what good
care
The Lord for me hath taken;
All in the dark to leave me there,
By all I owned forsaken.

" Wind, Fox and Lion, each one came,
And Angels, to stand by me
And guard my life—blest be His name !
Thus harm did not come nigh me.

" If at the inn I'd lodged at night,
A corpse they would have made me,
And in the wood the torch's light
Would surely have betrayed me.

" The cock's loud crow, the ass's bray,
My death-knell would have sounded;
My God ! I own Thy wondrous way,
Thy wisdom is unbounded."

Take pious Nahum, dear young friend,
And make him thine example,
Then shalt thou be right in the end,
And build up Zion's temple.
                                    J. T.

GOOD WORKS.

THREE sorts of friends man possesses in this world, namely: his children, his wealth, and his good works.

When the hour of dissolution is at hand, man in the agonies of death calls his children and grandchildren to his bed and says: "Oh, can you not mitigate my sufferings and save me from the pangs of death?" ·

And the afflicted children answer: "Thou knowest, dear father, that nothing can prevail against death; neither children nor relatives, nor friends are able to redeem man from death." The Divine word has gone forth (Dan. xii: 13): "Go, sleep in peace, and prepare thyself for the day of judgment." Then the dying man thinks of his wealth and calls it to his assistance. "Oh, save me from that terrible sentence of death." And his wealth answers him: "Gold and jewels are powerless in the hour of God's wrath; the Divine word has proclaimed it." (Mishle xi: 4.)

Whereupon the dying man calls his good works and says to them: "Oh! save me from the horrors of the pains of death; leave me not to myself; come, accompany me and save me, for I was always your friend."

And the good works answer: "Depart in peace, dear friend! Even before you arrive there for judgment, we will already have reached that place," for the Divine word has gone forth to man: "Thy virtue precedes thee on the way, even till heavenly bliss receives thee."— Isaiah lviii: 8.   TALMUD.

KINDNESS AND FORGIVENESS.

RABBI NECHANIA was asked by one of his disciples which were the virtues best to perform in regard to a long life granted unto him?

The Rabbi answered: "I never ventured to degrade my associates for the purpose of advancing my own honor—a wrong done me never went to bed with me—with my wealth I dealt liberally.

"The first I acquired from another learned man, who one evening returning from his fields with a hatchet on his shoulder, when a friend of his tried to take it from him in order to carry it in his stead. The other, however, prevented him, and said: 'If you are used to carry such implements, I am willing to submit to it, but if it is not your habit to do so, then I do not wish to procure any honor at the price of thy degradation.'

"The second one my friend, Mar Sotra, taught me, who prayed every night on going to bed: 'My God, pardon all those who have done me wrong.'

"The third virtue I derived from Job, who, whenever he engaged laborers to do some work for him, increased, of his own accord, their small wages, although their pay had previously been agreed upon."
                                          TALMUD.

CHARITY.

A LEARNED man wandered one day amidst the ruins of Jerusalem, and a friend quietly followed him. On arriving at the place where the Temple once rose in its majestic splendor, he commenced shedding tears and calling aloud: "Woe to us! The Temple where our sins were expiated is destroyed! Woe to us! How shall we atone for our sins?" The friend who had followed him said: "Do not trouble about it, O master! There is yet one not less powerful medium left for expiation; there is still charity remaining to us."
                                          TALMUD.

CHARITY.

CHARITY is like perfumed flowers,
Or heaven's manna sent on earth,
Or like the dew of dripping showers,
Refreshing nature and giving birth
To growths of beauty and thoughts
divine,
To the Great Hereafter to bloom and
shine.

Charity is a mantle gemmed with
tears,
Which wraps the donor in rays of
light,
And in its ample folds appears
To gather misery, and make life
bright;
It is a garment of purest snow,
It is a diadem upon the brow.

Charity is bounteous as the sea,
The winds of heaven waft it here and
there;
It is the honey in a human bee,
That sweetens grief and trouble
everywhere;
It is the excelsior, and the soul's device,
It is God's essence, culled from Paradise.

Charity, stretch forth thy supple hands,
Be just, yet generous in thy gift,
It will bear fruit for thee in brighter
lands,
And to a heavenly sphere the soul
uplift,
Where angels in advance shall bring
the deeds,
Which to a life of everlasting leads.

EMMA SCHIFF.

DIADEM—A tiara; an ensign of royalty bound about the head of Eastern monarchs.

MANNA—Food sent from heaven, to provide for the Israelites in the wilderness.
EXCELSIOR - More lofty; higher.

JUDAISM IN METAPHOR.

COUNTLESS are the figures under which Judaism appears in the Bible and the writings of the sages. Now it is compared to water, because it cleanses men from what is animal and low, and dulls and cools the passions ; and now to wine, because time cannot injure it, nay, it increases in power with advancing age ; to oil, because it mixes not with foreign elements, preserving ever its distinctiveness ; to honey, because it is sweet and lovely, free from religious hatred ; to a wall, because it protects its professors from the violence of the wicked ; to manna, because it proclaims human equality before God, and asserts His justice ; and lastly it is compared to a crown, because it invests every son of earth with sovereignty, and raises him higher than all nature. A. JELLINEK.

DR. A. JELLINEK—An eminent Jewish divine and orator, minister of one of the chief Congregations in Vienna; author of several important works, and a writer of great repute.
METAPHOR—A simile comprised in a word.

IMPERISHABLE GOODS.

A LEARNED man was once a passenger on a vessel where there were also some great merchants, who carried their merchandise to a large distant city. They took the learned man to be also a man of business, but as they could not obtain any clue as to what kind of goods he was dealing in, they inquired of him, jeeringly, " What part of the ship are your goods stored away, or do they indeed require no warehousing at all?" " Better by far, and more valuable, are the goods," replied the offended man, "I carry with me, than any you can boast of." But curiosity prompted them to make fresh inquiries, and they even went so far as to search every part of the ship, but being unable to gain any information, they considered the learned man's assertion to be an untruth, and revenged themselves by annoying him continually. The vessel, however, was afterward captured by pirates, who possessed themselves of the whole of the valuable cargo. The passengers were all sent on shore, and had to travel to the next town, where they suffered great hardship, for no one was willing to believe their statement that they had lost all at the hands of pirates. But how did the learned man fare? He went at once to the chief academy of the place, where he delivered several discourses, which, being found interesting and instructive, caused him soon to be taken care of, and all his wants were well supplied. Being a man of great talent, he became known all over the town, and all the rich and influential men bestowed money and presents on him, and continually invited him to their houses. In the meantime his travelling companions, the merchants, being penniless, had to suffer great want, and in hearing accidentally of his renown, and the success he had hitherto met with, they came to the scholar, related to him what they had to suffer and undergo, and begged of him to intercede for them with his rich friends, in order that they might thus obtain some help, otherwise they should have to starve and never be able to get away from the place and so reach their home. "The loss of your so much praised goods," replies the scholar, "brings you now to me, whom you considered to be without any possessions. A man of tender feeling cannot behold tears of sorrow without being moved to compassion, if it is in his power to mitigate the grief that gives rise to them. You shall obtain succor, but let this misfortune teach you that it is not the quantity but the durability of the goods which constitutes the value thereof, and points to the truth of the Solomonic proverb: ' A good and useful doctrine I give unto you, my instruction, never to forsake my knowledge.' "

H. A.

PIRATE—A sea-robber.

CHANUKAH.

We welcome thee joyfully, glorious night;
We hail thee with pleasure, O Chanukah light !
Its lustre, so brilliant, invites us to joy;
Invites us to praise Him, the great Adonay.

He was our Redeemer, and Helper in woe,
When cruelty pressed us, a merciless foe,

Who sought to destroy our religion, so dear,
And solace in danger, in trouble and cheer.

The faithful and pious, who died without fear,
Exclaimed with their last breath, "Hear, Israel, hear !"
So Hannah, the mother, and sons good and true,

All sealed with their life-blood their faithfulness too.

But Israel's God never slumbers nor sleeps;
He ever is near him, who mournfully weeps.
He saw our oppression, and hearing our pleas,
Awaked, to redeem us, the brave Maccabees.

They fought like true heroes, for God, law and land,
To victory leading their heroic band.
The enemy dreaded the name Maccabee;
He perished or fled, and Judea was free !

Once more was Jerusalem happy and gay,
When Judah returned in triumphant array;
Then songs of victorious joy and of praise
Arose from God's Temple, all brilliant ablaze.

Be welcome, then welcome, O glorious night;
We hail thee with pleasure, O Chanukah light !
Its lustre, so brilliant, invites us to joy;
Invites us to praise Him, the great Adonay !

REV. L. STERN.

THE TWO STRANGERS.

HAVE you ever been at Worms, dear reader, and there paid a visit to the venerable synagogue celebrated for its antiquity and architecture? There you will have seen in front of the holy ark a lamp, from which two flames throw their reflecting light upon the curtain of the Ark of the Covenant. Centuries have already elapsed into the inexhaustible realm of the past, generations have entered and left in continual alternation the stage of life, but the lamp never gets empty, nor do the flames ever become extinguished, and the rays of light always illumine the inner space of this house of God, as if the obscurity of night should never prevail in its walls, nor spiritual darkness ever penetrate here ! And why do those lights never become extinguished? Because the everlasting shining faith kindles them. Once, tradition tells us, the much-hated quarter of the Jews (Judengasse) was entered by a rabble, led by the Bishop of Worms, charging the Jews with having poured water from the roofs of their houses upon the Bishop and the holy flags carried before him in procession. The noise and fury of the rabble, proceeding from all sides, was like the roaring of a terrible hurricane, and overreached the loud prayers and sighs of the inhabitants of that street, who, from fear and terror, had shut themselves up in their dwellings. " Death, death to all Jews!" was soon the dreadful outcry of the rabble, who persisted in their false accusation, and demanding a sacrifice to appease an offended divinity, as their Bishop was pleased to style it, in order to rouse the enraged multitude to excessive measures. All houses were broken into or destroyed, and the unfortunate inhabitants, both old and young, without exception, were dragged to an open place before the synagogue, being maltreated on the way. Hereupon the Rabbi began to address them in a loud

voice : " Dearly beloved and unfortunate brethren in Israel!
Blessed be God, the true Julge ; He gives life and takes it away.
He be praised in eternity. Have we been in anyways guilty and
deserving of our woe--and God does not punish in vain—then let us
gladly accept our lot from His hands, and joyfully to offer ourselves,
like our forefather, Isaac, as a sacrifice unto Him ; but, in case we
are not guilty, and God has ordained for us this heavy trial, then let
us remain steadfast and trust to His mercy. Is not to-day the
seventh day of the Pesach festival, on which our ancestors went
through the dried-up sea? We also should not fear the currents
which seem to surround us, for God is able to free us from the most
powerful floods. If, however, some one be amongst us who is guilty
of the charge we are accused of, then let him at once appear and
confess the deed, in order to avert the calamity from our entire
harmless congregation, and not do like Achan, who once brought
misfortune upon the innocent. He will have no share in eternal
life, and he is here and there condemned, who, by his guilt, causes a
guiltless life to be destroyed." The Rabbi was silent; but no one
came forth, for no one felt guilty of the accusation. Solemn silence
prevailed for a moment, and even the furious mob seemed almost to
have come to their senses ; but it did not last long, and very soon
the noise commenced afresh. " A sacrifice! a sacrifice !" shouted
the Bishop and the rabble; "an offended God requires it," and
already the enraged mob began to get ready their murderous
weapons, during which the loud and heart-rending cry of "Shema
Jisroel, adonay elohenu, adonay echod !" was sent on high, when two
men, tall and powerful, pressed through the throng and made their
way to the open place in front of the synagogue. Here they shouted
in a loud voice : " Stay, stay, for here are the guilty, and no one in
this congregation has offended your God." Surprise took hold of
the congregation, and the bloodthirsty mob felt satisfied and yet
dissatisfied. But quickly some wood was procured, a stake erected,
and the two men soon disappeared in the blazing flames ...not
a word more escaped their lips. Who these men really were, no one
ever knew. What their names were, or where they came from, no
one ever could tell. But the congregation was saved, and in gratitude therefor the two lights of that lamp are kept turning at all
times, which you, my dear reader, will perceive in the synagogue in
front of the Ark of the Covenant, and upon which the word,
"Shnee Orchim," are perceptible.

L. PHILIPPSON.

DR. L. PHILIPPSON, OF BONN, GERMANY—A
Jewish divine of great repute, editor of the
Allgemeine Zeitung des Judenthums; and
author of many other useful works, and
especially well-known for his untiring zeal in
all that concerns Judaism.

WORMS—A city on the left bank of the Rhine.
TRADITION—Accounts delivered from mouth
to mouth orally, from age to age.
ACHAN—An apostate in former times.
SHNEE ORCHIM (Hebrew)—Two strangers.

NARE TAMID.

CRUEL death, so wondrous mighty in thy power,
What harrowing sting is thine, in that last hour,
When human aid and skill no longer dare
Detain thy victims? Then, in wild despair,
We call upon our Maker to receive
The human soul so loved, for which we grieve.
And when the last faint sigh hath taken flight,
When the dear spirit, clad in garments white,

Sueth for admittance at the gates of heaven,
From which repentant mortal ne'er was driven ;
'Tis then we burn in memory of our dead,
As symbol of the soul so lately fled,
The sacred light ; to us it would appear
That, while it lasts, our dear ones still are near
In spirit ; and e'en though the frame may be
Enshrouded in the tomb, the soul is free.

J. M.

NARE TAMID (Hebrew)—Perpetual light.

THE BIBLE.

THE Bible, what a book! Large and wide as the world, based on the abysses of creation, and peering aloft into the blue secrets of heaven; sunrise and sunset, promise and fulfillment, birth and death, the whole drama of humanity are contained in this one book. It is the book of God. The Jews may readily be consoled at the loss of Jerusalem, and the Temple, and the Ark and the Covenant, and all the Crown jewels of King Solomon. Such forfeiture is as naught when weighed against the Bible, the indestructible treasure that they have saved. That one book is to the Jews their country, their possessions—at once their ruler, and their weal and woe. Within the well-fenced boundaries of that book they live and have their being; they enjoy their alienable citizenship, are strong to admiration; thence none can dislodge them. Absorbed in the perusal of their sacred book, they little heeded the changes that were wrought in the real world around them. Nations rose and vanished, states flourished and decayed, revolutions raged throughout the earth—but they, the Jews, sat poring over this book unconscious of the wild chase of time that rushed on above their heads.

HEINRICH HEINE.

H. Heine, one of the most renowned poets of Germany, whose numerous works are well known and have been translated into almost every European language.
ABYSS—A great depth.   To ABSORB—To swallow up.
DRAMA—A poem.   ALIENABLE—Withdrawn from.

SELF-SUPPORT.

WHOEVER has no possessions may be compared to a suckling babe which has lost its mother. Poor creature! It is handed about from one woman to another, but it does not thrive, because the love of the mother no one is able to supply. The man who is supported by others, were it even by his own father or mother, or his children, never feels that unspeakable contentment which he would otherwise experience in maintaining himself by his own exertions.

TALMUD.

PRIDE AND HUMILITY.

It requires but a slight breeze of ill-luck to cast down the proud, and quite right, too; for the immense ocean, which consists of many million drops of water, is nevertheless disturbed by the slightest breeze; and will there be anything more necessary to humble man, in whose veins only one drop of blood is flowing?

TALMUD.

JUSTICE.

Rabbi Samuel crossed a river in a boat, and, on reaching the shore, a man stretched his hand out, in order to help him to get safely on land. The same man appeared before him in a lawsuit. "Friend," said the learned Rabbi to him, "I cannot be your judge, because I am indebted to you for a service you have formerly rendered me."

TALMUD.

THE THREE NAMES.

Three names are given to man; one by his parents, another by the world, and the third by his works—the one which is written in the immortal book of his fate. Which of these names is the best? Solomon teaches us, when he says (Koheleth vii. 1.): "A good name is better than the sweetest oil."

TALMUD.

HAGAR.

The brazen, fiery sun is sinking now,
Yet in hot gusts the lifeless desert air
Scorches my throbbing temples through my hair,
And beats like burning kisses on my brow.

Athirst, I pant to taste the cooling breeze,
As, with spent breath and eyes with weeping dim,
I watch my little son and pray for him,
Where he lies fainting on my weary knees.

Young, princely face, grown strangely pale and mild,
Young limbs so motionless, young lips so dumb;
Oh! that some gracious angel would but come

And lay strong hands of healing on my child.
I see no place of rest on either hand,
I see no rock, I see no cooling well;
Jehovah will not pity Ishmael,
And we shall die in this accursed land.

Yea, hungering and thirsting, shall we die,
Like a fierce desert tigress and her young,
Who lie, with panting side and parched tongue,
On the hot stones, beneath the burning sky.

Yet, outcast, friendless, homeless, as we be,
Death is more merciful than life, I know,
And with submissive heart I wait to go
Into the pitiful eternity.

J. M.

THE KING OF KINGS.

THE King of Syria, at war with the King of Egypt, having conquered Palestine, became sole ruler of that country, for after the return of the Babylonian captivity the strife between the two countries continued, and only by paying tribute the people of Palestine were permitted to carry on their worship, and to serve the invisible God.

Thus, the King of Syria one day requested the High-priest to relate to him the wondrous powers of his God, and then remarked: "I honor your God, because I am told that He is great and mighty, but as He has allowed me to vanquish His people, I believe that my power cannot be altogether deficient, and therefore I deserve honor as well. I shall order a great feast in order to convince your God of my esteem, and I invite Him to be my guest on the occasion, and as I am sure that no one would decline my invitation, I hope you will not fail to attend to my commands, otherwise I shall hold you and your people responsible for the consequence." The High-priest, who had no chance to make a reply, raised his eyes on high to offer up a fervent prayer for the preservation of his people.

Everything was now got ready, great preparations were made in the palace garden adjacent to the sea-shore, where numberless tents, tables, chairs and all other necessaries had been arranged, whilst a variety of viands and luxuries were not wanting. When all was completed, the king informed the High-priest that he and his guests were ready to receive his God, to which the High-priest, who was occupied in prayer, made no reply. But amidst the festivities, made brilliant by splendid sunshine, there arose on a sudden a slight breeze, which gradually increased until the wind blew with some violence, and all at once a gust came, carrying away tents, tables, chairs and all the remaining portion of the preparations, sweeping them clear into the sea, the waters of which soon covered them. The king trembled and inquired of the High-priest the cause of this phenomenon. The High-priest answered: "My God is approaching; his servant, the wind, has just arrived in order to clear the place for his Almighty Master." The king grew pale, and fearing another gust would perhaps sweep him and his guests away, quickly replied: "Never mind. Your God need not come, for if the power of the servant is so great, what must be that of the Master?"

TALMUD.

UPRIGHTNESS.

RAB SAFRA had a valuable jewel for sale, and some merchants had offered him five gold pieces for the same, but he declined and demanded ten, which the merchants refused to give, and left him. After second consideration, he, however, resolved upon selling the jewel for five pieces. The next day, the merchants unexpectedly returned just at the time when Rab Safra was at prayers. "Sir," said they to him, "we come to you again in order to do business after all Do you wish to part with the jewel for the price we offered you?" But Rab Safra made no reply. "Well, well! don't get angry, we will add another two pieces." Rab Safra still remained silent "Well, then, be it as you say; you shall get the ten pieces, the price you require." By this time Rab Safra had just ended his prayer, and said: "Gentlemen, I was at prayers, and did not wish to be interrupted in my devotions. In regard to the price of the jewel, I have already resolved upon selling it at the price you offered me yesterday. If you then pay me five pieces of gold, I am satisfied; more I cannot take."   TALMUD.

FILIAL LOVE.

DAMA, a son of Netina, was a heathen, to whom once some customers came to buy goods for which they offered him a very high price, on account of being much in want of the articles for a certain purpose. "Friends," said he, "the key of the place where this particular kind of goods is stored away lies just under the pillow whereupon my father is now asleep; I dare not disturb my father's rest, and, therefore, cannot comply with your wish at the present moment, however tempting your offer may appear."   TALMUD.

SAUL AND THE WITCH OF EN-DOR.

Thou whose spell can raise the dead,
Bid the prophet's form appear,
"Samuel, raise the buried head!
King, behold the phantom seer!"

Earth yawn'd; he stood the centre of a cloud;
Light changed its hue, retiring from his shroud,
Death stood all glossy in his fixed eye;
His hand was wither'd, and his veins were dry;
His foot, in bony whiteness, glitter'd there,
Shrunken and sinewless, and ghastly bare;
From lips that moved not, and unbreathing frame,
Like cavern'd winds, the hollow accents came.
Saul saw, and fell to earth, as falls the oak,

At once, and blasted by the thunder stroke.

"Why is my sleep disquieted?
Who is he that calls the death?
Is it thou, O King? Behold,
Bloodless are these limbs, and cold;
Such are mine; and such shall be
Thine to-morrow, when with me;
Ere the coming day is done,
Such shalt thou be, such thy son.
Fare thee well, but for a day,
Then we mix our mouldering clay.
Thou, thy race, lie pale and low,
Pierced by shafts of many a bow;
And the falchion by thy side
To thy heart thy hand shall guide:
Crownless, breathless, headless fall,
Son and sire, the house of Saul!"

                        BYRON.

LORD BYRON was born in London (England), January 22, 1788, and died April 19, 1824, at Missolonghi, Greece. One of England's greatest poets and r voluminous writer.
FALCHION—A short crooked sword.

JOYOUSNESS.

How pleasantly and with what happy results we journey on through life, if we always endeavor to be joyful in all our daily actions! We increase, moreover, the happiness of our neighbor by pouring the balm of consolation into suffering and devoted hearts. The weary laborer, returning from his daily toil, finds joy in his household whenever his family are cheerful toward him in all their intercourse. He remembers with pleasure, then, that a joyful soul is ever resigned to the lot marked out for him by a merciful Creator; and that if he bears up under all his misfortunes his joy in the life to come will be such as never can be conceived by man until he enters the kingdom of joy, so great will be his happiness.

It is, moreover, always in our power to do something to alleviate the miseries of those around us. The friendless, for instance, we can comfort by trying to elevate their condition in all that concerns their welfare in this life; the ignorant we can assist by giving them our best admonition, instructing them in every way possible for their temporal happiness. The broken-hearted and dispirited we can console by a kind word of sympathy, telling them that it is a holy resolution to assist their fellow-being in every way—for their advantage through life – telling them of the reward which the Creator has in store for them; and thus we can in several ways assist every one needing our advice, ever believing that God will reward us, and that He never will be outdone in generosity to all His faithful servants.   H. O.

GOD'S LOVE TO ISRAEL.

A GREAT king informed his friend that he would come to visit him on a certain day, and the friend made up his mind that the king would surely come incognito or at night, inasmuch as his poor hut was too miserable a place to hold such greatness. But, think of his astonishment, when one day the king made his appearance, sitting upon his noble steed, clad in purple, and accompanied by a numerous retinue. "I have come," said he, "in all my splendor, in order to show you before all the world how much I am attached to you."

Thus it was with Israel, when God announced to them that He would dwell in the Tabernacle; they still thought, Will God in His whole glory condescend to dwell among men here on earth?

And, behold! scarcely was the Tabernacle consecrated, when the Divine cloud beamed forth, and the Divine light surrounded and enveloped the same; it was in like manner when the same Divine cloud appeared in its whole mysterious grandeur on Sinai, and thus God bestowed on Israel the greatest token of His love.

TALMUD.

CHARITY RECONCILES MAN WITH GOD.

He who is unfortunate and is continually struggling with poverty, is often enticed, on account of his sufferings, to murmur against an all-wise Providence. He frequently thinks: "Am I not also God's creature? Why does there exist such difference between myself and the wealthy. He sleeps quietly in his splendid mansion, and I have to lay in my miserable hut; he sleeps in his soft bed, and I am obliged to take my rest on the hard floor."

The charitable person by his liberality pacifies the complaints of the poor, and thus puts him to silence at once. God says to these charitable persons: "By your liberality you reconcile the poor man with Myself; you make peace between us." Talmud.

CHEER UP.

Cheer up! my friend, cheer up, I say;
Give not thy heart to gloom, to sorrow;
Though clouds enshroud thy path to-day,
The sun will shine again to-morrow.

Oh! look not with desponding sigh
Upon these little trifling troubles;
Cheer up! you'll see them by-and-by
Just as they are—like empty bubbles.

So come, cheer up! my friend, cheer up!
This is a world of love and beauty;
And you may quaff its sweetest cup
If you but bravely do your duty.

Put gloom and sadness far away,
And, smiling, bid good-bye to sorrow;
The clouds that shroud your path to-day
Will let the sunlight in to-morrow.
Adapted.

ISRAEL'S PRIVILEGE.

A certain king constantly reminded his servant to take care of a purple cloak, to clean, to brush, to fold it properly and to pay great attention in preserving the same ; and this caution he repeated to the servant continually. One day, however, the servant could not refrain from addressing the king in these words : "Great king, thou hast hundreds of purple garments not less beautiful than this, and yet thou always remindest me in regard to this particular cloak only?" The king replied : "This one I like best, because I wore it on the day when I was placed on the throne."

In the same manner said Moses, when God gave him hundreds of commandments for Israel. "Oh, my God! Thou hast hundreds of nations on earth, and yet Thou speakest continually to me of Israel, and it is always Israel to which Thou callest my attention?"

Whereupon God said : "They are all my people, but this one nation I love best because it was the first to proclaim My kingdom upon earth." Talmud.

TWOFOLD JOY.

Two vessels sail on the ocean at one and the same time ; the one is leaving, the other entering, the harbor. For the one which is leaving a number of friends had prepared a great feast, and with clapping of hands, and loud vociferations of joy, they celebrated her departure, whilst the one which entered no one seemed to notice. An intelligent man, who was a spectator of what passed, said: "Here quite the reverse appears to take place, as otherwise ought to happen. They rejoice over the one which departs, and feel indifferent toward the other which returns. What a fallacy! Rejoice over the one which has accomplished its voyage, and is returning from many dangers in safety; and bewail rather the vessel which is departing, for she will thus be exposed to the storms of an inconstant sea." The same when man is born, great rejoicing takes place, whilst at his death much grief is expressed. One ought to weep at his birth, because no one is certain whether he will be able to overcome the dangers and temptations of life; whilst at his death one ought to feel pleased, if he only leaves a good name behind him. At his birth, man is entered in the book of death; when he dies he is entered in the book of life. TALMUD.

THE BEAUTIES OF NATURE.

PAUSE awhile, ye downcast and disconsolate tenants of earth! Raise your bowed heads and look upward! Behold the vast panorama which nature has spread out for your study and contemplation! If you look at the blue concave heavens over your heads, on a clear night, you will behold it bedecked with myriads upon myriads of sparkling gems, outvying in beauty the most resplendent coronet that ever adorned the head of any earthly potentate.

"The heavens declare the glory of God, and the firmament showeth His handiwork." If these are glorious, what must be the glory of Him who created them! What a magnificent temple for the worship of that Almighty Being "who stretcheth out the heavens like a curtain, and who laid the foundations of the earth that it should not be removed forever."

Look abroad over the earth. What a prospect is spread out before you! What an endless variety of configuration—hill and valley, mountain and plain, rivers, lakes, seas, cataracts are presented to your enraptured view! If you look over the illimitable ocean, and behold its heavings, its turbulences and ceaseless agitations, the mind is overwhelmed with awe and admiration at the works of the Lord, and His wonders in the deep! Look at the earth in the various changes of the seasons. Now it reposes for a while in the icy embrace of winter; now it is decorated with the verdure and flowers of spring; now it smiles in the luxuriance of summer; anon it is laden with the rich bounties of autumn, affording sustenance for every living creature.

Look up, ye desponding children of earth, to that kind and beneficent Father whose watchful care is ever over you, and whose faithfulness is pledged to supply your every need. He opens His hand and supplies the wants of every living thing. Surely the earth is

full of the goodness of the Lord ! Let His wisdom and goodness fill
your hearts with gratitude and love !   ADAPTED.

ILLIMITABLE—Without limits.
PANORAMA—Complete or entire view.
CONCAVE—Hollow.
MYRIADS—10,000; proverbially, any great
number.

RESPLENDENT—Bright, beautiful lustre.
CORONET—An inferior crown worn by no-
bility.
POTENTATE—Monarch, prince,

THERE IS A GOD.

THE one who says there is no God,
  Should study nature's laws;
From worlds in space, down to our sod,
  There's naught without a cause;
The laws which govern earth and sky,
To God's existence testify.

Look at the earth, see how plants grow
  Out of a little seed;
If one would only wish to know
  His God, this he would heed;
For plants all grow by certain laws,
Of which our God's the only cause.

Let him who doth his God deny,
  The stars of heaven trace;
See how each world doth occupy
  A certain part of space;

There're made and moved by certain
  laws,
Of which our God's the only cause.

Year after year, from west to east,
  Our planet round doth go;
And ev'ry star, to say the least,
  Some motion has, we know;
These laws of motion tidings bring
Of God, the everlasting King.

Who made the laws which govern
  space ?
  Who maketh grow each seed ?
Who gives each starry world its place,
  And bids it onward speed ?
'Tis God, the King of earth and sky,
Who lives on earth and dwells on high.
                              M. LEHMEYER.

HOPE.

MAN's dearest possession is hope. When that which we hold
most precious is taken away from us, and all the chords of the heart
mourn and bewail the loss, then after awhile from the most hidden
recess of our bosom proceeds a low, but sweet whisper, which
silences the wild outbreaks of despair, and softens down the grief
to faithful submission and willingness of the heart to be afflicted.
These sacred sounds, with their soothing power, are the language of
hope in the soul of man. Hope is like a nurse. If she is mercenary, I would not trust my soul to her charge; if she is the true, devoted friend, then she will never break faith toward her trusted
nursling.

Mercenary hopes are the whimsical expectations of a covetous
heart. They never satisfy, and never are to be satisfied; the more
you give them the more they ask, and forever they keep the minds
of their votaries in a morbid state of suspense. Genuine hope is the
child of faith, and, therefore, proves always faithful. It does not make
its promises dependent on vague uncertainties that may and may
not come to pass. It relies on the unfailing wisdom and mercy of
Providence, and therefore it never fails. Mercenary hope makes us

impatient, passionate, and thereby undermines the strength to endure and causes the loss of success. Spiritual hope arms those that enlist under her banner with the irresistible weapon of resignation; she enables them to withstand the tribulations of the present, and wait patiently and quietly until the tempest is followed by more genial weather, and thus spiritual hope is a more reliable guide even to material results.

The patriarch Jacob sends his favorite child on a short errand; he will see him soon again. The beloved son, however, never returns; all that is left to him is the bloody coat, which is brought to the unhappy father with the cold question, Acknowledge whether it be thy son's coat or not? Jacob mourns his son for a long, long period. He hopes to meet him only in that land where there is no parting. He abides patiently his time until his Maker will call him. Twenty-two years have passed since that terrible moment when he exclaimed, " I must go down unto my son mourning into the grave;" and, after these many years, behold! like cold water to a fainting soul, comes from a far country the good news to him, " Joseph is yet alive, and he is governor over all the lands of Egypt." His heart gave way under these tidings, but his spirit soon revived. The heart is weak, but the spirit is strong. Spiritualize your hopes and that will strengthen your hearts, and will bring a never-failing fulfillment to your cleansed expectations. In the sultry hours of your life, approach with love the sacred shrine of your sanctuary, and the word of the Lord will prove its effect on you. As cold water is to a fainting soul, so will be the glad tidings of the spiritual region to your minds.   Dr. HUEBSCH.

[Adapted from a lecture delivered by Dr. Huebsch, Minister of " Ahavath Chesed," New York.]

THE FUTURE OF THE JEW.

What has prevented this constantly migrating people, this veritable Wandering Jew, from degenerating into brutalized vagabonds, into vagrant hordes of gypsies? The answer is at hand. In its journey through the desert of life, for eighteen centuries, the Jewish people carried along the Ark of the Covenant, which breathed into its heart ideal aspirations, and even illuminated the badge of disgrace affixed to its garment with an apostolic glory. The proscribed, outlawed, universally persecuted Jew felt a sublime, noble pride in being singled out to perpetuate and to suffer for a religion which reflects eternity, by which the nations of the earth were gradually educated to a knowledge of God and morality, and from which is to spring the salvation and redemption of the world. The consciousness of his glorious apostolic office sustained the sufferer, and even stamped the sufferings as a portion of the sublime mission.

Such a people, which disdained its present, but has the eye

steadily fixed on its future, which lives, as it were, on hope, is, on that very account, eternal like hope.   H. Graetz.

Degenerate—Base.
Apostolic—A person sent with a charge.

To Perpetuate—To continue.

THE BETTER LAND.

" I hear thee speak of the better land,
Thou call'st its children a happy band;
Mother! Oh, where is that radiant
      shore?
Shall we not seek it and weep no more?
Is it where the flower of the orange
      blows,
And the fire-flies dance through the
      myrtle boughs?"
" Not there, not there, my child!"

"Is it where the feathery palm trees rise?
And the date grows ripe under sunny
      skies?
Or 'mid the green islands of glittering
      seas,
Where fragrant forests perfume the
      breeze,
And strange, bright birds, on their
      starry wings
Bear the rich hues of all glorious
      things?"
" Not there, not there, my child!"

" Is it far away in some region old,
Where the rivers wander o'er sands of
      gold,
Where the burning rays of the ruby
      shine,
And the diamond lights up the secret
      mine,
And the pearl gleams forth from the
      coral strand?
Is it there, sweet mother, that better
      land?"
" Not there, not there, my child!"

" Eye hath not seen it, my gentle boy!
Ear hath not heard its deep sounds of
      joy,
Dreams cannot picture a world so fair,
Sorrow and death may not enter there;
Time does not breathe on its fadeless
      bloom,
Beyond the clouds and beyond the
      tomb;
It is there, it is there, my child!"
                         Adapted.

WOMAN'S FRIENDSHIP.

The love of women for women has frequently been sneered at by shallow minds. The idea of lasting affection between them has not seldom been the subject of cheap satire and pointless wit. Pliant argument has been used to give support, or the appearance of it, to the theory. The impossibility of sincere friendship between women is explained upon the fact that not being schooled in the ways of the world, in the art of disguising their sentiments, mere passing dislikes and groundless suspicions are uttered forth to the destruction of lasting intercourse. In a word, woman's honesty of speech is declared to be the bar to the honesty of her friendship. A preposterous paradox, and one that reflects severely upon the friendship of men toward men. If such be the pillar on which man's friendship rests, sung by poets, extolled by philosophers, eulogized by our own David, woman may scorn friendship based upon deceit. But, in reality, such critics are like the ignorant people who trample on the sand or the grass without a thought of the thousand marvels which cluster around each grain. each blade, but which are enough to stagger wise men. Woman's heart, a common thing, contains marvels that we may wonder at, but not explain. Woman's un-guarded speech? As if all the hasty utterances in the world, as if the most bitter expressions that tongue ever fabricated, ever killed a mother's love for her daughter. Say that men cherish hasty words, brood over them, nurse them like torpid vipers in their bosom, till the warmth of their own vengefulness and unforgiveness rouses them to life, to lacerate them unto death, but say not that women treasure hasty speech.

That a daughter's love can be undying, too, Ruth shows us. All a woman's holier instincts are toward matrimony. Not for her own good was she made, but to perfect man. Ruth had lost her hus-band; the cup of wedded happiness had been dashed from her lips; she renounced all hope of future wedded bliss to follow an old and broken woman. Naomi bade her stay and marry in Moab; she refused. Her sister did remain; she refused. Animated with true friendship, with woman's friendship, the world's literature, which has had centuries to improve on it, can furnish no more touching response: the refined feeling of enlightened age has never brought out a holier devotion than in the reply, " Urge me not to leave thee ; whither thou goest I will go. Away with all thoughts of my welfare ; whither thou goest, I will go, broken and heart-stricken, sad and desolate, where God's hand and man's are surest upon thee. Urge me not to leave thee ; whither thou goest I will go !" Long may these words be preserved to fire the souls of such women as Ruth. You may not have the same opportunity, but each, in your own degree, can emulate heathen Ruth. Aye, a heathen she was—an unenlightened, idolatrous heathen—but she married into our faith, adopted it, and her great-grandson, David, inherited his ances-tor's nobility. The material is in our women—it needs but the spark to fire it—and I fear not that when sad misfortune lowers, we have yet to hear of many a noble Ruth. Long may this Book, the personification of woman's devotion, be preserved, to be read and reread, to make us meditate upon the life and deeds of Naomi's granddaughter, Moabite Ruth. Dr. Mendes.

[From a lecture delivered by Dr. F. De Sola Mendes, minister of Congregation " Shaary-Teflla," N. Y.]

Paradox—An assertion contrary to appear- | Preposterous—Wrong, absurd.
ance.

THE SHUNAMITE'S REPLY.

II. Kings iv. : 13.

" And she answered, ' I dwell among my own people, I dwell among my own.' "

Oh ! happy thou !
Not for the sunny clusters of the vine,
Nor for the olives on the mountain's brow ;

Nor the flocks wandering by the flow-ing line
Of streams, that made the green land where they shine

Laugh to the light of waters ;—not for
these,
Nor the soft shadow of ancestral trees,
Whose kindly whisper floats o'er thee
and thine.
Oh ! not for *these* I call thee richly
blest,
But for the meekness of thy woman's
breast,

Where that sweet depth of still contentment lies ;
And for thy holy household love, which
clings
Unto all ancient and familiar things,
Weaving from each some links for
home's dear charities.

MRS. HEMANS.

FEMALE INFLUENCE.

WHEN we analyze the various remedies which have been recommended to heal the disease which afflicts Israel, undermining its
spiritual health—indifference—after the most minute analysis one
must arrive at the conclusion that female influence is the best
remedy that can and should be employed. Religious education has
its advocates, and will tend in a great measure to benefit the col-
lective body ; but must inevitably fail to produce the desired effect
unless strengthened by the wide-spreading influence of the "mothers
in Israel." Let not mothers or daughters exclaim, "What can we
do ? We are willing to contribute our portion to the alleviation of
Israel's spiritual condition, but we are subjected to the control of
our husbands, and it is they that should be admonished and
reproved, not we. Their indifference on religious matters has such
an influence that, even with the best intentions, we find our efforts
frustrated, until at last we act as they do, and banish religion from
our homes, doing this for the sake of peace." Have the women of
Israel yet to be told that true peace can only be found where
religion prevails, and that their influence rightly directed establishes
concord and happiness on a permanent basis.

From our earliest records we find that women exercised an influence indescribable ; as said by one of our sages : "But for woman,
Moses would never have been our law-giver." What nobler example
need we adduce of woman's influence in a semi-barbarous period,
and has woman's influence degenerated in our so-called enlightened
age ? We will not, cannot believe it. We are well aware that they
have difficulties to encounter. There appears to be a determination
with some thoughtless beings to surrender all that was wont to be
held sacred ; but knowing woman's influence, we entreat them to
exercise their power to check this spirit of error, and their efforts
cannot fail to be beneficial. Let them exercise their undoubted
power over their husbands, and their efforts, if directed in the cause
of religion, will ultimately prevail. The men, struggling against the
foaming stream of society, unsuccessful in their transactions, often-
times come home to their families morose and discontented. It
becomes women to soften what is hard, make smooth what is rough,
and send a ray of light through the clouded sky. By their words

they can teach their husbands resignation ; by their influence and their example they can instruct them in religion, and cause them to say in the midst of their despondency: "It is well to be nearer to God." Let them not mistrust their power, and employ their trite expression : " What can we do ?" By their example they can bring back to religion and worship the spirit which only needs a true woman's guide. Do they doubt this? Let history dispel all such misgiving, for it clearly proves their influence. Need we demonstrate this by what they did for the living? How often they caused the waverer to become strong in the faith ! See what woman did for the dead ! How Ayah's daughter took sackcloth, and sitting upon the rock from the beginning of the harvest, guarded those who had been executed, so that neither the birds of heaven nor the beasts of the field should rest on them. Would any man have performed so herculean a task? It was woman, totally regardless of self, who watched them by day and by night ; and so powerful was her influence, that David took not only their bones, but also that of Saul and Jonathan, and buried them in the sepulchre of Kirsh. But why require further evidence? The last chapter of Proverbs, written by the sapient king, fully portrays the influence of woman.

As it was in days of old, so it is now. If women employ the golden key of religion and benevolence, they will impress the heart by their influence ; if they permit the key to corrode, the heart will remain closed against every attempt to open it. It was not without an object that King Solomon said, "Forsake not thy mother's laws." This was directed to husbands as well as to children. Of husbands we have already spoken, but women's influence over their children requires especial attention. If by their pious example and their never-failing persuasive language they bestow upon their children religious knowledge, they will accustom them to religious acts, and their exertions will not be in vain. They will reap a harvest of blessings ; their children will become such as our religion requires— enlightened, strong in their faith, unshaken in their observances ; they will honor God, love their parents, and their affection will give every comfort to those who educate them by their example. But if, on the reverse, mothers neglect their sacred duty, or, as an excuse for their shortcomings, blame their husbands—and, with regret be it said, the fathers often deserve the blame then they will be punished by the indifference and probably by the disrespect of their offspring, who in maturer ages will probably say: "We knew nothing of our religion or its ceremonies ; the voice of prayer never illumined our dwellings ; everything prohibited by Jewish law was permitted in our homes ; our mothers taught us nothing of our religious duties." Will not these words be a reproach that will torment them and follow them to the grave ? In making this appeal to woman, knowing their influence, we would not, even in the remotest degree, re-

flect on them as being unmindful of some portion of a woman's
duty, but we would have them use their power and example to promote the observances of their religion. The true Jewish woman
who can be pious without bigotry practices them with punctuality
and devotion. If she will but employ her immense influence, she
will exercise such irresistible attraction that she will succeed in winning her whole family over to her ideas and convictions, and their
words will be : "Only the woman who fears the Lord shall be
praised."   S. M. ISAACS.

Rev. Samuel M. Isaacs was born in Lewarden, Holland, in 1804, and died May 26, 1878. He
was for many years Rabbi of Shaary Tefila Congregation, New York, and the founder of the
Jewish Messenger. He was noted for his piety and the blamelessness of his life, which endeared him to people of all classes and creeds.

ANALYSIS—A solution of anything into its several parts.

HERCULEAN—Having extraordinary strength.
SAPIENT—Wise, sage.

RESOLUTION OF RUTH.

FAREWELL? Oh, no! it may not be ;
My firm resolve is heard on high ;
I will not breathe farewell to thee,
Save only in my dying sigh.
I know not that I now could bear
Forever from thy side to part,
And live without a friend to share
The treasured sadness of my heart.

I did not love, in former years,
To leave thee solitary now ;
When sorrow dims thine eyes with tears,
And shades the beauty of thy brow,
I'll share the trial and the pain ;
And strong the furnace fires must be
To melt away the willing chain
That binds a daughter's heart to thee.

I will not boast a martyr's might,
To leave my home without a sigh ;
The dwelling of my past delight,
The shelter where I hoped to die.
In such a duty, such an hour,
The weak are strong, the timid brave,
For love puts on an angel's power,
And faith grows mightier than the grave.

It was not so, ere he we loved,
And vainly strove with Heaven to save,
Heard the low call of death, and moved
With holy calmness to the grave,
Just at that brightest hour of youth,

When life spread out before us lay,
And charmed us with its tones of truth,
And colors radiant as the day.

When morning's tears of joy were shed,
Or nature's evening incense rose,
We thought upon the grave with dread,
And shuddered at its dark repose.
But all is altered now : of death
The morning echoes sweetly speak,
And like my loved one's dying breath,
The evening breezes fan my cheek.

For rays of heaven, serenely bright,
Have gilt the caverns of the tomb,
And I can ponder with delight
On all its gathering thoughts of gloom.
Then, mother, let us haste away
To that blessed land to Israel given,
Where faith, unsaddened by decay,
Dwells nearest to its native heaven.

We'll stand within the Temple's bound,
In courts by kings and prophets trod ;
We'll bless with tears the sacred ground,
And there be earnest with our God ;
Where peace and praise forever reign,
And glorious anthems duly flow.
Till seraphs learn to catch the strain
Of heaven's devotions here below.

But where thou goest, I will go,

With thine my earthly lot is cast ;
In pain and pleasure, joy and woe,
Will I attend thee to the last.
That hour shall find me by thy side,

And where thy grave is, mine shall
be;
Death can but for a time divide
My firm and faithful heart from thee.

ADAPTED.

To PONDER—To consider. | ANTHEM—A holy song.

PERSONAL RELIGION.

POLITICAL eminence and professional fame fade away and die with all things earthly Nothing of character is really permanent but virtue and personal worth. These remain. Whatever of excellence is wrought into the soul itself belongs to both worlds. *Real* goodness does not attach itself merely to this life; it points to another world. Political or professional reputation cannot last forever; but a conscience void of offence toward God and man is an inheritance for eternity.

Religion, therefore, is a necessary and indispensable element in any great human character. There is no living without it. Religion is the tie that connects man with his Creator, and holds him to His throne. If that tie be all sundered, all broken, he floats away, a worthless atom in the universe, its proper attractions all gone, its destiny thwarted, and its whole future nothing but darkness, desolation, and death. A man with no sense of religious duty is he whom the Scriptures describe, in such terse but terrific language, as living "without God in the world." Such a man is out of his proper being—out of the circle of all his duties, and out of the circle of all his happiness, and away, far, *far* away, from the purposes of his creation. DANIEL WEBSTER.

Daniel Webster, a lawyer and statesman, was born in Salisbury, New Hampshire, Jan. 18, 1782, and died October 24, 1852 He was for 30 years in the public service, as a Representative in Congress, or Senator, or Secretary of State. He was a man of great intellectual powers.

EMINENCE—Distinction. | To THWART—To oppose.
REPUTATION—Honor. | TERSE—Neatness of style.

THE GREATEST TREASURE.

A THIEF once broke into a palace. His feet were arrested on the threshold by all the splendor that he beheld. There were so many valuable articles of silver and gold that he could not decide which to choose. Here shone precious stones set in a crown of gold; while there lay a diadem studded with most valuable diamonds. Riches on all sides wherever his eyes wandered. From time to time he stretched forth his hands to grasp something, but always hesitated, as his sinful, avaricious eyes fell on something that seemed more valuable. Presently he spied another door; he opened it, and entered another chamber. What did he see? Could such things be real, or was he dreaming? No: here were displayed all

the riches the world affords. Tables, chairs, ottomans, and vases
of solid gold, ornamented with myriads of pearls and other precious
stones. The brilliancy dazzled the thief's eyes; he thought he was
in fairyland. But he did not stay long; wandered from room to
room, lost in amazement and admiration. He could not decide
what to choose, because he feared that if he took some of the splendid articles he might leave the richest. While he was hesitating he
heard loud footsteps on the stone pavement in front of the palace.
His comrades called to him to come out. Day had dawned, and he
must fly. Leaving all the treasures he had beheld, he made his
escape, rejoicing that he was able to save his life and get out of the
palace undiscovered. A rabbi once told this to his congregation,
and as they looked up into his face inquiringly, he continued: "So
it is with man. God, the Almighty, gives him life. He enters the
world - the magnificent palace. Is there anything more beautiful
and more valuable than life itself on this wonderful earth, with its
green mountains and hills, its sunshine and fresh air? But men fly
from one pleasure to another, always seeking for more and more. The
possession of one blessing only makes them desire another, and fills
them with discontent if they cannot obtain it. They become satiated,
and, like the thief, throw away the pearls only to seize the diamonds.
Virtue and justice, charity and humanity, are more to be desired
than all the pleasures and luxuries of life. While men spend their
time striving after wealth and position, death overtakes them, as day
did the thief, unawares, and they are called to appear before their
Creator, naked as they came into the world, without the treasures
that once lay within their reach, lamenting their lost hopes, their
lost, wasted lives. '   S. F. P.

SHABUOTH.

Let praise and song and psalmody   It leads us to the realms of light
In chorus rise to God on high !   Upon our path through earthly night,
For He hath made this glorious day !   And sanctifies our life and will.
Be glad ! Rejoice ! Hallelujah !   Our duty ever to fulfill.

From heaven came in brilliant rays   Let praise and song and psalmody
The law, which shines on all our ways;   In chorus rise to God on high !
Its gentle light now casts its beams   For He hath made this glorious day !
On all that dark and hidden seems.   Be glad ! Rejoice ! Hallelujah !
                                              JAMES K. GUTHEIM.

Rev. James K. Gutheim, minister of the Sinai Congregation, New Orleans, is noted for
his beautiful compositions and translations of devotional hymns.

SELF-MADE MEN.

ONE of the most common excuses which young men make for not
trying to improve their talents is that they are poor, and have no
means of acquiring an education, and no rich or influential friends to
assist them in life.

Young man! You need no assistance. It would hinder rather than facilitate your progress. If you have the will and resolution which you ought to possess, and that manly self-reliance which is indispensable to success in every department of life, you have all the assistance you need. With these you may overcome every obstacle, and attain to eminence in any position which you may be called to fill.

Let any young man select from his acquaintance a number of the most prominent men of any profession—men who are distinguished for talents or public usefulness—and he will find that they are all, with scarcely any exception, men who began the world without a dollar. Look into the public councils of the nation; and who are they that take the lead in all its controlling interests? They are men who began the world with nothing, and have made their own fortunes.

The rule is universal. It pervades our Courts, both State and Federal, from the highest to the lowest. It is true of all the professions. It is so now; it has ever been so since we became a nation; and will be so while our present institutions continue. And the history of the prominent men of this country is but a repetition of the history of the most distinguished men of all other countries.

A young man must be thrown upon his own resources in order to bring out his capabilities. The struggle which is to result in eminence is too arduous, and must be continued too long, to be encountered and maintained voluntarily. It must be a struggle, as it were, for life itself. He who has a fortune to fall back upon will soon slacken his efforts, and finally retire from the contest.

It is, therefore, a question whether it is desirable that a parent should leave his son any property at all, if he desires him to rise to eminence in any department of life. Said an eminent jurist to a young man of fortune, who wished to enter upon the study of the law, "You will have a large fortune, and I am sorry for it, as it will be the means of spoiling a good lawyer."   ADAPTED.

To FACILITATE—To make easy.   FEDERAL—Relating to a league or contract.
EMINENCE—Loftiness; reputation.   CAPABILITIES—Capacity; power.

AN ANECDOTE OF CREMIEUX.

IN the year 1823, Adolph Cremieux, then thirty-two years of age, made his first trip to Paris. Near Lyons he began a conversation with a man who was party to a divorce case which was to be tried in that city. The man greatly feared that he would lose his case. "I have already paid my lawyer," said he to Cremieux, "and that's what bothers me. He looks at things in the wrong light—I will be defeated."

"When is your suit to be tried?" Cremieux asked him, as they left the mail-coach at Lyons.

"To-day—this morning."

"Very well; go at once to your lawyer and make him return your documents; I pledge myself to bring you out of your troubles."

Two hours later, after he had hastily glanced at the evidence, Cremieux electrified the Court by a brilliant and fiery speech. He wins his case and leaves the court-room immediately after the session, in order to proceed on his journey.

His client accompanies him to the coach and offers him a fee of two thousand francs. Cremieux declines it, saying, "Give the money to the poor; I don't want any of it ; I have conducted your case as an artist, merely to relieve the tedium of the journey; and now shake hands—good-night."

The Lyons journals printed full accounts of the occurrence, and before he arrived Paris had heard of it. As he entered the Palace of Justice, he received an ovation, and the younger lawyers held a meeting and tendered him a banquet.   ADAPTED.

ADOLPH CREMIEUX was born in the year 1796, and became one of the foremost lawyers belonging to the French bar. He defended the famous Polignac, Prime Minister of Charles X. In 1848 he was chosen a member of the Provisional Government under Lamartine and was Minister of Justice and Religion. He is the founder of the "Alliance Israelite Universelle," pleaded the cause of his co-religionists on all occasions both at home and abroad, and there are few names more endeared to the hearts of Israelites than that of the late Adolph Cremieux.

CARVING A NAME.

I WROTE my name upon the sand,
  And trusted it would stand for aye;
But soon, alas ! the refluent sea
  Had washed my feeble lines away.

I carved my name upon the wood,
  And, after years, returned again;
I missed the shadow of the tree
  That stretched of old upon the plain.

To solid marble next my name
  I gave as a perpetual trust;
An earthquake rent it to its base,
  And now it lies o'erlaid with dust.

All these have failed. In wiser mood
  I turn and ask myself, "What
    then ?"
If I would have my name endure,
  I'll write it on the hearts of men

"In characters of living light,
  From kindly words and actions
    wrought,
And these, beyond the reach of Time,
  Shall live immortal as my thought."

ADAPTED.

THE PROGRESS OF HUMANITY.

LET us, then, be of good cheer. From the great Law of Progress we may derive at once our duties and our encouragements. Humanity has ever advanced, urged by the instincts and necessities implanted by God, thwarted sometimes by obstacles which have caused it for a time a moment only, in the immensity of ages—to deviate from its true line, or to seem to retreat—but still ever onward.

Amidst the disappointments which may attend individual exertions, amidst the universal agitations which now surround us, let us recognize this law, confident that whatever is just, whatever is humane, whatever is good, whatever is true, according to an immutable ordinance of Providence, in the golden light of the future, must prevail. With this faith, let us place our hands, as those of little children, in the great hand of God. He will ever guide and sustain us—through pains and perils, it may be—in the path of Progress.

In the recognition of this law, there are motives to beneficent activity, which shall endure to the last syllable of life. Let the young embrace it; they shall find in it an ever-living spring. Let the old cherish it still; they shall derive from it fresh encouragement. It shall give to all, both old and young, a new appreciation of their existence, a new sentiment of their force, a new revelation of their destiny.

Be it, then, our duty and our encouragement to live and to labor, ever mindful of the future. But let us not forget the past. All ages have lived and labored for us. From one has come art, from another jurisprudence, from another the compass, from another the printing press; from all have proceeded priceless lessons of truth and virtue. The earliest and most distant times are not without a present influence on our daily lives. The mighty stream of Progress, though fed by many tributary waters and hidden springs, derives something of its force from the earlier currents which leap and sparkle in the distant mountain recesses, over precipices, among rapids, and beneath the shade of primeval forests.

Nor should we be too impatient to witness the fulfillment of our aspirations. The daily increasing rapidity of discovery and improvement, and the daily multiplying efforts of beneficence, in later years outstripping the imaginations of the most sanguine, furnish well-grounded assurance that the advance of man will be with a constantly accelerating speed. The extending intercourse among the nations of the earth, and among all the children of the human family, gives new promises of the complete diffusion of Truth, penetrating the most distant places, clearing away the darkness of night, and exposing the hideous forms of slavery, of war, of wrong, which must be hated as soon as they are clearly seen.

Cultivate, then, a just moderation. Learn to reconcile order with change, stability with progress. This is a wise conservatism; this is a wise reform. Rightly understanding these terms, who would not be a Conservative? who would not be a Reformer?—a conservative of all that is good, a reformer of all that is evil; a conservative of knowledge, a reformer of ignorance; a conservative of truths and principles whose seat is the bosom of God, a reformer of laws and institutions which are but the wicked or imperfect work of man; a conservative of that divine order which is found only in movement, a reformer of those earthly wrongs and abuses which spring from a violation of the great law of Human Progress. Blending these two characters in one, let us seek to be, at the same time, Reforming Conservatives, and Conservative Reformers. CHARLES SUMNER.

CHARLES SUMNER was born in Boston, January 6, 1811, and graduated at Harvard College in 1830, and admitted to the Bar in 1834. He was chosen Senator for Massachusetts in 1851, and noted for his learning, his eloquence and his peaceful sentiments against the war system of nations; and all institutions of slavery he assailed with his utmost rigor.

JURISPRUDENCE—Science of law.
PRIMEVAL—Original, that which was at first.
To OUTSTRIP—To out-go.

To ACCELERATE—To hasten.
CONSERVATISM—The desire of preserving the established laws and customs.

JEWISH EMANCIPATION.

(Maiden Speech of Alderman David Solomons, in the British Parliament, July 18, 1851.)

"I SHOULD not have presumed to address you, sir, and this house, in the peculiar position in which I am placed, had it not been that I have been so pointedly appealed to by the honorable gentleman who has just sat down. I hope some allowance will be made for the novelty of my position, and for the responsibility that I feel in the unusual course which I have judged it right to adopt; but I beg to assure you, sir, and this house, that it is far from my desire to do anything that may appear contumacious or presumptuous. Returned, as I have been, by a large constituency, and under no disability, and believing that I have fulfilled all the requirements of the law, I thought that I should not be doing justice to my own position as an Englishman or a gentleman, did I not adopt that course which I believed to be right and proper, and appear on this floor, not meaning any disrespect to you, sir, or to this house, but in defence of my own rights and privileges, and of the rights and privileges of the constituents who have sent me here. Having said this, I beg to state to you, sir, that whatever be the decision of the house, I shall abide by it, provided there be just sufficient force to make me feel that I am acting under coercion. I shall not now further intrude myself upon the house, except to say that I trust and hope that, in the doubtful state of the law, such as it has been described to be by the eminent lawyers who addressed you, no final order or resolution in reference to me or my constituents will be adopted without giving me the fairest opportunity of addressing this house, and stating before the house and before the country what I believe to be the duty of this house. I hope this house will not refuse that which no court ever refuses to the meanest subject of the realm, but will hear me before its final decision is announced. L. I. CH.

ALD. DAVID SOLOMONS was a pious Israelite and a native of England, and by profession a lawyer. He was elected Lord Mayor of London, became M. P. for Greenwich, and made a Brt. by Queen Victoria. He was also during a number of years president of the London and Westminster Bank, being the largest Joint Stock Bank in the world.

CONTUMACIOUS—Obstinate.
COERCION—Penal restraint; check.

REALM—A king's dominion.
BARONET—A title of honor that is hereditary.

LIFE.

Ah, Life is like the ocean wide,
It has the *storm*, the *calm* and *tide*,
It has the *lightning* and the *gale*,
And o'er its deep do mortals sail.

And *Faith*, this is the vessel brave,
In which we breast the stormy wave;
The life-boat, *Truth*, lies on the deck
To save us from a fearful wreck.

The *Compass*, God, does never change,
Although the waves with fury range;
The pilot, *Virtue*, knows the way,
And guides us safe through foam and
　　spray.

The mainmast, *Hope*, lifts high its head;
On it the sails of *Peace* are spread;
The *Passions* are the seamen bold.
And to our will must we them hold.

For if they e'er their bonds do break,
Destruction's course the ship will take,
And o'er the sea of life we steer.
Full many a wave its crest does rear.

And many a ship has found its grave
Upon the stormy ocean wave;
For *Envy's* billows, white with foam,
The trackless sea of life do roam.

They rush before rude *Discord's* blast,
Which from the shores of *Hate* outcast,
But the whirlpool of *Vice* is the worst
　　of all
The dangers that with fear appall.

The current of *Indolence* to it doth lead,
Which rushes along with frightful
　　speed,
And all o'er life's proud sea must sail,
And all must battle with storm and gale.

And though the sky is black with clouds
And the wind doth roar through all the
　　shrouds,
If we make our *Pilot* and *Compass* the
　　guide,
The foaming waves in safety we'll ride.
　　　　　M. LEHMAYER.

COMPASS—An instrument whereby mariners steer.
INDOLENCE—Laziness.

PILOT—An officer who steers the ship in and out of harbor.

JEWISH RESERVE.

THE social coherence of the Jews, which continues in spite of the acquired civil equality, still puzzles the Gentile observer. To the theological mind it argues a divine purpose with the chosen, but temporarily rejected, race; to the philosopher, the astounding pertinacity of traits of character; to those hostile to the Jews it is a proof of a secret conspiracy against the welfare of their Christian nations; and the most general impression is that pride of race lies at the bottom of the strange fact. Even Mr. James Freeman Clarke has no other explanation to offer. He says: "Hereditary and ancestral pride separated them (the Jews), and still separates them, from the rest of mankind."

How singular, indeed, that when the Jew attempts to quit his reserve and mix freely with his neighbors, he is repelled and unceremoniously shown back to his own tribe; and, if he keeps there, he is accused of hereditary and ancestral pride! We need not strive for an explanation to great depths; the reasons lie much nearer the surface; so near, indeed, that even "he who runs" may see them, perchance in the accuser much more than in the accused

Be it remembered that most of the heads of families are of foreign birth, and were of mature age when they pitched their tents

on this free soil. They had contracted their social habits, which to
abandon they saw no reason whatever. They readily fell in line for
the discharge of their civic duties; but their private life, their domestic customs, which were of the German-Jewish type, they could not
all at once change without causing a rent in their most intimate relations. These are far too precious for such experiments. People
whose strongest affections centre in their homes are naturally
tenacious of their manners and usages; and none should understand
this better than those of the Anglo-Saxon stock, who themselves
carry their household gods with them wherever they go. Besides,
recreation after the exacting labors of the day a man can find nowhere except in places where he may move in perfect ease and freedom; and these, again, the society of his equals in temperament,
language, and taste, alone will afford him. The Jews do not differ
in this respect from other foreigners, all of whom show a decided
preference for their own circles.

In the civilized countries of the old world the seclusion of the
Jews has almost entirely disappeared, and it would cease here much
sooner but for the ecclesiasticism which enters so largely into the
formation of American society. Christianity, although not legally
dominant, is yet practically so. Where the spirit has departed, the
phraseology still remains. Everywhere the tenets of that faith are
assured as beyond question, making conversation often embarrassing
to the dissenting Israelite. No matter how much or how little the
Gentile believes of the dogmas, their assumption does not incon-
venience him; no need for him to guard against the charge of
supineness and insincerity, to which, however, the Hebrew lays himself open if he fails to record his dissent. Nor is it the dogma alone
which enjoys such a pre-eminence. The laws of morality, the
motives of kindness, the graces of conduct, are also marked with the
device of the Church. We are not speaking now in the way of
censure; we simply state facts which are potent to all. But let the
candid reader realize for a moment the feelings with which an
Israelite must hear every virtue under heaven—manliness, candor,
honor, humility, love, forbearance, even charity and the sanctities of
home, nay, courtesy itself—a matter in which the coarse Norseman was
the disciple of the polished and courtly Oriental—stamped with a
name that degrades him and makes him appear a graceless intruder
into the circle of the elect—and the problem of Hebrew retirement
will lose much of its mystery. It will then appear why the Hebrew
philanthropist does not yet take that personal share in the benevolent
labors of his fellow-citizens which he is most willing and unquestionably able to bear. Where his money is welcome his faith is proscribed. Dear and near to his heart as many of the beneficent
efforts for the amelioration of the conditions of the poor are, he can
do no more than aid them with his purse, for he knows that his just
sensibilities will not be consulted. We readily admit that often no

insult is intended, but that does not take the sting from a reproach, pronounced or implied. If long habit is pleaded for extenuation, our answer is: The time has surely come to conquer it. Some think that the Jew himself ought, by abandoning his reserve, to remove the obstacle in his way. That may be so, but such missions do not ordinarily inspire men with the courage to face prejudice. We do not for a moment pretend that the Jews are blameless in that respect, and never indulge in religious arrogance. We have no excuse for them, beyond this, that the fault is a little less reprehensible in those who have suffered so much for their faith's sake. It certainly is for the *dominant* religion, rather than for that of a small minority, to lead the way in this very desirable reform.

If social alienation is undesirable on general grounds, it is especially so for this reason, that it prevents both Jews and Christians from correcting their views of their respective religions, a thing as yet much needed on either side. Nothing brings man nearer to man than the sacred community of good work; nothing strengthens faith in the Father more surely than the growing sense of the brotherhood of His children. Probably unbelief itself will not object to be conquered by the logic of such facts. If churches and synagogues must needs preach the same truth under different aspects, and worship God in diverse tongues, may they not learn to praise Him also in the universal language of good deeds on the broad fields of our common humanity? Meanwhile, we shall do what in us lies to make ourselves known, not only outwardly, but inwardly too; we shall let the reader into all the mysteries of our faith, as far as we ourselves know them. For, after all, the chief interest which the Hebrew race offers to the eye of the student is its religion. As the propounders, witnesses and soldiers of a new faith, the Jews appeared in history and have steadfastly pursued their course, from the call of their first father, "the friend of God," in the plains of ancient Chaldea, to this day, when their presence is felt in so many lands. Through light and darkness, through victory and defeat, through glory and shame, their faces remained firmly set toward a goal which the ancient seers planted on the heights of a redeemed and perfected humanity. Their contributions to the intellectual and industrial achievements of the past were of no mean importance, but they all had their root in the religious genius which they developed, and it is their religious mission from which they derive to this day both the right and the duty to remain outside the dominant religions. Dr. G. GOTTHEIL.

[Adapted from an article in the "N. A. R." by Dr. Gottheil, minister of "Emanu-El," New York.]

RESERVE—Modesty.
COHERENCE—Resisting separation.
PERTINACITY—Stubbornness.
TRAIT—A touch.
HEREDITARY—By right of inheritance.
TENACIOUS—Inclined to hold fast.
PHRASEOLOGY—Peculiar in expression.

ECCLESIASTIC—Relating to church.
DOGMA—Established principle.
PRE-EMINENCE—Superiority.
TO PROSCRIBE—To censure.
DOMINANT—Presiding; prevailing.
ALIENATION—Change of property or affection.

FRIENDSHIP.

How sad, without a friend to be,
While sailing o'er life's stormy sea,
For without friends man cannot steer,
As dangers do too oft appear.

When in the gale his vessel reels,
When thunder loudly o'er him peals,
When in the air the lightnings flash,
When masts are shivered with a crash,
When waters swell and whirlwinds roar,
And breakers sound far from the shore;

When round him fly the foam and
    spray,
And succor is too far away,
And when for help he loudly cries,
And to his shouts no voice replies;

Some one he needs to give him cheer,
To calm his mind, dispel his fear,
To help him through the tempest's blast,
To aid him till the storm is past,
To mind the compass—trim the sail,
And with him weather out the gale.

In short, we see man needs a friend
To stand by him until life's end;
But in the world true friends are rare,
Friends sail with man when all is fair,
But when clouds lower o'er his head,
He seeks his friends, who then have
    fled.
Yet true friends stay, who bid him know
That they in danger friendship show.
          M. Lehmayer.

TALMUDIC ALLEGORY.

THE SONGS OF THE NIGHT.

As David, in his youthful days, was tending his flocks on Bethlehem's plains, God's spirit came upon him, and his ears were opened, and understanding enlightened, that he might comprehend the songs of the night. The heavens proclaimed the glory of God; the glittering stars all formed one chorus; their harmonious melody resounded on earth, and the sweet fullness of their voices vibrated to its utmost bounds.

"Light is the countenance of the Eternal." says the setting sun. "I am the hem of His garments," responded the rosy tint of twilight.

The clouds gathered and said, "We are His nocturnal tent;" and the waters in the clouds, and the hollow voice of the thunder, joined in the chorus: "The voice of the Eternal is upon the waters; the God of glory thundereth, the Lord is upon many waters." "He did fly upon my wings," whispered the wind; and the silent air replied, "I am the breath of God, the aspiration of His benign presence."

"We hear the songs of praise," said the parched earth; "all around is praise; I alone am silent and mute!" And the falling dew replied, "I will nourish thee, so that thou shalt be refreshed and rejoice, and thine infants shall bloom like the young rose."

"Joyfully we bloom," replied the refreshed meadows. The full ears of corn waved as they sang, "We are the blessings of God; the hosts of God against famine."

"We bless you from above," said the moon; "we bless you," responded the stars; and the grasshopper chirped, "Me, too, He blesses in the pearly dewdrop."

"He quenched my thirst," said the rose; "and refreshed me," continued the stag; "and grants us our food," said the beasts of the forest; "and clothes my lambs," gratefully sang the sheep.. "He heard me," croaked the raven, "when I was forsaken and alone." And the turtle dove cooed; and the swallow and all the birds joined in their song. "We have found our nests; we dwell on the altar of the Lord, and sleep under the shadow of His wing in tranquillity and eace."

"And peace," replied the night, and echo prolonged the sound, when chanticleer awoke the dawn, and crowed, "Open the portals, the gates of the world! the King of glory approaches. Awake, arise, ye sons of men! Give praises and thanks to the Lord; for the King of glory approacheth!"

The sun arose, and David awoke from his melodious rapture.. But, as long as he lived, the strains of creation's harmony remained in his soul, and daily he recalled them from the strings of his harp.

J. R.

CHANTICLEER—The cock; the male to the hen.

HASTY WORDS.

How many, many words are said
  Which we would quick recall,
And substitute kind words instead
  Had we a chance at all.
A hasty word may wound the soul;
To guard such words is self-control.

A man, before he speaks, should think,
  The passions should not reign;
A hasty word may break a link
  Within the social chain.
The most sublime relations may
By hasty words drop in a day.

The wounds which hasty words inflict
  Will never, never heal;
We would not wound, could we predict

How tender others feel.
The passions give to language rise
Which we should keep if we were wise.

Men may forgive a hasty wrong.
  But words are not forgot;
The memory takes the words along,
  And time recalls them not.
Deliberately men will not say
What time can never wipe away.

Before we speak we should reflect.
  And guard the passions well;
A word is cause, cause brings effect,
  And every word will tell.
The language is at least a waste
Which comes to life by hate or haste.

B. J. CH.

FROM DARKNESS UNTO LIGHT.

THE great problems of death and immortality have in all ages attracted a large share of thought. In the truth and reality of the ssues involved, all mankind have a common interest. Men, unaided by revelation, have sought to determine the nature of our final destiny by appealing to the teachings of philosophy, and although their conclusions have occasionally verged upon the truth, still they can, at best, only be regarded as the uncertain ventures of speculation. Revelation clearly shows forth the truth of the doctrine of immortality. Nevertheless, men have complained that the Bible says nothing of a hereafter. Some have striven to apologize for what appeared a weighty omission. Others, again, have sought for reasons to justify the wisdom which they imagined exists in the exclusion of all mention of a future world from the sacred page. But if we turn to the Bible we shall find that not only is the truth of a future existence distinctly asserted, but Scripture goes further, and even sets forth the *nature* of the world beyond the grave. It is not to be expected, however, that a subject which occupies but a very small place in its connection with the duties and obligations of man's daily existence should be so fully treated as the questions of morals and religion, with which our daily life is identified. The information which the Bible gives concerning another world must appear meagre in comparison with principles of right and wrong, of human failings and transgressions, of man's duty to his God, his fellow creatures, and himself. The sacred writers lift but a corner of the veil which hides the Unseen from our view, and let into our dark abode but a few rays of the coming glory. But enough is told to assure us of its *reality*, and to create expectation and desire in our breasts, till death shall rend the veil and mortality be swallowed up in life. Then, perhaps, we shall " see God," and comprehend the Divine nature. We shall be able to realize the greatness of the reward which has been reserved for the righteous. The glories of the reward could only suffer by comparison with things of this world.

But we know something of the *nature* and *duration* of that reward ; the only points on which we could seek to be enlightened. We know that the righteous will be "received in glory ;" "everlasting joy ;" that they will enjoy "pleasures for evermore" at the "right hand" of God ; that God is to be to them " a crown of glory and a diadem of beauty ;" and that they " shall shine as the brightness of the firmament, and as the stars forever and ever."

King David's conception of the nature of our reward is indeed sublime : "I shall be satisfied in awaking in *Thy likeness*." Whatever be the state of the soul while the body is in the grave, whatever be the nature of our sleep, the awakening from it will be a revelation of infinite glory. By what simile can we bring it home to the mind ? By what figure can we realize it ? Were we entombed alive, and after having been left to death and despair, we were to be suddenly borne upward into the dazzling sunlight and to the arms of our relatives, our joy would indeed be great. But who shall describe the infinite glory of man awaking in the perfect likeness of his Heavenly Father ? What Micah beheld when he said : " I saw the Lord sitting upon His throne, and all the hosts of heaven standing on His right hand and on His left ;" what Isaiah beheld when he said : " I saw also the Lord sitting upon a throne high and lifted up, and His train filled the temple. Above it stood the seraphim ...and one called unto another and said, Holy, holy,

holy is the Lord of Hosts ;" what Ezekiel beheld when he tells us : " I looked, and behold, the glory of the Lord went up from the cherubim . . . and the court was full of the brightness of the Lord's glory." All this, all indeed which the most favored of the prophets were permitted to see, must fade into nothing in comparison with the glory of the future ; for has not one of God's messengers told us : " Eye hath not seen, O, God, beside Thee, what He has prepared for him that waiteth on Him."

How full, how bright are the evidences of a future world ; how weak the arguments which skepticism arrays against it !

The evidence of Scripture leaves room for only one objection, if it may be so called ; and this arises from the very *greatness of its truth*. To think of ourselves as existing through all time, as surviving the giant mountains of our world, as exempted from every imperfection of our nature, as being clothed with an angel's glory, and enjoying eternal happiness, appears a blessedness almost too great. But to all is this blessedness offered. And what is its price? Simply the price embraced in the words of the preacher : " Fear God and keep His commandments, for this is the whole duty of man."

Reader, we have shown you but one side of the picture—the bright one. We have endeavored to set before you some of the blessed promises of Scripture for the practice of righteousness. But the book which speaks of the rewards of virtue, tells us with equal precision of the punishments of vice. Let us, however, practice virtue not from hope of reward, or from fear of punishment, but for its own sake ; and be of those who serve our Master " not for the sake of receiving a reward." Let us remember that the priceless blessing of a good conscience waits upon the performance of duty ; and whatever be our struggles and self denials in the course of religion, we are but fitting ourselves for that glorious day when we shall pass " from darkness into light." L. J. A.

REVELATION—Communication of sacred and mysterious truths.
FIRMAMENT—The sky; the heavens.
DIADEM—A tiara; a mark of royalty worn around the head.
CHERUBIM (Hebrew) — Plural of cherub; a celestial spirit.
SERAPHIM .Hebrew —Plural of seraph.
SKEPTIC—One who doubts; or pretends to doubt everything.

LIGHT OUT OF DARKNESS.

God moves in a mysterious way
His wonders to perform ;
He plants His footsteps in the sea,
And rides upon the storm.

Deep in unfathomable mines
Of never-failing skill,
He treasures up his bright designs,
And works His sovereign will.

Ye fearful saints, fresh courage take !
The clouds ye so much dread
Are big with mercy, and shall break
In blessings on your head.

Judge not the Lord by feeble sense,
But trust Him for His grace ;
Behind a frowning providence
He hides a smiling face.

His purposes will ripen fast,
  Unfolding every hour ;
The bud may have a bitter taste,
  But sweet will be the flower.

Blind unbelief is sure to err,
  And scan His work in vain ;
God is His own interpreter,
  And He will make it plain.

ADAPTED.

HEBREW CHARACTERISTICS.

My son, give God all honor and the gratitude which is his due; for He it is who made thee and brought thee into this world. Thou hast need of Him, but He needs thee not. Put no trust in thy mere corporeal well-doing here below! Many a one has lain himself down to sleep at nightfall, but at morn risen not again; many a one hath gone to his couch at nightfall sound in health and of high cheerfulness, and has waked up to agonies and terrors. Fear the Lord, the God of thy fathers; fail never at eventide to pronounce the great word wherein Israel is wont to proclaim that He is, and that He is One, and One only; at dawn fail never to read the appointed prayer see that thou guard well thy soul's holiness; let the thought of thy heart be saintly when thou liest waking in the bed, and profane not thy soul, even in the hour of most intimate communing with others, with words of impurity. Be thou cleanly in things that concern the body; wash well thy hands ere the morning be far gone; and when thou seest that they are clean and pure, fold them then in prayer. Praise thy Creator when thou puttest on thy clothing, and when thou takest the nourishment that supports life. Be among the first to reach the house of God; enter it with reverential awe. Think well before whom it is thou standest there. When thou goest to the place where the law and the truth are studied, let no idle word pass thy lips; note well in mind the words of the sages there; deem not that anything there is small and of slight account, and beware that thou never allow thyself to look down on any one. Visit the sick and suffering man, and let thy countenance be cheerful when he sees it, but not so that thou oppress the helpless one with gaiety. Comfort those that are in grief; let piety where thou seest it affect thee even to tears; and then it may be that thou wilt be spared the grief of weeping over the death of thy children. Respect the poor man, by gifts, whose hand he knows not of; and when he eats at thy table, gaze not on him too much, lest he doubt his welcome; be not deaf to his beseechings, deal not hard words out to him, and give him of thy richest food when he sits at meal with thee. When thou prayest, be lowly and think thyself nothing before the Almighty, and use all thy soul's energy and force to hold in check what evil desire there may be in thine heart. Greet every man pleasantly, speak truth only, forget not modesty, and in thy eating be moderate; rather feed thyself with the vilest weed than make thyself dependent on other human beings; and seek not greedily after power and pre-eminence in the world. From a wicked neighbor, from a person of ill-fame, see that thou keep aloof, and spend not much of thy time among people who speak ill of their brother-man; be not as the fly that is always seeking sick and wounded places; and tell not of the faults and failings of those about thee. Take no one to wife unworthy to be thy life's partner, and keep thy sons close to the study of divine things. Dare not to rejoice when thine enemy comes to the ground; but give him food when he hungers; be on thy guard lest thou give pain ever to the widow and the orphan; beware lest thou ever set thyself up to be both witness and judge against another; and when thou passest judgment, see that thou invoke counsel from another mind. Never enter thy house with abrupt and startling step, and bear not thyself so that those who dwell under thy roof feel dread when in thy presence. Purge thy soul of angry passion, that inheritance of fools; love wise men, and strive to know more and more of the works and the ways of the Creator. Forget not that the hope of pious souls is that concealed paradise prepared by God before the foundations of the world; that consecrated place where pure spirits and holy enter at last into their rest.   L. Zunz.

Dr Leopold Zunz a native of Detmold, Germany, a Jewish divine of great eminence, was born in 1794, studied philology at Berlin, was preacher at the Berlin Synagogue from 1820 to 1822, was editor of the *Spenersche Zeitung*, one of the principal journals of Berlin, from 1824 to 1832, and was head of the Jewish Seminary for teachers in Berlin from 1839 to 1850. He is regarded as having been the first in Germany to treat Hebrew literature in a scientific manner, and the Jewish community of Berlin has bestowed on him an annuity, in respect for his services. He has written many useful and important works, which have gained for him a world-wide reputation.

THE WESTERN WALL.

Do you see this shattered wall,
    And will the sight not break your
        heart?
The stones seem to lament their fall,
    Grieve that the glory did depart.

Alas! the Temple was destroyed,
    This broken fragment but remains;

Time lingers to fill up the void,
    A lasting monument it contains.

Israel, thou resemblest this wall;
    And although nations pass away,
To you belongs the divine call,
To remain God's witness for aye.
                    H. Vidaver.

Rev. H. Vidaver, formerly Rabbi of Emanu-El Congregation, San Francisco, Cal., was a Hebrew scholar of great repute.
Western Wall—The only fragment still remaining of the Holy Temple in Jerusalem, and is chosen at the present time as the wailing place of pious Israelites, who mourn for their sad loss.

THOUGHTS OF A WANDERER.

There is unspeakable joy in the heart of the wanderer who, after long years of strange vicissitudes, returns unto his father's home. The glad fulfillment of the home-sick yearning, the dear familiar aspect of objects enshrined as holy remembrances; it is as if, not retrograding, but advancing, the grey hairs crowned themselves with the rose-garlands of youth, renewed for evermore. Along the path of the spring-time the footsteps lead again, and unforgotten fragrance fills the air, and vivid sunshine illuminates, not only the sweet welcoming earth, but the gladdened soul that rests in its ancestral home.

And so it is with the heart and spirit of the Israelites, who for years have wandered in alien paths, among strange people, mingling with the crowd or dwelling in enforced seclusion. But from the inner depths ascended unto Him who is the Father of us all the cry for help and strength, the supplication for " His mercy that endureth forever." And the prayer was spoken in the language sacred to us all, and the Sabbath holiness enfolded the lone, sad wanderer, even as it rested on the happy faces assembled in the place of worship. And when the strains of contrition and penitential sorrow were poured forth as incense before Him on the day of Atonement and Prayer, there mingled with the universal accord of Israel's homage to the *Only One* the weak but unfaltering offering of a soul that felt its banishment, but still rejoiced in its kinship with the adoring multitude that call upon His name throughout the world.

And so, amid trials, pangs and disenchantments of this changeful life, the soul held fast to its allegiance and kept intact its sacred faith. It failed in outward observance, but the vital breath of true religion animated the daily effort and guarded the spirit from idolatrous seeking. In this, our modern, matter-of-fact life, there glowed the bright reflections of ancestral glory, and the foregleams of Israel's future came in glimpses of beauty to one who prayed and labored and waited for deliverance. Out of the slavery of uncongenial surroundings He led the soul that trusted Him out of the Egyptian servitude to circumstance; He guided through bleak deserts of the heart and mind to the smiling valleys of content, to the inviting heights whereon His Majesty abides.

By the glad seas of deliverance let us sing His praises, we who feel His nearness and know his Father-love. Our cheerful, sustaining, ever onward, ever upward-leading faith is founded on eternal truth; we live beneath no terror-shadows of fear, no encircling mists of superstition appall us, for " He who was, who is, will be for evermore," is narrowed down to no human conceptions, embraced in no mystic covering of flesh, revealed by no mediator, but through Himself alone! With reverent awe comes trustful, ever present peace, for He is Love as well as Power, and blessings descend from His divine Omnipotence. To the heart filled with the sense of human duty incumbent on the Israelite crime is an impossibility and deception an abhorrence. For no honors of place or position will the true Jew sell his birthright, the inheritance handed down to him from dim, remotest time.

And the world, cold and callous as it is called, has still warm heart-throbs for heroic deeds and noble purposes; it looks upon the achievements of our race in the present day, at first with incredulous wonder, at last with unrestrained applause. We stand amid the foremost in the vanguard of true liberty; we lend the hand to all the researches of science, we welcome every discovery in nature. Our sons are found amid the statesmen and the *literati* of every land that gives them the privileges of an equal citizenship; in art, in music, in all intellectual attainments, the genius of our people shines; a proof to those that doubt our past glories, shadowed, but never swept into oblivion; a token of what Israel yet may be, a nation great and powerful, that shall be as a beacon-light unto the world.

And to claim kinship with this wonderfully preserved people, to feel the pride of alliance with the best, purest, most unselfish minds of the day, to live to behold even the present enfranchisement, is a bountiful compensation of Divine love to the wanderer come home at last. CORA WILBURN.

MISS CORA WILBURN—An American lady of the Hebrew persuasion, possessing great literary attainments, and a writer of note, having the welfare of Israel at heart.

CONTRITION—Sorrow for sin.
PENITENTIAL—Repentant; bent on amending life.
INCENSE—Perfumes exhaled by fire.
HOMAGE—To pay respect.

APPALL—To afright; to depress.
MYSTIC—Obscure, secret.
CALLOUS—Hardened, insensible.
OBLIVION—Forgetfulness.
VANGUARD—The front.

THE EXILES' LAMENT.

Ps. CXXXVII.

By the rivers of Babylon sadly we wept
  At the thought of returning to Zion
    no more;
And the harps of our gladness all
    silently slept
On the boughs of the willows that wept
    on the shore.

For heartless they came, who had borne
    us afar,
  And their mandate was, "Mirth and
    melodious lays!"
And they who had spoiled us with revenge and war,
  Cried: "Sing us a song in Jerusalem's praise!"

But how shall we sing in the alien's
    land,
  The songs that Jehovah once hearkened to hear?

O Zion, let perish my ready right hand,
  If fades from my bosom thine image
    so dear!

Thou home of my heart, if I cherish not
    thee,
  Let my tongue sink in silence, my
    gladness be o'er,
If high o'er all treasures, possessed or
    to be,
  I place not Jerusalem, blest evermore!

On Edom and Babylon terrors shall
    fall,
  Who mocked when Jerusalem's woes
    followed fast;
Forever the same that they measured
    withal,
  Shall be the return the Lord gives
    them at last! ADAPTED.

TO EXILE—To banish, or drive from a country.

ALIEN—One born in a strange country.

THE HEBREW LANGUAGE.

WHAT can give a greater dignity to this language than its being the first language of mankind; its being the language of God, the language of angels, the language of prophets; for God Himself breathed this language into the first parents of mankind—Adam and Eve—at their very first creation, that they might explain their sentiments to one another, and in proper and convenient terms express whatever is comprehended in the whole universe of nature. This God made use of to manifest his boundless grace and will to men. In this language the holy angels talked with mere men. In this the prophets copied out the Divine word concerning the eternal salvation of man. But if antiquity procures esteem to things of a durable nature, what bears an earlier date than this language, that is coeval with itself? And if the dignity of the author enhances the dignity of a thing, what deficiency can there be here? In a word, if the excellency of the subject-matter that is laid down in these writings conduces anything to the dignity of the language itself, what can be imagined more worthy than that which leads us to the saving knowledge of God Himself, which shows the manner of attaining eternal salvation? Oh, truly laudable and worthy study! An industry beyond all praise! whereby a man is enabled in the same language knowingly to converse with God, with holy angels, with patriarchs, and with prophets, and clearly to unfold to men the mind of God from the language of God.   J. BUXTORF.

DR. JOHANN BUXTORF was born at Camen, in Westphalia, 1564, and died in Basel, 1629. He was the author of a Hebrew and Talmudic Lexicon.
COEVAL—Of the same age. | ANTIQUITY—Old times.

OBSERVE THE LAW.

I DO not see how those who were born in the house of Jacob can in any conscientious manner disencumber themselves of the law. We are allowed to think on the law, to inquire into its spirit, and, here and there, where the lawgiver assigned no ground, conjecture one, which, perhaps, was governed by times, circumstances and local situation; and, perhaps, will undergo modification according to times, circumstances, and local situation—whenever the Supreme legislator shall be pleased to make known to us His will thereon; and make it known to us as loudly, publicly, and as utterly beyond doubt and hesitation, as He made known to us the law itself. As long as that does not take place, as long as we cannot produce so authentic a discharge from the law, all our fine reasoning cannot exonerate us from the strict obedience we owe to it, while the awe of God will always draw a line between theory and practice, beyond which no conscientious person will permit himself to go. Who can say: "I have entered into God's holy of holies; I have seen through the whole system of His purposes, and can fix its measure, aim and bounds? I am at liberty to suppose, but not to decide. Why, even in human matters, I dare not presume to act on my own supposition, and explain away laws without the legislator's or judge's leave; how much less, then, in things divine?" Laws necessarily connected with the possession of land, and with local institutions, carry their dispensation with them. Without a temple and a priesthood, and out of Judea, neither sacrifice, nor a law of purification, nor contributions to the priests, as far as they depended on landed property, any longer remain. But personal commandments, duties which were imposed on a son of Israel, without any consideration of the Temple service or landed property in Palestine, must, for aught we can see, be observed strictly to the letter of the law, until it shall please the Most High to make our consciences easy by loudly and openly proclaiming their abrogation. MOSES MENDELSSOHN.

A BICCURIM PROCESSION.

BICCURIM are called the firstlings of the productions of agriculture, which God consecrated, and had to be brought to the Temple. The country was divided in twenty-four districts. At a fixed time, those who wished to bring the firstlings to Jerusalem, met together at the capital of the district, where, without going under shelter, they spent the night in the street, in order to be ready early in the morning as soon as the call goes forth from the captain of the district, "Arise, let us go hence toward Zion to the house of the Lord our God!" Such a Biccurim procession has just made halt at Northgate, to announce from here to the Temple that they have arrived, and in the meantime to get the firstlings in proper order and readiness, placing the most beautiful fruit in wreath-like form around all other productions. Already the delegates from the Temple are approaching. These are the representatives of the officiating priests and Levites, and also the treasurer of the sanctuary. And now the cheerful playing of flutes can be heard at a distance, whilst a sweeter rapture of humor in which Jerusalem is placed to-day cannot be imagined. The Israelites' national feeling, depressed by a tyrant's rule, raises itself at such a spectacle, and it is true that it answers his mind and disposition by far better than stage-playing and the Grecian music of the theatre, or the gladiator games and animal-baiting at the Amphitheatre with which Herod presented Jerusalem. Those in front of the procession carry in their baskets, which are either of gold, silver, or willow twigs, new figs; although it is now only the end of June, yet they have already also fresh grapes. Those behind carry dried figs and other fruit, and to their baskets pigeons are attached, having the wings tied to serve for burnt offerings. A bull, destined to become the thank-offering for all in common, forms the head of the procession. Its horns are covered with gold, and upon its head rests a wreath made from olive-branches. It is a long procession which enters Jerusalem, amidst the sweet sounds of many flutists. The procession comes from Sebaste, the ancient Samaria. Wherever the procession passes, the tradespeople, sitting at work before their houses or in the lower stories, rise respectfully and accost them in the words : "Achenu, anshe Sebasti bathem leshalom !"—(" Dear brethren, men of Sebaste, ye are welcome to us !")

Arrived under the sound of music at the Temple-mount, every one takes his basket on his shoulder, and thus they proceed till they reach the fore-court for men, and here the Levites begin to chant, with musical accompaniment, the following psalm : "I praise Thee, Lord, for Thou hast heard me, and sufferest not my enemies to rejoice over me." The pigeons hanging on the baskets are now taken for burnt-offerings, and whatever they bring besides they hand to the priests, whilst, in doing so, they speak, according as contained in the five books of Moses, the confession of the firstling-deliverers. All this takes place the same day, at the time of the evening service, and a multitude of people, men and women, old and young, have met at the Temple to be present on the occasion. The most of the visitors receive a friendly reception from their relatives and friends, whilst the rest are eagerly sought for, and almost a struggle takes place in order to show them hospitality.

PROF. F. DELITZSCH.

* HEROD (see biography) is meant by the tyrant spoken of.
PROF. F. DELITZSCH—Professor of Hebrew and Oriental Literature at the University of Leipzig (Germany), and considered the greatest Christian Hebrew scholar in the world.

ESTHER.

How it flashes in the darkness
  Of ages long ago,
The sweet brave soul of Esther,
  With strong heroic glow !

Not all the pomp of Persia,
  Nor all a tyrant's art,
Could silence the hot throbbings
  Of her Jewish heart.

A simple, wayside violet,
  Plucked from humble stem,

She never lost her fragrance,
  Clad in many a gem.

We need to-day thy shining,
  O star, forever set,
Lest we, amid our grandeur,
  The ties of race forget !

Despise the past that's golden,
  And spurn the lowly stem,
Enraptured by the glamour
  Of wealth's diadem.   J. M.

TYRANT—A cruel master. | GLAMOUR—Charming the eyes.

ETHICS.—Never was a people more tried with adversity than the Jewish nation; adversity overcome is the greatest glory, and willingly undergone is the greatest virtue; sufferings are but the trials of gallant spirits, of which Judaism has given ample proofs.

SPEECH ON "JUDAISM."

(Prussian Chamber of Deputies.)

HAVING combatted the arguments of Herr v. Sybel, who opposed the motion before the house, Herr Lasker continued:

"I should never have given my assent to the law should I fear that it would endanger the stability of the Jewish religious fellowship. Not only do I belong externally to its communion, but I find its nucleus in the highest ideal expression, which, according to the testimony of all history, for the first time has been announced to mankind in the form of a religious confession. And because I believe that the essential contents of Judaism lie in the adhesion (bekenntniss) to the only God, for this reason I am filled with the idea that the power of this living conviction will always suffice to give duration as long as religious fellowship will exist to that communion which first entered with this exalted religious idea on the stage of universal history. If one sees confirmed this view, by a history extending over thousands of years under the most adverse circumstances, one is justified to cherish this confidence, and to act accordingly. What justifies this mistrust of the power of Judaism, that it cannot maintain itself on its own ground? What compels us to have recourse to law courts for its protection that it may be able to stand? Historical testimony speaks against it. Until the year 1847 this protection did not exist in several districts of Prussia. Then the compulsory means recommended by Herr v. Sybel were necessary to preserve Judaism and the Jewish communities. They have maintained themselves from their internal vigor.... What justifies the assumption that Jews to any considerable extent will give up the ties of fellowship from mere love of pelf, or sheer obstinacy? In America there is no compulsion for the formation of communities, and yet nowhere are they more closely knit together than in this very America. They mostly consist of persons who have immigrated from these parts, and have joined, forming a communion.... Gentlemen, whatever your decision may be, I am much gratified and grateful for the sympathies in which supporters and opponents of this bill have been united for the interest of Judaism. This is especially gratifying at a time in which the most absurd attacks have been made upon the Jews from various parts. I now perceive by way of contrast in the lively interest of this house a testimony which the Jews will certainly receive with thanks, and which will doubtless serve them as an encouragement.... Judaism deserves to be protected from external danger. It trains, in common with the other creeds, good citizens, and does not fall morally below the level of other denominations. Its moral precepts are free from those curiosities which the enemies of Jews have gathered together from casuistical writings to mold from it a displeasing image.

PART I.—C.

Whoever would take the trouble to make similar collections from the casuistical teachings of other creeds, as, for instance, from the practical business treatises of the Jesuits, and also, as I do not doubt from similar casuistical treatises of other religions, could easily produce the impression that the morals of those who follow such directions must be very low. But the intelligent are aware that in practice a majority of a religious body is not penetrated by the moral instructions given by individual casuists, but by the innermost marrow of its faith. For this reason it is clear to me why Judaism meets with the deserved sympathy calculated to avert from its dangers. But I maintain that the power of Judaism is not less than the power of any other living religious confession. Through millennia the Jews have shown how to behave themselves in fellowship, despite hostility from without. For the same reason I have faith in the future that they will cling to the law and fellowship even when the state withholds from them the hateful privilege of coercion and pressure, compelling those to remain within the communion who from their innermost being and conscientious scruples strive to get out of it. . . . It is my conviction that the effect of such a law would not be a dissolution of communities. A change perhaps will take place. Reforms will not be undertaken with levity, and attempt made to force a certain public worship upon communities, numerous members of which may not participate in the service. There are several religious bodies in Prussia which do not enjoy the protection arising from coercion, for instance, the Mennonites. Their fellowship rests on voluntaryism. Have you heard that a Mennonite Congregation became dissolved from selfishness or quarrelsomeness? Why should Jews not possess the same public spirit? Of a surety the Jews cannot be reproached that they are cool or indifferent toward religion. Probably no other religion has had so many martyrs as the Jewish, whose followers have sacrificed all their worthy interests, and they have not even had the comfort that their martyrdom was rewarded by the outward acknowledgment of their courage. On the contrary, they have, in addition to the loss of their property and lives, had to bear taunts and scorn, and yet they have proved faithful to their creed. Do you really believe that the few *thalers* (dollars) which legal compulsion obtains for single congregations would prove to them a powerful tie?" A. I.

Dr. Edward Lasker was born Oct. 14, 1829, in Jarocin, Prussian Poland, studied law, entered the Prussian Civil Service as assessor in 1846, and was appointed to a position in the Berlin Register's Office a few years later. In 1865 the voters of Berlin sent him to the Reichstag, and on March 27 he delivered his maiden speech. He has since distinguished himself as a powerful writer and orator, and as statesman he holds the foremost rank in Prussia.

NUCLEUS—Kernel.
PELF—Money; riches in an odious sense.
CASUISTICAL — Relating to cases of conscience.

JESUITS—A society belonging to the Catholic Church founded by Ignatius Loyola.
MILLENNIUM—A thousand years.
VOLUNTARINESS—Optional.

ROSH HASHANAH.

(NEW YEAR.)

A SPIRIT haunts the year's declining
hours,
And renders them pathetically grand,
The year's events recalling by its powers
Events so often touched by sorrow's
hand.

For though fond Love is God's most
lasting gift,
Its cherished objects ever but a loan,
Which often, when in peace we onward
drift,
Falls off, and grieving, Love is left
alone.

This is the heavy curse of time. Alas!
But few there are, in that sad grief
unlearned;
Full many through whose doors grim
death did pass
From whose dear homes, some went,
but ne'er returned.

The old year's dying, and with it, what
is lost?
A little joy, much care, much trouble
and much woe.
Hopes oft deferred, and plans full often
crossed,
And struggling manhood's last despairing throb.

Yet others are, whom retrospection
shows
No happier year, and none more
sweetly bright,
In which the tide of time more smoothly
flows,

On which fond memory dwells with
more delight.

To those so blessed may the coming
year
Bring unalloyed and still continued
bliss,
Their eyes undimmed by sorrow's doleful tear,
Their lips untouched by Death's cold,
chilling kiss.

To those woe-stricken, may the coming
year
Bring solace to the weary heart and
brain;
Life seems more bright, to whom it erst
seemed drear,
And all who suffer be released from
pain.

And, as each coming year succeeds the
past,
May Prejudice her vicious hold relax;
Full liberty, equality, at last,
Efface her hidden, still lingering
tracks.

Sweet liberty shall foremost stand and
shine,
Illumine our days and enliven our
dreams,
And turn to scorn, in proud accents divine,
The enslaver's thraldom, and the
despot's schemes.

DEBORAH KLEINERT.

ROSH HASHANAH.

(NEW YEAR.)

IN the period which has elapsed since the *shophar* last sounded,
what changes have taken place for good and for ill! We survey the
rapid current of time, and we realize with the Psalmist that we are
carried away as with a flood. Surely, then, Rosh Hashanah is a day
for serious reflection; one of those "solemn days" which bids us
pause amid the turbulent cares of business or the exciting allurements of pleasure to question ourselves as to our use of the past, our

prospect for the future. It is wise, then, to take a survey of the present, and to inquire, in the words of the prophet of old, "Watchman, what of the night?" Night is the symbol of sorrow. Its terrors can be displaced only by returning day, when the gloom of grief will be enlivened by the light of hope, for "weeping endureth only for the night, but joy cometh on the morrow." The times are full of portents, social, political, and religious. Let us look them in the face and endeavor to answer the interrogatory of the prophet's ejaculation. If danger confronts us, let us marshal our forces, take good heart and possess ourselves of strong resolves to meet the emergencies which may threaten, and if there be before us a sea of troubles let us, by opposing, end them. By courage and firmness we will thus, with God's help, be enabled to conquer.

It is the part of wisdom to examine the past, with an eye to the advantage of the future; in the night to endeavor to discover when the bright hues of morning will dawn, how and under what conditions. At the onset let us admit there has been night for many of us. Homes have been darkened during the year with sorrow; sickness and misfortune have been unbidden guests, and robbed us of many dear ties. But as night passes away before the morning's dawn, so the darkness of suffering and grief gives place to the holier and better feelings of hope and faith.

Who does not remember and grieve at the night of anxiety which hitherto beset our co-religionists in different parts of the world in their peaceful homes? It was, indeed, a period of dark suspense, but wisdom, discretion, and patriotism prevailed. The night passed away and light came, and the fruits thus earned are a part of the gains to be enjoyed in the new year. As in Egypt, so the hand of God, through the influence of advancing civilization, has brought them forth "from thick darkness unto resplendent light." "Watchman, what of the night?" Glorious tidings—in the disenthralment of conscience in those benighted countries—the realization of civil and religious liberty for every man.

Nor must we overlook the promise which the new year brings to us religiously. We have labored under the incubus of indifference to spiritual things on the part of some. Infidelity, too, has attempted to storm the fortress of Judaism. Some of the stoutest hearts yielded to apprehension and despondency. The outlook was indeed gloomy, but it was not a night without the morning's dawn. I look around and have reason to perceive a happy awakening; I recognize the noble and united stand on religion's side made by our best and ablest men all over the globe. Ask them, "Watchman, what of the night?" and they will reply in encouraging tones that they despair not. Their unwavering faith gives them courage and strength, fills them with hope that light is at hand to dispel the shadows of the night. Let us not, then, be affrighted by the enemies of religion. Judaism has encountered stronger foes in the past, and yet her flag waves triumphantly.   REV. H. JACOBS.

[From a lecture by the Rev. Henry S. Jacobs, Minister of " B'nai Jeshurun."]

SHOPHAR (Hebrew)—Ram's horn.
DISENTHRALMENT—Emancipation from slavery.

BENIGHTED—Involved in darkness, physical or moral.
INCUBUS—The nightmare.

HYMN FOR YOM-KIPPUR.

From Thee, O God, no thought I hide;
  O Judge of present and of past,
My penitential soul now guide,
  And let Thy mercy hold me fast.

What refuge have I but with Thee ?
  Changed is the spirit once so proud,
From Thy rebuke it dares not flee,
  But waits Thy mandate, crushed and bowed.

The gods on earth I've worshiped, too,
  Oh ! wicked, hardened, have I been,
Omitted deeds Thou badst me do—
  And sought concealment from each sin.

Just and holy as Thou art,
  I am false and vain and weak;
Oh ! Father, cleanse my wicked heart
  And make it like a child's, as meek.

Though all my faults before Thee lie,
  Behold me not with angry look;
Oh ! hearken when to Thee I cry,
  And write me in Thy holy book.

I cannot live without Thy light,
  No strength but Thine can now restore;
Drive not Thy servant from Thy sight,
  But help me that I sin no more.

My soul is humbled in the dust,
  And yet I dare approach Thy throne !
For Thou art merciful and just
  To all who earnestly atone.

Oh ! let Thy love my tongue inspire,
  God of my fathers, Thee to praise,
And let my heart henceforth desire
  Humbly to walk in virtue's ways.
                          S. A. DINKISS.

YOM KIPPUR (Heb.)—Day of Atonement; to atone, to expiate, to atone for.

ADORATION.

DAY OF ATONEMENT.

WE are strangers before Thee, O God; sojourners as our fathers were; like shadows our days vanish on earth—unresistingly. The wise man and the fool, the poor man and the rich, the king and the slave—they all are under the same bond of finiteness; they all go there, where the weal and woe on earth find their end forever, where the great and the little, the master and the servant, the wolf and the lamb, rest in peace, side by side; the silver cord is torn which unites body and soul for a while, and the jar is broken at the fountain. This, O God, thy inscrutable wisdom has ordained, and is the unavoidable end of us all. When the roots of the tree grow old in the earth, and its stock dies in the ground —being refreshed with water, it buds anew, and brings forth boughs like a fresh plant. The rock that falls is not sterile, though removed from its place; the stone crushed by the flood, and swept to the earth, is yet a soil for plants. But when man dies —his strength is gone, and though the skies

grow old above him, he awakens not, never rises from his sleep.
And rapidly we pass away; we walk not, we fly to the goal, whether
walking or sleeping, whether intoxicated with joy or prostrated with
woe, we know not when we are to arrive there. Our heart often
trembles with the desire to know when the end is to come, how long
the measure of days will last; but surely they are but a handful, and
our existence is like naught before Thee. But this speedy flight of
our life and the gloom of the grave ought not to frighten us, but
teach us wisdom, teach us to put our trust in Thee, who sufferest not
Thy followers to see corruption. For only the dust returns unto dust,
but the spirit which Thou hast implanted in us is Thine, and returns
to Thee, its everlasting Father; and all those who walk here below
before Thy countenance, and sow their seed in due time—though
with tears—go home laden with sheaves, when the harvest comes,
and joyfully re-enter the paternal house. He who sows but wind
may tremble at the whirlwind which he has to reap; he who toils
only for vain things and makes flesh his strength, may dread the
grave in which death is to tend him, and where his idol is to moul-
der; for the record of his life is—an epitaph; his monument—a mound
of clay; his support—a fragile reed, a spider's web. But he who trusts
in Thee, and seeks his salvation in Thee, renews his strength in his
last struggle on earth; his soul Thou refreshest, that it becomes like
a watered garden, like an ever-flowing spring; to him death is like a
High-priest, who, at his appearance, offers up a double sacrifice,
sending the body, the receptacle of sinful lust, away into the wilderness, but causing the spirit, which proceeds from Thee, to shine and
flame on Thy altar, and to rise toward Thee, to find peace, and see
felicity forever. He that has clean hands and a pure heart, and
loves and does good to his fellow-man, will enter Thy abode, when
taken from his earthly dwelling; and yet, even this earthly place
will not deny him, surely not. It will loudly acknowledge the blessings of which he was the promoter, and preserve his name in blooming freshness in the loving memory of mankind. Oh, that we too
may die the death of the righteous, and that our end may be like
theirs! Oh, Judge of life and death! teach us to count our days,
and to hasten to make good use of the brief hours ere they vanish.
Gird us all—the great and the little, the old and the young—with
strength and understanding, that we may not be slow in removing
from our midst all that is repugnant in Thy sight, in reconciling ourselves to Thee, O God of Mercy, and also in reconciling all men
whom we may have offended in word or deed; let us put our house
in order, faithfully doing our duty toward Thee, toward our family,
toward the community, toward Israel, the father-land, and mankind;
that our men may see in Thee their strength, and our women their
ornament; and that also our youth may understand how vain even
the very dawn of life, and that it is good to remember the Creator in

the early hours of our existence, before the years approach when the sun and the light, the moon and the stars, become darkened, and snow covers our heads, and earth—ultimately—our whole frame. Grant, then, merciful Father, that every limb of our body may assert its dignity as a tool in Thy service, and be to us a step in the ladder that rises from earth to heaven. · And when we reach there—at Thy side, you will embrace Thy image with paternal arms, and under the shadow of Thy wings he will be new-born and rejuvenated, and his felicity, like Thy love, will last forever.

DR. EINHORN.

[From the "Ritual" compiled by Dr. David Einhorn, late minister of Beth-El, New York.]

FINITENESS—That which is limited.
INSCRUTABLE—Unsearchable.
MOLDER—To crumble.
FELICITY—Happiness.

TO IMPLANT—To establish, to fix.
RECEPTACLE—A vessel, or place to receive.
STERILE—Barren.
REJUVENIZE—To render young again.

PART SECOND.

—o—

HISTORICAL AND BIOGRAPHICAL.

—o—

Voila ce que les Juifs
ont fait pour la civilisation.

BEUGNOT.

THE PROPHET JEREMIAH.

[586 B.—2402 A. M.]

I.

THE lot of the prophets was peculiar. During their lifetime they were seldom listened to, but often scoffed at and maltreated ; whilst after death, although venerated and held sacred, they were not less ill-used. The wrongs which their mortal bodies experienced appear but trifling compared with the torture applied to their immortal spirits and the divine outpourings of their sacred nature. Agadists and typologists, indifferent to the accomplished work of art, have with emulation often pulled and dragged the beautiful organism of the prophetic literature and dismembered it limb from limb, in order to produce an artificial preparation ; or, without speaking figuratively, they have used the works of the prophets as a cloak for their own fancies.

The pulpit nowadays is in nowise any better. It tortures and torments the writings of the prophets to give a drastic effect to its eloquence. To the real nature of the prophets, their designs and works, their struggles and sufferings, there is but little attention paid to inculcate it upon the people's conscience. Few, indeed, can form a proper picture of those heralds, with their clear-sighted views, overflowing hearts, and fiery language. Hellas had its artists and poets, who poured over life the charm of beauty. Rome had its warriors, senators, and statesmen, whose will was forced upon the people of the historical world to make it their law, and who yoked kings to their triumphal cars. But the prophets of Judea are, by far, more eminent, inasmuch as morality and religion stand higher than art and conquest.

The prophets, however, were no gloomy censors and blustering preachers, with narrow boundaries and limited views, such as superficiality often represents them. Their views reached, by far, beyond their people, although their immediate calling was for the purification and improvement of their race ; nay, it extended even beyond the period in which their mortal existence was confined, although they made use of the prevailing ideas of those times. They were mostly the counsellors of kings and the leaders of the people ; and their intelligence was even sought by heathen princes, for their advice was always correct and striking, and being never dazzled by the appearance of things, they could penetrate the better into the nature and depth of all affairs and circumstances. The prophets knew well the effect of words and poetically-arranged speeches upon the human heart, and, therefore, their ideas were generally illustrated with powerfully drawn pictures, and they spoke in well-articulated phrases. The poetry of the prophets is the more powerful because they never adopted the false aesthetic principle, that the beauty of poetry rests on inventions, fables, and lies, but always clung to truth as the sheet-anchor of their poetical eloquence.

It is therefore remarkable, although nearly half a century has passed since the European Jews have come to consciousness, and the intellectual portion feel no more ashamed of Judaism, but take pride in their doctrine and the past, that they are, nevertheless, better acquainted with Greek and Roman literature than with the prophetical, and more familiar with every mythological character than the radiant heroic figures of the prophets. The fault principally rests with authors. Any one able to delineate the life of these godly men vigorously and without bombast, merely in their simple greatness, with historical facts, from which their efficacy may be discernible, would soon silence the complaints that we do not possess popular writings for Jewish families.

In the following sketch an attempt is made to bring before the reader a picture of the life of Jeremiah, as partly related by himself, and partly by his disciples. If, therefore, the copious life and character, the profound and cultivated mind of this prophet, together with the fullness of his afflictions, and his hope amid ruins, should not be able to captivate the reader's interest, then nothing but misrepresentation could be at fault. A biography of the prophet of Anatot is at the same time an apology in his behalf, in order to disprove the charge that this lofty genius could have thought and acted unpatriotically, and even been guilty of betraying his country.

The ideal picture of Jeremiah, Bendemann's palette has already made popular. His creation—the aged man with almost super-terrestrial forehead, a throne of thoughts, convulsed with heavy clouds of afflictions—requires only to be seen to be never forgotten. But in the whole of his efficiency he appears still more eminent. This hoary man never knew youth and gladness. Already at an early age the prophetic impulse laid hold of him to oppose the wide-spread demoralization, and to place himself with high-spirited courage against kings, princes, priests, false prophets, and the mass of the people. "Never I sat," Jeremiah himself relates, "in the circle of the gay and merry, but, mastered by the prophetical power, I sat solitary and desolate." In his early years, he felt burning grief over a people endowed and favored by God, who, hastening their own downfall, deprived him of all love of life.

On him, bashful and inexperienced, the task was imposed to overcome his weakness, and to step forth with firmness. From him, the tender-hearted and sensitive, who could not refrain from tears at the misfortune of his enemies, and who even prayed for those who conspired against his life, the prophetic call went forth, unsparingly to proclaim the awful fate threatening his nation. His nature often strove against this impulse; he exerted himself to see nothing and say nothing. This, however, he was not capable of doing; it being stronger than his will. "Thought I," speaking of his inner experience, "not to speak in the name of God; then a fire kindled in my heart, which within seemed to consume me, and I could not bear it; could not keep silent." No worldly motive, or the aspiring after gain, not ambition, or a spirit of contradiction, determined him to put on the prophetic cloak; but solely the impulse felt within; the voice of God, the "hand of God," only urged him on, even against his will, and unmindful of the consequences it might draw upon him.

Jeremiah was opulent, possessing many acres of land and ample means for purchasing more. According to his temporal affairs, he might have looked at the degeneration quietly and indifferently, and without being necessitated to conjure up the potent powers of religion and state against him. As one of the priesthood, it was even his own interest (the same as all priests of his time) to desire the continuation of the Temple worship, however inconsistently it was carried on, as well as to promote the prerogative of the state, or at least to bear disinterestedly the prejudices of his caste and its further duration.

But his actions proved the very reverse. No station in life he chastised more than the priesthood; scourging, in spite of its antiquity, the religious practice brought hither, with words and acts unsparingly, which may be applicable at all times. Jeremiah not only renounced advantages, prerogatives and honors, but also the delights of wedlock, and the gentle feelings of family life. The voice of God spoke to him: "Do not take a wife and beget no children," and he obeyed and brought the sacrifice, which, by the Orientalist and the Israelite, is felt the harder to perform. Jeremiah is the only one, as far as is known from Jewish history, who remained unmarried. Already, these few traits in his character, taken even at a human standard, show us Jeremiah as a remarkable appearance, a personality whom nature destined to a modest, noiseless activity, but who was drawn from his career and launched into a whirlpool of complicated circumstances, in order to show energetic action in the same. What may, indeed, have been his real motive? The answer to this question is seen only in the course of his biography; but so much, however, to begin with.

Jeremiah, like the prophets before and after him, bore within him an ideal picture of Judaism, and this ideal he desired to see in classes of the population, under all conditions of state and religion, in the kingdom and the Temple, in the priesthood and in social life, to be set at work and to become realized. But owing to reality being the obverse of this ideal, he declared against idolatry, superstition, thoughtless hypocrisy, immorality, every kind of perverseness and the persons who represented them, inexorable war. He proved that morality and sincere piety were the fundamental conditions which decide the welfare of a state, and that a commonality which lacks this support is thoroughly rotten, and must sooner or later break down. The final result proved his words only too correct. During half a century nearly (625-580) Jeremiah thought in this manner under severe persecutions and constant danger of his life. His importance, however, becomes more evident in connection with the historical circumstances and events in Judea during the last ten years of its existence, which we have to delineate in brief outlines, as far as they encroach upon the biography of the prophet.

At the time when Jeremiah came forth as prophet, scarcely twenty years old, there sat upon the throne of David a youth but a few years older than himself. Josiah, who at the tender age of eight wore a crown, had neither power nor penetration to govern the general religious and moral degeneracy which bore date from his grandfather, Manasseh. A dissolute idolatry, like garb and manner, had been installed as fashion, and, on account of its long duration and habit, had attained right, authorization and sanctity. Judea had become a Pantheon, the same as Rome at the time of its downfall; and every abominable worship was not only suffered, but also fostered. The temple dedicated to the holy God of Judaism, and in which the Levitical choirs were chanting the psalms, was a place for the lascivious worship of Aphrodite. In the valley of Hinnom (Gehinnom) westward from Jerusalem, there existed a permanent funeral pile (Tophet). Jeremiah himself says: "As many towns in Judea, as many gods," and the priests, the sons of Aaron, with but few exceptions, paid homage to this confusion; and the lying prophets, a sort of prostituted press, led the discourse under the existing state of things.

The moral condition of the people was at that time likewise quite discouraging, being brought about by political disorder. The king-

dom had become a kind of caliphate, which ruled, but did not reign;
and which the aristocracy, the chief of families, the commanders and
priests, had kept in complete dependence and in a minority. The
princes of Judea oppressed the people, the same as every aristocracy,
whose egotism, boundless impudence and arbitrary inclination are
not restricted by those placed either above or below them. They
suck the marrow of the nation and degrade them to a brutalized horde.
·They appropriate to themselves the sons and daughters of the lower
classes, and treat them with that rudeness generally perpetrated by
the strong over the weak, as long as they are not subdued by law, religion or custom. The bad example set by those in higher places had a
demoralizing effect upon the mass of the people. Perversion of law,
violence, oppression, deceit, and falsehood, were the general order
of the day. With one single stroke, Jeremiah sketches the entire
demoralization (previous to the reform of the empire) of the reign
of Josiah: " Run to and fro through the streets of Jerusalem, look
about you and seek in the places thereof whether you can find one
only who executeth judgment and teacheth truth, and I will pardon it."

II.

Demoralization within is generally an exponent of weakness abroad.
The small neighboring nations, formerly dependencies of Judea, the
republican coasting states of the Philistines, Idumæans in the south,
the Moabites and the Ammonites in the east, perpetrated with impunity a deal of mischief all over the country. It became a matter
of difficulty for the kingdom of Judea, with but a small territory, to
maintain its independence against the two great rival powers of
Assyria on the one hand, which even in its last moments under
Sennacherib's descendants, and Sardanapalus, was still powerful,
and Egypt on the other, whose reformatory king, Psammetichus, left
his isolated position, in order to strive for the mastery of Asia. Josiah,
or rather the reigning aristocracy, without support from within, betrayed their weakness in the face of these two kingdoms through a
vacillating policy. At one time they entered upon negotiations
with Assyria, at another with Egypt, and thus their wavering became
apparent to both powers.

When Jeremiah arose to be a prophet, and for the first time spoke
in the fore-court of the Temple, the Forum of Jerusalem, he laid
particular stress upon these three points: the idolatrous perverseness, the moral degeneracy, and the political weakness; which stood,
according to his view, in alternate operation. His first speech is a
pattern of popular eloquence. For in this respect he distinguishes
himself from his predecessors, that he spoke in a distinct manner
and yet in an elevated tone, avoiding always obscure and enigmatical
phrases. Here Jeremiah is the very opposite of the prophet Hosea,

with whom he otherwise has much similarity. It would lead too far to follow the train of thoughts of his first oration. A few quotations, however, may suffice to give the reader a slight conception of the same. Of the religious decline, he spoke in the following manner:

"The priests do not point to God, and those who have the care of instruction do not know Him. The leaders resist Him, and the oracle of the prophets is for Baal. Go ye but to the isle of Kittyim (Cypern), and send only to Kedar (the nomadical Arabs), and see whether you can find any people who have changed their god; but my people have bartered the Sublime God for mere nothing."

Pointing to the immorality of the day, one reflection produces the words:

"Upon your vestment, O Judea, adheres the blood of the innocent you have slain, whom you never caught in the act of transgression, and yet you maintain that you are free from sin."

Referring to the political situation, Jeremiah thus spoke:

"What about your journey into Egypt? for to drink the waters of the Nile! and also concerning your travels to Assyria? for to sip the waters of the Euphrates! Exert not your wandering foot fruitlessly, and let not your voice languish for thirst (through the wilderness); but you say never mind, I love the strangers, and I will follow them. How you degrade yourself by your continual changes! You will come to confusion by Egypt, as well as Assyria."

On account of the obduracy of the people, partly owing to the youth of the prophet, the impression was lost, which, otherwise, this speech must have made. The threatened punishment of the nation through a northern power, which he saw in his prophetic foreboding, and even predicted for a certainty, produced no terror in the mind of the people, because it was a boy that prophesied. If anything could establish the truth of the prophecy, then the proof thereof lies in the prophet's own dark features, delineated in undefined outlines by the threatening catastrophe. Writes Jeremiah:

"I look at the earth, and all is waste and void; I behold the heaven without splendor. I see the mountains, how they stagger; I view the hills, how desolate; I remark the cornfields turned into a desert, and the towns destroyed; no man can be met with, even the birds of heaven are migrating."…. "God sends upon Judea a nation dwelling afar off, a people as firm as iron, whose language thou wilt not understand, and whose quiver opens like a grave; a nation of heroes, who will annihilate thy crop and thy bread, thy vines and thy fig trees, thy sons and thy daughters, and who will destroy thy fortified places in which thy trust is put."

Jeremiah did not know at that time either Nebuchadnezzar or the Chaldeans, the existence of the kingdom of Babylon being then only in embryo; but in the soul of the prophet it waved already before his eyes as a crushing power, and he struggles to find expressions in order to evidence what to himself seemed still to be a mystery. He did not, however, deceive himself, for he knew that his words, although issuing from the depths of his soul, nevertheless died away fruitlessly, and yet he never shrank from continuing his exhortations. In another of his speeches at the commencement of his career he remarks:

"To whom do I speak? is not their ear closed, that they cannot hear, and the word of God used as a mockery, for they do not want it? I thought (at first) the people are low and ignorant, not knowing the way of the Lord; and, therefore, I turned to the great, for they must surely know the way of the Lord; but these have broken the yoke and torn the band."

What self-denial it must take to form a clear conception of the incorrigibleness of all classes of the people, without feeling discouraged either with the stupidity of one, or the insolence of another! But to approach again and again these deluded and deaf men, in order merely to get sneered and scoffed at; herein consists the true greatness of the prophet, the greatness of Jeremiah. In another of his speeches, delivered about the same time, he draws an excellent picture of the perverseness of the people: "Even the crane in the air knows its time, and the migratory birds the hour of their arrival, but my people know nothing of a return."

It seems, however, a few years after Jeremiah's appearance, as if the prophet had been mistaken in regard to the capability of improvement of the then existing circumstances; for a return took place quite unexpectedly, which banished idolatry from Judea. A warning omen terrified King Josiah, and he introduced an amended constitution for the empire (621). He called the people, the priests, and the prophets to Jerusalem, and made a fresh covenant, by accepting the law of God as the only precept in life, and annihilating all idolatrous worship. In this change, however, Jeremiah had no direct participation, for Josiah never consulted him, probably on account of his youth; but the prophetess Hulda was applied to. Yet this return was neither fundamental nor lasting.

III.

The king's intention was sincere in regard to reform, but he was unable to banish from the heart the inclination after strange worship which favored sensuality and vulgarity. Thus the state was carried on for nearly thirteen years during the reign of Josiah, and when this last noble king, in the unfortunate battle of Megiddo, had to succumb to Necho, the king of Egypt (608), then the old disorder in its full hideousness again appeared. Schalum-Joachas, Josiah's second son, was placed on the throne by the anti-Egyptian party, but, after governing three months, he was dethroned by the conqueror Necho, and exiled into Egypt. In his stead he crowned Josiah's eldest son, Jojakim, owing to his friendly intentions toward Egypt. From this time there was an end to the independence of Judea; it had become a province of Egypt, in order to pass later to another master.

Under this profligate king, a second Manasseh, began Jeremiah's real and proper prophetic activity. Then Jojakim not only indulged in the former idolatry, but, in order to please his sovereign, also introduced the Egyptian animal-worship. In a hall of the Temple there were all kinds of animals placed on the walls, and incense was distributed by a band of priests. Again the funeral-piles in the valley of Hinnom were filled with all sorts of victims. A certain prophet, Urijah, having expressed his indignation against these insane proceedings, by threatening Jerusalem with destruction, he was persecuted by Jojakim and had to fly into Egypt; but was remanded, delivered up, and executed. Freedom of speech, which up to now had been respected, was utterly suppressed. What courage did it require for Jeremiah to swing the lash of his word against the perverseness of the people, and yet, without the least chance of success! His speeches delivered about this time we do not possess completely; they became a prey to the flames afterward. In one of the speeches which were saved, he reminds of the covenant entered upon under Josiah, to put aside idolatry, and he denotes the relapse as a breach of the covenant and perjury.

"There exists a conspiracy in Judea and Jerusalem; they have returned unto the sins of their fathers. Therefore I will bring about (says the Lord) a misfortune, which they will not be able to escape; then they will supplicate *Me* without being heard, and they will also call upon their idols; which, however, in time of need will not help them. Then once more are the idols of Judea as many as the towns. What does my beloved people in my Temple? there to commit crimes? Shall vows and sacred flesh take away thy sins? Thou wouldst indeed rejoice over it!"

The indifference and even the contempt expressed against the thoughtless, mere outward sacrificial rites, in these masterly ironical observations, are certainly not peculiar to Jeremiah. His predecessors, the prophets Amos, Hosea and Isaiah, all spoke in the same style; but none of them has, like Jeremiah, made this theme repeatedly the object of his admonitions. "Put your burnt offerings," he once said, "to your palatable offerings, then you may at least eat the meat thereof; for not on account of the sacrifices have I spoken to your ancestors." "What use is your incense to me," he said at another time, "which comes from Sabæa (Jemen), for which purpose you fetched that fine spice-reed from a far country? Your burnt offerings are disgusting, and your sacrifices unpleasant unto *Me* (says the Lord)." Through such frank expressions, Jeremiah started the whole of the priesthood against him. His own countrymen, the priests of Anatot, became his worst enemies. But friends also he did not lack, although perhaps his gloomy disposition was not exactly suited for promoting an intimate acquaintance. Yet the uprightness of his manners, his intrepidity, and power of mind, gained him many admirers. His disciple, Baruch, was with full resignation attached to him, and had no part in the persecutions against him. Another follower of Jeremiah happened to be Achikam-ben-Schafan, a man of high birth, who saved him from many perils at different times.

As soon as his prophecy that from the north misfortune would befall Judea and the neighboring powers seemed to become sad reality, he grew even bolder than ever. Nabopolassar, governor of Babylon, had, in conjunction with Kyaxares, of Media, revolted against Sardanapalus, the last Assyrian king, and conquering Nineveh, had thus put an end to the kingdom of Assyria (606). Nebuchadnezzar, the son of Nabopolassar, advanced thereupon with a numerous army against the lands on the Euphrates. Before even the result of the battle became known, Jeremiah prophesied, in presence of the Egyptian ambassador, the defeat of the Egyptian army:

"I behold the Egyptians, faint-hearted, retreating: their heroes are cut down, they give way, they fly without turning about. Move to Gilead and fetch yourself balm, daughter of Egypt. In vain I have prepared remedies, for you there is no cure."

Very soon after, the news spread that by Circesium, on the Euphrates, the mass of the Egyptian army was entirely destroyed (605). This was the first ratification of Jeremiah's prophecy, whereby he gained the confidence of his race. Nabopolassar soon died, and the conqueror, Nebuchadnezzar, became king over the new empire of Babylon (604). Before, however, any one was acquainted with the daring plans of conquest of the young king, Jeremiah already made mention thereof, as if it were an accomplished fact. He told the ambassadors of the different states that their countries must be prepared to acknowledge the supremacy of Babylon. His speech concerning Egypt, in which irony and bitter sternness interchanged, must be considered a pattern of phrophetic eloquence, deserving to be placed side by side with those of the prophet Isaiah.

One day Jeremiah approached some foreigners of different nations, handed to each poisoned wine, and signified unto them, symbolically, that intoxicating poison and an ignominious end are imminent to all of them: to proud Egypt, to the liberty-loving republics of the Philistines, to wise Idumæa, to seafaring and trading Phœnicia, to desert-navigating Arabia, and to all states near and far off. "You will have to drink the poison, and, becoming intoxicated, you will reel and fall to rise no more." But for Judea, to whom he had already preached three-and-twenty years, without finding a willing ear, he announced the threatening disaster in quite comprehensible expressions. "Nebuchadnezzar will, with the Chaldeans and northern nations, approach and turn the country into a desert; every sound of joy will become mute." The proclaiming of this judgment before the people, and evidenced by symbols, produced a perfect panic. Judea had just now fostered sweet hopes, after the defeat of Necho, that its independence appeared to be more secure than ever, and thus, all at once, its happiness was menaced by a kingdom only just risen. The incorrigible and deluded portion of Judea showed their indignation toward the prophet, pretending not to mind the punishment thus announced. Jeremiah was taken into custody, probably to check his influence among the people.

IV.

But it was just as important to him not to let pass by this favorable opportunity, in order to induce the people to return; and being hindered from speaking in person, he at least made his mind speak. All speeches in full which he delivered from the commencement of his appearance, were written down by his disciple, Baruch, whom he ordered to read them before a large assembly on some holiday. Baruch did accordingly; and the effect which these simple poetical words, resting upon truth, produced on the hearers, was really marvellous. A young man belonging to the aristocracy, a certain Micha, ran trembling and quite animated from the Temple to the palace, communicating to the assembled princes what he heard, and was so overcome whilst relating it that it aroused their attention, and all were willing to lend their ear for a similar purpose. Thus they ordered that Baruch should be called to read the scroll to them. Even these heart-hardened men, amongst whom was Elnathan, who seized the prophet Urijah in Egypt, and led him to the scaffold, were all overwhelmed and petrified after having listened to Baruch. It was a great triumph which truth celebrated over uncultivated minds. The same princes who previously made merry over Jeremiah, were now quite changed, and consulted together what plan to adopt in order to acquaint King Jojakim with the contents of Jeremiah's speeches, as well as how to protect him and his disciples against the wrath of the king, should he remain unmoved. After placing Jeremiah and Baruch in safety, they went to Jojakim and acquainted him with the exciting effect which the prophet's written speeches had produced upon them. The king, on expressing his desire to hear them read, was supplied with the scroll, and one of his servants read it to him in his winter palace, whilst he stood before the fire warming himself (604). During the reading the princes were closely watching his features to see what impression these powerful words would produce upon the king, who coolly took from the scroll one leaf after another and threw them quietly into the fire. Quite stunned, the princes adjured him not to become hardened against it, but Jojakim simply ordered the reading to proceed, thus burning the scroll leaf by leaf. Hereupon he charged his son, with some other faithful servants, to seize Jeremiah and his disciple, intending probably to take their lives. But as long as those high in position felt an interest in their behalf, they could remain safely in their hiding-places without any fear of betrayal. The lurking-place of the fugitives was in a deserted spot, in order not to fall into the hands of these myrmidons, but they were compelled to change their refuge continually. Jeremiah bore his fate with the greatest resignation, but his disciple, Baruch, less courageous, complained "he cannot find rest," and his master was obliged to encourage him to perseverance.

During the last six years of Jojakim's reign nothing is heard of our prophet, probably on account of his absence from the capital. in the meantime, another portion of his prophecy came into fulfillment. The fate awaiting Judea, according to his prophecy, drew nearer and nearer. Nebuchadnezzar, "the lion who rushed from his thicket," held with his armies the whole of the territory from the Euphrates to Egypt entirely in his power, and had subdued whatever nations would not submit to him. Jojakim acknowledged his supremacy (600), but his heart still favored Egypt. Psammetichus II. induced him to desert Babylon, owing to which Nebuchadnezzar declared war, and Jerusalem, which for half a century, since Menasseh, had not seen an enemy, was besieged. Jojakim died soon after—whether in his palace or in captivity is still doubtful—and the capital of Judea surrendered to the conqueror (597). His son, Jojachin (Jechonja, Konjah), was called to the throne, probably by Nebuchadnezzar himself. During his reign, we find Jeremiah once more in Jerusalem ardently engaged in his prophetic charge. Jojachin, only eighteen years old, had no foreboding of the dangerous situation of Judea ; and being frivolous beyond measure, as well as a great spendthrift, he settled down for a long reign, ordering cedars from Lebanon, and building an extensive and splendid palace, playing the part of a Solomon. Whilst he thus found delight in raising the structure, his mother, Nechushta, carried on the government. But she soon found that, in these critical times, she could not handle the nation like her spinning-wheel. It appears she was engaged in political intrigues with Egypt, and it cannot be said that she was a model of a queen.

Against this king and queen-regent, Jeremiah spoke with such boldness that it is astonishing the court suffered his attacks. From this the conclusion must be drawn that Jeremiah had already gained many adherents among the people and those high in position; that the court felt afraid to venture upon violence and seize the prophet. "Tell the king and the queen-regent," he once said, "step down from your throne, and place yourself low (into dust), for your diadem is sinking as well as your pompous crown." Another time he announced to the king in person, without the least digression, that he and his mother would be cast into a strange land, where they would find their grave. His successor, however, would be a just king, a worthy son of the house of David, under whom Judah will dwell in safety, and who shall be called (Zidkijah), "God is our righteousness." Very soon after, this prophecy came to be fulfilled, for Jojakin's reign lasted exactly but one hundred days, and owing to Nebuchadnezzar's being informed of the treachery of the court of Judah, he laid siege to Jerusalem once more, and this time invested the place so closely that the king was obliged to deliver himself up. He, his mother, his eunuchs and servants, the noblest amoust the people, the armorers and fortress-builders, the treasures of the Temple and the sacred vessels, all were carried to Babylon (597). Jeremiah's influence as a true prophet rose with every fresh catastrophe. The banishment, which he foretold long before, had now happened, for the exiled were considered by those remaining as the flower of the nation.

Nebuchadnezzar, whose mildness had been continually opposed by manifold faithlessness, proved the nobleness of his character as a ruler by permitting also the continuance of the throne of David, in placing upon it Josiah's third son, Zidkijah (Zedekiah), who had to take a solemn oath that he would remain a faithful vassal, and not turn his mind to Egypt. Zidkijah was possessed of a few qualities which, in time of peace, would have made him a good king. He was mild, tender-hearted, manageable and susceptible to receive good advice; an enemy to oppression, he had no special inclination toward the prevailing idolatry. Jeremiah was confident that he surely would lend a helping hand for the improvement of both public and private life in the sense of ideal Judaism.

But one single trait in his character neutralized almost all his good qualities. Zidkijah was governed by weakness and inconstancy, and thus those who were continually about his person made use of him as a play ball. To-day, he was quite ready to accept Jeremiah's advice, whilst to-morrow, already he lent his ear to just an opposite opinion. This weakness left the princes of Judea ample scope for their selfish motives, and, instead of keeping them in check, the king feared them, and condemned himself for his non-independence. Jeremiah developed an extraordinary activity during the eleven years of Zidkijah's reign, in order that a decline, if possible, be prevented. He not only had to struggle with the king's fickleness, and the strong temerity of the eye-service of the false prophets, together with the frivolousness of the people, and the influence of the neighboring states, but also, and above all, with what seemed the most difficult part, the patriotic feeling in his own breast. His prophetic charge enlarged even to the sphere of a statesman.

V.

Jeremiah formed in a certain manner the centre of a political party to which the better class—Achikam, his son Gedaljah, several princes, and at times even the king himself—belonged. The clear-sighted views of the prophet penetrated the obscure complications of his time, and his upright mind was for honest statesmanship. But this policy was nevertheless entirely subordinate to the object he strove for, that of ameliorating the moral and religious condition of the people.

Yet, as his views of existing circumstances ran counter to public opinion, he was placed every moment in danger, and his life was, as it were, hanging on a thread. The acquiescence of his friends, and even the favor of the king, could only with great difficulty protect him. All this, however, did not deter him for a moment from speaking his mind with indiscreet freedom. Soon after Zidkijah came to the throne he insisted upon abolishing animal worship, and the immorality closely connected with it. At the same time he expressed himself in respect to the highly honored Temple, which was considered a kind of talisman against all perils, in such a manner that it produced the utmost indignation in all circles. He cautioned the people that they should not depend on the Temple for protection: "Indeed, you steal, murder, commit adultery, take false oaths, and sacrifice unto idols. You came to the Temple, believing that here is deliverance!—is then the Temple a den of thieves?" He announced the same fate to the sanctuary in Jerusalem as at Shiloh, which, owing to the degeneracy of the people, had been destroyed.

These decided threats expressed against the Temple sounded in the ears of the stone-and-wood-worshipers like blasphemy, and they treated him as a sanctimonious slanderer. The priests and prostituted prophets seized him, accused him of blasphemy, and delivered him into the hands of the public authorities, shouting, "Kill him! kill him!" This caused a great commotion in Jerusalem, and every one ran to the Temple, where Jeremiah had suffered ill-usage. As soon as the news became known at the palace, the princes hastened to the place of tumult. But no sooner were these men of high-standing seen than the enemies of the prophet began repeating the accusation brought against him, and insisted that he should suffer death for his blasphemy. The wicked accused piety, and those stained in vice impeached innocence. Jeremiah defended himself in a worthy and dispassionate manner: "I speak in the name of God against the town and the Temple, and it rests with you to avert the misfortune. I am in your hands; do with me whatever you please, but beware of shedding innocent blood." So powerful was the effect of these few simple words, that those in high position soon felt favorably disposed toward him. They even tried to pacify the people, saying: "The man does not deserve death, for he speaks to us in the name of our God." Some referred them, as an example, to the King Chiskijah, in whose time the prophet Micah prophesied in a similar manner, that the Temple would become a desert, and yet no harm was done to him. The wrath of the people was appeased, and Achikam was enabled to withdraw Jeremiah from the vengeance of the priests and the lying prophets.

But idolatry had taken root to such an extent that removing it this time was as difficult as ever. In fact, by the intercession in his favor Jeremiah only gained freedom of speech and nothing else. This freedom Jeremiah made good use of, in order to steer the state against political errors. Almost every one was dissatisfied with the Chaldean-Babylonic sovereignty. It was considered disgraceful to submit to an upstart like Nebuchadnezzar. His conquest seemed things of the past, the same as those of the Scythians, a kindred race to the Chaldeans, who formerly attacked and devastated the whole country from the Euphrates to Egypt as far as Asia Minor, and afterward deserted it again, without leaving a trace behind them. A similar end it was believed the Chaldean conquest would soon share. The court of Egypt, concerned for its own independence, kindled the spark of dissatisfaction, in order to procure the alliance of Judea in the expected struggle with Nebuchadnezzar. The neighboring countries sent again their embassadors to Jerusalem, for the purpose of inducing Zidkijah to desert Babylon. Most of the provinces were in favor of it. Quasi prophets, among whom was Chananje-ben-Asur, commanded in the name of God that the exiles of Judea would soon return from Babylon to their fatherland, and bring with them all the vessels of the Temple which had been taken away as booty. The slightest occurrence was considered by the credulous a sure foreboding of the speedy fall of the Chaldean empire.

This fancy, as if Nebuchadnezzar's established power were but an ephemeral appearance, which would melt into nothing over night, Jeremiah was obliged to destroy, inasmuch as a great deal was depending on it. In order, however, to make his words effective, he put on a yoke of wood, and thus placed himself before the foreign ambassadors. This symbol appeared evident enough. He announced therewith that it had pleased the God of heaven and earth to choose Nebuchadnezzar as executor of His will, bestowing on him dominion that all nations should come under his yoke, whilst further resistance would prove useless, and only lead to harder servitude or total decline. "The Chaldean empire, strengthened by God, and appointed to receive power and dominion, will last three generations, and then only their turn will come to be subdued." To the king and the people of Judea he announced the evil consequences of their opposition to the Chaldeans with still greater force: "Instead of listening to the allusions of the prophets, that the vessels of the Temple will soon be brought back, let them rather pray that those yet remaining may not also be taken to Babylon."

VI.

Owing to Jeremiah's powerful eloquence, strong energy, and indefatigable watchfulness, he actually succeeded for a time to frustrate all machinations, and to induce Zidkijah to remain faithful to Nebuchadnezzar. Thus Judea enjoyed a few years' rest and calmness. Jeremiah proved also successful in affecting the emancipation of the slaves. The king called an assembly of nobles and slaveholders, and prevailed on them to set at liberty all Jews who had been enslaved by mere force, or through want; and he also made them take an oath never to subject in future one of their own brethren. Even the zeal for idolatry seemed to have received a check through the prophet's influence. Those who still carried on a perverse and unbecoming worship had to hide themselves with it, and even seek the darkness of night (vid. Jer. xliv: 18, and Ezek. viii: 12).

However, the independence idea continually turned their heads, and if Judea had not over-rated its strength, feeling satisfied in being a vassal, then Jeremiah and his disciples might have succeeded, if not exactly in realizing ideals, at least in bringing about times like the days of Chiskijah, that the fear of God and a moderate and simple state of things would have been established in Judea. But he was opposed not only in Judea and Egypt, but in Babylon as well. The exiles in Babylon were anxious to return to their fatherland. Two evil-disposed persons, Zidkijah and Achab, professing to be prophets, and being believed in their statements, made known that the hour of redemption from the Chaldean dependency was at hand, and the exiles would return in great triumph. Jeremiah was, therefore, compelled to forward a letter to the exiles, in order to disperse these vain hopes. He urged upon them not to deceive themselves with mere delusions, but to settle down in Babylon, and to help forwarding the welfare of that hospitable kingdom, for they would have to abide there several generations.

This advice, however, did not meet the expectations of the exiles, and the most violent amongst them became mortal enemies of the prophet. One of the exiles, Sherajah, wrote to the High-priest in Jerusalem, that he should silence Jeremiah at home, and that it was his duty to have this madman placed in custody, in order to prevent his discouraging the men of independence. Nothing but delu-

sion could and can descry in Jeremiah a man of no patriotic mind,
an enemy to independence, who, instead of exciting to mortal combat against the foreign government, advises thus cowardly submission. In times of loose morals and general degeneration the counsel
of an Aeschines, to submit to what seems unavoidable, to prevent
still greater misfortunes, is by far more patriotic than the extrava-
gancies of a Demosthenes with insufficient means to run blindly
against a Colossus, in order to break your soul into pieces. Jeremiah was the Judean Aeschines, but without his vanity. He could,
therefore, advise moderation, the more so because he knew Judea
had another task than that of governing, being convinced that all
hopes of the untenableness of the Babylonian kingdom, and the
expected succor from Egypt, promising horses and armies, rested
entirely upon mere delusions. Nebuchadnezzar was also no
Caligula or Nero, for Chaldea did not oppress the Jewish nation
the same as Rome did afterward. They enjoyed perfect freedom,
and in the interior even autonomy, possessing their own king and
their own judges. Nebuchadnezzar desired nothing but tribute,
and that they should remain hostile to Egypt. Jeremiah, who
recommended submission toward Babylon, would himself, perhaps,
have unfurled the flag of revolt in the same manner as Isaiah urged
to resistance against the Assyrians.

It was no trifling task for Jeremiah to prevent the fickle Zidkijah
during nine years, against his own inclination, and foreign intrigues
as well, from becoming faithless to the alliance with Babylon (597-
588). But fate is mightier than individual design. The Jewish
nation was doomed to wander into exile, in order to lose its stately
power, and thus become purified. Zidkijah now entered upon an
alliance with the Egyptian king, Chofra (Apries), and informed
Nebuchadnezzar that he could not show him any further obedience
(winter 588). The rejoicings in Jerusalem in expectation of a
speedy independence were but of a short duration. Nebuchadnezzar, enraged at the violation of faith of the king of Judea, ordered
his troops to enter Judea; and conquering one stronghold after
another, he surrounded Jerusalem with redoubts and bulwarks (10
Tebet, Jan., 587). The besieged fought courageously, their hope
being centered in the army of relief which they expected from
Egypt. Jeremiah was then compelled, the day of punishment for
so many perverse actions drawing nigh, to repeat his admonitions.
Zidkijah was induced to send messengers to him, to beg him to
pray to God for victory over the Babylonian army; but Jeremiah
replied: "Whoever remains in the town will perish either by sword,
pestilence, or hunger, whilst those who will join the enemy shall save
their lives." Nevertheless, he was not detained from praying fervently for the unfortunate, but to offer resistance he could not advise
them. A whole year passed before Egypt made a stir, and the dead

covered the streets and boundaries of Jerusalem. At last an Egyptian army entered Judea, and Nebuchadnezzar raised the siege. A frantic joy seized the inhabitants of Jerusalem; but the gloomy prophesies of Jeremiah soon dispersed the same. Jerusalem's destruction was inevitable in spite of favorable aspects: "Should there be even but a few of the wounded remaining from the whole Chaldean army, these few will set fire to the capital."

On account of Jeremiah's perseverance in announcing the misfortunes of Judea, his sufferings had now reached the utmost point. One day, in leaving Jerusalem for Anatot, in order to settle there some private matters, he was arrested by the town-captain, Jerijah, who led him back under ill-usage, accusing him that he was going to join the Chaldeans. It was in vain that he proved his innocence in having never harbored the thought, being resolved to share the sufferings of his nation. The judges had him lashed and thrown in a narrow, damp prison, where he was exposed to hunger and the greatest hardships. In the meantime, the Chaldean army had defeated the Egyptians, and the siege of Jerusalem was renewed by them. Only too late did Zidkijah now awake from his delusions, ordering secretly Jeremiah before him and adjuring him to reveal unto him God's will. He told him that captivity should be his lot. At this interview Jeremiah complained of the sufferings he had to undergo in prison, and the compassionate king had him placed in safety in the guard-house of the fore-court of the palace (mattarah), and gave him liberty of conversing with the people. Day by day he urged the surrender of the town to the enemy, in order to procure forbearance, inasmuch as further resistance was quite useless. At length his words had the desired effect.

VII.

In spite of the king's attempt to rescue Jeremiah, his enemies demanded impetuously that the prophet should suffer death. Zidkijah could not save him, and left him to the mercy of his enemies. But in order not to lay hands on him, whom they thought in nature a superior being, they threw him into a deep cistern filled with mire, that he might thus perish without their further interference. A peculiar sophistry that Crime should be horrified at his own deeds! In this place death seemed unavoidable, had not an Ethiopian felt more compassionate than an Israelite. A servant of the king, Ebed-Melech, from Ethiopia—whose name was immortalized by Jeremiah—adjured the king not to allow this holy man to perish so miserably. Zidkijah was roused to pity, and ordered that he should be saved; and Ebed-Melech, with thirty men, succeeded, by means of long ropes, in drawing from his grave the half-dead prophet, whom they carried again to the watch-house of the fore-court. Here Zidkijah deliberated with him about the steps he should have to take, and the prophet answered that he should pass over to the enemy without the least fear. Jeremiah also quieted his fear of being maltreated in the Chaldean army by those who belonged to Judea. The king was so illiberal as to force a promise from Jeremiah not to divulge this interview to the princes, and for which in return he assured him of his protection. Both kept their word. Jeremiah remained in the watch-house of the fore-court, receiving daily a loaf of bread, till the famine made its appearance.

While God's judgments were raging in Jerusalem, and the three plagues, sword, hunger, and pestilence, were destroying its forces, while mothers from sheer desperation were consuming even their own children, and every one was feeling that the last glimmer of hope had been extinguished, then was Jeremiah's breast filled with bright aspirations. Previously he had only misfortunes to announce, but amid the deep sorrow of the present he could see the aurora of a better future. The subversion of the independence of the state, which, through the general demoralization, had been undermined ; the desolation of the Temple, stained with horrors and crimes, the voice of God had told him were all to lead to a holy life. Jeremiah's speeches the night before the destruction were of a cheerful and encouraging nature. His prophetic effusions at this time rose from the elegy to the hymn.

"A voice is heard at Rama, a bitter, sorrowful crying, Rachel weeps for her vanished children. Thus then speaks the Lord : Quiet thy tears, mourning mother! far better things are stored up for thy children, they shall return home one day from the enemy's country; there is hope for thy posterity, they will return to thy fatherland.".... "The day will come, when I (God) shall make a fresh covenant with Israel and Judah, a covenant not like that of Egypt, which they destroyed, and owing to which I had to reject them. The law which I gave them I shall write into their heart, and all, from the greatest to the least, will be filled with the knowledge of God. Inasmuch as the light of day and the regular change of the constellation at night will ever cease, as much will Israel ever cease to be a people before God."

Such is the style of Jeremiah's eloquent speeches, proceeding from the watchtower of the fore-court. In confirmation of his prophetic consolation, he bought at that time, when the enemy was almost master of the whole country, a piece of ground belonging to his cousin at Anatot. To this act he added the prophecy that, although the country is now passing into the enemy's hands, the time will, nevertheless, not fail to arrive when Judea shall again buy and sell fields and vineyards, and exercise a busy and active life. Probably about this time he made the short but flourishing speech :

"Thus saith the Lord: I remember, Judah, the attachment of thy youth, the love of thy betrothment, when thou didst follow *Me* through the inhospitable wilderness. Holy is Israel unto the Lord, being His first fruit, and whoever lays hands on it has forfeited punishment."

At length Jerusalem's last hour appeared. After a siege of sixteen months the walls received a breach, by which the enemy entered, and Zidkijah with his warriors escaped through some subterranean passages (9 Tamus, July, 586.) The king was captured, blindfolded and taken into captivity. A month later, the Temple and the palaces became a prey to the flames, and all the prisoners were placed in shackles. Jeremiah was amongst them awaiting his fate, but he did not remain a prisoner very long. The victor knew Jeremiah's character well, and he ordered one of his generals, Nebusaradan, to set him at liberty. In rending the chains which held him, he was informed that he was at liberty to choose either to emigrate to Babylon or to remain in Judea. Jeremiah had no desire yet of leaving his fatherland, although it was in ruins, and therefore he preferred to stay. He joined the small number which the victor left behind him under the Governor Gedaliah-ben-Achikam. Upon the smoking ruins of Jerusalem Jeremiah was breathing forth his immortal lamentations. But it was not reserved for him to die in the land of his ancestors. The small number left behind, which could have become the kernel of a rejuvenated nation, were soon dispersed after Gedaliah had lost his life. The remaining few, under Jochanan-ben-Kareach, in doubt whether to remain in the country or emigrate to Egypt, consulted Jeremiah in the matter. But, although he reminded them not to leave their fatherland, and assured them they had nothing to fear from the Chaldeans, they rejected his counsel after all ; for these unfortunate, helpless men fancied that it was his disciple, Baruch, who induced Jeremiah to give them such advice, believing that Baruch intended to deliver them to the Chaldeans for punishment. They then emigrated to Egypt, and Jeremiah, in order not to remain behind entirely by himself, joined them also (about 584). They had a friendly reception in Egypt, and settled in different parts of the country. Jeremiah probably resided at Daphne, a part of Lower Egypt.

Here he had still to contend against the indelible idolatry which seemed rooted in the hearts of almost all the exiles. The Jewish women took to the worship of Isis, persuading the men to follow their example. Yet it is remarkable that the emigrants in Egypt still hoped to return to their fatherland and see the Temple rebuilt once more. These hopes were grounded upon Egypt's preparations for war with Nebuchadnezzar. Jeremiah, whose last breath was still an exhortation for improvement, gathered together all the Judeans in Egypt, and addressing them in affecting language (probably his dying strains), endeavored to destroy the delusions under which they labored. He inquired of them whether they had not had enough of misfortunes, and if they could not see quite clearly that the destruction of the state and the Temple was owing to idolatry and demoralization, and whether they had any desire to call upon them the wrath of God even still more. But the women were impudent enough to reply that they expected better success from the worship of Isis than the adoration of the blessed God. Jeremiah hereupon announced to them inexorable punishment from on high. To the unfortunate prophet it was not granted to gather around him even a small congregation of God-fearing men, whose true piety would have revived his drooping soul. The day of his death is not known. It is said that he was stoned to death by those who belonged to his own race.

But whatever his living word could not accomplish the writings he left effected afterward; and his admirers collected them both in Babylon and Egypt. These writings were diligently read and taken to heart. The exiles, through this valuable heirloom, and through the prophet Ezekiel, who probably was his disciple, and laboring in the same direction, were drawn nearer to a spiritual attachment toward God, and gradually abandoned idolatry. The rejuvenated and purified nation felt so grateful to Jeremiah that everything wonderful related of him was readily believed. But singular traits in his character, which veneration toward him affirmed, are here out of place. The historical facts of his life are sufficiently corroborated to make his loftiness worthy of admiration, and himself a model whose confidence in God was unshaken and devoted to the last.

Dr. H. Graetz.

Bendeman—A celebrated German painter.

Prerogative—An exclusive privilege.

Oriental—Belonging to the Eastern part of the world.

Ideal—Mental, intellectual.

Pantheon—A temple at Rome for idol worship.

Caliph—A title assumed by the successors of Mohamed, the Saracenes.

Forum—Court of justice, any public place.

Enigmatical—Darkly expressed.

Obduracy—Hardness of heart.

Embryo—The state of anything yet unfinished.

Sanctimonious—Saintly, appearing as such.

Ephemeral—Which lasts but a day.

Colossus—Enormous, magnitude.

Autonomy—To live according to your own mind.

Isis—An idol worshiped by the Egyptians.

Typologist—The science of types.

Emulation—Rivalry, contest.

Organism—Various parts co-operating with each other.

Drastic—Powerful.

Figuratively—In a sense different from that which words generally imply.

Herald—A forerunner, a harbinger.

Hellas—Pertaining to Greece.

Aesthetic—Impressing the senses and feelings of our nature.

Mythological—Relating to fabulous history.

Incense—Perfumes exhaled by fire in honor of some god.

Myrmidon—A rude ruffian, so named from the soldiers of Achilles.

Quasi—As if, as it were.

Sophistry—Anything subtle, corrupt and not genuine.

Aurora (poetically)—The morning.

BELSHAZZAR.

The midnight hour was drawing on;
Hushed into rest lay Babylon.

All save the royal palace, where
Was the din of revels, and torches'
    flare.

There high within his royal hall
Belshazzar, the king, held festival.

His nobles around him in splendor shine,
And drain down goblets of sparkling
    wine.

The nobles shout, and the goblets ring;
'Twas sweet to the heart of the stiff-
    necked king.

The cheeks of the king, they flashed
    with fire,
And still as he drank his conceit grew
    higher.

And, maddened with pride, his lips let
    fall
Wild words, that blaspheme the great
    Lord of all.

More vaunting he grew, and his blas-
    phemous sneers
Were hailed by his lordly rout with
    cheers.

Proudly the king has a mandate passed;
Away hie the slaves, and come back
    full fast.

Many gold vessels they bring with them,
The spoils of God's house in Jerusalem.

With impious hand the king caught up,
Filled to the brim, a sacred cup;

And down to the bottom he drained it
    dry,
And aloud, with his mouth afoam, did
    cry:

"Jehovah! I scoff at Thy greatness
    gone!
I am the King of Babylon!"

The terrible words were ringing still,
When the king at his heart felt a secret
    chill.

The laughter ceased, the lords held their
    breath,
And all through the hall was still as
    death.

And see, see there! on the white wall,
    see!
Comes forth what seems a man's hand
    to be!

And it wrote and wrote in letters of
    flame,
On the white wall—then vanished the
    way it came.

The king sat staring, he could not
    speak,
His knees knocked together, death-pale
    was his cheek.

With cold fear creeping his lords sat
    round;
They sat dumb-stricken, with never a
    sound.

The magicians came, but not one of
    them all
Could interpret the writing upon the wall.

That self-same night God put an end
    to his reign!
And Belshazzar, the king, by his nobles
    was slain.

HEINRICH HEINE.

SIMON THE JUST AND HIS TIMES.

[332 B].

A STRANGE feeling seizes the inquirer into Jewish history, in leaving the last writings of the sacred historic records, Ezra and Nehemiah, in order to follow the thread in the books of Josephus—a feeling of desolation and regret. Hitherto he has moved in a rich world, a host of distinguished names rustled around him, eminent personalities have captivated his interest, and, all at once, everything becomes quiet; he merely hears some isolated sounds, he meets during an interval of two centuries only now and then some dismembered persons, who appear neither acting nor speaking, and differ only from each other by their names. It is as if one would suddenly be transposed from a tumultuous rising of the people into a heath, where, after a long space of time, he alights on a living being. To this isolated feeling is added that of obscurity, for the inquirer is looking in vain for a hold to cling to from which he could reconstruct the long period. Josephus, in recounting the events after Nehemiah's time, merely rehearses the names of the High-priests: Onias I., Simon the Just, the fabulous Eleasar, a Menasse, Onias II., remarkable for his avarice and apathy, Simon II., Onias III., whose grave was scarcely closed, when the bloody combat for the dignity of High-priest commenced between the Nationals, true to the law, and the faithless Hellenists; only at the time of Simon II. the scene becomes somewhat more lively, without getting, however, in anywise brighter.

And yet one can hardly be persuaded that this long period should resemble a plain tablet, upon which merely a few names and fragmentary occurrences are notched. Does not there happen in this period a turning point strictly marked in the history of mankind—the downfall of Persian rule, and the victory of Greece over the Orient? Alexander the Great, the youthful Macedonian hero, with his gigantic schemes and his generals, those men with hearts of steel, filled the world, from the Danube to the Indus, with the deafening noise of their arms; and the shock which these wars and bloody contests brought about were also heavily felt in Judea. The inner change which the Orient experienced, owing to this ferment, did not pass Judea traceless. The Jewish nation, also, although of extraordinary tenacity, and full of stings against the pressure of foreign elements, could not escape Hellenizing influence. Hellenism, which left deep wounds on Judaism, but, at the same time, roused it to its own perception, had, during the above-named line of high-priests in Judea, spread its first seed, which, owing to unfavorable times, grew up to a poisonous plant. How was the Judaism of that period situated, when first Greekism entered upon Jewish soil? The historian, Josephus, does not answer this question, and we should not be able to form the least conjecture, had not fortunately the Talmud, the gnome poet, Jesua Sirach, and some odd records, left us a few intimations respecting it. This period forms (what we have told at the outset), to a certain degree, the transition of the Biblical state, as impressed in the writings of Ezra and Nehemiah and the Chronicles, to the Maccabean epoch, influenced by Greekism, or under circumstances reaching against it, and which may be safely distinguished by the individuality of the High-priest Simon the Just. The life of prominent personalities is reflected most distinctly by the disposition of the time, especially if these are placed officially at the head of a people or community. In the following, we gather the few traits which are still cognizable of Simon the Just and the commotion of his time, and which we give here as a representation of that period.

Simon the First, son of Onias I., has left to posterity some good impressions, which we can infer from the honorable surname "the Just" (or "the pious"), even if historic authorities mention nothing else respecting him. At this simple period, names of honor were not thrown away extravagantly, in order to bestow them undeservedly, and Simon, even if High-priest and Regent of the Jewish community, was, nevertheless, not powerful enough to have had flatterers who would have invented this epithet. "He is called the Just," says Josephus, "on account of his pious conduct toward God, and his benevolent intentions for his race." Some Talmudic authorities are almost at a loss to do proper justice to his deep piety; and a single trait, which has been handed down to us, shows that he was animated with pure piety, and had no opinion of an obscure, life-hating, ascetic religiousness. The gnome-poet, Sirach, who has written a commendatory poem on Biblical heroes, and bringing it down to his contemporary, Simon, calls him "the chief of his brethren, and the crown of his people." His outward appearance, also, must have been imposing; the same poet gathers together the most lovely and brilliant similes, in order to celebrate in his song this worthy and grave high-priest. "How beautiful he appeared in quitting the Temple, or when he had left the Holy of Holies! Like the morning star, surrounded with clouds; like the full moon in the days of spring; like the sun brightens the Temple of the Most High; like the rainbow from out the clouds; like the rose in the time of spring; like the lily on the rim of a rivulet; and like the Lebanon flower in the days of summer." In such representations Simon's delineation is continued. That cannot have been an unimportant person who could thus influence the poet's mind to such flourishing ecstacy.

Simon administered as High-priest when Alexander the Great undertook his triumphant march. The Macedonian hero, although but slightly affected by Grecian civilization, was no barbarian, no Sennacherib or Nebuchadnezzar, to allow, merely for the sake of taking delight in destruction, the innocent to be put to the sword, to lay cities in ashes, to turn flourishing countries into deserts, or even subjugate nations by tearing them away from their soil, and transplanting them to a distant region. He demanded merely submission; and, perhaps, some supply of their natural productions for his numerous army; and the Asiatic people of the interior, as well as Judea, had no cause to oppose him, especially as they felt no particular attachment to the Persian despots, being continually oppressed by the satraps, in order that a change of rulers may not be welcome to them. When Alexander, after his first victories over the Persian army, came to Syria, to go to Egypt, no country, except Tyre and Gaza, resisted him, but all the kings met him and did him homage. Simon the Just, as the chief dignitary and representative of the

Jewish nation, went as far as the sea-shore to meet the Conqueror, wearing the attire of a high-priest, and being accompanied by a number of priests in their ornate robes, and by the noblest of the nation. Report has it, Alexander was so overcome with awe at the sight of the High-priest, that he at once approached to greet him; and, when his courtiers expressed their astonishment at his condescension, he observed that he once saw in a dream the likeness of this High-priest, clad in the very same attire, and he then promised him victory. Alexander, thereupon, on the application of the High-priest, granted to the Jews religious freedom, and freed them e en of all contributions in the Sabbatic year; because, there being no harvest during that period, they could not supply any natural productions. After Alexander's departure for Egypt (333), he gave the government of Syria, to which now Judea and Samaria belonged, to his general, Andromachus.

While Alexander carried on his conquests in Egypt, disturbances took place in Samaria, the cause and extent of which are unknown; but so much is certain, that they originated between the religious Jews and the Samaritans, and not with those originally of one race. But as soon as the governor, Andromachus, interfered, in order to settle the animosities, the Samaritans revolted, and killed him by committing him to the flames. Alexander, on receiving the news of this horrid deed, hastened to the spot, demanding that the perpetrators of the awful crime should be delivered up to him; this being done, he punished them and destroyed the town of Samaria; or, as others would have it, put a Macedonian garrison in the place. As he punished the Samaritans for their rebellion, the Jews were rewarded for their restraint and moderation; it is even said that he added Samaria to Judea, and declared it free of all taxes. Probably Alexander thought proper to declare that, for the future, merely a border district with the towns Lydda (Ramatain) and Ephraim (Apherema) should belong to Judea, which was, perhaps, the cause of the quarrel; for, under Simon's son, the Samaritans afterward took revenge, and gained possession once more of the same district.

Thus the first meeting of Judah and Javan was a pleasant one, accompanied by mutual kindness. Alexander favored the Jews, and they entered his army and assisted him in his conquests. Simon the Just was the mediator between the two antagonistic nations. Both had no foreboding that, before long, they should have to undergo together a hard combat, and that the Jews would be instrumental in bringing about the ruin of Grecian rule, both in Syria and Egypt.

The peace and comfort which Judea enjoyed under Alexander lasted only until his death. Hereupon two decades followed, during which his generals kept up a destructive war, from which Judea also had to suffer much. The columns of the army of Antigones, of his son, Demetrius, the city conqueror, and Ptolemæos Lagi crushed the blessings of this land and filled its inhabitants with horror. Ptolemæos took Jerusalem by storm on a Sabbath, and the walls of Jerusalem, which were great strongholds since the time of Nehemiah, were pierced again, for the first time since the existence of the second Temple, with many breaches. Judea had only just regained proper rest, when it was annexed to the Egyptian empire in continuity. All these occurrences Simon the Just lived to see, which gave him ample opportunities of confirming his trust in God, in order not to succumb under these misfortunes, and to prove his love toward his people, to alleviate their miseries, and to heal their wounds as much as he could.

> "He cared for his nation
> And saved her from ruin,"

the poet Sirach sings of him. Through this poet we are also told in what manner Simon showed his activity for his people. He made Jerusalem, which had suffered much through the wars, a great stronghold, in order that it might not be so easily taken, concerning which many gloomy prospects continually sprang up. The Temple Simon also fortified, repaired all damaged places, and raised the foundation of the fore-court. The reservoir in the Temple, holding the water, he enlarged to the dimensions of a pond, in order that the inhabitants might not suffer from scarcity of water in case of a siege. After that time the Temple had always large quantities of water in store, which, in a hot climate, and a dry soil like that of Jerusalem, was looked upon with great astonishment.

If Simon thus cared for the material interests of his people, he was not the less severed from the idea of Judaism, that Israel's strength does not depend upon such means. "Of three things Israel's salvation is composed," as taught by the choice sentence preserved to us; "upon observance of the law (Torah), upon reconciliation with God by virtue of means of grace, which the Temple-worship furnishes (Abodah), and upon works of charity (Gemilath Chessodim)." His piety was a purified one, free from ascetic excess. His period being full of wars and troubles, brought about many evils, and the strictly pious sought, as during the time of the prophets, to withdraw from human society altogether, and to consecrate themselves in vowing to lead a Nazarean life—the first onset to the sect of the Assideans. Simon did not like this mode of life, and showed his protest against it by not allowing the priests to use the pieces due to them from the sacrifices of the Nazareans. Only once he made an exception in favor of a young, beautiful shepherd, who came to him as a Nazarean. "Why do you wish," inquired the High-priest of the youth, who was adorned by a splendid head covered with ringlets, "to destroy thy beautiful head of hair?" To which the shepherd replied: "Because my headful of ringlets has nearly enticed me to sin from mere vanity. I once saw my reflection in a clear stream, and, as my likeness thus met my eye, the thought of self-deification took hold of me; wherefore I consecrated my hair unto the Lord through the Nazarean vow." In hearing these words, Simon kissed the young shepherd of such morally pure simplicity, and said to him: "Oh, if there were only in Israel many Nazareans like yourself!" At that time the whole nation was penetrated with a religious feeling for which Ezra paved the way, while Nehemiah, in conjunction with the great assembly, had strengthened it. During the time of Nehemiah the people in general cared but little for the Sabbath, being often engaged in the fields on that day, and, in Jerusalem, even the weekly market was held on the Sabbath; yet, in Simon's time, all had undergone a great change. Agatharchides, a Greek historian of that time, cannot avoid admiring much the strictness of the Jewish Sabbath. "The Jews are accustomed to rest on the seventh day; they carry neither arms, nor do they occupy themselves with field-work, or any other business matter on that day, but spend the whole of the day until evening sets in with praying, and, when Ptolemaeos Lagi laid siege to the town, they did not protect it, but protected their law."

Simon the Just was unequaled as High-priest, and, on account of his acquaintance with the law, president and active member of the great assembly, and in an efficient manner effected the strengthening of religiousness, and participated zealously in all institutions belonging to it, although these are only partly known to us. But whether the writings of the prophets received under him the character of being sacred documents (first canonical collection), and that also the reading of the prophets on the Sabbath was then introduced, can neither be affirmed or denied. Forty years, it is said, Simon administered as High-priest and benefactor of his people, and announced his death beforehand, after completing the service of the Day of Atonement. In entering the Holy of Holies on that day, he used to perceive, every year, an apparition in snow-white garments, which generally followed him; but as soon as he once missed this apparition, he considered it a harbinger of his approaching demise. He died seven days after the festival (about 300). Posterity honored him as a holy being, and related of him that during his lifetime the visible tokens of God's mercy never ceased. After his death the levity of Hellenism began gradually to corrupt the people; his grandchild, Joseph ben Tabia, was infected by it, and his great-grandchildren showed their bad example by deserting Judaism entirely, and thus brought about the troublesome times under the tyrant Antiochus Epiphanes. Soon after Simon's death the pious resolved, in presentiment that degeneracy and desertion seemed to be imminent, that the sons of Israel should discontinue uttering the sacred name of God. The priests only, when they concluded the daily sacrificial service, pronounced from the Duchan the blessings over the people, or when the High-priest on the Day of Atonement uttered his confession of sins for himself, his house, and the nation, then they made use of the four letters of the sacred name (Tetrigzammatau), collectively and in a devotional disposition of mind. Dr. H. Graetz.

HELLENIC—Pertaining to Hellenes or inhabitants of Greece.
EPITHET—Denoting any quality good or bad.
ASCETIC—Employed wholly in exercises of devotion and mortification of the flesh.
GNOME—An imaginary being, supposed to inhabit the inner parts of the earth.
DELINEATION—To represent a true likeness.
SATRAP—A nobleman in ancient Persia who governed a province.

ECSTACY—Rapture, enthusiasm.
ORNATE—Decorated.
SABBATIC—Resembling the Sabbath, bringing intermission of labor.
ANTAGONIST—An opponent.
CONTINUITY—Uninterrupted cohesion.
NAZAREAN—One who gives himself up entirely to devotion.
DEIFICATION—The act of deifying or making a god.

ISRAEL'S BANNERS.

Ye true sons of Israel, e'er faithful, undaunted,
  Whose hearts still are burning with love and with pride,
For the faith which, sublime in its power and its grandeur,
  The storms of long centuries has nobly defied.

Raise high the bright banner of Judah's proud glory,
  The emblem of honor, the symbol of light,
The flag that has braved every peril and danger,
  On whose folds are engraven truth, justice and right.

Aye, raise the proud ensign with glad acclamation,
  Let it kiss the proud zephyrs of morning once more,
For grandly it waved over sages and martyrs,
  And beneath it have stood kings and prophets of yore.

Vain, vain were the efforts of despots and tyrants
  Its brightness to sully, its beauty to mar;
In adversity's clouds, in the gloom of misfortune,
  It shone like a beacon and glowed like a star.

It guided the Hebrew through cruel oppression,
  Through darkness and sorrow, injustice and wrong,
With fortitude grand and with courage heroic,
  With a faith e'er unfaltering, unyielding and strong.

Antiquity's nations are lost in oblivion,
  Proud kingdoms have moldered in dust and decay,
And empires that once were the pride, and the glory,
  And the wonder of earth, have long passed away.

But our flag is still waving, as pure and and as stainless
  As when ages ago 'twas in grandeur unfurled,
When a nation received the commands of Jehovah,
  When the lightnings of Sinai illumined the world.

In the glorious lands of the radiant tropics,
  Where the palm and the cedar are kissed by the breeze,

Which, laden with perfumes and sweet-
scented flowers,
Blows gently and soft o'er the bright
Southern seas;

In the climes of the North, where the
frost-king eternal
Bears sway, and the storm-winds in
fury e'er blow,
Where the pole-star looks down in its
radiant effulgence
On ice-plains, bright, gleaming, and
mountains of snow;

In the countries renowned of the far-
distant Orient,
In whose seas and whose mines lie
treasures untold;
On the Occident mountains that tower
in proud grandeur,
Where the sun sinks to rest behind
billows of gold;

In America's beautiful meadows and
valleys,
E'er in nature's fair garments of
holiday dressed;
In the isles of the sea, o'er the sands of
the desert,
In the North and the South, in the
East and the West;

There, there is the banner of Judah
still floating,

In brightness and beauty, in glory
and might,
In its triumph o'er time and o'er tyrants
proclaiming,
The victory sublime of truth, justice
and right.

Proud flag of our fathers, wave on in
thy splendor,
Till sin and corruption from earth
shall depart,
Till man shall bow down before truth's
sacred altar,
And love and good-will reign supreme
in each heart!

Wave on—till all men shall know and
acknowledge
That honor alone is the token of
worth;
Till grief shall be lost in gladness un-
ending.
And the angel of plenty shall smile
on the earth.

Wave on—till like roaring of ocean's
great billows,
Like heaven's mighty thunder, the
glad cry shall ring,
From zone to zone—from nation to nation—
"The Lord is our God, and the Lord
is our King!"

MAX MEYERHARDT.

SYMBOL—A type; that which comprehends in
its figure a representation of something else.
ZEPHYR—The west wind
DESPOT—An absolute prince.
ANTIQUITY—Old times.
OBLIVION—Forgetfulness.
TROPICS—The line at which the sun turns

back, of which the north has the Tropic of
Cancer, and the south the tropic of Capricorn.
ORIENT—Rising as the sun, Eastern.
OCCIDENT—The West.
ZONE—A division of the earth, with regard
to heat and cold. There are five zones, viz.:
the torrid, two frigid and two temperate.

THE MACCABEAN WAR OF LIBERATION.

I.

175-140 B.

AFTER many of the wealthy in Judea had come into contact with the
Greeks, and had grown acquainted with Grecian life and manners
at the courts of Alexandria and Antioch, there arose an irresistible
desire among them to draw Greek influence into Jewish circles.
Yet so low was their sympathy with Hellenic genius and taste, that
it was not the refined part of the Grecian nature which enticed them;
but they were allured by the debauchery, pomp and the inordinate

enjoyments of the demoralized Asiatic Greeks. At the Jerusalem
gymnasium (a tilt-yard, where, in naked form, old and young practiced gymnastics), their principal effort was directed to strip off from
the Jew everything whereby he is recognized, firmly believing that
they would thus succeed in being considered of equal birth with the
Greeks. But as Judaism with its morality and earnestness proved
an impediment to this childlike occupation, they conceived a passionate hatred toward their faith ; and Judaism being likewise intimately and indissolubly associated with nationality, they became thus
the most bitter enemies of their nation. Without faction among the
people, these Hellenists were obliged to apply for aid to the Syrian
potentates, in order to enable them to effectuate their perversities ;
and thus they became traitors to the nation they belonged to and to
their paternal doctrines and morals as well. Alas! that they should
have counted men among them who were functionaries of the Temple, priests, and many a one of old and respectable lineage, for their
acts caused thus the long chain of affliction which befell Israel under
the Syrian king, Antiochus Epiphanes, of whose tyranny toward those
who steadfastly adhered to the God of Israel we scarcely find a parallel in history. But as a disease threatening to destroy the whole
body miraculously displays all at once some vital spark, inflaming
anew the oppressed vital powers and forcibly driving out the destroying spirits, till with cheerful and lasting vigor the body assumes
again its former activity, in the same manner there was yet a seed
of solid nature germinating in this almost dissolved nation, which
grew up amidst the storms, uniting everything afresh.

Passing over the foul murder of the noble High-priest, Onias (Jech-
anja), and that of the pious Eleasar, together with the slaughter of the
devout mother and her seven children, as well as the many thousands
of other victims who, for the sake of truth, suffered martyrdom, it
happened that Appellas, a delegate of the Syrian governor Phillipus,
came to Modin (Modaim), a place near Jerusalem, in order that the
Jews residing there, who were still persisting in their faith, should
be forced into subjection. In the same place there lived a highly
respectable family of priests, whose ancestral name was Hasmonai.
The descendants of this family then living were Matatia, the father
of five sons, bearing the names of Jochanan, Gadi, Simon Thassi,
Jehuda Maccabee, Eleazar Havran, and Jonathan Haphus. Owing
to this family being one of great influence, Appellas was in hopes that
in gaining them for his purpose it would enable him to execute his
plan more easily. Therefore, he directed his first summons to them,
requiring them to offer sacrifices on an altar he had erected, and
holding out tempting promises of what the king would bestow upon
them should they comply with his request. But they steadfastly refused compliance, declaring even publicly their indignation in being
thus called upon to transgress their holy law. " If all nations should

obey Antiochus," said Matatia, "and every one felt ready to desert the law of their fathers, I would, nevertheless, together with my sons and my brethren, still cling to the law of my God."

It occurred, however, that one of their confederates was induced to sacrifice on the altar, whereupon their zeal overpowered them, and with one stroke the old man brought the apostate to the ground; whilst his sons, assisted by others, destroyed the altar and slew Appellas with his accomplices. This was the first signal for revolt, and being once put in motion it soon grew of sufficient strength. In order to adopt proper measures, Matatia and his sons fled to the mountains, leaving their possessions in Modin; many others who also could not endure their oppression took refuge in the desert, where they spent a miserable existence by living upon roots and herbs. Thus the mountains and steep rocks of the middle-lands, where the caverns offered a safe retreat, were soon filled with rebels, who desired nothing but inflexible resistance. A Syrian captain marched against them and soon came upon a body of about 1,000 men, whom he summoned to surrender. But as his challenge was not listened to he awaited the next Sabbath, and then massacred all these defenceless men, who, on that holy day, would not fight, nor even throw stones, or barricade the entrances of their caverns. "We will die innocently," they called aloud, "and heaven and earth shall bear witness that, in taking our lives, you are guilty of an act of great injustice." Being terrified by this fresh misfortune, Matatia resolved, in case of an attack, upon fighting even on the Sabbath day. Gradually Matatia and his sons brought together a small army of brave and pious men, who were ready to lay down their lives for their faith. In self-defence they now proceeded as the attacking party. Small bodies appeared here and there, entered several towns and villages and defeated their persecutors, killed the apostates, and destroyed the altars of the heathen, circumcised the remaining uncircumcised children and insisted upon the immediate restoration of the synagogue worship.

A few months after the commencement of the revolt, Matatia, already an old man, felt his end approaching, and therefore called his children unto him, inspiring them with fresh courage, and urged them to adhere faithfully to the law of God, and to risk their lives for the preservation of the covenant. "Consider only," said he, "what happened generation after generation, and you will find that all who put their trust in God never succumbed under their afflictions. Your brother Simon is wise, and him you shall obey as father; but Judah, in his vigor of youth, is strong, and he shall become the leader of the army to carry on the war for this holy cause." These were the last words of this high-minded old man, whom his sons buried in Modin, and mourned for by every one in Israel.

With lion-like courage Judah now commenced the struggle. Appolonius, Governor of Naples, became the first victim of these desperate combatants. He scarcely had advanced when Judah went to meet him, massacred his troops and slew him also. His sword, which became Judah's booty, never left the hand of the young hero. Soon after this Seron advanced against him with a larger force. They met upon the heights of Bet-Horon, and the Syrians suffered a terrible defeat, and lost also their commander. The news of these disasters irritated Antiochus; the more so, because there were still other causes which placed him in difficulties; inasmuch as by his dissipation his treasury had become exhausted, and, besides, many provinces, feeling encouraged by the step Judah had taken, refused to pay tribute and threatened to shake off the oppressive yoke of the Syrians. His embarrassment increased his rage, and whilst he himself advanced northward, he ordered his minion, Lysias, to enter Judea, there to annihilate all the Israelites, and to colonize the country with a strange people. An army of 40,000 foot and 7,000 horsemen advanced, and he felt so sure of victory that Nicanor, one of the commanders appointed under Lysias, made publicly known that a rich and well supplied slave market was to be opened, and that he would be ready to sell ninety Jewish women and children for one talent. These boasting proclamations actually enticed many merchants to the spot in order to buy the Jewish prisoners. Judah, however, could only muster 6,000 men. After dividing his army and placing each division under the command of one of his brothers, and holding a solemn service at Mizpah, he moved to meet the enemy. Although his army was small, he nevertheless issued the order prescribed according to law (Deut. xx: 5), that all who had built a new house and had not yet consecrated it, and those who had planted a vineyard and had not yet kept the first vintage, together with those who had affianced themselves to a woman and had not yet been wedded, and, besides, also those who lacked courage to go into battle, were at liberty to quit the army. "It is better for us," the army replied, "to die in battle than to behold our nation in misery."

One evening Judah announced that a battle was to take place the next day; but being informed that Georgias, a Syrian general, had left his camp with 5,000 foot and 1,000 horsemen to surprise the Jewish army in the flank that very night, he at once set out with all his forces and surprised the Syrian camp. The confusion which this unexpected night attack brought about caused the Syrians a loss of 3,000 men, whilst the rest took to flight. Judah waited now the return of Georgias, who, to his astonishment, found his camp in flames. Great was the terror which beset his warriors; they shunned fighting, and many threw away their arms. Judah pursued the flying enemy, whereby several thousand lost their lives, and thus almost the whole of the Syrian army was destroyed. Nicanor, disguised in the dress of a slave, escaped to Antioch. After this great success they kept a joyful Sabbath day, thanking God for the victory thus obtained, and imploring his further mercy. Other divisions of the Syrian army were also defeated. On all occasions rich booty was gained, and Calisthenes, who, by the taking of the Temple, had burned the gates, was made prisoner in a hut where he had taken refuge, and committed to the flames. All these happy results won for Judah much influence, and thus more and more able fighting men joined his flag. The next year Lysias himself advanced against him with an army of 60,000 foot and 5,000 horsemen, and Judah, who had now 10,000 men under his command, met him at Betsur, westward from Jerusalem, where he obtained a decisive victory over Lysias.

But, to crown the work which he had begun, Judah resolved upon another daring enterprise. While he fortified Betsur, to be safe from the hostile-disposed Idumæans, he advanced with his brothers and the best of his troops against Jerusalem, in order to restore the solemn service of the Temple. On their arrival they found the altar desecrated, the places overgrown with grass and bushes, and the dwellings of the priests falling to pieces. This sight had such an effect upon them that they rent their clothes, scattered ashes on their heads, fell upon their faces, sounded the trumpet, and cried aloud to the heavens above. Hereupon they begun their work. The Syrian fortification, situated on a hill opposite, was invested by a number of brave warriors, who resisted every sally, and soon a strong bulwark was erected opposite the Temple, whereby the laborers were kept from molestation. From the booty they restored the golden vessels, whilst the priests cleansed the Temple and the fore-courts, and prepared everything for the service of God.

On the 25th of Kislev, when all was properly arranged, they kept the feast of dedication during eight consecutive days, offering sacrifices, and singing praises and thanksgivings unto the Holy One in Israel. The finding of a jar of consecrated oil, with the seal of the Temple upon it, must be considered a miracle of Divine providence, as the same proved sufficient for lighting the Temple during eight days, when fresh oil was then ready. From that time it became a law in Israel to celebrate yearly these eight days (Chanukah) by illuminating the houses and synagogues, and also by praising and giving thanks to Him who had vouchsafed unto Israel all these mercies.

II.

The news of the restoration of the Jewish Temple, with its divine services, brought all the hostile heathen nations against the Maccabees, so that Judah and his brothers had to fight on all sides, in order to protect their people from persecutions; but they proved successful everywhere. Antiochus was on a journey when the news reached him that Lysias as well as the generals under his command had been defeated; that the Jews had fortified Betsur, which was now occupied by a garrison, and that the Temple had been restored. He resolved, therefore, to advance once more against the people he so much hated, taking a vow that he would turn Jerusalem into a pit for their dead bodies. However, it never came to this, for the Almighty decreed otherwise. Antiochus was stricken with sickness, suffering excruciating pain, from which no medical aid could free him, so that he was obliged to use great haste on his journey. In his hurry he fell from his carriage, thus aggravating the disease from which he suffered. Under these afflictions he soon changed his resolution, promising not to molest the holy city, to bestow rich presents on the Temple, and to proclaim everywhere the power and greatness of God. But God, from whom no secrets are hid, knew well that it was not true repentance, and he suffered a painful death far away from his home. In this manner the prophesy of the youngest of the seven brothers, whom he had innocently slain, became thus fulfilled: "Thou wilt yet, under pain and torture, acknowledge that the God of Israel is the only true God."

However, neither the restoration of the divine service nor the death of the king brought this terrible war to an end. Judah had hitherto been victorious, but now heavy trials awaited him. Eupator, the son of Antiochus, a mere boy, succeeded to the throne, and undertook, with Lysias, an expedition against Jerusalem. His army counted 100,000 foot and 2,000 horsemen, besides thirty-two elephants. With this enormous power he advanced against Betsur. Judah hastened to its relief, but was unable to stand against this overwhelming strength. He, therefore, retired upon Jerusalem, and Betsur surrendered under favorable conditions. In this last battle he had to deplore the loss of his brother Eleasar, who, wishing to secure victory, ventured, in his daring bravery, into the midst of the enemy, when he mistook a full-equipped elephant for the one upon which the king sat, and, creeping under the same, stabbed it until it fell dead upon him, and thus the thoughtless hero was crushed to death.

After Betsur had surrendered the Syrian army advanced as far as the Temple-mount, where Judah had to defend himself, and where his ruin became almost a certainty, had not another fortunate occurrence saved him from his difficulties. A message reached the Syrian camp that Philip, a friend of the deceased and guardian of the present king, had attempted to seize upon the throne, on account of which Lysias urged a peace, which was soon accomplished. The Jews took the oath of fidelity toward the Syrians, under the condition that religious freedom and all the fortified places should be granted them. The last condition, however, Lysias soon broke, for he immediately gave orders that the wall which protected the Temple should be demolished; showing, nevertheless, that he was in earnest in keeping peace by having Menelaus executed as the author of all mischief and the instigator of the war. Alkim (Jakim), a friend to Hellenism, took his place, and, being of priestly descent, he was made High-priest. He was, however, to the Jews just as corruptible as his predecessor. But scarcely had Demetrius Soter, son-in-law of Antiochus (to whom the Syrian throne really belonged, already before Antiochus returned from Rome, where he lived as hostage), ascended the throne after the assassination of Eupator and Lysias, when Alkim applied to him to bring Judah under subjection.

Demetrius granted his request and sent a strong army, first under Bacchides, and then under the command of the well-known Nicanor, in order to attack Judah. A battle was fought, and Nicanor lost 5,000 men. A second time the opposing forces met at Bet-Horon, for Nicanor had received reinforcement, whilst Judah had only 3,000 men under his command. The Syrians, however, were defeated, and Nicanor lost his life on the battle-field. That day—Nicanor's day—which happened on the 13th of Adar, was instituted as a holiday, but the same, having become obsolete, is not celebrated at the present time. Judah, who now plainly saw that he had but little to expect from the Syrians, sent an ambassador to Rome, who succeeded in entering upon an alliance with that great power; but, as regards advantages which the Jews may have gained by this league, we are left without information. Thus, while Judah was engaged in taking these steps for the welfare of his people, the end of his eventful life was approaching, and the time was near when his unfortunate nation should have to lose his strong arm.

Enraged at the defeat of Nicanor, Demetrius sent once more with the High-priest, Alkim, under the command of Bacchides, 20,000 foot and 2,000 horsemen to make another attack upon Judah, who had now only 800 men at his disposal. The only chance he had was flight, but he preferred death to this humiliating expedient. With lion-like courage he threw himself upon the enemy, who, at the commencement, gave way on all sides. But he was soon obliged to succumb to the overwhelming strength continually brought to bear against him, and he finished his eventful career on the field of battle, dying for his religion, his people, and his country. His brothers buried him in the family sepulchre at Modin, and all Israel mourned for him, for, by the death of this hero, it had indeed become an orphan.

After his death the people became dejected, and many yielded to Bacchides; a famine forcing submission. But the remaining three brothers soon took courage, and their resistance against the Syrians was continued under Jonathan's leadership. He was no less brave than Judah, and in prudence and sagacity he was even his superior.

These advantages came very useful to him. About this time the strife for the possession of the throne brought many troubles on Syria, which were very beneficial for Israel. A certain Alexander

Bolas, pretending to be a son of Antiochus Epiphanes, arose against Demetrius, in order to displace him. Demetrius, fearful of losing Judea altogether, resolved upon acknowledging Jonathan. He gave him permission to raise troops and to procure arms, and ordered the Syrian garrisons to withdraw from the fortifications. Jonathan now commenced rebuilding Jerusalem, erecting a fresh wall on the Temple-mount, strengthening Mount Zion by square stones, and other places were fortified. But Alexander also sought Jonathan's assistance. He sent him a purple cloak, a golden crown, and the appointment of High-priest. This offer Jonathan accepted also, and on the feast of Tabernacle (153) he, for the first time, entered the sanctuary as High-priest. Demetrius now held out still greater and better promises; but, being disliked by the people, Jonathan remained an adherent of Alexander, by whom he was much esteemed. Alexander, however, did not abide on the Syrian throne, which changed its possessor continually.

Jonathan and his brother Simon made good use of these circumstances, in order to make Judea still more independent and self-subsisting. They also sent, the same as Judah had done, an ambassador to Rome, and received many friendly and peaceful assurances from that quarter. But, alas! Jonathan, generally so prudent and heedful, had to succumb to craftiness, and fell into the hands of the treacherous Tryphon—a Syrian commander—who had him executed, after he had already taken Jochanan prisoner, who had to share the same fate. Judah had executed more heroic deeds, and his fame in war was more splendid than Jonathan's, who, however, had raised his people to might and influence, and made his generation one of great repute, on account of having gained the dignity of High-priest. To seek for a similar picture of both brothers from the past history of the Israelites, we should have to compare Judah with one of the Judges, but Jonathan with Saul, the first king in Israel. Simon had his earthly remains entombed in the family sepulchre at Modin, and the whole people mourned for their wise hero, who fell a sacrifice for Israel, which he led again into the ranks of free and independent nations.

Simon Thassi, the fifth heroic son, undertook now the guidance of the Jewish nation. Although already advanced in years, he still possessed the fiery courage and vigor of youth, as at that time when his dying father recommended him as counselor in the war then pending. Four sons, full of hope, were ready to assist him. He at once declared himself independent of Syria, and did not wait, as was usual, to have the dignity of High-priest confirmed by the king. He also obtained for Judea a discharge from paying taxes, and now they ceased counting the change of the year after the Syrian kings, but commenced from the year 142, according to the princes belonging to the family of the Hasmonæans. Another matter of importance was that he expelled the yet remaining Hellenists, who could still be met with at the fort in Jerusalem and in several other fortifications, and thus the last vestige of those who brought so much misery upon Israel was entirely extirpated. Simon thought to secure the independence of the Jewish state by placing himself under the protection of the Romans. Therefore he sent an ambassador to the Roman Senate, who were not disinclined to enter upon an alliance with the Jewish nation. But the intercourse, as was proved afterward, had more evil consequences than Simon really expected.

As the Syrian power over Israel was now entirely broken, the people resolved in public assembly to choose Simon as hereditary prince in Israel, and as High-priest as well. This resolution was engraved on brazen tablets, which were deposited in the Temple. Simon also coined money in proof of the independence of the Jewish state. In many collections we find, now and then, Jewish coins, which are of great value for their antiquity. Simon fell by the hand of his own son-in-law, Ptolemæus, governor of Jericho, with whom he was staying at the time. Thus ended the last brother of the Hasmonæans, none of whom died a tranquil death, but all expired for the cause of the people and the sanctuary. Judah and Eleasar died on the field of battle; Jochanan, Jonathan and Simon, less fortunate than their brothers, had to succumb to the craftiness of the enemies of their people. But their memory will forever be blessed in Israel, for, by their blood, they have saved the most sacred of all possessions, God's revealed law unto Israel. LUDWIG STERN.

Dr. LUDWIG STERN—Noted as a writer of many useful works for educational purposes.

GYMNASTICS—The performing of athletic vigorous exercises.
INDISSOLUBLY—In a manner resisting all separation.
FACTION—A party in a state.
APOSTATE—One that has forsaken his religion.
MINION—A favorite.

"HANNAH AND HER SEVEN SONS."

ALL is desolate and dark ! To me there's no light,
Since they took from the world my treasures so bright,
My children ! my children ! beats yet my heart,
When all of its strings are thus riven apart !
Yet for Israel's God this suff'ring I bear,
And would bear a greater, if greater there were.

Oh, how the whole scene is burned into my brain !
I see the vile Syrians, with faces like Cain,
Rush over my threshold and ruthlessly seize

All my seven fair sons, while I on my knees,
With tears and implorings, beseech them to wait—
Hope whispers that Time might avert their dread fate—

I knew 'twas but yesterday the old scribe they slew,
The old Eleazar, to Israel so true—
On my knees I implore them to wait but a day;
They mock at my pleading; then drag us away
And cast us in prison; but leave us not long;
The bigot his triumph will show to the throng.

With wickedest pleasure, he calls for
the first
Of my beautiful boys, the one that I
nursed
In the flush of my youth, when Judea
was free;
O God, keep his heart firmly true unto
Thee!
Ha! The king commands homage to
him and his gods;
He looks up to heaven, nor falter his
words:

"God forbid that homage to thee I
should show"—
"Israel's God is my God! to none else
will I bow!"
They lead him to death, my first born!
my pride!
And now tear my second fair boy from
my side,
And place him in front of the conqueror's throne;
Thou wilt not, my son, thy religion dis-
own!

His answer is ready; he quick makes
reply,
"My brother bowed not, and no more
will I."
"Why not?" asks the tyrant. "Be-
cause," says my boy,
And his face glows resplendent with
heavenly joy,
"Our second commandment tells all—
even thee—
'No other gods shalt thou have before
Me.'"

Death follows his brave words; my
third boy they take;
Be still, my wild heart—not yet must
thou break.
My third one! my hero! How princely
his port!
"No other gods shalt thou worship, is
taught
In my pure religion; more gladly I meet
The fate of brothers than bow at thy
feet."
These proud words the death-blow as
guerdon receive.
My fourth boy they take; will the
tyrant achieve
Any conquest over his soft, gentle heart?

Fear not, my sweet son, bear bravely
thy part!
Yes; he, too, is faithful. He utters
these words:
"He that sacrificeth to all other gods,
Save the Lord only, shall be wholly
destroyed."
Alas! he, too, is slain! How widens
the void
In my sore stricken heart. Ha! now
my fifth lad
They drag to the tyrant, who, already
mad,
Becomes doubly enraged at the words
of my son:
"Hear, O Israel! The Lord our God,
He is One."

With this watchword of faith he yields
his young life.
Now they come for my sixth; his spirit
is rife
With scorn and contempt for the despot's vain power,
Nor scourges nor threats will cause him
to cower.
"Why so obstinate?" asks the tyrant,
more mild;
Waver not, my dear son, thou'rt Judea's
true child.

"Think'st thou I'm affrighted? My
God is still here;
He is mighty and terrible; Him only I
fear.
And thou, too, wilt one day acknowledge
His might,
And suffer that thou hast usurped His
right."
They take him to death, in his fresh,
joyous youth,
That thus he pronounces the stern
words of truth.

What horror is this! My youngest
ye'll take—
My baby! My darling! Oh, for the sake
Of the mother who bore you, spare me
this son!
My six have ye murdered! Will ye
leave me not one?
They heed not my pleading, but drag
him away.
Oh, Father of Heaven, is this but one
day?

But see, the base murderer speaks
kindly to him.
My sweet, precious child, do nothing to
dim
The lustre that shines from thy six
brothers gone.
Be true to thy God, e'en though thou'rt
undone.
Now the king hands him treasure and
tells him to live,
And promises all, if allegiance he'll give.

See, now does he cast his ring on the
ground,
Now shows him his dead brothers lying
around,
And tells him their fate will be his if he
dare
Refuse to stoop for it. Still lies the
ring there.
"Think'st thou that I fear thy threats?"
says my boy;
"Our God is the great King of kings.
Then why
Should I give allegiance to other than
He?"
"If thy God is so great, why saves he
not thee
From my power?" asks the king.
"Because," he replies,
And in his young face a grandeur doth
rise,
"I am not worthy redemption from thee,
And thou art not worthy God's great-
ness to see."

"Slay the lad like his brothers," the
tyrant commands.
Oh, cruel king, ere thou steepest thy
hands
In the blood of my little one, let me be
slain,

I cannot endure this mountain of pain.
"Nay, thy own laws forbid," the tyrant
doth say;
"Sheep nor cow with its young shalt
thou kill in one day."

Oh, woe to thee, murderer, our laws to
pervert!
The God of our race will inflict thy
desert.
Come, my sweet angel, my lamb, ere
we part,
Kiss thy poor mother! Come nearer
my heart!
Oh, courage! my dear one, tell Abra-
ham there
My sacrifice hath his much exceeded;
where
He built one altar, I have built seven!
He offered one Isaac; all mine have I
given!
A little longer! A little longer! Fare-
well, my son!
'Tis for God's glory; His will be done.
There, there are my children, my dear
treasures, all!
They see me! and now they beckon
and call
To come and join there in that beautiful
place.
Yes! Yes! my beloved ones, quick,
quick will I trace
My steps to our house-top, and thou
canst reach there,
And with thy strong arms, draw me up
through the air.
We'll cheat the mad tyrant, and dwell
in our home;
Yes! Yes! my beloved, I'm coming!
I come!

MRS. M. D. LOUIS.

GUERDON—Reward, recompense.

THE MARTYR MOTHER.

WHERE in the vast tomes of history, sacred or profane, shall we
find a deed more heroic, a fortitude more sublime, than is recorded
of Hannah, the Hebrew mother, during the persecution of Antiochus?
We read in the second Maccabees, chap. vii., confirmed also by all our
Hebrew writers, that a mother and her seven sons were taken, and
brought before the tyrant, who, in the wantonness of cruelty, commanded them to eat the forbidden meat, commencing first with the

more moderate torment of whips and scourges, but heightening them gradually to tortures, which we leave our readers to peruse in the chapter we have quoted; for the soul sickens to dwell upon them, as deliberately to write them down. We will content ourselves with repeating the words they spake in the midst of those appalling sufferings, for surely they are in themselves witness of what the religion of the Eternal taught.

"What wouldst thou ask or learn of us?" the first said; "we are ready to die rather than transgress the laws of our fathers." And as his brethren beheld his lingering torments, instead of failing, they exhorted one another, and their mother, to die manfully, saying thus: "The Lord God looketh upon us, and in truth hath comfort in us, as Moses, which in his song, witnessed to their faces, declared; and he shall be comforted in his servants." To the second the question was put, "Wilt thou eat?" under threat of similar tortures which he had witnessed, but in vain. "Thou, like a fury, takest us out of this life," he said, in the very agonies of death, "but the King of the World shall raise us up, who have died for His laws, unto everlasting life." The third himself stretched forth his limbs for the torture, saying: "These I had from Heaven, and for His law I despise them, for from Him I expect to receive them again." Inasmuch as the king and those that were with him marvelled at the young man's courage, for that he nothing regarded his pains. The fourth then suffered, and he said:" "It is good, being put to death by man, to look for hope from God to be raised up again for Him; as for thee, thou shalt have no resurrection to life." And the fifth, in his dying agony, calmly looked upon the king, and said: "Thou hast power over men, but art corruptible; thou doest what thou wilt, but think not our nation is forsaken of God, but abide awhile, and behold His great power, how He will torment thee and thy seed." And the sixth being ready to die, emulating his brothers' constancy, addressed the tyrant: "Be not deceived without cause; we suffer these things for ourselves, having sinned against God, therefore marvelous things are done unto us; but think not thou, who takest in hand to strive against God, that thou shalt escape unpunished."

Nor was it one alone who thus endured. The Hebrew mother witnessed these agonizing tortures, done not unto one but unto six of her cherished offspring. Yet how do our elders speak of her? "The mother was marvelous above all, and worthy of honorable memory; for when she saw her seven sons slain within the space of one day, she bore it with a good courage, because of the hope that she had in the Lord. Yes, she exhorted every one of them in her own language, filled with courageous spirit, and stirring up her womanish thoughts with a manly stomach, she said unto them, 'I cannot tell how ye came into my womb, for I neither gave you breath nor life; neither was it I who formed the members of every one of you; but, doubtless, the Creator of the world, who formed the generation of man, and found out the beginning of all things, will also of His own mercy give you breath and life again, as ye now regard not your own selves for His law's sake.'"

Quaint and terse as this language is, and devoid of all ornament, yet how emphatically it breathes of the extent of this mother's trial, the struggle with her "womanish feelings," and her triumph over nature, over humanity, through that superhuman faith! Nor is the trial over. One still remained—her youngest born, probably still the tender and best beloved of his mother—one round whom the bleeding tendrils of her lacerated heart must have clung in such unutterable love; her last, her loveliest, and, evidently, from the tyrant's own words, one in the first and freshest prime of youth, when life has so many rich enjoyments, it seems doubly hard to turn from them to the cold, dark grave, and Heaven's perfected happiness to such ardent spirits feels dim and distant, compared to the present joy of earth. We know he was of such an age, and such aspirings, else the temptations of the tyrant would not have been couched in promises to make him a rich and happy man, and take him for his friend, and trust him with affairs, only on condition of his deserting the law of his fathers; and when the young man would not hearken to him, the king called upon the mother, and exhorted her with many words to counsel him to save his life. He believed nature, in such a case, must triumph, for he knew not the hope beyond the grave, which could still the throbbings of maternal love, and bid, even on earth, the angel triumph over the human, the immortal shine above the mortal!

Calmly she listened to the tyrant's "many words," and then bowing to him as about to obey, addressed her son in her own language: "Oh, my son, have pity on me who love thee, and gave thee suck three years, and nourished thee, and brought thee up unto this age, and endured the troubles of education. I beseech thee, my son, look upon the heaven and the earth, and all that is therein, and consider that God made them of things that were not, and so was mankind also. Fear not this tormentor, but, being worthy of thy brethren, take thy death, that I may receive thee again in mercy with thy brethren." And even while she was yet speaking, the young man said: "Whom wait ye for? I will not obey the king's commandment, but I will obey the commandment of the law that was given unto our fathers by Moses. And thou, that hast been the author of all the mischief against the Hebrews, shalt not escape the hands of God; for we suffer because of our sins, and though the living God be angry with us a little while for our chastening and correction, yet He shall return, and be again with His servants. But thou, O most godless man, and of all others most wicked, be not lifted up without cause, nor puffed up with uncertain hopes, lifting up thy hand

against the servants of God; for thou hast not yet escaped the judgment of Almighty God, who seeth all things. For our brethren who
now have suffered a short pain, are dead under God's covenant of
everlasting life; but thou, through the judgment of God, shalt receive just punishment for thy pride. But I, like my brethren, offer
up my body and life for the laws of our fathers, beseeching God
that He will speedily be merciful unto our nation, and that thou,
by torments and plagues, mayest confess that He alone is God, and
that in me and in my brethren the wrath of the Almighty, which is
justly brought upon all our nation, may cease." Then the king,
being in a rage, handled him worse than all the rest, and took it
grievously that he was mocked, so this man died undefiled, and put
his whole trust in the Lord. Last of all, after the sons, the mother
died. "Let this be enough," the writer concludes, "now to have
spoken concerning the idolatrous feasts, and the extreme tortures."

Enough? It is enough indeed for every Israelite to dwell upon,
not with shuddering horror, not with that squeamish kind of affected
feeling which pretends incapacity to look fearful truths in the face,
but with emotions of intense thankfulness, that such a record has
been left us, bearing such faithful witness as it does to the true
Israelite's belief. It is not merely a record of superhuman heroism,
alike in male and female. It is not merely a proof of the little
moment in which torture and death were held by the Hebrews, compared with which the far-famed firmness of Spartan and Roman
mothers sinks into nothing. It is the doctrines betrayed throughout, which, revealed at such a moment, must have impregnated the
very existence of the Israelite; and these doctrines may be treasured
up as invaluable evidences of all which was taught by our holy law,
however some may disbelieve the actual tale, of martyrdom in
which they are disclosed. The books of the Maccabees in the Apocrypha are on all points the exact counterpart of the same history in
Josephus, and also of Antiochus Epiphanes in Rollin.

There can be no doubt that the books were written by a Hebrew
for his countrymen, and therefore the words put into the mouths of
the sufferers must have been the exact transcript of the Hebrew's
true belief. If the doctrine of immortality—that hope beyond death
and the grave—was, as it is reported, unknown and unrevealed to
the Israelites, what could have inspired, not only the hope itself, but
the expression of that hope, in the very midst of torture and anguish
which human nature of itself could never have sustained. We have
quoted the words of the sufferers at full length, only to illustrate
this doctrine; to prove that all of immortality, of resurrection, of
being with God in heaven, of reunion there with our beloved ones,
of the transientness of the severest agonies below compared to
the permanency of bliss awaiting us above—that all was revealed
to us, all was known to every Hebrew, male and female, childhood

and age, believed in, acted upon, ages before the advent of that religion which was the first, her followers believe, to inculcate such doctrines. In a work like the present, we may not dilate on this glorious subject as much as inclination prompts; but, oh! let us not, by present indifference, by stagnant ignorance, or fearful shrinking from the idea of death, give our opponents only too much reason to believe that to them alone has been revealed the consolation, the glory, the blessedness of the belief and hope in immortality.

Great emergencies will often create great characters; but in the narrative which we have been considering we read something more in the character of the Hebrew mother than even the heroism which she displayed. By her close connection with her sons, in being brought before the tyrant, and condemned to share their fate, it is clear that though a woman in Israel, her influence must have been supposed of some consequence. That her sons owed their all to her, even to their education, and that her influence on them was very great, we read alike in her own words, and in the appeal of the king to her to save by her exhortations her youngest born. There is no mention of a father; she had probably been, from the infancy of her children, that especially beloved of the Eternal, a widow in Israel. And in the calm courage, the noble words of each of her sons, we learn the education she had given. They had probably been amongst the valiant though unsuccessful defenders of their land; amongst the faithful few who, in the very face of the persecutor, dared to obey the law of Moses, and refused every effort to turn them from their God. Would this patriotism, this devotedness, have come at the moment needed, had it not been taught, infused from earliest boyhood, by example as well as precept. A mother in Israel could be herself no warrior, but she could raise up warriors; she could be no priest, but she could create priests; she could not face the battle's front, or drive the idolatrous invader from God's holy land; she could not stem the torrent of persecution and of torture, but she could raise up those who would seek the one, and, by unshrinking death, bear witness to the fruitless efforts of the other; and it was these things this heroic mother did. She had trained up her boys in that faithfulness, that constancy, which could only spring from virtue. She must have taught them, aye, infused it with her very milk, that the pains and troubles of this world are, in their sharpest agony, but of a moment's duration, compared with the everlasting blessedness awaiting them in heaven. She must have taught them that death itself was but a darkened portal, opening into an infinity of glory; that man might, indeed, have power over this present life; but over the future, what mortal could have dominion? That all they possessed, even to the members of the body, life itself, they had had from God, to whom they were ready to resign them, knowing that from Him they would be received again; that even in that extremity of bodily

PART II.—9.

torture, their lot was happier than that of their tormentor, for their heritage was everlasting, but his was corruptible, and vanishing with a breath. She must have taught them in the true spirit of the law, that, however persecuted, however sinful in themselves, their nation would never be forsaken by God, yet that it was for their sins they suffered; not to gratify the exulting tyranny of their persecutor, but for themselves, for the sins of their hapless countrymen. Their sufferings in the flesh .were to make manifest to the whole world God's judgment upon His children for their national sin; but that still to the virtuous even such a death had no sting, for their earthly sufferings bore witness to the justice, and their Heavenly reward to the mercy of their God. She must have infused within them that pure, beautiful spirit of self-devotion which is woman's own, and can only be imparted by woman to the more selfish, more calculating man, else we should not find the last and youngest martyr beseeching God, even at that terrible moment, to turn His just wrath from His people, and that the sacrifice of himself and his brethren for the laws of their fathers might be so accepted as to cause the national misery to cease. All this (and in such doctrines, how much more is comprised than we can trace in a brief survey!) she must have taught her boys. We hear her herself refer to the labors of education as an additional incentive to her sons' obedience, and we must be convinced that all their heroism, firmness, self-devotedness sprang from her, and had become part of their very being, years before such exalted principles were thus called upon to be displayed.

Will not this narrative then strongly confirm all that we have stated in the second chapter of our second period, as elevating the position and marking the duties of Jewish mothers? Will it not prove that the mothers of ancient Israel were perfectly aware of all the responsibility attendant on them in the education of their sons, and that they really were included in the charge of Moses, contained in Deut. vi: 20–25. The education given by this martyr-mother to her sons is an exact illustration of the manner in which these ordinances were obeyed, including also the instruction in the history, theocracy and claims of Israel down to the times in which they lived. And how could this be, if the Jewish female were lowered by social treatment to the position of a slave or a heathen, on whom no responsibility, no religious duty, devolved. Be the narrative itself truth or tradition, it matters not; the ancient fathers would never have given a woman that influence and elevation in tradition which had not its foundation in truth; would never have made her occupy that position in tradition which the ordinances of the law forbade. This consideration is most important to us; for we are now rapidly advancing to the period whence it is said modern Judaism, in contradistinction to ancient Judaism, takes its rise. There will be many perhaps to agree with the theories formed on Scripture already brought forward, but to declare it is modern, or what is termed Rabbinical Judaism, which they condemn. We hope to satisfy such inquirers that even in Rabbinical Judaism there is no foundation whatever for the degradation of woman.

And what were the "wages" received by the Martyr-Mother for thus "nursing her boys for God"? Could it be their earthly tortures, their agonizing deaths? Alas! what female heart, in its first natural weakness, will not shrink and quiver, and feel, if such must be her wages, how can she nurse her child for God! How may she instill such feelings, if torture and death must be their reward! Why are obedience, constancy, allegiance, virtue, said to be acceptable to the Most High, when such is their earthly end, and the sinful, the faithless, the apostate, are spared and enjoy? Let us ponder on what was the support, the hope, aye, even at that moment, the triumph of Hannah. Did she feel as if that trial's intolerable agony were indeed her "wages"? We know not how a frail, weak woman could thus have looked on, and instead of unnerving them by cries and sobs, encouraged them to suffer still. God gave her power (it was not in humanity), and so increased the strength, the might, the vividness, of those hopes beyond the grave, which she had felt and realized so long, that the blessedness awaiting her children with their God seemed palpably revealed. The veil of flesh, of corruption, was rent from her mortal eyes, and all which the Lord had prepared for those that love them, unseen by human eye and unheard by human ear, was through her pure faith disclosed; nothing else could have so sustained her, or given the immortal spirit such dominion. We are expressly told "she stirred up her womanly thoughts with a manly resolve." Consequently we know and feel that she had all a woman's nature. "Take thy death," she bade her youngest born, "that I may receive thee again in mercy with thy brethren." Had an angel from heaven spoken in her ear these words she could not have believed more strongly. "The Lord will of His own mercy give you life and breath again," she had before said; and if she had fear when she exhorted her youngest born, it was not that he should pass away from her earthly love, but by his acceptance of the tyrant's proffers be lost to her in heaven. Faith, trust, hope, these then were her sustainers: she had brought up her children not for earth, but for heaven, not for time, but for eternity; and she knew that she should receive her wages, not from earth, but in His presence for whom her boys were martyred. And can we doubt for a single moment that those "wages" were received? Can we believe in the God of love, whom Pentateuch, Psalms, and prophets all reveal, and yet allow the faintest shadow of an unbelieving thought to come across our minds? Can we with a skeptic's fearful scorn refuse faith in another purer, lovelier world, where such noble and faithful spirits receive their promised recompense,

because to the finite sight, hearing, and wisdom of frail, poor
humanity it has not been visibly or palpably revealed? No! no!
Stagnant and indifferent as Israel may sometimes appear, it never
has thus fallen, never can reject that unutterably consoling revelation of immortality, which became its own glorious heritage long,
long ages before it was vouchsafed to the Gentile world.   By the
words, "Last of all, after the sons, the mother died," and no mention
of tortures, we may hope that, if the tyrant commanded her death,
it was comparatively easy, or, which is our own belief, that the
Eternal, in His infinite mercy, Himself called her to rejoin her sons,
never, never more to be separated from them.   The spirit might be
supernaturally strengthened, to make manifest such firmness and
faithfulness as would exalt the glory of the Lord; but the physical
powers must have sunk beneath it.   And if the tyrant did indeed
put the seal to the work of butchery by slaying her, he did but forestall
the death which would inevitably have come; and his cruelty in this
instance was mercy.

It may be said that, striking as this narrative is, it cannot bear upon
us now, either as guidance or example, and that, even if it could, it
would be impossible for us to imitate the heroism of which we read.
Earnestly we trust that such manifestations of faithfulness are indeed no longer needed.

Yet that mother's lessons may still be to us as guidance; may
teach us how we should instruct our children, so as to provide them
against the arrows of misfortune, which, ere life close, may assail
them, either through bodily affliction or mental woe.   Religion, real
spiritual religion, will not find resting in the human heart unless infused, unless made the first great object in childhood ; not to affect
with gloom, but inexpressibly to deepen the enjoyment and hilarity
of youth.   Affliction may do the work for us in riper years, and bring
the soul to its God, because earth has become a void, its former
pleasures dashed with poison ; but, oh! it is a fearful thing, when
we wait for affliction to teach us our God; when sorrow must be
sent to bring us to Him.   If the mother would but look forward;
would but sometimes think that the sweet and smiling babe upon
her lap, the laughing girl and merry boy, now playing in such shad-
owless glee around her knee, may one day be bowed down in sorrow,
exposed to bodily pain, to bereavement, to one or more of the
numberless sorrows ever incidental to humanity ; nay, to privation
of health, of sight, of use of limb, will she not, must she not seek
to provide them with some unfailing refuge, some fadeless hope and
inward consolation?   Why is she so anxious to provide for their
temporal welfare, to secure provisions for their earthly wants, resources of education, enjoyment, ambition, wealth? Why fill the infant mind with every branch of learning, and train it to think, and
calculate, and act ?   Why be so careful of all these things did not

the thought of the future guide the workings of the present—did not love itself become ambition, and future hope inexpressibly heighten present enjoyment? And these thoughts, these hopes, are natural and right ; but why provide only for a future of success and of joy? These things may be. It may please our Father in heaven to fulfill the mother's every wish, and make her child's future as smiling as its present ; but it may equally please Him to try that cherished darling in the ordeal of adversity ; and then, if he has only been provided for a future of prosperity, oh! what shall sustain him? How may he bear up against the trials which may be his, as well as of thousands of his fellows? No! mothers of Israel, let us ever train our children for a future, and strengthen them for sorrow as well as for joy. Should we think our duty done did we provide them only with summer clothing, and expose them unprotected to the wintry blast and howling storm? Might they not with justice reproach us in the first tempest, if we bade them thus set forth on the journey of life? However smiling as far as the eye can pierce, is not the horizon enveloped in such mists that we know not whether it conceal sunshine or storm,and shall we send forth our beloved provided only for the one?

Let it not be thought that to inculcate piety—that clinging love of and confidence in God, the only support of mental or bodily affliction—demands a relinquishment of the bouyant, light-heartedness of childhood. Far from it. The peculiar susceptibility of childhood to emotions of gladness and love renders the task easy and most blessed (if the right moment be seized) to lift up the young spirit to the kind and loving Father who has given so many things to love and to enjoy. And when the young mind has expanded to a consciousness of the temporal enjoyments it has received from God, let it rise still higher, in the tale of that world where there is no sin, no pain, no change, but where joy and love live forever; where their souls will be with God and His angels, if they seek to live there, and in all they do, and think, and feel, pray and seek to love and serve the heavenly Father, who is so good to them in this world, and has provided such a home for them with Him. Teach them that sorrow and pain are not proofs of their Father's wrath, but of His love; that all He does is love, however we may not understand it; that much, very much, must puzzle us while we are on earth, but that we shall understand it all in heaven; and, till then, if we will but believe He loves us, and all He does is love, we may be sorrowful and sad for a time, but we know He will once more give us joy.

Lessons like these, united with a firm observance of the ordinances and commands of Judaism, will, indeed, be blessed to our children, even though we see not their fruit till long, long years after the first seeds were planted. Let us not suppose, because we can discern nothing in the heedlessness, the levity, the occasional faults, even the

apparent indifference to spiritual things, in our offspring, that we
have worked in vain. Let sorrow, let sickness come, and our children will bless the parental love which, under God, has provided
them with such hopes, such thoughts, that pain itself is comparatively easy to be borne, and sorrow is assuaged. Better, far better,
provide for adversity a hundred times, and the provision be not
needed, than one case in which the sufferer shall need religious
comfort, and in vain and in bitterness of anguish exclaim, "Why
was I not taught to know and love God? Why not guided in my
childhood to that holy consolation of which I hear others speak, but
which I cannot feel?" How, in the midst of suffering can we teach
that God is love? How can the bruised and broken spirit lift up its
thoughts to heaven, when it has until that moment been chained
to earth? If the soul, in health and joy, has not been taught that it
has wings wherewith, even in its earthly shell, to fly to heaven, how
may we hope to use them when they lie crushed and broken beneath
the heavy hand of woe? It is vain to hope it! Then, oh! would
we do our duty to our children; would we indeed provide for their
future; would we have them recall us, with the tenderest love and
deepest gratitude, long, long after we may have passed from earth ;
let us imitate the Martyr-Mother, and, clothing them for affliction
as well as joy, nurse them from their infancy for God ; and we shall
indeed receive them once again in mercy from His hand, and in
His presence for everlasting.   GRACE AGUILAR.

GRACE AGUILAR was an English lady of the Jewish persuasion, noted for her talents,
her great literary attainments, and her unflinching attachment to Judaism. She was the
authoress of many valuable works for religious and educational purposes.
HERITAGE—Inheritance in religion, the | SUPERNATURAL—Being above the power of
people of God).   nature.
VOUCHSAFED—To grant.   MANIFESTATION—Discovery.
PHYSICAL—Relating to nature.

THE RABBI AND THE ROSE.

THE Rabbi Mayer was old,
The Rabbi Mayer was grey,
The snows of four-score years had shed
Their silvery spray upon his head.

His form was bent with age,
His cheeks were wan and pale,
But in his eyes there glowed a fire
To which few mortals could aspire.

In contemplation rapt,
The live-long day he prayed;
And in the pauses of his prayer
The song of learning filled the air.

The years swift hurried on,
And Death impatient grew;
He donned the monarch's crown and
crest,
And faced the Rabbi at his rest.

But weary Rabbi Mayer,
Unruffled, read and prayed;
Not all the monarch's pomp or look
Could wean the Rabbi from his book.

Next Death assumed the form
Of woman in her pride;
In soft, alluring robes she came
To tempt the Rabbi to his shame.

The Rabbi softly sighed
As him the tempter neared;
Then Death heard his words of prayer,
And, baffled, vanished into air,

Beneath the casement low
There bloomed a fragrant rose,
And the Rabbi loved that flower,
For it consoled his study-hour.

It chanced, one sunny day,
The Rabbi opened wide

The windows of his casement low,
And stood admiring in the glow.

*   *   *   *

Upon his forehead pale
The winds disport at ease;
For in the fragrance of the flower
Fate had softly used its power,
And, bathed in the rose's breath,
The Rabbi gently met his death.
                                    ADAPTED.

To Don—To put on. | Unruffled—Calm.

THE RELIGIOUS SECTS.

During the last centuries of the existence of the second Temple, various sects existed among our ancestors, with which we ought to become acquainted, in order to understand in some measure the history of those times.

The Pharisees can only improperly, and in antithesis to the Sadducees and Essenes, be called a sect, inasmuch as the principal part of the nation were of this class. The leading principle of their thoughts and actions was that the preservation of Judaism, that is to say, the law and morals of their fathers, must be the only guidance for the state as well as for the individual; this being the sole purpose for which precious blood was spilled upon the battlefield, and under the axe of the executioner. In deviating in the least degree from this principle was, to the Pharisees, a violation of sacredness. When their Sadducean opponents maintained that, in regard to political circumstances, a different rule must be adopted, then Pharisaism answered: The destiny of the state, the same as of the individual, does not depend on human activity, but entirely on Divine rule, as plainly proved by certain facts which they lived to see lately, when large armies were brought to ruin by trifling numbers, experienced warriors by timid weaklings, and the wicked by the pious. Not the power of man, not the strength of armies, are able to determine the weal and woe of the Jewish nation, but only Divine providence. Everything happens according to the everlasting determination of the Divine will, and only the acts of the individual, his moral conduct, devolve upon human discretion; the issue of human activity and the consequence lies by no means within the reach of human calculation. The peculiarity of Pharisaic teaching is certainly a fundamental doctrine of Judaism.

Another doctrine of the Pharisees was probably directed against an objection raised by the Sadducees. If the fate of the individual or of the nation is not depending upon its conduct, then Divine justice would thus become arrested; for the just has often enough to struggle with misfortunes, while the unjust has generally the sun of serene happiness smiling upon him. This objection the Pharisee removed through the principle that the Divine justice is not confirmed in life, but only after death. One day God will rouse the dead from their slumber in the grave, in order to reward the just according to their conduct, and to punish the wicked for their deeds. "Those will rise to eternal life, and these to everlasting shame."

These views, however, relating merely to an inner conviction, formed no such decisive antithesis as the third doctrine of the Pharisees concerning the extent and the validity of religiousness. Many precepts of the law, especially those referring to the practice of religious doctrines, which in the law are but briefly hinted at, were introduced by common consent by the leaders of the nation, the prophets, and the men of the Great Synagogue. All lived without written instructions, through oral tradition among the people, whose vital breath always was their religion. The supporters and defenders of these oral traditions, and the interpreters of the law, were also the Pharisees. This outward piety, however, did in no wise shut out the inner one. The Pharisees were considered strictly moral, chaste, abstemious in enjoyments, mild and benevolent toward everybody. Indifferent to worldly possessions and worldly honors, they never hesitated to sacrifice, for conviction's sake, all their wealth and even their life. Therefore, the whole nation clung to this sect with deep veneration, readily submitting to their decisions, and always willing to defend them and make their cause their own.

But the greatest influence the Pharisees possessed in consequence of their profound knowledge of the law and its application to life; hence they alone were considered acquainted with legal knowledge and theology. The degrading names of eye-distorters and hypocrites, wherewith, in later times, their enemies designated them, they by no means deserved; otherwise, the people would never have become so attached to them, nor would subsequent rulers have intrusted them with the most influential offices, which placed the entire interior administration of the state and of the Temple in their hands; it is especially absurd to say that a whole class of men is composed of hypocrites.

In case any individual belonging to them practiced outward piety for the sake of self-interest, the entire sect showed their indignation toward the hypocrite, styling him the "Plague of the Pharisees," who commits evil, like Zimri, and expects God's reward, like Pinchas. There were seven distinct sects of Pharisees, but only those were considered legitimate who practiced the law out of pure love to God. Thus it is entirely wrong to charge the Pharisees with being hypocrites; they were, rather, the most noble preservers and representatives of Judaism and strict morality; even their opponents, the Sadducees, could not avoid bearing testimony to this fact: "That they pine away in this life, but will hardly find reward in a future one."

The antagonists of the Pharisees pursued a national political tendency. To the Sadducees belonged the Jewish aristocracy, the brave warriors, the generals, the statesmen, who in the wars with Syria and other nations had gained renown and riches, and in their contact with the outer world had accustomed themselves to more liberal and worldly views of life. Their name they probably obtained from the founder or leader, named Zadock. The interest the Sadducees took in the Jewish commonality surpassed their concern in the Jewish doctrine and law. Glowing patriotism was their predominant feeling, and piety took the second place in their hearts. They seemed to have fostered the worldly view, that the mere confidence in the strict practice of religious laws cannot suffice to maintain the independence of the Jewish state; but believing that man must exert his temporal and spiritual powers for that purpose, one must not be prevented by religious considerations to enter upon political alliances, or to carry on wars whereby a violation of religious precepts cannot be avoided. Altogether, they were of opinion that God purposely endowed man with a free will, in order that he himself may establish his welfare, to be the master of his own destiny, inasmuch as God does not meddle with human affairs. On the deeds and acts of man alone depend his weal and woe, and it is folly to remain idle, in expectation that God will intervene to direct the circumstances either of the individual or of the state. Reward and punishment for just and unjust actions are the result of these very actions, and one need not expect for that purpose a resurrection after death, when God shall judge the acts of mankind. Without exactly denying the immortality of the soul, the Sadducees refused the acceptation of an equalizing justice after death. (It requires but a slight knowledge of Scriptures in order to perceive how much these principles are opposed to the plain word of God. Deut. xxxii: 39; I Sam. ii: 6; Ps. xxxi: 20; Ps. xvi: 9, 11; Ps. xvii: 15; Dan. xii: 2; Jes. xxvi: 19; Jes. xliv: 3.)

In the same manner the Sadducees denied the general validity of religious statutes; maintaining that only those law-appointments which the Pentateuch plainly and fully contains are binding; and others, which rested upon oral traditions, or sprung up at various periods, have but a subordinate value, and cannot therefore claim an inviolable sacred support. They would only allow the barren letter of the law, and the consequent carrying out of this view led them sometimes to assert a greater religious strictness than the Pharisees, who were decried for their severity. The Sadducees, for instance, took the appointed punishment of the Pentateuch in regard to bodily injury, "Eye for eye, tooth for tooth," in its literal sense; while the Pharisees, according to tradition, showed more lenity in such cases, and only determined upon an indemnification in money for any bodily injury. Besides, the Sadducees could not help consenting to many traditions.

But in spite of the relief which the views of the Sadducees offered, their sect found but little favor among the people, who disliked that any one should find fault and bargain with the living convictions within them, and what they saved with their heart's blood was dear and precious. It was sufficient for them to practice what they themselves had seen practiced from generation to generation, or what was pointed out to them as important by the teachers of the law. Moreover, the Sadducees were thrust off by the people, owing to their proud and unfriendly manner, their rigid proceedings in law, on account of which they could never gain in public opinion, but had to use force in order to see that their principles be respected; therefore their ruin was hailed by the people with joy, as a deliverance from a heavy yoke. The views of the Sadducees, the same as those of their later twin brothers, the Karaites, tending to worldliness and enjoyments of life, never proved penetrating.

The origin of the remarkable order of the Essenes, which evoked even the admiration of the Greeks and Romans, happened also during the great commotion which the resistance against Syrian tyranny brought about. The Essenes, from the commencement, never formed a political party; but, on the contrary, they always avoided the noise of public life; they stood also in no antagonistic opposition to the Pharisees, but constituted rather a class of Phariseeism, with which originally they were of one caste. Their ideal was to obtain the highest sanctity of priestly consecration; but they desired, by and through the external observance of the Levitic precepts, to attain an inner holiness and consecration, and to mortify the passions of life. These considerations forced them to associate only with those who were of one mind with them, and to unite themselves, in order not to experience any trouble in their consecrated condition; thus they had to form themselves into an order whose first rule was based upon a conscientious observance of the strictest care to purity. Only those who held the same opinions with them could prepare their food and clothing; tools and other utensils were bought of those whom they felt convinced manufactured them with the strictest adherence to the laws of purity. Thus they were assigned for each other, and thought it advisable to take their meals in common, in order to dispense with every help from those less strict in their observances. How could they in their severity, even in those warlike times, maintain themselves amid society? Every warrior who in battle had become defiled by the corpses would have thus destroyed all their precautions.

This embarrassment may have led them to retire to a lonely part of the country, in order to remain unmolested by these commotions, which proved detrimental to their mode of life. They selected for their abode the deserts of the west, the Dead Sea, the oasis of Engedi. The date trees, so plentiful about these parts, could, by their simple mode of life, supply them in some measure with food. Women could not submit to the rigid manner of their life, and, as it is natural that family life causes trouble, they lived unmarried. On account of their living together, they were led to divest themselves of all property. Every one gave his property to the treasury of the order, from which the expenses of all necessaries for members were defrayed. Thus there were neither poor nor rich among them, which placed them in a position free of care, and consequently their mind was entirely bent to religiousness, renouncing more and more all that is temporal, and following an ideal design. The Essenes distinguished themselves also by other peculiarities; they always used white linen clothing. They also wore a kind of apron, which served them as a drying towel. They bathed every morning before prayers in fresh spring water, as did the priests previous to the service of the Temple. No profane word escaped their lips during their meals, which they kept as a kind of service unto God, and generally all was silent in that interval. Only after many preparations, and by degrees, did they admit fresh members; these novices received the marks of distinction of their order, as already mentioned, with great solemnity, after being sworn to observe the Essenean mode of life, and to preserve the secret doctrines conscientiously and to hand them down faithfully.

These external appearances, however, were only a preparatory step for obtaining that inner piety, that close union with God, by which they tried to reach even to prophetic inspiration; unadorned simplicity in food and dress, sobriety, modesty, ever ready to make sacrifices for others, were certainly virtues which adorned the Essenes; yet they were not peculiar to them, inasmuch as they shared them with the Pharisees. They, however, distinguished themselves by their aversion to the taking of an oath, by frequently praying, and by their mystic doctrine. Owing to their peculiar mode of life and fanatic aim, the people not only considered them as holy, but also as workers of miracles. They indeed engaged in affecting miraculous cures, which, in those times, were well liked, and adjurations and the expulsion of spirits were executed by them. Their means of effecting cures consisted in speaking quietly certain verses of Holy Writ, and partly in the use of certain herbs and stones of supposed hidden powers. Thus the Essenes had combined in themselves the highest with the lowest; the efforts after a pious conduct and holy inspiration with the most common superstition. On account of these excrescences, the Pharisees paid them not so great a veneration. They were much displeased with the miraculous cures and expulsion of spirits, and it seems that there was a slight difference existing between the two sects. It was a foreboding that they should later become enemies; for Esseneism concealed in its lap a contradiction against the existing Judaism, of which its followers and opponents had but an obscure presentiment, but which, in the course of history, has been substantiated as correct.

Dr. H. Graetz.

PHARISEE—One who adheres strictly to all the rites and ceremonies.
SADDUCEE—One who denies the resurrection and the belief in angels or spirits.
ESSENES—A sect professing extraordinary purity of life and devotion.
INVIOLABLE—Not to be broken.

EVOKE—To call forth.
DETRIMENTAL—Causing loss.
ADJURATION—The act of proposing an oath to another.
EXCRESENCE—Contrary to the common order of production.

PSALM XV.

I.

Lord, God, who shall abide and dwell
  Within Thy holy hill?
Who in Thy tabernacle shall
  Enjoy Thy gracious will?

II.

He who walketh in uprightness,
  And worketh righteous lore;
Who full of truthful consciousness,
  Speaketh for evermore!

III.

He who backbiteth not with tongue,
  Nor will he evil sow,
Nor say reproachful words among
  His neighbors to and fro!

IV.

He in whose eyes contemned stands
  A person vile and rude;
Who honor'th those all o'er the lands
  Who love and fear the Lord!

V.

He who sweareth to his own hurt,
  And will reverence God,
And firmly stand, and changeth not,
  To act within His word!

VI.

He who not in usury lent'th
  His money on a term,
Nor taketh bribe 'gainst innocence,
  Will stand eternal firm!

Max L. Guttman.

ALEXANDER JANNAI AND SIMON BEN SHETACH.

Alexander the Third, son of Jochanan Hyrkan, began to rule when he was twenty-three years old, and was, like the family he sprang from, of a warlike disposition. Thus the twenty-seven years of his reign passed in strife and war, and were not calculated to enhance the welfare of the nation.

He first turned his hostilities against the seaport towns, which, under circumstances now unknown, were in the hands of the Greeks. But Lathuras, an Egyptian prince, who was also at war with his own mother, the Queen Cleopatra, completely defeated him. Another time, this same Lathuras destroyed Alexander's whole army, consisting of 50,000 men, and afterward marched through Judea, murdering and destroying everything before him, and showing no mercy even to women and children. Then Queen Cleopatra formed an alliance with Alexander, and he was thus enabled to continue the war in which he defeated Lathuras, obtaining, at last, possession of the seaports as well as of other towns.

This war lasted nine years, and Alexander being thus fully occupied, never interfered in the internal affairs of the country. He was not on the side of the Pharisees, yet he suffered them to exist, doing nothing to injure them, in order not to excite the people who felt attached to them. Simon ben Shetach, the chief of the Pharisees, stood well even at court, and was regarded by Alexander with great favor, owing to being a blood relation of Queen Salome, and on account of his wisdom they were pleased with him. But this intimacy did not last long; for as soon as Alexander returned as conqueror, he, in his arrogance, thought himself absolute lord and master, and thus brought on a change for the worse. The cause, however, was never exactly known, but it was thought to be the Pharisees, who, true to their principles, were continually urging upon him, according to the law of Moses, rather the improvement of the state within than agrandisement from without, and were thus opposing his war policy. Alexander, therefore, unexpectedly turned against the Pharisees, showing his animosity in the following manner: Once, when during the feast of Tabernacle, he was officiating as High-priest, he, according to tradition, had to pour water from a silver vessel upon the altar, as a symbol of fertility; but instead of doing so, he poured the water down before his feet, in order to show his contempt for this religious custom of the Pharisees. More was not necessary to rouse the people who were assembled in the forecourt of the Temple; they threw their festal-fruit (Etrog), which most of them held in their hands, at the king, calling him unworthy to be their High-priest on account of being the grandchild of a captive. He then sent for his troops, who seemed to have been ready as if by appointment, and nearly six thousand men lost their lives in this unfortunate affray. Besides, it brought on an irreconcilable hatred between the king and the Pharisees, which the Jewish nation continually paid for with their blood, and thus reducing them to that extent that they felt unable to withstand any pressure from without. The dissension of the realm under Rehobeam and Jerobeam was repeated in the bitter party hatred of the Pharisees and Sadducees.

Alexander, however, did not notice the harm which in his arrogance he had thus brought on the state, but was still occupied with his high-sounding plans of conquest. He conquered twelve towns to the east of Jordan, but was soon after defeated, losing his whole army, and feeling glad to reach Jerusalem in safety. The people were imbittered against him, and nothing but bloodshed followed the next six years, during which the whole country had become quite exhausted. But being thus prevented from carrying out his plans abroad, Alexander at length held out the hand of peace and friendship. His opponents, however, would not listen to any proposals, except under the condition that he should suffer death. Nay, they even committed the great mistake of applying for a Syrian army to assist them in putting down Alexander. He was defeated, and was obliged to fly with his hirelings into the mountains, where his pitiful condition after all roused the people to mercy once more. Six thousand men left the Syrian camp and went over to Alexander, and thus he succeeded in driving the Syrians from Judea and in defeating the rest of his opponents. At this juncture the Sadducees persuaded him to revenge himself on his enemies, and he had 800 of the Pharisees executed—a cruelty which brought him the surname of "Men-slayer." About 50,000 men were sacrificed during these six years; the Pharisees suffered most, and they considered themselves no longer safe in the country, and fled the night after the execution of their 800 brethren. About 8,000 left the country, partly for Syria, where many were killed by the heathen, and partly for Egypt, where their co-religionists gave them a hearty reception. Among the latter was also Jehuda ben Tabbai, who, in later years, became a noted personage. Simon ben Shetach also got into great difficulties on account of this persecution, and he was compelled to become a peddler in order to find a livelihood. His disciples, tradition states, presented him with a camel to ease his labors in peddling his goods about the country, and finding accidentally after the purchase that around the camel's neck there was a very valuable collar, they presented it to their teacher, congratulating him upon the luck in finding such a treasure; but the Rabbi replied that he could not accept of it, inasmuch as the collar not being included in the purchase-money, it must be returned to the Saracen of whom the camel was bought.

In spite of all troubles Alexander's propensity for war had not diminished yet, and once more he carried on a three years' campaign, proving on the whole very successful, and, entering Jerusalem as a conqueror, was received with enthusiasm.

During the last year of his reign he undertook an expedition against the country east of Jordan, but at the siege of Regaba he became seriously indisposed, and was thus obliged to give up his design. In his last hours he felt great regret about his deeds and estrangements with the Pharisees, and therefore he advised the queen, who was much concerned about the future of her sons, that she should hold strictly to the Pharisees, and do nothing without their consent. He died in his fiftieth year, after reigning twenty-seven years, leaving two sons, Hyrkan and Aristobul, and his wife Alexandra as Regent. It was a fortunate circumstance for the Jewish nation that a woman, of modest and pious character, ruled the state at a time when a man's impetuosity had just left it in a dilapidated condition. Thus she produced a change like a refreshing dew upon blighted, sun-burned fields.

But in a spiritual point of view also everything seemed to prosper in these few years, bearing abundant fruit which for centuries to come proved a blessing to the nation. This state of things was brought about by two husbandmen, whose names belong to the most renowned in Israel.

Simon ben Shetach, already mentioned, was regarded with the highest favor by the queen, who bestowed on him the first place in the Sanhedrim. But Simon was not ambitious, and he therefore summoned also Jehuda ben Tabbai, a man of superior knowledge and character, who was then sojourning in Alexandria. The words Simon addressed to the latter ran thus: "From me, Jerusalem, the holy city, to thee, Alexandria, my sister: My husband dwells in your midst, and I am sitting desolate." Jehuda ben Tabbai did not hesitate to accept the invitation, and those two men now labored uninterruptedly for the welfare and amelioration of the nation. Like Ezra and Nehemiah, they accomplished the regeneration of Judaism, and with them begins the control of lawful Judaism in accordance with the view of the Pharisees. Thus they were called the restorers of the law, who again placed the crown upon the Thora in its former splendor.

Both of them were noted for their extreme strictness, and it is related of Jehuda ben Tabbai that, in his ardor to fulfill the law, he once had a man executed on account of being charged with a certain crime; and when afterward Simon ben Shetach sifted the matter, and found that according to traditional law the accused man did not deserve death, and charged Jehuda ben Tabbai with having spilt innocent blood, Jehuda felt so deeply affected and grieved, that he at once resigned his seat in the Sanhedrim, and showed his remorse by throwing himself daily upon the grave of the executed man, calling unto God for a speedy death, in order to expiate the judicial murder he was guilty of.

Of Simon ben Shetach a case is also related, of which history has probably no similar example to show. On account of his extreme strictness he made many enemies, especially among those families whose members were executed under his jurisdiction. The latter, in order to take revenge, procured two false witnesses who accused his son of a heavy crime, owing to which he was found guilty, and Simon himself, who presided at the trial, passed sentence of death upon him. On the way to execution, the accused son continually expressed his innocence under the most heartrending protestations, so that even the two false witnesses felt perplexed and confessed their guilt. When hereupon the judges were ready to set the accused son at liberty, he himself reminded them that their proceeding must be considered illegal, for, according to law, the witnesses, even in retracting their former assertions, can no more be relied on. " Wilt thou," said the unhappy son, turning to his father, "that the salvation of Israel be established whilst in your hands, then make me the threshold over which it enters." And father and son showed themselves worthy of the important task to be preservers of the law; the one laid down his life, the other his parental love, for the saving of the law. Simon had the law carried out against his son, although he and all the judges were convinced of his innocence.

One of the most important services of Simon was especially the improvement of imparting instruction, for he knew well that Judaism does not consist in strength from without or mere vain splendor, but in the unfolding and spreading of truth, which, proceeding from the house of Jacob, should pass over to all mankind, and help to establish the salvation of the world.

There were as yet no schools in Judea, and the father alone instructed the youth according to Biblical principles. In Jerusalem a high school existed, but was only accessible to the wealthy; and therefore Simon ben Shetach, to supply the want thus felt, established high schools in all the large towns of the country.

But after Salome's death the country was plunged into war again, and once more the spirit of Judaism fled from the peaceful schoolrooms, where thousands of disciples sat at the feet of one of the most renowned Rabbis. Thus fresh places had to be found for the teaching of Judaism, which always became renewed by the continual succession of generations. This arrangement has outlived all other institutions, proving the most efficient measure to save Judaism from the shipwreck of time.

H. GRAETZ.

THE MYSTIC TIE.

THERE is a mystic tie that joins
    The children of the Hebrew race
In bonds of sympathy and love,
    Which time and change cannot efface.

When, 'mid the world's abuse and scorn,
    The sons of Israel bravely stood,
That bond was holier, stronger still—
    Cemented by their martyrs' blood.

And though to-day the Hebrews dwell
    In every clime and every land,
Yet, joined by that immortal tie,
    A holy brotherhood they stand.

Go to the North, where Polar stars
    Look down on fields of ice and snow;
Go where, in sunny tropic climes,
    The gentle breezes softly blow;

Go to the countries of the East—
    Arabia and the Hindoo land;
Go where the calm Pacific sweeps
    'Gainst California's golden strand;—

And there, in reverent tones, is heard
    The sacred cry, always the same,
"O Israel, hear! our God is one,
    Blest be for aye His holy name!"

This is the mystic tie that joins
    The children of the Hebrew race;
This is the grand and holy bond
    Which time and change cannot efface.

MAX MEYERHARDT.

JUDEA UNDER ROMAN SWAY.

[63 B.]

I.

WHEN, in later times, inquiry was instituted as to the cause which brought about the decline of the Jewish state, no other reason could be assigned than the bitter hatred existing between the two sons of Alexander, which being continually on the increase proved fatal at last. The death of Queen Salome was the first signal for this strife, dividing the nation into two camps, and making an end to the happy days of the second Temple.

The dying mother, according to the law of primogeniture, gave to the eldest son, Hyrkan, the crown; but although endowed with many virtues in his private capacity, and there is no doubt that in times of peace he would have made a very fair ruler, yet he was in no wise fit for those agitated times, and his good nature did more harm than another's tyranny could have accomplished. His younger brother, Aristobul, was the very reverse; the cowardice of Hyrkan stood in strong contrast to Aristobul's impetuous courage. The chief aim of the latter was to become the mighty ruler of Judea and to subjugate all the neighboring countries; but instead of laurels, he heaped disgrace upon himself and the nation. Scarcely had Queen Salome closed her eyes and Hyrkan ascended the throne, when Aristobul, with mercenaries and his Sadduceean adherents, marched against the capital in order to dethrone his brother. On Hyrkan's side were the Pharisees and the troops which the deceased queen had maintained. At Jericho the two hostile brothers, with their armies, met, when Hyrkan was defeated and fled to Jerusalem, whilst the principal part of his followers, to avoid a civil war, joined Aristobul. But the two brothers soon became reconciled, and in the Temple they both agreed, upon oath, that Aristobul should receive the crown, and Hyrkan wear the diadem of High-priest, the latter thus losing his crown after a reign of three months. To give to this agreement a kind of guaranty, Aristobul's son, Alexander, married Alexandra, Hyrkan's daughter, whose children and grandchildren were to end miserably in later times.

Perhaps the peace now brought about could have proved of some duration, procuring also for Judea better and happier days, had not all at once a man encroached upon this state of things, who was full with ambitious designs and personal interest, and who, together with his family, became the vampire of the Jewish nation, draining their noble blood to the dregs. This man was Antipater, a descendant of a respectable Idumæan family, who, like other Idumæans, were forced under Jochanan Hyrkan to embrace Judaism. Never was there a perverse action more quickly and more energetically punished than this proceeding. The fanaticism of Hyrkan I. was

now to bring misfortune on his house and his nation. Hyrkan II.,
being in want of a leader, had placed his confidence in Antipater,
who misused it in the most shameful manner. He embraced every
opportunity to remind Hyrkan of his humiliating position; that he,
although called to the throne, was obliged to abdicate in favor of his
younger brother. Besides, he continually tried to convince him that
Aristobul was plotting against his life, believing that his throne
could never be safe as long as the true heir remained among the
living. By these means he succeeded in persuading the timid
Hyrkan to break his oath, and to adopt the malicious plan of calling
a strange nation to his assistance. Antipater was cunning enough
to have everything arranged beforehand. In the darkness of night
Hyrkan and Antipater fled the city and sought refuge with Aretas,
King of Arabia, who received them kindly and consented to assist
Hyrkan in his operations; having previously received from Antipater many valuable presents in order to gain his adherence to the
plot; besides, Aretas was glad of the chance which gave him an opportunity to get possession of twelve towns in the eastern part of
the Dead Sea, which formerly the Hasmonæans had taken from him.
Aretas, with an army of 50,000 men, and Hyrkan with his followers,
who had joined them, offered battle to Aristobul, who was defeated
and had to fly to Jerusalem.

Thus, owing to Antipater's artful ambition and Hyrkan's boundless imprudence, Jerusalem had to contend with another siege,
which its strong walls prolonged for a time, otherwise Aristobul's
handful of followers must soon have succumbed. Antipater was the
chief of the besieging army, and many atrocities were committed.
In the city the want of sacrificial animals was soon felt, and Aristobul appealed to the pious feeling of the Jewish besiegers in order to
buy of them the necessary animals. Every day baskets filled with
money were lowered from the wall in return for lambs which were
drawn up. To vex the besieged and to force them to capitulate the
sooner, the cunning Antipater (for no doubt he was the perpetrator)
had the audacity one day to have a pig substituted for one of the
lambs. At that time the pious Onias, generally known as "Honi
Hameagel," was living, who, in times of emergency, sent his prayers
on high, which were often favorably answered. This pious man
was requested by Hyrkan's soldiers to pray for the destruction of
Aristobul. Onias obstinately declined at first, but when hard
pressed, he, in the full strength of his moral greatness, said: "Lord
of the Universe! as these standing around me here are the people,
whilst the besieged are Thy priests, then I pray you may not fulfill
the imprecations which they pronounce against each other." The
coarse soldiers, insensible to such elevated sentiments, stoned him
to death like a common criminal. The people felt enraged at this
atrocious act, and considered the earthquake and hurricane which

just then raged all over Palestine as a sure sign of God's wrath. But a still greater misfortune than earthquake and hurricane began for Judea "The animal with iron teeth and brazen claws and stony heart, that should consume much, and trample the remainder under foot," invaded Judea's territory. The hour had arrived when the Roman eagle should in speedy flight throw itself upon Israel's plains, to encircle the Jewish nation, already bleeding from her many wounds, in order only to inflict on her fresh hurts till she became a cold corpse.

II.

At that time Rome ruled over the destinies of the nations composing the anterior part of Asia, and Scaurus, a Romish official, sent on a mission to Syria, came also to Judea, and to him, as if he were a messenger of peace, the two brothers made their appeal. The Romans never despised gold, and Aristobul sent 300 talents (about $400,000), whilst Hyrkan held out very favorable promises. But the interest of Rome was for Aristobul. Thus Scaurus demanded of Aretas to raise the siege of Jerusalem at once, in case he valued Rome's friendship. Aretas then immediately withdrew with his army, as well as Hyrkan and his followers, and Aristobul really believed for a short time that he was indeed victorious and sole king of Judea. But Aristobul was no match for Antipater's inventive mind, and in picturing the unsafe condition they were placed in, he played into the hands of the Roman general and conqueror, Pompey, whom he pretended he had gained for the cause, and thus Aristobul felt satisfied. Pompey then received from Aristobul a present, consisting of a solid golden vine, with golden branches, grapes and leaves, valued at half a million dollars, and which Alexander had established in the Temple. It was a masterpiece in every respect and admired by everybody, so that Pompey had it sent as a trophy to Rome, where it became an ornament amongst the idols in the temple of Jupiter. The Jewish Temple, however, did not miss this embellishment very long, for the impulse of piety soon supplied another one, which was also placed in the same spot at the entrance hall of the building. This beautiful present did certainly satisfy Pompey's vanity, but he was, nevertheless, not on Aristobul's side. He called the two brothers to Damascus to settle their affairs, but came to no conclusion, trying to prolong the proceedings till Judea, weakened by civil war, should fall a prey to Rome.

In the meantime, the people, tired of shedding blood, did not wish either for Hyrkan or Aristobul, but demanded, in a modest way, the same as at the time of Persian supremacy, that they should live peaceably under the leadership of a High-priest, according to Divine law. Therefore the Jewish patriots closed the gates of Jerusalem against the Romans, and thus the city had to endure another siege, which, however, Hyrkan's followers soon abandoned.

The patriots, nevertheless, retired to the Temple-mount, destroyed the bridge, and there defended themselves with astonishing bravery. After a siege of three months a tower, one of the strongholds, was at length, on a Sabbath in the month of Sivan, entirely destroyed. The Roman legions then penetrated into the forecourt, slaying everything before them, even the priests at the side of their sacrifices. The priests never shrank for a moment, never felt perplexed in their sacred occupations, but faced death courageously and quietly. Pompey penetrated as far as the interior of the Temple, in order to satisfy his inquisitiveness as to the peculiarity of Jewish worship, and felt surprised to find that there was not a single representation of the Divinity to be met with. Whether it was timidity, from the impression made upon him of the sublimity of the Temple without a single image, or from caution, not desiring to be decried as temple-marauder by his enemies; whatever it may be, it is singular that Pompey could subdue his greediness for money, for he left untouched the Temple treasury, which contained not less than 2,000 talents, amounting to as much as two and a half million dollars. This, then, was the prelude to the destruction of the Temple which Judea had to witness. Pompey ordered the leaders, or rather the foremost among the Jews, to be executed, and the remainder he sent to Rome. The Jewish princes, Aristobul, his son, Antigonus, his two daughters and his uncle, Absolon, were obliged, among other vanquished kings and princes of Asia, to walk in procession before Pompey's triumphal car in Rome.

Alexander, Aristobul's eldest son, escaped whilst a prisoner, and arrived in Judea, where he raised an army; but Antipater soon arrayed the Romans against him and defeated him; and only to the entreaties of his mother, who threw herself on her knees before the Roman general, had he to thank his escape from the executioner's axe.

Aristobul, with his son, Antigonus, also succeeded in escaping from Rome, reaching Judea once more. Here he also raised an army, but it was of no avail, for he was soon defeated, and was sent a second time to Rome. His son, Alexander, who had also ventured upon a fresh revolt, met a similar fate.

Once more was Aristobul inspired with hope that he might again obtain the throne of his ancestors. When Julius Cæsar, the greatest man Rome can boast of, tried to come to power, he, in order to weaken Pompey, gave Aristobul his liberty, and at the same time intrusted him with two legions to operate for him in Judea and Syria. But Pompey's adherents soon became aware of it, and got rid of the Jewish prince by poisoning him, and his eldest son, Alexander, was ordered by Pompey to be beheaded.

Thus the fraternal war ended, and what was Hyrkan's benefit in appealing to Roman justice? Pompey deprived him of royalty, but left him the honor of being High-priest, with the ambiguous title of national prince under the guardianship of Antipater, who was made governor. But Antipater, as usual, misused his office, and brought upon Judea unspeakable misery. He drained the Jewish nation to the last drop of blood, and with the sweat of Judea he assisted the Romans, whose aid he so much needed, on account of the people's deadly hatred, who looked upon him as the destroyer of their liberty. But the hour of retribution at length arrived, and a certain Malich poisoned him, when he was just on the point of depriving Hyrkan of his throne. The walls of Jerusalem were demolished, and Judea, considered vanquished, was obliged to pay tribute once more to a strange power, after enjoying freedom for half a century; the boundaries also were limited to the extent occupied previous to the time of the Hasmonæans. While Rome felt intoxicated with victory, Zion wrapped her head in mourning, for the independence had disappeared from the moment the Roman set his foot upon holy ground. Just a century after the Maccabees had overcome Syrian tyranny, their descendants brought Roman tyranny to rule over Judea. DR. H. GRAETZ.

PRIMOGENITURE—Seniority; state of being first-born.
MERCENARIES—Hired; sold for money.
FANATICISM—Religious frenzy.

JUPITER—The chief deity amongst the Greeks and Romans.
VAMPIRE—Used as imaginary beings, who tormented the living by sucking their blood.

ISRAEL.

How great, O Israel, have thy sufferings been
Since doomed in every land and clime to roam,
An exile and a wanderer on the earth,
Without a country and without a home!

Throughout the world men scorned the Hebrew's faith—
That holy creed of origin divine;
They stamped as crime his sacred, pure belief,
And mocked his worship at Jehovah's shrine.

"Cursed be the Jews!" this was the fearful cry
That followed e'er the Hebrew where he fled;
Proud monarchs were his deadly foes, and popes
Hurled their anathemas upon his head.

And Israel, once a nation proud and great,
From whom sprang sages, kings, and prophets grand;
Earth's mightiest race, the chosen of the Lord,
Was mocked and scorned and jeered in every land!

In sunny Spain, the Inquisition dread
Cast him in dungeons terrible and dire,
And with a thousand tortures racked his form;
Then led him forth unto the death of fire.

Oh, shame! that such a fearful blot as this
Should stain the history of the Spanish land;
And deathless infamy forever rest
On Torquemada and his hated band!

Where'er the Hebrew roamed, on land
  or sea,
Did persecution follow in his path;
And furious mobs deemed it a noble act
  To vent on him their hatred and their
    wrath.

Ten thousand martyrs died for Israel's
  cause,
  With fortitude sublime, 'mid smoke
    and flame,
And while their cruel foes stood mock-
  ing 'round,
  They called on God and blessed His
    sacred name!

Through all the horrors of that fearful
  time,
  Through gloom and death, the He-
    brew saw afar,
With faith's unfailing and undying eye,
  Beyond the clouds, hope's bright and
    glorious star.

He knew that God would rise 'gainst
  Israel's foes
As, long ago, upon the Red Sea coast,
With miracles He saved His chosen
  race,
  And in the sea whelmed Pharaoh's
    mighty host.

And gloriously was that bright trust
  fulfilled,
  For Israel triumphed over every foe,
And marching on with undiminished
  zeal,
  Emerged in triumph from the night
    of woe!

Yes, Judah proudly stands, 'midst all
  mankind,
  Once more as beautiful, sublime and
    grand
As when, in blessed days of old, she
  stood
  A mighty nation in the Holy Land.

Weep not, O Israel, for thy martyred
  ones;

For though no monuments rise o'er
  their tomb,
Yet fame upon the sacred spot shall
  shed
  Her fairest garlands and her bright-
    est bloom.

Their names are graven on honor's
  deathless page,
  And on the scroll of glory written
    high;
And though earth's proudest monu-
  ments decay,
  Their deeds sublime will never, never
    die!

Mourn not, O Israel, for thy glorious
  past;
  The future holds a destiny more
    grand;
For 'tis thy mission great to teach God's
  laws
  To the inhabitants of every land,

And cause the nations of the world to
  know
  That unto Him alone shall prayers
    ascend,
And that before His great majestic
  throne
  All men in reverent suppliance shall
    bend.

Oh! may the time soon come when o'er
  the earth'
  In thunder tones the glad acclaim
    will ring,
And nations, taking up the shout, shall
  cry,
  " The God of Judah is our Lord and
    King!"

Thus Israel's ancient glory will return,
  And Israel's banner be again un-
    furled;
Thus will the star of peace and promise
  dawn,
  And shed its radiant lustre on the
    world!"

                    MAX MEYERHARDT.

ANATHEMA—A curse pronounced by ecclesiastical authority.
INQUISITION—A court established in Spain
and Portugal during the reign of Queen Isabella for the detection of heresy, as pretended
by its votaries.

TORQUEMADA—Grand inquisitor and confessor to the Queen of Spain, a man noted for
his cruelty and hatred to the Jews.
To WHELM—To cover with something; to
bury.
ACCLAIM—Acclamation, shout of praise.

JOCHANAN HYRKANOS.

[153-106 B.]

ONE of the noblest of the illustrious race of the Hasmonæans was Jochanan Hyrkanos. He not only continued the work of his father, who went forth as independent prince from the heroic combats against the Syrians, but crowned it also with the stamp of completion. At the commencement of his reign, Judea was again threatened with a great deal of danger, it having but just obtained its freedom, and enjoying some rest. Antiochus Sidetes, who had not forgotten yet the grief which its desertion from Syria caused him, advanced with a large army, destroying everything in his march, and was approaching the capital. Hyrkanos must have felt too weak to give him battle, for he shut himself up in Jerusalem, depending on the strength of its walls. Antiochus therefore laid siege to the city on a very extensive scale, but, in spite of the seven camps, the wide and double trenches, and the hundred towers with which he surrounded the town, the besieged made continual sallies, defeating, with great bravery, all preparations for storming the city. Thus the siege was protracted; the besiegers had no water, and the besieged were in want of provisions, which made both parties feel disposed to seek for peace, especially as the wet season was at hand. Hyrkanos made the first step toward it, in asking for a suspension of hostilities during the eight days of the feast of the Tabernacles. Antiochus not only agreed to this, but sent also animals with gilt horns, and golden vessels with sweet scent, for sacrificial purposes. Hereupon negotiations for peace commenced, and Antiochus was urged by his friends to use the utmost severity; but it was fortunate for the Jews that this one was neither so cruel nor powerful as his predecessor, Antiochus Epiphanes, otherwise the old struggles would have been renewed. A favorable peace was the result, and the design of Antiochus that Jerusalem should receive a Syrian garrison Hyrkanos decidedly rejected.

Antiochus, soon after this, lost his life on the battle-field, and Hyrkanos, who, as his ally, had to assist him with auxiliaries, immediately made use of the state of weakness into which Syria was placed, owing to the many disputes that arose as to the right of succession, not only to become independent of Syria, but also to adopt the offensive, in order to wrest from it all the towns and fortresses formerly belonging to the land of Israel.

But Judea was still confined on three sides by a foreign population; in the south by the Idumæans, whose territory extended far into Judea; in the middle by the odious Samaritans, whose dominions prevented the Jews of Galilee from taking the shortest road to Jerusalem whenever they visited the Temple; and then, also, the district beyond the Jordan, the shores of which were entirely inhabited by Greeks, who always proved inimical to the Jews. Hyrkanos therefore considered it his task to reduce these territories to subjection, and either to banish the hostile population or to unite them closely with the Jews. He turned first to the land east of the Jordan, conquering, after a siege of six months, Madaba, a town which always proved hostile to the Hasmonæans, being well fortified, and defended bravely. Afterward the army moved south of the Jordan, where Samega was taken, a town situated on Lake Tiberias, and of great importance to the Jews. Then he commenced with the towns belonging to Samaria, Sichem being the capital, which was destroyed, together with the temple on Mount Garizim.

At one time Menasse—grandchild of the High-priest Eliashib, whom Nehemiah drove from the temple, because he had married a daughter of the Samaritan governor, Sanballat, and would not separate himself from her—built this temple, which was similar to the one in Jerusalem, at the request of his father-in-law, and over which he officiated as priest. This aggravated the dissension already existing between the Jews and Samaritans, and thus the temple always proved a great stumbling block to the Jews. It stood nearly three hundred years, and its destruction caused so much joy that the event was celebrated annually as half holiday. Ever since the splendor of the Samaritans has disappeared; for, although they preserved their peculiarities for thousands of years, and even to this day they exist, and still continue to sacrifice upon a simple altar on Mount Garizim, their substance, nevertheless, is wearing away more and more, owing to the want of a proper centre.

After this victory over the Samaritans, Hyrkanos turned against the Idumæans. This people who, for ages, always proved hostile to the Jews, had been already subjected by Judas Maccabee, but owing to their peculiar tenacity, they had become strong again, possessing themselves of the south, to the great detriment of the Jews. Hyrkanos thought himself powerful enough to make them harmless, laying siege to their fortifications and razing them, and then offering them conditions, either to embrace Judaism or to go into exile. They accepted the former, submitting to circumcision, and from now they externally adhered to Judaism. For the first time Judaism showed, under this Prince Hyrkanos, intolerance toward other worshipers, by imposing religious restraint upon them; but it soon had to learn, under painful experience, how disadvantageous it is to carry the zeal of self-preservation so far as to force others to conversion. While Simon, though becoming an ally of the Romans, laid the first *germe* for the dissolution of the Jewish realm, his son contributed largely to that step by the forcible conversion of the Idumæans, and in less than half a century it fostered the most bitter fruits. Romans and Idumæans were the parties who dethroned the reigning family of the Hasmonæans, and brought about the decline of the Jewish realm.

Hyrkanos also sent ambassadors to Rome, who took many presents, among which was also a golden shield weighing 1 000 ounces, which had the desired effect upon avaricious Rome. The senate repeated their assurance of remaining a true ally, forbidding the Syrians to make further inroads into Jewish territory, and ordering them to deliver up all the towns which they conquered at the commencement of the reign of Hyrkanos, and especially the town and port of Joppa. The town of Joppa was for Judea a source which yielded money abundantly, inasmuch as the superfluity of the different productions of the country, especially of wheat from the fields of the Ephraim mountains, as well as oil from Galilee, and balsam from Jericho, were exported in large quantities into foreign ports, from which the revenues were immense. The treasures thus obtained supplied Hyrkanos with ample means to carry on the war energetically, for already in those times gold was the nerve of conquest.

Being thus protected by the Romans, and well supplied with money, Hyrkanos was enabled to follow up his plan of enlarging the Judean territory, and after succeeding in a series of wars, the power of all his opponents was crushed, the far-extending plans of the Hasmonæans realized, and their work crowned at last with success. Judea felt safe in its independence, and had risen to the eminence of the neighboring states. The enemies who had threatened it on all sides, the Syrians, Idumæans, and Samaritans, had been for the most part subdued, and the country at large had overcome those barriers which prevented its development. The happy times of the Israelitish people under David and Solomon seemed to have returned once more, and strange nations were compelled to pay homage to Jewish rulers. The old hatred between the brotherly races of Judea and Idumæa was destroyed, Jacob and Esau had become twin brothers again, and the old prophecy confirmed; the elder served the younger. The shores on the Jordan, the sea coasts, the caravans, which led from Egypt to Syria and Asia Minor, were entirely in the power of Judea. Hyrkanos was brought up according to the principles of the Pharisees, and he lived and acted in the spirit of that sect. He faithfully tried to establish again the worthiness of religion, which, during the war, had become neglected in many instances; he was really a pious high-priest, as well as an excellent guardian and promoter of Judaism. Besides, he could not venture to oppose the Sadducees; they were his co-workers, his generals, and counsellors. But Hyrkanos always understood well how to solve this difficult task; even when an old man, he knew how to keep the two distinct parties in tolerable amity; but, uttering an inconsiderate word, this zealous adherent of Phariseeism was induced to become its bitter opponent. In the last years of his life, he entirely inclined to the Sadducees.

The cause which brought about this change was unimportant. Hyr-kanos had returned home from a great victory. Feeling exceedingly happy at the great result thus achieved, and the flourishing con-dition of the country, he arranged a splendid meal, to which he invited, without exception, all the leaders of the Pharisees and Saddu-cees. Upon golden tables, meals were served up, among which were also desert-plants, in remembrance of the suffering during the time of the Syrian subjugation, when the nobles of the people had to hide themselves in heaths and deserts. Amid the good humor prevailing among the guests, Hyrkanos all at once asked whether the Pharisees could anyway reproach him of having ever committed himself against the law; and, if such was the case, they should confess it frankly, for it was his earnest desire to make the law the basis of all his actions. Whereupon a certain Eleasar ben Poira (according to others, Jehuda ben Giddin) rose, and, without further ceremony, said: "Hyrkanos should be content with wearing a princely crown, but the diadem of a High-priest he should transfer to a more worthy person, inasmuch as his mother, at a surprise which the Syrians made upon Modin, was taken prisoner before his birth, and the son of a captive was disqualified for a priest, much more for High-priest."

Although deeply affected on hearing this defamatory assertion, Hyrkanos possessed discreetness enough to yield to an investigation into the matter, and the accusation soon proved void of all truth. But when the Sanhedrim, whose members consisted of Pharisees only, fell away from their principle that before the law all are alike, in condemning the offender of the prince to pay merely a fine for slander, instead of suffering death for high treason, as Hyrkanos had expected, then he was persuaded by the Sadducees that the whole affair was purposely arranged by the Pharisees in order to abase him; and thus he renounced the Pharisees altogether, becoming a Sadducee in word and deed. The Pharisees were displaced from all high offices; the officials belonging to the Temple, the Sanhedrim, and the courts of law, were all filled by men holding Sadduccean principles.

The historians of the Pharisees, however, do not detract anything from Hyrkanos' high merits, and even state, in spite of their dismis-sal, that this prince reached the ideal; the three highest dignities of Judaism, that of prince, High-priest, and a thorough acquaintance with the law, were all united in his person. But this occurrence had sad consequences, and Hyrkanos did not survive long, but died soon after in his sixtieth year, and the thirtieth of his reign. The Sanhedrim, now composed of Sadducees, put upon the people, Pharisees generally, restraint of conscience; the freedom and inde-pendence of the high-council, who had to preserve the law against the encroachments of the crown, were entirely abolished. The princes of the Hasmoneans, who rose by freedom of election, had become despots. It was then no wonder that hatred began to show itself against the house of the Hasmonæans, which consequently plunged the nation into civil war, and reduced them to a state of weakness. This single act was sufficient to carry the cheerful days of the Hasmonæans to the grave, and thus the Jewish nation now began a retrograde movement; for the second time the Jewish realm sadly realized that in reaching the pinnacle of power, it could not keep its ground by external greatness.

Dr. H. Graetz.

Siege—Any continued endeavors to gain possession.

Defamatory—Calumnious.
To Abase - To bring low.

THE CHILDREN OF HYRKAN THE FORTUNATE.

THE aged Hyrkan, prince in Israel and High-priest, who so triumphed over many enemies that he received the proud name of the Fortunate, could, nevertheless, not triumph over death. His enfeebled head rested upon the gold-embroidered cushion, his eye was raised toward the canopy, and the sacred priest's cap, with its golden escutcheon, was placed on a table beside him. Around his couch stood his wife and five robust sons. But in casting his eye downward, it seemed to hover over them sorrowfully, and his soul apparently could not depart without foreseeing what the future would bring forth. "You have no desire for peace," he at length exclaimed, with feeble voice, "which I command you to observe in the name of the father. Then you will perish, one after the other, so that it will be said of the house of Hyrkan: It was! But you, Aristobulus and Antigonus, who are the eldest, you who ought to be the support of the house, on your heads the punishment will fall. Ere a year has passed you will have to give an account to me." Thus saying, he died, and in his eyes reproach could still be seen.

The corpse of the prince was soon interred; the tears of those belonging to him were soon dried; and his wife demanded the regency, according to the will of the deceased. But suddenly the trumpets sounded in the streets of Jerusalem, armed men rushed to the place before the Temple, and, separating the people, called aloud, "Aristobulus is king over Israel." A period of 471 years and three months had passed, after Israel's return from captivity by the waters of Babylon, when Aristobulus for the first time again as an Israelite wore upon his head the royal crown. But poisonous serpents of vice he twisted into it, for he threw his mother and three of her sons into a dark dungeon, while his beloved brother, Antigonus, remained with him, and was declared co-regent. About midnight, lamentations sounded through the royal palace; a dark figure, adorned with the sacred priest's cap and the golden shield, dragged itself through the different chambers; but for the princely widow the gates of the dungeon would not open. She had a terrible guest in her cell, attacking her with an iron grasp, and killing her by starvation. Till midnight she lingered, and then her soul departed with insane imprecations against the whole race of matricides.

The king was stretched on a bed of sickness, but Antigonus, dressed in robes of triumph, which he brought from his successful campaigns, and accompanied by heroes and nobles, entered the Temple of the Lord, in order to thank the God of Israel for his victory, as well as to offer prayers in behalf of the king. At the gates of the Temple stood an old man with a white garment, in his hand an axe, his loins covered with an apron, an Essenean, Judas by name, endowed with the gift of prophecy, which came over him in the seclusion of his life. "Who desires to live," he exclaimed indignantly, "when truth has died? The voice of Heaven speaks within me. To-day, Antigonus dies in the Tower of the Straton; but from the coast of the sea which touches upon it, are 600 stadia to the Temple of the Lord, and the fourth hour of the day has already arrived; the voice of the Lord fails within me; the house of Hyrkan continues to exist."

Then intriguing courtiers approach the sick bed of the king. "Where does my brother Antigonus tarry?" inquired he; "has he not yet reached the gates of Jerusalem? I am longing to behold the smile of his lips, and the tears of his eyes."

"Antigonus enters in triumph with weapons and army into the Temple of the Lord, in order to be anointed as the only king. Thou wilt no more behold the smiles of his lips, or the tears of his eyes, but the threatening sword of his hand, which strives after your heart."

"Antigonus! Antigonus!" the trembling king called aloud, wringing his hands in despair; "brother, come to my heart, but not with the sword. My heart feels desolate, thou shalt fill it up; graves seem to open around me, thou shalt cover them."

"Hail, hail, unto thee, Antigonus!" the people and army exclaim; but, as to the bed-ridden king, no one thinks of him.

The king kept silent for some time, but, at length, he called for the chief of his body-guard, commanding him to place himself with all his confidants in the secret passage which leads from the Temple of the Lord to the king's palace, called the Tower of the Straton. There he should await Antigonus; if he came unarmed, then he might pass unmolested; but if armed, then the deadly weapon should be plunged into his bosom. Whereupon he sent his chamberlain to Antigonus, to request him to appear unarmed before the king.

At the same time intriguing courtiers were hastening to the queen, saying to her, "The king demands to see his brother in the splendor of arms he has conquered, and ·how they become his beloved one." The queen hereupon sent her chamberlain, even quicker than the former, to acquaint Antigonus with the instructions she had received. Antigonus hurried to comply with his brother's request, leaving the Temple of the Lord to walk through the Tower of the Straton to the king's palace, in the Castle Antonia. There the hidden assassins lie in wait, and as the rays of the sun through the apertures of the vaults fell upon the bright weapons of the royal brother, a deadly stroke brought him to the ground, upon which his blood flowed.

The trembling king sits upon his bed listening to approaching steps, but those of his brother, which he watches for, do not draw near. Suddenly the gray-headed Judas, in his white garments, makes his way through weapons and chamberlains. "Antigonus!" he calls aloud, making the walls shake, and swinging his axe; "Antigonus has fallen in the Tower of the Straton, although not where the sea washes the coast, but between the Temple of the Lord and the king's palace. The voice of the Lord deceives not; the house of Hyrkan becomes a ruin." The king faints on hearing this, and a stream of blood begins to flow from his mouth, filling all the vessels that are brought to receive it, which are carried from the palace into the Tower of the Straton, where the chamberlain stumbles, and the blood of the king becomes mixed with the blood of his brother on the ground into which it flowed. Then the hearts of the chamberlains began to tremble, and their lamentations reached the king's chamber. In vain did the king continually inquire after the cause of these lamentations, and only by threats he succeeded in obtaining information. "Well," said the king, in a feeble voice, "thy blood has become mixed with mine; thy death demands also mine; graves open around me, we both will fill them."

It was the very day on which Hyrkan died that the royal mausoleum at Gethsemane received the corpses of the two kings. One year only had they reigned over Israel. On the same day when the graves closed upon Aristobulus and Antigonus, the gates of the prison also opened for the three confined brothers. Alexander came to the throne, but true to the curse of fratricide, he killed the one, while the other had to take an oath before the altar of the Lord that he would continue to live a private life. Alexander ruled twenty-seven years, cruel and revengeful, till he died in consequence of his debauchery.

The house of Hyrkan continued in its evil ways. Alexander's sons, Aristobulus and Hyrkan, fought with each other all their lifetime. The former died of poison by the hand of a Roman, and his son was executed for high treason. Hyrkan had ruled twenty-three years, lived three years in captivity, when he was condemned by Herod to die the death of a common criminal. The house of Hyrkan was no more!   Dr. L. Philippson.

ESCUTCHEON—The picture of the ensigns armorial; the shield of the family.
MATRICIDE—A mother-killer.

FRATRICIDE—The murder of a brother.
DEBAUCHERY—The practice of excess.

FAITH AND TRUST.

HAVE faith and trust, ye wavering,
  God's ways we may not see,
What may seem chaos in our view,
  To Him is harmony;
And when deep anguish fills our hearts,
  And tears well from our eyes,
The ill that causes them may be
  A blessing in disguise.

The noisome poisonous weed which
    grows
  Without a single charm,
May hold in its obnoxious stem
  A medicinal balm;

And tempests that o'erwhelm us
  And fill us with dismay,
May render pure the fetid air
  And drive disease away.

Then faint not when reverses come;
  Have faith, and hope, and trust,
That all is ordered for the best—
  That God is kind and just;
Dwell not on evils that may come,
  Nor mourn o'er evils past,
But nurse the precious hope that God
  Will comfort you at last.
                              B. J. CH.

THE JEWS IN ALEXANDRIA.

I.

THAT fairy-land on the Nile, once the school of affliction of the Israelitish people and the cradle of Judaism, became, in later times, the school of wisdom for the Jewish nation. Whether Alexander, the conqueror of Asia and Egypt, the founder of Alexandria, transplanted a Jewish colony into Egypt, or the first Ptolemæan removed many Jewish prisoners to Egypt, who received their freedom of his successor, or even a remnant of those emigrants who sought refuge in Egypt after the destruction of the first Temple, had preserved themselves there, it remains certain that the Jewish population was very numerous, amounting, a hundred years after Alexander's time, to as many as a million.

They had spread all over Egypt, from the Lybian desert in the north to the borders of Ethiopia in the south. In Egypt and Cyrene the Jews enjoyed the same privileges as the Greek inhabitants, because both having settled there at the same time, they were even preferred to the Egyptian aborigines, who, being once vanquished, were treated as such by their rulers. The Alexandrian Jews felt very proud of this equalization. The greatest number of Jews resided in Alexandria, which was, next to Rome, the second town for commerce and political importance, and, in the same manner, next to Athens, the second for arts and sciences. Among the five parts of Alexandria, the Jews occupied almost two; especially the quarter called Delta, situated on the sea-shore, was entirely inhabited by them. As an Egyptian ruler had granted them the right of inspection over the navigation of both sea and river, they availed themselves of the opportunity thus offered in carrying on a larger trade by sea; and prosperity, together with a refined mode of life, were the fruits of activity. But commerce was in nowise their exclusive occupation. There were among the Alexandrian Jews tradesmen and artists; if any artists were wanted for the Temple in Jerusalem, they were always called from Alexandria, the same as they were formerly obtained from Phœnicia. They acquired also the Grecian art of war and policy, as well as the melodious Greek language, and at length absorbed themselves in Greek erudition and philosophy, so that many of them understood Homer and Aristotle quite as well as Moses and Solomon, while others, as statesmen and generals, rendered great services to the rulers of Egypt. Thus the Jewish congregation of Alexandria was admitted to be a strong pillar of Judaism. At the head of the Egyptian Jews was a Chief President, who was of priestly descent, with high judicial powers, bearing the Grecian name Alabarch; he had to see to the proper payment of taxes of all the Jews, whom he was bound to protect under all circumstances. Besides himself, there existed also a high council, a *fac-simile* of the Jerusalem one, being composed of seventy members, who managed all religious affairs.

In every part of the town, houses of prayer, called Proseuchen, were erected, among which the building of the chief synagogue was noted for its artistic style, elegance and beautiful endowments. The same was so extensive that a functionary, especially appointed for the purpose, had to swing a flag as often as the congregation had to respond "Amen" to any of the blessings uttered by the chanter, who, otherwise, could not be heard all over the synagogue. The synagogue also contained splendidly gilded seats for each of the members of the high council, while each guild had its own place, in order that every stranger entering the synagogue might at once recognize his guild and be able to join his colleagues. The houses of prayer in Alexandria were also houses of instruction, for on all Sabbaths and festivals discourses were held by those well versed in Scriptures, who explained in the Greek language the appointed portion of the Pentateuch which had previously been read to the congregation. During the Syrian oppressions many prominent Jewish emigrants came from Judea to Alexandria, and the most eminent among them was Onias, the youngest son of Onias III., the last legitimate High-priest, who, when his aged and venerable father was murdered, thought himself no more safe in the mother country. The King of Egypt received him very favorably, and Onias rendered him, as general, many important services.

When, soon afterward, the Temple was defiled by the Syrians, and especially when Alkimos was made High-priest illegally, then Onias resolved to erect a lawful Temple in Egypt, instead of the one defiled in Jerusalem, and whose High-priest he himself would be. In order to obtain the consent of the Jews, he backed his proposition by referring them to the prophecy in Isaiah, which should thus become fulfilled: "One day an altar of the Lord will stand in Egypt." (xix: 19.) The then reigning king, Philometer, gave him, for the purpose, a plot of land in the neighborhood of Heliopolis, four and a half geographical miles northeast from Memphis, in the land of Goshen, where once Jacob's descendants dwelt till the departure from Egypt. In the small town of Leontopolis, on the ruins of an Egyptian idol-temple, where once animals were idolatrously worshiped, Onias built a sanctuary for the only One God. The exterior of the same did not entirely correspond with the Jerusalem Temple, but was more in the form of a tower, and built from fire-bricks, while the interior contained the vessels of the Temple, after the model in Jerusalem, except that the standing candlestick of seven branches was replaced by a golden chandelier, fixed on a golden chain. Priests and Levites who had escaped the persecution in Judea served in Onias' temple. For the support of the temple and the priests, the king resigned, in the most generous manner, all the revenues of the Heliopolitanic country. This happened about the year 160. Although the Egyptian Jews considered the temple of Onias as their centre, whither they all went on pilgrimages during festivals and brought their sacrifices, yet they never placed the same on a par with the one in Jerusalem. They, on the contrary, honored Jerusalem as the most sacred capital of all Judaism, and its Temple as a divine place. As soon as it recovered its former dignity after the Syrian wars, they fulfilled it toward it all their religious obligations, in sending yearly their contributions by their own deputies, and also sacrificed there now and then. But in Jerusalem they were nevertheless dissatisfied with this foreign temple, and although they did not exactly condemn it, yet they maintained that the same was opposed to the express determination of the law (Deut. xii: 13). The priests of the temple of Onias were not permitted to do service in Jerusalem, but they were not deprived of their priestly dignity, and received their share of contributions belonging to the priests.

Another still more important occurrence, encroaching deeply on the world's historic fate, also took place at that time, and upon the same spot. On account of many refugees coming from Judea to Egypt, who, owing to their great attachment to the paternal law, gave up their fatherland, after suffering innumerable afflictions, a desire rose in the Egyptian king to become acquainted with this so much honored law, especially as Antiochus, the persecutor of the Jews, was also his enemy. He ordered, therefore, that seventy-two theologians should come from the Holy Land, to whom he gave the commission of translating for him the law of Moses into Greek. In order that they should be undisturbed in this important work, and that no communication should take place between them, he brought them to the Isle of Pharos, situated a short distance from Alexandria, where he placed each of them in a separate apartment. Yet their separate labor is said to have agreed, proving to the king the correctness of their interpretation. This translation is therefore generally called "the translation of the seventy" (Septuaginta). In course of time, also, the remaining books of Holy Writ were translated; nay, even independently of these, some other books, *fac-similes* of the Biblical ones, were composed, such as the "Book of Wisdom," and mostly the so-called Apocrypha, except the Book of Sirach, which was originally written in the sacred tongue. The completion of this work caused great joy among the Jews of Alexandria and Egypt. They were proud that the Greeks, boasting so much of their wisdom, at length perceived how much more sublime and ancient the wisdom of Judaism is than the doctrines of Grecian philosophers. It pleased them to be able to say: "Behold, Moses is greater than your philosophers." Therefore, in remembrance of this event, the day on which the king received the translation was kept as a jubilee on the Isle of Pharos.

II.

Although the Greek translation of Holy Writ proved rather successful in making the heathen acquainted with Judaism, the pious in Judea were no more pleased with that event than with the establishing of Onias' temple. They hated already the Grecian system, which brought so much evil upon the nation and sanctuaries, and therefore this translation increased only their apprehension. Would not their foreign brethren become thus more estranged from the mother country and the mother tongue? Was a clear study of the law possible from such a translation? Is it at all likely to execute a translation into a language so radically different that the right sense of each expression could be properly rendered? How could the Greek text of the law be always watched, that no one should venture upon making alterations in the attempt to effect improvements? It was indeed the case that, after a few generations, the Jews of Alexandria cared but little for the original sacred writings, and thus they forgot the sacred tongue, and in their translation many arbitrary alterations, additions and omissions crept in. Yet, all these errors they deemed the word of God. Therefore the pious of Judea considered the day of translation—which the Egyptian Jews kept as a jubilee, as a national calamity—like unto the day when the golden calf was placed before the Israelites in the wilderness as their god; it is even said that the day (8th Tebeth) was instituted as a fast day.

But affliction, heavy affliction, the Jews of Alexandria had once to endure. The prosperous state, which their diligence and industry had produced, the established renown of the Jews, which their accomplishments and knowledge had procured for them, the favor in which they stood among the Egyptian governors, and later the Roman rulers—all this raised the most violent envy among the Greek inhabitants of Alexandria. The hatred of the Greeks was the greater because they thought the Jews had lured away their beautiful language, art and science, and yet they took care not to become infected by their heathenish immorality, but persisted in their belief in only One God, while all the people of the East believed in the ridiculous fables of their mythology. Certain writers inimical to the Jews—especially the false Apion—spread among the mob the most absurd reports respecting Jews and Judaism. The order given by the Roman emperor, Caligula, that in all the temples of the empire his statue should be put up, and divinely worshiped, was a welcome opportunity for the enraged mob to fall upon the Jews. They stormed the synagogues, placing therein the statues of the emperor as idols. The Jews were expelled from all parts of Alexandria and pressed together in the quarter Delta, which was inhabited by them only. Their houses and workshops, which they had left, were soon entered by the bloodthirsty mob, who robbed and destroyed what diligence and industry had gathered together during centuries. The quarter Delta was surrounded, in order to prevent the Jews from leaving the place, and the mob thought they would have to succumb to heat and hunger in being kept together in so limited a space. · If the want of provisions forced any to leave the besieged quarter, the mob seized them, maltreating them most cruelly, putting them to the rack, and pitilessly throwing them into the fire; even to the female sex no mercy was shown. The members of the High Council were attacked in their houses, dragged to the theatre and publicly lashed. It was the Roman governor who was guilty of these acts of violence, which were the more so wholly barbarous, because the privileges granted to the Jews by the emperor ought to have protected them from such degrading punishment; besides, the lashing took place on the emperor's birthday, which brought even to criminals a delay of punishment. The same governor also deprived the Jewish inhabitants of their citizenship, which they had exercised with pride for centuries before, it having been guaranteed to them by all the emperors, but now they were declared strangers and outlaws, although they contributed to the advancement of science, art, trade and navigation quite as much as the Greek population.

The despotic command of the emperor might have put a stop to all the differences, but he was ill-disposed toward the Jews, because they refused in Jerusalem—as well as in Alexandria—to pay divine honors to his statue. A deputation sent to him he would scarcely listen to, receiving them with the words: " You are also those who despise the gods, and would not acknowledge me as god, but you deify an anonymous one, while, except yourself, all worship me." When the deputies replied that they sacrificed for the emperor, he observed: "What use is sacrificing for me, if it is not to me." At the departure of the deputation he said: "These people seem to me less wicked than ignorant in denying my divinity." Thus the Jews had to commit their just cause unto God, and it has not transpired how the quarrel ended. On the death of Caligula, in the year 41, who suffered an awful death at the hands of his soldiers, this occurrence brought to the Jews of Judea deliverance, and also better times for those of Alexandria.

Although most of the Alexandrian Jews remained under their afflictions true to the paternal religion, there were, nevertheless, many who seemed to care but little for Judaism. They esteemed the Grecian philosophy quite as much as the word of God—became frivolous and immoral. The Alexandrian interpreters of the law believed that the contents of Holy Writ, both historically and legally, must be taken in a symbolic sense; that the divine laws should awaken in us certain thoughts and sentiments, which make the actual observance of the religious laws, such as Sabbath, festivals and circumcision, quite superfluous. Such views caused many to feel indifferent toward practical Judaism. This lukewarmness was opposed in word, deed and writing by a man whose name ought to be known to every Jew — Philo. In excellent, animated language he spoke of the continual obligation of the law, and thus inspired his contemporaries with fresh love for it. In decided and severe tones he expresses himself against those who felt satisfied with the sublime sentiments met with in the law, but who treated the law indifferently; he called them frivolous and superficial. The Holy Law teaches us, indeed, to elevate ourselves to a more sublime mode of thinking, but without leaving anything undone of the rites and ceremonies. Should we, he remarked, because we know the importance of the Sabbath, keep the same no longer? Should we cease with circumcision, because we know its signification? Then we should lose the law, and in the end the sense thereof as well.

He descended from an eminent priestly family, and was a brother to the Alabarch. Everything which at that time belonged to science he had thoroughly studied from his earliest days, and he was considered the greatest scholar and most profound thinker of his time; but only to Judaism, he remarked, belongs true wisdom. Therefore he was continually absorbed in its Scriptural works, and the glorification of the same he considered to be his life's task, for which purpose he published his numerous works, which partly have been handed down to us. He lived a temperate, plain and retired life; virtue he esteemed as the highest ornament of man. Only for the sole purpose of serving his brethren would he leave his studies. He was the spokesman of the deputation sent to Caligula, and when an aged man he traveled to Rome in behalf of the Alexandrian Jews. One of his most important works is the refutation of Apian.

After the destruction of Jerusalem the zealots tried to renew the rising against the Romans in Alexandria, but their plan was defeated. Vespasian, the emperor, who was afraid Egypt would become the hearth of fresh resurrections of the Jews, ordered them to close the

SCHOOL AND FAMILY READER

Onias temple, in order to deprive them of their religious center. All the sacred vessels went—like those of Jerusalem—into the imperial treasury, and the Egyptian sanctuary, after existing 233 years, was closed forever in the year 73.

DR. JOST.

ABORIGINES—The earliest inhabitants of a country.
TO ABSORB—To swallow; to suck up.

PHILOSOPHY—Knowledge, natural or moral.
MYTHOLOGY—System of fables.

CONTRAST BETWEEN JEWS AND SAMARITANS.

THE gratification of the Alexandrian Jews at having disclosed to their Greek neighbors their sacred monuments of literature, awakened the ill-will of a sect which always was the irreconcilable enemy of the Jews. There lived in northern Palestine a not very numerous small nation, comprised of the remnants of the late kingdom of the Ten Tribes and heathen emigrants from the other side of the Euphrates, and called Samaritans, or Cuthim. Though in most points adherents of the Jewish creed, yet, owing to reminiscences of old hostilities, they hated the Jews bitterly; and the ill-feeling was mutual. What chiefly offended the Jewish heart was the existence of a rival temple with sacrificial ceremonies on the mountain of Garizim, for the sacredness of which the Samaritans claimed the authority of a Biblical verse.

This mutual antipathy followed the adherents of Jerusalem and of Garizim into foreign countries, where they continued their contest with that peculiar jealousy which stimulates religious communities removed from home to watch over their domestic traditions.

The translation of the Torah into Greek, favored as it was by King Philometar, appears to have given fresh food to their hatred. It must, indeed, have deeply grieved the Samaritans to see the sacredness of their temple impaired by the septuagints, since the Greek text did not contain the verse, "And thou shalt build an altar on the mo unt of Garizim," which they had smuggled into their Bible. The Samaritans of Alexandria, it appears, protested against the translation, which they alleged contained a forgery of the text; and as probably some of them were well liked at the royal court, their influence prevailed upon the mild monarch to arrange a religious disputation between the contesting sects for the sake of deciding the question of superiority between the temples of Jerusalem and Garizim.

This was the first religious debate that ever was held before a secular authority. It differed from those which subsequently were of frequent occurrence in the course of Jewish history, in that the arbiter was entirely impartial as to the pending question; and, accordingly, the contestants were at full liberty to bring forth their arguments without restraint or reservation.

Each party selected its best scholars for spokesmen. Andronicus ben Messalem, otherwise unknown, pleaded for the Jews; while the Samaritans were represented by two men, Sabbai and Theodosius, who are not without learned reputation in Samaritan history; the latter, whose name appears variably changed into *Dositai, Dostai* and Dostan, being reported as the father of a Samaritan sect, which, except as to the sacred character of Mount Garizim, very nearly met the Jewish views, and which, under the name of Dositeans or Dostans, held its ground against the old Samaritans for a considerable length of time. In what manner the disputation was conducted and how it resulted, the legendary character of the extant reports makes it impossible to ascertain. As there was never a tangible result arrived at in the way of religious disputations, so in this case each party claimed the victory; and each in its reports has exaggerated its success. According to the Jewish account, a condition was laid down (which is certainly untrue) that the king should have the right and the duty to execute the defeated disputants, and when, therefore, Andronicus had cited the long succession, from Aaron down to the present day, of High-priests who had officiated in the Jerusalemic temples, and furthermore pointed out the fact that the King of Asia had frequently enriched the same temple with costly votive offerings, while the Garizim temple could not boast of any similar honor, the defeat of the Samaritans was publicly proclaimed, and their execution performed in conformity with the agreement.

The contrary reports, however, which are of a much later date, and still obscurer nature, assign the victory to the Samaritans, who advanced the argument that Moses, the law-giver, could not possibly leave in abeyance a matter of such importance as the national place of worship (Kiblah); it was therefore certain that in his last benediction, when alluding to a mountain belonging to the tribe of Joseph, he meant to distinguish the Mount Garizim, whereas no proof could be adduced against them from the other Jewish writings, because they denied their sacred origin, and refused to acknowledge their authors as prophets. By these arguments, the Samaritan reports say, convinced of the holiness of the Samaritan temple, the king forbade the Jews, under penalty of death, from ascending the mountain of Garizim.   J. R.

[From a lecture by Rev. Dr. Jastrow, minister of " Rodef Shalom," Philadelphia.]

ANTIPATHY—A natural repugnance against anything.

SEPTUAGINT—The old Greek version of the Old Testament.

ARBITER—A judge appointed by parties, to

whose determination they voluntarily submit.

VOTIVE—Given by vow.

ABEYANCE—A fee or right in consideration of the law.

HYMN TO THE DEITY.

In the dim twilight of the leafy woods,
Where the light zephyr stirs the cano-
   pies,
And sways the foliage of dark forest
   trees;
On the wild waste of waters, when the
   floods
Lift up their voices, and in grief
   or glee
Still touch the heart with nature's
   minstrelsy—
There, even there, let the soul turn
   to Thee,
And thank Thee for the beauties of
   this earth,
For all the glorious things to which
   Thou gavest birth.

O'er the wild desert's sandy solitude,
Where the sirocco breathes its withering flame,
And the lone traveler treads with
   wearied frame,
Thou bringest his heart to Thee, Giver
   of Good;
There the oasis springs, leafy and
   green,

Like a sweet fairy isle, in slumber
   seen;
Gladdening his heart when every hope
   was past,
And every death-fraught moment seemed his last.

Thou holdest the mighty thunder in
   Thy hand,
And the frail leaflet of earth's mean-
   est flower;
The writhing waves own and obey
   Thy power,
And check their fury at Thy dread com-
   mand.

Oh! turn our hearts to such piety
As all inanimate creation bears;
Let that instruct us in our daily
   prayers,
And teach us how to raise our thoughts
   to Thee,
In forest, desert, ocean, everywhere,
Turn Thou the heart to Thee, O God!
   in prayer.

REBEKAH HYNEMAN.

ZEPHYR—West wind; any calm wind.
SIROCCO—The southeast or Syrian wind.   OASIS—A fertile spot in a desert.

THE SPREAD OF JUDAISM.

THERE is no people extant to whom even in the cradle the song of endless wandering and dispersion had grown more familiar than the Jews; and this awful cradle-song has really become fulfilled to the very letter of its frightful utterance. There was not a corner in the two empires of Rome and Parthia where Jews did not reside, and where they had not grown into a religious community of their own. The borders of the great basin of the Mediterranean Sea, and the mouth of all the principal streams of the old world— Nile, Euphrates, Tigris and Danube—were all populated by the Jews. Like an inexorable fatality, the sons of Israel were driven continually further away from their center.

But, however scattered the body may have been, its limbs were, nevertheless, not loosened from another; they had a point of union in the Jerusalem Temple, as well as in the Sanhedrim of that place, to which the dispersed ones clung with all their heart. To this spot their attention was directed, thither their contributions went, to enable them at least to participate in the sacrificial worship.

Their religious and moral life was ruled by instructions received from the Sanhedrim, and these were the more willingly observed, inasmuch as they were not applied by force. The Sanhedrim sent deputies from time to time to all parts, in order to acquaint the people with their most important decrees. Even Jews not natives of Palestine possessed their own places of worship in Jerusalem, where they met for service. There were in the capital synagogues for coreligionists from Alexandria, Cyrenæa, Sicily and other places. It is said that the number of synagogues amounted to 380, and this is probably no exaggeration, considering that during the Passover festival there were often as many as two millions of people gathered together here from all countries; and to form a proper estimate of the great number of Jews of those times it is only necessary to state that in Egypt alone, from the Mediterranean Sea to the borders of Ethiopia, nearly one million of Jews resided.

In Syria, and especially in the capital, Antiochia, the principal part of the population were Jews. The congregation of Antiochia had a beautiful synagogue, rich in costly gifts, all dedicated to the service of God. In Rome, the metropolis of the world, they resided in such great numbers that they even exercised some influence in politics; and as those formerly resident there, as well as the ransomed prisoners, were entitled to vote in popular assemblies, they often succeeded, by their unanimous, active, cool and dispassionate conception of all affairs, and perhaps even by their power of mind, in determining many a popular decree. In fact, they were possessed of so much influence, that even the eloquent Cicero, in attempting once to speak against the Jews, felt afraid to utter his hostile opinions, in order not to incur their displeasure. Yet still larger than in Europe, Syria and Africa were the number of Jews in the Parthian countries, the remaining portion of former exiles, who were possessed of whole districts of land in Mesopotamia and Babylonia. In the countries beyond the Tigris, in Media and Persia, many Jewish congregations existed, and the president of the Sanhedrim issued to them also a missive, which has been preserved for us, and runs as follows :

"To our brethren, the exiles in Babylon, Media, Greece, and to all other exiles in Israel, greeting : We herewith make known to you that the lambs of this year are still tender, doves have not fledged yet, and the spring being retarded, it pleased myself and associates to prolong the current year for thirty days."

The towns of Athens, Corinth, Thessalonia and Philippi had Jewish congregations. It is also certain that Rome sent Jewish colonies westward, to the southern parts of France and Spain, although we cannot exactly trace them in those countries previous to the destruction of the Temple.

But this dispersion was a blessing as well as the work of an all-wise Providence. The indelibleness of immortality of the Jewish race was thus secured. In one country persecuted and crushed, they gathered in another, always forming fresh establishments for the doctrine which continually became more and more endeared to them. They were like scattered grains of seed appointed by Providence to transplant everywhere a true and pure knowledge of God, as well as a more enlightened civilization. As the colonization of the Greeks contributed toward awakening among different nations an appreciation of art and science, as the settlements of the Romans served to forward in many countries well arranged commonalities, based upon principles of right and justice and established law, so the widespread dispersion of the Jews had the indisputable, effect of counteracting the false notions and the brutalizing vices of heathenism.

The first impression which Judaism made upon heathen nations was of a repulsive nature; the Jews appeared to them, in reference to their peculiar mode of life, customs, and in all their religious views, a somewhat singular, enigmatical and mysterious race. They were unable to fathom them, and looked upon them now with profound aversion, and then again with the utmost irony. The antithesis between Judaism and heathenism was so decidedly put forward that it became manifest in every act. Whatever was holy to the heathen, was to the Jews abomination; and whatever the former considered as a matter of indifference, became to the latter an object of piety. The separation of the Jews from the common dining-table, their aversion to intermarrying with heathens, their abstinence from hog's flesh, and also their objection to make use of warm food on the Sabbath day, all these matters the heathen considered perverse doctrines, and the restrictions in regard to social intercourse as misanthropy. The covenant of circumcision was to the heathen a special object of astonishment and derision. Even the seriousness of the Jews, who would never take part in the childish amusements of the theater and its bloody combats, seemed to them the effect of a gloomy temper, which finds no pleasure in such beautiful pastimes. Therefore all superficial minds considered Judaism a barbarous superstition, which teaches mankind nothing but uncharitableness; while the more profound looker-on, in contemplating the pure adoration, free from all idol worship, of the only One God, as well as the other attachments and sympathies prevailing among the Jews, together with their chastity, temperance, and firmness, readily confessed his admiration for the many excellencies which characterized them.

The penetrating and moral minds among the Greeks and Romans soon came to this conviction, turning away in disgust from a religion which, besides its unworthy representation of a divinity, seemed to justify even a vicious life according to the model of their idols. The want of religion, which was much felt among the people of the ancient world, caused many a heathen, who sought after religious and moral truths, to embrace Judaism, the nature of which became more apparent to them by their intercourse with intelligent Jews, partly through the Greek translation of the religious system of Judaism, and partly also through the Greek-Alexandrinean literature. During the latter part of the century previous to the decline of the Jewish realm, more proselytes existed than at any other period, all of whom embraced Judaism, not for the sake of worldly advantages, but entirely from pure conviction. In Judaism they found ease of mind for all their doubts, and food for their spiritual and temporal welfare. Philo states that, from personal experience in his fatherland, he is able to testify as to the alteration of conduct of all the heathens who embraced Judaism. They led a life of virtue, moderation, benignity and humanity; and especially the women were attracted by the filial yet sublime representations of the Bible. In Damascus almost all the heathen women embraced Judaism. In this manner Judaism found access to all the Asiatic courts, and the royal members remained true followers of the Jewish faith during several generations. H. GRAETZ.

INEXORABLE Not to be moved by entreaty.	ANTITHESIS—Contrast.
FATALITY Decree of fate.	MISANTHROPY—Hatred of mankind.
SANHEDRIM—Seventy elders of the Chief Council of the Jews.	SUPERFICIAL—Shallow; without learning.
MISSIVE—A letter.	CHASTITY—Purity of body.
COUNTERACT—To hinder.	VICIOUS—Given to vice.
ENIGMATIC—Obscure.	BENIGNITY Actual kindness.

THE LORD IS NIGH.

WHEN the storm-shattered vessel is toss'd by the gale,
And each billow speeds on, bearing havoc and death,
Till the courage grows weak and the strength waxes frail,
With the wild sky above, and the wild waves beneath;

When the young heart is crushed 'mid its early delights,
And the soul is bowed down with a weight of despair,
And we turn from a treacherous world, that requites
Our warmest heart-treasures with anguish and care;

When the one whom we cherished turns coldly away,
And we weep o'er the dream that has cheated our youth,

And mourn that no longer one love-beaming ray
Will return to illumine our pathway with truth;

Then! then in our anguish we fly unto Thee,
When the false world is fading like dreams of the night,
And the idols to whom we have bended the knee
Have fallen to earth, and are hid from our sight.

And Thou! oh! Thou hearest the suppliant's voice,
Whether tossed on the ocean, or wrecked on the earth;
And Thy mercy can cause the sad heart to rejoice,
Tho' surrounded by perils and storms from its birth.
REBEKAH HYNEMAN.

HEROD, KING OF JUDEA.

[37 B.]   *

ANTIPATER had left four sons and one daughter, all of whom surpassed him in effrontery; and especially one, Herod, whom history, as if in mockery, surnamed the Great, proved an evil demon for the Jewish nation. Like his intriguing father, he sought at any price to gain the honor of the Romans, and he despised no means, however bad, if they only led to this object. He knew well how to cringe and to flatter, and to extort money, in order to corrupt with it. Yet fortune seemed to favor him amazingly, so that from all difficulties he always emerged with still greater power. His life offers a picture of audacity from the first, as this incident in his early days shows:

A small troop of Aristobulus' army had succeeded in keeping their ground in the Galilean mountains, and were only waiting for a favorable opportunity to hoist the flag against the enemies of their fatherland. They were considered by the Romans a band of robbers, and their leader, Ezekias, was termed a captain of robbers; while the Jews looked upon them as avengers of their honor and liberty. In order to gain the favor of a foreign government, Herod undertook an expedition against them, made Ezekias prisoner, and had him executed without trial. This was a great violation of the law, for whether Ezekias was innocent or not, the right over life and death belongs to a court of justice only. Some men of high standing, indeed, appealed to the weak-minded Hyrkanus not to permit any longer that Idumæans should deride the law in this manner; and, however reluctantly this weakling felt, he was at length obliged to order that the audacious Herod be summoned before the Sanhedrim, over which Shammai and Abtalion presided. But how did he appear? In purple and in arms, and surrounded by a body-guard, he, the descendant of a prisoner of war, clad in princely garments ! This deprived the judges of their courage, and only Shammai took heart to say, " Does not the prisoner who stands accused of murder appear before you, as if ready to put us to death, should we declare him guilty ? But I am almost inclined to attach less blame to him than to you and the king, that you suffer justice to be thus abused. Know, then, that the man at whose presence you now tremble will, one day, deliver you all to the axe of the executioner." These spirited words roused the judges, who now threatened to pass sentence upon the accused. But Hyrkanus ordered the trial to be adjourned, and he thus gave Herod a chance to make his escape.

When the power of Herod began to increase, and found the nation daily more oppressed and weak, Antigonus, son of the unfortunate Aristobulus II., succeeded in raising a strong army, entered upon alliance with the Parthians, Rome's most powerful enemies, and then advanced on Jerusalem. Phasael, Herod's brother, and Hyrkanus fell into their hands; the former committed suicide in prison, and the latter had his ears cut off, to make him unfit for the office of High-priest, and, mutilated in this manner, the Parthians took him prisoner to Babylon; while Herod fled, and the curses of the whole nation followed him. Thus Antigonus, who bore the Hebrew name of his great grandfather, Mattathias, was again upon the throne of the Asmoneans; Judea cleared of foreign troops; and, after a hard struggle of thirty years, they could venture upon enjoying momentary repose, having thus regained independence.

But it was only a dream, a short dream, for Antigonus was no match for Herod, either in intellect or energy. In his flight, deprived of all means, he traveled through the wilderness, and, after a stormy sea voyage, at length arrived in Rome. Here they acknowledged that he deserved the respect of Rome, and promised to assist him in his troubles. The Roman Senate declared Antigonus an enemy of the Roman Empire, and made Herod King of Judea; in gratitude thereof, Herod sacrificed upon the Capitol to the Roman tutelar-idol Jupiter. In returning, however, he was obliged to conquer first his kingdom, carrying on war for seven years, aided by Roman troops. Jerusalem was besieged, and upon a Sabbath it was occupied. The Romans entered the city and the Temple, cutting down all unsparingly without regard to age or sex, and even the priests at the sacrificial altar shared the same fate. Antigonus was made prisoner, and upon Herod's urgent request the Roman general led him to the stake, an ignominious death, opposed to law and custom, and causing, even among the Romans, the utmost indignation. He was the last of the eight princely High-priests belonging to the house of the Asmoneans, who at first, for twenty-six years, governed Judea with splendor and renown, but in disgrace and misery afterward. Herod, or as the people styled him, the Idumæan slave, had now reached the goal of his ambition, and his opponents had to feel his vengeance. By crowds the followers of Antigonus were massacred, among whom were forty-five families of the highest standing. The Sanhedrim, who, twelve years before, were on the point of passing sentence of death upon him, were all executed, with the exception of their chiefs, Shammai and Abtalion, who had been opposed to Antigonus. All the property of those who were condemned he confiscated for his treasury, and the accumulated wealth thus obtained served him for purchasing the favor of the Roman rulers, who alone were capable of protecting him against the bitter hatred of the Jewish nation. From the hostile disposition of the people, Herod never thought his throne safe, especially as long as any one of the Asmoneans lived; for, in spite of the misery which latterly they had brought upon Judea, the nation, nevertheless, clung to them with great attachment. Therefore, like a bloodthirsty tiger, he murdered every member of this unfortunate family, although he was connected with them by the closest ties; inasmuch, as in order to banish all fear of Herod, Hyrkanus gave him his grandchild, the ill-fated Mariamne, in marriage, who, on account of her virtue and her beauty, became celebrated and loved in Judea. Herod, in an unmerciful manner, turned away his wife Doris, and wedded Mariamne.

Mariamne had a brother, the High-priest Aristobulus III., a youth of eighteen, of unsurpassable beauty, and the idol of the nation. This young man, Herod thought, might become dangerous, and therefore he strove to rid himself of him; but it was impossible for Herod to seize openly this virtuous young man, and therefore he had recourse to his usual cunning. He invited Aristobulus to Jericho, which was his favorite residence. After an entertainment, which he had given in his honor, the king walked with his brother-in-law about the extensive grounds, and, as if by chance, they came all at once upon a large lake, in which several youths belonging to the court were bathing. Herod prevailed upon Aristobulus to share in the pleasure; but scarcely had he plunged into the water, when those who were bathing seized him, and pretending to sport, held him so long under the water that he died. However much Herod feigned to mourn his loss, ordering a splendid funeral, it was all of no avail; for there was not the least doubt that he had previously planned the deed, and everybody looked upon him as the murderer. But who would dare to make such an assertion? With Aristobulus died the last support of the house of the Asmoneans.

Now came the turn of old Hyrkanus, to whom the Parthians had generously granted freedom, who being overloaded with honors by the Babylonian Jews, could have thus easily finished his troublesome life in peace and quietness. But, with his peculiar dissimulation, Herod invited him to return to Jerusalem, to share with him both throne and power, and, above all, to receive his thanks for the many favors he had rendered him. In vain did the Babylonian Jews dissuade the credulous Hyrkanus from departing. He felt an ardent desire to see the Temple and the Holy Land, and easily went into the golden trap set for him. Arrived at Jerusalem, Herod did indeed receive him in a friendly manner, calling him his father, and gave him a place of honor at his table, and in the council-chamber. Under a shallow pretence that Hyrkanus had formerly been in harmony with Malich, the assassin of Antipater, he summoned him before an arbitrarily composed court of law, which acted cowardly enough to pass sentence of death upon Hyrkanus.

These murders perpetrated on Mariamne's brother and grandfather were certainly not calculated to fill her heart with affection toward Herod; yet this virtuous woman would have borne all without a single word of reproach, had not Herod, in a remarkable manner, taken care to change her dove-like meekness into the most bitter hatred. Since his marriage with Mariamne, he was twice compelled to visit

Rome, in order to show, on the one occasion, that he had no hand in the death of Aristobulus, and on the other to seek the favor of Octavius, who had dethroned Antonius, Herod's great patron, and who now, under the name of Augustus, declared himself sole monarch of Rome. On both occasions he knew well that his life was in jeopardy, which made his return uncertain. Therefore, his inhumanity made him each time give the order to one of his accomplices, that as soon as the news of his death became known Mariamne should be assassinated, in order that none should have the fortune to possess her after his death. Fortune did not forsake him on these two occasions, returning each time in safety, and being even furnished with still greater power. But his cruel orders had, nevertheless, been betrayed to Mariamne. He had the traitor executed, and although he assured Mariamne of his unaltered affection, it proved of no avail, for this noble woman treated him now with icy coldness, and in a manner becoming her virtue she frankly confessed that she hated him, and charged him with the death of her brother and grandfather. Herod's wrath on hearing these words knew of no bounds, and his cruel sister Salome made use of his rage in persuading him to believe that Mariamne had bribed his page to poison him. Hereupon he called a special court of justice, and he himself, with the utmost vehemence, accused her, the virtuous descendant of the Maccabees, of adultery and conspiring to assassinate him. The mercenary judges thought to please the king, and condemned her to death. Thus the most beautiful of Judea's women, the pride of the whole Jewish nation, was led to the place of execution. With firm resignation she met her fate.

Yet not even Mariamne's death eased the spirit of revenge in Herod's breast, but only kindled in him a still greater rage. He could not bear the thought of having lost her, and he grew sick and delirious, being so ill at his palace in Samaria that his physicians despaired of his life. This opportunity induced his mother-in-law, Alexandra, to try whether she could not possess herself of Jerusalem and remove her mortal enemy. The mad attempt was betrayed to Herod, and Alexandra paid for it with her life. She was the last scion of the Asmoneans, and died after beholding her father-in-law, Aristobulus II., her husband, Alexander, her son, Aristobulus III., her father, Hyrkanus II., and her daughter, Mariamne, one after the other, suffering ignominious deaths.

Herod's fondness for building was truly remarkable, through which he intended partly to flatter the Romans, and partly to become celebrated and immortal in the heathen world, for as to the Jewish nation their hatred toward him was ever strong. In Jerusalem and other places, he introduced the Grecian system, in order to establish gradually idolatrous customs and manners. He was even not afraid to build upon Judea's consecrated soil several temples for idol worship, in order that these follies might procure for him the admiration of foreign nations, while he impoverished the Jewish people to the last they were possessed of, in order to carry out his obnoxious plans. This fondness for building, and desire to gratify the Romans, induced him to alter the old Temple, which had stood five hundred years—a small edifice, and built in antiquated style. The representatives of the nation, to whom he communicated his resolution, did not trust him, feeling afraid that he would pull down the old Temple without building another in its stead, and they only gave their consent after all the necessary materials were at hand for commencing the work. The interior of the temple was finished in a year and a half, but the exterior, the walls, the porches and colonnades took several years for their completion. Herod's temple was considered a magnificent building, admired by every one for its beautiful architectural style; but Herod had placed it under protection of the Romans. A golden eagle—symbol of Roman power—was placed over the principal entrance, causing a great deal of vexation among the Jewish patriots. It entirely rested with the Romans to decide how long the Jewish sanctuary should exist; in less than a century this work of splendor was turned into a heap of rubbish and ashes.

We must not believe, however, that Herod buried his old life under the ruins of the old temple, and commenced a new life with the new one; he remained the same character to the very last. Mariamne had borne him two sons, Alexander and Aristobulus, who had been brought up in Rome, and were already married. Salome was their bitter enemy, as she had been Mariamne's, while the people loved these Asmoneans for their mother's sake. This circumstance Salome made use of, and together with Antipater, son of the expelled Doris, tried to make the suspicious king believe that Mariamne's sons hated their father on account of their mother's death, and that they were striving to slay him and seize his crown. Upon this false accusation Herod had them both executed. The old sinner, who was now nearly seventy years of age, was at last stretched upon a bed of illness, being attacked by a painful and loathsome disease, from which his sufferings were so great that he was on the point of taking his own life. Yet even this miserable condition, which would have caused any one else to grow better, had not the least moral effect on him. Upon a false rumor of his death, several young men entered the temple court, cutting down the hated eagle. Herod had them all burned alive. At this instance the sixth High-priest was arbitrarily installed by Herod.

Antipater, son of Doris, was a prisoner in the palace of Jericho, where Herod lay ill, and was convicted of having prepared poison for his father, and causing the innocent death of his brothers. Augustus left it to Herod to say whether he should be executed or not, and five days before Herod breathed his last he had him put to death. Although Antipater was deserving of a tenfold death, his execution caused, nevertheless, great indignation, that a father should pronounce sentence of death upon his third son. Herod's last thought was occupied with further orders for assassinations, for he invited a number of Judea's most eminent men to come to Jericho, where he had them confined in a race-course, and put under a strong guard, while he instructed his sister Salome that, after his death, his body-guard should cut them down, in order, as he said, that the whole nation and every family may have to lament the loss of those near and dear to them, and thus be prevented from rejoicing over his demise.

From the first moment of his public career, until he breathed his last, he was possessed of evil and bloody thoughts. Herod was in his seventieth year when he died, thirty-four years after dethroning the last ruler of the Asmoneans, and in the thirty-seventh year of his reign. His corpse was taken to Herodium with great pomp, being followed by the so-called Augustean troop, and the Thracian, Germanic, and Gallic body-guards. But the Jewish nation kept that very day as a half-holiday.   DR. JOST.

HEROD—An Idumæan by birth, a sect which under Jochanan Hyrkanos became Jews.
GALLIC—Pertaining to Gaul or France.
DEMON—A spirit; generally an evil spirit.

CAPITOL—Temple of Jupiter in Rome; the Senate-house.
TUTELAR—Having the charge or guardianship of a person or thing.

HEROD'S LAMENT FOR MARIAMNE.

Oh, Mariamne! now for thee
The heart for which thou bled'st is bleeding;
Revenge is lost in agony,
And with remorse to rage succeeding.
Oh, Mariamne! where art thou?
Thou canst not hear my bitter pleading;
Ah, couldst thou—thou wouldst pardon now,
Though Heaven were to my prayer unheeding.

And is she dead?—and did they dare
Obey my frenzy's jealous raving?
My wrath but doom'd my own despair;
The sword that smote her's o'er me waving.

But thou art cold, my murder'd love;
And this dark heart is vainly craving
For her who soars alone above,
And leaves my soul unworthy saving.

She's gone, who shared my diadem;
She sunk with her my joys entombing;
I swept that flower from Judah's stem,
Whose leaves for me alone were blooming;
And mine's the guilt and mine the hell,
This bosom's desolation dooming;
And I have earn'd those tortures well,
Which unconsumed are still consuming!

BYRON.

HILLEL AND SHAMMAI.

[40 B.]

WHILST Herod on his throne was trying hard to annihilate Judaism, two men, in the seclusion of scholastic life, were effectively engaged in preserving it, of which the Idumæan tyrant had not the least foreboding. Hillel, who could trace his ancestry, which had remained in Babylon after the exile, as far back as David, came to Jerusalem in order to study law, and became the most ardent disciple of Shemajah and Abtalion. He at the same time had to struggle with the most abject poverty, and from the pittance he earned as day-laborer half went to pay for admission to the academy. One day—it was on the eve of Sabbath and in the midst of winter—he could not find work, and having no means he was unable to pay the usual fee, and was therefore refused admission to the academy. In order, however, not to miss the discourse, he climbed from outside one of the windows of the school-room and there placed himself to listen to the instruction. Here the cold soon benumbed him, and during the night a heavy snow-storm covered him with snow three feet deep. The two teachers entered the hall in the morning and Shemajah said: "Brother Abtalion, it is here very dark and the heavens seem to be cloudy." But they soon perceived a human being sitting in one of the windows and exclaimed : "Indeed, he deserves that, on his account, one may venture to violate the Sabbath!" Whereupon they took him down, placed him before the fire, and tried every expedient to restore him to life. The stranger, until now but little known, was soon to become one of the foremost in their ranks. Shemajah and Abtalion were no more. By the executioner's axe of Herod many hundreds of learned men breathed their last or were frightened away into strange countries. And it came to pass that the eve of Passover happened on a Sabbath, owing to which the question arose whether the Pesach-offering abolishes the order of the Sabbath or not. Hundreds of thousands had come to Jerusalem for the festival, but the Synhedrion were at a loss to solve this pungent question of the day. Then Hillel arose and decided the question in the affirmative, proving the correctness of his decision not only by certain precepts according to the interpretation of Holy Writ, but also by appealing to the traditions of his teachers, Shemajah and Abtalion. In consequence of this occurrence Hillel was chosen president of the Synhedrion.

Hillel, far from being proud of the high dignity thus conferred upon him, felt rather dissatisfied on account of it, and began to reproach the members of the Synhedrion: "What could have caused the appointment of an insignificant Babylonian to the presidency of the Synhedrion but your inactivity in not paying proper attention to the instructions of Shemajah and Abtalion?" Besides Hillel, Shammai's efficacy must also be mentioned. He was just the counterpart of Hillel, and yet a necessary complement to the same. Hillel's predominant character consisted principally in that cordial, dove-like meekness which never permitted the ebullition of ill temper, even for a moment, to gain the mastery over his mind; that thoughtful philanthropy which arises from one's own humility and the favorable judgment of others, and lastly that calmness which emanates from the deepest confidence in God, and in the face of approaching misfortune always remains steadfast. In later times no more perfect ideal of charitableness and modesty was ever known than the Babylonian Hillel.

His liberality knew no bounds, showing the utmost delicacy not to shame the receiver, but to respect him rather, according to his station in life. He esteemed the doctrine of Judaism so highly that he felt excited when he saw the same misused in becoming the means for satisfying ambition and greediness of fame. The same as Hillel was, on account of his great virtue, taken as ideal by those who came after him, in the same manner he was considered next to Ezra the spiritual restorer of the Jewish doctrine, who saved it from the decaying condition it was placed in. The attachment which the people showed him extended even to his descendants; the presidency of the Synhedrion was ever since hereditary in his house, and it has continued to maintain this dignity during four centuries.

Of Shammai's biography but little is known. He was for certain a Palestinean, and therefore took a sincere interest in all political and religious complications of his native country. His religious views were very rigorous, but he was nevertheless of no morose, misanthropic temper, urging rather to meet everybody in a friendly manner, as shown by the motto preserved of him: "Make your occupation with the law your chief object, speak little, but perform much, and receive every one with a friendly air."

Each of these two members of the Synhedrion, Hillel and Shammai, formed schools of their own (Bet-Hillel, Bet-Shammai), both of which proved of great influence and importance.

DR. JOST.

SYNHEDRION—The highest council at Jerusalem, composed of seventy Elders and presided over by the High-priests.
COMPLEMENT—Perfection.
EBULLITION—Act of boiling up with heat.

PHILANTHROPY—Love of mankind; good nature.
BET-HILLEL (Hebrew)—Signifying *house* of Hillel.

THE AIM.

I QUESTIONED a leaf as it rustled past,
Borne along with the autumn's blast,
Its life full spent and unknown to
fame :
Whither goest thou, fluttering leaf?
Can'st thou tell in thy voyage so brief,
This life's aim?

I measured a rainbow's fleeting span—
Its arch from heaven down to man,
Transient beauties ever the same,
And sought to seek in the magical bow,
Ere it lost its fervor and glow,
This life's aim.

I gazed in the eyes of a matchless face,
Divinely dowered with every grace
That might a heart of stone inflame !
Pray tell me with thy art of speech,
What I would learn if thou wouldst
teach—
This life's aim?

I looked at a rushing silver stream,
Whose breast was decked with a dia-
   mond gleam
That ever went and ever came,
And questioned it—as dashing through
The flow'ry mead it onward flew—
     This life's aim?

A thought I plucked from a busy brain—
A note I caught from a sweet refrain—
A laurel leaf from a wreath of fame—
A broken sod from a nameless grave

I asked (but no response they gave)—
     To this life's aim.

*   *   *   *   *   *

Within the shrine of the silent soul,
Lies the Aim of Life we all control—
  The nobler instincts of the men,
That rise like stars to shed their light
On travelers weary with their night—
  To lavish all the *good* they can!

                    JACOB G. ASCHER.

THE SIEGE OF JOTAPATA.

[69 A.]

I.

SURELY if the people of Israel stood in need of any glorification, then the history of their decline as an independent nation would demonstrate it beyond measure. In the eventful history of this decline, the siege of Jotapata stands prominently as an incident which should never be allowed to be forgotten. This terrible occurrence furnishes many instances of what a handful of spirited men could accomplish for religion and fatherland, even against the bravery and pride of a well-disciplined army accustomed to war; the issue between both could only be determined, as often is the case, by way of treachery. Let us then tarry for a moment on this blood-saturated ground—we are standing upon the graves of the bravest of our ancestors—the second Temple was yet on Moriah's height. Thirteen Roman procurators brought upon the Jews in Palestine unspeakable oppression ever since the animosities of the Asmoneans in self-destroying manner had called the enemy to the country; and thus the patience of the people had become entirely exhausted, owing to impoverishment, mockery, and the withdrawal of all rights and privileges. The invaders installed by force the god of the insane Roman emperor, together with his worship in the Temple at Jerusalem, the sacred place of devotion of the One Incorporeal God, introducing the same also in every house of prayer belonging to the Jews, and were even impudent enough to set up the statues of the emperor on the altars. On this, the rage of the Jewish people burst forth, and under the guidance of able leaders they succeeded in driving the Romans with great loss from the country. The governor from Syria, Cestius Gallus, who hastened with a strong army to Jerusalem, was also obliged to withdraw under disgraceful circumstances, and more than 6,000 Romans were slain. On the 8th of Marchesvan, in the year 66 (according to the usual chronology), not a single Roman could be found in Judea proper.

The emperor, who was traveling in Greece, commanded at once his most tried general, Vespasian, to subdue the Jews. He led into Syria above 60,000 of the bravest and choicest troops. His well-laid scheme was to conquer first the Jewish provinces, then to invest Jerusalem in order to cut off all resources, and thus forcing the place to surrender, to destroy it ultimately. However, it took three campaigns (67, 68 and 69) to accomplish his plan, and only in the fourth year did his son Titus succeed in reaching Jerusalem.

The northwest province of Galilee was singled out to become his first spoil, and his success was facilitated by the Jewish general of that province, who was wavering between the Jews and the Romans. It was the same Josephus who became afterward the Jewish historian, but also the partisan of the imperial Flavian. Sepphoris fell, we will merely say by the neglect of Josephus, into the hands of the Romans. Vespasian marched from Ptolemea (that is, Acco, now Jean D'Acre) with the flower of his army, being well supplied with war materials, and a number of mules and horses, carrying artillery and siege trains. On account of the undetermined policy of Josephus, there was no Jewish army present in Galilee to defend this province. Those who did not wish to show resistance to the Romans would not fight. Thus only a few towns remained which held out against the Romans. The town of Gabara also fell into their hands, all able-bodied men having left for more important places, while those who stayed behind were put to the sword, and the towns and villages were laid in ashes.

Vespasian now turned against the mountain fortress Jotapata. Jotapata was but a comparatively small town, situated on a rock, and surrounded by very deep valleys. On the north side only the town was accessible, being built here upon the projected part of a hill, which, however, was well secured by strong redoubts and towers. The town being surrounded by hills, it became visible only on a close approach. But who were the defenders of this mountain fortress? No veterans, no well-trained garrison, no tried warriors; only the simple citizens of the place, merely reinforced by patriots who had escaped from the provinces. Already, previous to this, Placidus had undertaken an expedition against Jotapata, in order to surprise the place. But the citizens received a timely warning, and courageously went to meet the Romans, who had to retreat with great loss. From the smoky ruins of Gabara to Jotapata was but two hours' distance, yet it took the Roman pioneers four days to clear away the many obstacles which nature and cunning had furnished, before the roads could be made passable for the army. In the meantime, Josephus had gone to Jotapata. It was in the first week of May that the Romans commenced the siege, establishing their camp upon a hill near Jotapata, and investing the entire town by a double line of troops. Promptly on the next day, Vespasian attacked the place in great force, but the Jews defended themselves with energy, having six hundred wounded and seventeen killed. The attack was repeated by the Romans during the next five days without intermission, and the sallies of the Jews brought on heavy fighting outside of the walls, the besieged never feeling dejected or weary in the least degree. On the one side was desperation, on the other shame, and both parties showed the greatest coolness and utmost valor. If then the Parthian king, Vologeses, the most powerful sovereign and enemy of the Romans in Asia, had crossed the Euphrates, and if the Jews, instead of being divided into factions, could have formed a proper regular army, and thus surprised the Roman troops in the defiles of Jotapata, what a turning point in the history of mankind!

It was not to be. The besieged of Jotapata were abandoned to their fate. As all the assaults made upon the town proved fruitless, Vespasian resolved upon throwing up ramparts, from which the town could be better bombarded. Enormous quantities of wood and stones were procured, a kind of basket-work was stretched over palisades, in order to ward off the arrows thrown constantly from the city walls; also a dike was erected, and one hundred and sixty catapults were set up. The catapults threw lances and stones of heavy weight, and the ballisters swarms of darts as well as fire. The Jews were obliged to leave the walls, but they continually made sallies, tore away the covering which sheltered the Romans, killed the workmen, destroying partly the dike, and setting fire to the posts which held the basket-work. At length Josephus had the city wall raised in proportion to the dike opposite, which continually grew larger. He ordered hedge poles to be rammed into the city wall, over which he extended the hides of fresh stripped oxen, which slackened in receiving the stones thrown, and also protected the Jews from the fire. Behind these the workmen felt more secure, and were thus enabled to work day and night in raising the wall till it reached a height of forty feet. This accomplished, they were now by far safer, and felt encouraged to attempt fresh sallies, in which they always proved successful, destroying the enemy's works, who on all occasions sustained great loss. Vespasian soon perceived that all his attacks, however well planned, must prove of no avail, and that only a regular state of siege, to bring on famine, would force the place to surrender. He then ordered that the passes leading into the town should be occupied, and that all its communication should be cut off. However, the inhabitants of Jotapata had a plentiful supply of provisions, but water was scarce. There was no well in the town, and they had to depend upon rain water, which was not plentiful at the season when the siege took place; therefore the water was parcelled out in rations, which generally caused the longing for it to be the stronger. The Romans could perceive the place where the water was served out, and thus killed many a one in fetching it, as their catapults reached as far as that spot. But in order to blast the hopes which Vespasian enjoyed in thinking that, owing to the want of water, the place would soon have to surrender, the Jotapateans hung large pieces of cloth over the walls, which were so wet that the water dripped down in large quantities. Vespasian then took to arms again, which made the Jews rather glad, inasmuch as they preferred to die in battle rather than from hunger and thirst. They even became the attacking party, after Josephus attempted to escape with some of the most distinguished inhabitants of the place, which, however, was frustrated by the people.

The Jews fought desperately, and in their sallies nothing could withstand their boldness, which compelled Vespasian to withdraw his heavy troops, putting in their place the Arabian archers, the Syrian slingers and stone casters, and all the heavy artillery. Indeed, for a time Vespasian considered himself the besieged instead of the besieger. In the meanwhile the Romans had advanced the dike close to the city wall, and now the "ram" was to be made use of. This was an enormous beam, the size of a ship-mast, being at one end overcast with heavy iron in the shape of a ram's head, and in the middle were attached strong ropes like a beam-scale on another large crossbeam, which rested upon strong posts. A number of workmen drew the ram backward, and then, with united strength, thrust it again forward, which caused the ram's head to be driven into the wall. No tower, no wall, could resist the constant attacks of this machine; and then the catapults and ballisters moved forward together with the archers and slingers, clearing the city wall of its defenders. Then the scaffolding of the ram was brought thither, and at the first shock the wall quaked, causing a cry of lamentation in the city.

II.

Josephus, not in the least alarmed, ordered that large bags filled with chaff be let down the walls where the ram was striking; and no sooner did the ram begin to play, than the bags were placed from the breastworks against the thrusts of the ram, which caused them to rebound without doing the least injury. However, the Romans found out a remedy in making for themselves long pikes wherewith they cut off the bags; whereupon, the new wall, from the many thrusts made upon it, began to give way, and the besieged had to renew their exertions. They then furnished themselves with dry wood and firebrands, and thus attempted another sally. But previous to this one of the Jewish combatants executed a miracle of heroic bravery. His name was Eleazar, son of Sameas from Saab, in Galilee. He placed himself upon the wall, and, taking an enormously large stone, threw the same with such precision and power down the breastwork that it hit the machine, and entirely demolished the ram's head.

But not yet satisfied with his achievement, he jumped down the wall, and in the midst of the enemy he took the ram's head, and carried it to the wall. Being unprotected, and without armor, he was pierced by five arrows at the same time; yet, unconcerned about his wounds, he mounted the wall again, and there placing himself proudly before the enemy, held up the ram's head for every one to behold, causing a cry of admiration in both armies, lasting just long enough to see this noble patriot falling dead from the wall, still clinging to his trophy. Now, without a moment's loss, Josephus sallied forth with his troops, carrying the firebrands, and led by two brothers, Netiras and Philip, who made a dash against the Tenth Legion with such impetuosity that they broke their lines, and entirely routed them. Machines, palisades, outworks, utensils — everything was burnt, and all the redoubts destroyed.

The same evening, Vespasian himself was wounded in his leg by one of the Jewish archers, which caused great consternation among the Romans; but the general tried to suppress his sufferings by showing himself the next morning to the army and encouraging them to fight and avenge their defeat. The Romans then commenced to storm the place with such violence that the besieged considered this assault far more dangerous than the previous ones. The Romans kept up the storming of the place the whole night, and with such success, too, that the besieged were obliged to hold firebrands in order to defend themselves and to take proper aim, as the enemy almost remained invisible to them. The power of the catapults and scorpions was so great that several persons were pierced at the same time, while the mass of stones cast into the place destroyed the breastwork, and dashed the towers to pieces. To be able to judge of the effect of this artillery, it is only necessary to remark that a warrior standing close to Josephus had his head torn off by a sling-stone, and the head was thrown a distance of a quarter of a mile. It was a terrible outroar, to which were added the dull sounds of the numberless corpses of combatants rolling down the wall, the heartrending cry of the women, together with the groaning of the wounded and dying. The Jews fought with lion-like courage, the blood flowing in streams from the wall, which could now be reached by heaps of dead bodies. Everywhere the Jews stood out; not a single one left the wall, and no sooner did the number of combatants diminish, than the gaps were filled up again. It was impossible for the Romans to hold out against such bravery, and although the wall had given way during the night, the besieged had already thrown up fresh redoubts. The night passed, and Jotapata was still unconquered. The next morning, Vespasian was obliged to give his soldiers some rest, and then he again led them to the assault. In well arranged order, they advanced to that part of the wall which was already destroyed, and at the sound of the trumpeters of all the legions, the army raised a

horrible battle-cry, and commenced the attack with such violence
that the sky darkened from the arrows and stones thrown on all
sides. But the Jews continued to fight bravely, cutting down all
who stood in their way. Yet even the most splendid deeds of bravery
could not prevent their becoming fatigued in the struggle, for while
the Romans continually brought fresh troops to bear against them,
they had now but a small number to depend upon. Vespasian then
formed his men into close columns, and protecting themselves by their
shields from above, they advanced in a body close to the wall. Under
these fearful circumstances, Josephus all at once ordered that seething
hot oil should be poured upon the columns of the Romans. It did not
take long to supply the oil, which had been kept ready, and which
easily became heated. It was poured upon the soldiers from the
wall. The effect was terrible; the columns were soon broken, and
under awful pain they rolled down the wall. But this only made the
Romans more enraged; they cleared the roads of their suffering comrades, and made another advance. Whereupon the Jews cast boiled
Grecian hay upon the boards of the storming bridges, which caused
the storming parties to slip and to fall, and those who could not keep
on their legs the Jews easily cut down. Thus the combat lasted till
evening, and, although it was a fearful day for the Jews, it ended nevertheless gloriously, for the Romans had to retreat under heavy loss.
This battle happened on the 20th of June, and had caused the ranks
of the Romans to become much reduced. After this, the fighting became insignificant, the Romans being principally engaged in raising
the rampart, which at length exceeded the wall. They also erected some
towers fifty feet high, which were covered with iron, and from which
they could dislodge the combatants who defended the wall. Thus
forty-seven days had been spent in this memorable siege; a solitary
mountain fortress occupied by unpracticed citizens, being bravely defended and holding out against an army of 60,000 of the bravest and
best warriors of Rome. The spirit with which the besieged were animated is proved by the fact that one of the Jewish prisoners from Jotapata defied all the torments of the rack, and smilingly met his death,
without betraying in the least how matters stood in the fortress.
Nevertheless Jotapata's last hour had struck. A deserter went to the
Roman general, and offered himself as a guide to bring him into the
town at a time when he would meet with the least resistance. Small
was the number, and weak the strength of the besieged. A surprise
after the last night watch is put on duty would be the safest time,
for then the Jews considered themselves out of danger, and, owing
to great fatigue, permit themselves some rest. Vespasian resolved
to trust the traitor. Exactly at the appointed hour, they quietly
approached the wall. Titus, with the Fifteenth Legion, entered
the place first, killed the guards, and then took possession of the
citadel. The Romans stood already in the midst of the town, and

the invaded had not yet the least presentiment of danger. The Romans knew of no mercy, of no forbearance. The people at length awoke, and in the confusion which ensued they were murdered without being able to offer any resistance, while many were thrown down the declivity to prevent them from defending themselves. Many of these brave men preferred to die by their own hands. The Romans spared no one, and during several days they searched every hiding place and every spot in the subterranean passages and caves, slaying every one they could find except women with their babes, to whom they showed some mercy. Not less than 40,000 lost their lives in the siege and by the conquests, while only 1,200 prisoners were made. Vespasian ordered the town to be razed. Thus fell Jotapata on the new moon of July and in the thirteenth year of Nero's reign.

But the tragedy was not yet ended. In the confusion which took place at the occupation, Josephus stole away through the enemy, and being well acquainted with the locality, he made his escape by throwing himself into a deep cistern, which he was aware led to a large cavern. Here he found already forty others, who also knew this hiding-place, and were well provided with provisions. Josephus was ready to leave the spot, and commence negotiations with Vespasian. But the others hindered him from carrying out his intentions. "Thou wishest to go," they said to him, "because thou desirest to live, and behold daylight as a slave. Well, if thou wilt die voluntarily, then thou endest as general; but, if not, thou wilt die as a traitor!" And with their swords drawn they surrounded him. Josephus tried hard to persuade them to save their lives by submitting to the Romans; but all proved of no avail. They wished to die as heroes, as independent men, and as they could not do so now in battle, after once leaving the cave, they would prefer rather to die by their own hands. Josephus, by his cunning, hit upon a fresh plan, and, pretending to submit to the proposal, said: "Well, if you think that death is the only expedient, then the casting of lots shall bring us to our decision, that by turns one may die at the hands of another." They agreed to it. The lots were drawn, and accordingly, with the exception of Josephus, only one of the forty was left, all ending their existence. The one left Josephus easily persuaded to leave the cave, and throw himself upon Vespasian's mercy. They left the cave, and Josephus fell upon his knees before the Roman general, prophesying unto him his approaching greatness. Vespasian considered Josephus serviceable in finishing the war, and gave him many valuable presents. The ruins of Jotapata have long since changed into dust and disappeared; but the heroism of its defenders will ever be admired, reflecting its golden rays upon the solitary rocks.   L. PHILIPPSON.

PROCURATOR—Manager; one who transacts affairs for another.
PARTISAN—An adherent to a faction.
PALISADE—Poles set by way of inclosure or a fence.

CATAPULT—An engine used in ancient times to throw stones.
BALLISTER—A cross-bow.
RAM—An instrument to batter walls.

ISRAEL'S POWER.

There is a reminiscent glory, shedding
Its light upon To-day,
That brightens life as with a benediction,
Sweet peace and heavenly sway;
Upon the Sabbath's sweet and festal beauty,
There gleams a jeweled ray

That, in the centuries past of wild oppression,
Lighted our wandering race
Over the rugged paths of faith and duty,
To Freedom's resting-place.
The Beautiful and True was Israel's guidance,
'Neath Thy sustaining grace!

In this dear land of conquering peace and plenty,
We share the honored name
Of patriot, statesman, all the nation's glory,
Time's laurel-bringing fame;
Heart-linked to noblest deed and aspiration
Is Israel's world-wide aim.

And still the reminiscent light is beaming,
The Sabbath's festal glow;
To Truth's triumphant anthem-peal the nations
Respondent onward go;
And Israel wields the sceptre, love empowered
For Evil's overthrow.

CORA WILBURN.

THE DESTRUCTION OF JERUSALEM.

[70 A.]

JERUSALEM was never before so populated, so beautiful and so fortified, than at the time when it was doomed to destruction, as if the Jewish capital should verify that external strength and outer splendor are of no avail. The circumference of Jerusalem within the wall encircling it was about four English miles, besides the suburbs at the foot of the Mount of Olives, such as Bethphage, Bethanian and others which also belonged to it, and which offered excellent accommodation for many of the guests who visited Jerusalem during the festivals. In regard to the number of inhabitants no certainty exists, but it is supposed that it amounted to at least 600,-000 at the time we speak of. But considering also the mass of people who continually flocked to the capital from abroad, the result, in counting the inhabitants once on a Pesach festival by means of an offering-piece, which every society participating in a Pesach-lamb had to deliver, clearly proved that the astonishing number of the population amounted to more than 2,000,000 people. The fortifications made Jerusalem appearingly a gloomy looking place, but it made it also so formidable that it was considered almost impregnable. Even was the Temple a great stronghold, which Pompey and Sosius had to fight hard for. All the fortifications were well supplied with numberless warriors, inasmuch as Jerusalem, since Galilee had been disarmed, became the meeting-place of all who, either for noble or ignoble purposes, expressed their desire of taking part in this final struggle. The love for fatherland, the impulse for liberty, ambition, vengeance, despair, the noblest virtues, the basest passions, all had sent their representatives—men with hearts of steel, of whom the most had already given proofs of heroism and disregard for death. The just cause for which the Jews fought, the great number of warriors who resolved to conquer or die, the excellent means of defence; everything seemed to point to a successful issue, especially as the state of Rome just then was rather endangered, several legions in different parts of the empire having revolted, and each choosing an emperor of their own.

Had these death-defying Jewish combatants acted like one man in attacking Rome, which was then already tottering—had Agrippa taken the lead in the movement and made the Asiatic nations his ally against Rome—who knows whether not at that time the Roman Colossus would have been crushed, or whether not, at least, the Romans would have offered favorable conditions to the Jews. But instead of adopting this plan they extirpated their own ranks in mortal party strife, thus giving the Romish general ample time to turn first almost the whole country into a wilderness, so that Jerusalem, being now isolated, could obtain no succor, not from any part, while in the meantime the circumstances in Rome became more settled, and the emperor's crown rested safely upon Vespasian's head.

There were about 24,000 men, all foolhardy heroes, forming four different parties, who could have executed extraordinary deeds of bravery had they been united against a common enemy in the field of battle; but instead of which each party intrenched themselves in a separate part of the town, made continual sallies against the other, as if fighting an inexorable enemy, in order that one might crush the other to become master of the situation. Their leaders were Eleazar ben Simon and Simon ben Jair, belonging to the Jerusalem zealots; also Jochanan of Gischala, of the Galilean zealots; whilst Jacob ben Sosa and Simon ben Kathla led the third party, consisting of Idumæans, all eager combatants, and the fourth party, the so-called Sicareans (robbers), were commanded by the wild Simon Giora. The struggle, which was renewed almost every day, destroyed many buildings and a vast quantity of stored-up provisions. The greatest havoc was perpetrated by the followers of bar Giora, who, being composed of the worst class of the population, were used to an adventurous life, and committed plunder and devastation with the utmost coolness. In this manner two years passed away, which gave ample time to the enemy to desolate all parts of Judea, especially as Vespasian took good care not to attack the lions in their places of concealment, although many deserters tried to persuade him that it would be merely an easy task to do so. He preferred to abide his time, till the different parties should have extirpated each other, and in the meantime he subdued those parts of the country which still held out.

Vespasian was just approaching Jerusalem when he was declared emperor. He went to Rome to be crowned, and Titus, who was appointed successor to the throne, came to Jerusalem to take the command of the army.

Titus now brought together about 80,000 men, and procured such quantities of siege materials as no other general ever had before him. At the approach of danger an approximation between the contending parties in Jerusalem took place. From all sides, from Judea and other foreign parts, especially from the countries on the Euphrates, very many flocked to the capital to lay down their lives in its defence. The walls and all other strongholds were well fortified, in order to withstand the many battering machines brought to bear against them. But all exertions could not prevent the fall of Jerusalem, for the struggle of the different parties, which had lasted so long, had deprived the city of its vast resources, without which it was impossible to hold out long. Before the war Jerusalem was well supplied with all sorts of provisions; all the storehouses in the Temple and in the city were well stocked with corn and other necessaries. Three of the richest men in Jerusalem, ben Tsisit, Kalba-sabua and Nicodem ben Gorion, had stored up such a quantity of provisions, that it was sufficient for the whole city, even for a period of ten years. But, owing to the continual struggles which took place within its walls, all these resources had become a prey to the flames; and the destruction thus caused had produced an enemy who in exorableness vied with the Romans, and against whom heroism could prevail nothing. In April (70) the Roman army encamped before Jerusalem, surrounding it on all sides. The Jews continually ventured upon making bold sallies, which almost frightened the Romans, for already, on the first day, Titus himself had but a narrow escape from being captured. Yet all these skirmishes proved fruitless, and the Romans at length succeeded in placing their battering machines on three sides in proper position, the same being directed against the outer wall of the city, and fixed on ramparts which reached to the height of the wall. The Romans now began to throw their arrows, slings, and blocks of stone into the city, and upon the defenders posted on the walls. On three sides battering rams and iron ram's heads played against the wall in order to effect a breach; but scarcely had the enemy commenced the attack, when the Jews sallied forth like demons, destroying the machines and all their preparations. Even women took part in the fight, giving thus to the men unexampled proofs of courage and their defiance of death. The besieged in their turn threw blocks of rock upon the enemy, poured seething hot oil upon their heads, and, after a while, they also understood to handle heavy artillery, turning the ordnance which they captured against their former possessors. After a lapse of fifteen days, however, the Romans forced the besieged to leave the outer wall (7 Jiar.), and now a terrible combat commenced for the middle wall, which the defenders had erected behind the outer one, and of which the Romans gained possession after four days of hard fighting, when also Bezetha, one of the suburbs, fell into their hands. This made the besieged fight the more desperately, for they had no other alternative but to conquer or die, being well aware that they had no mercy to expect from the Romans. The prisoners of war and those who intentionally fell into the enemy's hands in order to escape starvation, which was now staring them in the face, Titus put to the stake, and five hundred of them suffered thus in one day, to show to the obstinate defenders the consequence in prospect for them. The Romans now attacked the Antonia, and only on the third day they succeeded in becoming masters of the place. The defence of this bastion brought to light such heroism of the defenders, that Titus gave up all hope of a speedy termination of the war, and began to prepare himself for a protracted siege. Starvation, which now made its appearance in all quarters, should thus become his ally. In order to prevent all egress from the town he erected a wall a mile in circumference around the whole city, destroying all the gardens and fields about Jerusalem, making the entire neighborhood for two miles around resemble a wilderness. By the mass of people within the town, food became more scarce every day, and as all the resources to procure provisions from without were cut off, hunger was now raging on all sides, snatching away its victims in great numbers. The poorest class, whose pittance was soon exhausted, were the first who had to succumb to this dreadful scourge; making all compassion grow dumb, and stifling even parental love. The houses and streets began to fill with corpses, whom their own relations did not care to bury, and had to be removed at public expense. The living who were lingering about the streets had their faces swelled and resembling specters. This terrible state induced many to desert to the Romans, where another death was in waiting for them. The Romans had some suspicion that many of the deserters had swallowed pieces of gold to serve as a kind of palliative when in captivity; but as they acted like cannibals toward the prisoners, they cut them up alive in order to find the hidden treasures.

In spite, however, of starvation, as well as treachery with which they were surrounded, the zealots of all parties never shrank or tired in carrying on the defence. On the 17th Tamus, the daily offerings had to cease for want of animals. Titus embraced this opportunity for the purpose of making peace; but the appearance of his ambassador, Josephus, only increased the wrath of the combatants. After the fall of the Antonio, it became necessary to defend the Temple. As soon then as the Romans turned their artillery against the Temple, the Jews were compelled to destroy the colonnades which connected the Antonia with the Temple.   They set fire to the eastern portion, and pretending to fly from the disaster, many of the Romans climbed the colonnades, and thus lost their lives either by the swords of the combatants, or in the conflagration.   The fire extended to the whole western part of these beautiful structures, which all became a prey to the flames on the 27th Tamus; and the next day the Romans set fire to the northern portion, which was also destroyed.

In the meantime the destroying angel of starvation strode through Jerusalem's population, enervating with eagerness all vital spirits, abolishing every barrier between rich and poor, and unfettering the lowest passions.   Money had lost its value, for one could no more procure bread for the same.   For the sake of a little straw, a piece of leather, and things even by far worse, the starving inhabitants contended with each other to get possession of them.   The rich Martha, wife of the High-priest, Josua ben Gamala, who once walked on carpets from her house to the Temple, was now seeking, the same as the poorest inhabitants, whether she could not pick up in the streets some nauseous food, in order to satisfy the cravings of hunger even for a moment only.   As if not one incident in the awful picture of the admonition of the great prophet should remain unfulfilled, a deed of the greatest horror happened, which made even the enemy shudder.   A woman, Mirjam, who, from the country, had taken refuge in the capital, killed her baby and consumed its flesh. The heaps of corpses, which soon became putrid at this season of the year, filled the whole place with a nauseous smell, causing pestilence all over the city, and which, with war and hunger, vied with each other in snatching away the population.   Yet the brave warriors bore all these dreadful troubles with undiminished courage; they entered the battle-field with empty stomachs, and surrounded by the gloomiest pictures of death, they showed nevertheless the same impetuosity as on the first day the siege commenced.   The Romans brought their siege trains to bear against the outer works of the Temple, but after six days (2-8 Ab.), continually bombarding the place, they could not succeed in shaking the foundation of the wall.   They then commenced storming the place, trying to climb the wall by means of ladders, but were repulsed with great loss. Titus then gave up his plan to save the Temple, and ordered to set fire to the outer works; but, as if repenting the step he had thus taken, he all at once countermanded his orders, and directed his soldiers to extinguish the conflagration, which had raged already for thirty-six hours, doing a great deal of mischief.   On the next day (9 Ab.) the Jews boldly attempted another sally, but had to retire on account of meeting the enemy in great force.   At length the last hour of the fall of the Holy City had arrived, leaving in the memory of the nation a sad grief even for thousands of years to come. The besieged ventured again upon another sally on the 10th Ab., trying to dislodge the Romish artillery in charge of the siege train, but they were repulsed and pursued by the enemy. In the confusion which now ensued a Roman soldier took up a large firebrand, and being lifted by one of his comrades, he threw it through the so-called golden window into the Temple. The wood of the Temple cells soon caught fire, and spread the flames to the next compartments, causing the conflagration to rise to a great height. This awful sight brought on discouragement for the first time, and even the most courageous shrank back and felt disheartened in beholding the Temple on fire. Titus now advanced with his troops, for resistance had almost ceased, and he at once ordered that the conflagration should be extinguished. But his command was not listened to, and his furious soldiers now filled all parts of the Temple, in order to plunder, to set fire to the remaining places, and to murder everybody they met with.

Titus himself, drawn by curiosity, entered the Holy of Holies, felt delightsome at the sight, and never left the spot till the dense smoke compelled him to make his retreat. Once more, now, the Jewish warriors made their appearance in the midst of the burning scene, and one of the hottest combats began. The shoutings of victory of the Romans, the lamentations of the Jews at the sight of ruin, the crackling of the fire, made the earth and the atmosphere tremble, and the echo carried the sad news even to the mountains beyond the Jordan, while the sea of fire imparted to the inhabitants round about that the Temple stood in flames, and that all further hope had ceased. Many of the Jews in their despair threw themselves into the flames—they desired to live no longer than the Temple; others, many thousands, men, women and children, had remained, in spite of the approaching enemy, and the continually increasing flames, in the southern portion of the colonnades. The Romans fell upon them, and they were all massacred without mercy. The Temple, except the foundations and some odd ruins of the wall, became entirely a prey to the flames. Some of the priesthood, who had taken refuge upon the wall, where they held out several days in spite of hunger and thirst, were at last forced to leave their retreat, and Titus had them immediately executed. "Priests ought to perish together with the Temple," were the words which the tyrant uttered in cloaking his evil deeds. The victorious legions made offerings to their gods upon the Temple-place, hoisted their standards, and proclaimed Titus for their emperor. But the fighting had not yet ended, for even the last stone must be contended for, and only on the 8th of Elul the Romans took possession of the last quarter of the city, which they also set fire to. All the walls except a small portion of the western wall were destroyed; the three towers, Hippicos, Marianne and Phasael, were spared by Titus, in order that they might be a sign of the great victory he had thus achieved.

Amid the ruins of Jerusalem and the Temple the last residue of Judea's stately independence was gone. Above a million of people lost their lives during the siege, and in considering those also who had sacrificed their lives in Galilee, Peräa and other Jewish towns, it may almost be concluded that the Jewish race on native soil was for the most part annihilated. Once more Zion sat upon the burning ruins and wept; her sons had perished, and her daughters had been led into ignominious captivity. She was even more unhappy than after the first destruction, for now no seer was at hand to inform her of the end of her widowhood, and when the days of her mourning should cease. But the time will arrive when again aged men and women shall sit in the streets of Jerusalem, each having his crutch in hand to support him in his old age; the open places of the city will again be filled with boys and girls, who will be playing in the streets. (Zach. viii: 2.)　　　　　　　　　　　　　　　　　　　Dr. Graetz.

Dr. H. Graetz—Noted for his great erudition; a man of letters; professor at the University of Breslau; Lecturer at the Breslau Jewish Theological Seminary; chief editor of the Monatschrift; author of a Jewish history and many other works which gained him a world-wide reputation.

Legion—A body of Roman soldiers, about 6,000 men; a great number.

Colossus—A statue of enormous magnitude.

THE FALL OF JERUSALEM.

My hapless country's woes I weep,
The land of song and golden lyre,
Where sages, seers, and prophets sleep,
Whose harps did heaven inspire.

I mourn her fall from regal state,
From high and lofty pride;
No more among the nations great—
We're scattered far and wide.

Nor wine, nor fig, nor olive hills,
In blooming verdure crowns;
The deserts choke her healing rills,
And nature forever frowns.

Her lofty piles and towering domes
Are shrouded in the dust;
And Israel o'er the wide world roams,
A captive, dumb to foul lust.

And where is now her holy fane,
Where angels and seraphim dwelt?
Alas! the Pagan rites profane
Where priests, kings and people knelt.

The Lord hath turned away his face!

For this we weep and mourn our fate;
We pray, in mercy, love and grace,
Once more restore our glorious state.

When shall Thy temple 'gain appear,
Its ample courts on Zion's hill,
And nations all, both far and near,
Thy shrine and tabernacle fill?

When shall Thy children 'gain return,
With song and harp and sacred lyre;
The lamps of heaven deeper burn,
And light their path with pillowed fire?

An exile made by God's command,
We will not murmur at His will,
But ne'er forget the promised land,
Which His divinity doth fill.

This solace only have we left,
To weep, and mourn so long for Thee;
Of this we cannot be bereft,
We know she shall again be free.

J. M.

THE FATE OF THE CAPTIVES.

[70 A.]

Who is able to delineate the sufferings which the prisoners met with who fell into the hands of the Romans? More than 900,000 were made prisoners in the war. Those taken in Jerusalem, Titus had penned together and closely watched by a certain Fronto, a liberated slave. Two officials belonging to the Temple received their pardon, on account of having delivered to Titus the robes of the High-priest and the vessels in use at the Temple. All those who were recognized or betrayed as combatants were immediately executed by Fronto's orders. Those remaining envied their speedy end ; for 17,000 died of hunger, their scanty allowance not being sufficient to keep them alive. Many of the prisoners refused to accept anything of the Romans and soon perished. Of those still remaining, Fronto picked the finest and most vigorous youths to serve the purpose of fighting wild animals, and for accompanying Titus on his triumphal march to Rome ; others, again, who were above seventeen, were sent to the mines in Egypt, in order to spend their lives in constant labor, the same fate as the Galilean prisoners formerly met, who were condemned to do socage for the Isthmus of Corinth. There were yet 40,000 left, of whom Titus presented a large number to his friends to serve as slaves, and the remaining male and female prisoners under seventeen were sold for a mere bagatelle to slave-dealers. Thus were the sons and daughters of Zion dragged about as slaves all over the Roman Empire. What heartrending scenes have not these unhappy ones experienced! The terrible anguish they had to undergo has found no pencil to preserve it for posterity! Only a slight consolation was left to the unhappy captives, consisting in the possibility of being sent to some spot where a Jewish community existed, when they could make sure of meeting with brotherly sympathy, where also their co-religionists would not fail to pay almost any ransom to procure them their freedom. When Titus left the scene of devastation, he left the Tenth Legion, commanded by Terentius Rufus, in charge of the country. The vigorous Jewish youths were put in fetters and sent after him. In Cäsarëa Philippi he and his courtiers held a grand court-day, when amusements, according to Romish customs, were prepared for his friends. Wild animals were led into a well-secured place, and the Jewish prisoners were compelled to fight with them till they became overpowered and torn to pieces by the furious brutes. Sometimes the spectacle underwent a change, by making use of the Jewish prisoners in a tournament, in order that they might pierce each other to death. The same kind of amusements Titus ordered to be instituted in Cäsarëa on the sea, in honor of his brother's birthday, when more than 2,000 Jews lost their lives in this horrible manner. He then went to Berytus, where he celebrated the birthday of his father, and in the combat of beasts and men which took place here also, the sand of the arena soon become red from Jewish blood thus spilt ; in every town he granted to the Syrians, whose hatred to the Jews was well known, the mischievous joy of delighting themselves with the agonies of the unfortunate Jews. This was Titus' levity and inhumanity; this the man whom flatterers styled the bliss of the human race.

At length he got ready to proceed on his triumphal march to Rome. For this occasion he took with him 700 Jewish prisoners, who were all picked men of the finest caste, and the leaders Jochanan, of Gishala, and Simon bar Giora, were also of his retinue. The former, forced by hunger, submitted to the Romans, and the latter, not able to make his escape in the subterraneous passages of Jerusalem, and becoming also short of provisions, placed himself suddenly, wrapped in a white garment and purple cloak, before Rufus, announcing himself to him as Simon bar Giora, the leader of the zealots. He was immediately put in fetters, and, as he knew but too well what he had to expect from the Romans, he awaited his fate with the utmost resignation. What became of the third leader of the zealots, Eleasar ben Simon, has not transpired ; but it is probable that he ended his heroic existence on the battlefield, which, however, the knavish historian, grudging him immortality, has avoided mentioning. The two heroes, Jochanan and Simon, accompanied Titus upon his triumphal march through Palestine, Syria and Alexandria, and they were singled out for magnifying his entrance into Rome.

In the meantime Vespasian expected his son with torturing impatience, not because he wanted to press him to his paternal heart, but rather to get rid of the trouble which a certain report caused him, in regard to Titus' intentions to dethrone him. In order to divert his father's fear, Titus' first salutation in meeting his father was : " Behold, I have not failed to come." Whereupon the father and his two sons, Titus and Domitian, celebrated their triumph over Judea. In the procession which they arranged, the vessels of the Temple, the golden candlestick, the golden table, and the scroll of the law belonging to the Temple, were carried before them; the prisoners, all in fetters, followed, and drawings of all battles and devastations were shown to the merry, show-seeking people. Simon bar Giora was dragged through the streets by a rope, and at length, according to Roman custom, which required a human sacrifice, he was executed. Medals were struck, the impression of which represented unhappy Judea as a contrite woman in a despairing attitude, under a palm tree, before a warrior standing upright, and bearing the inscription: " The Captured and Conquered Judea." Later a triumphal arch was erected for Titus, upon which all the vessels of the Temple taken as booty may be seen even unto this day. The Romish Jews for a length of time tried to avoid this arch, preferring rather a round-

about way instead of beholding it. The booty taken from the
Temple remained for a long time in Rome, deposited in the Temple
of Peace, which Vespasian had erected, while the scroll of the law
was kept in the Imperial palace. But afterward, when the time
arrived for Rome to suffer for its manifold sins, these remnants of
the Jewish sanctuary were carried off into other countries, and all
further knowledge of them has thus ceased.

Dr. Honigman.

Dr. Honigman—An eminent Jewish Rabbi in Hungary known as a pulpit orator and writer
of note.

Socage—Husbandry services to be performed to the lord of the fee.
Levity—Idle pleasure.

Isthmus—A neck of land joining the peninsula to the continent.

THE NINTH OF AV.

(From the Lamentations of Jeremiah.)

How does our city sit forlorn,
　Once regal in her pride;
Become a mourning widow now,
　Who was the nation's bride.

Alas! the tears are on her cheeks,
　By night she weepeth sore;
Her lovers come to comfort
And her friends to cheer—no more.

Hush'd is the harp in Judah's halls,
　For she is captive led;
Her kings, her prophets, and her priests
Are powerless as the dead.

Her warriors and her mighty men
　With chains the foemen bind;
Her princes are like timid harts
　That can no pasture find.

The chosen of the Lord of Hosts
　Are wanderers on the earth;
The heathen rules the Holy Land
　Which gave our fathers birth.

Yet Zion well remembers
　In this, her tearful day,
The pleasant things she had of old,
　Her temples—far away.

Abroad the sword bereav'd her;
　At home it was like death,
When her sacred fanes fell prostrate
Before the Almighty's breath.

When in the wine-press of His wrath
　Her patriarchs were cast,
Her youths and virgins swept away
　Like chaff before the blast.

Oh! God hath cover'd Zion
　With a dark and stormy cloud,
And the beauty of proud Israel
　From heaven to earth hath bowed.

With His right hand he bent his bow
　'Gainst Jacob in His ire,
And the Lord hath pour'd His fury out
　Like a swift and flaming fire.

Arise, afflicted Judah,
　And never cease to cry,
Till all thy sins are pardon'd
　And His anger hath passed by.

Pour out thy heart like water
　Before His shrouded face,
Until again His smiles shall beam
　On all thy fallen race.

Behold, O Lord, in mercy,
　When thy people pray to Thee;
Tho' we have sinn'd against Thee,
　Unbind and set us free.

And lead us, we implore Thee,
　To a Canaan of delight,
With a cloud of purest snow by day
　And a fiery cloud by night.

Then shall our song exulting rise,
Our harps harmonious sound,
When Israel's tribes are gather'd home
From nations all around.

And the remnant of Thy children
Shall joyously record
Thy wondrous, loving works anew,
And the pardon of the Lord.

L. J. Ch.

RABBI JOCHANAN BEN SAKKAI.

[70 A.]

· It is certainly a highly interesting question to consider, how it happened that, after the second destruction of Jerusalem and the ruin of all the institutions which existed in that center, after the dispersion of the Jews in every direction, Judaism was so saved that, instead of perishing, only a new great era commenced, which has already outlasted seventeen centuries. It would be exceedingly partial to ascribe this great phenomenon to a single motive, or even to a single personality. All was a mighty web of Divine providence, of which the threads, centuries ago, were knotted and spun without interruption. A satisfactory explanation could only be obtained from glancing at the entire history of Judah during its second life, in conjunction with the whole condition of the world at that time.

One great cause consisted essentially in the faithfulness of belief, which the Jewish colonies, both sides of the Euphrates, on the Nile, the Tiber, the Ebro, and on the Rhine, had preserved long before the downfall of Zion, enabling them to grant unto broken and exiled Judaism a place of refuge. But that in this process only single personalities were called to handle this gigantic work, in drawing together into fresh joints the scattered members, is not the less evident. Rabbi Jochanan ben Sakkai stood foremost in accomplishing this work.

Jochanan was a disciple of Hillel. During forty years, it is said, he was engaged in business. As long as the state existed, he was a member of the Sanhedrim, occupying his time in teaching, as his academy in Jerusalem became very important. During the troubles of the war of liberation, he belonged, on account of his peaceful character, to the peace party; continually urging the people and the zealots to surrender Jerusalem, and submit to the Romans. "Why should you wish to destroy the town, and expose the Temple to the flames?" he remarked to the war party. But they despised his exhortations, owing to their love of independence. Fearing the rageful fanaticism of the zealots, or on account of wise precaution, to insure to instruction a place of refuge, Rabbi Jochanan passed over to Vespasian's camp. But the distance leading out of town was rather difficult to traverse, considering the careful watch kept up by the fervent patriots. Jochanan therefore resolved, being in league with one of the chiefs of the zealots, Ben Batiach, who was his relative, to be carried out of the town as a corpse. Placed in a coffin, his pupils,

Eleasar and Joshur, carried him at the hour of twilight to the gates of the city. A piece of rotten meat was also placed in the coffin, in order that the bad odor might deceive the guard at the gates. But the guard hesitated to let them pass, and was on the point of examining the coffin, when the pressing warning of their leader, Ben Batiach, not to violate the corpse of the venerable teacher, had the effect of preventing them from carrying out their intention. Vespasian received him kindly and gave him liberty to ask a favor of him. Rabbi Jochanan very modestly prayed for permission to establish a school-house at Tabneh, and Vespasian felt no objection to a wish which appeared to him not very captious, never thinking that, through this simple act, Judiasm would be placed in a position to outlive Romanism with all the boasting of its power and iron-like vigor, even for thousands of years to come. Vespasian's kind reception arose, perhaps, from the circumstance that Jochanan prophesied to him his elevation to the dignity of emperor. In making this statement beforehand, it was not the gift of prophecy with Rabbi Jochanan, but it rested upon conviction, taken from the words of the prophet, that "the Libanon (Temple) should only succumb to a crowned head." (Isaiah x: 35.)

Jochanan with his pupils settled in Tabneh, or Tamnia, a town close to the Mediterranean, and situated between the port of Joppa and the town of Asdod, formerly belonging to the Philistines. At the outset, Jochanan's activity found but little practice, as long as exasperated warfare was raging under the walls of Jerusalem, in its streets, and around the Temple. When the sad news arrived that the town had succumbed and the Temple was in flames, Jochanan and his disciples rent their clothes, mourning and lamenting as for the death of a near relative. But the master did not despair in the same manner as the disciples, being aware that the nature of Judaism was not indissolubly bound with the fate of temple and altar. He consoled his sad pupils on the loss of the expiatory place, in making the striking remark that, " Charity makes up for sacrifices, as stated in Holy Writ; for I have pleasure in charitableness and not in sacrifices." This view concerning the value of sacrifices made him clearly perceive that it was above all things necessary to establish a fresh center in place of the Temple. He ordered the formation of a Sanhedrim in Tabneh, whose president he was selected to be; the more so, because he was the only one left of Hillel's disciples, as Gamaliel, the son of Simon, the active patriarch during the war of liberation, was under age. The fresh-gathered Sanhedrim was surely not formed of exactly seventy members, and was probably appointed to fill a sphere of activity different from that exercised in Jerusalem during the war, which had full power assigned to them under all circumstances, and in the most important political affairs of the day. On the Tamnian Sanhedrim its founder conferred above all religious sovereignty, such as possessed by its predecessor in Jerusalem, and at the same time all the judicial functions of a high tribunal were combined with it. Only Jochanan's full authority could accomplish such a work as the formation and strengthening of a Sanhedrim under the existing unfavorable circumstances. The most important functions, which operated decidedly upon the foreign congregations, were the arrangements of the new moon and festivals, which always proceeded from Tamnia.

Jochanan's exertion as teacher also proved highly efficacious, and he was constantly surrounded by a large number of pupils. At that time he was admitted to be the living bearer of all oral precepts. Halacha, Midrash, Talmud and Agada he so handled in his discourses that the benumbed body of the nation soon revived. The prohibition to use no iron tools at the building of the altar, he explained thus : " Iron is the smybol of war and strife, the altar on the contrary, the symbol of peace and expiation; and therefore iron should not come in contact with the altar." From this he inferred the value of peace. Besides Rabbi Jochanan, seven Tanaim constituted the doctrinal office. The fifth—Abba Saul ben Botnit—was formerly a wine merchant in Jerusalem, and in his business was so extraordinarily conscientious, that he would not even keep the sediment for himself, because he thought it belonged to the buyer. He saved it up to a quantity of three hundred quarts, and then took it to the treasurer of the Temple in Jerusalem. Although told that he was entitled to it, he declined making use of the same. Upon his deathbed he could hold out his hand and boast of "the hand which was always scrupulously honest in giving measure."

Of these Tanaim, Rachum of Gimso became a man of special importance. Rapoport has made him the hero of many wonderful adventures, of which however, all seemed to have turned in his favor, so that even the name of his birthplace was altered, in suggesting the motto—"This even will tend to some good"—(Gamsule toba). But when an old man, the dreadful misfortune befel him of becoming blind and palsied. In order not to reproach the justice of Heaven, he claimed that this misfortune was a just punishment, and to all who visited him he observed that he was deserving the affliction in consequence of his own crime. One time he carried his father-in-law many presents, which were packed upon asses, and having met a poor man who begged of him some assistance, he kept him waiting till he had unloaded ; but in looking for him afterward, in order to relieve him, he found him dead. On account of the grief he suffered in having thus been the cause of the death of this person, he wished himself to become blind, and that his hands and feet should get palsied, because they had not shown more compassion for the poor man ; and, consequently, very soon after this imprecation he thus became afflicted. His disciples in beholding his sufferings could not guard against expressing their grief. "Woe to us, to see you in this state!" but Rachum replied : "Woe to me, if you were not to behold me in this condition."

Jochanan was also, in a political point of view, a protection for all the new communities of his time. His friendly and mild character, in which he resembled his teacher, Hillel, he made also use of toward the heathen. He saluted them always in the most friendly manner wherever he met them. But as much as the Flavian emperors were inclined to show benignity to Jochanan's kind disposition, many oppressions nevertheless took place. Many acres of land the Jews were deprived of, and bloody banditti made great havoc among them.

Rabbi Jochanan, in describing the state of things, makes use of these striking words : "I saw once a woman belonging to the rich and respectable house, Nicodemus ben Garian of Jerusalem, how she was gathering at Maon some barley corns from under the horses' hoofs, in order to support herself with this food. This scene made a most painful impression upon me; the more so because I could bear witness to her former fortune and splendor. 'Unhappy people,' exclaimed I ; 'you would not serve your God, so you must now be subject to strange nations; you would not contribute half a shekel toward the Temple then, you are compelled now to pay fifteen shekels for supporting the state of your enemies; you would not keep in order the roads and streets for the pilgrims who came to the festivals, and so you must now keep the watch-houses in the vineyards, to which the Romans have laid claim.'"

The unanimity of the Jewish nation in their dispersion is entirely the work of Rabbi Jochanan, who well understood how to unite even the most distant congregations. Jochanan died upon his bed in the arms of his disciples. His conversation with them before his death gives some insight into his inner feelings. The disciples were astonished to behold their high-spirited master despairing and pusillanimous in the hour of death. He told them that he did not fear death, but the appearing before the Eternal Judge, whose justice is incorruptible. He blessed his disciples previous to his death with these significant words : "May the fear of God be as efficacious in all your acts as the fear of men." He died at the age of one hundred and twenty, and it is said of him that, after his death, the brilliancy of wisdom became extinct. Thus lived and died a man who possessed energy enough not to despair at the sight of ruin and decay, but in the downfall of his nation gathered anew all that was suitable for building, and upon a firmer basis rebuilt the edifice of his fathers.

L. PHILIPPSON.

CAPTIOUS—Given to cavils; ensnaring. IMPRECATION—Prayer by which any evil is wished.

SHEKEL—An ancient Jewish coin, in value about two shillings and sixpence.—*English.*

THE ROSE OF JERICHO.

Tenant of the trackless waste,
Thou crouchest 'neath the sand,
And should I pluck thee in my haste,
Thou shrivelest in my hand.

The hot sun scorcheth all thy growth,
And when eve's shadows creep,
The hoarse cries of the prowling fox
Lull thee off to sleep.

I seize thee, tiny floweret,
And bid my servant bring
A goblet full of water pure,
Fresh from the foaming spring.

I bathe thee, gentle flower mine,
In the liquid crystalline,
And each pearly rootlet feels
The impulse of a power divine,
While the leaflets swift assume
The grandeur of their tinted
   bloom.

Not alone the rose can dwell
Confined in a sandy shell;
Frequently a faith divine
Is buried 'neath the crust of time.

And men deify the crust
As they grope amid the dust,
While the truth that hidden lies
Is lost amid the centuries.

Till the hero, prophet, bard,
Boldly grasps the flower,
Plucks it from its pent-up cell
And unfolds its power.

Shows the truth in fossil faiths,
In rites and dogmas dear;
When translated into *life*
The blossoms bright appear.

J. M.

Rootlet—The fibrous part of a root.
Deify—To praise excessively.
Bard—A poet.

Fossil—That which is dug out of the earth.
Dogma—Settled notion.

RABBI AKIBA BEN JOSEPH.

[118 a.]

R. Jochanan ben Sakkai was like a cautious gardener who carefully separates the sound germen, although in a vigorous state, from the dropping mother-stem, transplanting and fostering it in a favorable soil, till he can make sure as to its future by having raised a powerful growing stem. But how different was the character of Rabbi Akiba ben Joseph, who shone in the next generation. Fiery, energetical, ingenious and armed with the sword of intellect, he shunned not even the sword of iron, although dripping with the blood of martyrdom! The history of his youth is traditional. According to some he was a proselyte, and it is a certain fact that Rabbi Akiba, even at an advanced age, was very ignorant, for he himself afterward relates, that in his state of utter ignorance he hated all those who were acquainted with the law. That he lived with his wife in penurious circumstances is a certainty; from trustworthy report it is known that she sold her braids of hair in order to procure the necessaries of life. All these obstacles, which would have proved disheartening to any one else, served only to impress him with the stamp of magnanimity; his robust nature conquered all obstacles, overcame all difficulties, and placed him before the world as one of the most celebrated teachers and scholars.

He married the daughter of Akiba Calba, one of the richest and most respectable men in Jerusalem, who being against the marriage, deprived the daughter of her dowry, and thus they had to put up with the greatest misery. But they nevertheless felt happy and contented, and one day the pious wife urged upon her husband the necessity of obtaining wisdom and knowledge, and that he should for that purpose depart, to seek amid the wise and learned men in Israel to improve his mind, and to make himself acquainted with the teaching of the holy law. He at once took her advice, left his beloved wife and remained away twelve years, and during this long period the pious wife had to endure many a hardship, besides becoming the scorn of her neighbors, who upbraided her for her levity in contracting such a marriage, trying to shake her confidence as to her husband's return. "As far as it rests with me," she always replied, "he may even stay away another twelve years, till he has fathomed the depth of our holy law, and is able to return as a wise man in Israel." Akiba, hearing the opinion of his pious wife, really returned once more to the wise men in Israel; passing among them another twelve years, and then made his way home, followed by a host of pupils, all listening respectfully to the instructions of the highly-renowned teacher, who during his long absence had stored up much wisdom and learning, thus gaining for himself fame and reputation, so that now the whole town came to meet him. His beloved wife also, who had thus waited so long and endured so much want and hardship, did not hesitate to go to meet him; but the wicked neighbors again sneered at her, saying that, poorly clad as she then was, she should certainly feel ashamed to venture upon such an errand; but she did not mind their reproaches, and merely replied that the pious well knew the heart of the needy. At his approach some of his pupils tried to prevent his wife from accosting him, but Akiba said: "Pray, let her be! Whatever wisdom and learning I may possess, whatever you may have acquired of me, we have to thank her for." Her father also, to whom the news of his son-in-law's fame, together with the faithfulness of his daughter, had become known, was so moved that he at once freed himself of his vow, so that he might be able to reinstate them in their possessions.

From this time Rabbi Akiba lived in affluence, and his gratitude toward his much tried wife was quite equal to the sacrifices which she so readily had made for him. Everybody was surprised, dazzled and animated by Rabbi Akiba's great erudition. Rabbi Tarphon, who surpassed Rabbi Akiba, formally observed to him in a respectful manner: "Whoever forsakes you, forsakes life eternal; and whatever tradition neglects, you supply by your interpretations." Rabbi Josua, his former teacher, also spoke of him with admiration: "Who will take the clod from the eyes of Rabbi Jochanan ben Sakkai, so that he may see how his apprehension was but vain, that one day a Halacha might be given up for want of support in the scriptural text, and now, behold! Rabbi Akiba has found a proper hold for it." One was obliged to confess that the law had been forgotten, or at least had become neglected, if Rabbi Akiba had not sought to sustain the same.

His home was in Bene-Berack, where he also kept his academy; but he often came to Tabneh, on account of being a member of the Sanhedrim, and it happened but seldom that anything was resolved upon without his presence, for they said: "In his absence, the want of law is felt." He was, however, in spite of the homage paid him on all sides, not the least proud, and always showed the same, as previously, due regard for his former teachers and colleagues. Owing to his modest character his influence under Rabbi Gamaliel's patriarchate, and later under Rabbi Josua's management, did not become very prominent; but later, after the demise of the latter, he was considered the chief of the Jewish body, and he it was who principally assisted during the last decade of that century in bringing about those terrible occurrences which, under the name of the revolt of Bar-Kochba, threatened to shake the whole of the Roman Empire.

This is the period in which Rabbi Akiba, with the same ardor he always administered the law, also tried to transform the political position of the Jews, although to the ruin of himself and numerous others. These events, however, made an end of the past, for this last explosion of the Jewish love for liberty settled the future so far, that the Jews should henceforth exist among the nations as members of a civil community.

The history of the revolt of Bar-Kochba cannot be delineated here, and it will be sufficient to say that Rabbi Akiba took an active part in the whole preparations, which lasted nearly twelve years. He undertook long journeys, visiting almost every spot where Jewish congregations could be met with, in order to rouse them to action, desert Rome, and re-establish the Jewish realm. It is stated that he himself raised 24,000 men full of courage and expectations, and the revolt spread afterward to such extent that Dio Cassius mentions the number of Jewish warriors at 580,000 men. The war lasted three years and a half, and finished with the siege of Bethar, which lasted twelve months before it was taken on the 9th Ab., 135.

After this the most awful persecutions awaited the Jewish nation, and the enemy resolved upon annihilating not only the Jewish people, but also Jewish nationality altogether. They were threatened with the severest punishment if they should venture to keep circumcision, the Sabbath, or occupy themselves with Jewish law any further. Thus, numerous were the victims; ten especially who suffered martyrdom (of whom seven are named to us) have become solemnized even unto this day. Soon also the turn of the aged Rabbi Akiba came, who was the third of these ten martyrs, being charged with having held discourses secretly. He was, according to the "Calendar of these unhappy days," thrown into a dungeon on the 5th of Tishri, and Ticinus Rufus, the governor, treated him with unsparing severity. At length the melancholy hour of his execution arrived, and Rufus, a pliable tool of Hadrian's vengeance, ordered the agonies of death to be increased by other painful tortures, and the skin was torn off his body with iron horse-combs. His noble soul expired with the confession of faith in the Eternal One, "Adonai Echad."

Rabbi Akiba's death, which was, like his life, extraordinary, brought about a terrible emptiness among his contemporaries, who mourned that, with him, the arms of the law were broken, and the springs of wisdom shaken. He left but one son and a few pupils, who made his name the most celebrated of the day. Thus died Rabbi Akiba.

From his grave bloomed a time of peace, for in a spiritual point of view he prepared the path for Jewish posterity; and as to political matters, the Vesuvius of the Jewish nation had now ceased burning, the last eruption was over, and three centuries of rest, of civil equality and honor, began to dawn.

Dr. Sachs.

Dr. Michael Sachs was born in Glogau, 1808, and died in Berlin, 1864. He was an eminent pulpit orator, a man of great literary attainments, whose works were much sought for among co-religionists, and who, on account of his kind and amiable disposition, was much esteemed and honored by everybody.

Proselyte — One brought over to a new opinion; a convert.
To Fathom—To penetrate.

Erudition—Learning.
Decade—The sum of ten.

HOLINESS.

Be holy, man, the Lord commands,
  Like angels, goodness, love;
Lift up thine eye, thy heart, and hands,
  To God enthroned above.

In yonder sea of starry light,
  Where pure seraphim shine,
Immerse thy soul with pure delight—
  Let holiness be thine.

To man, to God's own image, cling
  With love's refulgent fire;
The true and good to man to bring
  Let be thy heart's desire.

For wisdom live, for virtue glow,
  With God thy soul entwine;
An angel be on earth below—
  And holiness be thine.

The choicest gifts, all joys divine,
  By holiness are won;
It's bliss from virtue's sacred shrine,
  Salvation's precious sun.

The hallowed soul with rapture sings
  The Lord's eternal praise,
She soars aloft on golden wings
  To heaven's purest grace,

A. J.

THE SCHOOLS OF PALESTINE AND THE MISHNA.
[70–200 a.]

The Jamnensian Sanhedrim became, after the destruction of the Temple, the heart of the Jewish nation; since, from this source, life and activity flowed to the remotest congregations, who in case they looked for approbation and sacredness of character, were obliged to adhere strictly to all fixed regulations and religious appointments proceeding from that body. The people considered the existence of the Sanhedrim as a residue of the state, and they paid the president thereof (Nassi), who was a descendant of Hillel and of the royal blood of David, almost princely honor and homage. The Greek appellation seems to point out that the Patriarchate amounted to a princely dignity, being styled Ethnarch, signifying a prince of the people—a position almost as high as royalty; even the usual title of Patriarch includes a function belonging only to the sovereign. Next to the Patriarchs were their representatives (Ab-bet-din) and their Chacham (the wise). The authority of the Patriarch allowed, however, an undiminished independence to a few managers of schools, to enable them to declare their disciples judges and teachers of the people without requiring the sanction of the Patriarch. This dignity was bestowed upon the disciples in a solemn manner. In the presence of two members, the master placed his hand upon the head of the selected pupil, not as was the case with the disciples of the prophets; it was but a mere acknowledgment that the one thus initiated was worthy of undertaking certain duties, for which his capacity had been sufficiently proved. This form of consecration, and the placing of the hands upon the head, was called Semicha, signifying as much as nomination or ordination. The one ordained was styled Soken (old), which is almost similar to the title of Senator; for, by this ordination, they also obtained the privilege of becoming members of the High Council, if ever chosen for that purpose. The Jewish nation, owing to the differences of sects and parties, must have become dissolved, had not thus the inner unity been constantly maintained.

The principal efficacy of the Patriarch consisted in presiding over the solemn assemblies of the Sanhedrim. He was the foremost in these great meetings, surrounded by the most important members, sitting in a semi-circle before him. At the back of the members, who, in those times amounted to seventy, there sat in rows those who passed the ordination, and behind these again, the pupils were standing; while the last of all were the people, lying on the floor, and listening to the proceedings. The Patriarch opened the meeting, either by choosing from the code of laws some subject for discussion, or, by making use of the form "question," he called upon the members to speak. In his own harangue, he quietly communicated a few sentences to the speaker (Meturgeman) standing next to him, which the latter had to expound and to illustrate in a rhetorical manner. Everybody was at liberty to start subjects for debate, even the people who were listening to the discourse. A special and important business of the Patriarch was the fixing of the festivals, there being no calendar in those days; and in possessing the right of regulating the same, the remotest congregations were entirely dependent on the Patriarch, and thus a bond was effected whereby the dispersed of Israel were continually kept together.

In general, the religious life was arranged by the Sanhedrim and Patriarch together. The destruction of the Temple had not wholly embarrassed the Jewish nation. Constant prayers, the study of the law, and charity, atoned for the sacrifices; and, except the observance of sacrificial worship, the whole of the law was performed in the strictest manner. The insurrection under Bar-Kochba, and the persecutions on account thereof, indeed, for a time, disturbed the existing state of things; but the Jews being already humble through misfortunes, were not yet annihilated. They were reduced in numbers, but in no wise exterminated, for they still continued to exist in one idea, which always kept on generating as long as one only was left. Besides, the Romans did not contemplate the extermination of the guiltless, their existence being found necessary for enriching the capital. The teachers very soon raised their voices again in all the synagogues, assuming once more the care of the religious life in a vigorous manner.

The most important among them, whom we shall notice here, were Rabbi Meier, highly accomplished, sagacious and bold; Rabbi Jehuda ben Ilai, brave, tender-hearted, vigorous, and yet amiable in appearance; Rabbi Simon ben Jochai, sensible, penetrating, but gloomy and stern on all occasions; Rabbi Jose ben Hilephta, serene, and well-balanced; and Rabbi Simon ben Gamliel, who was very young, when he escaped from Bethar at the time. All these men, except the last named, carried on a handicraft, the same as all teachers before that period, and yet they could find ample time for expounding the law which they inherited. Rabbi Meier, of non-Jewish descent, was the favorite pupil of Rabbi Akiba, and maintained himself by copying the Holy Law, which he was able to write from memory. His delivery was animated, owing to his great sagacity, and the illustrations he gave by means of fables and allegories. His wife, Bernniah, was also celebrated for her erudition. Rabbi Jehuda ben Ilai was a cooper, and deserves the praises of the rabbis, on account of his zeal and his frugality, although he was in affluent circumstances; and by reason of his demeanor under misfortunes, and the excellent method he adopted in the way of instructing his pupils. Very often he made use of a barrel for a pulpit, and he never failed to speak in great praise of industry. The clothes he wore were all made by his wife; and when it happened that his new garments were not finished, he neglected to attend a festive meeting, in order to avoid dressing himself in a suit borrowed from another. On the day when his beloved son died, he delivered a funeral discourse in spite of his sorrow. Of his excellent knowledge of Judaism and his acuteness in decisions, every page of the Mishna bears ample proofs. Above 600 of his sayings are there recorded. Rabbi Simon ben Jochai made study his sole occupation, and attended especially to private instruction; he was a rigid teacher of morality, as all his utterances of dissatisfaction with this world corroborate, and having always some higher aim before his eyes. He was sent to Rome by the rabbis, in order to entreat the emperor to recall the prohibitions which were of an oppressive nature. His exertions in this matter proved very successful. The prohibitions were removed, and he received great honor on his return, for it was entirely attributed to his influence that this great favor was granted; yet through him they had unfortunately to suffer persecution afterward. He spoke once against the Romans, on account of which he was betrayed, condemned to death, and had to make his escape to some hiding-place, where he remained for a length of time.

Rabbi Jose ben Hilephta, a currier by trade, was a model of prudence, clearness, and modesty. "I am," said he, "more ready to listen than to teach others; to die in the midst of my duties, rather than in my bed ingloriously; to do too much than too little; I prefer gathering alms for the poor, instead of spending my own; suffer wrong, instead of practicing it myself." Concerning knowledge he said, "Whoever honors science, is worthy of honor; but he who despises it, is worthy of contempt."

But Tiberias had now become the seat of the high-school and the Sanhedrim. Tiberias was in a flourishing state, a splendid town, pleasantly situated, and receiving continually, ever since the destruction of Jerusalem, more Jewish inhabitants. At first, these were mostly Galileans, whom the rabbis despised, and were generally looked upon as belonging to a different nation, on account of their different dialect, vulgar manners, and aversion to the law. Therefore the rabbis came much later to this place, and only after many inhabitants from the south had settled there. The newly-formed Sanhedrim were a *fac-simile* of the higher Council of Jerusalem. Rabbi Simon ben Gamliel became here Nassi; Rabbi Nathan, Ab-betdin; and Rabbi Meier, Chacham. Tiberias soon received the honor of being named Jerusalem, Zion, and, by preference, the Sanhedrim were called the great Law Court; it was a fresh center for the total guidance of all the Jews in the Roman Empire. Very soon the youths flocked to this place, in order to satisfy their cravings after knowledge.

II.

THE school at Sepphoris, established by Rabbi Jose ben Hilephta, soon enjoyed the fruits of its labors, as well as great renown. Many others were established. The knowledge of the law was the only branch taught. The Pentateuch especially was expounded, and the traditions concerning the precepts of the law, such as the Scriptures did not fully contain, were continually imparted to the pupils; but other attainments, as auxiliary science, were also necessary for that purpose. Therefore, the rabbis engaged in the study of physics, medicine, mathematics, etc. The number of accomplished scholars who received their training and education in these schools, after the destruction of the Temple, and during four generations, may be counted by thousands, and hundreds of venerable names occupy niches in fame. After receiving the Semicha, they proceeded to the congregations, in order to assume the instruction and the religious guidance of the people. The sacrifices which these God-fearing men brought on all occasions saved the nation from becoming ruined through misery and ignorance. The congregation of Simonias, south of Sepphoris, petitioned the Patriarch for a person to deliver public lectures, decide points of law, preside over the synagogue, execute acts belonging to the code of laws, instruct the youth, and perform all the general duties of the congregation. This list of duties proves sufficiently what was required in those times of a public teacher.

All teachers of the law, commencing with Simon the Just, were generally known under the Chaldaic name of Tanaim, which signifies "repeater" of the law, because their principal occupation was to impress upon the memory the interpretation of the received oral law, and in making it clear to the mind.

At the head of the fourth and last lineage of Tanaim, after the destruction of the Temple, stood Rabbi Jehudah the Holy, who, in fact, was the most celebrated of the Tanaim and the most powerful Patriarch. He was the seventh member of the house of Hillel, and under his care it reached the highest point of splendor. Rabbi Jehudah was favored with extraordinary blessings, and it was proverbially stated of him, "Rabbi Jehudah's stalls of cattle have more value than the treasury of the King of Persia is possessed of." He led a life of frugality, made little selfish use of his wealth, spent it for the maintenance of his disciples, both native and foreign, who flocked round him during his Patriarchate, in great numbers, and were kept entirely at his own expense. At the time of the terrible famine, which, with the plague, raged all over the Roman Empire, this Jewish prince opened his storerooms, and distributed corn among all classes who stood in need of his assistance. The seat of the Patriarchate was at first at Bet Shearim, northeast from Sepphoris, but was afterward removed to Sepphoris. In consideration of his high repute, he was plainly called Rabbi, as if no other teacher of the law but himself had proved of any importance, and that he was the law exclusively. But the principal act, however, whereby his name has obtained a lasting reputation, was owing to his representing the close of an epoch, which brought about the completion of the Mishna.

The law handed down, and the interpretation thereof, were hitherto transplanted through oral communications from teachers unto pupils, without being written down or properly classified. But the pressure of adverse times just commenced, and this prevented many from studying the law, for Israel became dispersed more and more, even to all the corners of the earth. It was greatly feared, hence, that the law was in danger of being forgotten. In order to prevent such a catastrophe, Rabbi Jehudah the Holy went to work and gathered the debates and disquisitions of the different schools on the law as handed down to them, examined their correctness, divided them according to their contents into six volumes, and these again into chapters and sections. This collection of the law contained everything that could only be expected of such a work; completeness, brevity, clearness of expression, and especially proper order, so that the whole could easily be reviewed. The Mishna of Rabbi Jehudah soon attracted great attention, and his numerous disciples diffused the same over the remotest parts of the country. Thus it became exclusively the text and guide of the instruction imparted at the schools. Rabbi Jehudah managed the Patriarchate during thirty years. With great resignation he awaited his dissolution. He ordered his sons and his schoolfellows to appear before him, and impressed upon them his last will. The Sanhedric college he instructed to avoid all ceremonies at his funeral, not to permit in the different towns any funeral solemnities, and that after a lapse of thirty days the reopening of the assembly of teachers should take place.

Great numbers of the population from neighboring towns had come from Sepphoris, on hearing of the approaching end of the Patriarch, in order to show their sympathy. As if such an event were impossible, the mass of the people really began to threaten any one who should venture to bring the mournful news of his death. The eagerness and the excitement were indeed very great, so that a fearful outburst of grief was apprehended. Bar Kappara, celebrated as rabbi as well as poet, acquainted them, however, with the sad news without using any words for the purpose. With his head wrapped up, and his clothes rent, he told the people, "Angels and mortals struggled for the ark of the covenant. The angels conquered, and vanished is the ark of the covenant."

Upon this announcement, the people raised a cry of grief: "He is dead." Bar Kappara answered: "You said it." The lamentations of the population, it is stated, could be heard as far as Gabbata, a distance of three parts of a mile from Sepphoris. The funeral was largely attended; a vast concourse followed the deceased from Sepphoris to Bet Charim, and funeral orations were delivered in eighteen synagogues (200).

The management in the schools was now different from that since the Mishna was expounded, all Mishnaic doctrines which seemed contradictory were solved, and these were made to agree with the traditional law definitions, which, in the collection of Rabbi Jehudah the Holy, had not been received. Such traditions were collected by

some of Jehudah's disciples, and were called Boreitha, foreign
Mishna, and Tosiphta, supplements to the Mishna. The teachers
were now called Amoraim, orators, expounders, and their expositions,
Gemara, completion.

The Patriarchate and the Tiberian schools remained yet for two
centuries, adorned by many a man of great intellect, as well as by
flourishing seminaries of learning. However, their bloom seemed to
fade more and more, and in course of time they lost almost all their influence and reputation. The Patriarchate being very much restricted
in its authority, through Roman extortions, resolved to resign in consideration of higher motives, and even denied itself the important
privilege of regulating the appointments of the calendar, which, from
the Patriarch Hillel II., had abided unto this time (359). At the
commencement of the fifth century, the Patriarch Gamliel was dismissed, on account of having aided in the building of new synagogues. He died childless. Then the Jews did not appoint any
other Patriarch, and an imperial decree declared this dignity to be
extinguished(429). The oppressions increased continually, and the
further existence of the Palestinean schools became a matter of impossibility.

But ere even the sun of the law had disappeared in the west, there
was already a fresh day dawning in the east. The different schools
in Babylon, which, after the death of Rabbi Jehudah the Holy, had
been established, had become of the same influence and importance
as those of Palestine.

I. M. JOST.

Dr. ISAAC MARCUS JOST was born February 22, 1793, at Bernburg (Anhalt), and died quite
unexpectedly, almost in the prime of life. He was a colleague of Leopold Zunz, and became
one of the most renowned Jewish scholars of modern times. He studied at Göttingen and
Berlin, was a writer of great note, and published many valuable works, and his history of
Judaism gained him a world-wide reputation. He was a great philanthropist, a strict observer of Judaism, and he made his name immortal by establishing the well-known orphan
asylum at Frankfurt on the Main. In him mankind lost an excellent man, science one of
her honest disciples, and Israel one of her most beautiful ornaments.

RESIDUE—That which is left.
NASSI—One who presided over the Sanhe-
drim.
AB-BET-DIN—Vice-president of the Sanhe-
drim.
METURGEMAN—Interpreter.

To INITIATE—To enter; to instruct in the
rudiments of an art.
RHETORIC—Speaking with art and elegance.
To DEBATE—To deliberate.
DISQUISITION—Disputative inquiry.

THE SOUL.

THERE is a vital spark of heavenly
flame,
That fills a   permeates the mortal
frame,
Which He with sacred thoughts doth oft
inspire,
Who filled Isaiah with poetic fire.

Such thoughts, whose influence the
glowing mind

Hath oft disturbed, delighted, raised,
refined,
Thoughts so ineffable, soothing, yet
great,
Thoughts of the life-sustaining Potentate.

And this same spark that in us dwells,
Through which our heart with prayer
swells,

Whence comes it? Whence its origin divine? Whence but from Him from whom all glories shine!

His living breath has reached our bosoms, too, As shines the sunbeam in a drop of dew; The effluence of His presence divine,

Pervading worlds, doth in our spirit shine.

From Him, who plants in the immortal soul The spring of love, and power of self-control; From God, who doth all motion guide, The only God!—there is no God beside.

DEBORAH KLEINERT.

EFFLUENCE—That which issues from some other principle.

POTENTATE—Monarch, prince.

THE SCHOOLS OF BABYLON AND THE TALMUD.

[200–500 A.]

I.

DURING the patriarchate of the second Rabbi Jehuda (grandchild of Jehuda the Holy), we find in Babylon a real historical life developing itself, which, in course of time, placed that country in the foreground of Jewish history, effecting a condition so flourishing, and of such accomplished ripeness, that it prevailed beyond a period of a thousand years. Babylon proved a second mother to the Jewish nation after being deprived of its first, and it was but seldom that she behaved toward her like a stepmother. By the name of Babylon, of which we speak here, is generally understood the shores of both sides the Euphrates as far as the shores of the Tigris, comprising, therefore, the southern part of Mesopotamia, the territory of ancient Babylon, and a part of old Chaldea. These countries were inhabited by Jews to that extent that the name "Land of Israel" was given to it.

Four towns were of great importance, forming prominent centers for the whole country. Nahardea occupied the first place, being a fortified town on the Euphrates, and entirely inhabited by Jews. The town of Nahardea was for a time the Babylonian Jerusalem. During the existence of the Temple the treasury of all the Babylonian congregations was kept here, from which the contributions toward the Temple were paid, and which were sent under a strong escort to Jerusalem. As long as the Temple stood the Babylonian Jews contributed largely toward its support. Pumpadita, situated on one of the many canals of the Euphrates, was also entirely a Jewish town, and had a very ancient congregation. The place was noted for its many palaces. Several smaller towns and a few fortified places were in its immediate neighborhood. Thirteen geographical miles, and in a southern direction from Pumpadita, the place of Mata-Machassia was situated on an extensive lake, called Sura, which properly was the Euphrates. From this lake the town of Sura received its name.

Here we find a mixed population of Jews and heathens, and as Pumpadita was noted for its palaces, and the cunning character of its inhabitants, in the same manner was Mata-Machassia distinguished for its poverty and the uprightness of its residents. A common saying points out the properties of the two places to each other: "It is better to dwell upon the dunghills of Machassia than in Pumpadita's palaces."

Besides Nahardea, Pumpadita and Mata-Machassia, there was a fourth one, vying with these three towns on the Euphrates, which was Machurza on the Tigris, about three miles distant from Otesiphan, the capital of the Parthians. It had close by a citadel. In spite of the importance which Machurza with its forts offered to the reigning Parthians and Persians, the inhabitants thereof were nevertheless entirely Jews, and an Amora felt astonished that the gates of the fortress were not furnished with proper door capsules, according to the usual regulations. The most respectable Machurzanic families were descendants of proselytes, which made their national character peculiar, entirely differing from the rest of the Jewish population of Babylon. They were termed a frivolous people, given to pleasure and more addicted to temporal than spiritual matters. Thus they were styled "Candidates of hell." The same is related of the Machurzanic women, who often sought after pleasure, and spent their time in idleness.

The whole stretch of land, with its many canals, which connect the Euphrates with the Tigris, resembled a cluster of islands; and, being also noted for its fruitfulness, the country appeared like a garden of great extent. Large groves of date trees were so plentiful that it had become proverbial to say of a Babylonian: "A basket full of dates for a Denarius, and they shall not occupy themselves with the study of the law!"

The land around Sura was considered the most fertile in the country, being of a low level, and thus the Euphrates, with its by-rivers and canals, overflowing the same yearly, produced an Egyptian fertility. The occupation of the Babylonian Jews was mostly agricultural and trades of every description; but living in a country depending on canal irrigation, they made it their business also to build and to clean canals applying themselves as well to the breeding of cattle, and carrying on commerce, navigation, and in many instances even some of the arts were not neglected by them.

The number of Babylonian Jews being very large, it made them somewhat independent, and they felt almost as much at home as in their own country. The position they occupied in respect to the reigning power was a very liberal one, and consisted merely in paying certain contributions for poll-tax and ground rent. In attending to this regulation, they were permitted to have their own governor, who was styled Prince of Exile (Exilarch, Resh-Galuta.)

He was considered one of high dignity in the Persian Empire, and was, next to the king, the fourth in rank of all the Persian magnates. His position to the Parthian and Persian kings was something similar to the petty princes in Germany. The exilarchs were vassals of the Persian crown, being, however, not chosen by the crown, but merely ratified. The mark of dignity was a silken gown and a sash, and in later times they were surrounded by princely splendor, driving in state carriages with a large retinue of servants, and an outrider to announce their arrival. Whenever they had a solemn audience of the king the royal servants received them with due honor, and they transacted their business with the king in person. Every exilarch was a descendant of the house of David, and thus the people gladly submitted to their sway, feeling honored in having their own ruler. In a chronicle of ancient date we find their number and their names correctly stated, and their descendants being proved as far back as Zerubbabel, grandchild of the Jewish King Joachim.

These exilarchs were chief justices of the Jewish congregations, not only in matters of civil law, but also in all criminal cases; they themselves executed judgment, or appointed a tribunal for that purpose. The main force against offenders was the use of the cudgel, according to Oriental custom. Also the functions of keeping up a magistracy in the different towns, of watching over proper weights and measures, of attending to the canals and the public safety in general, were entirely in their hands, as well as the appointments of the different officers for that purpose. The business of the Resh-Galuta was entirely concerning worldly affairs, while the religious matters were regulated by proper authorities from Palestine.

Before these historical times, or, rather, previous to the transplanting of the law and its establishment in Babylon, there was but little learning to be met with in these parts. But it was ordained that this barren field should soon become a flourishing and fruitful plain. More numerous than in former times were the Babylonian youths of the last lineage of the Tanaim, under the patriarchate of Rabbi Jehudah I. Thirsting after knowledge, they flocked to the different schools in Galilee, as if they intended to catch the last rays of the setting sun of the doctrine of the ancestral country in order to illuminate therewith their native land.

Two men especially are noted for having traced out a fresh path, whereby Babylon obtained the reputation of Judea. Abba Arreka, commonly called Rab, returned to his native country from Palestine, where he sat at the feet of Rabbi Jehuda the Holy, and became a man of great renown, on account of which he was invested with office by the Resh-Galuta, in which capacity he was obliged to travel much about different parts of the country. Thus, to his great surprise, he soon learned that the people were living in a state of great ignorance, and that the greatest carelessness prevailed about Sura. Therefore he resolved upon opening a school on this very spot, in order that his pupils might be able, in their coming and going, to spread the knowledge of the law. In this great undertaking he proved very successful, for Sura became, during eight centuries, the seat of Jewish science. The school was opened by Abba about the year 219. The great name which Rab bore soon brought twelve hundred pupils together, who arrived from all parts of Babylon, to attend to the teaching of this new establishment. Above one hundred renowned scholars have spread his utterances and decisions far and wide. The throng of attendants who daily listened to his discourses became so large that the garden had to be added to the school-house in order to enlarge the same. The love and respect with which his disciples regarded him were so great that they used the common title toward him of Rab (teacher), the same as they called the patriarch Judah Rabbi, or Rabbenu, which became the prevailing expression. All the pupils were entirely maintained by Rab, in case they were without means, he being a man of great wealth, and possessed of extensive property, which he cultivated himself. All his arrangements were so wisely conducted that those who listened to his discourses had still ample time left to attend to their daily occupations and provide for the support of their families.

Two months in the year (Adar and Ellul), in autumn and the beginning of spring, the pupils gathered together at Sura. In these two months, which were called the months of assembly, the instruction was carried on daily, lasting the whole of the day, so that the pupils could scarcely find time to take their meals. Besides these two months public discourses were always held by Rab a week previous to the chief festivals, which were attended, not only by his disciples, but almost by the whole nation. Even the exilarch came to Sura about this time, and received the homage of all the people, who had thus come together for the occasion. The throng was immense, and very many could not find shelter in the houses, but were obliged to encamp on the shores of the Sura Lake.

The system of Rab's instruction was not only for the education of his disciples, but it provided at the same time for the cultivation of the ignorant population. With energetic earnestness he labored uninterruptedly for the improvement of morality, which, as well as religion, were at a very low standpoint among the humbler classes of the people. The virtues which Rab possessed, together with his perseverance and patience, his suavity and modesty, recall to mind those of Hillel. When, during the days that he held his discourses, a multitude were following him into the school-house, he used to repeat to himself the verse in Job: "When the grandeur of man reaches to the heavens, it passes away quite as suddenly." Previous to his entering a court of justice, he usually said: "Freely I resign myself unto death; the affairs of my household I do not manage here, for empty I return from this place to my home, and my wish only is, that I may be quite as guiltless on my return as I am on my arrival." Rab wrote poetry on religious matters to great perfection, being able to handle the Hebrew language in a most masterly style. Many of his religious effusions, especially the sublime and effective prayer for the New Year, have been received under his name in the regular order of prayers offered up on that day. For twenty-eight years did Rab continue to labor at his school in Sura. When he died (247), all his pupils followed his corpse to the grave, and all the Jews in Babylon mourned for their eminent Amora for twelve months.

II.

Rab's friend and co-worker for the elevation of the Jews of Babylon was Samuel, or Mar-Samuel, with the surname Arioch or Jarchinai, who had arrived at his native home before Rab, and was principal of the school of Nahardea. Not much is known of him, except that he obtained great repute as a physician and an astronomer. In Palestine he cured his teacher, Rabbi Jehudah the Holy, of an eye disease from which he suffered for many years. Being also a great astronomer, he compiled a calendar for sixty years, which was considered no mean task in those days. He also had numerous pupils.

With the death of Rab and Samuel, the founders of a real active and scientific life in Babylon, diligence and activity increased even to a greater extent. During the half century of their efficacy the knowledge acquired had taken root so deeply that the seed transplanted into foreign ground throve even better than upon native soil. A lively, indestructible emulation seized upon all classes of the population, in order to make themselves fully and perfectly acquainted with the Halacha, and to regulate their lives accordingly. To be well versed in the law was considered a great honor, while ignorance therein became a matter of disgrace. The former immorality and ignorance among the Jews of Babylon vanished more and more, and domestic, as well as public life, formed itself according to the ideal which the two great chiefs of scholastic life (Rab and Samuel) had conceived in so masterly and animated a manner. Babylon assumed in many respects the character of the Holy Land.

Rabbi Huna (born about 212, died 297), who became Rab's successor in Sura, was the most renowned man of his time, and one to whom the Jewish Amoraim gladly submitted. His biography supplies us also with a characteristic picture of this, in which especially untiring zeal for the study of the law went hand in hand with worldly occupations, such as agriculture and many other branches of industry. Rabbi Huna, although a relative of the Prince of Exile, was not of rich descent; and he himself cultivated the few acres of land he possessed, without feeling ashamed of his occupation. Whenever he was chosen judge by any party he used to remark to them: "Find me first a laborer to attend to my fields, and I shall then be your judge." He often returned from the fields carrying his spade on his shoulder. Thus he was once met by Chama ben Anilay, who was the richest man in Babylon, and at the same time a most liberal and benevolent person.

This very Chama, in practicing the Jewish virtue of being a father to the poor, had realized an ideal but seldom experienced. In his house, both day and night, the preparing of provisions for the poor was carried on. His dwelling was provided with several entrances, so that all who stood in need of help might enter at once, and not leave it until their wants had been fully supplied. Whenever he left his house, he continually kept one of his hands in a bag filled with money, in order not to keep the poor waiting, should he happen to meet any. During the famine, he ordered that, at night, wheat and barley should be placed in different public thoroughfares, so that the respectable poor, who felt ashamed to mix with beggars, might have an opportunity of providing for themselves. At all times, whenever a large sum, or some heavy tax, was required, it was a certainty that Chama was ready to bear the heaviest burden. Yet, with all his riches, he was so humble and modest in his character that he, out of respect to Rabbi Huna, continually desired to carry his spade for him, whenever he met him coming home from the field. But Rabbi Huna would not consent to it, and generally replied: "You are not used to do such a thing in this place, and therefore I cannot acquiesce in your demand."

In after years, Rabbi Huna became very rich, employing many laborers for tilling his lands, to whom he gave a share of the crops. He also possessed large herds of cattle, which grazed on the heaths of South Babylon. But he made proper and noble use of his riches. On stormy days, when the winds, coming from the Syrian coast, generally proved very disastrous, he had himself carried to all parts of the town of Sura, in order to investigate the damage done, and repair it. During meal time, all the doors of his house were opened, and a crier shouted the words: "Whosoever is hungry may enter at once and eat." Many noble illustrations of his untiring benevolence are related. All destitute pupils of his school, who were rather numerous, had their wants supplied during the school months. The whole number of his pupils amounted to eight hundred, and he made use of thirteen expounders, whom he placed in different parts of the school-house, so that all should be able to hear and understand his expositions.

About this time, a school was opened at Pumpadita by Rabbi Jehudah ben Jecheskiel, which became the center of Jewish life and activity in the north of Babylon, the same as Sura was for the south. This scholastic establishment became a high school of great eminence, maintaining its high position more than eight centuries. Other similar establishments sprung up at Nares and Machurza. The number of men of talent, all well versed in the law, were several thousand, and many hundreds of these glorious names have been transmitted to us.

The mode of instruction in the Babylonian schools was, in the main, similar to that employed in Palestine. The Mishna formed generally the foundation of the discourse which was expounded, the sense of every word and sentence being illustrated and compared with the Boraita and Tosephta. But the social condition of the Jewish population of Babylon, as well as their conduct of life, was essentially different from that in Judea. Therefore hundreds of religious questions sprang up, which were not expressly provided for in the Mishna. In such cases, the schools sought to make use of the doctrines of the Mishna; and even matters which were not under immediate consideration were discussed, in order to know how to decide them, should they ever come to pass. The attractive play of the mind concerning acute questions, answers, comparisons, whereby these questions were solved; the lofty train of thought, proceeding from certain points, and measuring, with the swiftness of lightning, the gradation of a series of conclusions; all this excites astonishment, and cannot be made comprehensible to the uninformed.

In the meantime, the great migration of nations had commenced (375). The uncouth Huns, the scourge of God, drove before them horde upon horde, nation upon nation, too difficult for the mind to behold, or for the tongue to repeat. These times verify almost literally the words of the prophet: "The earth staggers like a drunkard, heavy sins rest upon her; she falls, and cannot rise again; and the Lord Zebaoth on high punishes the bands above and the kings of the earth here below." This remarkable change of the decay and rise of nations impressed the reflective Jewish mind with the full conviction of the perpetuity of the Jewish nation. "A nation arises, another vanishes, but Israel remains forever."

In these hard times which made the coming morning insecure, the leaders of Judaism felt a sudden impulse which urged them to bring into safety the treasure with which they were intrusted, and not to endanger it by the many changes which every day brought to light. The time had arrived for the gathering of that which their ancestors had sown. The whole matter of the traditions had now to be put into proper order, and this important business was commenced by Rabbenu Ashi (born 372, died 427). In his younger days, he was the chief of the Surianic school, for which he rebuilt the school-house that Rab, several centuries before, had established. In order that the building should not be neglected, he had his bed brought therein, spending both day and night in the house, and never leaving the spot until all was completely finished.

Possessing the learning and the influence which once Rabbi Je-huda the Holy was noted for, Rabbi Ashi was capable of an under-taking which, in regard to the destiny and the development of the Jewish nation, has proved of indisputable consequence. He began this gigantic work by gathering and arranging all explanations of the Mishna which had been discoursed at the public schools since the compiling of the same. His labor of love was facilitated by an all-wise Providence granting him a period of more than half a century to accomplish the difficult task he had imposed upon himself. Every year, when all the disciples and pupils met, several sections of the Mishna, with the different Talmudic explanations and complements, were thoroughly sifted, so that the sixty sections took about thirty years for a proper arrangement and classification. During the re-maining second half of his activity, Rabbi Ashi reviewed once more the whole of the matter which had been arranged and disposed of. This second review, sifted and examined, has been accepted as a fixed rule, and the work thus accomplished bears the name of the " Babylonian Talmud" (Talmud Babli), in opposition to a similar work of much less importance, which was compiled in Palestine, and known as the Palestinian Talmud (Talmud Jerushalmi). Therefore Rabbi Ashi, having collected the Talmud, was considered the accomplisher of that work which Rabbi Jehuda the Holy had commenced two centuries previously. But Ashi's undertaking was by far more diffi-cult, and it was not in his power to finish it. His son, Mar, continued the same; but heavy afflictions, which the hitherto happy Babylonian Jews had now to experience, forced them to close the work, and thus Rabina brought the same (about 500) to a conclusion.

After the closing of the Talmud, the Babylonian schools still flour-ished another half a century, especially those of Pumpadita and Sura. During the next generation, the teachers of the law bore the name of Saburaim. By degrees, the head masters of schools were called Gaon; wherefore the whole period, till the decline of the schools, is called the Gaonaic period. The decline was at length brought about by different circumstances. The whole country, inhabited by Jews, was conquered by the Islams. Under the dominion of the Caliphs, they lived at first very contented, but in later days they had heavy afflictions to experience. The dignity of the Resh-Galuta was cor-rupted, and fell into evil hands. This caused unpleasant and injuri-ous disputes with the Gaonim, till at last, about the year 1030, the schools, the Gaonate, and the dignity of the Resh-Galuta, became extinct.

But the Jews in the meantime had removed more and more from their cradle-land on the Jordan and Euphrates, to parts in the east beyond the Indus, as well as to the west, on the shores of the Tajo, the Loire, and the Rhine, in order to dwell in those countries. They had taken the Talmud with them, which became now the educator of the Jewish people; and this education was not of an inferior kind, for, in spite of all disturbing influences, exceptionable positions, humiliation and premeditated demoralization, it fostered a degree of morality which even its enemies could not gainsay. It maintained and promoted the religious and moral life of Judaism; it was the standard furnished to the congregations, far and near, in order to preserve and cement the community. It has acquainted the descendants of the Jewish nation with its history, and has also brought about a thoughtful and active life, in lighting the torch of knowledge for the enslaved and stigmatized sons of Israel.

I. M. JOST.

PATRIARCH—One who governs by paternal right, or one who holds a high ecclesiastical office.
PROSELYTE—One brought over to a new opinion; a convert.
IRRIGATION—The act of watering.
MAGNATE—A person of high rank.
VASSAL—A dependent.
SUAVITY—Sweetness to the mind.

PERPETUITY—Something of which there is no end.
ISLAM—The faith according to Mahomet.
PREMEDITATE—To contrive beforehand.
DEMORALIZATION—The act of corrupting morals.
TO STIGMATIZE—To mark with a brand; to disgrace.

THE SABBATH LAMP.

Shine, Sabbath Lamp, oh, shine with tender ray!
Pierce the soft wavelets of the fading light;
Speed the faint footsteps of the waning day,
And greet the shadows of the coming night!

Cast thy rays upward—cleave the darkening air,
And lift a stream of brilliant light on high;
Shine on the wings of faith, and may they bear
The wavering, wandering heart from earth to sky.

Fling thy beams forward—may their radiance meet
The welcome presence of the heaven-sent guest;
Illume the path she treads with glistening feet;
The Sabbath bride of Israel's panting breast.

Cast thy gleams backward, six days' toils are tolled;
Soothe with thy smile the wearied breast and brain;

And may thy glittering lustre change to gold
Each seventh link in life's dull iron chain.

Shed thy rays downward—may their sacred ray
On life's rough road of earthly travel shine;
And strew the crags that fret the rugged way
With sparkling gems which breathe a light divine!

Cast thy beams inward—may they pierce the fold
That each one gathers round his secret breast;
Show forth the idol in its godless mold,
That we may crush it in our bosom's nest!

Shed thy rays outward—lest at last we grow
Centered in self—and life's best purpose mock;
And dwell, unmindful of a brother's woe,
Like callous limpet on the weed-bound rock.

Ah, shine afar! and may thy waves of light
Bring near the absent dear ones far away;
Show us our loved ones in our dreams to-night,
Our dead who rest in Heaven's bright Sabbath day!

Shine on the Past—and, as the rain-drops gleam
With rainbow tints where'er the sun-beams rest;
So may our tears grow bright beneath thy beam,
And every grief be sanctified and blest.

Shine on the Present—may thy beacon light
Beam on life's sea where mists and tempests reign;

And may its radiance guide our course aright,
And fling its silvery track across the main.

Shine on the Future—lead these hearts of ours
Far beyond home and clime and native strand.
Light up the East—gleam on yon ruined towers;
And rend the gloom that veils our long-lost land.

Shine, Sabbath Lamp, with ray of heavenly birth,
Emblem of Faith and Hope in mercy given;
Gleam on the rude, dark path we tread on earth,
And light our souls to find the road to heaven.

L. J. CH.

WAVELETS— To move loosely; to waft.　　　LIMPET—A kind of shellfish.
CRAG—A rough, steep rock.　　　　　　　CALLOUS—Hardened; insensible.

SAADJA GAON.

[892-942 A.]

RABBENU SAADJA GAON was born in the year 4652 (892 A.) in the Province of Pithom, in Egypt, and died in 4702 in Sura. His earthly existence was but of short duration, yet significant and wonderful are the works he accomplished during that period; but all this must be looked upon as trifling, if we consider what he really could have achieved for his nation, had he not been cut off in the midst of his eventful career. Never before him was there any learned man appointed Gaon, except that he belonged to Babylon, and was one of the academical teachers of that country; but he was called to office by the Prince of Exile David ben Sakkai, inasmuch as he found that the academy at Sura decayed more and more every day, and the learned men belonging to it becoming scarce, he was compelled to seek for help in a foreign country. But Rabbi Saadja's name had already reached the remotest parts; his renown as a learned man was not limited to his knowledge of the Talmud and the sciences only, but he had also gained great reputation as a brave man full of lion-like courage, who shunned no obstacle, and was no respecter of persons.

In the month of Ijar, in the year 4688, he came, at the age of thirty-six, to Sura, was appointed Gaon, and commenced at once spreading knowledge in all directions, which soon increased the number of pupils, and the Academy at Sura became famous throughout the whole country. But the period of his greatness did not last long, for after two years a dispute arose between him and the Prince of Exile, whose legal sentence on a certain occasion was upset by the Gaon, who without regard of the person, immediately censured the same. The son of the Prince of Exile, who wanted to force Rabbi Saadja to acknowledge the opinion of his father, was abused by the people and even wounded. This brought the quarrel to a climax, and the Gaon made an attempt to persuade the king to dismiss David ben Sakkai, putting his brother, Jashia ben Sakkai, in his place as Nassi; but he was unsuccessful, for David remained at his post, and the Gaon was obliged to fly and hide himself from him during seven years. In this unfortunate period, which the Gaon had to spend secluded from all human society, his mind found great enjoyment in the pursuit of the sciences, and he also occupied himself with the study of ancient authors. He imbibed the honey of their wisdom, drank from the fountain of their doctrine, with which he watered his co-religionists. During the same period he composed his numerous far-famed works, the like of which never before appeared in Israel, for previous to him but few existed who wrote down their thoughts in order that they should remain for the benefit of future generations, and it amounts to even less, what is still preserved to us from former authors. After an elapse of seven years, a noble minded man, Cassar ben Harum, exerted himself to make peace between him and the Prince of Exile. He succeeded in his plan, and on the fast of Esther, both concluded a treaty of peace in Cassar's house; lots were cast who should dine with the other on the Purim festival, and the chance fell on Rabbi Saadja, who thus became the guest of the Nassi, with whom he spent Purim and two more days very comfortably. However, the quarrel with David and many other disputes with the Caraits had already taken root in his heart, so that it was almost next to impossible to get rid of them easily. He lived only five years more, and died at the age of fifty, mourned by all the great and wise men in Israel. Although many whose opinions he disliked had to feel the satire of his language, the remembrance of him after death was nevertheless honored by the learned and God-fearing men of all classes. There were certainly some whose opinion was at variance with his, especially in regard to the pursuit of science and philosophy; yet he did not mind them, but continually imparted to the world his researches, for the fear of God was with him the groundwork of all wisdom. Also the celebrated scholar, Abraham ben Esra, called him "the chief of all cities who is entitled to your suffrage." The good he did for Israel is described in the book Gillug, and in a letter of his son, Rabbi Dossa, in addressing Rabbi Chisdai, Nassi Jizchak ben Shafrut in Spain; neither of these works, however, are in our possession now. His works on law and science, religious teaching, Scriptural expositions, style and grammar of the sacred tongue, were very numerous, and were written in Arabic, the language in general use at that time, and in which the works of most all the Gaonim were written. The three smaller works, Asharoth, Iggaron, and a piece of poetry concerning the number of letters in Holy Writ, were an exception to this rule. All were well known to the learned men in Israel, yet only a few have come down to us, for the most of them the ocean of time has swept away.   S. RAPAPORT.

REV. S. RAPAPORT, Chief Rabbi of Prague, noted for his piety and great erudition; a man of great research, as his numerous works sufficiently prove. He was one of the greatest Hebrew scholars of modern times, and all his writings are written in that language.

RABBI MOSE AND RABBI NATHAN IN CORDOVA.

[980 A.]

ONE of the most interesting parts of the history of the Israelites after the destruction of the second Temple is the history of the Jews in Spain. In early times, and, according to some, even as far back as King Solomon, the confessors of the Mosaic faith settled on the soil of the Pyrenean peninsula. With the Romans especially many Israelites fixed their abode here, and the Jewish congregations became in course of time more numerous, attaining here and there strength and influence. Yet they lived to see unhappy days 'as soon as the Westgoths, during the fifth century, entered Spain. At a later period, however, they experienced better treatment, for in the year 711 the confessors of Islamism landed in Spain and founded there a Moorish Empire, during which the Spanish Israelites experienced the happiest times. History records but very few instances of persecution which Jews had to suffer from the Moorish race in Granada. They were permitted to carry on every kind of trade and profession, many occupied high offices and dignities, not only among the Moorish kings, but also in Arragon and Castile, while others again became noted for their erudition in Arabic literature. Until the middle of the sixteenth century the Spanish Jews acquired their Talmudic learning in the Orient, but a remarkable circumstance proved of such advantage to them, that they could soon dispense with the Babylonian schools, which were then already fast declining. Four eminent rabbis who undertook, for religious purposes, a voyage in the Mediterranean Sea, fell into the hands of pirates, who had captured their vessel, and treated them as common slaves. Rabbi Mose, the most renowned among them, had his wife and child with him. The pious woman, who could not find means to escape the violence of the pirates, threw herself into the sea, not without the hope of resurrection with which her pious husband supported her in her last moments, by reminding her of the Biblical passage, where God says:

" I bring back from Basan, even from the depths of the sea I bring back."

Rabbi Mose and his son Henoch were brought to Cordova, where his co-religionists paid a ransom for them, without, however, becoming further acquainted with their circumstances. Rabbi Mose, who was still wearing his slave dress, went at once to the Temple, and after the service entered the school-room close by, where, according to custom, discourses were daily delivered. The Chief Judge of the congregation, Rabbi Nathan, was the speaker, and every one was permitted to put questions to him, or raise any objections as to the point in dispute. Rabbi Mose listened to all attentively, but on finding an observation made by Rabbi Nathan, which, in his opinion, was opposed to Talmudic teaching, he ventured upon some remarks on the subject, thus causing great astonishment among the audience. They all agreed that his objections were correct, and he was now called upon to continue to speak on the very same subject, and to give his explanations without reserve. He readily complied with the request, showing at once his great erudition, especially by answering satisfactorily a number of intricate questions put to him. Scarcely, however, was the discourse finished when two parties stepped before Rabbi Nathan to have a certain question set to right; but he immediately observed to them: " I am no longer Judge here; this stranger in his slave dress is my teacher, and I am only his pupil; choose him for your Judge!" The great humility of Rabbi Nathan met the approval of every one present, and with his consent Rabbi Mose was accordingly elected Chief of the Cordova congregation.

The pirate who had disposed of him, all at once got to know what an important personage he had thus sold for the mere price of a common slave, and feeling dissatisfied with the bargain, brought the matter before the king, Hasham the Second, who, however, decided in favor of the Jews, and at the same time confirmed the appointment of Rabbi Mose the more willingly, because he was given to understand that, on account of his great erudition, the Jews from henceforth would need no longer to travel to Asia for the sake of acquiring a knowledge of the Talmud. Rabbi Mose became afterward a great favorite with the king, who ordered the Babylonian Talmud to be translated into Arabic, for he himself desired to become acquainted with it, and wishing also to supply his Jewish subjects with the same, in order that all questions might be settled according to its contents. Rabbi Joseph bar Isaac ben Stanas completed the task to the great satisfaction of the king. This event, however, brought about a new epoch for Spanish Jews, inasmuch as it severed the connection which from the year 100 had existed between Spain and the Orient. But the consequence also was that the Jewish inhabitants from the north coast of Africa settled in France, even as far as the Rhine provinces, and thus gradually all intercourse with Babylon ceased, and its celebrated schools soon decayed. Yet this occurrence gave to the Jews in Spain peculiar conspicuousness, for the liberty they enjoyed under the Moorish kings, and the esteem which their great and learned men met with, raised the consciousness even of the humblest among them, and thus forwarding every accomplishment which so much distinguished them from all other European Israelites. JUD. PLUTARCH.

THE MISSION OF ISRAEL.

THROUGH ancient prophets was the promise given,
Whose glad fulfillment by the hand of Time,
Onward to harvest fields of ripened beauty,
Beckons the race with destiny sublime.

The crown has fallen from the brows anointed;
The scepter passed away from Israel's hand;
Yet, in the vanguard of Truth's mighty legion,
Our laureled statesmen, heroes, poets, stand.

The victor genius of that olden wisdom,
That gave its inspirations lasting worth,
Blossoms anew, linked to the heart of Science,
Interpreted by lofty souls on earth.
And Israel fears not Nature's revelations,
Eternal Truth can ne'er be overthrown;
The Only One, the spirit only worships,
By glorious ministry of love is known.

That love is banished of superstition,
Of all the idols ignorance reverses;
Upon the Unseen Altar, light-enkindled,
The guiding flame of Holiness appears—
Its radiance leads out of the mists of error,
Out of the valleys of law, unwinged thought
To amethystine heights of templed beauty,
To life-achievements long and vainly sought.

The ancient glory is not dimmed, resplendent,
Freighted with power and treasure manifold,
Its benedictions rest where truth ascendant,
The pages of His Wisdom's love behold,
A mightier sceptre in the hands of Judah,
Benignant sway and holier council wields;
The watchword is for "Universal Freedom!"
The trophies gathered in life's widening fields.

The heart of Israel, faithful and heroic,
Answers the questions of this restless age;
Its sky of faith no fabled terrors darken:
Over its path no fear-born phantoms waige.
Life's inner conflict; that, His love denying,
Enthrones great evil 'mid the multitude;
Its fearless soul enshrines the grand ideal
Of the world's consecrated brotherhood.

This is the mission of the ancient people,
Long in oppression's cruel shackles bound;
With rosy dawn of the new morn of freedom,
The clarion tones of glad awakening sound.
The soul of Israel rouses from its slumber,

The True Republic is its crowning aim;
Once more amid the great, enfranchised
nations,

Unfold our standard in His holy
name.

CORA WILBURN.

AMETHYST—A precious stone of violet color,
almost purple.

SCEPTER—The ensign of royalty borne in
the hand.

PHANTOM—An apparition; a fancied vision.

TROPHY—Something taken from an enemy
and kept as a sign of victory.

SHACKLES—Fetters; chains.

CLARION—A trumpet.

SALOMO GABIROL.

[1021-1070 A.]

SALOMO BEN JEHUDAH IBN GABIROL, or Gebirol, also called by the Jews "Solomon the Spaniard," the hymnologist, and "Rashbag," from the initials of Rabbi Shlomeh ben Gevirol, by the Arabians, Abu Ajjub Suleiman Ibn Jachia ibn Djebirne, and by the Christian schoolmen, Avicebrol, Avicebron, etc., a very distinguished Jewish philosopher, commentator and grammarian, as well as hymnologist, and of whom Alcharisi said that he supposed all Hebrew poets before him, and that all since his time have taken his works for their models, was born in Malaga, in Spain, about the year 1021, and died in 1070. His life was as short as his talents were brilliant, and his end tragical His death is said to have been caused by the sanguinary envy of an Arabian rival in song, and the legend tells that the young poet was buried by his murderer under a fig tree, which in consequence produced so great an abundance of fruit of such exquisite flavor as to attract the attention of the Caliph, and led to the discovery of the body and detection of the crime which had been committed. When only nineteen years of age he evinced his great skill as a poet and his thorough acquaintance with the Hebrew grammar by writing a grammar of the Hebrew language in verse,* a work which Aben Erza has since pronounced worthy of the highest praise. The following ideas, taken from the introduction, may lead us to form some estimate of the poetical imagination of its author.

In this part of the work the author complains "that the study of the sacred tongue, honorable above all others, had been too long neglected, so that by a great multitude of his brethren the words of the prophets were no longer understood." At this thought the consciousness of his own youth neither could or would restrain him. A voice cried within him, "Gird thyself for the work, for God will help thee! Say not I am too young; the crown is not exclusively reserved for old age." He will make use of poetry to render this labor attractive to the eyes, like a garden of flowers; for his hope was great that the language may again be studied in which the inhabitants of heaven sing the praises of Him who clothes Himself with light as with a garment; this language formerly spoken upon earth by all men, before the foolish ones were scattered and their speech confounded; this language became the inheritance of God's people under the tyranny of Egypt; in this language the law of God was promulgated, and the prophets brought healing to the afflicted nation. He would they were jealous like Nehemiah (xiii.: 23-25) for the purity of the language of Israel. He then expresses his indignation that the mistress should have been reduced to the state of the servant, and the lawful wife to that of the concubine.

At the age of twenty-four (1045) Ibn Gabirol published his ethico-philosophical work, "Tikkun-middot ha Nefesh," which was translated by Ibn Tibbon into Hebrew (published in 1550 and often since). In his work Ibn Gabirol propounds "a peculiar theory of the human temperament and passions, enumerates twenty propensities corresponding to the four dispositions multiplied by the five senses, and shows how the leaning of the soul to the one side, may be brought to the moral equipoise by observing the declarations of Scripture and the ethical sayings of the Talmud, which he largely quotes, and which he intersperses with the chief sayings of the 'Divine Socrates,' his pupil Plato, Aristotle, the Arabic philosophers, and especially with the maxims of a Jewish moral philosopher called "Chefiz Al-kuti."† But as his work contained also personal allusions to some leading men of Saragossa, he was expatriated in 1046. After traveling from one place to another, he finally found a protector in the celebrated Samuel Ha-Najid, a Jew also, then prime minister of Spain, and he was enabled to continue his philosophic studies, as the result of which he produced his greatest work, called in Hebrew Meckour Hachajim, "The Fountain of life," and in Latin "Fons Vitæ"‡

The influence which Ibn Gabirol exercised on Jewish philosophy cannot be too highly estimated. He certainly deserves to be called "the Jewish Plato," as Graetz chooses to name him; but the assertion that he was the first philosopher of the middle ages, and that his philosophical treatises were used by the scholastic philosophers, is an error, as Lewis ("History of Philosophy," II. 63) fully proves, although Munk, and after him Graetz, fell into the same mistake.§

From frequent quotations in Aben Ezra's commentaries, it seems that Ibn Gabirol must also have written some expositions of the Old Testament Scriptures, though none such are known to us at present to exist. But what gave Ibn Gabirol a lasting fame were his poetical talents, which were exercised on many different subjects--hymns, elegies, confession of sins, descriptions of the future. In all these we find a noble and affecting echo of the poetry of his ancestors. The Kether Malkuth, "The Royal Diadem," a grand devotional and didactic hymn in 841 verses, giving a poetical *résumé* of the Aristotlean Cosmology, is looked upon as his masterpiece. This beautiful and pathetic composition of profound philosophical sentiments and great devotion, the pious Israelite recites during the night passed in watching and prayer before the great day of Atonement. After a brilliant introduction, this poem, in honor of the goodness and power of God, contains first a description of the universe, rich in details which give us much interesting information on the ideas held by the Talmudists concerning the laws of creation; then follow praises of the greatness and wisdom of God, as manifested in the construction of the human body; he then dwells, with equal richness of language and poetry, on the nothingness and misery of human nature, and the necessity for humiliation before God on account of sin. The whole closes with a prayer for the temporal and eternal preservation of Israel, their restoration to their country, and the rebuilding of their sanctuary, and this is followed by a magnificent doxology. Gabirol is also the author of another work on ethics, entitled "Mibchar Happeninnim," a collection of ethical sentences from Greek and Arabian philosophers, which has been translated into English by B. H. Asher, under the title "A Choice of Pearls," London, 1859.

---

* This grammar, which originally consisted of four hundred verses, has never been printed entire, but parts of it have been published by Parchan in his Hebrew Lexicon (Paris, 1844), and by L. Dukes in "Shire Shelomo" (Hanover, 1858).

† This philosopher was probably the composer of an Arabic paraphrase of the Psalms in rhyme, cited by Moses Ibn Ezra, by whom he was called once Al-Kuti, and once Al-Futi, a variation easily explained by the Arabic characters. Steinschneider, "Jewish Literat." (London, 1857.)

‡ Fragments of a Hebrew translation and an entire French version were published by Munk in his "Melanges de Philosophie Juif et Arabe." (Paris,1857-59.)

§ It is more proper to call Ibn Gabirol as Ueberweg does in his "History of Philosophy," I., 424, "the earliest representative of philosophy among the Jews."

HYMNOLOGIST—A composer of hymns.
CALIPH—A title assumed by the Saracens in succeeding Mahomet.
ETHICS—The doctrine of morality.
COSMOLOGY—The science of the universe.

EQUIPOISE—Equality of weight, equilibration.
PATHETIC—Affecting.
DOXOLOGY—A form of giving glory to God.

MEDITATIONS.

BY GABIROL.

Forget thine anguish,
  Vexed heart again.
Why shouldst thou languish
  With earthly pain?
The husk shall slumber,
  Bedded in clay,
Silent and sombre,
  Oblivion's prey.
But, Spirit immortal,
Thou at Death's portal
Tremblest with fear.
If he caress thee,
Curse thee or bless thee,
Thou must draw near,
From him the worth of thy works to
  hear.

Why full of terror,
Compassed with error,

Trouble thy heart
For thy mortal part?
The soul flies home—
The corpse is dumb.
Of all thou didst have
Follows naught to the grave.
Thou fliest thy nest,
Swift as a bird to thy place of rest.

What avail grief and fasting
Where nothing is lasting?
Pomp, domination,
Become tribulation,
In a health giving-draught,
A death-dealing shaft.

Wealth—an illusion,
Power—a lie.
Over all dissolution

Creeps silent and sly,
Unto others remain
The goods thou didst gain
With infinite pain.

Life is a vine branch,
  A vintager, Death.
He threatens and lowers
  More near with each breath.
Then hasten, arise !
  Seek God, oh, my soul !
For time quickly flies—
  Still far is the goal.
Vain heart praying dumbly,
Learn to prize humbly
  The meanest of fare,

Forget all thy sorrow—
  Behold, death is there !

Dove-like lamenting,
Be full of repenting,
Left vision supernal,
To raptures eternal.
On every occasion,
Seek lasting salvation;
Pour thy heart out in weeping,
While others are sleeping;
Pray to Him—when all's still,
Performing His will.
And so shall the angel of peace be thy
  warden,
And guide thee at last to the heavenly
  garden.   EMMA LAZARUS.

RASHI.
[1030-1105 A.]

RABBI SOLOMON BEN ISAAC, known as Yitzchaki Jarchi, but better known as Rashi, was one of the most talented and voluminous writers and commentators belonging to our race; but while his works have been handed down to us, and have been multiplied in almost innumerable copies, yet the known incidents are so few that there is scarcely sufficient to provide materials for his biography; indeed, so little is known, that the very place and date of his birth are matters of dispute.   There are some who contend that he was born in Lunel, and that he died at the age of sixty-four.   According to the best authorities, however, he was born in Trayes, ancient Trescis, a town in France, about the year 1030, and he lived to the age of seventy-five.   Passionately devoted to the attainment of knowledge, he pursued it with energy; and in order to gain instruction, at the best possible sources, he spent a great portion of his life traveling through Germany, France, Italy, Greece, Egypt, Palestine, and Persia; conversing with the learned in every city he passed through, and thus continually adding to his already wonderful store of knowledge.   During his travels he occasionally gave lectures in the various schools and synagogues he visited.   He finally settled in the city of Worms, where he married and established a school, and where his lectures, from which partly arose his writings, were attended by hosts of pupils, who ardently received his instructions.   At Worms there is shown to the visitor the chamber where his pupils assembled, and the stone seat in the wall where he sat.   His life, although passed in labor, was nevertheless graced by many noble virtues, and was remarkable for its purity and religious fervor.   He had three daughters, who were united in marriage to men foremost in the ranks of the Jewish literati; and his grandsons were famed as

skilled commentators on the Talmud. By his deep learning, and his
zeal in teaching, he acquired a most remarkable reputation. The
terms, "the Great Luminary, *par excellence* the expounder of the
law, and the chief of the tribes of Judah," were all applied to him,
but the name Rashi is the one by which he is best known.

The most stupendous labor of Rashi was his commentary on
the Talmud, a work without which the Talmud itself would almost
be a sealed book. This commentary explains in a lucid manner the
difficulties found in the text, the many technical terms employed,
and throws at all times a ray of light on the subtle arguments of
the Rabbins. Next to the Talmud may be classed his commentary
on the greater portion of the Bible, a work which, although written
in an abrupt and concise style, and quoting largely from the Talmud
and Midrashim, is, however, of the greatest value to the student,
and largely aids him to understand the sacred text. The principal
portion of this work has been translated into Latin, and the whole
of his commentary on the Pentateuch has been translated into German. The ethics of the fathers, the Mishna, and 100 chapters of
the Bereshith Rabba, a Midrash, received also a commentary from
his prolific pen. Among his original writings were Lecute Hafardes,
a work on rites and ceremonies, and eight penitential hymns. A
detailed list of his writings, and the dates of publication, will be found
in the catalogue of Hebrew works in the British Museum Library,
under the head of Solomon Ben Isaac of Trayes.

It is a fact worth remarking, that Maimonides, who lived shortly
after Rashi, while advising his son to pay special attention to the
study of the exegetical works of Aben-Ezra, merely alludes to Rashi,
by saying: "That he had abstained from writing certain commentaries, from finding that he had been anticipated by a Gaul." The
only solution to this reticence is the great dislike that Maimonides
had to the French Rabbins, a dislike that may almost be termed a
prejudice, for he advised his son entirely to avoid them. The more
modern and gentler Mendelssohn, however, renders him the justice
his works merit, and speaks of him in terms of the highest praise.
It is, however, only possible thoroughly to appreciate the labors of
Rashi by a deep study of his writings. Then, and only then, will
be discovered the value of those works which have immortalized
him, and which have spread through every clime the name of one
who, not only as an author, but as a pious, good man, has been the
means of showering honor upon the race to which he belongs.

J. T.

VOLUMINOUS—Consisting of many volumes or books.
FERVOR—Zeal.
LITERATI—The learned.
TECHNICAL—Not in common use.
PROLIFIC—Productive.

TO ANTICIPATE—To take something sooner than another.
GAUL—A native of France; ancient name of France.
RETICENCE—Concealment by silence.
TO IMMORTALIZE—To perpetuate.

THE LXVIII PSALM.

God will arise, and then his foes
Will find fulfilled, predicted woes;
As smoke dispersed goes out of sight,
Their joys die out in dismal night.
Like wax that melts near glowing coals,
Strength melts away from godless souls,
But saints in might shall rise from dust;
Triumphant songs await the just.
    Raise deserts to highways for God,
    Bedeck his way with flow'ry sod;
    Behold him marching. praised as Jah,
    Renew the hymn of Deborah.
Father of orphans, widows' Judge,
Thou seest as wrong man's rankling
    grudge;
Homes free, enlarged, thou giv'st Thine
    own,
But rebels live 'mid wilds alone.
    When Thou, O God, didst lead Thy
      flock,
    Their drink supply from smitten rock,
    The earth convulsed and Sinai's flame
    Proclaimed Thy holy, awful name.

Thy holy law from highest heaven,
At Sinai was to Israel given;
All laws of nature prostrate fell
When came Thy law with men to dwell.
    Thy gifts will come in plenteous
      showers,
    How precious such reviving hours !
    Thy tribes at home from roving
      cease,
    And poor men's homes are blessed
      with peace.
The Lord sends word—the publishers
Are women's choirs, blest messen-
    gers.
    Kings, with their hosts, break forth in
      flight,
    Some Heber's wife will close the
      fight.
When peace restored make prospects
    bright,
The dove's back, silvered, will be white,
With gold for lining of each wing—
With chantings such glad patriots sing.
    When God gave kings their cup of
      woe,
    Then Salmon black seemed white
      as snow;
    The peaks of Hermon are sublime,
    Zion their name, in ancient time.

A mount of God is Hermon Mount,
Its peaks may guard an envious fount.
Do envy's eyes watch Israel's hill?
God's holy throne will be here still.
    For God's march chariots are pre-
      pared,
    Ten thousand doubled, thousands
      squared.
    As once Mount Sinai saw His power,
    That same law beams from Zion's
      tower.
Thou hast ascended on Thy throne
Made captives many, all Thine own;
Even rebels yielded to Thy will,
And hailed Thee King upon Thy hill.
    The Lord Most High ! Him bless
      each day;
    Our heaviest loads He takes away.
    God saves, in His omnipotence,
    From death's deep pit—from dark-
      ness dense.
Besides, He'll crush proud hairy scalps,
Defying him, like oaks on Alps;
His arm brings down from Hermon's
    height,
No ocean depth eludes His sight.
    His foot will crush tall foes in blood,
    And leave to dogs the purple flood;
    Then hosts in triumph march around
    The hill of God with trophies
      crowned.

Singers in front, with harps behind,
And both with virgins, drumming, lined;
Bless ye the God of Israel,
Ye chosen tribes, His wonders tell.
    Thou Benjamin, thou small yet
      fierce,
    Will armies great with terror pierce;
    From Judah's sling hosts vanquished
      fly.
March ! Zebulun and Naphtali.
Strengthen, renew, else all is naught
Which Thy strength, Lord, for us
    hath wrought,
Jerusalem will be Thy seat,
Where kings lay tribute at Thy feet.
    Rebuke the beasts where grows the
      reed,
    Egyptianbulls and calves they lead;
    Let each one pay some silver coin,
    And laws accept which peace en-
      join.

Princes whose homes are on the Nile,
Will seek the Lord, obtain his smile.
Rich Ethiopia will bring
Her heart and gold to God, the King.
  Yet kingdoms of all lands, praise
    God,
  And deprecate his angry rod.
  Most ancient heavens His footprints
    bear,
His voice! What matchless strength!
  Beware!

Ascribe ye strength to God most High;
His helping hand is always nigh,
Yet dwells His power above the skies—
Beyond all reach of mortal eyes.
  God's palaces impress with awe,
  He gave to Israel His law,
  Bless God, our fount of strength
    and force,
  Bless God, of perfect gifts the
    source.

A. I.

RABBI JUDAH-HA-LEVI.

[1140-1190 A.]

RABBI JUDAH-HA-LEVI BEN SAMUEL was one of the greatest geniuses of whom the Jews of his period and of all other times can boast. Thoroughly acquainted with Rabbinical and Arabic literature, he sought to impart his knowledge also to the laity by means of verses. All other Jewish poets were inferior to him, and he exhausted the whole profundity of poetical treasure; in his commendatory poems prevails an apprehensive ardor; in his elegies the most austere feelings of grief, which irresistibly transports every perception; in his letters the most splendid clearness; in his representations the most sublime view of the world.

This Rabbi Judah is also the author of the religious-philosophical book Cosri; it is written in Arabic, and aims at defending and protecting the Jewish religion. A king, Bulan the Chasarean, is engaged in conversation with a Rabbi and thus becomes healed of his doubts, gets converted to the Jewish views of a Supreme Being, and his ruling of the universe. He endeavors to show how the whole Jewish religion agrees especially with human reason, and whatever Judaism possesses in a particular or exclusive manner, serves only to maintain and to strengthen its confessors in true religion.

At the age of fifty he undertook a journey to the Holy Land, which was then the usual custom. In doing so, he had no further intention than to satisfy his heart, which was longing to behold the Holy Land of his fathers. What he saw made a deep impression on his soul; the emptiness of the formerly populous country, the barrenness of the once fruitful soil, the barbarism and the misery of the few inhabitants, he could not behold without breaking forth into loud lamentations. Being thus once placed in the deepest grief concerning his nation, he, in a public thoroughfare, began to tear his clothes, threw away his shoes, and commenced singing an elegy on the fall of Jerusalem, which he himself had composed for the occasion. An Arabian who happened to see him in this state, tried all means to disturb him in his devotion, by heaping upon him all manner of scorn and threats; but finding his evil intentions unheeded, he became so enraged that he set spurs to his horse, and rode over the obstinate man. Unfortunately the horse's foot hit the poor poet in such manner that he almost immediately breathed his last. He wrote a great deal of poetry, which found admission into the Liturgy, and among which is the celebrated elegy, the Zionide ("Zion, don't you care for the lamentations of your captives?").

Many of his writings, which are very valuable, have been handed down to us, and it is said that his daughter, the only child he had, was married to Aben Ezra.   Jud. Ehrentempel.

ELEGY—A mournful song; a funeral song; a short poem with points or turns.

ON THE VOYAGE TO JERUSALEM.
BY JUDAH-HA-LEVI.

My two-score years and ten are over,
Never again shall youth be mine,
The years are ready winged for flying,
What crav'st thou still of feast and wine?
Wilt thou still court man's acclamations,
Forgetting what the Lord hath said,
And forfeiting thy weal eternal,
By thine own guilty heart misled?
Shalt thou be never done with folly,
Still fresh and new must it arise?
Oh, heed it not, heed not the senses,
But follow God, be meek and wise.
Yea, profit by thy days remaining,
They hurry swiftly to the goal.
Be zealous in the Lord's high service,
And banish falsehood from thy soul.
Use all thy strength, use all thy fervor,
Defy thine own desires, awaken!
Be not afraid when seas are foaming,
And earth to her foundations shaken.
Benumbed the hand then of the sailor,
The captain's skill and power are lamed,
Gaily they sailed with colors flying,
And now turn home again ashamed.
The ocean is our only refuge,
The sand bank is our only goal,
The masts are swaying as with terror,
And quivering does the vessel roll;
The mad wind frolics with the billows,
Now smoothes them low, now lashes high—
Now they are storming up like lions.
And now like serpents still they lie.

And wave on wave is ever pressing.
They hiss, they whisper soft of tone;
Alack! was that the vessel splitting?
Are sail and mast and rudder gone?
Here, screams of fright; there, silent weeping,
The bravest feels his courage fail.
What stead our prudence or our wisdom?
The soul itself can naught avail.
And each one to his God is crying.
Soar up my soul, to Him aspire,
Who wrought a miracle for Jordan,
Extol Him, oh! angelic choir.
Remember Him who stays the tempest,
The stormy billows doth control,
Who quickeneth the lifeless body,
And fills the empty frame with soul.
Behold! once more appears a wonder,
The angry waves, erst raging wild,
Like quiet flocks of sheep reposing.
So soft, so still, so gently mild.
The sun descends, and high in heaven,
The golden-circled moon doth stand;
Within the sea, the stars are straying,
Like wanderers in an unknown land.
The lights celestial in the waters
Are flaming clearly as above,
As though the very heavens descended,
To seal a covenant of love.
Perchance both sea and sky, twin oceans,
From the same source of grace are sprung;
Twixt these, my heart, a third sea, surges,
With songs resounding, clearly sung.   Emma Lazarus.

ALACK—Alas; an expression of sorrow. | STEAD—Use; help.

ABEN-ESRA.

[1120-1195 A.]

EMINENT as Halevi, but in another way, was Rabbi Abraham Ben Maier Aben-Esra, born at Toledo, in Spain, where he belonged to a highly respectable family. He was possessed of much learning, but his excellent mind, which gathered it, is still more remarkable than the bulk of the gathering. The two languages, Hebrew and Arabic, he understood more profoundly than any one before him, and he handled both as expert inquirer and grammarian; the whole extensive field of Rabbinical theology he had thoroughly investigated, and into the spirit of the Bible he had penetrated deeply; mathematics and astronomy he had completely studied also, without which there was no learning in those times. Maimonides esteemed him and his writings so highly, that he, in one of his letters to his son, advises him to study principally the writings of Aben-Esra, which, he adds, are especially distinguished for elegance, learning and correct opinion. De Rossi says of him: "He was a renowned Bible interpreter and theologian; he was celebrated as physician, philosopher, mathematician and astronomer, as well as grammarian, philologist and poet." Charisi, himself a first-rate poet, bestows on him great praise for his poetic talent. Richard Simon says, quite plainly, that among the Jews there was no other who inquired into the literal sense of the Bible so successfully, and has especially explained it with so much wisdom and profoundness as Aben-Esra. His grammatical works show deep meditation; they were greatly admired, and during many centuries could be met with almost everywhere. His mathematical writings show great acuteness of mind; in astronomy he is considered the inventor of the way and manner of dividing the celestial globe through the middle of the equator into two equal parts; besides several other successful discoveries in this branch of science, which were readily acknowledged by the most eminent mathematicians of the day. His exegetic works are remarkable for their careful etymology, acute judgment and great learning. But all this knowledge was placed in the shade by the light of his genius; his wit was inexhaustible, and the refined satire of his pleasantry made him conspicuous to the greatest advantage. He undertook many journeys to different foreign lands, sojourning in the year 1145 at Mantua, in 1156 in Rhodes, in 1159 in England, and in 1167 at Rome. Wherever he spent his time he always sought the society of the most respectable and learned men. Some of the localities where he stayed for any length of time became the birthplace of several of his literary productions. In fact, it made no difference which place he chose for his residence; the fame of his talent always reached there before him, and thus he was everywhere received with esteem, while at his departure nothing but admiration and gratitude followed him.

The Caraites maintain one of their learned rabbis, Rabbi Japhel Halevi, to be the actual tutor of Aben-Esra. This perhaps is only so far possible, inasmuch as the great progress of the Caraits in Spain just at that time may have offered an excellent opportunity for his own cultivation, and of which it seems he made good use; but he never belonged to that body, a fact which the numerous sallies directed against them in his writings must sufficiently corroborate.

His works are many, all of them written in a pure and concise style, and in an ingenious and instructive manner; his poems are beautiful, full of wit, and his sallies against rejectable opinions acute and striking. He proves in all his works that a strict adherence to Rabbinism well agrees with the plainest explanation of Holy Writ, which the Caraits, as is well known, entirely deny. It is supposed that at the age of seventy-five he died in the Isle of Rhodes.

Jud. Ehrentempel.

PHILOLOGIST—A critic: a grammarian; a linguist.
EXEGETIC—Explanatory.
SATIRE—A poem against vice, folly etc.

CENSORIOUS—Severe; to censure.
CARAITES—A sect of Jews, now only to be met with in Russia and Austria.
SALLY—Extravagant flight; frolic; sprightly.

SONGS OF THE NATIONS.

Among the Arabs in their fiery way,
The song doth breathe alone of love's sweet sway;
The Roman sings exultant of war's spoils,
Of battles, sieges and warrior's toils;

In wit and spirit doeth the Greek excel,
And India's bards of curious riddles tell,
But songs devoted to the Maker's praise,
The Jews alone among the nations raise,

Aben-Esra.

MAIMONIDES.

[1131–1201 a.]

Rabbi Moses Ben Maimon Iden Joseph, better known to the literary world as Maimonides, and to the Jews as Rambam, from the initial letters of his name, was born in the city of Cordova in the year 1131. He descended from an illustrious line of ancestors, tracing his lineage to the celebrated Rabbi Judah Hanassi, the Patriarch of Tiberias, from him to the pious Hillel, the elder, Chief of the Sanhedrion, in the time of Herod, and through Hillel, by the female side, to the royal house of David. His father, Maimon, was a Judge in Cordova, a man of high rank, exalted position and great learning—a fit parent to so illustrious a son. Maimonides never experienced the love and tender care of a mother, she having died in giving him birth; but he received the watchful attention of his father, by whom he was instructed, aided, however, by the most celebrated teachers of that period. Legend has been busily employed to cast a mystery around his boyhood days, but a career like that of Maimonides requires no fables to elevate it. Stripped from all extraneous circumstances, it appears that his boyhood did not give promise of the celebrity he obtained in manhood. Dull in acquiring knowledge, and slothful in his habits, he was outshone in his youth by his brother. The praises the latter received for his diligence aroused all the slumbering energy of his nature, and brought to light the latent talent he possessed. He now applied himself to study with untiring zeal. It is said that he left his home and traveled to Lucena, then noted for its famous school, and that he was admitted as a pupil under an assumed name. Here he made such rapid and almost marvelous progress in all branches of study, that his reputation began to be noised abroad, and the dull, slothful boy was changed into the famous scholar. He returned home to Cordova, where his fame had preceded him. He received permission to deliver a public discourse in the synagogue, which was thronged to hear him. His address was so full of learning and so eloquent, that he called forth the admiration of all present, among whom was his father, who was afterward delighted to find in the renowned scholar his own son. His stay in his native town was attended with disaster, as both he and his father were compelled, under penalty of death in the event of refusal, to embrace the Mohammedan religion. This they did outwardly; but he, however, shortly afterward escaped from Cordova, and, after many trials and anxieties, arrived in Egypt, where he at once professed Judaism, and where he for a time maintained himself by following the business of a diamond merchant. Maimonides, however, could not long remain in obscurity. He established a college, where he delivered philosophical lectures, and he also practiced as a physician. His fame soon became as established in Egypt as in his native town, and he was appointed by the celebrated Saladin as his physician. His career now became prosperous, but his success was only obtained by the most unremitting labor. He, however, found time for literary pursuits, and his writings on nearly every subject he touched bear the stamp of the greatest genius. He was married, and had one son, and one daughter, who died young. His son Abraham was the object of his greatest care, and his well-known letters addressed to him remain to this day as models of excellence, both in composition and parental forecast. He died at the age of seventy, mourned by thousands; indeed, so great a calamity was his death deemed that "wailing and lamentation resounded on every side, and public fasts and mourning were ordered everywhere." In complying with his dying wish, his remains were interred in the Holy Land.

As a writer, Maimonides may be ranked with the first of any age, and his well-deserved reputation is as great and bright now as in the days when he lived. His principal work is the Yad Hachsacah, "The Strong Hand," or Mishna Thora, a repetition of the law, wherein he endeavored to "arrange the chaotic materials scattered through the two Talmuds." This work is written in pure Hebrew. His other great work is the Moréh Nebuchim, "Guide to the Perplexed," a work which called down an excommunication on the writer, but which has outlived its puny adversaries. In this work Maimonides attempted "the reconciliation of religion with philosophy." Parts of the Yad Hachsacah have been translated into Latin and English, and the whole of the Moréh Nebuchim into Latin by Buxtorf, and into French, from the original Arabic in which it was written, by the celebrated Munk of Paris. As it would extend this article too much to give a list of all his works, we shall reserve that for a future publication; and we shall conclude by saying that Maimonides well deserved the tribute of honor paid to him, that "from Moses, the law-giver, until Moses, the son of Maimon, none has arisen like Moses."   J. T.

EXTRANEOUS—Belonging to a different substance, foreign.
LATENT—Hidden; concealed.
To FORECAST—To foresee.
CHAOTIC—Confused.

SANHEDRION—The Chief Council among the Jews, composed of seventy elders, over whom the High-priest presided.
PHILOSOPHY—Knowledge, natural or moral.
To RECONCILE—To compose differences.

A SONG OF PRAISE.

PSALMS CXLV.

MAKER and King of all I see,
My grateful praise to Thee;
Forever be Thy name adored,
Awake my powers to bless the Lord.

Each rolling day, to Thee belong,
The morning and the evening song;
The greatness of Thy mighty deeds
The deepest search of thought exceeds.

Thy wondrous works, from age to age,
In worship will the world engage,
And future nations shall unite
To praise Thy majesty and might.

Nations "Thou madest of one blood"
Shall freely own the Lord is good;
And children's children shall confess
The wonders of Thy righteousness.

Thou openest wide Thy bounteous hand,
To spread Thy grace o'er every land;
The Lord is good to every soul,
His tender mercies crown the whole.

All His vast works shall give Him praise,
And saints the grateful anthem raise,
The sons of men in songs to tell,
"Jehovah hath done all things well."

Thy kingdom, Lord, safe and secure,
Throughout all ages shall endure;
The weak, supported by Thy hand,
In strength and vigor firmly stand.

Thy bounty, Lord, most freely gives
The food of everything that lives;
Righteous art Thou in all that's done
Beneath the circuit of the sun.

To all who call upon the Lord,
In truth, shall be a sure reward;
To all who fear, He'll grant supplies
Of all they wish, when troubles rise.

All they that love the Lord shall share
The gifts of His preserving care;
While they who walk in wicked ways
"Shall scarcely live out half their days."

My mouth, O Lord, shall speak Thy | Revere Thy name, Thy truth extol,
praise. | Long as the sun and moon shall roll,
And let all flesh in swelling lays | H. S.

DON ISAAC ABARBANEL.

[1437- 1509 A.]

I.

Among the many eminent men of the Jews of Portugal none ranks higher than Don Isaac Abarbanel, who, owing to his position, his upright character, his sincere love for Judaism, his philosophic and exegetical accomplishments, his political adroitness, his practical usefulness, and his embittered fate, is unquestionably the most renowned of the Jews of the Middle Ages, and especially of those Jewish statesmen who, in centuries past, rendered many extraordinary services to their country, and thus contributed much toward its prosperity.

Abarbanel traces the descent of his most noble family in a direct line from David. Yet it cannot be denied that his mind and his whole conduct bear the stamp of true nobility. Of his renowned ancestors, the worthy grandchild counts upward of six, whose names, like sparkling stars, he adds to his own, although concerning them nothing remarkable has been handed down to us. Seville was their home. Here lived his learned great-grandfather during the reign of the pious and wise Alphonso of Castilian. By the explanation of the simple word *Nochri*, which he gave to his learned Christian friend Thomas, a confidant of the wise Alphonso, he averted many evil consequences which threatened his co-religionists, and became afterward a great favorite with the king. Here also resided his grandfather, Samuel Abarbanel, who in the same manner was noted as a high-minded and distinguished man; he was a promoter of the sciences and rendered every assistance to men of letters. Menahem ben Arou ben Serach, who escaped in a wonderful manner from the massacre which befell the Jews of Estella, and in his flight found a home with Abarbanel, wrote a book in his honor, which is even unto this day highly valued. For reasons which we cannot trace, Samuel's son, D. Jehuda Abarbanel, went to Portugal and settled in Lisbon. His riches as well as his talent soon brought him into notice, and all the nobles of the land honored and esteemed him. Like his ancestors he soon used his influence in behalf of his co-religionists, and his energy proved a blessing to many. He became treasurer to D. Fernando, brother of King Duarte, a fanatically pious Infante, who, by his limited income, was continually obliged to have recourse to the rich D. Jehuda. Before he undertook his campaign against the Moors he, with a presentiment of his approaching death, ordered a testamentary letter to be written, that "the Jew Abarbanel, an inhabitant of Lisbon," should receive promptly 506,600 Reis blancos, which is the sum he had obtained from Abarbanel as a loan.

This happened in the year 1437, and about the same time his son Isaac was born in Lisbon. His education was carefully attended to, and the Lisbon Rabbi, Joseph Chajun, exercised a weighty influence on the cultivation of his mind. While but a young man, Abarbanel conceived the plan for his commentary to the Pentateuch, and began soon afterward with that on Deuteronomy. Already in his *Ateres Sikenim*, which he himself styles his juvenile composition, he cites his commentary on Deuteronomy. He was of a precocious nature, of a clear, penetrating mind, animated by a rare love for knowledge and full of zeal for Judaism. Even in his youth he became the associate of kings and nobles, but all this did not prevent him from prosecuting his studies with the utmost vigor. The works of Aristotle and those in Arabic of Ibn Roshd, Ibn Sinai, Algasali, and others. he studied thoroughly; and also with Maimuni's *More*, Jehuda Halevi's Cusari and Levi ben Gerson's (Gersonide's) philosophy, he soon became acquainted, of which he gathered certain portions, compiled them into a comprehensive pamphlet, and thus his first production, "The Original Form of Elements," which may easily be called his own dissertation, was presented to the public. Soon after a second one, much larger and by far more important, followed under the title, "Crown of the Ancient "(Ateres Sikenim), and its twenty-five chapters treat upon the chief points of faith, the special providence of God toward Israel and prophecy, etc., all in a very clear and pleasing manner. About the same time he also published his *Machse Shadaj*, in which he principally discusses prophetic subjects, but it has been lost to us, and we only find it quoted in his commentary on Joshua.

But far greater renown he obtained on account of his political usefulness than through the short philosophical writings hitherto published, which after all were merely his juvenile productions; and while engaged in writing the "Crown of the Ancient," he could already boast "that under God's blessing he is possessed more than any one before him of riches, wisdom and greatness, male and female servants, who eat his bread and clothe themselves from his wool and linen." Alphonso knew how to appreciate the political talent of Abarbanel, and, therefore, he did his utmost to keep this rich, amiable, and gifted Jew at court, especially as on account of his enormous warlike undertakings such a man was of great importance to him. In fact, Abarbanel soon became the favorite of every one at court. With all the members of the house of Braganza he was on intimate terms; princes and nobles were the daily visitors at his palatial mansion; all the learned men of Lisbon sought his acquaintance, among whom was the well-known Dr. Sezira, who unremitingly labored in behalf of the Jews.

Thus Abarbanel passed his time cheerfully and happily, as he himself relates in the preface to his commentary on Joshua: "Contented I sat in my native country, in a patrimony rich in possessions, in a house filled with the blessings of God, and surrounded by riches, honor and friends. I built for myself houses and beautiful balconies; my house was the meeting-place of all men of learning, and from here we diffused knowledge and the fear of God. I was liked in the palace of the King D. Alphonso, this mighty and far-ruling king, who reigned over two seas, and was fortunate in all his enterprises; the king who sat upon a throne of justice, exercising all over the country right and righteousness, who trusted in God, avoided evil and always sought the welfare of his people, and under whose government the Jews also enjoyed freedom, peace and safety. I loved to dwell under his shadow, I felt attracted to him, while he considered me his support, and as long as he lived I went in and out of the palace as if it were my own home." Yet in spite of his fortune and the high position which he occupied he never forgot his co-religionists for a single moment; he was to them, as his poetic son Jehudah Leon of him says, "shield and rampart," for he saved the sufferer from the power of his adversary, healed his wounds, and kept off the ferocious lion. When King Alphonso conquered the seaport Arzilla, in Africa, 250 Jews of different ages and sex were exiled, and most of them sold for slaves all over the country. Such proceedings the compassionate Abarbanel could not look upon with indifference; he at once formed a committee of twelve of the most eminent men of the Jewish congregation in Lisbon, placed the case before them, proposing that without delay these unfortunate brethren should be freed from their captivity. In a very short time he had raised 10,000 gold doubloons, and 220 of the slaves received their freedom. They were all clothed and supported until they had acquired some knowledge of the language, and then situations were procured for some of them, while the others were enabled to find a livelihood for themselves.

But the fortune and peace which Abarbanel, with his excellent wife and three hopeful sons, enjoyed, were suddenly interrupted by the change of the regency in Portugal. The good King Alphonso died in August, 1841. His son, Ioao II., became his successor, who was a morose, heartless, selfish man, and aimed at establishing an absolute government. The Duke of Braganza, the richest and most agreeable man of the country, and also a relative of his, was the first who fell a victim to his treachery. The Duke's brothers and many of the nobles sought refuge in foreign lands, while their rich possessions fell to the Crown. The victims being all intimate friends of Abarbanel, his turn soon came, for Ioao charged him with being in league with them. "Also against me," relates Abarbanel, whose hands and mouth were without wrong or deceit, "he vented his rage because I had lived with these persecuted nobles on terms of tender friend-

ship. In the midst of these complications I received the unlucky
message to appear before the king without delay. I obeyed the
command, and started at once, without having any presentiment that
evil was in store for me. But on my way a man came to me and
said: 'No further! Save thy life; bad reports are in circulation,
fear prevails everywhere, and against you several have formed a conspiracy.' This friendly advice I took to heart, and resolved to
leave my hereditary portion, the wife whom the Lord appointed
unto me, my children, whom the Lord bestowed on me, and all
that belonged to me. I sought safety in flight. In the night I
went away, and as my misfortune had come upon me as suddenly as
a storm scatters chaff, I could save nothing of all my possessions
except my life. The next morning the news of my flight was already
known at Pharao, Ioao's palace, and upon the king's orders a number
of horse soldiers were immediately dispatched in all directions, in
order to trace me and to slay me at once should they overtake me.
God's mercy did not permit any evil to befall me. At midnight I
departed from Egypt, the kingdom of Portugal, and entered Castilian
territory, namely, the border town of Segura della Orden. When
the king saw that he could not rob me of my life, that I had gone
the way which God pointed unto me, then his rage knew no bounds,
and he treated me as his enemy; he put his hand on all my wealth
and possessions and left me nothing at all. (October, 1483.)

II.

The impoverished Abarbanel now began to reproach himself that
he as a statesman, and under the fortunate circumstances he had
been placed in, had entirely neglected the study of the law. Being
free now from public life he praised the Almighty for His mercy,
and with his wife and two of his sons—the third remaining in Portugal—once more united, he devoted his time to the services of the
Lord. He then commenced carrying out his former intention
of supplying the historical books of the Old Testament with a
copious commentary. To a large circle of men, all full of zeal and
desirous of knowledge, he delivered his explanations verbally, and
afterward wrote them down in a surprisingly short time. In sixteen days (from the 10th to the 26th of Marcheshvan, Nov., 1483),
the commentary on Joshua; in twenty-five days (from the 1st till
the 15th of Kislev, Dec., 1483), the one on the book of Judges, and
in three and a half months (from the 1st of Tebeth until the 13th
of Adar II., Jan. till April, 1484), the commentary on both books of
Samuel were finished. For these exegetical productions Abarbanel
was well prepared; he so masterly solved his task that his great
merits, even to the present day, are readily acknowledged and highly
valued by both Jews and Christians. But seldom have the writings
of a Jewish scholar of the Middle Ages received so large a circulation,
even among Christians, as have those of Don Isaac Abarbanel.

More than thirty Christian theologians, among whom we find such men as Alting, Buddeus, Constantin L'Empereur, Hulsins, Carpzov, Surenhus, and especially Buxtorf, were continually occupied with his writings, translating some parts of his commentaries, and furnishing extracts from almost all his works.

Abarbanel was a man free from prejudice, by far more so than any of his contemporaries and successors. More than six months, however, were not granted unto him for carrying on at his leisure his studies and literary pursuits, for he was persuaded to accept public office once more. He was just on the point of commencing his commentary on the book of Kings, when he was appointed by Ferdinand and Isabella to the office of a Royal Commissioner of Taxes. He was again fortunate and accumulated great wealth, besides gaining the affection of the royal couple, as well as of all the grandees of the state. Eight years he was in the Castilian service, and so far as his official duties allowed him, he never neglected his studies, or his co-religionists, or his duty toward his Creator. But he was filled with fear for the future, with apprehension for his brethren.

Like a flash of lightning from a clear sky, the edict of the 31st of March, 1492, came upon the Jews, that all of them should with their wives, sons, and daughters, male and female servants, of every age, station and sex, emigrate within five months, otherwise they should forfeit their lives. Don Isaac Abarbanel, an account of his position at court, was one of the first who received the evil, inhuman, and sad news. He took courage, went to the king, beseeching him to act in a humane manner with the poor Jews, and to recall the harsh decree. " Impose rather upon us," he implored, " that we should bestow contributions and gifts, and whatever any one of the house of Israel is possessed of, he will surely and readily give for the sake of his country." Abarbanel went to his numerous Christian friends, who were favorites at court, and they all interceded for the Jews with the royal couple, and tried their utmost to persuade them to annul their wrathful orders. But, like a deaf adder, they closed their ears against all supplications, and listened to none. The queen, especially, was inflexible, being the tool of her audacious confessor, Torquemada, who said to her: " Judas Iscariot was the first who sold the Lord for thirty pieces of silver, and your highness wishes now to be the second in disposing of him for thirty thousand ducats."

As soon as the news became known to all the Israelites of the land, great lamentations were heard everywhere, such as never had been known since Judah was exiled from his country; and one said to the other: " Let us find support and strength in our faith and in the holy law of our God, which will surely save us from the voice of the slanderer, and protect us against the raging of the enemy. If they let us live, then we live; and if they slay us, then we perish; let us not disgrace our covenant, and depart from it in our heart, but continue in the path of the Lord our God !" Like heroes they all clung

to their faith when the day of departure was approaching, and, in
spite of their pitiful and desperate situation, only a few were enticed,
by despicable ambition after money and honor, to forsake their religion. How great Abarbanel appeared compared with such men who,
for the most part, all belonged to the upper classes! Already before
the respite granted had expired he left the country, against which—
could it be otherwise? he nourished in his heart a deep resentment,
and, taking sail together with his wife and children, and the fragments of his wealth, he soon reached Naples in safety. Here he took
up again his commentary on the book of Kings, which he left unfinished while in Castile, and, in September, 1493 (the last day of the
year 5253), brought the same to a close. Ferdinand, King of Naples,
was soon informed of the presence of the exiled Spanish statesman,
even by Ferdinand and Isabella themselves, who told the Neapolitan
king that many rich Spanish Jews had taken refuge in his country,
and demanded of him, in a peremptory manner, not to spare them,
but to have them sentenced to death, and to deliver their possessions
to the Spanish treasury. Without, however, heeding in the least the
threats of the Spanish rulers, King Ferdinand did not hesitate to
persuade the experienced Jewish statesman to enter his service. As
long as this humane monarch lived, Abarbanel enjoyed days of happiness, for he soon earned again wealth and renown, lived in quietness
and peace, and had joy and superfluities in all things. But also here
it was not granted him to enjoy rest for any length of time. The
following year, Charles VIII., of France, declared war against Naples.
Alphonso II., successor of the noble Ferdinand, was obliged to fly
from the country, and Abarbanel accompanied him to Sicily, remaining with him till his death (1495). Deprived of his property, and
even of his valuable library, the much tried Abarbanel began to experience "need instead of plenty, and his joys were turned into
days of mourning;" feeling, however, grateful to God that, after a
troublesome journey, he could at length settle in Corfu, one of the
Ionian islands. A feeling of awe and pity overcomes one who puts
himself in the sad position of Abarbanel, nearly sixty years old, separated from wife and children, a stranger in a strange country, with
a shattered constitution, without means or help! Thus placed,
he sought for consolation in his studies, and found peace in the
consoling and animating prophecies of the prophet Isaiah, on which
he, in July, 1495, began his commentary. A peculiar circumstance,
however, induced him to lay aside the work just begun, for, singularly enough, he found here, to his great joy, his commentary on
Deuteronomy, a work he had already commenced in his youth, and
which he had given up for lost. Therefore, he now continued the
same with the utmost zeal, and, in Monopoli (in the kingdom of
Naples), to which he soon removed, he completed his Deuteronomy
in January, 1496. And now his great literary activity began to develop
itself, for most of his works appeared in Monopoli. About two

months after, his commentary on the Pesach-Hagada was completed, and, in July, the same year, for his youngest son, Samuel, now twenty-three years old, his commentary treatise on Aboth, and, in December, 1496, the commentary on Daniel. Then some other writings followed, being explanations of particular chapters only, also a commentary on More, April, 1498, as well as one on prophecy and redemption; January, 1498, on articles of faith, or resurrection, recompense, punishments and on the creation. His commentary on Isaiah, August, 1498, was also completed at Monopoli. Some of these were published at Venice, Constantinople, Amsterdam, Salonichi, and other places, while others were in MSS., and were not printed until many years after.

Abarbanel remained in this place until the latter end of 1502, when he, in compliance with a request of his second son, Joseph (born in Lisbon, 1471), who was then a physician, and a man of great renown at Venice, removed to that place. In this rich town of the Doges, the venerable old man spent the latter part of his eventful life in peace and happiness. He was once more drawn into politics, for all statesmen felt glad of his counsel; and, therefore, he was chosen as mediator between the republic and Portugal, in order to bring about an honorable peace between the two countries. Here he also had the fortune of becoming once more united with his eldest son, Jehudah, whom the father considered the greatest philosopher of his time. He completed also before his death the commentary on Jeremiah, Ezekiel, and the twelve minor prophets, as well as a commentary on the first four books of Moses, besides several revisions. These comprehensive commentaries became favorite works among his co-religionists. They liked these productions, on account of the system Abarbanel adopted in arranging them. Every book had a special introduction, and each section or chapter was headed by a certain number of questions. His easy and simple presentation of truth, his fresh and piquant style, his vast knowledge from other sources, and the peculiar bent of his mind—it was this which made him popular.

He died at Venice in the year 1509, at the age of seventy, and all the eminent men of that place followed his remains to Padua, where he was buried next to the renowned Rabbi Jehudah Minz. But the whim of fate pursued him even beyond the limit of his mortal existence, for his resting-place was destroyed after the lapse of a few weeks, the whole country being in commotion on account of war, which was everywhere raging.   PH. PHILIPPSON.

Dr. PHŒBE PHILIPPSON, brother of Dr. Ludwig Philippson, residing at Madgeburg, reputed as pedagogue and philologer.

EXEGETICAL—Explanatory.
PRECOCIOUS—Ripe before the time.
DISSERTATION—A discourse.
NOCHRI (Hebrew – A stranger.
REISS—A Portuguese coin.

MSS.—Manuscript.
DOGE—The title of the chief magistrate of Venice and Genoa.
WHIM—A freak; a caprice.

THE SONG OF THE WELL.

NUMBERS XXI : 17.

As they wandered in distress,
Through the weary wilderness,
To our fathers came a voice,
Which bade their anxious souls rejoice,
And treasure thro' the centuries
The song that from the well did rise.

It was the fountain of our sires
Before they turned to foreign fires;

And as we wander in distress,
Through another wilderness,
O wayside well, O joyous song,
Thy gladsome notes in us prolong,
That in my bubbling waters pure
The strains of faith which shall endure
May thrill the modern Jewish heart,
And to his deeds a glow impart.

J. M.

PORTUGUESE DISCOVERY AND THE JEWS.

[1492 A.]

I.

Ioao I., Henry the Navigator, Alphonso the African, Ioao de Menezes, Azambuja, Vasco de Gama, Columbus, Albuquerque, Cabral, Cortez, Pizarro—what names of clever and valiant men! What histories and achievements belong to these adventurers and conquerors! With what charm and rapture do not both young and old listen to the narratives of their discoveries, their battles by sea and land! No people on European soil were more animated with a spirit of enterprise than the Portuguese. Should, then, these heroic names, the discoveries of which caused that small, narrow strip of land of Portugal to become a great power, have no reference to Jews? No one has ever had any doubt about it, and yet no one has at any time thought proper to bring these seemingly widely remote facts in connection with the Jews and their history.

Ioao I. began with the discoveries in Africa and its partial conquest; Ceuta, that immense city, the chief fortified and most beautiful populated town of Mauritania, was occupied; and the Portuguese Infantes, longing after heroic deeds, had thus reached their goal, to attain which had been their earnest desire for many years. Ceuta was the key to all the countries of Islam, the terror of the Mohammedans, and the central point for further conquest along the African coast. At the storming of that place, many Jews belonging to the Portuguese Armada were present, and one of them lost his life on the occasion.

After the occupation of Ceuta, the Lusitanian discoverers commenced their first distant voyages, being led by an extraordinary man, the Infante Henry, called the Navigator, who was the third son of Ioao I. With the zeal of a lover, he lifted the veil of the coast of an unwieldy continent, and Jews, with their knowledge and experience, rendered him many services in his enterprise. Through Jews engaged in commerce, who had traveled through the unknown regions, he received the first news, which confirmed his supposition that a road from Europe to India could be found; and every Jewish traveler from a distant country received from this affable prince, when he resided in after days at his observatory, a kind and hearty reception.

Ioao II. also took much interest in the discoveries along the western coast of Africa. With the head-money, which Jewish emigrants driven from Spain and settling in his country had to pay, he intended to carry on the campaign so gloriously begun by his ancestors. He, however, undertook nothing; but, being avaricious and fond of gold, he seized upon the work of discovery with the utmost zeal, in order to outdo his great successor. He employed many Jews to make all possible inquiries by land, feeling convinced that, by their close observation and penetrating mind, he would find means to venture with more safety upon the pathless element, and thus enable him under an unknown sky to steer toward the obscure but much desired object of all his wishes. In order to avoid the danger of deviating from the right course upon an unknown sea far away from the coast, Ioao ordered the most eminent mathematicians of his realm to find out some means to show clearly the direction to be retained, and if possible also the proximity of coasting land already known, besides pointing out the whereabouts of the position as near as could be calculated upon. The celebrated knight, Martin Behaim, a navigator belonging to Nurnberg, was chosen for this important business, and he consulted a Rabbi, Abraham Estrolico (the astrologer), renowned for his mathematical knowledge, and Joseph and Roderigo, the two Jewish physicians in ordinary to King Ioao, who were also employed by the navigator Pedro de Carilhao for manufacturing a globe, and became afterward men of great renown in the history of Portuguese discoveries.

About this time a Geonese appeared before King Ioao, making him the offer to take a fleet across the ocean to those lands whose riches and high civilization were so temptingly depicted by Marco Polo. This Geonese was Columbus. The king placed the proposal before the nautical authorities, who, as already mentioned, were just assembled, consulting upon the best means for starting upon fresh enterprises. The Jewish members, Joseph and Roderigo, considered Columbus' demand foolish, believing that the whole of his statements rested on the mere whim of Marco Polo concerning the Isle of Tipango. D. Pedro de Menezes, the old Count of Villa-Real, sided with the advice of the physicians, prevailing upon the king not to listen to the dreams of Columbus, and thus the king dismissed him. Spain, the neighboring country, was to enjoy the fruits of his discoveries. On August 3, 1492, a day after the royal decree was issued ordering all Jews to leave Spain, Columbus set sail from Palos to discover a new world. Among the ninety adventurers who accompanied him in his perilous enterprise, there was also a young man of Jewish persuasion, Luis de Torres, who, in the town of Murcia, had acquired a knowledge of Hebrew, Chaldaic and Arabic, and he it was whom the great navigator, on November 1, 1492, before leaving Prio de Mares, sent into the interior in order to obtain further information, and especially in regard to the "mother-plants" of spices supposed to abound in that region.

While Columbus occupied America in behalf of Spain, Portugal fixed its attention upon India, which was yet unknown. In order to obtain some information about this secret realm of the royal priest Johannes, Ioao II. sent the knight Pedro de Cavilhao to Jerusalem. The knight visited Goa, Calcutta, and other large cities in India, even as far as Sofala, and was on the point of returning to Portugal without having succeeded in his object, when he met in Cairo two Jews from his native country. The one was Joseph from Lamego, a shoemaker by trade, and the other Rabbi Abraham from Bija. They brought the knight letters from the King of Portugal. Joseph, who had formerly been in Bagdad, and there had heard about Ormuz, the celebrated market for spices and other riches possessed by India, on his return told all he knew of it to the monarch, who then ordered him in company with the Rabbi Abraham to go in search of the knight. Pedro was to send by him alone all the information he had gathered, while Pedro himself and Rabbi Abraham were to depart for Ormuz, in order to inquire into the state of India. The knight obeyed Ioao's commands, and went with Rabbi Abraham to Ormuz, while Joseph joined a caravan bound for Aleppo, and from thence returned to Portugal.

The plan Ioao formed respecting India, his successor, King Manuel, who was considered the blessing of his realm, embraced with much zeal. He sent a fleet under the command of the well-known navigator, Vasco de Gama, to discover a passage to India. It was then for the first time that the Portuguese flag was seen on India's shores, and he landed on the coast of Malabar, remaining for some time in Calcutta. He left the town, and on the heights of Andjediva he had to defend himself against a sudden attack of pirates, when unexpectedly an European made his appearance, who accosted them in Italian, which he spoke with fluency. This white man was a Jew from Poland. Some years before he had been sent as a slave to India, and was enlisted now in the service of the Governor of Goa. As soon as the Jew perceived the variegated colors of the Portuguese flag, he started to inform his master that a nation was approaching the shore "who dwells at the utmost end of the Christian countries, calling themselves Portuguese, and are deserving of esteem and honor on account of their bravery." He was ordered to go and meet them, and in the name of the prince to offer them the hand of peace and friendship. He entered a boat and was soon close to the Portuguese fleet, when he called aloud to the steersman that he desired to speak with the admiral. Gama heard it, and pretending friendship he enticed him to come to him. But scarcely had he put his foot on board when Gama, recognizing him as a Jew, immediately made use of the rack, and torturing him so long that the poor Jew was forced to accompany him upon his voyage. He implored Gama to behave with clemency toward him, and with tears he briefly related the history of his eventful life. Vasco de Gama, not satisfied yet, was determined that he should be baptized, and gave him the name of Gaspar de Gama. He returned with him to Europe, and as a skillful pilot he rendered for many years valuable services to all the Portuguese fleets.

II.

The important services which Jews rendered in all these discoveries were also much enhanced both by their fitness as interpreters, and their scientific knowledge of languages, a fact which proved of the greatest importance to many an admiral. Thus the great Alfonso de Albuquerque, who completed in India what Vasco de Gama begun, experienced many favors from Jews, which no one else in his camp could have rendered him. One day the royal priest Johannes sent him a letter written in the Chaldaic language, and, to the great joy of Albuquerque, he found in Cairo an exiled Jew from Portugal who understood several languages, and at once translated the royal epistle into Portuguese. He afterward found in Calcutta two engraved tablets of very ancient date, which no one was able to decipher; but on hearing of a Jew who was noted for his learning, he went to him, and, producing the tablets, it did not take long before the Jew informed him that they were written in the Chaldaic, Malabar and Arabic languages, which he readily translated into Portuguese. On his voyage to Goa the admiral fell in with a Spanish Jew residing at Cairo, who petitioned him in behalf of five Portuguese prisoners kept at Aden; and, when at Beja, another Jew came to him upon the same errand, advising him besides to seize Aden. We now enter with the cunning Azambuja upon Murritanian territory, and in following him on his expedition we begin at first with the ancient coasting town of Safi. This old town, according to Arabian authors, founded in hoary times of yore, had, at the time when Azambuja entered it, more than four thousand houses, four hundred of which were inhabited by Jews. These contributed much toward the prosperity of the place, and by their enterprise Safi had become an important place of business. To the Portuguese it was a matter of great consequence to obtain possession of the place, and only by the assistance the Jews rendered them did they at length succeed in accomplishing their object. Azambuja entered the town with but a few followers, and a Jew (Rabbi Abraham) served him as interpreter, to whom he was also indebted for his life, as a conspiracy arose, which was betrayed to the Rabbi. Being thus in danger of his life, he thought best to leave the place for a time, and he returned to Castello Real. But on August 6th, 1507, he re-entered Safi, according to instructions received from his monarch, who ordered Garcia de Melo to join him and to aid him in his task. They made good use of the dissensions then existing between the different members of the Moorish family, in regard to the regency, and the cunning Azambuja adopted the plan of increasing the mistrust between the two contending parties, and brought the town under Portuguese subjection in the following manner: The associate of Azambuja (Garcia de Melo) was dangerously ill, and a Jewish physician from Safi attended him, who was also acquainted with the two Moorish parties. The Portuguese admiral succeeded in gaining over the doctor to his plan, and persuaded him to carry letters to these two leaders, in such a way that one should not become aware of the other's communication thus sent to him. Both were informed of the impending danger which their opponents had in store for them, and to each of the leaders the assurance was given that if he would only place confidence in the Portuguese, and make common cause with them, he would become co-regent together with the governor appointed by King Manuel. No one but these few persons were acquainted with the strategy, and the Portuguese at length succeeded, each leader entering into the snare, in occupying Safi. It is very rare to find Jews, always and everywhere the most faithful subjects, siding with the enemy. The Jewish physician, however, had the welfare of his fellow-citizens and of his brethren at heart. He wished to see the town freed from tyrants, in the hope that under Portuguese rule the inhabitants would get rid of the yoke which heavily pressed upon them.

When Nuno Fernandez d'Atayde was governor of Safi, the town was once unexpectedly surrounded by 100,000 men, and he found himself in the greatest danger. Two Jews from Azamor heard of it, and resolved to assist their friendly-disposed countryman. Isaac Benemero, and a certain Israel, furnished at their own cost two vessels with co-religionists, and sailed without delay for Safi. In the darkness they succeeded in effecting a landing, and were received with great joy by Atayde, who was indebted to them for the deliverance of himself and army, for a battle was fought in which he was the victor, and the enemy retired.

In 1359 the Xarife of Morocco appeared again before Safi with a considerable force, and one of the exiled Spanish Jews, living then in Fez, gave a surprising example of Jewish faithfulness and bravery. Samuel Valenciano is the name of this Jewish general, who soon after his arrival in Fez gained for himself the love and esteem of all the inhabitants, and especially of the ruler of the place, who belonged to the family of the Marines, and was very much attached to him.

In after days the Xarifes rose against the Marines and drove them from the country. The princes, thus deprived of the throne, placed themselves under Portuguese protection. The noble Samuel staked his life and property in order to serve the family which he considered the lawful rulers of the land. Besides the Marines, the Alcaldeans—who had remained true to the former sovereignty—all united under Samuel, who had equipped some vessels; and being selected as leader, he lost no time in sailing for Ceuta. He reached the place in safety, and at once landed his men, consisting of no more than four hundred all told, and with these he ventured a night attack upon the enemy's position, entirely defeating him. The opposing army numbered 30,000 warriors, of whom about 5,000 were slain in the battle, while Samuel did not lose a single man. Ceuta was delivered, and before the morning began to dawn the Xarife retired upon Fez. With the same heroic bravery and extraordinary boldness, he also defeated the enemy encamped before Safi, and thus raised the siege of that important town. The Jewish hero now went to Azamor, which became his abode.

Azamor is but a few miles distant from Fez, and next to Safi the chief town of the province Duccala. Here King Manuel possessed a few trustworthy friends, who, with the assistance of Rabbi Abraham, the head of the Jewish inhabitants, were so successful that the town in the year 1512, with the consent of the governor, submitted to the King of Portugal. But Muley Zeyan, the governor, being a great tyrant, soon violated the treaty, and thus King Manuel resolved (1513) upon occupying the town. He equipped a large fleet, and under the command of his nephew, Duke of Braganza, sailed for Azamor, which they reached in a very short time. Muley Zeyan, assisted by his two sons, met them with a considerable force, and a great battle was fought here. The Moorish warriors fought with lion-like courage, but great lamentation soon proceeded from the town, for their brave leader was killed, having been struck by a shell. This sudden loss soon deprived them of all their courage; in haste they left the place, and in passing through the city gates, the throng became so enormous that eighty of them were crushed to death. The day had hardly began to dawn, and in Azamor a death-like silence was prevailing, when all at once a voice was heard proceeding from the city wall: "Diego Verrio! Diego Verrio!" It was the voice of a friend, an old acquaintance from the native country, that of Jacob Adibe, who had been exiled from Portugal. Without delay Jacob wished to be led before the duke. Diego Verrio consented to lead him. "The town is free!" With these words Jacob fell on his face. "Azamor is delivered, O Duke! Azamor is free! I entreat you for my life, for that of my brethren and co-religionists!" The duke raised the Jew up and promised him protection and support, and then sank upon his knees, thanking

God for His mercy in giving him this large, important town. Jacob Adibe had the promise of the duke, and full of joy returned to his family, with whom he soon left the town.

This short sketch will undoubtedly suffice to show that in the history of discoveries and conquests Jews have played no insignificant part. M. KAYSERLING.

DR. M. KAYSERLING—A noted Rabbi of Pesth in Hungary, a man of great research and literary talent, taking a true interest in all that concerns Judaism, and author of many useful works.

INFANTA—A princess descended from the royal blood of Spain or Portugal.

ARMADA—An armament for sea.

NAUTICAL—Pertaining to sailors.

CARAVAN—A troop or body of merchants.

STRATEGY—The science of military command.

PSALM XXIV.

THE Lord possesses all the earth,
And gives to life on earth its worth;
The land He raised from depths of seas,
Earth's floods transgress not His decrees.
    Whom will the Lord on Zion meet.
    And welcome on that holy seat ?
Hands pure and heart, the Lord requires,
Abhors all lips profane and liars.
This pure man God will strengthen, bless,
Admit to heights of holiness;
His righteousness is from the Lord,
Assured salvation his reward.
    This is the generation pure
    Who shall to earth's last day endure.
Who seek the Lord, the pilgrims true;
Their guide is Jacob's star all through.

Raise high your heads, ye gates sublime;
Eternal doors! make way in time.
Of heaven's great scenes this is the sum:
The King of Glory—He will come.
    But who ? this King of Glory ! who ?
The Lord Omnipotent to save or crush,
Omnipotent the raging war to hush.
    Lift, oh, ye gates, your heads on high!
Eternal doors ! His steps are nigh !
Of heaven's great scenes this is the sum :
    The King of Glory—He will come.
    But who ? the King of Glory ! who?
The Lord of hosts who worship Him above:
He is the King of Glory—God of Love.
                                        A. I.

ANTONIO JOSEPH.

[1650 A.]

IT is a well-known fact that, among the many victims of the Inquisitions of Spain and Portugal, the greatest number belonged to the Jewish nation, who were best calculated to satisfy the greedy desires and passions of their persecutors, and especially to furnish a rich booty for their avarice. But these Jewish martyrs counted also many eminent men, who, owing to their vast knowledge in every branch of science and literature, roused the envy of the inquisitorial body. While, then, some of these men are known to posterity, others have, thanks to the ardor of the Inquisition, found their way so swiftly from earth to heaven, that their names are never mentioned except in Spain and Portugal.

At a distance of about nine miles from Braza lies the Abbey St. Martin de Tibaens, which is considered the greatest and richest in the kingdom. This establishment possessed at the time we speak of an extensive library, which comprised, among other works, all the writings of every man of importance in Portugal. Each publication contained also the author's biography, and a treatise, or critique, was added to each work; but those whose knowledge of Portuguese literature is limited to the Lusiade of Camoens would really feel surprised were they to know anything of the long catalogue of names, and the immense variety of literary and scientific productions, with which this collection abounds. Among the authors whose works have been carefully preserved, and are still held in great esteem, are many Israelites, who spent their time and labor for the enlightenment of a people whose grateful tribute consisted in committing them to the funeral pile.

Among the most eminent we find especially mentioned Antonio Hornem, a jurist, and professor at the University of Coimbra, who distinguished himself by his writings, which are still preserved in the University library of that place. He, with many others, was accused of being a faithful follower of the Jewish religion, and condemned to death. He suffered death at Coimbra, his native place, and where his house once stood a monument was erected, on which his name was engraved, with the inscription "Praeceptor Infelix." In the same manner may be mentioned Freyre Mascarenhas, who, as he had traveled over the world, understood all European languages, was a member of the learned societies in Portugal, and published the best political works of his time, in which he fully describes the battles, sieges, earthquakes, assassinations, the life and death of renowned men, treaties and alliances, which he himself everywhere witnessed, and wherein he played a prominent part. "He saw everything he wrote, and wrote everything he saw." He was the first who, in 1705, established newspapers in different parts of Portugal. In short, many of our co-religionists could be mentioned who became celebrated by their writings, which, as already stated, are still preserved in the library of Braza.

Among the dramatic writers, the foremost of all is the man with whom we are now concerned, Antonio Joseph, who contributed more to the rich and manifold treasures of Portuguese literature than any one else; and enriched the Portuguese stage with so many valuable dramatic works, that no one has ever produced the fourth part only of what he wrote; and yet we find that this celebrated author, a man worthy of immortal renown, who manifested a heroic courage until death, is hardly known by name among his co-religionists. Of his younger days very little is known, except that he became a widower at the age of thirty, the period when he first commenced writing for the stage. Five years later he entered a cloister, according to all appearance upon his own determination, wishing to crush the suspicion which he was aware had been stirred up against him on account of his being inclined to Judaism. His writings gave rise to this suspicion. But he remained here only a very short time, and soon left the country for the Brazils, where he stayed eight years. He then returned to Portugal once more, and immediately after his arrival was cast into a dungeon by the Inquisition on a charge of having openly confessed, on two different occasions, his adherence to Judaism; yet he escaped with a slight punishment and a heavy penance. He, however, committed himself for a third time upon a similar accusation, and was then sentenced to die on the funeral pile; but especially for asserting that he was all his lifetime convinced of the truth of Judaism, feeling regret that he only embraced that faith when he was already forty-seven years of age. He was then circumcised, for which, previously, he could not find a proper opportunity.

After the tribunal had passed sentence of death upon him he addressed the inquisitors as follows: "I own that I belong to a faith which you yourselves acknowledge to be of divine origin! God loved this religion, and He, according to my belief, is still attached to it, while you think He has ceased to be so; and because your belief differs from mine, you condemn those who are of opinion that God continues to love what He formerly loved. You accuse the Mohammedans that the spread of their religion was accomplished by the sword, and in this you are quite right; but do you not diffuse yours by the funeral pile? You strive to prove that your religion is of divine origin, pointing to the persecution or destruction of the heathen, that blood spilt by martyrs, as the causes of its growth; but now you occupy the place of a Dioclesian, and let us take your place. You demand that we should become Christians, and yet you are far from being Christians yourselves. Be at least men, and act toward us as reasonably as if you had no religion at all to guide you, and no revelation for your enlightenment. If Heaven really loves you so much and has favored you so much, in revealing unto you the truth, then you are indeed its beloved children; but is it proper for children who are in possession of their paternal heritage to hate those who are not participating in this hereditary portion? When, at some future period, one should be bold enough to maintain that, during our age, the nations of Europe were enlightened, then you will be quoted in proof of the fact that they were barbarians."

His biographer, who was an eye-witness to his execution, gives the following description of the awful spectacle: "I felt some desire," says he, "to be present at the auto-da-fe, which the people wished for with feelings of delight. On such a day women were permitted to dress in their best attire, and to appear at the windows, ornamented with jewels, and all manner of precious trinkets ....On the arrival of the king, the procession began to move from the holy office to the Church of St. Dominic, where the sentence was read before the criminals. There were many more doomed to share the same fate, the most, if not all, of them being Jews. I could not refrain from admiring the king's kindness, who condescended to turn to these sinners and admonish them to repentance.

"The Jews remained steadfast to the last, and his majesty showed great benignity and kindness, especially in addressing Antonio Joseph, who treated him with silent contempt; a few, however, implored the king's mercy, and were pardoned. In spite of Antonio's silence, the king continued earnestly to urge upon him to save his life and to submit to baptism. The kindest expressions were used to move his obstinacy, and the king went so far as to offer him his special protection, with the promise that he would provide for his subsistence, if he would only confess his errors and return to the arms of the Church, which will surely receive him with the paternal love of a mother. Everybody who listened to the king was astonished at his kind condescension toward this unfortunate man, who preferred to be burned alive to uttering a single word in defence, or in reply to the king's remarks; and, although he was already about sixty years of age, he betrayed not the least fear or weakness, and nothing but an ironical smile on his lips could be perceived, whenever the monks called upon him to repent and become baptized.

"Before he was placed on the funeral pile the skin of his fingers was torn off, and his nails cut out, because these fingers had once, in a sinful manner, touched the 'host,' which had thus become violated. He bore all these horrible tortures, and the agonies of the funeral pile, with the greatest fortitude; and only once he called out that it was an infamous shame to act in this cruel and wicked manner toward a man who, on account of his firm belief in the existence of one God must thus suffer death. In uttering these words, he, with his handkerchief, tried to keep off the flames, which now threatened him on all sides, and soon deprived him of consciousness. All at once some of the spectators began to shout " Osscitaro barbaro " (clip his beard), and immediately one of the executioners took a long brush, and, dipping the same in a mixture of pitch and turpentine, besmeared the venerable beard and set fire to it, whereupon the mass rejoiced and clapped their hands. Amid oaths and imprecations the people dispersed; many folding their hands and lifting their eyes on high, called aloud, " Blessed be forever the goodness and mercy of the holy office, blessed be the holy trinity, the sister of the Virgin Mary."

Thus died one of the noblest sons of Israel, who, although but little known among his co-religionists, has not been forgotten in

Catholic Portugal, where the performance of his dramatic pieces draws tears even to this day.

Z. Frankel.

Dr. Zacharias Frankel was born in Prague, 1801, and died in 1874; was noted for his piety and his great erudition. He was chief Rabbi of Dresden and Leipsic, author of many useful works on science and theology, editor of the *Monatschrift* and principal of the Breslau Seminary.

Martyr—One who by his death bears witness to the truth.

Inquisition—The court established in some countries for the detection (as they say) of heresy.

Auto da-fe.—The execution of a sentence of the Inquisition.

Host—The sacrifice of the mass in the Roman Church.

REMEMBER ME.

Creator of the world of light,
  Thou Sovereign, high and holy One !
'Mid cherubim and seraphs bright
  Thou sittest on Thy sapphire throne.
Low from the dust my voice.I raise,
  And lift my trembling heart to Thee;
Thou searcher of our silent ways,
  Thou Lord of Life, "Remember me."

Remember me when sorrows roll
  With tumult through my troubled
    breast,
When darkening cares o'erwhelm the
    soul,
  And earth can give nor peace nor
    rest;

And when the storm is in the sky;
  Thy bow of promise let me see,
Then hear in heaven the suppliant cry,
  My Father, still "Remember me."

When false allurements meet my eye,
  And hidden snares my steps surround,
Oh, be thy presence ever nigh !
  At my right hand be ever found.
Guide me secure from every foe,
  Help me from every sin to flee,
In conflict, sorrow, weal or woe,
  Through life's short hour, "Remember me."

J. M.

MANASSEH BEN ISRAEL.

[1604 1657 A.]

I.

It is well known with what fanaticism the descendants of the Jews were persecuted in Portugal from the middle of the sixteenth century. Every one is aware that many terminated their lives on the funeral pile and in the gloomy dungeons of the Inquisition; that also many, in order to escape the constant snares and to abide in their native country, which brought them a rich support, pretended to acknowledge the Christian religion, and under this cloak they often existed during many generations, without, however, extinguishing their love for their true religion. Those among them who grew tired of this pretence, and of the constant watch of the Inquisition, into whose hands they fell after all, sooner or later left the country and sought to dwell among their brethren in Italy and Turkey.

For those clandestine Jews who remained behind, and who were still very numerous, a hard time was approaching at the commencement of the seventeenth century. Portugal had ceased to be an independent state, having been annexed by the cruel Philip to the Spanish monarchy; and his deep hatred toward the descendants of the Jewish race induced this new monarch to apply all means in order to discover these secret Jews; and, wherever they could be traced, confiscation of property, torture, and a miserable death, became their unfortunate lot.

When Philip III. ascended the throne the Inquisition, which during several years discontinued making sacrifices in Portugal, commenced again its activity, and even with more rigor than on previous occasions. In the presence of the regent it came to pass that, on August 3, 1601, two women and five men, one of whom was the lay-brother, Diego de la Assension, were publicly burned in the capital of Portugal on the charges of being clandestine Jews; but it was merely a prelude to the great auto-da-fe, which took place on January 16, 1605, in the market-place at Lisbon. One hundred and fifty persons, men and women, appeared in their penitential garments, and confessed publicly that they were guilty of having lived according to Jewish law. The king regent had compassion on the poor sufferers, and by paying down the enormous sum of one million of gold florins (800,000 ducats, and 500,000 cruzados)—so much only for the charitable disposition of the monarch—besides another 100,000 cruzados for the clergy, he exerted himself to procure for them indulgence, and thus their lives were spared.

Deprived of their property, and their health ruined from the tortures they had undergone, they resolved, together with many others afraid of meeting a similar fate, to leave the country, and, with their families reduced to the most abject poverty, they took the road to Holland, the land which had opened its hospitable gates to these unfortunate refugees for the last twenty years.

Among those persons deprived by extortion of everything they possessed, and now wending their way, sorrowful and dejected, toward Amsterdam, the rich capital of Holland, there was also a man, with his wife and a boy of tender age. This was Joseph ben Israel, who, although poor and ill, felt nevertheless happy in being the father of Manasseh ben Joseph, born in Lisbon about the year 1604, and commonly called Manasseh ben Israel. Of Manasseh's childhood and his youth we know no more than the statement he himself has given us. Arrived in Amsterdam, his education was intrusted to Rabbi Isaac Usiel, an emigrant from Fez, who was the rabbi of a small congregation just formed. He was, however, noted for his Talmudic and mathematical knowledge, and also as a physician and poet he gained great celebrity; and, under his care, the gifted boy, anxious for learning, soon made such progress that he was enabled, when not yet fifteen years old, to come forth as preacher; and, before he was eighteen, to occupy the place of his teacher, who died in 1620. About this time Manasseh was married to Rachel, a great-grandchild of Don Isaac Abarbanel, who was of an ancient noble family, and stood in high honor with their Spanish majesties. He was proud in having formed this engagement, and always adhered to the opinion that the Abarbanels descended in a direct line from the royal house of David. The youthful Manasseh was now rabbi and preacher of the "Neve Salom" congregation, and imparted to the growing generation a knowledge of the Talmud, or, using his own expression, of Jewish theology. From his earliest youth he always had a special predilection for rhetoric, so that he very soon surpassed as orator all his other colleagues; and after officiating eighteen years, he boldly maintained that his discourses were listened to with pleasure, and they were on all occasions received with approbation. By the harmony which at that time prevailed among the different congregations of the free states-general, it was in no wise strange that also Christians and their men of talent very often visited the synagogue, and that especially Manasseh's friends, Barlaeus, Vossius, and others, of whom we shall speak hereafter, were constantly among his audience; also the most renowned pulpit orator of his time, Father Antonio Vieyra, a countryman, and, as rumor will have it, formerly a co-religionist of Manasseh, visited at different times the synagogue at Amsterdam during his stay in Holland, in the years 1646 and 1647, in order to listen to the discourses of the man who had already become known to him as a scholar by the different religious disputations he had hitherto carried on with him. This Portuguese minister attended also the discourses of Isaac Aboab, who was renowned as a clever preacher as well; and, being once asked which of the two Jewish preachers pleased him most, he, in order to avoid offence and to do justice to both of them, very ingeniously replied: "Manasseh says what he knows, and Aboab knows what he says." Aboab may have surpassed Manasseh in richness and depth of ideas, while Manasseh's discourses were more instructive and popular, and even more acceptable to the public at large; he was the "gran rio de eloquencia," and thus became the favorite of his congregation.

Nevertheless, the extraordinary busy mind of this young man was not free from heavy cares for sustenance, with which he had to struggle all his lifetime; for, in spite of the approbation which his discourses met with, as well as in spite of his indefatigable official activity and exemplary sense of duty—giving daily eight hours' instruction—he was by his rich congregation not placed in a position freely to devote himself to study and science, his salary being barely sufficient to support himself and family respectably. The poor rabbi had therefore no other alternative than to turn his mind to material advantages. He resolved upon establishing a printing business, and, without loss of time, he entered upon the execution of his plan. On January 1, 1627, he finished the first impression of his printing house, consisting of a Hebrew prayer-book, according to the Spanish ritual. This was the first of those works for which Amsterdam afterward became so famous, owing to its important typographical establishments. In this prayer-book it is stated that Manasseh was induced, on account of the worn-out state of the Bambergeau types, to cast fresh ones of beautiful finish, according to the plan of Michael Jehudah Leon, the well-known Sopher, which probably gave rise to the tradition that in Amsterdam the types were cast of gold and silver. Thus Manasseh is considered the founder of the Hebrew printing-press in Holland. Soon after the publication of this prayer-book a Hebrew grammar of his teacher, Uziel, followed, and a few months later appeared an Index to Rabbot, a small publication by the proprietor of the printing-office himself, to which he gave the title "Pnai Rabbot," being his first attempt, not yet twenty-four years old, in entering upon a literary career, and in which he successfully persevered till the end of his life. Manasseh ben Israel understood thoroughly ten languages; he wrote Hebrew, Portuguese and Spanish with elegance, and English with surprising dexterity. Although unable to speak Latin with the fluency he could master other languages, his knowledge thereof nevertheless cannot be denied, or in the least doubted, inasmuch as the Latin works he published (of which we possess his own authority that they were written by himself) must have emanated from his pen, and perhaps only a slight assistance of some of his learned friends may have come to his advantage. That he was, however, an expert in that language is sufficiently proved by his trying his skill also as Latin poet; for he wrote an ode, a paraphrase of the 126th Psalm. But his early reputation became established with the publication of his "Conciliador," of which the first part appeared in 1632 at the sole expense of the author. This was the first of his larger publications with which he ventured, at the age of twenty-seven, to come before the public. Perhaps at no time has a book composed by a Jew received such a reception and general approbation as the "Conciliador." The Rabbinical College at Frankfort-on-the-Main, over which the well-known Sabbatai (Schaftel) Hurwitz presided, approved the work of this "great man, well known for his erudition and the sacredness of his character;" the philosopher, Abraham Cohen de Herrara; the Licentiate, Daniel de Caceres, and the celebrated physician, Zacuto Lusitano, recommended the work to their Spanish and Portuguese co-religionists. Dr. Joseph Bueno and Immanuel Nehemias, the intimate friend of the author, immortalized the occasion in some beautiful verses; Dionysius Vossius translated the work into Latin, and Marco Luzzato into Italian.

In this work, published in the Spanish language, Manasseh imposed upon himself the difficult task of "conciliating" various seemingly contradictory passages of Holy Writ, and also of the Pentateuch, which extend over his first volume, to equalize and to remove all contradictions by weighty reasons. Extraordinary assiduity he spent upon this composition, and he himself confesses that it took him five years to accomplish it; and every page of his extensive book gives plain proof of his being well read in holy as well as profane writings of different literatures; here Euripides and Virgil, there Sohar and Midrash; here Maimonides and Leon Febreo, there Plato and Aristotle; Scotus and Albert Magnus; next to Gabirol and Nachmanides; Paul de Burgos and Nicolaus de Lira, in a range with Isaac Luria and Moses Cordovero; above two hundred and ten Hebrew works and fifty-four Greek and Latin, Spanish and Portuguese authors are in the first volume alone made use of and quoted. But the manner in which he solves his task leaves all expectations, I may almost say, quite disappointed. In the "Conciliador," as well as in all other works in which he treats upon theological and philosophical matters, Manasseh appears but as a learned and clever compiler; very seldom only does he tender an idea of his own matured within himself; it is sufficient for him to gather the heterogeneous opinions of his predecessors, and to place them side by side ; a real philosophical value none of his works can claim.

Yet Manasseh wished to be regarded as a philosopher, and was fond of wrapping himself in the philosophical garb, and, with a sort of self-satisfaction, styled himself "Theologian, Philosopher, and Doctor of Physics." If a knowledge of various subjects of philosophy, an acquaintance with a compendium of a history of philosophy alone, is sufficient to stamp any one as philosopher, then, of course, Manasseh must be counted as such. It is absolutely impossible that a man whose views were deeply rooted in the Cabala, to whom mystics and blind heroes of faith appear as higher God-inspired beings, who takes every allegorical representation in its literal sense—it is impossible that a man who found pleasure in cipher-playing and the mystic formation of words, who allows his fancy the widest scope, and in visions has intercourse with the Deity; that such a man, in spite of his great gifts and endowments, could have raised himself to free thoughts and a pure philosophic activity of the mind. Manasseh allowed himself to be drawn on by the prevailing spirit of the age, and with his works attached himself closely in matter and form to the Hollanders, his present countrymen. Whoever is acquainted with the scientific management emulated in Holland, especially during the seventeenth century, will soon perceive that there is not the slightest difference between his writings and those of the learned men in Holland. After this short and general criticism, which was necessary to precede the estimate of Manasseh's literary activity, we will now consider the various writings of which he was the author. It is almost impossible to bring these under proper classification; but, taking them as a whole, they may be analyzed in the three following main groups: Theologic-philosophical, theologic-hermeneutical, and historical writings.

II.

Under the first group of Manasseh's writings, the theologic-philosophical, we count all those works which treat upon the soul, immortality and resurrection; on sin, the creation, and similar themes. For several years the learned men of Holland were engaged in a controversy, started first by the physician and senator, Beverovicius, of Dortrecht, whether the termination of the life of man is subject to mere chance, or guided by a higher power. The aged Vossius, Hugo Grotius, and, above all, the learned Episcopius, had already stated their views upon the question, when the physician of Dortrecht applied also to Rabbi Manasseh ben Israel, whom Rosales had recommended to him, in order to obtain his opinion as well upon this significant theme. Manasseh, according to his own statements, hesitated at first to comply with this honorable summons; but, after much persuasion by his friends, he published, in 1639, his "De Termino Vitæ," being written in Latin, and sixty years later translated into English by Pococke. The answer of the pious man, as may be expected, had the tendency to show that the termination of life is not from God prefixed or determined, but depends upon the natural condition of man, his temper, and the influence of climate.

To this production, we may add, in regard to its contents, his work "On the Resurrection" (De Resurrectione Mortuorum), published in the Spanish language, and soon afterward rendered into Latin. It is said that the infidelity of some of his co-religionists, who were emigrants from the same country, induced him to come forth with this publication, consisting of three volumes. In the first, he collects all parts of the Pentateuch, the prophets and sacred writings, in which the views of the rabbis in respect to the doctrine of immortality and resurrection are hinted at, and proves, as he expressed himself, *ab experienta*, but, in fact, in a mystic-cabalistical manner, that the departed rise again to a new life. He is led in this connection to refute the contradictory views of the Sadducees, and speaks his mind upon reward and punishment accordingly. The second volume treats upon the most notable forms of resurrection, while the third contains a compilation of views of the Cabalists in regard to eternity and the heavenly abode of the righteous.

A few years later, he was induced to take part in a controversy which originated in the Church, and was carried on with great spirit, in regard to sin and grace; and he published his work "On Human Weakness and the Inclination to Sin" (De la Fragilidad Humana, e Inclinacio del hombre al Peccado). In this work he speaks principally upon the doctrine prevailing in the Church in regard to original sin, and proves especially that only the impulse to sin is innate in man, who enters the world clear and free of all guilt; but that this impulse may, through the law and the duties incumbent upon every one, become checked and subdued.

As partly proceeding from these writings may be considered his larger Hebrew work, entitled "Nishmas Chajim." Having had tact enough in the above writings, destined for Christian readers, to keep within limit his extravagant views, he now makes up for it in the latter publication, presented to his co-religionists, in setting forth his wisdom, as drawn from the Sohar and the Cabalists, about dreams, visions, angels, etc., calculated only for the uneducated of the Portuguese Jews, who were already inclined to superstition, and were becoming still more confirmed in the same. His pamphlet concerning the creation, previously alluded to, must also be brought under this class of publications, especially as it obtained some importance on account of Barlaeus having celebrated it by a poetical effusion, which caused a dispute among the learned men of that time, lasting several years.

To the second class, the theologic-hermeneutical works, belongs chiefly the already quoted "Conciliador," of which the second volume appeared in 1641; then, in 1650, the third; and the fourth and last part in 1651. As supplement to this work, so much praised by Jews and Christians, appeared in 1655 his "Piedra Gloriosa o de la Estatua de Nebuchadnesar," published in Spanish, and dedicated to his friend, Isaac Vossius. In this work he explained Daniel's interpretation of the dream of the Babylonian king, without, however, producing anything new upon this subject; but it has gained a lasting reputation, even unto the present time, on account of Rembrandt, the greatest and most original master of the Dutch school of painters, having executed for the same four etchings, which Manasseh himself explains in the preface. The exceedingly industrious Manasseh intended also a similar publication on the "Seventy Weeks of Daniel," but it never appeared in print. Several of his theological works also remained unpublished, and, among others, one on the "Divine Origin and the Authority of the Mosaic Doctrine", which was already commenced in 1641; also a work entitled the "Ichnography of Jewish Theology," as well as a "Polemical Philosophy," on the "Science of the Talmudists in all its Branches;" another, too, on the "Necessity of Tradition," and others besides, which, although they never came before the public, must, nevertheless, be taken as proof of the ardent endeavors with which Manasseh was animated. He wanted to do his utmost, and touched upon almost every topic. With a "Bibliotheca Rabbinica" in its widest scope, and a "Hebrew-Arabic Dictionary," he intended to surprise the world, and many of his fertile thoughts would have been brought into practice, if this restless, active man had been placed in a more comfortable position, without being obliged to seek material advantages. He intended to bestow upon his co-religionists a book containing ample instructions in respect to all their religious obligations, and in consideration of which he was especially induced by the elders of his congregation to publish his "Thesare dos Dinim" (1645–47). This work, of which the fifth and last volume treats upon the duties of women, on wedlock, etc., was dedicated to the brothers Abraham and Isaac Pereyra, besides to the "very noble learned and women of the Portuguese nation," and was written in four weeks. It embraced the entire six hundred and thirteen rituals in a simple and plain form, without the author indulging, as often has been the case in modern times, in useless bombast, or falsely attributing any symbolic signification to the same. We have now only to mention his rendering of Phocylides into Spanish verse, furnished with musical notes, which procured him a place in the ranks of Spanish poets; also his intended Hebrew translation of the Aphorisms of Hippocrates, which belongs to the third class of his historical works. It is to be regretted that the promised "Heroic History" (Heroyca Historia), as he calls it, on which, according to his assertion, he spent much time, never reached the public. His intention, however, deserves acknowledgment, for he not only wished to explain and to correct Josephus, but to add also, as it were, a continuation of the same Jewish history from the destruction of Jerusalem up to the time in which he lived. "In my continuation of Josephus, I have faithfully noted the names of persons, the places, and the time where and when every occurrence has happened," he states in a pamphlet ("Deliverance of the Jews") which he published shortly before his death. In paying due honor to his statements, we believe, nevertheless, that the few historical fragments which we possess in the "Deliverance of the Jews," in "Israel's Hope," and in his published "Address to the English Nation," are the best part of the whole material which Manasseh had collected for his "Heroic History." Manasseh was in nowise suited to become the historian of the nation; his manifold occupations would never have allowed him to give that attention and assiduity which such a work really requires. A most necessary requisite of the historian is the critical mind, of which he was entirely deficient; his publication, "Israel's Hope," amply proves how he was inclined to all that is fabulous and mystic, even in writing upon historical subjects.

Relying mainly on a statement of a certain Aaron Levi (or Antonio Mantesino), who came to Amsterdam on the 18th of Elul,

5404 (Sept., 1644), he believed the wonderful tale thus communicated to him by that individual, who asserted that he met in America a wild race of men who read the Shemah, adhered to many Jewish customs, and therefore must be Jews; whereupon he immediately published in Spanish "Israel's Hope," which he himself translated into Latin. In this work he inquires into the history of the ten tribes, and at length comes to the conclusion that the aborigines of America were descendants of those lost brethren, and, consequently, that the wild Indians were of Jewish origin. This remarkable work caused, nevertheless, on account of its being piquant and new, some sensation among the public at large, and became soon translated into several languages. A few years after its publication, Theophil Spizelius refuted Manasseh's statements, and also Simon Luzzato censured him on the same account.

The remaining works which belong to the historical class we shall have occasion to refer to afterward, and for the present we shall proceed to speak in relation to Manasseh's social standing and disposition.

Manasseh ben Israel was as upright in character as he was dignified in appearance. He formed not only the center of the intellectual Jews of his time, but, owing to his comprehensive knowledge, drew also the attention of learned Christians to such an extent that his reputation reached Paris and London, Silesia and Poland, and other remote places. They considered him a phenomenon, inasmuch as the learning which one met with in the Rabbi was quite unexpected, and with all his piety he showed toleration enough to win him the hearts of all classes of the population. Letters reached him from the most distant parts. He was continually called upon to give his opinion about the most difficult theological questions of the day. It is no boast of Manasseh when he states in the second volume of the "Conciliador" that he had answered more than two hundred letters to different learned men in Europe. His works caused a great stir in the literary republic, and the mere name of the author was everywhere a sufficient recommendation. He was considered a Polyhistor, and very seldom did any man of learning pass his dwelling without paying Manasseh a visit, in order to make the acquaintance of the "Rabbi of Amsterdam." The circle of his Christian friends and acquaintances was very extensive.

A natural consequence of the tolerance which the free States-General exercised toward the professors of the Jewish faith was that Christians came more in contact with Jews, who accordingly assisted Christians to the utmost in all their scientific endeavors, both trying to forward each other's views. It was especially to the Christians of that time, the same as formerly, a matter of importance to make the study of Hebrew a necessary element of education; and even women acquired Hebrew knowledge, such as the celebrated and notorious Anna Maria von Schurmann, who wrote even Hebrew poetry with ease, and also Henrietta Catharina Frisia, who was acquainted with the Greek, Latin, Italian, Dutch, Hebrew, Arabic and Ethiopian languages. Thus it proved a much-wished-for opportunity to associate with learned Jews, and owing to Manasseh's personal amiability he received many calls, every one being aware that he could give all possible information, and always felt glad to do so. Even women of rank and talent did not fail to visit him; and the just-named Schurmann continually sought his advice, and even borrowed books of him on several occasions, for which we have her own statement in the Hebrew grammar she published. In his "Deliverance of the Jews" he says: "I have become familiarly acquainted with various great, wise and eminent men in Europe; they came from numerous places to visit me, and we had much friendly intercourse together; yes, Caspar Barlaeus, the Virgil of our time, and many others, have written poems in my praise; but I do not make this statement (far be it from me) out of vain-glory."

The renowned poet and historian, Caspar Barlaeus, who suffered much persecution on account of his liberal religious views, and of whom Manasseh speaks so affectionately, was one of his oldest and most intimate friends. When Manasseh published his "De Creatione," he composed in his honor a Latin poem, full of genius and grace, and in which he did not deny his liberal views. Although nothing unsuitable could be found therein, he was nevertheless accused of being an atheist, and Videlius, a pious clergyman, wrote a whole volume against him, calumniating him and his Jewish friend.

III.

Among other intimate acquaintances of Manasseh were all the members of the Vossius family. Gerhard Vossius, the father of the family, was not only friendly disposed toward the Jews, but sought Manasseh's acquaintance, as he himself confesses (Vossi Epistolæ I.), on account of the assistance he rendered him in his studies; and in course of time felt so much affection for Manasseh that he continually honored him with his visits, and recommended him to his friends. Vossius writes to Van der Linder, a professor at Leyden:

"Yesterday I had a visit from Manasseh ben Israel, accompanied by Isaac Rocamara, a Portuguese Jew, who was born about 1600 in Valencia, and trained for the ministry. He lived many years under the name of Fray Vincente de Rocamara, as Dominican monk, and was confessor to the Empress Maria of Austria, a Spanish princess, who held him in great esteem. In 1643 he went over to the faith of his ancestors, and performed with his own hands the operation which brought him again within the pale of Judaism. For two years he studied medicine, and has made such progress that he considers himself capable of obtaining the dignity of Doctor from your university.   He was highly recommended to me by Manasseh, your kind friend, whom, as you know, I exceedingly love and esteem."

The friendship of the father reverted to the sons, who also honored and respected Manasseh as their teacher.   Dionysius translated under his care several parts of Maimonides, and, as already mentioned, he rendered the "Conciliador" into Latin.   Isaac Vossius kept up correspondence with him, and in his capacity of chamberlain to Queen Christina of Sweden did him many important services.   With Hugo Grotius, too, an eminent theologian and profound philosopher, was Manasseh on friendly terms.   Grotius was not bashful in putting numerous questions to him, which Manasseh never wearied in answering in a prompt and satisfactory manner. This readiness soon procured him the attachment of this eminent man, who otherwise, in spite of his "Benevolentia," upon which his law of nations is based, and in spite of the theory that men should practice benevolence and love toward each other, could not shake off his old prejudices against the Jews; but Manasseh seemed in some kind of a manner to have extorted from him that esteem which he so undeservedly withheld from his nation.   With what esteem and veneration he always treated Manasseh, his letters (ib. Epistol., 564) addressed to him while Swedish Ambassador at the French Court, sufficiently prove.   These letters were, however, not a vague compliment; Hugo Grotius did, indeed, think so of his learned Jewish friend.   On October 30, 1638, he mentioned to Vossius: "Manasseh, who has my best wishes, is a useful man both to state and science;" and in the same letter to Vossius he makes the confidential remark: "I am writing again to Manasseh, whom I do esteem not only for his learning, but also for his judgment; he is treading successfully in the footsteps of Eben Ezra, Maimonides and Abarbanel.   His well-known publications are much read here and highly valued." Others, too, like Episcopius, Vorstius, Meursius, Blandel Bochart, etc., esteemed Manasseh on account of his vast knowledge and excellence of character.

Another, who made his personal acquaintance during his stay at Amsterdam, was the skeptic Huet, the violent opponent of the Cartesian system, and the most fierce enemy of the "wretched, horrible" Spinoza, as Malebranche likes to call him.   He had read the works of this learned Jew, and heard much of his reputation, and said "he desired to fathom the mental powers of the Rabbi, and obtain, if possible, his opinion about the Christian religion."   The principles of faith were mostly discussed during their long and continual interviews.   During one of these scientific conversations he all at once resolved upon being, for the sake of his faith, disgusted with all philosophy, and, even in contradiction with himself, to publish his "Demonstratio Evangelica," his most important work, in the preface of which he also mentions Manasseh, and was in hope that his book would put a stop to the increasing degeneration of his time. With the same intention as Huet, who took leave of Manasseh with regret, many others, such as Sobierre and Felgenhauer, Frankenborg and Mochinger, came to see him.

Sobierre, known as a great wit, came to Amsterdam in 1643, and visited Manasseh "because he deserved it, for he was the most learned man of his time, and well known through his works." One time during Passover they met at the house of their friend Episcopius, and Manasseh being invited to partake of some wine, excused himself on the plea that the goblet may also have been used for beer, and perhaps an atom of that beverage might have remained in the vessel. The enthusiastic Felgenhauer met Manasseh at the house of their mutual friend, Peter Serarius, and the conversation turned upon the Messiah, whose appearance was then looked for, and occupied the attention of many a learned man. This induced the former to publish his pamphlet, "A Happy Message for Israel," and to dedicate it to Manasseh ben Israel, the "Jewish philosopher and theologian." But Felgenhauer was not the only one who in those times comforted Israel in this manner; there was also Henry Jesse, a Dutch clergyman, who maintained the same views, which he laid before the public in his publication, 'The Salvation of Judah and Israel," dedicating the same also to Manasseh. An English preacher, Nathaniel Hommes, wrote also on the same subject, and many of the clergy of his nation entirely agreed with him. Abraham von Frankenborg, the most renowned man in Silesia, addressed several letters to Manasseh upon the same theme, and became so intimate with him that he sent him his likeness in bronze, bearing the emblem of a wandering man with a light, and having the inscription, "Thy word is a light for my path." Frankenborg's colleague and friend, Johannes Mochinger, who was revered in Prussia almost like a saint, was also in correspondence with Manasseh, and in one of his letters he makes the following remarks:

"I cannot say what desire after truth forced from Abraham de Balmes (a great grammarian and physician of Padua, who translated several of Averroe's works into Hebrew) these words: 'Science has perished on account of Israel's sins, so that they do not further even their native language, much less the sacred, in order to bring to light those works which captivate the public.' But with you, high-honored sir, is not only the study of the Holy Scriptures, but also the knowledge of the Latin language, to be praised and admired. I cannot recollect any one of your nation to be compared with you. In fact, one should point at you with fingers! I have ventured, therefore, to beg of you to continue your endeavors, and to remember the words of Hillel: 'At the place where no man is, be thou a man.'"

IV.

The circle of Manasseh's friends, as well as his correspondents, is so extensive that it is hardly possible to give the same in full; we will therefore only mention that many of his co-religionists were also intimately acquainted with the renowned Rabbi, and among whom we may notice here Immanuel Bocarro Frances y Rosales, a celebrated physician. He wrote in Manasseh's praise a poem entitled "Carmen Intellectuale;" also his most intimate friend, Immanuel Nehemias; the renowned physician, Joseph Bueno; Doctors Raphael Levi, Ephraim Bueno; his two relatives, Jonas and Daniel Abarbanel; Moses and Abraham Pinto; Daniel Abudiente (uncle of the great grammarian, Moses Gideon Abudiente); David Senior Henriquez, Zacuto Lusitano, a physician whose works gained great reputation; the Licentiate Daniel de Caceres; the Doctor Diego Barrasso, and many others. The latter here named was noted for his vast knowledge in astronomy, medicine and botany, as well as for his acquaintance with the Arabic and Syrian languages. He lived for some time in Castile, pretending to profess Christianity, till at length he came to Amsterdam and publicly acknowledged Judaism. To him Manasseh dedicated his work "De la Fragilidad Humana." The last and only one which now remains to be mentioned is the well-known Joseph Salomo del Medigo, from Candia, who in his travels visited Amsterdam, where he made Manasseh's acquaintance, who enabled him to publish a selection of his written works.

But whoever has friends, enjoying reputation and applause, is seldom without enemies, and thus many, who had become envious about the great success Manasseh had achieved, began to harass and injure him. Besides, constant want and trouble never left his abode, and all this was in nowise calculated to better his condition. His numerous occupations increased year by year, but he never shrunk for a moment from the task he had imposed upon himself, feeling always contented if he could satisfy the modest demands which life required of him. His printing establishment was certainly a great help to him during many years, having produced many excellent Hebrew and Spanish works, besides some of his own publications; but even in this branch he began to suffer on account of the great competition he afterward met with; so that he had no other alternative left, according to his own assurance, than to throw himself into the hands of Mercury, and thus the Rabbi, owing to want, was forced to become a merchant. To this purpose he had already sent one of his relatives, Ephraim Sociro, to the Brazils, hoping that, in the way of business, he might probably be able to ameliorate his condition. He now resolved upon leaving Holland altogether and making Brazil his future home. His preparations for the journey were soon made. He had just finished the second volume of his "Conciliador," which he dedicated to the Directors of the East India Company, and to several eminent co-religionists residing at Pernambuco, in expectation of a friendly reception. He obtained from the Prince of Orange some recommendations to the Prefects of the Brazilian Chamber of Commerce, and remaining firm in his resolution, he was ready to take his departure, to the utmost regret of his friends and almost all classes. Vossius the elder writes to Grotius (1640):

"Manasseh intends to depart for Brazil; he will probably show his learning in that country, but I believe it is principally business which urges him to this step. He is a man given to science, and thirsts after fame; but he is without means, and his family circumstances compel him to venture upon this undertaking." To which Grotius replied on February 2, 1640:

"My heart sincerely desires that Manasseh may prosper, and I am only sorry that his circumstances should oblige him to go so far away from us. Could I serve him for the favors rendered me, I would do it with pleasure. I always believed that the Jews of Amsterdam were rich and liberal, but now I find that I have been mistaken. I can hardly believe their statement. I think they like to be considered poorer than they really are."

In solemn manner he took leave of his congregation, and was on the point of "deserting the home which so often had been entered by noble and learned men," when, all at once, the Jews of Amsterdam began to see their folly, and, becoming aware of the great worth of this rare man, they now made efforts to prevent him from carrying out his plan. The great and opulent house of Abraham and Isaac Pereyra, who had just settled in Amsterdam, appointed him President of the Academy, of which they were the founders, and this, as well as other arrangements made by his congregation, placed him in a position to abandon his emigration scheme, and to carry on his literary and scientific pursuits still further. He now gave much of his time to the schools, in which he imparted instruction in the Talmud, the Pentateuch, and many other useful branches of education. His printing establishment was for a time carried on by his friend, Elias Aboab, from whom it passed into the hands of Joseph, one of Manasseh's sons, who was a great linguist and Talmudist, and who directed its affairs from 1646 to 1648. He afterward had occasion to visit Danzig, and also Lublin, in which place he died at the age of twenty, to the unutterable grief of his father.

In course of our reflections we have surveyed Manasseh, from a scientific point of view, as a productive author, poor rabbi and preacher of his congregation, as a greatly extolled friend of learned Christian men; but, in the splendor of his real greatness, he appears in his far-extending practical activity, in his efficiency for the welfare of his brethren, and as the representative of his nation. Manasseh wished nothing less than to procure for the Jews fresh places of abode, to gain liberty for his oppressed nation; being never afraid to appear before princes and potentates, and only with this noble intention he saluted queens and princesses. For no other reason than to obtain permission for the naturalization of Jews in the Scandinavian peninsula he, with the kind assistance of his friend Vossius, visited Queen Christina. This young queen was a thorough Hebrew scholar, and took great interest in all Oriental studies. Manasseh received her order to send a selection of Hebrew works and manuscripts to Sweden, the cost of which amounted to 360 imperials.

After her abdication, Manasseh continued to correspond with the queen, and during her stay in Antwerp he had an interview with her, after which he published his panegyric to her, written in Spanish, with a Latin translation placed opposite to it. But his whole exertion went to induce the queen to interest herself in behalf of his suffering brethren both at home and abroad. His endeavors, in connection with the admission of Jews into England, met with better success, for, after an elapse of three hundred and fifty-eight years, the Jewish question was once more revived in England, and Manasseh was successful in his efforts. The Jewish nation could not have wished for a better advocate to plead their cause than Manasseh, and his petitions in reaching London (October, 1655), which were addressed to Cromwell and the English nation, are admired even to this day.

But Manasseh was not destined to see the fruits of his never-tiring activity. Cromwell dismissed him in an honorable manner, bestowing upon him a yearly pension of £100 sterling. Before, however, he had reached his home, death overtook him at Middleburg, a town in Zealand, in the year 1657. His remains rest in Amsterdam. On all sides nothing but lamentations were heard when the sad news of his death became known, for there had died one of the most eminent and remarkable men of the Jewish nation.

M. KAYSERLING.

FANATICISM—Religious frenzy.
CLANDESTINE—Secret.
PRELUDE—Something that shows what is to follow.
DUCAT—A coin, in gold valued nine shillings and sixpence, English.
PREDILECTION—Preference.
RHETORIC—The art of speaking with art and elegance.
TYPOGRAPHY—The art of printing.
ODE—A poem written to be sung to music.
To PARAPHRASE—Not literal; not verbal.
LICENTIATE—A degree in a university.
To IMMORTALIZE—To perpetuate.

ASSIDUITY—Diligence.
HETEROGENEOUS—Opposite or dissimilar in nature.
PHYSICS—The science of nature or natural objects.
COMPENDIUM—Abridgement; summary.
ALLEGORICAL—Not real; not literal.
HERMENEUTICAL—Science of interpreting.
ICHNOGRAPHY—The ground plot.
POLEMIC—Controversial.
CARTESIAN—Pertaining to the philosopher Des Cartes, or to his philosophy.
PANEGYRIST—One that writes praise.

AN INVOCATION.

Oh, harp of Judah! wake again!
Can no one deftly touch thy strings
To scatter far the sacred strain,
Which from divinest patience springs?
Have all the strife sown, troublous
years
No joys for happy song to cast?
Can love distill no hope from tears,
Or steal no beauty from the past?

Has music lost its spell and power
To summon hopes that only rest?
Endowed with truths, our lasting dower,
That mock the ages' wear and test.
Can no heart-stirring melody,
Imbued with light and touched with
fire,
Flow from a nation proud and free,
Whose past *must* urge them to aspire?

Reproach, an ignominious sea,
Can follow in our wake no more;
The poisoned waves of calumny
Are washed away from Freedom's
shore;
The justice of a nobler age
Has reached and raised our scattered
race;
Our history shows a fairer page,
Our future wears a brighter face.

The rooted weeds of narrow thought
Which closely cling, or idly spread,
Which ignorance has sown and
wrought,

Are crushed and buried with the
dead;
A loftier sense of heavenly things,
A wider view of human life,
Have fashioned tolerance; which brings
Its own repose to cast off strife.

Beyond man's vain imaginings,
Is Israel's faith that never dies,
The boon of slaves—the pride of kings;
Its meanings make the nations wise.
And through the mists of ages gone,
Its God-stamped visions still appear,
As in the Bible's earliest dawn,
Supremely true, divinely clear!

And who asserts that Judah's claim
To any chosen land is o'er?
When all the earth contains her fame
That spreads and widens evermore;
The truths that sanctify her creed
Shall scatter hope where e'er they
shine,
Until all men shall feel the need
Of her own unity divine.

So wake, my harp, my fingers press
Thy rust-worn strings, while fancy
longs
To dower with melodiousness
The burden of unuttered songs;
My faltering touch may reach in vain
The music of my sacred themes,
Still Truth may charm the feeble strain,
And lends its sweetness to my dreams.
A. I.

INVOCATION—The act of calling upon in prayer.
DEFTLY—Neatly.

DOWER—Gift.
IGNOMINIOUS—Shameful.
TOLERANCE—Act of enduring.

MOSES CHAIM LUZZATO.
[1707-1746 A.]

THE learned Moses Chaim Luzzato, born in the year 1707, received his education from the erudite Rabbi Jeshaja Bassan, author of *Lachma Thoda*, the excellent Rabbi Jizchock Chaim Cantarini, author of *Pashad Jizchock*, Eth Kez, Pi Sefarim, and Ekeb Rab, as well as from other celebrated scholars, who, at that time, resided at Padua, and whose instruction he was fortunate enough to enjoy. At the age of seventeen he published, at Mantua, the first volume of his book, Leshon Limudim, and soon afterward Chanukhat Haaran,

containing among others seven hymns of the book of Psalms, which
he completed at a later period. Moses grew up amidst the wise
rabbis of his time, who then occupied the office of Judges, and he obtained thus a knowledge of the natural sciences in practice and religion;
acquiring also the Greek, Latin and French languages, inasmuch as
God had bestowed on him a comprehensive mind, enabling him to
conceive all science and knowledge in a thorough manner. He
opened an academy at his house, and soon obtained pupils desirous
of learning, attending daily to his instruction in the Bible, the Talmud and Midrashim, so that he and his establishment soon got into
great repute far and near.

Besides his learning he was also blessed with wealth, which he
appropriated to benevolent purposes, maintaining and assisting
everybody in whose heart God had planted a desire for knowledge.

The study of Cabala had, at that time, greatly advanced; every
aspiring mind was longing for something beyond the fetters of
earthly nature; every genius gifted with conception, despising the
common incidents of the day, and seeking for hidden secrets, turned
his study to the Cabala. But this science did great mischief in these
days, being made use of by perverse people, followers of the false
prophet Shabtai Zebi, who spun a web of mysteries and miscon-
structions, wherewith they tried to draw the inexperienced into their
net. The eminent men of that period, however, perceiving the
mischief which these extravagant notions brought about, soon commenced to subdue these cabalistic writings, and endeavored to pull
down the foundation, in order to destroy the phantom thus built
upon. The learned Rabbi Jehuda Arja, of Modena, rose like a lion,
and in his work, Shagath Arjectri Nohem, which in MS. is still in
existence, attacked with all might the study of the Cabala and all its
adherents, both of ancient and modern time.

But Moses Luzzato, a man who possessed all accomplishments and
capacities to perfection, and whose fullness of thought and action
animated him to soar unto higher regions, had acquainted himself
with cabalistic science, which is indeed more suitable for the heated
imagination than for a reserved mind, and had acquired all its mysterious doctrines and mysteries from the pupils of the celebrated
Moses Sakhut, in Venice. He then advocated the doctrine in public,
and published a work, in the form of a dialogue, controverting the
book *Ari Nohem*. This treatise he first submitted for a sifting examination to his celebrated teacher, Bassan; his father-in-law, then
administrator of justice at Mantua, the renowned cabalist, the author
of Amumath Chachamim, and the learned Gar Arje Zinzi. The work
met with great favor. Thereupon some of the Venetian rabbis rose
against Luzzato, for they had to defend the honor of their countrymen, the author of *Ari Nohem*, and thus heaped a mass of unjust
reproaches upon Moses, inasmuch as they maintained that he made

the law his study merely for the sake of ignoble intentions, and
that all his coadjutors in league with him are followers of the lying
prophet Shabtai Zebi. They also enticed the learned Chagies, a man
of zealous mind, to turn against him. He joined another German
scholar to fight the battle, and they succeeded in spreading among
the celebrated men of Germany the story that Moses really belonged
to the heretical party. This had many evil consequences, as delineated in the book Thorath Hakenaoth, published by Rabbi Jabetz.
He was a man who, with heart and might, fought for truth, yet was
not inclined to do justice to his opponents, but without examination
gave ear to everybody who complained about his enemies.

Thus Luzzato was attacked in an unjustifiable manner; he never
dreamed of setting himself up as the Messiah, as his enemies would
have it. and his treatise on redemption, written for encouraging the
faint-hearted, and to give them the assurance that God will redeem
Israel in due time, must be sufficient to silence his accusers. His
great teacher, Rabbi Jeshaja Bassan, who was the ornament of his
time, protected him against his opponents, to bear witness for him,
being a man of pure heart, noble mind, full of faithfulness toward
God and man.

The spirit with which, it is said, he often conversed—ridiculed by
many and considered a lie, while others speak favorably of Luzzato
and declare it possible that probably one of a thousand distinguished men may have had the privilege of a holy being revealed
unto him—was, however, nothing but his own spirit, that of wisdom,
with which he was so mightily endowed, and upon which the mass,
as generally is the case with all invisible divine powers, were ever
ready to bestow a name. Whatever, in his mode of life, they could
not understand, they thought of looking for in heaven; in the same
manner people carried on at all times, as history sufficiently corroborates. Also, in the Psalms and in the book of Sohar Thnijana,
which Luzzato wrote, his opponents found occasion to attack his
reputation and to put a stain upon his good name; but their eagerness and their attacks rose from a mean service. Who has ever
heard that men of sense, if they not intentionally aim at doing mischief,
would pass sentence on an intellectual giant because he produced
marvelous poems in masterly style? But to condemn him even for
the sake of the opinion of a man—that surely has never been ordained by God. I do not here pretend to become a judge between
Luzzato and his opponents, for this is not my intention in writing
these lines, but rather to lift the rose out of the mire of malevolence.
Among Luzzato's enemies there was not one who dared to attack
the purity of his actions and his efficacy. But the power which
animated him with a divine ardor, which became his share from
the sacred Sepharim, the eternal prophets of divine hymns, that was
the power of his poesy. His contemporaries, however, living in

darkness and incapable of understanding such a being, could not perceive that this power was the center from which, while he remained in the land of the living, all his acts proceeded and to which they again returned.

Luzzato was blessed with riches, and he possessed at Amsterdam an establishment for cutting and polishing diamonds, where the pious grandfather of Rabbi Girandi acted as manager. He relates that Luzzato at that time, when he had to battle with public opinion, made it a rule to sift minutely all his acts, even the most hidden, in order to effect a change for the better, in case something evil should have crept in unawares; but he knew that he was clear of all faults, and at length even public opinion became favorably disposed toward him. He had at Amsterdam a number of disciples, who all followed the light of his instruction. The celebrated poet, David Chofshi, called him, in the preface of the book Derech Chochma, the ornament of poetic talent, the crown of poets, master of the seven liberal arts. In conclusion he says : " His pure soul breathed its last in the Holy Land; he has attained salvation, and has prepared it for others with his numerous writings, which are full of wisdom, knowledge and the fear of God. Happy am I that I had the fortune of being one of his pupils." At the age of forty Moses departed unto God, in the land of Israel, in the sacred town of Tiberias, and was buried next to Rabbi Akiba. The rabbis and learned men of Tiberias sent to all Israelitish congregations a letter full of lamentation and grief, wherein it stated: "The teaching of truth was in his mouth, wrong was not found upon his lips; many he brought back from sin to the path of virtue, and none rose in Israel like Moses."

This short account of his career, which has been preserved to us, is sufficient proof of his estimable qualities. But his productions puzzled many great and learned men. What they saw astonished them. They could not conceive it; what his heart contained was unattainable for them. Moses understood his brethren, but they would not understand him. While he, upon the wings of his genius, soared to heavenly regions, they looked from the earth after him who was wrapped in clouds. Yet his valuable writings have established what he contrived and explained. They secure for him a remembrance forever blessed, and for his soul immortality.

DR. LETTERIS.

DR. LETTERIS, late of Vienna, a man of great learning and research; one of the greatest Hebrew scholars of his time; author and translator of many works into Hebrew, and whose translation of Göthe's "Faust" into Hebrew gained him a world-wide reputation.

CABALA—Tradition; a mysterious kind of science.

MALEVOLENCE—Ill-will; inclination to hurt others.

THE VOICE OF THE LORD.

The mighty voice of the Lord
Was upon the waters that day;
Like thunder it scattered abroad
The works that before it lay!

The voice of the Lord was heard
On the powerful ocean that night;
The billows arose, and the depths were
stirred
In their glorious power and might.

The voice of the Lord is grand!
It lifts up the waves on high;
They proudly sweep o'er the land,
And the works of man defy!

The voice of the Lord awoke
The slumbering ocean's tide;
That voice, "full of majesty," spoke,
And the sea in its roar replied!

The white cliffs trembled and shook;
They broke at its angry blast,
They shivered in pieces before His look,
And into the foam were cast!

The voice of the Lord flashed fire,
And bars of iron gave way;
They bent—they fell as the waves rose
higher,
And tossed them about in their spray!

Then the mighty sea had rest,
In its beauty, its clearness, its calm;
The voice of the Lord was hush'd on
its breast,
Which heaved 'neath His heavenly
arm!

ROSA EMMA COLLINS.

N. H. WESSELY.

[1725–1805 A.]

THE age of Mendelssohn will always be regarded as famous in Jewish history; for his name suggests a cluster of brilliant men, who were pioneers in the yet unbroken paths of science, literature, and social emancipation, and whose sturdy efforts cleared the road for a later generation. Of these, Naphtali Herz Wessely occupies a prominent place; for, like Reuchlin in the century of the Protestant Reformation, he too brought about a revival of the Hebrew language, not, however, as his prototype had done, in the Church, but among his own brethren.

Born at Hamburg in 1725, Wessely possessed so remarkable a talent for languages that he understood German, French, Danish and Dutch; in Hebrew he distanced his contemporaries; he was well versed besides in mathematics, history and natural science. His Hebrew style was pure, fluent and lofty. It abounded in graceful and sublime metaphors. His knowledge of Hebrew was so profound, and it responded so deeply to the sentiments of his mind and heart, that the comparative neglect in which it stood among his brethren filled him with dismay; and he resolved to devote his genius to its revival. He felt that loyalty to Judaism was indissolubly connected with loyalty to the Hebrew language. For forty years, from the appearance of his "Hebrew Synonyms" in 1765 to his death in 1805, his literary activity was continuous. A bookkeeper in Amsterdam, he published in 1765 his commentary on the "Ethics of the Fathers." In 1771 he went to Hamburg, and there married. In the day he was a lowly merchant; in the evening a Hebrew student. But his business not proving lucrative he settled in Berlin, entered into the service of a banker, and published in 1775 his translation of Ecclesiastes with a commentary, in pure Hebrew. In business he was far less successful than in literature, and soon after he had been dismissed by his principal, owing to the latter's advancing years, he fell into the greatest poverty. To gain an income, he was obliged to give public lectures on the Bible, which sufficed for his modest wants.

In Berlin he found a firm friend in Mendelssohn, and wrote for him a commentary on the last three books of the Pentateuch. Among the strict conformists he stood in high esteem, because he scrupulously observed the Rabbinical laws. But when the Emperor Joseph II. issued his famous Edict of Toleration, and Wessely was consulted on the subject of education by the Community of Trieste, he urged them to improve their system, to develop a higher culture, and teach the Hebrew at the same time as the mother tongue, but defer the Talmud until a maturer age. A storm then broke loose. The Rabbinical party strongly censured him, and there was heated discussion, until finally the Rabbis of Trieste, Venice, Ferrara, Reggio, and elsewhere decided in his favor. Without changing in the least his strict observance of Rabbinical laws, he taught now all the more tenaciously for enlightenment. In 1788 appeared his Sepher Hamiddoth, his "Book on Morals," superb in diction and style, and at last, after some lyrics, his epic on Moses, Shire Tefereth, in five parts, the sixth and last being written in 1829 by M. T Landau, of Prague.

This poem was an awakening for the Jews of the day. No one had imagined that the Hebrew language was capable of being made the medium for such lofty sentiment. That it should possess such a wealth of synonyms, such a smoothness of expression, such poetical power and brilliancy, was not dreamed by those who had associated the Hebrew language with the corrupt Jüdish Deutsch. But Isaiah, David, Ezekiel, Amos, were living voices to Wessely; and his tones couched in their language aroused a genuine revival. It began to be felt that the Talmud was not the only study for the Israelite. The poetical muse was now to be cultivated anew, and both in Hebrew and German Jewish minds were spurred on to worthy rivalry.

In February, 1805, Wessely died in Hamburg, in very needy circumstances, eighty years old. His whole life had been embittered by poverty, but he never faltered in his championship of Hebrew culture and enlightenment. He was gentle and modest in bearing, and loved his fellow-men.

It is suggestive to find that a century ago Wessely, in his "Words of Peace and Truth," addressed to his Austrian brethren at the time of the decree of Joseph II., gave advice which can be reflected upon with profit by his co-religionists to-day in lands where civil and social restrictions have petrified the Jew or converted him into a wandering Bedouin in life and morals. Wessely then said that the great mass of Israelites in Germany and Poland were wholly ignorant of a proper system of education. The grammar of the holy language was entirely unknown, its poetical productions were closed to them. The language of the people among whom they lived was similarly neglected. They knew little or nothing of science, history, ethics. It was jargon and chaos with which they were familiarized; and hence the ideals of Judaism were no longer cherished. The age demanded riper teachers and broader instruction, for it was an age of dawning toleration and liberty, and the Jew was to fit himself for the times in which he lived, and not be satisfied with lingering superstitions.

The purer his faith, the higher must be his education. A century has passed, and yet there are several millions of Jews in benighted lands that have yet to learn that God is not worshiped in a babbling of tongues, and that if their Judaism cannot be reconciled with the higher thought and refinement, the noblest efforts and achievements of a later age, it is so much the worse for their Judaism The age will exist and endure nevertheless. J. M.

To SYNONYMISE—To express the same meaning in different words.

BEDOUIN—A wandering trib e in Arabia who live in tents.

THE HEAVENLY LIGHT.

When Israel to the wilderness
Had fled from Pharaoh's cruel might,
The Eternal sent, to lead them on,
A cloud by day, a fire by night.

And, guided by that heavenly flame,
That beacon from Jehovah's hand,
The chosen people safely reached
Their destined goal, the Promised
Land.

Yet not alone in days of yore
Has God His wondrous mercy shown,
For still He grants to all mankind
A glorious light to lead them on;

A lamp of radiant, glowing hue,
By Israel borne in every clime,
Through fire and flood, through tears
and blood,
With courage grand and faith sublime.

When all the world was steeped in sin,
The Hebrews braved the nation's
wrath
And nobly followed still the guide
That led them on in virtue's path.

That beacon is the Decalogue,
Proclaimed from Sinai's flaming
height,
And burning, as each age rolls by,
With purer, grander, holier light.

Oh, glorious flame! Thy sparkling
beams
With radiant splendor shine to-day,
Nor time, nor change, nor tyrant's
power,
Can quench or dim one holy ray.

Oh, heavenly lamp! Thy light shall shine
Till sin and hate from earth depart,

PART II.—18.

Till wrong shall fail and right prevail.
And justice rule the human heart.

May that bright beacon guide us still,
E'en like God's own, unerring hand,

That we, when this life's storms are
o'er,
May reach with joy the heavenly land

MAX MYERHARDT.

DECALOGUE—The ten Commandments given by God to Moses.

LAZARUS BENDAVID.
[1762-1832 A.]

ABOUT forty years ago one could daily meet, almost at the same hour, in the shady walk, "Unter den Linden," in Berlin, a man of impressive exterior, taking a stroll by himself; his looks always downcast, and seemingly lost in deep meditations. He was of robust but short stature, dressed on all occasions in a suit of gray, and holding his hat in one hand. Rain and snow played unmercifully upon the bald head, and the wind sported with the few gray curls about his temples. His appearance brought everybody to an involuntary standstill, to glance at the venerable old man, with his high forehead and aquiline nose; while the Berlin people, to whom he was known, passed him respectfully, for they considered him a great genius. He was a pupil of Moses Mendelssohn, and afterward became a noted personage in Vienna, where his lectures and the teaching of Kant's philosophy procured him many admirers and friends.

The name of this Jewish savant and philosopher was Lazarus Bendavid, born in Berlin on the 18th of October, 1762. His father, David Lazarus, was a native of Brunswick, and his mother a daughter of J. Hirsch, the largest velvet manufacturer in the Prussian States. When three years old he could read Hebrew with some fluency, and translated a number of Hebrew and French words into German. His mother, a highly accomplished lady, being thoroughly acquainted with French and German, became his first instructor, and in his sixth year a Polish Israelite was engaged to teach him the Hebrew text of the Bible, and, according to the prevailing custom, to impart to him a knowledge of the Talmud as well; but this tutor, not giving entire satisfaction, was soon discharged, and he was sent to his grandfather, a man of talent, with whom he remained till his tenth year. By this time his father had procured him another teacher, also a Pole, who was well liked, possessing more tact; and his instruction comprised beside the Talmud, Hebrew grammar and the Aristotelian logic of Maimuni, of which Moses Mendelssohn had published a new commentary a few years before. After leaving this second tutor he was considered a very fair Talmudist, besides being well acquainted with the original text of the greatest part of the Bible, as well as possessing some knowledge of the Syrian and Arabic languages; he was also well versed in mathematics, French and Latin. His leisure time he spent in playing and reading, never satisfied with one author, or keeping to one and the same subject; but, without guidance or choice, he read indiscriminately the most varied books of his father's library, such as Abulfeda and the Koran, the New Testament and Rousseau's Emil, cabalistic and medicinal books, German poets and Wolf's metaphysics.

But who would believe that this intelligent boy, scarcely thirteen years old, all at once would turn his mind to business? It was, of course, done without the knowledge of his parents, and he now employed himself in selling a few wares from morning till night. In a very short time he had gained many customers, and was in possession of ninety dollars profit. What wealth! But this mode of life ended rather comically, as his own words show:

"I went one morning, a boy twelve years old, of morose aspect, with my package of dry goods and a yard measure under my arm, along Leipzig street, when a baker called me into his shop, inquiring of me whether I could sell him any good velvet; and as I really carried some of first rate quality, I could at once comply with his request. He then wanted to know how long a pair of breeches made of that material would last; to which I replied that it entirely depended upon the fact whether he goes often on horseback or not, and in the latter case they would surely last him four years. 'What!' the baker exclaimed, 'only four years! A pair of breeches made of good velvet ought to last forever.' This made me feel vexed, and being acquainted with metaphysics I commenced demonstrating to him, according to Wolf, that all that has a beginning must have an end, and that there is nothing in the world which is everlasting My baker listened to all this with a very phlegmatic air, then took in the same phlegmatic manner the four corners of the wrapper which contained my goods, and calling out, 'Nonsense! trickery' he shuffled me and my bundle out of doors, where I had the trouble of picking up my things in the greatest confusion. Nothing can describe the effect this insult made upon me; and sobbing like a child I ran to my Polish teacher, related to him what happened, and swore never to venture upon any kind of business again."

This accident caused Bendavid to show great dislike to commercial pursuits, and he accepted a bookkeeper's place with one of his relatives. Here he remained about a year, saving a few hundred dollars, and then resolved upon returning to his studies and becoming a man of letters. With the zeal of a dilettaute he now devoted himself to various scientific studies, and on account of his acuteness of mind it was mathematics especially which occupied his attention. His friend, Marcus, a native of Hamburg, who was then studying mathematics in Berlin, felt astonished at his rapid progress; for in a very short time he was able, without a teacher, to understand Euclid from beginning to end, and not only could he demonstrate every thesis and construe every lesson, but he was also able to quote exactly the number of each theme. Marcus, therefore, took him one day to Lambert, the celebrated mathematician, and after undergoing an examination and hearing that he acquired all without a master, this kind gentleman lent him some books, and assisted him in continuing his mathematical studies. Moses Mendelssohn, too, who had many valuable mathematical works in his library, rendered him assistance in supplying him with books and instruments. But in the midst of his mathematical studies he became acquainted with a Berlin clergyman, who urged upon him not to neglect the study of philosophy, and he began to read with him Des Cartes, Locke and Leibnitz. He owed much to this venerable clergyman, for he was the first who systemized his chaotic knowledge. Besides his scientific studies, to which he applied himself assiduously and regularly from five in the morning until late at night, he now bethought himself of learning a trade, an idea which his friend, the clergyman, had suggested, in order to procure him a livelihood in case of emergency, especially as, on account of being a Jew, he could not hope to fill any public situation.

Like Spinoza he resolved upon becoming a glass-cutter. But where to obtain a master was the next question. Moses Mendelssohn, and the afterward celebrated ichthyologist, Dr. Bloch, took a great deal of trouble to find him a master, in which they at length succeeded by paying a certain sum of money for his apprenticeship. The young scholar made even on the turning-lathe great progress, and soon acquired a perfect knowledge of that trade. But he lacked the requisite patience, and once more he returned to his studies, whereby he forgot all his troubles, for he also had to struggle with the malice of fate, as his parents had become reduced in circumstances. He lost his mother in early life, and he had now to find means to support his aged father and youngest brother. All his privations, however, only prompted him to make still greater efforts in his studies. He commenced with special predilection to study physics and astronomy, the science of a Herschel and Bode, and for that purpose he built himself an observatory. In March, 1785, *Biester's Berlin Monthly*, a periodical to which Mendelssohn, Friedländer and Solomon Maimon were contributors, published his first treatise on the subject, "Are the seven chief colors the simplest?" it being addressed to his friend Marcus, and a year later he wrote upon "parallel lines."

He soon became known in the republic of letters, and the aged Castilian rejoiced in having found a young man who thoroughly understood Euclid, for which he bestowed great praises on him, while the mathematician Kästner, in Göttingen, presented him with the epigrammatic testimonial stating: "Bendavid knows so much mathematics that he can lay claim to any professorship, only not to mine, as long as I am living." With this Kastner, with whom he kept up a constant correspondence, he became personally acquainted a year later, at the time when he published his work upon "Mathematical Infinity," which originated from the lectures he then delivered in Berlin. As companion and tutor to a young Dutch gentleman who was studying medicine in Göttingen, he soon gained the friendship of almost all the professors, and besides Kastner he clung especially to Lichtenberg, with whom he studied physics, but also Michaelis, Burgers, Feders and others befriended him. From there he went to Halle, where he continued his studies, and became intimately acquainted with Eberhard, for whose archives he elaborated the "Principles of Mathematics." Under Eberhard's management the philosophical faculty presented him with the honorable diploma of a Ph.D., an honor which Bendavid accepted in a very indifferent manner. He returned to Berlin and was engaged with Eberhard in publishing a comprehensive philosophical work, when all at once his philosophical convictions took such an opposite turn to those of his friend that they became more divided every day, causing the work which both in common had commenced to be discontinued. Bendavid unexpectedly appeared now as the apostle of Kant's philosophy, which had taken such effect upon him that he is considered, even to this day, one of the earliest who elaborated the philosophy of the great German. Full of ardor for the new philosophy of Kant, he went to Vienna, where he expected to find sensitive minds for the reception of his philosophic views, and in this he was not disappointed. Here it was where his impassioned readings met with the greatest success, where hundreds, composed of all classes, assembled in his lecture rooms, and where he for the first time received that rare pleasure of instilling knowledge in a people desirous of knowledge. Soon his public readings were interrupted, as numerous demands for private lectures were made upon him, and the most eminent men could be found among his pupils. His criticisms on plain reason, on the faculty of judgment, on practical reason, on the metaphysical rudiments of the sciences, on nature, and on the science of law, he published in quick succession for the use of his audience, while there was also no lack of some independent philosophical works. At the country seat of a friend, who resided in one of the most beautiful spots in the neighborhood of Vienna, he wrote, during the summer of 1793, his work, "Essay on Pleasure," in two volumes, one of which he dedicated to his friend Kastner, and the other to Aulic Counselor Herz, in Berlin. Bendavid had now become the fashion in Vienna; he was surrounded by the most eminent and learned men of the place, such as Baron von Retzer, the noble Count of Harrach, "whose mind was stocked with knowledge, and heart filled with humanity." The Prince Lichnowsky and many merchants of the highest standing were

among his pupils; also the poet Aixinger, in whose monthly his
novel, "Ferdinand and Madame Weber," appeared; the philosopher,
Michael Wagner, for whose "Philosophic Anthropology" he wrote
a treatise, and numerous others, too, with whom he was connected
by ties of the most sincere and intimate friendship.

In this manner Bendavid very pleasantly spent his time, but the
success he met with could not last long without raising a few opponents. Some of the professors of the University became envious, and
taking advantage of his liberal views, or, as Bendavid wittingly
observed, of all his attributes as philosophic-Kantish-Protestant-
like Prussian Jew, whom the government already suspected, they
succeeded in having his lectures prohibited, and thus his lecture
rooms had to be closed. His friend, Count von Harrach, immediately offered him a large hall in his own mansion, where he continued his readings for some time longer. But he received soon
afterward a second caution from a high state official, and as this
warning extended to some of his friends, owing to their liberal
views, he resolved upon leaving Vienna and returning to Berlin.
Arriving in his native place, he continued his lectures as well as his
literary activity, partly in works of his own composition and partly
as contributions to different journals of the day. His treatise,
"Philotheos; or, the Origin of our Perception,' was crowned by the
Berlin Royal Academy of Science (1802), but here also he was compelled to discontinue his lectures, because they encroached upon the
rights of the University.

Nearly thirty-five years he passed at Berlin in the society of numerous friends and acquaintances. He was never married, because
he stated that "the choice between simple innocence and guilty
prudence" is too difficult for him. To be independent he prized
above all things, and in the epitaph which he himself had ordered
he thanks God for his independency. He was, however, already an
aged man before he succeeded in becoming exempt from care. He
had employed many ways to obtain a livelihood; for some time he
was occupied as secretary to the Royal Widow Fund; then, during
the French rule, he became editor of the *Hande and Spener Zeitung*;
he also gave instruction in mathematics, and among his numerous
pupils was the afterward celebrated Börne.

His constant watchword was humanity, and nothing but humanity; enlightenment, and nothing but enlightenment; like
most of the disciples of the immortal Mendelssohn, such as Friedländer, Euchel, Linder and others. He attended regularly the
Sabbath meetings, which were held at the house of Mendelssohn,
from which those men sprung who thought with the master, or at
least through him only. They were, as Bendavid styled them, "the
retailers of the wares which they purchased at wholesale in the society of Mendelssohn." But these "retailers" were not satisfied with

a small profit, and wishing to become rich all at once, made such an onset upon their co-religionists that enlightenment received a check and lost much of its strength. These few words, we believe, will show Bendavid's religious worth. We have had enough of that superficial humanity, that false, all-denying liberty, which, as Riesser once observed, "upsets the support as well as the edifice."

Bendavid, indeed, received no proper religious training from his parents, and yet, after passing the day of confirmation when thirteen years old, he became almost a pious man; offering up his daily prayers with great devotion, and with the resignation of a fanatic he strictly adhered to all festivals and fast days. But his fanaticism soon cooled down, and scarcely had he reached his fifteenth year when he gave up all positiveness, while the belief in God, the immortality of the soul and a future state he still clung to, and which his "Moral Proofs of the Existence of God" sufficiently corroborate. Yet he never deserted his co-religionists, for his character, which had its point of gravity in the love of truth, was incapable of any kind of hypocrisy. If he ceased to take active part in their religious worship his interest in his oppressed brethren never rested, and he became their reformer and defender, even when twenty years old. His father died about this time, and as it was his sole desire to labor for the interest and welfare of his co-religionists, he thought it also his duty that he should conform to their rules, even if it were outwardly. So he attended the synagogue, in order to say the usual prayers for his father's soul, according to Jewish custom. For two days he read the prayers before the congregation, but on the third a deputation informed him that on account of his having violated publicly four ceremonial laws, which they named to him, they thought it not right to give him permission to be their reader, and that he should content himself with saying the Kadish to himself. He asked the deputation whether they considered him as belonging to them, or whether they excluded him altogether from the congregation. They replied: "God forbid that we should think so; but —" "Very well, I know what that 'but' is intended for," he answered. "They renounce my society. All right. I give them warning too," and, putting his tephilin together, he departed, never again to enter their synagogue.

This breach was the principal cause why he afterward discontinued living according to certain prescribed formulas, yet his excellent moral and religious character never left him. During his residence in Vienna, when the Emperor Joseph commenced his great work of emancipation and reform, of which the Jews, too, came in for a share, Bendavid immediately urged upon his co-religionists not to be idle in accomplishing their own emancipation, and to this effect he published "Something on the Characteristics of the Jews," wherein he proves that the real faults of his co-religionists originated from their oppressed state, and are the mere faults of slavery. This pamphlet brought him many enemies, his motive being misunderstood, and he was ordered to appear before Cardinal Migazzi, who addressed him in Latin, in the language of a Grand Inquisitor. Bendavid denied that his writings had any reference to the Christian religion, and proved him that the entire accusation rested upon some misunderstanding; whereupon the Cardinal dismissed him.

His next publication, "Inquiries into the Pentateuch," received no better reception then his "Characteristics," and he was obliged to give up the idea of publishing the whole in a complete form. Being the secretary of the Philomathic Society, he delivered a lecture before that institution on the 2d of January, 1812, which, from its tone, caused such excitement among Jews and Christians, that Bendavid states, in his preface to the published lecture, "These gentlemen would have liked to kindle with their heat a little funeral pile, in order to roast me for the honor of God, if they only had one to dispose of." To appease the public he next published "The Religion of the Hebrews before Moses," and it is doubtful whether, in doing so, he did not rather pour oil upon the flame. After this his treatise upon "The Written and Oral Law" followed; also, "The Belief of the Jews in a Future Messiah,' as well as "A Calculation and History of the Jewish Calendar," besides several other similar works. But more important than this side of his activity was his practical zeal for schools and all educational establishments. He was director of the "Society of Friends of Humanity," and his lectures before that body upon "The Instruction of the Jews" are a masterpiece of pedagogical science. In 1806 he undertook the superintending of the Berlin Jewish free school, established thirty years previously by David Friedlander and his rich brother-in-law, Isaac Daniel Itzig, a brother of the renowned Baroness Fanny von Arnstein, of Vienna. For twenty years he managed this charity in the most disinterested manner. Although he had many difficulties to contend with, he spared no sacrifice as long as he could only keep the institution in its proper state, which, owing to his exertions, continued to exist under the most favorable circumstances even after his death.

Bendavid died on the 24th of March, 1832. He was about seventy years old, and his tombstone contains the following inscription, composed by himself: "My name was Eliesor Lazarus Bendavid; God was my help, granting unto me independence, which I aspired after. Blessed be the name of God."			M. KAYSERLING.

Dr. Kayserling, Rabbi in Pesth (Hungary), an eminent scholar and author of various very important historical and theological works.

SAVANT—A man of learning.
INDISCRIMINATELY—Without distinction.
PHLEGMATIC—Dull, cold.
DILETTANTE—One who delights in promoting science, or the fine arts.
THESIS—Something laid down affirmatively or negatively.

ICHTHYOLOGIST—The doctrine of the nature of a fish.
EPIGRAMMATIC—Belonging to epigrams; a short poem terminating in a point.
INFINITY—Immensity.
PHILOMATHIC—Pertaining to the love of learning.

THE RABBI'S BLESSING.

"Why prayest thou not?" said Rabbi
Tarphon once,
As thunders rolled across the eastern
heights,
And lightnings flashed above. "Re-
peat the prayer,
And bless the God who rules the thun-
dercloud."
But quick the Rabbi Jacob made reply:
"Pray, brother, if thou willest, I save
my prayer
When noble deeds resound, and sim-
ple truth
Doth in my neighbor's conduct vivid
shine;
Then praise I God for having made it
so.

In thunder is no greater miracle
Than in the dew-drop or the opening
bud,
Or in an infant's upturned laughing
eyes.
When lightning flashes, bless God, if
it please;
But silence not a benediction brief
When thou shalt see, not transient as a
star,
Which shoots across the desert of the
skies,
But steady as an everlasting sun,
The light of noble purpose crowning
men,
And making human life the happier."
                                   J. M.

MOSES MENDELSSOHN.
[1729-1786 A.]

At the commencement of the eighteenth century there lived at Dessau a so-called Sopher (scribe) and schoolmaster, Mendel by name, an extremely poor but upright man, to whom in September, 1729, a son was born, who received the name of Moses. In the abject poverty of his parents, the chief object they aimed at was to procure for themselves and children the necessaries of life. The father, however, did not neglect his duty in a spiritual point of view, and did his utmost, as far as his limited knowledge would allow him, to advance the education of his son. He instructed him in Hebrew and the Talmud, and whatever the customary education of those times required; but, without being aware of it, he improved hourly his power of mind by every object that came under his notice. The deep impression which everything that was sublime, beautiful and good made upon his susceptible mind, caused the writings of the Old Testament, especially the poetical portion thereof, that grand and striking picture, never failed to influence his unprejudiced youthful heart. Moses was irresistibly attracted by all the writings of the Old Testament, especially the Psalms, which was the chief cause of his soon making an attempt at poetry. But the germinating inclination for poetry was soon suppressed by his proneness for penetrative inquiries, which developed itself in him, and induced him to destroy his poetic undertakings. This inclination showed itself in our Moses already in his youth, when all at once a lucky chance threw into his hands the writings of Maimonides. His "Guide for the Perplexed" soon became the favorite book of the aspiring youth. In later times he always called it the source of all his learning, but he was also obliged to confess that it was the source of his illness,

for it was no doubt the excessive diligence and the incessant thirst
after knowledge, with which he continually read this book, that ultimately brought on a severe nervous disease, from which, although a
recovery was effected, he subsequently suffered from a deformed
spine, and undoubtedly caused his early death.   He sometimes said:
"I must attribute it to Maimonides that my body has become so deformed; he alone is the cause, but I love him nevertheless, for he
has cheered me up in my bitter hours, and has thus amply repaid
that which he deprived me of unintentionally."   But the lot of a
poor Jewish boy of his time, which he had to share in being obliged
for the sake of a livelihood to hawk a few wares, also made his life
a great hardship, for he thus lost the whole of the day in this occupation, and compelling him to make use of the night for study, so
that very often he only extinguished his lamp when already the dawn
of morning began to appear in his miserable chamber.

Mendelssohn remained with his parents till he was fourteen years
of age, but as he had not the least desire to spend his life as a peddler, which was his daily occupation as long as he stayed at home,
he of himself proposed to his parents to try his luck at some other
place.   With feelings of the utmost pain and grief they at length
consented, coming at the same time to the conclusion that their son
would never find an opportunity in his native place to see his ardent
desires for furthering his studies fulfilled.   After a great deal of
consideration they resolved upon sending him to Berlin, on account
of the many acquaintances who, in matters of business, continually
visited that place, and trusting that some one might probably take
an interest in him and find him employment.   He then left his home
and arrived at Berlin in the utmost poverty, unacquainted with the
world, and the acquirements and pretensions of life; besides being
quite uncertain whether he should find here any favor among
strangers, or be enabled to satisfy his thirst after knowledge; while
a still greater obstacle was his debilitated body, which made his
situation the more deplorable, for who indeed would take pity on a
strange, poor, sickly Jewish boy, in order to open for him a path to
knowledge?

Confidence in an all-wise Providence, together with a true and
proper exertion of all faculties, will never disappoint.   Mendelssohn
was aware of this, and his persistent desire after knowledge inspired
him with hope that somebody would take pity on him; thus he
soon found a kind and benevolent Israelite, who took the poor
lost boy under his roof, where he gave him an attic to live in, and
allowed him also to dine at his table a few times every week.   For
the moment he was now right and safe, and his first step was to embrace every opportunity for the attainment of knowledge.   Being
one day informed that the chief Rabbi Fränkel, of Berlin, was the
same who formerly at Dessau was on intimate terms with his parents,

he overcame his natural timidity and went at once to this man, who immediately gave him a very kind reception, and after inquiring into his capacities, promised him that he would do his utmost in helping him to forward his views. He kept his promise, for he soon procured him an opportunity to study the Talmud in a clear and thorough manner, and, in order to assist him in a temporal way, he gave him all his manuscripts to copy, whereby Moses earned now and then a trifling sum, which enabled him at least to procure the most necessary requisites—they were indeed the most urgent, for he but very seldom got any further than procuring for himself a supply of dry bread, and even this he had to use with great economy, for which purpose he generally marked his bread as soon as he bought it, in order to make it last a certain number of days. About this time he had the fortune to meet with a certain Israel Moses, from Starizamose, a small place in Poland, between Krakau and Lemberg, in Galicia, who was then a Jewish schoolmaster in Berlin. This man was quite as poor as himself, but he, in the same manner, struggled hard against the vicissitudes of life, in order to search those truths which stimulate the mind of man. He also had studied Maimonides with great zeal, and conversed with his young friend according to the principles laid down by Maimonides. He gave him a Hebrew translation of Euclid, which soon stirred up an impulse for mathematics, causing the mind of the youth to become more acute and cultivated. A young doctor of medicine from Prague, Kisch by name, advised him to study first, Latin, otherwise he would not be able to read the most important modern books. It took him a long time to save up a sufficient sum to buy a second-hand grammar and lexicon. Kisch gave him daily during six months lessons in Latin, and in a very short time he succeeded, although with great exertions, in being able to read and understand Latin authors. About the year 1748 Mendelssohn became acquainted with a young Jewish doctor, Aron Solomon Gumperz by name, a man possessed of great talent and having an excellent knowledge of medicine, mathematics, philosophy and the modern languages, and who induced him to make himself acquainted with modern literature as well.

In this manner Mendelssohn spent his time, seeking wisdom and knowledge, without any encouragement, except what he drew from himself; even his livelihood was still a very precarious one, till a rich Jewish silk manufacturer, Bernard, took him into his house as tutor to his children, and finding also that he was an excellent penman, arithmetician and bookkeeper, a talent but seldom met with among men of learning, he appointed him in the course of time as overseer, then he became his foreman, and at length partner in the business. During the year 1754 Mendelssohn became acquainted with Lessing, to whom he was introduced as a first-rate chess player. This acquaintance proved the principal step toward the complete cultivation of his genius and the proper application of his rare talents. Lessing himself was thoroughly master of all the sciences, endowed with extensive reading and a perfect knowledge of historic erudition.

Up to this period Mendelssohn had never yet produced anything in German; but being urged to do so by some of his friends, he composed a philosophical dialogue, which Lessing soon ordered to be printed. He also joined his friends in their efforts to cultivate German literature, and he thus appeared as the admired German author, "to whom the German language is greatly indebted for its formation and dignity." This he brought to light by the publication of his chief work, Phædon, or concerning the immortality of the soul, which alone is sufficient to make his name, as long as the German language and philosophy will remain of any value, to be kept in veneration. The work, as soon as it appeared, produced such a surprise, that in a few years it was translated in almost all European languages, and from all sides statesmen and men of learning, theologians and warriors, women and men, flocked to Berlin, in order to make the acquaintance of the author. Neither his learning nor his intercourse with non-Jewish men of so high a standing could induce Mendelssohn to deviate in the least from his paternal religion, to which he strictly adhered till he breathed his last; although there was no lack of allurements, and even public calls made upon him to forsake his faith. But he disdainfully rejected all such summonses, and felt so vexed about it that he became ill and had to suffer several years in consequence thereof. His principal aim was directed toward educating and elevating his co-religionists, and thus his first step for accomplishing his object consisted in the improvement of all Jewish scholastic establishments. He translated the Pentateuch and other Biblical books into pure German for the use of Israelites, and wrote interpretations to the same, or induced his friends under his immediate guidance to do so. As one of the most faithful co-workers in all these excellent exertions, the pious and talented Hartwig Wessely deserves to be mentioned, who like himself took a heartfelt interest in all matters concerning his co-religionists.

Mendelssohn was also a lasting benefactor to his nation, in that he through blameless conduct and unshaken uprightness in his distinguished position destroyed the prejudice so much spread in those times, as if the Jewish character were not at all capable of these virtues. On the day when his funeral took place, every Jewish business house in Berlin was closed, which was generally the case only at the burial of a chief Rabbi; being thus a sure proof of the love he had gained for himself among his nation, who could not show their respect for one of their most eminent teachers in a more suitable manner than in the way they had chosen on this mournful occasion.

Thus we find that for centuries the persecution of the Jews did not cease. Fire and water, sword and rack, have, indeed, made great havoc in their ranks, but nothing was capable of destroying them. They were treated worse than cattle in order to wipe out the impression of divine resemblance; they made use of all possible means to put them to grief intellectually; to extinguish the last spark of modesty and morality; and at length they had recourse to coercive measures to induce them to forsake their God and their divine faith. All these machinations, however, never led their enemies to the object they had in view, but only brought upon the unfortunate Jew the most awful afflictions. The Jew, confined to his Ghetto, separated from the rest of mankind, differed from all other inhabitants of the country in dress, language and custom; and as recompense for his daily sufferings he found consolation in his faith. A remedy to cure the evil was anxiously looked for, but in vain, inasmuch as even the most enlightened minds of that period were full of prejudices against Jews and Judaism. It required, seemingly, some exertions from within, proceeding from the midst of their own body, that should bring the desired succor to their forlorn state. This, then, was only realized when the Mendelssohnian era set in and instilled fresh life into Judaism. But although Mendelssohn and his co-workers labored unremittingly for more than half a century to accomplish the great and difficult task, in seeing their brethren emancipated from the thraldom which beset them on all sides, they, nevertheless, succeeded only partly in their holy cause. The commotions, however, which the year 1848 brought about effected their complete emancipation, placing them in their full rights as citizens, granting them civil and religious liberty—a privilege they were long entitled to. A reaction now and then took place, but it was merely of a passing nature; and time has already sufficiently proved that the just laws thus established have carried rich fruit all over the world wherever Jews have found a peaceable home.

JUD. EHRENTEMPEL.

ELEGY ON THE DEATH OF MOSES MENDELSSOHN.

DARK torrent, Death! thou dismal stream of woe,
Wide o'er the world thy turbid waters flow;
The old, the young—ah! none can flee their doom,
A second Moses hast thou claimed to-day,
And borne him from the shores of earth away —
To God the soul, the dust unto the tomb.

Rest, weary laborer, rest; thy day is o'er;
Thy ardent soul shall toil on earth no more.
Hear, Israel mourns; thy orphan'd people wail,
For, like the prophet with his staff of old,
Thy right hand cleft the rocks, and from their hold
Waters of wisdom poured that ne'er shall fail.

Thy mind aspired, where'er the mind
   dare climb,
To all that is ennobling and sublime;
Thy knowledge was as gold refined
   from clay;
The truths engraven by thy pen divine,
The words that flowed forth from thy
   lips benign,
More soft than oil, than honey sweet
   were they.

The tree is withered, but the fruit remains;
Wrapped in the scroll of deathless
   truth, it gains
New, brighter fame as age succeeds to
   age,
He is not gone; he is not far on high,
His wisdom is the firm, enduring
   tie
That binds us ever to the immortal
   sage.

The great beheld in awe thy works,
   which shone
Fair, clear, and radiant as the sapphire
   stone;
As in a golden cup the sparkling wine.
Presumptuous foes in shame and ter-
   ror fled
When thou didst pour thy vengeance
   on their head—
Champion of Jacob, victory is thine!

Thy light dispelled the terrors of the
   tomb,
Vanished like mist the cold sepulchral
   gloom,
As a dark cloud before the sun it
   passed.
"There is a King, a God above the
   skies,"

The doubter echoed back with glad
   surprise,
And in the hours of morn found peace
   at last.

Yet was thy trust not fixed on thee
   alone ;
"Faith is to me," how proudly didst
   thou own ;
And faith, a fadeless garland, decks
   thy brow.
Oh, would that all might journey thus
   below
Securely by the dark abyss of woe,
Of God and man beloved—beloved as
   thou !

Praise ! sevenfold let praise to thee be
   given,
Who in a living form the word of
   heaven,
The sacred word of life, to Israel gave.
Still hadst thou labored ; yet it might
   not be—
The swift-winged angel came and pillowed thee
Among the slumberers in the quiet
   grave.

Sleep in thy narrow chamber, sleep in
   peace ;
Thy bonds have fallen, thy earthly
   sorrows cease,
To realms of bliss the spirit wings its
   flight.
But when the sleepers shall arise
   again,
Thou, too, wilt come with "Songs of
   David" then,
Servant of God ! robed in celestial
   light.

                                    DR. WESSELY.

PART THIRD.

——o——

SCIENTIFIC AND INSTRUCTIVE.

——o——

" Ein Volk, das man in Feuer,
Und in Wasser bringt hinein,
Muss Dir wieder theuer
Gereinigt von der Sünde sein."

JOST.

———

PALESTINE.

DESOLATE and sad is the present aspect of the Promised Land, but the past and the future make it remarkable to the intelligent of all nations, and to the Israelite sacred. On its soil our ancestors dwelt for centuries; on its soil prophets and holy singers proclaimed the divine words of revelation; on its soil thousands of our ancestry met a heroic death in defence of their faith; upon one of its mountains there twice stood a holy temple full of God's glory and splendor, and to which, once more, all nations shall flock on some future day.

By Canaan, the name mostly used in Holy Writ, is understood that part of Palestine lying westerly from Jordan, including Phœnicia and Philistria; while easterly, from the same river, the land was called Gilead. On the east it approached also the lakes of the Jordan; toward the south it bordered on the southern extremity of the Dead Sea, on the Idumæan mountains, and on stony Arabia as far as the Egyptian brook; in the north the Antelebanon, and in the west the Mediterranean Ocean were the boundaries. From the northern border town Dan, at the foot of Antelebanon, to the southern town, Beer-Sheba, the distance was about one hundred and eighty English miles, while the width measured about sixty English miles.

Palestine is a mountainous country. In the north we find Lebanon and Hermon, two far-extending, lofty and closely-connected mountains, with vast piled-up summits; the former rising rapidly from the seashore till it reaches a height of nearly nine thousand feet, and celebrated for its cedar forests and the uncommon fertility of its slopes and valleys—the picture of all that is grand and beautiful, sublime and commanding. Hermon is even a hundred feet higher than Lebanon, and rises solitary amid a chain of low mountains; it is the far-visible snowy landmark of Syria, and looks down like a venerable old man, the head wrapped in a snow turban, in majestic tranquility upon the country around. Mount Carmel (fruit field) is a continuation of Mount Lebanon, sloping toward the Mediterranean. Upon the mountains rivulets spring forth, which, with their crystal-clear water, irrigate a whole world of vegetation, and also appease the thirst of the wanderer, who is glad to repose here. The solitarily-placed Tabor, five hours southerly from Carmel, rises to a height of three thousand feet, and its flattened top of half an hour's circuit offers a splendid prospect over a large portion of the country. The mountain Ephraim, or Jisreel, extending as far as Jerusalem, includes the mountains Zalmon, Gerisim, Ebal, Shomron, Gaash and Zemarajim. The mountain-chain Jehuda, situated southerly from Mount Ephraim, between the Dead and Mediterranean Seas, is a fruitful landscape, and has many caves, which in time of war served the oppressed as a place of refuge. Part of this mountain-chain includes the Mount of Olives, half an hour from Jerusalem. To the east of Jordan is the mountain-chain Gilead.

But the country has also several extensive plains. The plain of Jisreel, or Esdrelon, so called from the town Jisreel, extending from Mount Carmel to the Jordan, where it leaves Lake Genezaret and, dividing the mountain chain, borders in the north on the Gallilean, and in the south on the Ephramitic mountains; it is irrigated by the waters of Kishon, and celebrated for the battles fought thereon. At present it is called Merdsh ebn Ameri, and is four hours long and eight hours wide. Along the Mediterranean, from Carmel to the Egyptian brook, extends a plain, of which the northern part, from Carmel to Joppa, was called Charon; its beauty and fertility is often praised; low, rocky flats and sandy downs intervene, having excellent vineyards, adorned with white and red roses, daffodils, lilacs, beautiful lilies and odoriferous evergreens. The southern part is called Shephela, a low-lying land, which is but of little fertility. The Jordan meadow, now called El-gour, is in extent twenty-five hours long from Lake Genezaret to the Dead Sea; it is at present very barren, surrounded by mountains, decreasing gradually in size till they reach Jericho, where they recede more, and the valley becomes a wide, fertile plain, noted for its palm and olive trees, balsam and rose bushes.

Real deserts, or any tracts of land untenable for men and refusing all cultivation, could not be met with in Palestine. Those deserts mentioned in Holy Writ—for instance, Jehuda, Tekoa Engedi, Beer-Sheba—are such parts which never received any culture, but, on account of the quantity of grazing land they produced, made excellent pasturage.

At the time when the eye of God still looked down upon Israel's inheritance in mercy, it was a land well irrigated; springs and brooks bubbled forth from hills and valleys; but now it is badly supplied with water. The Jordan (flowing downward) is the chief river of the country. It takes its source from several rivulets, which, with its principal spring, at the southern declivity of Mount Hermon, stand in subterraneous connection in Lake Phialy. After its outlet from Lake Phialy, it disappears under ground and runs thus for three miles, till it appears again by Paneas or Cæsarea Phillipi with great noise, and forms Lake Merom. This, however, is more like a morass than a lake, and is now called Bahrakel Huhlel. The Jordan receives its chief supply from the snow of Lebanon, on account of which it generally overflows in spring, and especially in March and April. After leaving Lake Merom it takes its course rapidly through a mountain pass into Lake Cineret or Genesaret. This pleasant lake, also called the Sea of Galilee, or Lake Tiberias. is three miles long and nearly one and a half wide. It forms one of the most charming parts of the Promised Land. The oval mirror of its dark-blue waters glances clear and brightly through the mountains, and thus the fanciful Oriental called it "The Eye of the Country." On the south, as well as north, it borders on fertile valleys; but in the east and west it is surrounded by hillocks and mountains of beautiful formation. From their steep, picturesque cavities spring forth rivulets in all directions, which flow into the basin of the "Sea of Galilee." Sometimes sudden draughts of air and whirlwinds will break forth from these mountains, setting the peaceable waters in wild commotion, resembling almost the force occasioned by the well-known "Fœhns" of Switzerland. The quantity of excellent fish found in the Galilean Sea is enormous, and the water is pure, cool and sweet; while the bottom, like the shore, consists of fine sand. The climate and soil of the surrounding landscapes are favorable to all kinds of fruit of the South, such as dates, citrons, pomegranates, grapes and melons, as well as for the culture of corn and indigo; and, by greater human exertions, the deep mountain basin of this sea would become a natural hothouse, where the most magnificent plants of Egypt, and even of Arabia, would prosper. Shrubs and thick forests, intermixed with cornfields, surround the northwest shore; like an "Aurora of the deep," flows the rose-colored sea of blossoms of oleander trees over hill and valley. From the bushes the song of thrushes and nightingales resound; and from caves of the rocks of Magdala is heard the voice of wild doves, which by hundreds fly about, making a rich meal of the prickly apple-like fruit of the lotus trees, here very numerous. To this blessed valley of the sea there flocked formerly a large concourse of people for busy intercourse. Prosperous cities and places of industry, with magnificent gardens, fields and forests of fruit trees which bore ripe fruit at any time of the year, surrounded the lake in beautiful alternation, like the costly setting of a rich jewel. More than one thousand two hundred fishermen found a livelihood here; three hundred and fifty vessels—fishing crafts, traveling boats, pleasure gondolas, and ships of burden—crossed this water-mirror in all directions; and thus it became a common place for commerce to all neighboring towns and villages. But now this magnificent landscape mourns like a widow. The forests and vineyards have disappeared from the hillocks; palm, fig and olive trees are but seldom met with; the balsam bush, which formerly with its verdure environed the sandy and gravelly shore of the lake, are nowhere to be found, and, instead of those hundreds of vessels, there is at present only now and then a solitary boat with her white sail to be seen passing through the mirror of the quiet waters, in order to fetch wood from the eastern coasts of Tiberias; and, in place of the fisherman, the pelican carries on its business in solitude.

As if tarrying in its course, the Jordan flows into the Dead Sea, the largest of the seas in the valley of the Jordan, surrounded by steep mountain walls from 1,500 to 2,500 feet in height, which on both sides skirt the shore, and especially on the west, with their deep crevices and narrow passes, presenting a very gloomy and desolate aspect; and thus the valley-basin is sunk 1,337 feet beneath the level of the Mediterranean Sea. This inhospitable lake is four to five hours wide, and about twenty hours long form north to south, and has therefore, on account of being exposed to the cloudless beams of a southerly sun, a climate and vegetation the same as Egypt. It is nearly to half its contents penetrated with salt, and therefore the water becomes heavy, quiet and scarcely stirred by wind—a perfect picture of death; and at the same time it has a bitter taste and is not transparent. No fish nor any kind of water-animals or sea-plants can exist therein, and its weight prevents man from sinking in it. Having no outlet, the water evaporates only from the heat of the sun, causing, however, no unhealthfulness, and covers thus the whole shore with a salt crust, upon which no green plants can grow. Only birds of prey, doves and swallows make their nests upon the surrounding rocks and enliven the sad wilderness. On the west side, nearly in the midst of it, lies the only place, Egedi, at the foot of an unusually steep pass, which from the south leads in zigzag along a steep rock to the top of the mountain, where a beautiful spring, which being once well supplied with palm and balsam trees, made this place a splendid oasis in the midst of a rocky desert. In the southerly part of the sea a small peninsula enters from the east, which is two hours wide, and owing to this circumstance a bay is formed at the south end of the shores, which are easily and very often inundated. Here was once the valley of Siddim, rich in water, beautiful and fertile like the Garden of the Lord (1 Mos. xiii: 10; xiv: 3.), with springs of a resinous substance, which are still to be found at the bottom of the sea (1 Mos. xiv: 10); here the towns of Sodom, Amora, Adma, Leboin and Zoar were situated. The weather in Palestine is less changeable than with us. There are indeed but two seasons. The winter begins in October with rain (early rain), and in December and January changes into snow, which easily melts away, and thereupon till the middle of April the late rain follows. The summer from the end of April is noted for hot weather, gradually increasing, a clear sky, dryness and a strong night dew. The regularity of the weather, the productive soil (consisting of clay and marl), and the extraordinary diligence of the inhabitants, made Palestine exceedingly fertile. It was rich in garden and field fruits, in forests containing tare-binth and oak trees, in excellent pastures, especially to the east of the Jordan, in oil and vineyards; and, upon the mountains, in balsam plantations; in Gilead, in palms, pomegranates, figs and other costly fruit; and there was not a month in the year which was without new fruit and flowers. The forests contained quantities of eatable game, and the waters abounded with fish. In minerals there was especially found limestone, clay, asphalt, mineral salt and sulphur, all of the very best quality; while metals in general were rather scarce, owing to the art of mining being but little carried on. The productiveness of Palestine, although sometimes visited by locusts, earthquakes, very hot east winds and inundations, was the cause, even three hundred years before the Israelites took possession, of the land being already covered with towns and villages, and the population also, before the Israelitish period, was very large.

But at present the traveler finds the country gloomy and disheartening. Agriculture, in less populated districts, lacks able and willing hands; besides, it is necessary to protect each harvest against the depredations of robbers. Commerce is insignificant, while there is great want of public roads, bridges, regular mails and accommodation for travelers. The arts and sciences are not in the least fostered, trades are still carried on in the olden style, and but few modern improvements can be met with. Splendid ruins put one in mind of the fallen greatness of former times; everywhere you behold, instead of the great bustle which in times past prevailed here, nothing but desolation and dullness. But the day will come when in the towns of Judah, and in the streets of Jerusalem, the voice of gladness and joy shall be heard again, and the desolate road to Zion will become lively from pilgrims singing new songs unto the Eternal.   L. STERN.

MONTEFIORE.

Oh, champion in thy Kentish home,
　Girt by the rushing sea,
Which rolls to every clime on earth,
　Glad praises sung of thee.

We dwellers on the Atlantic coast,
　Three thousand miles apart,
O'er breeze and billow reach across
　The offering of our heart.

We weave for thee no chaplet rare,
No lofty hymn we raise;
Thou claimest not the laurel-crown,
Thou seekest not our praise.

Let kings and statesmen on this day,
Their greetings send to thee,
From Europe, Asia, Afric's shores
A glad fraternity.

We, dwellers on American soil,
Fling flowers at thy feet,
Culled from the gardens of our hearts,
With love's own fragrance sweet.

The rapid years upon thy head
Have scattered wintry snows,
But deep within thy noble soul
How warm thy nature glows!

Oh, lofty soul, with childlike faith,
Strong, steady, calm and sure,

Thy tender heart and bounteous hand
Forever shall endure!

Thy name shall pass from land to land,
Thy deeds from tongue to tongue,
Thy virtues form inspiring texts
For aged hearts and young.

A noble life, a simple faith,
An open heart and hand ;
These are the lovely litanies
Which all men understand.

These are phylacteries of grace,
Though hidden to the view,
Which bind in sacred brotherhood
Christian, Turk and Jew.

The cries of creeds recalcitrant
On every side are sown ;
But no age is degenerate
Which claims thee as its own.

ABR. S. ISAACS.

DR. ABR. S. ISAACS, editor of the *Jewish Messenger*.
KENT—The County of Kent, England, in which the town of Ramsgate, where Sir Moses resides, is situated.
CHAPLET— A wreath.
LITANY—A form of supplicatory prayer.

RECALCITRANT— Obstinate.

EGYPT,

AND ITS CONNECTION WITH OUR NATIONAL HISTORY.

THE invention of railroads and steamboats has rendered it much easier for travelers to reach and examine Egypt than formerly; and I hope by the aid of their testimony to be able to explain to you how it is that we are beginning to find out that the connection of this wonderful Egypt with us Israelites, with Moses, and with a religion God taught him to teach us and the world, continues to this day, and that from Egypt we can still gather proofs of its truth, holiness and beauty ... The extreme productiveness of the soil accounts for the very frequent intercourse, to which the Bible testifies, between Mizraim and Palestine. Abraham, with Sarah, his wife, "went down thither" when there was "a famine that was grievous in the land," "and thence Sarah took her handmaiden, Hagar, who became Abraham's wife and mother of Ishmael, for whom, in her turn, she took a wife among the Egyptians." To Egypt went Abraham's grandson, Jacob, with his sons, "when the famine was sore in all lands," of which the disastrous consequences were averted by the judgment and foresight with which the God of Israel had inspired the agent of His divine mercy, the Jewish captive, Joseph. It was this very fertility which directed the steps of our chosen race to a land where abundant sustenance could be afforded them during the four hundred and thirty years "of their sojourn therein," and of their numerical increase, from a family of seventy, to a people numbering 400,000.... The recent traveler, Brugsch, affirms that portraits of the descendants of the Phœnician settlers differ greatly from those of the original Kopts, and this furnishes a strong historical ground on which the entrance and departure of the Israelites are based. Further evidence, according to the same authority, in the second edition of his learned works, has been obtained of the elevation of Joseph as Adom, or lord of the country. With this evidence before us, we can but deplore that several of those occupied during the last twenty years in Egyptian researches were in such haste to make known what they believed to be the outcome of their labors, that they were led to declare that outcome to be the absence of confirmation of the Biblical story of Joseph, and even of the existence of Moses.

Brugsch Bey, however, has discovered an inscription containing a remarkable confirmation of the Biblical narrative. It concludes with these words: "I collected corn, a friend of the God of Harvest. I was watchful at the time of sowing, and as there were several successive years of famine, I distributed corn in the town at every scarcity...." There is, besides, a most remarkable representation sculptured on the walls of the tomb of Khnumkept, in which certain Amu, or Semetic foreigners, are depicted arriving at his court, and being ushered into his presence. So striking a resemblance does this bear to the arrival of Jacob in Egypt, it has been deemed by some to be a picture of that event. The number of persons mentioned is not the same as of those who accompanied Jacob, and, therefore, others have doubted its representing that scene. The men are depicted as draped in long garments of various colors and wearing sandals, unlike those of the Egyptians. The features of these strangers resemble those of those Jews. The dress of the chief, named Abusha, is richer than that of his companions, and is ornamented with a fringe, and a meander round the neck; in his left hand he holds a short stick or crook, and with his right he offers a he-goat; seven others follow with their asses and their children.

On his death-bed, at the close of his long life, Joseph uttered these remarkable and trustful words, which form the concluding passage of the book of Genesis: "And Joseph said unto his brethren, I die; and God will surely visit you and bring you out of this land unto the land which he sware unto Abraham, to Isaac, and to Jacob." "And Joseph took an oath of the children of Israel, saying, 'God will surely visit you, and ye shall carry my bones from hence.'" "So Joseph died, being a hundred and ten years old, and they embalmed him, and he was put in a coffin in Egypt." After this event the stone-cut chronicles of the Egyptian tombs, and the written rolls, com-

posed of the leaf of papyri, and found in different places, are all
equally silent concerning the children of Israel during their continued sojourn in the land of Goshen, a period of 300 years. That
silence is first broken in reference to the stirring incidents preceding
and connected with the birth of Moses, and with the marvelous
events of which he was destined to be the God-chosen hero. But,
although no contemporary records have reached us of those three
centuries, we have abundant subsequent evidence of the powerful
influence exerted on the captives by the habits, manners, arts, attainments, customs and religion of the people among whom they were
condemned to dwell. When the curtain closed on the existence of
Joseph and his descendants, we quitted them as simple shepherds,
tending their sheep, believing wholly in the faith of Abraham,
Isaac and Jacob.

And we must briefly examine what were those manners, customs,
arts and religious notions, in order that we may comprehend the
changes in their nature and circumstances with which our great
Lawgiver had to contend. As we have already seen, the Egyptians
displayed great skill in sculpture and architecture. They possessed
an extensive literature, and to them the invention of the art of writing
appears to be due. The dress of the Egyptians was various; persons of high rank wore garments of fine linen, having sleeves, and
reaching to the ankles. The ornaments worn by both sexes were
nearly the same; coral, rows of beads, and chains of gold around the
the necks, armlets and bracelets of gold, inlaid with lapis lazuli and
turquoise, around the arms, and anklets of the same around the
ankles. Earrings were worn by women only; but both sexes loaded
their fingers with rings, some of which were used as signets.

Turn we now to the second great connecting link between the
early Hebrew and Egyptian annals—Moses. The very few brief and
salient points which I have just brought to your attention will make
it clear to you that the influence exerted by them on our ancestors
is no timaginary, though the fact of the Hebrews living apart "in the
best of the land," Goshen, secured to them the continued exercise of
their calling as shepherds, and the memory and use of their original
national language. We find that the unexplained divine command,
"Demand of the Egyptians jewels of silver, and jewels of gold and
fine raiment," was easily met; for, as we have just seen, these formed
part of the people's common apparels. And, as we are further told,
"the Lord gave the people favor in the eyes of the Egyptians, and
they spoiled the Egyptians," since they gladly divested themselves
of their ornaments, to free themselves from the trials to which they
felt, in the visitation of the ten plagues, the presence of the children
of Israel had exposed them. The arts thus learned from the Egyptians enabled the Hebrews to execute the previously unrevealed
divine purpose, for which the hitherto slaves denuded their masters;

for these very spoils furnished the materials for the erection and ornamentation of the Tabernacle, destined to be the national place for the worship of the Most High. Thus the arts learned from the Egyptians were exercised by those whom the sacred writings declare—"He hath filled with wisdom of heart, to work all manner of work, of the engraver and of the cunning workman, and of the embroiderer in blue and in purple, in scarlet, and in fine linen, and of the weaver, even of them that do any work, and those that devise cunning work."

Amid all this circumstantial evidence, with which the pages of the Pentateuch teem, it would seem impossible that the mere fortuitous circumstances of the non-discovery of the name of Moses should have caused any doubt of his having lived in Egypt to arise. Still more incomprehensible is it that a like doubt of his prophetic power having been given him by God himself could have subsisted, in presence of the testimony afforded by our dispersions, among all nations of the earth, as Moses foretold three thousand years ago, in the twenty-eighth, twenty-ninth and thirtieth chapters of Deuteronomy. But I think it not unlikely you may have heard that such a school of doubters among Egyptiologists did arise about twenty years since, among whom (I regret to add) the names of more than one of our own race were to be found. When referring to the connection of the two peoples being a permanent fact, I felt it would be my duty, before I close my address this evening, to place before you the results of the latest Egyptian researches, in the very words in which they were made known by the excavator and translator himself, Brugsch Bey, by the publication in German, last autumn, of a ponderous volume containing the narrative of this lengthy and laborious researches among Egyptian monuments and papyri. These are his words: "Directed by an order from His Highness, the Khedive of Egypt, to come to London, in order to represent his country at the International Congress of Orientalists, the desire of this Prince was, that I might communicate to the enlightened public in England, who interest themselves in Biblical questions, the results of my last researches on the sojourn of the Hebrews in Egypt. I have chosen for my theme their exodus from Ramses to their arrival at Elim. My researches were founded on the geographical indications of Egyptian monuments contemporary with the time of Exodus. I have arrived at the following conclusions, which I consider unquestionable: 1. That the town of Ramses differs in no way from the town of Zoan, which is spoken of in the Bible as the place where Moses performed the miracles before the Pharaoh of his time. 2. That the town of Pithon, likewise mentioned in the Bible, was the chief town of the adjoining district. 3. The third station, called in the Bible Ethom, bears the name of Hethom in the Egyptian texts. 4. From Hethom the Hebrews turned to the north and then arrived at Migdol, which was the fourth station. Setting out from Migdol the Hebrews encamped between Migdol and the sea, *i. e.*, the Mediterranean, opposite the Baal-Zephom."

As Pharaoh and his army pursued the Hebrews on the isthmus, between the sea and the lake of Sirbonis, they were swallowed up by the abysses of that sea. Once arrived at Mount Kasios, the eastern frontier of ancient Egypt, where "the way of the Philistines begins," the Hebrews traversed the desert to Marah, "where the water was bitter.' These are the bitter water lakes of our days. The sixth station, Elim, called in Egypt Alem, is to the north of the Red Sea. All these indications exactly correspond in Egyptian and in Hebrew. No student can separate them from one another or alter the site now fixed once for all.

Papyri inform us, likewise, that the Hebrews occupied during their sojourn in Egypt the districts of Ramses and of Pithon; that they were compelled to build certain constructions in both these towns, until Moses delivered them " out of the house of their bondage." The name of Moses, in Hebrew Moshé, is to be found in a place called "Isle of Moshé," which is situated on the right border of the Nile.

I have purposely deferred to the close of my address to bring before you the subject most important, most enduring, and, I may add, most disastrous in its influence on the Israelites. I refer to the idolatry of the Egyptians. Their religion was chiefly connected with the adoration of the sun and moon, with which were also associated deities too numerous, and a system of idolatrous worship too complicated, to admit of explanation this evening. To each of their gods and goddesses (some of whom were represented with human, some with animal's heads) a particular animal was dedicated. Ossiris and his wife, Isis, were after the sun and moon, the universal god and goddess of Egypt. The *bull* was the animal sacred to the sun and moon, and, in one temple, a *cow*.

If we consider that for 300 years the Hebrews had had no teacher of religion among them, no place of worship of the One God of Abraham, Isaac, Jacob and Joseph, instead of our surprise and condemnation being elicited by the first outbreak of idolatry which found voice, when a section of the people demanded that Aaron should make for them the god to which they were accustomed, the golden cow or calf of the vale of Sinai, we ought rather to experience admiration for the strong national feeling which bound the Israelites in the bond of their Abrahamic descent, and to recognize with prayerful gratitude that God was indeed "with Moses." We ought to see that it was the guiding hand of the Lord which enabled him to rule the hosts, but just emerged from the darkness of Egyptian bondage, to lead those who had reveled in the "flesh pots of Egypt," as houseless wanderers through the pathless wilderness, to the borders of that land which he was permitted to see, but not to enter. That this Moses, who (as Josephus tells us, on the testimony of Manetho, the Egyptian historian) was learned in all the learning of the Egyptians; that he had dwelt in the palace, and that he had, moreover, married the daughter of an Egyptian priest ; that this Moses had cast out of his mind all the religion, and all the false gods with which from his childhood upward it must have been filled ; that his life's thought and purpose were to execute his Creator's mission--is, indeed, incontrovertible proof that he had held spiritually direct communion and received direct inspiration and revelation from the Most High.

Those generations who followed him relapsed again and again, sovereigns and people, into the idolatry from the practice of which he ever sought to shield his beloved race. Yet this idolatry has shown itself still, amid all the boasted civilization of modern history, in various forms, and in many lands. Idolatry it was which armed the hands of the Crusaders in the bloody struggle for the possession of the so-called "Holy Sepulcher." Again, it was idolatry which, a century ago, in the time of Catherine of Russia, constituted the first phase of this fatal "Eastern Question." Once more, it is an idolatrous worship of a name in lieu of the thing which it is said to represent, that has enabled a cruel and despotic ruler to win approval and sympathy, even though but from a handful of the subjects of our high-minded and beloved Queen. An idolatry it is which has formed the hollow pretext for a fierce and aggressive struggle, carried on amid the groans and sufferings of victors and vanquished, in the blood-stained fields of Turkey.

For our great Lawgiver and Prophet, we had no " holy place " to guard. At His unknown grave we had, as says the Irish bard, but to

" Weep for him, the man of God,
  In yonder vale he sank to rest,
But none of earth can point the sod
  Which flowers above his sacred breast.
    Weep, children of Israel, weep !

His doctrines fell like Heaven's rain,
  His words distilled like Heaven's dew;

Oh ! ne'er shall Israel know again
  A chief to God and her so true.

Remember ye His parting lays,
  His farewell song by Jordan's tide,
When full of glory and of days,
  He saw the Promised Land and died.
    Weep, children of Israel, weep.''

Thus, my friends, I have, you will admit, proved the assertion with which I set out. Chronicles cut in the dark stone catacombs of Egypt 3,000 years ago, but only even now unearthed by the hand of the excavator, give their silent but imperishable testimony (one, however, which the diligent Bible student needs not) to the fact that the immortal agent of God's beneficent dealing with men—Moses— did live and work in the land. For assuredly the sacred and world-wide festival which we have just celebrated is in itself enough to prove that we were in, and came forth from, Egypt. Yet more, it should suffice to awaken in us all—men and women, youths and maidens, rich and poor, gentle and simple, learned and unlearned—the high resolve to fulfill throughout all time, and in all places, the task which he, Moses, bequeathed unto us ; to be God's laborers, His witnesses, His priests, to keep the holy places which He has given us to guard, hands with which to do justice, hearts with which to love mercy, spirits with which to walk humbly, souls to keep undesecrated sanctuaries, for the sole worship of the One Living God, at whose behest Moses called unto us, " Hear, O Israel, the Lord our God, the Lord is One."   M. A. GOLDSMID.

Miss M. A. Goldsmid, sister of the late Sir Francis Goldsmid, a lady of great culture, translator of the well-known French publication "The Deccides," author of several other works, and noted for her unremitting interest in the religious and moral training of the poorer class of her co-religionists.

MEANDER—Maze; labyrinth.
LAPIS LAZULI—A stone of an azure or blue color.
TURQUOISE—A blue stone among the meaner precious stones.
SALIENT—Leaping, bounding.
TO DENUDE—To strip, to make naked.

FORTUITOUS—Accidental; casual.
KHEDIVE—Title of the chief ruler of Egypt; vice-royal.
INCONTROVERTIBLE—Not to be disputed.
PHASE—Appearance.
BARD—A poet.

KIBROTH HATTAVAH.

NUM. xi: 31; Ps. cvi : 15.

Upon the sacred page that tells,
    With mingled grief and song,
The tale of Israel's journeyings drear
    Arabia's wilds among,

Are stories that we sometimes read
    With careless heart and cold,
But which the quickened spirit sees
    In characters of gold.

And chiefly now my mind recalls,
    Among these ancient tales,
How, in the wilderness, God fed
    The lusting Jews with quails.

The mighty hand and stretched out arm
    They had not learned to trust;
God's anger smote them while they ate;
    Theirs are the graves of lust.

Some unknown bard long after tried,
    Following the poet-king,
To set their chronicles to song
    For temple choirs to sing.

He wrote—some bitter memories
    Perchance lit up their scrolls—

"God gave them their request, but sent
    Leanness into their souls."

But those rebellious Jews are not,
    On Time's close-written rolls,
The only men that had their wills,
    With leanness in their souls.

He that believes shall not make haste—
    And herein lies our crime;
We strive for pleasure, fame and wealth,
    And cannot wait God's time.

His blessing makes His people rich,
    Nor sorrow adds withal;
While earth's best joys of Him unblest,
    To memory are as gall.

O God ! whose witness in our hearts
    Is that we turn to Thee;
Help us to trust Thee, that we may
    Thy faithful children be.

Could we so trust, we could not tire,
    Nor faint upon the road;
Fed, like the Jews, with angels' food—
    Our Guide, the mighty God !
           ADAPTED.

THE TEN COMMANDMENTS.

I.

Time and again it has been said that the revelation on Sinai, the ten words, or Decalogue, as recorded especially in Ex. xx., is the central doctrine of Mosaism, as well as the base of human civilization. Let us closely look at these Ten Commandments. Why are they of that paramount importance? Why have they become the patrimony of mankind? Under what circumstances, and with what aim have they been revealed?

A horde of laborers, sprung from an illustrious stock, but degraded by oppression, led by the greatest of prophets, the grandest legislative genius of antiquity, left, under the most arduous difficulties, now nearly 3,200 years ago, the country of their bondage, the then powerful Egypt. That host was to be converted into a nation, an everlasting, spiritual and monotheistic nation, or "kingdom of priests and holy people," at a time when all the surrounding tribes were ephemeral, coarsely material, and given to sensual idolatry. To be created, that nation needed, before everything, laws, morality and order; the ideas of right and sympathy, instead of physical force and selfishness, were to change the horde of laborers into a "kingdom of priests and holy nation," into a people where man and woman, young and old, high and low, shall be their own priests, their own mediators and intercessors with their Father in heaven.

That horde was, therefore, led to the vast and majestic Arabic desert, to the picturesque peninsula of Sinai. There they witnessed that grand and solemn divine act, the revelation on Sinai, memorable for all time under the most awful and tremendous phenomena of nature, only exhibited in those tropic latitudes; the terror inspiring outbreak of volcanoes; the lightning rending and wonderfully illumining the atmosphere; the crush and roar of tropic thunder storms pealing to the skies, majestically vibrating in the hundred ravines and hollows of the mountainous and craggy Sinaitic peninsula. All that re-echoed in the hearts of a whole people, standing around, trembling with holy awe, and awaiting their own salvation and the fate of their far future from that solemn hour. The deep waters of the Red Sea recoil in awe; the vast plains of the Sahara suspend their monotony; the imposing cataracts of the Nile interrupt their dashing and roaring falls; the innumerable tribes of Western Asia and Arabia, of Kush and Mizraim, forget their eternal wars. They all gaze at the spectacle on Horeb. Nature is in travail; she begets the nation of the spirit. Israel is coming to light; the skies are rent asunder. The holy angels stand in majestic array, chanting in eternal chorus, "Holy, holy, holy, the Lord, the Eternal Zebaoth; full of His glory is all the universe." The *Shechina* is descending on the summit of high Horeb, and there stands the grand prophet, Moses; rapt in silence he is awaiting the inspiration of the Most High. Kneel down, peoples of earth; fall prostrate, mortals! Lo, spirit is marrying matter! God is in common with men.

II.

"I am the Eternal, thy God, who has brought thee forth from the land of Egypt, the house of bondage. Thou shalt have no other gods before me." (2 M. xx: 2.)

Anochi, I. God is one, not two, as the contending principles of good and evil of the doctrine of Zoroaster; not three, as that of ancient Brahminism and later Christianity; not the four elements, not the many planets, not the entire physical world. The divine principle is Unitarian; no dualism, trinity, polytheism or pantheism. *Anochi, I am.* God is the Supreme Being, the eternal essence, the unchangeable and unextinguishable life of all existence, the cause, creator and preserver of the universe. *Anochi, I am.* God, the essence of all existence, the reality of all phenomena, is yet purely spiritual; he is self-conscious, all-intelligent and absolutely free. He is not the world itself, nor its order and harmony, nor its immutable law. This universe is God's free creation, not His necessary part. Thus no materialism and no Spinozism. *Anochi.* God is the living self-existence, not a mere abstraction of all the conscious intelligence of mankind. No Hegelianism! As a ray emanates from the sun, but is not the sun himself; as a drop of water is of the same nature as the ocean, yet not the ocean itself, even so are the free-will, the moral and the intellectual faculties of man, rays from the Godhead, but no entire God himself. Man and the world are resting in the lap of the great I Am, but He is not absorbed by the human intelligence. *Anochi, Adonaj.* I am the Eternal, the everlasting Being. God is uncreated, not composed of parts or persons, and not decomposable; hence a strictly and vigorously elementary Being, where birth and death are inadmissible—in contradistinction with Christianity.

Elohacho. He is also Elohim. The force, the innate essence of matter, as all the aggregate forces of nature, reside in Him. He penetrates, invigorates and preserves nature, as the heat of the sun is pervading and vivifying the plants. *Elohacho.* This is the God of Israel. Mankind's Lord is Israel's Lord too. Hence no national deities, no polytheism. "Who brought thee out of the land of Egypt?" He is a God of liberty. He breaks the chains of the captives and punishes tyranny. "Thou shalt have no other gods before me,' for there are none. The God of Israel is the Lord of mankind. He is enthroned on Moriah, and earth and heaven are but his footstool. "Make not unto thee any graven image or any figure." He being a pure spirit He cannot fitly be represented by any material object. Being all, He cannot be figured by a part. Being eternal, He cannot be imaged by anything final. In order to avoid idolatry there shall not be any material symbolizing of the Deity. The spirit shall be comprehended by the spirit, not by the senses.

"Utter not the name of the Eternal, thy Lord, in vain." The life, course and essence of all existence is the most sublime and most exalted conception of man. Hence, when in His presence, when in His temple, it shall be for the sake of prayer and instruction, for communion with Him, not for mere habit and imitation, pastime or fashion.

"Remember the Sabbath day for keeping it holy." Do remember it, brethren. Alas! you forget it but too often. For six days shalt thou work and provide for thy bodily wants, but the seventh day is a solemn rest, to be consecrated to the Eternal. That day is the patrimony of the mind; it shall be set apart for spiritual culture. Drudges as we are during the week days, we recognize on the Sabbath our noble birthright; we are rehabilitated into our human dignity. Hence is Sabbath-breaking a crime toward ourselves; it is a moral suicide.

"Honor thy father and thy mother." Honor and cherish, ye young ones; obey and respect your parents, who represent to you God on earth. They are your earthly providence from your very existence. You owe them your being, your education, your happiness. They sacrifice everything for you. They work and toil; they live and die for you; they sustain and educate, love and cheer you. You are their visible immortality, their hope and joy in the life to come. There are dangerous encroachments upon this commandment in our good America. How often does not liberty degenerate into license! What a tendency to be careless toward parents! What impatience at control! Remember, the noblest trait of the Jewish character, since times immemorial, has been the intimacy, the tenderness between the family members; the veneration, the implicit obedience of children toward their father and mother, and kindred. Let not, young Israel, this noblest laurel of Jewish family life be lost to you. Honor, cherish and reverence your parents on earth as you do your Father in heaven.

"Commit no murder, no adultery, no theft." Respect the life of thy fellow-man, the dignity and chastity of the family, and the prosperity of thy neighbor. These are the pillars of society. Upon them depends the salvation of the individual and of the State. "Bear no false witness against thy neighbor." Let never untruth pollute thy lips. Let sincerity, fairness and urbanity prevail among men. "Covet not thy neighbor's house, or his wife, or his property." Have no desire for anything not thine. Be pure and chaste even in thought, that thy deeds may ever be correct. The State punishes only bad acts; God forbids evil thoughts too.

This is an abrupt outline of the great and salutary principles

enunciated by the revelation of Sinai. You see these *ten words* bear
upon the whole man, as an individual, a member of the family and
of the State. This short and succinct expounding proves the Decalogue plainly to embody the entire essence of Jewish religion, as
well as all the chief features of human civilization. The more you
reflect, the riper you meditate, the wider will these words expand in
importance and comprehensiveness, till they simply become world-
wide.

The voice that resounded on Sinai, say our sages most profoundly,
was split and listened to in undertones and in seventy languages. This intimates that the Decalogue widens and deepens
in meaning and significance, the riper, the more profound and the
more exalted the expounder. Thus the ten words, the few verses
of Exodus xx., especially termed the revelation of Sinai, produced,
in the successive centuries, the Pentateuch, the prophets and the
holy writers; next the Mishna, the Gemara, the Cabala, and the
present modern phase of Judaism; next Christianity and Moham-
medanism, and in general the present civilization. On the other hand,
suggests again our Rabbinical saying, the Ten Commandments were
delivered not only to the Hebrews, but to mankind. To every
human being the doctrine of the existence of God, the Sabbath,
the respect to parents, the sacredness of life, matrimony and property, veracity and chastity, etc., is audible in every one's own
tongue, in the Horeb of our own hearts and consciences. Thus the
great doctrine of Israel is not dogmatic; no, it is self-evident; it
has been delivered, and is daily being repeated in the seventy human
tongues composing the civilized portion of mankind, in the Rabbinical metaphor.

And all the myriads of Jacob's house were present at the grand
scene. They beheld, trembling with awe, the thunder pealing, and
the lightning flashing, and the noise of the Shofar, and the holy
Horeb enveloped in azure clouds. "And the people together, as one
man, exclaimed, 'Whatever the Eternal has spoken we will perform.'" And all man's moral nature, indeed, entire mankind, and
even posterity, responded Amen.

III.

From that time on, until this very day, each generation of Israel
has subscribed to the Ten Commandments by exclaiming, as at
Horeb our sires did, "Whatever the Eternal has spoken we
will perform." This became the war-cry of our ancestors during
thousands of years and on a thousand battlefields; at whatever cost,
and whatever sacrifice, we shall not waver, and not hesitate, in spite
of all obstacles. March on, Israel, and no surrender, thou people
of the Decalogue! When, at the fatal battle of Waterloo, in 1815,
relates history, the French army was defeated and summoned to
surrender, the Imperial Guard answered: "The Guard dies, but

does not surrender." We, Israelites, had one hundred Waterloos in our career, and as the Swiss Guard of the Decalogue our ancestors responded: "Israel dies, but does not surrender. Whatever the Eternal has spoken we will do." During the long centuries of the first Temple our sires were enveloped, as with a brazen wall, by Paganism, and continually menaced to be swallowed up by the thousand-fold enemy. But they stood their ground, answering: "Whatever the Eternal has spoken we will do." Trinitarian Christianity, then, the Roman Pontiffs, threatened Israel with the hatred of rivalship and family feud. But our sires answered: "No surrender." ....Mohammedanism then made its appearance; first as a friend and ally, but soon as a bloody enemy, making a war of extermination upon our people, who yet did not yield, shouting: "The Guard dies, but does not surrender."

The seventh and thirteenth centuries came, when the Crusaders hastened to Jerusalem to conquer a grave; but before fighting the Saracens they let loose their fury against the inoffensive and defenceless Jews, giving them the choice between death and apostacy. They died with the old war cry. The fifteenth century appeared, and Spain and Portugal exhibited for the first time the immense tragedy of expelling, on account of religion, a million of Jewish subjects, who mournfully left their beloved homes, crying: "No surrender." The sixteenth century saw the same heartrending spectacle repeated over in England, France and Germany. Hundreds of thousands turned their weeping eyes to Poland, the Lower Danube and Turkey, yet defiantly shouting: "Whatever the Eternal has spoken we will do." In the seventeenth century the remainder of the Spanish and Portuguese Jews yet living in their old homes, under the mercies of the Inquisition, as the so-called new Christians or Marranos, were hunted up and discovered by those spiritual bloodhounds, and again placed between horrid death and apostacy. The Marranos answered: "The Guard dies, but does not surrender." In the eighteenth century Europe felt tired of killing and plundering on account of religion, but inaugurated the policy of pressing our fathers into the Ghetto, and excluding them from every honorable career. Yet Israel was not shaken in his constancy; submitting to everything but apostacy. The nineteenth century is soon past, but this war-cry is not silenced. Listen! The heroic shout re-echoes— there from Romania; here from Russia; now from Morocco, and again from Persia. Our brethren are required to abjure their faith, or be exiled and starved. And they, too, keep firm their banner with the old motto.

American Israel, should the occasion come to try your constancy in the Ten Commandments; should those fanatics succeed (they never will) in making our constitution trinitarian, I trust you and your children will answer the same, "Israel dies, but does not surrender." And Israel did not die; nor did he surrender. Israel lives, stronger in spirit and in number than ever. Israel will live to gain over mankind to the principles and practice of the Ten Commandments; will continue to battle for his Messianic mission, and his motto will be in the future, as in the past: "Whatever the Eternal has spoken we shall perform," and never surrender. Never, never, Amen. With the help of God!

MAURICE FLUEGEL.

Rev. MAURICE FLUEGEL, minister of Erie, Pa., well-known as a political writer in defence of his brethren, when and wherever they suffered persecution.

PATRIMONY—An estate possessed by inheritance.
MONOTHEISM—The belief in one God only.
EPHEMERAL—Beginning and ending in one day.
TO TRAVAIL—To labor.
SHECHINA—(Hebrew) Divine Spirit.
POLYTHEISM—The doctrine of plurality of gods.

DUALISM—The doctrine of the gods.
PANTHEISM—The doctrine that the universe is God.
SPINOZISM—The doctrine that God is not only the maker but the matter of the universe.
HEGELIANISM—The system of Hegel's philosophy.
DECALOGUE—The Ten Commandments given by God to Moses.

GOD KNOWETH BEST.

SOMETIME, when all life's lessons have been learned,
And sun and stars forevermore have set,
The things which our weak judgments here have spurned—
The things o'er which we grieved with lashes wet—
Will flash before us, out of life's dark night,
As stars shine most in deeper tints of blue,
And we shall see how all God's plans were right,
And how what seemed reproof was love most true.

And we shall see how, while we frown and sigh,
God's plans go on as best for you and me;
How, when we called, He heeded not our cry,
Because his wisdom to the end could see.
And even as prudent parents disallow
Too much of sweet to craving babyhood,
So God, perhaps, is keeping from us now
Life's sweetest things, because it seemeth good.

And if, sometimes, commingled with life's wine,
We find the wormwood, and rebel and shrink,
Be sure a wiser hand than yours or mine
Pours out this portion for our lips to drink.
And if some friend we love is lying low,
Where human kisses cannot reach his face,
Oh, do not blame the loving Father so,
But wear your sorrow with obedient grace!

And you shall shortly know that lengthened breath
Is not the sweetest gift God sends His friend,
And that, sometimes, the sable pall of death
Conceals the fairest boon his love can send.
If we could push ajar the gates of life,
And stand within, and all God's workings see,
We could interpret all this doubt and strife,
And for each mystery could find a key.

But not to-day. Then be content, poor
  heart!
God's plans, like lilies, pure and
  white unfold;
We must not tear the close-shut leaves
  apart,
Time will reveal the calyxes of gold.

And if, through patient toil, we reach
  the land
Where tired feet, with sandals loose,
  may rest,
When we shall clearly know and understand,
I think that we will say, "God knew
  the best!"

A. I.

WORMWOOD—A plant.
SABLE—Black.
CALYX—The outer covering of a flower.

To COMMINGLE—To mix, to unite with
another thing.

OBDURACY.

I.

THERE is perhaps no more marked feature in the national character
of the early Israelites than stubbornness of disposition. A state
of bondage had left this blighting heirloom, and years elapsed before
the people, who during their long apprenticeship to slavery had been
amenable to brute force alone, could be brought to yield to the milder
sway of reason and reproof. Yet had a cruel servitude rather de-
based than altogether corrupted their moral nature. Its finer
susceptibilities had, indeed, been deadened by the iron rule to
which they were so long subjected; nevertheless they could occasionally be roused to a sense of virtue, where the brighter side of
the national character was depicted. But here its darker pencilings
must necessarily be most visible, since we have to trace the doings of
a people not only sadly prone to evil, but who too frequently persisted
obdurately in their sinful course in utter disregard of the remon-
strances of their leader. Self-willed and perverse, they rarely sought
to quell their unruly passions and turn from their evil ways till they
had kindled God's just displeasure and brought on themselves the
chastisement of Heaven.

This dark outline we have now to fill up with incidents prominently figuring in the books of Moses, and the first which presents
itself is the murmuring of the people at the waters of Marah, which
spirit of discontent was the more culpable, as they had been but recent witnesses of God's miraculous interposition in their favor, as
we read, "And Israel saw the great work which the Lord did upon
the Egyptians, and the people feared the Lord and believed the
Lord and His servant, Moses." Again, a fresh cry of discontent
broke from them in the wilderness of Zin, and also at Meribah, notwithstanding God had just satisfied their cravings by sending them
"angels' food." The divine succor they thus repeatedly received
no way served to remove their mistrust. Though Moses expostu-
lated with them in these words, "Your murmurings are not against
us, but against the Lord," they nevertheless obdurately persisted in
upbraiding him, and further tempted God, saying: "Is the Lord

PART III.—2 ½.

among us or not?" Now, assuredly, while they could question God's continual presence and harden their hearts against proofs of His superintending providence, past lessons must have been singularly barren of good; indeed, discontent surged up at each new trial, and revilings were continually heard in the camp. Well, indeed, would it have been had the evil stopped there; but the next incident recorded is of a yet more painful character. The evident want of faith in God, and trust in their leader, which the people had manifested at repeated intervals, took a more tangible shape at the first opportune moment. They no longer confined themselves to murmuring against the All Wise, but "turned quickly aside out of the way which God commanded them."

Although, prior to the departure of Moses for the ascent of Mount Sinai, they promised to "do all that the Lord had said, and be obedient;" although they witnessed "the glory of the Lord, like a devouring fire, on the top of the Mount," yet, after the lapse of only a few weeks, they again turned aside from the path of duty. Impatience at the absence of their chief conquered all sense of fear, and in a body the people went to Aaron, and thus spake unto him, "Up; make us gods which shall go before us;" and having made a molten calf, they worshiped it and sacrificed thereunto, and said, "These be the gods which have brought us out of the land of Egypt." Thus it was that when Moses, after an absence of only forty days, again approached the camp, he found them dancing and shouting before their graven image, and enacting the vilest idolatrous practices. Now, mark his prayer thereon, "O Lord, remember thy servants, Abraham, Isaac and Jacob; look not unto the stubbornness of this people, nor to their wickedness, nor to their sins." Truly they were stiff-necked and obdurate, when they neglected the counsel of their great deliverer and preserver; when they forsook the living God, whose benefits and mercies they had so long experienced, and yet more so when they wrought gods after their own imaginings, and bowed before them in sterile and senseless worship. Greatly, indeed, did such a people need such an intercessor.

In the incident which followed shortly after the one just referred to, the self-will and perverseness of the Israelites is especially marked. The land of promise was before them—the land which "God had given them to possess it." They had only to advance, as commanded by Moses, yet they hesitated. Seized by sudden doubts and misgivings, they besought him to send forth spies to search the land, and "bring word regarding it." Devoid of faith and holy trust in their all-merciful Guardian, little was needed to dismay them, and the evil report brought back by the more timorous of these searchers threw the people into a state of consternation. Nothing that could be advanced by the brave and undaunted men, Caleb and Joshua, both of whom accompanied the expedition, nor the assurance given to them by Moses that "the Lord, who goeth before you, He shall fight for you," wrought any change of feeling. "The whole congregation murmured against Moses and against Aaron, and said unto them: "Would to God that we had died in the land of Egypt, or in the wilderness." Nor did their subordination stop here, for "they said, one to another, Let us make a captain, and let us return into Egypt." But their willfulness and obduracy became yet more apparent, since the interposition of the Lord alone prevented them from stoning the faithful Joshua because he thus mildly rebuked them: "Rebel not ye against the Lord, neither fear ye the people of the land, for they are bread for us; their defence is departed from them, and the Lord is with us; fear them not." Such perverseness, however, met its condign punishment. They who brought the evil report from Canaan died of the plague, while, notwithstanding the intercession of Moses, all who had murmured were excluded from entering the promised land. Thus spoke the Lord in His just anger: "Because all those men who have seen My glory and My miracles, which I did in Egypt, and have tempted me now these ten times, and have not hearkened to My voice, surely they shall not see the land which I swore unto their fathers. To-morrow turn ye, and get ye into the wilderness. Forty years shall ye bear your iniquities. I, the Lord, have said it; I will surely do it unto all this evil congregation that are gathered together against Me; in this wilderness they shall be consumed, and there they shall die."

Now, had not this people been obdurate beyond all belief, they surely would have sought, by conforming to the will of the Supreme, to merit His ever-renewing mercies, and thereby possibly avert the sad fate consequent on their past misconduct. On the contrary, however, they grew yet more perverse. As formerly they had been timorous when they might well have felt themselves safe under the protection of the wing of Omnipotence, they now believed themselves secure when, indeed, they had many causes for apprehension. Far from turning back at the distinct command of the Lord of Hosts, they determined on acting in direct violation of His will by advancing to attack their formidable enemy. Little regard did they pay to their leader, who thus addressed them in God's name: "Go not up, for the Lord is among you, that ye be not smitten before your enemies; *wherefore*, now, do ye transgress the commandment of the Lord, but it shall not prosper." With rebellion at their hearts, they were not to be deterred; but "they went up presumptuously against the Amorites, who chased them as bees," defeating them with great slaughter. Now, during the forty years longer they were thus doomed to abide in the wilderness, they too frequently disobeyed the word of the Lord by uniting themselves with surrounding nations and bowing down before their gods in idol worship. Fresh trials followed, but their stubborn spirit remained unsubdued, and

indeed no radical reform in their character could have been effected
even at the close of their long wanderings, else Moses would not
have addressed them thus: "Hear, O Israel, not for thy righteousness, or for the uprightness of thy heart, dost thou go to possess
this land, but for the wickedness of these nations the Lord thy God
doth drive them out from before thee, and that He may perform
the word which the Lord sware unto thy fathers, Abraham, Isaac
and Jacob."

This is truly a dark picture to draw, but how can it be otherwise
when obduracy and stiff-neckedness have to be held up to view?
Had the early Israelites only shown the same dogged determination
to adhere to the right path as they had manifested in the pursuance
of evil courses, such decision and stability of character would have
proved truly valuable qualities, deserving the highest commendation.
Desirable, however, as this would have been, yet, was it to be expected of them? Assuredly not. A hard, unbending spirit, born of
and long fostered by a cruel bondage, was little likely to lend itself
to good, more especially as several concurrent circumstances worked
in an adverse direction. Such, for example, was even the very boon
of freedom. An ignorant people, burning with ardent desires, thirsting after the pleasures of sense, could but regard their sudden liberation from thraldom as a fitting opportunity for those gratifications
which had been so long denied them ; the rebound was indeed all
the more violent from the low and prostrate condition into which
they had fallen. They did not even seek to control their hopes, nor
could they calmly brook any impediment which stayed them in the
way to the promised land, "flowing with milk and honey." Any
occurrence retarding the fulfillment of their sanguine expectations,
roused at once a strong spirit of discontent. They reflected not, or
at least gave no heed to the reflection, that their all-gracious Deliverer and Protector well knew what would most conduce to their
welfare ; they willfully ignored the penance they were to undergo by
God's all-just decree, and thence chafed at each new trial, each privation, nor could they be brought to bow before His wise dispensations in a resigned and tranquil spirit. Now, had they regarded
their moral rather than physical progress, and followed the path of
virtue to the desired goal, then assuredly they would never have
rebelled, nor seen the frustration of their sanguine hopes. The circumstances, however, which worked them most evil was the proximity
of idolatrous nations, who sought by every possible device to inveigle
and seduce them from the worship of the One only God. Every intoxicating temptation which could rouse their worst passions was
held up before them, and they but too soon learned to prefer these
orgies, which formed part of the rites of idol worship, to the pure,
calm delights which their own religion was calculated to afford. In
the paroxysms of their mad passions all holy and spiritual feelings

lost their attractions, while the licentious and material reigned supreme. Becoming thus a prey to their lower instincts, they rushed wildly on, abandoning themselves to every sensual indulgence.

Now, withal, and this is a bright spot in the history of the Israelites, they were reclaimable. Not wholly lost to a sense of the right, like the idolators who ensnared them, they could be brought to hearken to reproof. Obdurate and stiff-necked as they were, they yet made spasmodic efforts after self-restraint, and occasionally with some success. Indeed, had they not the All-merciful for their help and guide? He never failed to school the children of his love, and although He had again and again to reprove them through His servant Moses, because of their obstinacy, He never forsook them, nor shut his ear to their cry. Faulty as were His chosen people, He, in His wisdom, must not only have seen in them many redeeming qualities, but also have deemed them fitted to fulfill His gracious purpose. Indeed, the words of Moses, in one of his last addresses to the Israelites, lead infallibly to this conclusion. After exhorting to obedience, and bidding them "utterly destroy the idolatrous nations which were to be delivered into their hands, to burn their graven images, and make no intermarriages," he adds: "For thou art an holy people unto the Lord thy God; He hath chosen thee to be a special people unto Himself. He did not set His love upon you because ye were more in number than any people, for ye were the fewest of all people, but *because* the Lord loved *you;* and because He would keep His oath which He had sworn to your fathers." Wholly corrupt or iniquitous they could not possibly have been, thus to have gained God's all-gracious love. But yet more was required of them; they were to be a holy people, thence the moral training, the rude discipline, to which they were subjected during their long sojourn in the wilderness. Nor did this schooling fail to accomplish its purpose ; indeed, the very hardness and inflexibility which characterized the Israelitish nation became alike a virtue and a shield in succeeding generations, forming an everlasting bulwark to their imperishable faith.

Were it not that the distinguished traits of obduracy are as repugnant as they are marked, there could be no possible difficulty in detecting them both in ourselves and others, but if the natural aversion they inspire does not always suffice to make them shunned, it will at all events induce their withdrawal into the darkest recesses of the heart till they can issue forth to the light of day, either so guarded as to escape observation, or so disguised as to pass for virtues. Now, the knowledge that the hateful and repulsive features which characterized obduracy can be thus masked might well suffice to induce a vigorous inward search, and so whet our sagacity as to enable us to trace to its fount each questionable passion, each sentiment of the mind. But for this purpose it is essential we should learn to know in what obduracy consists; and may we doubt that it consists in a resolute persistence in wrong-doing, or, in its mildest form, in a laxity of principle frequently growing into a confirmed habit or temper of mind. And, again, it is characterized by a willful shutting of the mental eye to the blessings and mercies which are "new every morning," and by lending a too ready ear, on the one hand, to the voice of sensuality, which, making us the slaves of our selfish passions, draws us from our God; and on the other, to promptings of pride, which tempts us to rebel against the majesty of Heaven, and set at defiance God's holy law, our reason, and the admonitions of conscience. Indeed, obduracy takes its firmest root in the depraved and unfeeling heart, which, hearkening only to its own vile imaginings, its evil inclinations, and selfish desires, will, without scruple or compunction, seduce others to wrong, thereby darkening their future with sorrow and shame ; while it also flourishes in the fertile soil of the stunted and uneducated mind which seeks not, but rather shuns, the light of truth, and resists the force of argument, the teachings of virtue and religion. Now, once impressed with the conviction that obduracy is a willful deflection of the mind from the paths of justice and righteousness, also a hardening of the heart to moral principles and right feelings, we shall surely never be likely to mistake it for firmness, which is the true friend and stay of every virtue, and, therefore, itself a virtue. This indeed is a most valuable quality, and the indispensable foundation of all great and good deeds. Born of right principles, it will lead its possessor steadily and tenaciously to resist any deviation therefrom; it will keep him from trimming between God's will and his own inclinations; it will cause him resolutely and courageously to overcome every unruly impulse and temptation, while it will enable him in a noble, lofty, and generous spirit to throw his whole strength of volition into those duties which devolve on him in relation to his fellow-man and his Creator.

On proceeding next to consider the cause of obduracy, we find yet further evidence of the dissimilarity and antagonism which exist between it and firmness, or resolution, for which it but too frequently passes current ; nay, more, since firmness consists in a resolute resistance of evil, while obduracy is a willful persistence in sin, it is self-evident that the latter could have no existence if the mind and heart had remained unsullied through the sway of the former. Indeed, we have sown the first seeds of obduracy in our breast when we permit one guilty passion to gain supremacy over principle and duty. It is, therefore, to infirmity of purpose, or want of resolute will to cope with sin, itself so peculiarly hardening, that we must infallibly trace the primary cause of this signal defect. Nor do its baneful effects stop here, for it engenders a spirit of procrastination which seriously impedes all reform. Though conscience may tell us we are gravitating to ill, and that sin is becoming habitual, we, nevertheless, through its agency, find ourselves ever resolving an amendment, yet never accomplishing it, while becoming more and more callous under this system of self-deceit. Another cause is an insufficient or defective training of the youthful heart. When the loftier impulses are not cultivated, baser passions will assuredly attain luxurious growth ; the greed of gain and abuse of this world's pleasures will warp it from the right, the true, the holy. If lively gratitude to God be not made the predominant sentiment of the mind, softening, refining, and exalting it, unruly desires will enter, and usher in with them temptations; selfish indulgence will quickly follow, the sense of virtue and religion be speedily effaced and banished, and the heart, necessarily hardening, will finally petrify into obduracy.

II.

How to prevent, check, or cure so deadly a malady of the soul forms another important matter for consideration. If we will but early implant virtuous principles in the mind, and give to it a fixedness of purpose, based on a love of rectitude, and a love of God, we shall surely have accomplished our aim; moral firmness in youth utterly precluding obduracy in manhood. But if perchance the foundation of virtue has been shaken, and we have not been altogether proof to the seductions of sense, then must we set ourselves sedulously to the task of uprooting the evil propensities, and checking the distempers thus engendered. And here we must bear in mind that there should be no delay, no deferring to a future day; no one becomes entirely profligate at once. We deviate step by step from the path of virtue, and only by resolutely staying our downward course at an early stage, and directing our thoughts upward, may we hope to escape from the perilous position in which we have placed ourselves. If, however, unhappily through procrastination or stubbornness, we have persisted in wrong doing, to the prejudice of our moral health, and drank freely from the poisoned cup of intoxicating pleasures, let us remember while there be yet time that through God's infinite mercy we may find an antidote in penitence, a cure through contrition and amendment. And surely what will not sincere repentance effect for us! On each approach to the throne of God in prayer, the heart will sensibly soften, so that obduracy will be finally subdued, and we shall turn again with delight to the path marked out in that holy law, which He gave for the guidance and the good of his creatures. Heeding the soft voice of the conscience rather than the logic of vice, which declares, "I have done it once with impunity, so I may do it again," we shall resolutely abstain in the future from violating its dictates, though hitherto no ill results may have followed therefrom; indeed, having once strayed from the straight line of virtue, duty and religion, we should the more sedulously keep in view that heavenly bliss to which they point, and placing our de-

pendence on God, pursue the path of right manfully, hopefully.
And here it is essential to remark that there can be no permanent
reform without such dependence, coupled as it must ever be with a
keen perception of God's glorious attributes.   The obduracy which
pride and ingratitude engender is indeed only to be subdued and
conquered by a sense of our weak and erring nature, by a thorough
belief in God's goodness, His omniscience, His never-failing justice.
Let us but see and acknowledge our own weakness, and then shall
we feel how great has been God's forbearance; the heart will soften
into love at the thought of His goodness, His fostering care, His
solicitude for our well-being, and we shall be led to submit cheerfully to that restraint of our passions which He, in his wisdom, imposes for the general welfare.   Besides, the consciousness that His
all-seeing eye is watching over us with fatherly tenderness must
further tend to curb all rash presumption, and check us in the commission of evil.   But should the thoughts of our own unworthiness
or of God's benign attributes be powerless to subdue our obduracy
and kindle love, then may He, in His mercy, work on our hearts
through the sense of fear.   He will possibly force on our minds
the conviction that none may willfully disobey His holy law or obdurately resist His all-wise decrees without incurring a fearful penalty.
Indeed, though slow to anger, He yet holds the scales of justice with
an equal hand, and will not suffer the sinner to escape the chastisement due to his misdeeds.   With the object of promoting this
salutary conviction, we shall pass in review some few of the numerous
ills, mental as well as physical, which are inseparable from a course
of vice. Foremost, and possibly not the least distressing to the mind,
is the sense of self-abasement; indeed, so powerful is this feeling in
the yet unhardened heart, that if it be not made to subserve the
cause of virtue and reform, it will assuredly enlist on the side of evil,
and hurry its ready victim with ever-increasing celerity to the brink
of moral perdition.   Then, as sin gains upon us, and headstrong
passions obtain ascendancy, we shall find our physical powers and
mental faculties impaired; conscience, which cannot always slumber,
will at times make its warning voice heard, and rob us even of those
fleeting pleasures for which we have toiled and sacrificed so much.
Each fresh day, however, given to dissipation, will make the appeals
of the inward monitor less audible, and bowing under the yoke of
sin, the heart will harden, and be drawn further and further from its
God.   Now, how deplorable is the condition of him who, running
counter to the will of the Supreme, has ever to dread the show of
His displeasure !   Can, indeed, that man know aught of happiness
or peace, who sets himself in opposition to the will of his Creator ?
Must he not feel how abortive will be all his plans; how vain and
fruitless his desires; how certainly disappointment and misery will
attend on his senseless folly and disobedience?   Must not the con-

viction often flash across his mind that any evil committed recoils on the wrong doer, and that sure retribution awaits him who, taking advantage of the liberty God has given, rebels against His rule, perversely wronging his own nature, and injuring his fellow mortals?

Let, then, those who make pleasure the business of life—who tamper with vice, and permit the coil of sin to encircle the heart—stop short before "their cup of iniquity is full," and, through a moral reform and heartfelt repentance, stay the wrath of the infinitely merciful Lord, and avert the dire consequences incidental to the violations of His laws. Let them set themselves to the stern duty of self-correction before their misconduct and misdeeds call down upon them correction from above. This hopeful step once taken, a happy consummation will assuredly not be far distant. Learning to heed their spiritual interests, and remembering that God has offered heaven as a reward for virtue and piety, they will resolutely reject all such seductive pleasures as render the heart callous and obdurate, while they will gratefully seek and keep steadily in view these guardians of all true honor and peace of mind; these assured friends to happiness here, these faithful pioneers to the blessed realms above.

But if the precepts and teaching of Holy Writ bearing on this subject be not heeded, then will most surely follow the sad consequences of which Scripture so emphatically forewarns us.

III.

The later portion of the history of the Israelites now to be considered, and which commences with Joshua and the Judges, offers many a strong contrast with that which preceded it, yet none is more striking than their improved moral condition. Their wanderings, extended over a lengthened period, and accompanied with much suffering and many privations, had been prolific of good, as trials proceeding from Almighty goodness should ever be. Not only had the national character gradually improved under reproof and chastisement, but, further, the rising generation. had wisely profited by the errors and misconduct of their fathers, and taken salutary warning from the examples afforded by the backsliding propensities of their benighted parents. For undoubted evidence of this we have only to turn to the book of Joshua. Throughout its pages no single instance of idolatrous worship is recounted, nor one trait of that obduracy which in the past had been so prominent a feature in the conduct of the entire people; indeed, rebellion and contumacy had become most hateful to them, and was made punishable with death. In its place, however, happily figured its counterpart, firmness of will ever displaying itself in a staunch adherence to the right. Thus schooled, thus tempered, this defect of character had not only become a powerful auxiliary to virtue, but had actually grown into a virtue itself. Here, then, we have a people whom God deemed fitted to enter into, inherit and enjoy the good land of promise, the land for which they did not labor, cities to dwell in which they did not build, vineyards and oliveyards from which they might eat, but planted not. They could appreciate the rich blessings vouchsafed by the Lord in a grateful spirit, and partake of his bounty without in any way abusing it. Not to them, as to their stiff-necked fathers, could apply the words of Moses, " Jeshurun waxed fat and kicked." They repaid not God's benefits with rebellion, but with gratitude, and during " all the days of Joshua and all the days of the elders that outlived Joshua, they served the Lord."

In the next book, that of Judges, the history of Israel again enters into one of its darker phases. With the new generation a great change for the worse occurred. Their fathers, though serving the Lord with all their hearts, had overlooked or disregarded one important part of the commandment given by God through his servant Moses. Although they had themselves kept "the statutes and judgments of the Lord," they did not " teach them diligently unto their children, and to their sons' sons." For proof of this we have only to refer to the book of Judges itself, where we will soon perceive that this omission of duty was indeed a sad and fatal error on the part of the parents. Their neglect of one of the fundamental principles of the Mosaic code was indeed rife with evil consequences to their progeny, and to it must we, in a great measure, attribute their early fall into idolatry, with the subsequent relapses of each new generation throughout the whole rule of the Judges, lasting some three hundred years, as also their successive conflicts with surrounding nations, their many calamities and trials. And assuredly it would hardly be possible that a people who had never been taught either to love or fear God, who had never been led to feel how closely blended were mercy and justice in His all-wise dispensations, could altogether resist the contaminating influence and example of idolatrous neighbors. But, though they succumbed before the temptations held out to them, and forsook God and the right path, they were brought speedily back to the Lord and His holy worship, on being subjected to chastisement or even reproof. Indeed, those generations, criminal though they were at times, never displayed the inveterate obduracy which had characterized their progenitors; and when we consider they had not, like them, been witnesses of God's miraculous workings, or been made sensible of His immediate presence, through ocular demonstrations, we must clearly see that a decided improvement in the national character had taken place. Knowing much less of the All-merciful, they were nevertheless far more easily brought to bow down humbly before Him, and conform to His gracious will. Instances of this, as of the heartfelt repentance of the people, were rife under the rule of those noble patriots and national deliverers who figured in their history as judges.

We may now, however, turn not only to a brighter, but even a bright era in the history of the Israelites. The alternations which lasted throughout the whole period of the Judges had not been profitless; indeed, during their long rule the higher and nobler qualities of the entire nation were in course of development, and when it drew to its close the national character was altogether less faulty, even giving promise of future moral excellence. Nevertheless, the national failing had not unhappily become entirely extinct, and through the misrule of Samuel's sons they left the right path, became weary of their judges, and thence sought occasion to urge him to institute a monarchial form of government. They would not any further hearken to the gloomy predictions of their able seer, who could not deter them from following the bent of their inclinations. What cared they in their stubbornness and self-will for the prophecy: "Ye shall cry out on that day because of your king which ye shall have chosen, and the Lord will not hear you in that day." Heedless of after consequences, they refused to obey the voice of the Lord, and said: "Nay, but we will have a king over us, that we also may be like the other nations."

Now, willful as was such conduct, it formed a solitary exception; indeed, throughout the reign of Saul, whom Samuel presented to them for their king, and also during that of David, who succeeded him on the throne, and likewise in the early part of the reign of his son Solomon, not even one instance of obduracy or defection stands recorded. Truly, these were palmy days for the Israelites, and this the brightest era in their history. When, alas! Solomon, their king, impiously disregarding the injunction of the Lord, caused that fatal blight to fall upon the Israelites, of which they had been forewarned by Samuel, and though during the reign of some of their good kings its evil influence was sensibly lessened, it was never entirely dissipated, but finally gained such intensity as at times to deaden the heart of the nation, and depress their moral condition to nearly as low an ebb as that of their depraved and sinful neighbors. Indeed, their subsequent history is again of the darkest hue, and the incalculable evils foretold by the venerable seer came thick upon them. They followed their evil courses, while idolatry had, indeed, hardened their hearts, and rendered them as obdurate as they were criminal. Numerable proofs of this are manifested throughout the writings of the prophets, which furnish us with the last portion of the history of the Israelites, a period no less sad than eventful. Unhappily, all the efforts of these brave spirits proved of no avail. Thus, though many a "physician in Gilead" dispensed balsams of wondrous efficacy, the moral leprosy still remained unhealed; although the prophets were gifted with all the eloquence of truth, though fired by the keenest solicitude for the well-being of the nation, their words were powerless to work any permanent change in the hearts of corrupt kings and a hardened people; obduracy ever stood as an impassable barrier between them. Yet how sedulously these prophets of the Lord sought to impress the entire nation with a sense of God's goodness and justice, how earnestly they strove to bring the people to repentance and reformation, may best be judged from their several writings.

Then came their great calamity, their signal chastisement. Nebuchadnezzar besieged the famine-stricken city of Jerusalem till it was destroyed; the king was made prisoner, and afterward cruelly tortured; the nobles and the people, old and young, were put to the sword or taken captive; the treasures of the house of the Lord and of all the kingdom were appropriated; finally the Temple and palaces were burned, and the walls of the city broken down.

Thus did God's attributes of long-enduring mercy and fatherly tenderness finally yield before His no less fixed and certain attribute of strict justice. For three score and ten years had the Israelites to drink from the cup of God's wrath, and in a long, sorrowful, ignominious captivity expiate their past criminality, their perverseness and obduracy.   J. L. MOCATTA.

J. L. MOCATTA, an eminent merchant, residing in London, England, and well known for his benevolence and untiring exertions for the amelioration of the Jewish poor of the metropolis.

OBDURACY—Hardness of heart.
TO BROOK—To bear; to endure.
PENANCE—Infliction, as an expression of repentance for sin.
ORGIES—Mad rites of Bacchus.
PAROXYSM—A fit (disease).
LICENTIOUS—Unrestrained by law or morality.
SPASMODIC—Convulsive; violent.
INIQUITOUS—Unjust; wicked.
COMPUNCTION—Contrition, pity, repentance.

TO STUNT—To hinder from growth.
DEFLECTION—A turning out of the way.
VOLITION—The act of willing.
PROCRASTINATION—Delay.
PETRIFY—To change to stone.
ANTIDOTE—Medicine against poison.
LOGIC—The art of using reason well in our inquiries after truth.
CONTUMACY—Perverseness.
TO CONTAMINATE—To defile; to corrupt.

THE HEBREW.

A HEBREW knelt in the dying light,
His eyes were dim and cold,
The hairs on his brow were silver-white,
And his blood was thin and old!
He lifted his look to his latest sun,
For he knew that his pilgrimage was done.
And as he saw God's shadow there,
His spirit poured itself in prayer!
" I come unto death's second birth,
Beneath a stranger air,
A pilgrim on a dull, cold earth,
As all my fathers were!
And men have stamped me with a curse,
I feel it is not Thine,

Thy mercy—like yon sun—was made
On me—as them—to shine;
And, therefore, dare I lift mine eye,
Through that, to Thee—before I die!
In this great temple built by Thee,
Whose altars are divine,
Beneath yon lamp, that ceaselessly
Lights up Thine own true shrine.
Oh! take my latest sacrifice,
Look down, and make this sod
Holy as that where long ago
The *Hebrew met his God!*
I have not caused the widow's tears,
Nor dimmed the orphan's eye,
I have not stained the virgin's years,

Nor mocked the mourner's cry;
The songs of Zion in mine ear
Have ever been most sweet,
And always when I felt Thee near,
My 'shoes' were 'off my feet!'
I have known Thee in the whirlwind,
I have known Thee on the hill,
I have loved Thee in the voice of birds,
Or the music of the rill.
I dreamt Thee in the shadow,
I saw Thee in the light,
I heard Thee in the thunder peal,
And worshiped in the night!
All beauty while it spoke of Thee,
Still made my soul rejoice,
And my spirit bowed within itself,
To hear Thy "still small voice!"
I have not felt myself a thing
Far from Thy presence driven,
By flaming sword or warring wing,
Shut out from Thee and heaven!
Must I the whirlwind reap, because
My fathers sowed the storm,
Or shrink—because another sinned—
Beneath Thy red right arm?
Oh, much of this we dimly scan,
And much is all unknown—
But I will not take my curse from man
I turn to Thee alone!
Oh, bid my fainting spirit live,
And what is dark reveal,
And what is evil, oh, forgive.
And what is broken heal,
And cleanse my nature from above
In the deep Jordan of Thy love!
I know not if the Christian's heaven
Shall be the same as mine;
I only ask to be forgiven,
And taken home to Thine!
I weary on a far, dim strand,
Whose mansions are as tombs,
And long to find the father-land,

Where there are many homes!
Oh, grant of all yon starry thrones,
Some dim and distant star,
Where Judah's last and scattered son
May love Thee from afar!
When all earth's myriad harps shall
    meet
In choral praise or prayer,
Shall Zion's harp—of old so sweet—
Alone be wanting there?
Yet place me in Thy lowest seat,
Though I—as now—be there,
The Christian's scorn, the Christian's
    jest;
But let me see and hear
From some dim mansion in the sky,
Thy bright ones and their melody."

The sun goes down with sudden gleam,
And beautiful as a lovely dream.
And silently as air
The vision of a dark-eyed girl,
With long and raven hair,
Glides in as guardian spirits glide—
And lo! is kneeling by his side,
As if her sudden presence there
Were sent in answer to his prayer.
Oh! say they not that angels tread
Around the good man's dying bed?
His child—his sweet and sinless child—
And as he gazed on her
He knew his God was reconciled,
And this the messenger.
As sure as God had hung on high
The promise bow before his eye;
Earth's purest hope thus o'er him flung.
To paint his heavenward faith,
And life's most holy feeling strung,
To sing him into death;
And on his daughter's stainless breast
The dying Hebrew sought his rest.

                                    A. I.

THE SACRED TONGUE.

I.

The first period of the Hebrew language extends from the revelation on Sinai and the giving of the law, through the first founder, to the destruction of the Temple and the banishment to Babylon. Before that time we find no mention of the existence of the language, although it cannot be denied that it existed previously, and, according to the Scriptural narrative, from the beginning of creation, yet it is but in these that a remembrance of the language is kept up.

From the supposition generally taken, that the written memorials supply us with information concerning the condition of the language, we may with certainty conclude that the same must have reached, at that time, the highest state of culture, as it sufficed in all cases. Remarkable it is, however, amidst all troubles and hardships the nation had to undergo, during the time of the Judges, before they had a king, that poesy was nevertheless preserved to great perfection, as the song of Deborah sufficiently corroborates. But as soon as the kingdom was severed in two parts—when Ephraim deserted Judah, and the greatness of the house of David diminished—the language also began to decay, for Ephraim was opposed to Judah, and to his own detriment entered upon an alliance with strange nations. Amid such national dissensions, it is impossible that science could prosper, and in town and country every dogma fell into decline. Yet, in spite of all these drawbacks, the versatility of the language has not entirely ceased among the people, as long as the light of divine resplendence illumined the prophets, and poets and marvelous songsters were among them, such as Isaiah, Jeremiah, Hosea, Amos and Micah.

II.

The second period lies from the banishment to Babylon, to the return from thence, and from the building of the second Temple to its destruction, an epoch of about 500 years. We leave the preceding expulsion of the ten tribes unsaid, because they returned no more, and speak only of the banishment of Judah's and Benjamin's. Since the light and government in Judah had ceased, and the Israelites submitted to the Babylonian king, the language also lost its luster and color, for the Jews made no further use of the same, but acquired the language of the ruling nation, Aramaic and Chaldaic.

During the whole time of the second Temple we find not a single work composed in Hebrew except the book Ben-Sira, of which the Hebrew text was known, but this is not extant now ; it became lost, or is somewhere stowed away, and has thus remained unknown to our co-religionists. Perhaps, in course of time, even other works may have become lost, because in that period no such care was bestowed on them, which we find the scribe Esra, with his energy for the divine law, and his party, the society of the great Synod, have shown for the preservation and arrangement of the twenty-four books of Holy Writ. Through the Massora they had established the same firmly, and had secured them from arbitrary alterations, in order that evil hands may not bring about interpolations. Thereby these twenty-four sacred books are preserved to us in their correct form unto this day. Besides, these men of the great Synod have given us no fixed formulas for our prayers. From these works of theirs, to determine upon the state of the language, it appears that the same was at that time an object for study, and although they knew how to handle the language, it was with them nevertheless no more in that pure state as previously.

III.

The third period is from the termination of the assembly of the great Synod, the origin of the Pharisees in the third century of the second Temple, the body of Mishna teachers proceeding from the same, and the succeeding authors of the Talmud in explanation of the Mishna, till the completion thereof, a period of more than six hundred years. During this long period not a trace can be found for fostering or maintaining the language ; inasmuch as all the keepsakes their hands left us are the Mishna and the Talmud, containing laws and precepts. As these refer to objects which concern the acts of every individual from the mass of the nation, they preferred comparing the same in language well known and easily understood, as a pure Hebrew was to all accessible only under very great difficulty ; yet even during this period the existence of some odd clever man cannot be denied, possessing poetic talents, and who fostered the poesy of the Hebrew language ; for among a people endowed with knowledge, science and moral laws, it cannot lack poetical minds. As I have already mentioned, poesy is the sister of knowledge and culture, and where the latter is found the former is surely to be met with. In pursuing this aim, however, the authors of the Talmud have in their work found no opportunity, as their intention was limited merely to the proper arrangement of the law.

IV.

The fourth period is from the completion of the Talmud, the origin of the Seboraim, after them the Gaonim, and then the academical teachers, until the expulsion from Spain—a period of eight hundred years. This epoch especially had made great strides in the acknowledgment of the language. During this space of time the foundation was laid for the construction of grammar, which has been preserved unto this day ; for they breathed a spirit into the dry bones, that they have become a living being. To the latter, whose Hebrew works have been handed down to us, belong R. Abraham ben Esra, and the brothers R. Moses and R. David, sons of R. Joseph Kimchi. The most renowned is the latter, R. David Kimchi ; he is the pillar on which all succeeding authors leaned, and his two works, the Grammar and Lexicon, have served us for a finger-post in all improvements of the language, and all later works till the present time have drawn from this source ; for although an extension may be possible, it is not likely that anything can be taken away from them. But in regard to the productions of poetry during this period, we find two kinds: the one consisting of the ritual poesy, which is called Keroboth, as arranged and divided for the whole year, and in all Jewish congregations in Germany, Poland and other countries made use of. All these poesies have, with other poetic works, no other peculiarity in common, except the rhyme. The second kind includes the poetry which, from the Gaonim and the founders of grammar, have been composed, and which the Spanish communities have adopted. These are of sublime matter and of noble and poetic forms.

V.

The fifth period embraces the time from the expulsion from Spain until forty years before our time—about three hundred years. These are called the three hundred years of darkness in regard to language and sciences. With the expulsion of the Arabs from the western countries, Portugal and Spain, all science and also the Jews were expelled, and from that time their luster disappeared, and Jacob's honor became gloomy. They were tossed about from kingdom to kingdom, from one country to another, and at last they spread over Germany and Poland. There the sun of knowledge set for them entirely, the stars of perception became darkened, and the language went into mourning; for misfortune had broken their spirit, and the continual persecutions and expatriations made their mind cloudy, so that they turned their heart from all science and knowledge, and as they understood no other language, nor any other books than those of the Hebrews, and transferring the same into jargon peculiar to themselves, their expressions destroyed the meaning thereof, being unable to explain the Scriptures properly. Therefore the study of the same soon ceased to be an object for instruction, and thus the knowledge of the language and the art of poesy was lost to them. Yet, even in those hard times, Israel had not become an orphan, and not a few men of talent existed, who strenghtened the building of the language by clearing the stones of their rubbish and repairing the foundation.

VI.

The sixth period—the shortest and most changeable of all, because it comprises no more than forty or fifty years, and because in none of the previous periods do we meet with so strange a condition of the language so entirely opposite, now rising and now falling. The same as Mendelssohn in knowledge and understanding shone before his people, that people sought for him, and nations came to consult with him, so was also his friend, the energetic man in the law of God, the wise and renowned poet, Naphtali Herz Wessely, who spread a clear light, and raised by his excellent writings and invaluable poetry the value of the language and poesy. It was God who raised these two great luminaries and the stars—the members of the society for the advancement of all that is good and noble. But when Moses, the servant of God, had died, his works also came to an indifferent end; with the light of the divine man the sparks of desiring knowledge were extinguished, and the brightness of studying the language became darkened. The "Sammler" ceased to exist, its society soon dispersed, and the language lost its ornaments. Since the death of the righteous man the language has been sinking in proportion as the same rose during his lifetime. But we have retrograded in regard to language as well as all religious study, and the occupation with Holy Writ and the Talmud is unfortunately becoming year by year more neglected, till in due time God will once more ordain otherwise. JOSEPH ZEDNER.

JOSEPH ZEDNER was a native of Gr. Glogau (Prussian Silesia), a man of great literary attainments, a great Talmudist, assistant librarian at the British Museum in London, and author of several important works.

VERSATILITY—Easily applied to a new form or task.

RESPLENDENCE—Luster; splendor.

MASSORA—A Hebrew work on the Bible compiled by several Rabbis.

INTERPOLATION—Something added or put into the original matter.

SYNOD—An assembly, generally of ecclesiastics.

EXPATRIATION—Banishment.

JACOB'S PILLOW.

In the sea of Rabbinical lore,
Is a mystical legend of yore;
  Of Jacob who wandered afar.
In anguish of spirit, sore pressed,
He lay on the desert to rest,
  'Neath the light of a tremulous star.

And the moss-covered stones that he
    saw,
Grew still in their wonder and awe
  That the father of Israel's race
Should seek in the gloom of the plain
Surcease of his anguish and pain,
  "To lay himself down in that place."

Then they clamored in audible tones,
In the mystical language of stones,
  Each claiming pre-eminent right
To be chosen as Israel's bed,
To pillow the wanderer's head
  As he lay in the desert that night.

Each stone to the other laid claim
To the honor and marvelous fame,
  As contending they scattered his way;
But the presence of Jacob was there
Like the sanctified incense of prayer
  And in rapturous silence they lay.

But a marvelous destiny—true
To the grandeur of Israel's few
  Who invoked the religion of man—
Rewarded the rivaling stones,

In harmony blending their tones
  Like the hues of a rainbow's span.

For they merged and mingled in one
In the droop of the glowing sun,
  And from all but a single stone
Was molded for Israel's bed,
To pillow the wanderer's head,
  As he lay with his God alone.

And when morn shot her golden beams,
As seraphic as Israel's dreams,
  The pillow of mystical story
He knew in the depth of night
Had invoked the angels of light
  To compass the heavens in glory.

An altar to Heaven he raised,
And the God of his father he praised,
  As he set up the pillow of fame.
And the legend divinely has said,
That thus was the corner-stone laid
  Of the Temple to Israel's name.

Like the stones, so scattered and riven,
Was thus a heritage given
  To a race bearing proudly their pain;
But the fragments in one shall com-
    bine
To build up the faith of all time,
  And the Temple of God to regain.

JACOB G. ASCHER.

To SURCEASE —To stop, to put an end to.

THE STUDY OF HEBREW.

DAVID's description of our journeying beyond the borders of oppression is surpassing in elegance of style and loftiness of thought. The
frequency with which we repeat the hymn of the inspired bard cannot lessen its attractiveness. Our feelings are ever thrilled by the
bold apostrophe to the fleeing sea and the affrighted mountains;
and when the author, transported with religious enthusiasm, bids
the whole earth tremble at the presence of the Lord, coming to
overthrow the laws of nature, that He may miraculously sustain redeemed Israel, the effect is soul-stirring. Yet who would believe
that the daily recital of that sublime composition, upon the festival
we celebrated of late, awakened within me a sense of humiliation? I
fancied it provoked a contrast in our conduct between two periods,
which form two epochs in the annals of the world—the period of the
rule of tyranny in Egypt, and that of the rule of freedom in America;
for, if the concurrent testimony of history and tradition did not
show a brighter feature in the Jewish character, when the yoke of
the Pharaohs weighed us down, than when the freest government raised us up, a word ingenuously uttered by the Psalmist
would clearly exhibit it. Hear the opening sentence of his ode:
  "When Israel went out of Egypt, the house of Jacob from a people of *strange language*, Judah became his sanctuary." Were the
slaves in every deed unacquainted with the language of their task-
masters? Did not a residence of centuries in Mizraim enable our
forefathers to learn what was constantly spoken within their hearing?
None can entertain the supposition who has read the Scriptures attentively. The whole narrative in Exodus, from that part which
pictures Miriam accosting the gentle-hearted princess, and offering
to go in search of a nurse for the infant brother, to the other, in
which the leader urged the tribes, on the eve of their departure, to
ask the people who had robbed them of their children and their substance for objects of silver and gold, is a chain of evidence representing "the house of Jacob" as familiar with the vernacular tongue
of the land they inhabited.
  Not their ignorance of another people's language suggested the
term "Louas," in the sentence of the heaven-gifted poet, but
their retention of the ancestral language, their cherishing it and
setting thereupon a value, which made them consider strange what
was not Hebrew. The merit of having affectionately kept it as a
distinguishing characteristic is reckoned by the sages as one of the
virtues that purchased Israel's deliverance. But even if we are disinclined to accept the Rabbinical axiom, we cannot gainsay this truth.
Our predecessors, who responded to the victorious song of their
champion on the shore of the Red Sea; our predecessors, who stood
at the foot of Sinai to receive the divine mandate, must have treasured up a perfect knowledge of the language brought from Canaan

by the seventy persons who formed the nucleus of a future nationality; and that they accomplished in spite of a refined despotism,
bent upon extinguishing every sentiment of union among the enslaved. A marvelous preservation, because effected under the pressure of crushing hindrances. But that which came out of a fiery
furnace unscathed, a gentle stream has carried away.

"When Israel went out of Egypt, the house of Jacob from a people of strange language, Judah became his sanctuary." The nation
in whose midst the Divinity dwelt as in a sacred tabernacle, was that
who deemed strange the language which did not recall their origin
and belief. Such is, methinks, the burden of David's imperishable
hymn. Does it not sound like a reproach to the descendants of the
shepherd king, as a withering rebuke to the remnant of Judah?
To that portion, thereof, I mean, among whom *the Hebrew* has become
a strange language.... You know it, my hearers! The range of our
children's studies comprises a variety of studies, but that which ranked
foremost in the ancient "house of Jacob" occupies no place with us,
or it is put so far back as to be rendered almost invisible. I am
willing to concede much to the changes in time and circumstances.
Let us admit that our altered condition demands a broader culture
of secular learning than heretofore; that in order not to be lowered in
the social scale we must acquire a mastery of the language of the
country in which we live. Let us grant that we are instinctively
drawn to the literature of the people who have accorded to us the
right of liberty and the pursuit of happiness. But cheerfully making
that admission, we ought, nevertheless, to repel as impious the idea
of treating contemptuously the study of the Hebrew language. Aside
from the vital question, which our acquaintance with it—as a token
of recognition among the members of our race—has involved at all
times, but especially since the dispersion, our cultivation of it is im-
perative, because we must endeavor to maintain Holy Writ in its
original purity. We were celestially appointed its guardian, and
our having acted our part well in ages past prevented the designing
from tampering with it. As long as we keep the same jealous watch,
Gentilism will succeed as little as Samaritanism of old in its endeavors to foist in erroneous notions. But the moment we desert our
past we may open the way for the unscrupulous to mutilate and
corrupt, agreeably to the opinions wished to be palmed off on the
credulous as authoritative.

The knowledge of the Hebrew is then the golden hinge that our
national and religious existence turns upon. What Israelite will deliberately break it apart? Are we so infected with indifferentism
that we care not if it be shattered into pieces? Or are we so mate-
rialized, that our attention will be directed solely to that which procures some temporal gain? I will not so malign my people. No;
the Jewish community, small as it is in number, can point to men of

scholarly attainments, to individuals whose presence might grace any society. They can discuss the classics and the schools of philosophy; they can evince a due appreciation of arts and sciences. But has Hebrew literature no attraction for such Israelites? Can Homer and Virgil offer to a well-trained mind charms that exceed those abounding in Job and Isaiah? Has Aristotle displayed an acumen which has not been equaled by our Maimonides? And does not the Talmud contain what might profit even the scientist? Oh! that the Jew who immortalized his name by a writing proving his versatility of genius could address such among his co-religionists! Would that Emanuel Deutsch were living and in our midst! The depth of his learning and his impassioned eloquence might stir us up to the cultivation of a study reprehensibly neglected. But what a renowned fellow-believer might have accomplished by a richness of literary resources and persuasive words, I wish to perform simply by the resolve to do some good. We cannot disguise the fact that the number of Israelites in our community who can understandingly read from the text a portion of Scriptures is fast diminishing. So sadly have we degenerated from those who called strange what was not Hebrew, that a lad before reaching his religious majority, often devotes months to qualify himself for the recital of a portion of the Pentateuch; and only very few can be found able to rehearse faultlessly a chapter from the prophets. The prospect opening to our view is aught but cheering. If we proceed as of late, the next generation will, I fear, be incapable of making the declaration of faith in the now well known words of our inspired Moses.

As a palliative for the growing evil, a novel worship has been invented—a worship in which a *minimum* of Hebrew is interlarded with a *maximum* of German and English; a plan more fraught with mischief to the millions constituting "the house of Jacob" than any yet conceived ... I hold that the mission of the spiritual guides in Israel is to raise people up to their standard, rather than they themselves should come down to the level of their flock. It is not their mission, I say, to yield to the spirit of the time, and help in making the Hebrew a strange language, but to stand firm, laboring with might and main that the holy tongue may become household words. Had this plan been universally adopted we would not hear the humiliating confession that the divine service is unattractive, because recited in an unintelligible language. Had there been less preaching and more teaching we would not lament the consummate ignorance of a branch of learning as important as it is priceless. I have no desire, however, to reprove, but to improve; not merely to deplore a case of unpardonable negligence, but to implore your co-operation that it may cease to exist. "Ho! every one that thirsteth! Come ye to the waters; and he that hath no money, come ye, buy and eat." To contribute to the dissemination of a learning peculiarly ours, and which has held an empire over the heart of thousands of generations; to call into active life Judaism, through the agency of its handmaid, the Hebrew language, is my ardent wish.

Style it prejudice, if you choose, but I verily believe that to have drunk deeply at the fountain of a literature, whence heaven-bred poetry gushes forth, and sovereign wisdom wells out, is to have been filled with love for the religion of Israel. To be imbued with that knowledge, and desert that religion is impossible. Should the passions at times lure us away from it, we will still return to its fold, seeking it as we would seek a mother on whose breast we hope to find calm and repose.

The Hebrew language is holy, because it exercises that blessed influence. Flowing down from the hills of eternity, it restoreth the soul. The Hebrew language is an infusion divine. It holds the mirror up to nature, and reveals beauties undescribed. The Hebrew language is the treasure house of the poetry of the heart; now plaintive, anon joyous, but ever pure, ever noble, exalting. The Hebrew language is most holy, because it has been set apart by God as the receptacle of truths destined to sway mankind and humanize the world. Too long we have denied its supremacy. Let us crown it, and set a throne for it in the midst of the congregation. All eyes shall behold it, become enamored with it, and extol its peerless charms. No; the Hebrew must no more be strange to "the house of Jacob." Judah, the chosen sanctuary of the Lord, must enshrine it and make it glorious.
REV. S. MORAIS,
Minister of "Mikveh Israel," Philadelphia.

APOSTROPHE—A diversion of speech.
LOUAS (Hebrew)—The vernacular, the language of the nation.
AXIOM—Self-evident proposition.
MANDATE – Command; charge.
IMPIOUS—Irreligious; wicked.

TO PALM—To impose, to conceal.
ACUMEN—Quickness of intellect.
MATERIALIST—One who denies spiritual substances.
PALLIATIVE.—Mitigating, not removing.

BIBLICAL POEM.

"With human cords I drew them forward;
With leading strings, and bands of love."—Hos. xi: 4.

And who can say when first the silent cord
Moved onward thro' the spheres of infinite space,
To touch the heart, and lead it to the Lord,
All lesser powers of mortal to efface?

Whether by signal of electric fire,
Sent from eternal orbs of golden light,
Or silvery beams—to lift the soul still higher
Thro' grief and woe, to reach its destined height?

Or, if angelic beings, hence departed,
Weave, with soft music, 'neath their shadowy wings,
Those "cords and bands" wherewith God's tender-hearted

Are drawn to Him, who to His heaven
He brings?

What are they be—those silent cords of
love,
That bind us to His holy will forever.

And draw us, heavenly linked to those
above,
No earthly grief can shake—no death
can sever.

ROSA EMMA COLLINS.

THE HEBREW LANGUAGE.

IF we inquire into the excellencies which usually recommend the learned languages, we shall find the Hebrew to be an original and essential language, *that borrows of none, but lends to all.* Some of the sharpest Pagan writers, inveterate enemies to the religion and learning of both Jews and Christians, have allowed the Hebrew tongue to have a noble emphasis, and a close and beautiful brevity. The Hebrew is a language, for uniformity and simplicity, of all others the most easy; and yet at the same time so full of excellent wisdom and skill in the contrivance of it, as, considering it merely as a language, will afford exercise for the acutest parts and give pleasure to the most curious.

The Old Testament is the rich treasury of all the sublimity of thought, moving tenderness of passion, and vigorous strength of expression, which are to be found in all the languages by which mortals declare their minds. One word is often a good description, and gives you a satisfactory account of the chief or distinguishing property or quality of the thing or person named. It would be no difficult matter for a man of diligence and good taste, competently skilled in the Hebrew and classical learning, to prove that the Hebrew Bible has every beauty and excellence that can be found in all the Greek and Roman authors, and a great many more and stranger than any in all the most admired classics.

If it be objected that this representation seems to affect the Holy Bible, rather than barely the Hebrew language, and that the world is stored with a variety of excellent translations, it may be answered that this variety is an argument in favor of the study of the original, for amid a diversity of interpretations, how shall we be ascertained of the true one without the original? And, in short, after we have puzzled and perplexed ourselves with turning over and comparing the best translations, we can only know that the authors of such translations have acquainted us with the particulars we read in them, but cannot assure ourselves that the Holy Spirit has dictated such accounts in the Sacred Text. Add to this that every language has its idioms and peculiar beauties, which it is not possible to express or preserve in their native energy, when translated into any other language. This is more especially observable of the Hebrew, which is a language of a peculiar cast, both in the contexture of its words and the cadence of its periods, and contains expressions whose emphasis can no more be translated into another language than the water of a diamond can be painted without detracting from the original. PROF. THURLSTONE.

CONTEXTURE—The system. | CADENCE—The flow of verses or periods.

HEBREW POETRY.

THE art of the Hebrew is true art to those who can rise to the level of his passion. But religious conviction is supreme where it exists at all. And the æsthetic necessity that all things in heaven and earth shall bend to the divine purpose of salvation revealed to the poet's faith, is also the ethical necessity on which the whole religious life depends. That the things which are impossible with men are possible with God, is the first axiom of a religion that shall rise with triumphant assurance over all the powers of evil and all the woes of life. To assert with unwavering confidence the victory of spiritual certainties over all empirical contradiction, to vanquish earthly fears in the assurance of transcendental fellowship with God, to lay down for all ages the pattern of a faith which endures as seeing Him who is invisible—such is the great work for which the poetic genius of the Hebrews was consecrated by the providence and inspiration of the Most High. How nobly this work was served by that Hebrew intensity which carries one supreme conviction with irresistible poetic fire through all things in heaven or earth that rise up against it, may be read alike in the personal utterances of the Psalter and in the Messianic hopes of the prophets. Thus it was that the Psalmist, surrounded on all sides by the contradictions of sinners, bowed with sickness and grief, oppressed by the consciousness of guilt, was yet able so to cling to the unfailing certainty of his living fellowship with redeeming God, that danger, and sickness and sin itself were left behind, and he pressed forward beyond the fear of death to the assurance of immortality at God's right hand. Thus it was that the prophets, gazing on the certainties of Jehovah's righteousness and grace, saw the creation, now stained with sin, and blasted by the strokes of divine indignation, transformed in new perfection and holy loveliness, and instinct in all its parts with a sweet intelligence, so that from verse to verse of things now deemed inanimate the prayer of man goes up to God, and the answer of God descends on man.—*British Quarterly Review.*

AXIOM—A proposition evident at first sight. | TRANSCENDENTAL—General; pervading many
EMPIRICAL—Versed in experiments. | particulars.

WHAT IS LIFE?

"What is Life?" I asked of a wanton child,
As he chased a butterfly;

And his laugh gushed out all joyous and wild,
As the insect flitted by.

"What is Life?" I asked; "oh, tell
  me, I pray!"
His echoes rang merrily, "Life is
  Play!"

"What is Life?" I asked of the maiden fair,
And I watched her glowing cheek,
As the blushes deepened and softened
  there,
And the dimples played "hide and
  seek."
"What is Life? Can you tell me its
  fullest measure?"
She smilingly answered. "Life is Pleasure!"

"What is Life?" I asked of a soldier
  brave,
As he grasped the hilt of his sword;
He planted his foot on a foeman's
  grave
And looked "creation's lord."
"What is Life?" I queried; "oh, tell
  me its story!"
His brow grew bright as he answered,
  "Glory!"

"What is Life?" I asked a mother
  proud,
As she bent o'er her babe asleep,
With a low, hushed tone, lest a thought
  aloud
Might waken its slumber deep.

Her smile turned grave, though won-
  drous in beauty,
As she made reply, "Life?—Life is
  Duty!"

I turned to the father, who stood near
  by,
And gazed on his wife with pride;
Then a tear of joy shone bright in his
  eye,
For the treasure that lay at her side;
I listened well for the tale that should
  come:
"My life?" he cried; "My life is
  Home!"

"What is Life?" I asked the statesman
  grand,
The idol of the hour;
The fate of a nation was in his hand,
His word was the breath of power.
He, sickening, turned from the world's
  caress,
"'Tis a bubble!" he cried—"'tis emp-
  tiness!"

I turned and asked my inner heart
  What story it could unfold;
It bounded quick in its pulse's start,
  As the record it unrolled.
I read on the page, "Love, Hope, Joy,
  Strife—
What the heart would make it—such
  is Life!   ADAPTED.

THE PECULIARITIES OF ISRAEL.

ABOVE all things we must distinguish the people of Israel in their
peculiarities. This peculiarity consists, as every one must be aware,
in their religion. It is true that every nation of antiquity had its
peculiar religion, but the ancient popular religions were surrounded
by a common tie, and this joined character is opposed by the peculiarity of the Israelitish religion. While the others blend the Divine
Being whom they adore with the world, the Israelites distinguish
the God whom they worship quite differently from the world. The
plainest proofs can be found that every appearance of God was
always distinct from His being, and every representation of God, however well meant, was considered desecration. Closely connected with
this is also that the heathens conceived the Deity as a multiplicity,
while the Israelites always used the utmost rigor and severity in

adhering to the view of the indivisible unity of the Divine Being. The Israelites were conscious of this religious distinction in which they possessed the purity and truth of religion for all nations and unto all times. From of old they ascribed unto themselves the priesthood through which all the nations of the earth should be led unto God (Exodus xix: 6); and when, one day, the blessing of God through Abraham will have reached all races and nations, it was considered by them as the object and end of all history. (Genesis i: 3.) The Hellenes could not conceive a dignified human civilization and culture without being consecrated by their science and art; and to the Romans the world appeared without state and power if the nations and countries of the whole universe were not encompassed by their laws. History itself has impressed these universal historic presentiments of the three-named nations with the stamp of truth and right.

Art and science of Grecian antiquity have become the school as well as the lasting model for the cultivation of the mind at all times; and the Roman's legal system remained, both for government and code of laws, the strong frame in which the civil arrangements on this and the other side of the ocean were set. As the historic rules of the two named nations have reference to the development of worldly life, the ideal as well as the real, the Israelitish nation imparts the perpetual type for the religious life, for the relation between the Deity and mankind; and as confidence is the more necessary for this most intrinsic and tender relation than for worldly circumstances, so the Israelitish consciousness of their future destiny became the more self-confident and certain. While the two other nations possess only an instinctive foreboding of their future destiny, there stands by the Israelites their universal historic future in the form of prophecy and hope indubitably firm. In this light of futurity have all the gifts and advantages which Israel enjoys their final design upon the whole body of nations. These distinctions of the chosen people cannot, therefore, be given to them just merely for enjoyment and for fame; they require a rigid and holy service through which these treasures and gifts of sublime life, after being intrusted unto Israel, are to be made accessible to the whole world.

Among the many errors which have been diffused in regard to the people of the Old Testament, and which are propagated, it is said to be a characteristic of the Israelites, in conceited vain-glory and with haughty disdain over all other nations, which they denominate heathens, to boast upon their special covenant with Jehovah, the supreme God. The caricature of national vanity walks along everywhere and at all times beside the rightful and dutiful consciousness of national peculiarity. But if one wishes to know what by the name of Israel is really meant, then let him inquire and search for those which history itself has authenticated as representatives of their nation, and one will perceive that these are indeed penetrated with the consciousness of the highest superiority which fell to the lot of their nation; but by no means is this consciousness combined with anything like self-importance. On the contrary, the environment of that Israelitish consciousness consists in rigid self-denial, sincere humility, ready and capable for the severest troubles, the utmost exertion of all vigor of both body and soul, so that every one must say in them is reflected the truth of that consciousness.

Another misconception must also vanish which is generally circulated in reference to the God of the Israelites, as if He were a limited and partial being, attached to His chosen people with fond love, while the heathens are always treated by Him with rage and vengeance. It is incredible how, in times of civilization, one generation can belie another as long as it is flattering to the ruling prejudices. Whosoever really wishes to glance at the books of the Old Testament, will soon become convinced that a greater severity than that which God exercised toward His own people it is impossible to conceive. "Behold, among His servants is no one without fault, and upon His ground He finds folly." (Job 4: 18.) If Eliphaz speaks thus of God's heavenly spirits, it is no wonder that every page of the Old Testament proves how God punishes those whom He loves the most. If one wishes to know how the peculiar nation is nowhere spared, how the best and highest in the nation, without the least regard to person, are humbled. then one must peruse the literature of the Old Testament. Such inconceivable prejudices as those just named could not anywhere spring up, much more take root, if the Old Testament history and literature were not by preference possessed of a religious character, and thus subject to a fate which religiousness everywhere has to endure. Since the true and essential ideas of religion are but seldom conceived and understood, it becomes much easier to confound religiousness with any other appearance of life, with its phantoms and degeneracies. Religiousness in the Israelitish nation and in its history is the absolute fixed basis, and just on this account all other accomplishments of this nation, in a general and historical point of view, remain subordinate and unimportant. But even this circumstance is wrongly understood in believing that it is a characteristic of the religion to despise the world, and that Israel's deity is lowering the world to a vanishing, worthless moment. In taking in a superficial manner simple expressions from the Old Testament, and separating their connection, then one can only fall in with such conceptions. But if the connection and statements of the Old Testament are strictly adhered to, then is heaven and earth created of God, and man placed on earth in order that the divine destiny appointed at the creation of heaven and earth may be realized. From this point of view, undoubtedly, heaven, earth and mankind are depending, but in that case created through the word of God and animated by His spirit.—*From "David the King without Equal."* PROF. BAUMGARTEN.

INDUBITABLY—Undoubtedly.
CARRICATURE—A figure or description in which beauties are concealed and blemishes exaggerated.

PHANTOM—A fancied vision.
DEGENERACY—A forsaking of that which is good.

LONGING FOR JERUSALEM.
AFTER JEHUDAH-HA-LEVI.

Thou blooming joy of all the world,
    thou fortress proud and royal,
To thee from out the far off West my
    soul turns true and loyal.
My heart on thoughts of olden time
    groans up in plaints unspoken,
That all thy glory and thy pride should
    shattered be and broken?
Ah, could I like the eagle, free to thee
    my flight be wending,

How could I water thy hot dust with my
    fresh tears descending.
E'en though I found no royal throne
    upon thy site lamented;
E'en though the scorpion's breath in-
    stead of air sweet-scented,
With ardent love I'd kiss each stone
    by cruel foeman beaten,
And every clod of earth for me the
    grief of old would sweeten.

DR. HONIGMAN.

JUDAISM AND ITS RELATION TO MANKIND.

THE central thought and moral texture of our religion, its very warp and woof, is an all-comprehensive monotheism, and the natural result of which is, and must be, the breadth of its teaching and the universality of its application. Monotheism from a Jewish point of view ignores at once the possibility of regarding the God of nature—the first, the sustaining and the last cause—as a tribal God. No argument to the contrary, howsoever speciously put, can apply. Every line of the Holy Scriptures is intended to disabuse the mind of such a heresy. God declared Himself, through the Hebrew prophets, to be the God of all nations—good to all, and whose mercy extendeth to all His creatures. The Jewish teaching of Messiah is essentially world-embracing. It prophesies a golden age, not for Jews alone, but for the human race. The logic-chopping, the crafty sophistry, the counterfeit persuasion, the bigoted obtuseness, that would so libel Judaism as to narrow it to the puny dimensions of a tribal religion, can only be founded, to say the least, on an *argumentum ex absurdo* growing out of an obstinately cherished ignorance.

Judaism, I mean its saving dogma, addresses itself as its direct *sequitur* not simply to Jews, but to mankind at large. "Ye shall, therefore, keep My statutes and my judgments; which if a man do, he shall live in them." (Leviticus xiii: 4.) In commenting on these words, the Talmud and post-Talmudical words, without exception, infer in several places. Rabbi Mier asserts, hence we learn that even the non-Jew who studies and respects the moral laws stands side by side with the high-priest of the nation.   For, does it not especially say in the law, "Which a man shall do and live."   It does not here restrict the blessing neither to the priest, the Levite, nor the Hebrew, but, in the highest sense, confers it on man as man; hence the non-Jew who studies and respects these moral laws is on a level even with the high-priest himself.   Institutional Judaism alone is, and must be, from its nature, tribally Jewish.   Judaic discipline must inevitably be co-ordinate with racial habits, local requirements, historical traditions, and political necessities.

The canon of Judaic catholicity is, however, written by God himself, not only in the Holy Scriptures, but in the very constitution of man's moral being.   One God having created all men, all men have one common Father.   Thus, inasmuch as Judaism proclaims the unity of the human family, it follows that no matter how divergently its members may be grouped by race, climate, color, religion and consequent civilization, "the one touch of nature makes the whole world akin."   This is Judaism—the Judaism of the Bible of the Talmud and of history.   Yet we are told, to our utter dismay, that Judaism, from its very inception, inculcated a narrow and unnatural polity; that its spirit is even now impiously selfish and degradingly tribal.   This assumed to the satisfaction of our detractors, we "hard-shelled" Jews are declared to be *ex-necessitate* morally unfit to have a voice in the council of nations, that we cannot be intrusted to deal wisely, fairly or safely with the destiny of States.   *   *   *

In vindication of our faith, we may here quote and cannot quote too often, the maxim of the great Hillel: "Do not do that to others which from others would be grievous to you."   This is the gist, said Hillel, of our religion; all the rest is but its commentary.   Learn this, and become a Jew, said he to the heathen who desired to be converted.   This self-same maxim is the guiding principle of all sensible religions.   The proto-martyr Akiba asserted that "to love your neighbor as yourself" was the axis on which Judaism turned. Such utterances as these might be supposed to cover the whole ground.   Our sages, however, fearing—and well were their fears justified—that cavillers might desire to restrict the terms "*your neighbor*" and ask who is your neighbor? and answer the Jew only —members of the same race and religion—quote and urge the dictum of Ben Azai.   This Rabbi summed up the divine intention of the laws as inculcated in the scriptural phrase standing (in Gen. v: 1) as an exordium of the whole Bible: "This is the book of the generations of man.   In the day when God created man, in the likeness of God made He him."   By thus giving one common origin and parentage to the human family, the Bible gives the golden key that opens the wide portals of Judaism to all men.   Inasmuch as all men have one fashioner, and, therefore, one God, and as there is but one world here below for the whole physical human race, diversified though we are, so we are taught by Judaism that there is but one heaven hereafter to all born in the moral image and spiritual likeness of our beneficent Creator, and to whom we are responsible, not so much for what we in our weakness may think, but for that which in our moral strength we strive to do.

A. L. GREEN.

REV. A. L. GREEN, of London, England, late minister of one of the chief congregations of the metropolis; a self-made man.

TRIBAL—Belonging to a tribe.
SPECIOUSLY—With fair appearance.
HERESY—An opinion of private men different to the established orthodox faith.
OBTUSENESS—Bluntness; dullness.
ARGUMENTUM EX ABSURDO (Latin)—Inconsistent arguments.
SEQUITUR (Latin—Following ; succeeding.

To INFER—To draw conclusions from foregoing premises.
INCEPTION—Beginning.
EX NECESSITATE (Latin)—To make necessary; forced by others.
PROTOMARTYR—First martyr.
EXORDIUM—A formal preface.

RECOGNITION.

How shall I know thee, in the sphere which keeps
The disembodied spirits of the dead,
When all of thee that time could wither sleeps
And perishes among the dust we tread?

For I shall feel the sting of ceaseless pain,
If there I meet thy gentle presence not;
Nor hear the voice I love, nor read again
In thy serenest eyes the tender thought.

Will not thy own meek heart demand me there ?
That heart whose fondest throbs to me were given.

My name on earth was ever in thy prayer,
And wilt thou never utter it in heaven ?

The love that lived through all the stormy past,
And meekly with my harsher nature bore,
And deeper grew, and tender to the last,
Shall it expire with life and be no more ?

Shalt thou not teach me, in that calmer home,
The wisdom that I learned so ill in this—
The wisdom which is love—till I become
Thy fit companion in that land of bliss?

WILLIAM CULLEN BRYANT.

W. C. BRYANT was born in Cummington, Mass., 1794. He was admitted to the bar, but soon changed that profession to become one of the proprietors of the New York *Evening Post.* As a poet he is the delight of his countrymen and his style is distinguished by the perfect finish, elevated tone, dignity of sentiment, and the lovely pictures of American scenery.

MARVELS OF ISRAEL'S HISTORY.

CAN the world show anything like it ? Twice 1800 years old, they saw the proud Egyptian perish in the waters of the Red Sea ; they heard the fall of great Babylon's power ; they witnessed the ruins of the Syro-Macedonian conquest. And now they have outlived the Cæsars, and outlived the dark ages. They have been through all civilizations, shared in all convulsions, and have kept pace with the entire progress of discovery and art. And here they stand to-day, as distinct as ever, occupying no country of their own, scattered through all countries, identical in their immemorial physiognomy, earth's men of destiny, before the venerableness of whose pedigree the proudest escutcheons of mankind are but as trifles of yesterday. But have they suffered severely? One convulsive groan of agony breathing through eighteen centuries, and heard in every land but our own. At the siege of Jerusalem by Titus, besides the tens of thousands led into captivity, it was as if in a single action of a great war the slain on one side should amount to 1,300,000 ; and when, the remaining Jews having been expelled their country, they attempted, sixty years afterward, to return, a half million more were slaughtered. For centuries they were forbidden, on pain of death, even to set foot in Jerusalem. Under King John of England, 1,500 were massacred at York in one day. Under Ferdinand and Isabella 800,000 by a single decree were forced out to sea in boats, and the most of them perished in the waves. They have been fined and fleeced by almost every government known to history. They have been banished from place to place : banished and recalled, and banished again. By the codes of Justinian, they were incapable of executing wills, of testifying in courts of justice, of having social and public worship. The Koran of Mohammed stigmatized them as wild dogs ; the Romish Church excommunicated any one who held intercourse with them ; the Greek Church uttered anathemas still more severe. They have been forced to dissemble to save their lives, and in Spain and Portugal have even become bishops and have governed in convents. In the prophetic words of the Old Testament, they have been "a reproach and a proverb, a taunt and a curse ;" they have been "taken up in the lips of talkers," and have been "an infamy of the people ;" and the general estimate of them has ripened into the intense contempt of that dramatic conception—Shylock, the Jew of Venice. And now in this nineteenth century they are a suffering people still, but still as indissoluble as ever But now all this is not according to the established course of nations. The Northern tribes came into Southern Europe, and are now not at all distinguishable. No Englishman can say that he derives from the Britons and not from Normans. On the contrary, the Jew is a Jew still. Even our own all-appropriating country, which denationalizes Germans, Irish, French, Spaniards, Fins, Swedes, has left untouched this wondrous people. Here they are, holding fast to that one tell-tale face, keeping up the sacred learning of their traditions, self-conscious in their isolation, irrepressible in their love of Jerusalem, sublime in their singular patriotism, evermore looking and longing for their Messiah, the same intense individuality as when, lord of the soil, he plucked his fruit from the trees of Judea. And, what is more, these world-wanderers of the centuries, these tribes of the weary foot, have not only survived, but have now risen again as an element of power among mankind. The Jew is the banker of the world; he is among the foremost, whether in science, or literature, or government. In witchery of song unsurpassed, he enchants the world with some of the sweetest music it ever heard. Surely, he is the standing miracle of the world's current history; the bush of Moses, ever burning, yet never consumed; an ocular demonstration of how God may energize the secret springs of a people's life, yet without disturbing individual freedom or social characteristics; an unanswering refutation of that godless philosophy which would turn the Almighty out of His own universe. And for what have they thus been borne in the hands of God all along the ages? Beyond a peradventure, if so literally have been fulfilled the prophecies which foretold their sufferings and their preservation, equally sure are the predicted grandeurs of their future.

BISHOP NICHOLSON.

GRASS AND ROSES.

[From the Persian.]

I LOOKED where the roses were blooming,
  They stood among grasses and weed,
I said, "Where such beauties are grow-
    ing,
Why suffer these paltry weeds?"

Weeping, the poor things falter:
  "We have neither beauty nor bloom;
We are grass in the roses' garden,
  But the Master gives us room.

"Slaves of a generous Master,
  Born from a world above,

We came to this place in His wisdom
  We stay to this hour from His love.

"We have fed His humblest creatures,
  We have served Him truly and long,
He gave no grace to our features,
  We have neither color nor song.

"Yet He who made the flowers
  Placed us on the self-same sod;
He knows our reason for being—
  We are grass in the garden of God."

SAADI.

THE WORK OF HEBRAISM.

THE Hebrew religion is full of vitality; it is not one of enervating mysticism, but an intellectual faith which nourishes itself with all pertaining to the realms of culture and science. It reinvigorates itself with the realities of life, not aspiring to the indefinite, but hungers and thirsts for the positive triumph on earth of justice and law; and for the space of two thousand years Judaism has not ceased a single hour from this work—from longing and from combating with all its powers for the triumph of the right. The modest work of the Hebrew, silent and peaceful, carried on in the Eastern and Western world from the barbarous to the mediæval ages, forms the subject of a longer discourse than these fugitive pages are equal to. Let it suffice here to recall how he was the bond of union between the East and the West, between the ancient and modern; how to him is due the preservation of the treasures of literature; how he is the living embodiment of his story, of tradition; how to him, in the times of universal darkness, we owe it that the lamp of knowledge burned with no uncertain light; that judicial, medical, philosophical and economical science still flourished among men.

And not alone for this have the nations of the earth to thank the Hebrew race. When no one else worked they ceased not their indefatigable journeyings to and fro in pursuit of commerce among diverse people; and when the world, a prey to barbarisms, to feudatories, to the privileged robbers of the Church, was only an area of rapine and destruction, these people ceased not to work, to point out the great avenues of commerce, and to open up the true sources of social wealth. And when, in virtue of the great revolving wheel of time, a new epoch dawned, no people were found in a better condition to comprehend the change than the Jews; none better prepared to profit by their improved social positions. But under these happier circumstances they have continued with greater ardor than ever to work for the promotion of the principles of justice, of liberty and of labor; principles which were their strength in the past and are their most lively hope in the future.—*From the Italian.*

DAVID'S LAMENT FOR ABSALOM.

Alas! my noble boy, that thou shouldst
    die!
Thou who wert made so beautifully
    fair!
That death should settle in thy glorious
    eye,
And leave his stillness in this cluster-
    ing hair!
How could he mark thee for the silent
    tomb,
My proud boy, Absalom!

Cold is thy brow, my son! and I am
    chill,
As to my bosom I have tried to press
    thee;
How was I wont to feel my pulses
    thrill,
Like a rich harp string, yearning to
    caress thee,
And hear thy sweet "My Father!"
    from these dumb
And cold lips, Absalom!

But death is on thee. I shall hear the
    gush
Of music, and the voices of the young,
And life will pass me in the mantling
    blush,

And the dark tresses to the soft
    winds flung;
But thou no more, with thy sweet voice,
    shalt come
To meet me, Absalom!

And, oh, when I am stricken, and my
    heart,
Like a bruised reed, is waiting to be
    broken,
How wilt its love for thee, as I depart,
Yearn for thine ear to drink its last
    deep token!
It were so sweet, amid death's gathering
    gloom,
To see thee, Absalom!

And now, farewell! 'Tis hard to give
    thee up,
With death so like a gentle slumber
    on thee,
And thy dark sin!—Oh, I could drink
    the cup,
If from this woe its bitterness had
    won thee.
May God have called thee, like a wan-
    derer, home,
My lost boy, Absalom!

ADAPTED.

SCIENCE AND RELIGION.

IT is often said that there is warfare or contest between science and religion. Some of those who profess to have studied the different sciences assert that they are in opposition to divine revelation. It is true that at all times the Bible has had to sustain the assaults of men with sharp wit and acute intellect; geologists have ransacked the bowels of the earth, and astronomers tracked the stars of heaven to deny, attack, villify, and throw doubt upon the truth of Holy Scriptures. But perhaps no time has been so bold as ours in the attempt to revile and refute the Bible. And as, in our time, young men study other subjects more than the holy word of God, we cannot be astonished to find that doubts and uncertainties bring about indifference and apathy toward religion. However furious this antagonism be between science and religion with respect to those creeds in which faith is opposed to reason, such a contest must be slight or superficial in Judaism, where faith and reason go hand in hand. And, indeed, we are about to show how, in Judaism, science and religion are allies, co-operators, or in the words of the Bible, "two roes that are twins." It is true that the domain of science has become so large that no man can master it all; but when the comparison between religion and science is to be made, not with the *floating* theories of the hour, but with well-established truth, we may venture to convince you that our holy faith has nothing to fear from its attacks.

If we take Exod. xix: 24, we find that Moses and the people came near to Sinai; when the Lord prepared the latter for the great event; when he ordered them to make bounds round the mountain, a circumstance from which the three next days are called the "Days of the Bordering;" the Lord warned them once more that they should not break violently through, else when they would be anxious to gaze at the divine glory, it would cost them their lives. We hear the same warning from above—addressed now with respect to the dangers which may arise from the contest between science and religion, if we do not regard them from the right standpoint. I will venture to indicate to you this standpoint in as brief a manner as possible.

The knowledge of the Lord has at all times been regarded as a high mountain, which can be reached by sciences that form the steps thereto. Maimonides says, in the beginning of his great work, Yad Hachazakah:

" How can we fear and love God? When we consider and reflect upon the works and marvelous creations of the Lord, which have no limit or boundary—works which cannot be compared with anything wrought by man—we must feel a thirst to know God, and regard ourselves as insignificant creatures before Him who is perfect in wisdom."

Moses reached the highest point in this knowledge, because of him it is said, "In all my dominion he is faithful." The Psalmist and the prophets obtained a high standard, for they abound in reflections upon and pictures of nature. Again, of Solomon it is said, "He spoke of trees from the cedar, the tree that is in Lebanon, even unto the hyssop that springeth out of the wall; he spoke also of beasts, of fowls, of creeping things, and of fishes," which means that physical science was at his command. The teachers of the Talmud also made science the Hagar—handmaid—to Sarah, the mistress of theology. And, indeed, they ought to be regarded thus ancillary. Science teaches astronomy; but who is it, we ask with Job, that built the universe, ordained the sun's motion, projected the comets, placed the moon and stars in their orbits, "each in its proper station, service and charge," like the tribes in wilderness? Science teaches geology; but who has created the rocks of ages, the hills of the earth, "who removeth the mountains and they know not, and shaketh the earth so that the pillars thereof tremble"? Science teaches botany, but who gave such wondrous beauty and fragrance to the herbs, shrubs and flowers? Science teaches zoology, but "who provideth for the raven his provision, when his young ones cry unto God, and wander about for lack of food"? You must admit that all these sciences, rightly understood, are not antagonists, but helpers and aids to the knowledge of God.

The same is true with regard to the providence of God, which also can be better understood by the help of science. There is not a leaf that moves, not a wave that rises and sinks, not a ray of the sun that beams, not a whisper of the wind, that does not teach the providence of God. And we ascend higher up to man, who can deny the argument which the Psalmist adduces to prove God's direct and immediate providence? "He that planted the ear, shall he not hear? He that formed the eye, shall he not see? He that fashioned the brains and the reins, shall he not be able to reflect? He that teacheth man knowledge, shall he not know?" He knows our thoughts, every word before it is on our tongue, nay, the smallest incident, since they are often the cause and origin of the greatest events.

But do you need a proof of God's providence? Can you want any proof? Is it not abundantly demonstrated by the fact that you are here as Israelites, still existing, and prospering, and flourishing after all the trials and persecutions which our nation has for so long a time borne, compared with which those of Roumania are almost light. Yes, history, our history, gives evidence of God's direct and special providence.

Revelation on Sinai regards science, not as its rival, but as its ally. What do we generally hear urged against the Bible? That the teachings of geology are opposed to its statements. For, according to that science, the world must have already existed millions of years. According to a statement in the Talmud, the world was from the beginning created in its finished state, with all its strata and with all its layers. "The whole creation was called into existence in its full growth, beauty and development"— a theory by means of which all the objections will fall to the ground. This, moreover, I would say, that belief in revelation can be obtained either by faith or by science. When obtained by the latter method, it is like a mountain, the top of which will afford an excellent view in ascending, while there are some positions in which this view is hidden, concealed or seen only by a kind of optical delusion. Geology is a growing science. We know what our forefathers never dreamed of; that, for instance, the diamond which flashes on your finger is but a piece of coal; that the water which extinguishes fire is composed of two elements which burn with light and heat. A boy is now familiar with facts which would have astonished Newton. At present, it seems to the geologists that their science is in opposition to the Bible; but do we know whether our children will not laugh at their speculations, as they laugh at those of their forefathers, and then will be brought into harmony with the word of God?

But two conditions are required in the study of science and revelation. Do not violently break through; do not climb the mountain too boldly, lest the Lord might break forth upon you. We may study science to make ourselves acquainted with nature, but it must lead to nature's God. We may earnestly seek for second causes, but they must lead to the first cause. Forget not that after all the *Torah* is like the sun, the greater luminary, and science like the moon, the lesser luminary; and we may apply to them the well-known legend that when at first two great lights had been created, the moon said, "Two kings cannot have one crown," and rule at once over the same area. When you find that a theory of science will undermine your belief in God and revelation, follow the greater and not the lesser light. "Come not to gaze at the holy things with arrogance and presumption, lest ye die." When the spies presumed to go up to conquer the Holy Land, and the ark and Moses were not with them, they were smitten and discomfited even unto Hormah. When four of the wise men entered Paradise, which is perhaps another word for the garden of science, only Rabbi Akiva entered and went out in peace, delighting in its flowers; but Acher, who plucked them, turned an infidel.

The second condition is, that when any speculation of science will lead you away from any duty toward God, from keeping the Sabbath, or observing the dietary laws, be firm; obey the divine law and abandon the speculation. Forget not that any theory which is opposed to religion is but a floating theory, resting on the surface. And it will fail either in its premises or in its conclusion; for the fault lies not in religion, but in those who promulgate that as science which is not science, and give forth theories which deprive you of all means of self-control, while the Torah makes you better physically, mentally, morally and spiritually. For this reason our forefathers said at Mount Sinai, "we will do," before "we will inquire." Knowledge is required, but good works have the precedence. It is not what we know, but what we practice, which is important. What Aristotle said of his book, "That book is written not for knowledge, but for action," is much more true of the Torah. Bear in mind that at all times skepticism wanted to do its dangerous work. Our forefathers also saw the Torah attacked and villified, and brought in collision with the science of their day. Still they shed their blood, laid down their lives, sacrificed that which was near and dear to them, rather than trangress one important law of God. Especially this day forms the anniversary of the period when hundreds of our fathers and mothers became martyrs for their God and their religion; when, according to our history, the wives and mothers died more cheerfully and resolutely than the fathers and husbands, because their faith was stronger. Study science, study religious knowledge. Should a doubt enter and take root in your heart, give the benefit of the doubt to the Torah—do not throw aside any of God's commandments. Beware of your heart, keep it with all diligence, that nothing may find lodgment therein which might break through the boundaries which God hath set. Then the law will protect and shield thee.

"When thou goest it shall lead thee, when thou sleepest it shall keep thee, and when thou awakest it shall commune with thee."

NATHAN MARCUS ADLER.

REV. DR. N. M. ADLER, Chief Rabbi of Great Britain and noted for his erudition and extreme piety. He is the author of several works which gained him a European reputation. THORA (Hebrew)—Law; Scriptures: Holy Writ.

HYMN.

(BY GABIROL.)

ALMIGHTY! what is man?
But flesh and blood.
Like shadows flee his days,
He marks not how they vanish from
his gaze—
Suddenly must he die,
He droppeth, stunned, into nonenity.

Almighty! what is man?
A body frail and weak,
Full of deceit and lies,
Of vile hypocrisies.
Now like a flower blowing,

Now scorched by sunbeams glowing.
And wilt thou of his trespasses inquire?
How may he ever bear
Thine anger just, thy vengeance dire?
Punish him not, but spare,
For he is void of power or strength.

Almighty! what is man?
By filthy lust possessed,
Whirled in a round of lies,
Fond frenzy swells his breast.
The pure man sinks in mire and slime,
The noble shrinketh not from crime.

Wilt thou send on him the charms of
 sin?
Like fading grass
So shall he pass,
Like chaff that blows
Where the wind goes.
Then spare him, be Thou merciful, O
 King,
Upon the dreaded day of reckoning.

Almighty! what is man?
The haughty son of time,
Drinks deep of sin,
And feeds on crime.
Seething like waves that roll,
Hot as a glowing coal.
And wilt thou punish him for sins in-
 born?
Lost and forlorn,
Then like the weakling he must fall,
Who some great hero strives withal.
Oh, spare him, therefore! let him win
Grace for his sin.

Almighty! what is man?
Spotted in guilty wise,
A stranger unto faith,
Whose tongue is stained with lies.
And shalt thou count his sins—so is he
 lost?
Uprooted by thy breath,
Like to a stream, by tempests tost.
His life falls from him like a cloak,
He passes into nothingness like smoke.
Then spare him, punish not, be kind, I
 pray,
To him who dwelleth in the dust, an
 image wrought in clay!

Almighty! what is man?
A withered bough;
When he is awe-struck by approaching
 doom,
Like a dried blade of grass, so weak,
 so low,
The pleasure of his life is changed to
 gloom,
He crumbles like a garment spoiled
 with moth.
According to his sins wilt Thou be
 wroth?
He melts like wax before the candle's
 breath,
Yea, like thin water, so he vanisheth.
Oh, spare him, therefore, for Thy
 gracious name,
And be not too severe upon his shame!

Almighty! what is man?
A faded leaf.
If thou dost weigh him in the balance
 —lo!
He disappears—a breath that thou
 dost blow.
His heart is ever filled —
With lust of lies, unstilled.
Wilt bear in mind his crime
Unto all time?
He fades away like clouds sun-kissed,
Dissolves like mist.
Then spare him! let him love and mercy
 win,
According to Thy grace and not accord-
 ing to his sin!

EMMA LAZARUS.

EMMA LAZARUS, a lady of high talent and noted for her literary contributions both in
prose and verse to some of the leading papers and periodicals of America, and greatly esteemed
on account of her sincere attachment to Judaism.

THE REJUVENESCENCE OF THE HEBREW RACE.

THE first test which a nationality has to stand in order to show
durability and power in developing an unimpaired existence, is its
capability of rejuvenescence, after having once overcome the weakness of old age. If, therefore, any proofs of its resurrection from its
grave-like slumber are once given, then its immortality is thus
clearly established. It must be able to rise, if at any time made
low, and it must preserve in adverse times vital power like an inex-
tinguishable spark amidst a heap of ashes. The Talmud has an in-

genious allegory concerning the resurrection of the body. When death and putrefaction have dispersed the atoms of the human frame far and wide, there still remains in the spine a small bone that resists all destruction, and that cannot be demolished even by the anvil. It is from this indestructible solid part the resurrection develops itself. If, therefore, a people be possessed of such a precious kernel, then neither iron, nor fire, nor any corrosive acidities, can destroy it, but the same will expand even when pressed down by gravity into the smallest compass.

The Hebrew race is now quite plainly entering upon a process of rejuvenescence, of which we have had hardly any presentiment. The enemies of Judaism perceive it with suppressed rage. Jews who consider themselves cosmopolitans, shake their heads doubtfully, while those pious to the very letter do really place their hope therein; but all are startled at the appearance. Is, therefore, this apparently incredible movement real palpitation of the heart, or merely the galvanic short-lived motions of a corpse? Is it possible that diseased and dispersed bones could revive again? This question, in the very same form, was once started by a Hebrew seer, at a time when the Jewish race resembled a corpse, even more so than the case is now ; and the spirit which came over him showed him how bone moved near to bone, and these became covered with flesh, a skin stretching over the same, and at last a vital spirit entered these bones, which made them in living form. The fact is that the Hebrew race experienced such a resurrection from death during the Babylonian captivity, and it is highly suggestive to note how this process, from an almost imperceptible beginning, has brought about an era which is now exciting the greatest astonishment. This rejuvenescence of the organism of the Jewish race offers also in many other respects an interesting analogy, and deserves to be known in its proper light.

In times past, of the five to six millions of Jews belonging to the Israelitish nation, almost two-thirds were transplanted, one and a half centuries before the beginning of the Babylonian captivity, to Media, Bactria, and the country of the Caspian Sea, and there, amidst the natives, their total decline took place. Even the most strenuous inquiries proved unsuccessful in discovering only the slightest trace of the ten tribes. "As the day gone by will never appear again, so will the ten tribes never return," was the sober observation of Rabbi Akiba seventeen centuries ago. Everything which at the present time is fabled about the existence of the lost tribes is either a mere whim of learning or nothing but ignorance. The principal stem of the remaining third—the tribe of Judah— was transported to the left shore of the Euphrates. Small parties thereof separated as far as Egypt, or were sold for slaves by the Greek and Phœnician pirates at the coast towns, and the islands situated on the Mediterranean Sea. Slavery commenced when dispersion took place. "To become scattered to all the four corners of the world," was the sorrowful thought which the prophets imparted to the Jewish race in early times, even when the state was still in existence as an unbroken power.

The exiles in Babylon formed the nucleus and the heart of the national organism weakened already on all sides. In their midst was the Jewish nobility, as far as they did not succumb to the Chaldean conqueror in defending their fatherland and the capital. There were also some descendants of the royal family, and among them one who wore the crown of David during a hundred days, in order to wander from the throne to the prison, and to be freed from it when near the end of his life. There were the priestly Levites of the house of Aaron, who, after the temple was laid in ashes, became the bearers of the portable sanctuary, the holy law, which was then their sole care. Those who were already settled there a half century, possessing land, herds, and slaves, felt home-born in Babylon, forgot the lost fatherland, the destroyed Jerusalem, and the destruction of the Temple. These then soon adopted the Babylonian worship of idols, being used from home to idolatry, under a coloring of Israelitish worship.

Besides this class, doing homage to whatever seemed practical and the fashion of the day, were some who, with all their attachment to what they received from their forefathers, were dolefully despairing of the possibility of a restoration of the Jewish state, and the rebuilding of the sanctuary. They declared of themselves, " Our nature is faded, our hope is vanished, we are doomed to perish." God Himself, thought they, who sent so much misery upon His holy people, delivering his sanctuaries unto the enemy; God Himself has deserted, cast off and forgotten Israel. In ancient times the idea was indelible that people, soil and Deity are inseparable, and a nation, severed from its mother country, has lost all support, and even God Himself, however high Israelitish consciousness may have placed him, stands in a certain relation to the country, which he promised to the patriarchs, and presented unto their sons. With the banishment of this holy nation and the estrangement of the holy land, the band which united the Temple with heaven seemed forever broken. In this manner they resigned themselves to their fate; and, although they did not worship the customary idols of the day, they had nevertheless no confidence in their own affairs.

But the situation of the Babylonian captives was, just during the last years previous to their deliverance, of such a nature as to deprive them of all courage, and to make them consider it mere folly to hope for a restoration. At that period the Jewish nation experienced for the first time that frightful form of servitude, by which it became a mockery to the thoughtless multitude, who, adhering to externals, tried to provoke it to self-contempt. Already, in the Babylonian captivity, Israel was obliged "to hold forth his body to be flogged, and his beard to be plucked." The haughty conqueror told him already at that time, "Kneel down that I may crush thee," and he acquired the endurance of seeing "his body exposed to the feet of his oppressors." At that time the outer world said of the people of the Jewish race, "She has no form, nor appearance, nor comeliness, that we should fall in love with her; she is despised, abandoned by men, affected with pain, with sorrow." She was then already beaten and tortured without opening her mouth. "Like a lamb she was led to slaughter and shorn like a sheep, but remained dumb and never opened her mouth." The school of suffering oppression, hatred, contempt, scorn, flogging, ill-usage and misapprehensions, which the Jewish race was to undergo at a later period, even through many centuries, and which impressed her history with tragical appearance all this commenced during the Babylonian captivity.

But just amid these innumerable sufferings, and in spite of the apostacy of the one party and the dejection of the other, there rose a circle of ardent adherents to the God of Israel, whose hope in a brighter future never ceased. These were the "men of endurance," unmindful of their sufferings, sad in mind and broken hearted, and who, in their entire devotion, in their humility and self-denial, cleaved to God and left everything to His divine will. It was the circle of those who "mourned for Zion," and sat weeping on the rivers of Babylon, as often as they remembered the desolation of the sanctuary ; who suspended their harps on the willows and would not sing Zion's song in a foreign country. The famous poet who sang, "I will forget my right hand if my remembrance of thee does not surpass all gladness," also belonged to this circle. A few Judean servants of the court, and the eunuchs who kept the Sabbath, and adhered to the Israelitish covenant, were likewise of this order. This then was the precious kernel of the "indestructible bone" from which the rejuvenescence proceeded.

But how was this wonderful fact, so rich in consequences, and showing its after-effect even unto this day, brought about? Not perhaps by the return from the Babylonian captivity, for this event was the result of preceding causes, and would have been but of little use had not the half dead Jewish race been called into fresh existence previously. And to whom is this resuscitation to be attributed? It proceeded from a single person, who certainly was a God-fearing man, and who understood the signs of the times in order to adopt the right plan. He knew how to raise the slumbering echoes in every one's mind, whose powerful and inspired, at times encouraging and at times warning voice, was well calculated to transform depression into courage, despair into hope, timidity into confidence, indifference into participation, and even lethargy to sensibility. The pencil of history has not preserved the name of this prophet, and, therefore, he is commonly called the Babylonian or exiled Isaiah. This name he deserves, at any rate, for in loftiness, beauty, and impressiveness of prophetical poetry he was surely not inferior to the son of Amos, and his views extended even further than those of 'the latter.

But as soon as the historical work was undergoing a fresh change by the hand of the daring but mild conqueror, Cyrus, who led his strength of Media and Persia against the all-governing Chaldaic-Babylonian kingdom, in order to destroy it and to establish a newer empire, than the exiled Isaiah sounded the word Zion! giving it an inimitable magic, now in a sorrowful, tragic tone, and then again in an excited strain of triumph, so as to make it vibrate in the innermost recesses of the people's hearts. He represented Jerusalem as a widow shrouded in mourning, who had drained the cup of sorrow to the dregs. "She is the unhappy, distracted, disconsolate widow, who has borne so long the shame of being childless." But he called unto her "to shake off the dust of lowliness, to expand her tents largely; for her dwelling will become too small for the multitude of her own admirers, as well as of strangers, so that she herself shall be surprised as to who has born all those for her, childless, forsaken, banished and desolate as she has been." But in spite of the unbelieving, the scorners and the despisers, he foretold a speedy redemption through "Koresh" (Cyrus), whom God has called and chosen, and to whom He will impart strength in his conquests. No prophet has, the same as he, poured consolation into the heart of the sufferers and hope into the mind of the exhausted. The balm of his words is able even unto this day to heal the wounds of many a broken spirit.

Israel, however, should not enter upon the approaching redemption in a state of contamination, but should merit the same through self-excellence and nobleness of mind. He should seek God, for His help is close at hand. He should undo the knots of malice, loosen the fetters of slavery, discharge the oppressed from servitude, bestow bread on the hungry, give shelter to the suffering poor, clothe the naked, and not to turn away from the afflicted kinsmen of his own race. Then shall light of Israel rise Aurora-like, and his cure will speedily be brought about. Israel's heavy afflictions were conceived by the great prophet of the exile in a very high point of view. The painful martyrdom was requisite for his cure. Not only Israel himself, but also the sinful world of heathenism, shall be expiated thereby. God himself denied Israel's humiliation. "If he considers himself a guilty sacrifice, then he will see a long-abiding posterity, and through his instrumentality God's purpose will be promoted. Because he is ready to consecrate himself to die and is counted with the criminals, he thus bears the sins of many, and appears as mediator for those who have gone astray."

No one better conceived and represented Israel's ideal vocation than did Isaiah. The Jewish nation is the apostle whom God sends to the idolatrous, wicked, morally corrupted world. She shall be a light unto all nations, in order that God's salvation may reach to all the corners of the earth. Israel, "the servant of God," has a mouth like a sharp-edged sword, and is destined to be the chosen arrow. God has poured out His spirit upon this race, that it may possess the power of conveying right unto all nations, but "she shall not scream aloud, nor become proud, nor allow her voice to be loudly heard in the street. She shall not act by way of force, nor even break a bent reed, nor extinguish even a glowing wick, but through meekness she shall promote justice according to truth." Israel is anxiously looking for the great event of the coming of a Messiah, the anointed of the house of David, upon whom the spirit of God will rest. In him all the ardent hopes of the Jewish race are centered; hence every Israelite is composed of the matter to be a Messiah, for God has ordained that through his instrumentality universal harmony shall be established in the world, when all its inhabitants shall pay homage to the Lord, who is king over all the earth. Thus Israel will become the savior of the world, and he will announce the word of deliverance. The sorrowful, despised, crushed and servile form is called for a higher purpose, just on account of its suffering condition. The crown of thorns which this Messianic race bears so patiently makes her worthy of a kingly diadem. A nation which through affliction and death shall be aroused unto a resurrection, even through the gates of the grave unto life, such a nation is really praiseworthy!

The exiled prophet quickened the minds of his contemporaries in regard to another matter. The enemies of Israel will become his friends and confederates. Many of the prophets in their inspired views have indeed prophesied the participation of the nations in Israel's future welfare, but none have given such a correct and clever description of the universality of Judaism as the exiled Isaiah: "The neighbors, the strangers, the sons of heathenism shall not say the Lord will separate us from His people. But the strangers who will join Him, to serve Him, to love Him and to be His servants, He will rather lead them to His holy mountain, for His Temple will be a house of prayer for all nations." These noble thoughts, flowing from the heart and the most profound conviction, and spoken with eloquence, must all have died away in the air, had not the few remaining exiles of Judea sufficient susceptibility that they themselves labored to bring about their rejuvenescence. Under this inspiration the people consented to be aroused unto a resurrection.

The apparently dry bones moved one unto the other, became

covered with flesh and skin, and took within them the breath of life. The circle of the "ardent men of the word of God" became larger day by day. The more Cyrus approached the Chaldean capital, the more did the hope revive of the recovery of the lost independence and nationality. The "Eunuchs" of the tribe of Judea, the descendants of the house of David, Zerubabel, "the strangers," who joined Judea from pure love of God, became all very active to realize the words of the prophet. Self-examination soon began; and the idolatry, with which many exiles were still affected, was thoroughly and forever abolished. It was the work of inflamed inspiration which executed the miracle which many previously thought impossible. As soon as Cyrus made an end to the Babylonian kingdom, he in a wonderful manner fulfilled the hopes of the exiles by proclaiming: "Whoever is willing to return to Jerusalem is permitted to do so." There were above 40,000 families who resolved upon returning home, at the head of whom moved a king's son of the family of David, and a high-priest of the house of Aaron. This small number formed a state once more, producing again its heroes—heroes of the sword and of intellect—who became noted in name and in deed even unto the whole world. This small number has poured its healthy and nourishing sap into the veins of mankind.

H. GRAETZ.

REJUVENESCENCE—A renewing of youth.
PUTREFACTION—The state of growing rotten.
CORROSIVE—Having the power of wearing away.
COSMOPOLITAN—One at home everywhere.
GALVANIC—A kind of electricity invented by Dr. Galvani, an Italian.
ANALOGY—Resemblance between things.

DOLEFUL—Sorrowful.
INDELIBLE—Not to be blotted out.
CONTAMINATION—Defilement; corruption.
LETHARGY—A drowsiness.
UNIVERSALITY—Extending to the whole.
SUSCEPTIBILITY—Tendency to admit.
INSPIRATION—Infusion of ideas into the mind by a superior power.

THE SEVENTY-SECOND PSALM.

Oh God, with judgment bless the king,
His son, beloved of Thee, we sing,
All time shall prove him faithful, true.
All honest poor shall have their due.

From Eastern river, Eden's bower,
Through Western worlds men own his power:
Wild men, subdued, approach his seat
His foes lie prostrate at his feet.

The mountain peaks, in peace, no less
Rejoice thou hills in righteousness.
He'll judge and bless all humble folk,
And save poor children from the yoke.

The kings of Tarshish and the isles
Where blind idolatry defiles,
Both Sheba's kings and Seba's, too,
Shall give up all his will to do.

The oppressor's power, he'll crush outright,
And sooner fades noon's orb from sight,
And moons no longer wax and wane,
Than the oppress'd seek help in vain.

Yea, all earth's kings shall to him bow,
All gentiles serve him under vow,
And why? because he saves the poor,
All helpless ones have his help sure.

As rains revive the shorn-off mead,
And showers quicken covered seed,
His grace revives all upright hearts,
And endless peace His name imparts.

He'll save the contrite and the poor.
Assist them their trials to endure;
Redeemed from fraud and violence,
Their blood he counts of worth immense.

To him shall Sheba's gold be brought,
And for his reign all blessings sought,
The saved in gratitude shall sing,
All time with daily prayers ring.

Blessed be Jehovah, Israel's king,
His praise let every creature sing,
Whose love suspends primeval law,
Whose miracles impress with awe.

A mountain peak may have some corn,
Which spreads till rustling stocks adorn
A towering ridge like Lebanon;
So grows the realm of David's son.

With blessings of eternity
Crown his one name eternally.
Great name ! too brilliant for man's ken !
All earth shall sanctify. Amen.

His name shall bloom in Israel's rhymes,
The vernal blossom for all times.
Blessings shall hang upon his name,
All tribes his blessedness proclaim.

All prayers of David have their end
In blessings such as God will send.

                          A. I.

TOKEN—To know.

PERPETUITY AND IMMUTABILITY OF THE MOSAIC LAW.

THE words found in Exod. xix: 9 place us in immediate connection with the astounding revelation at Sinai, upon which the festival of Pentecost is based. They call back our minds to a scene, full of majesty and awe, over which more than three thousand years have closed. But if thrice that number of years had been marked by the register of time, this scene would be as vivid and its glory as bright; for of no occurrence on this earth has Almighty Providence left a stronger and more enduring remembrance. The words cited in the above Scripture passage invite us to survey the lowest of a range of mountains, at the base of which a whole nation of more than two millions of souls is assembled. Scarcely seven weeks have passed since these human beings, now awaiting the declaration of God's holy will, were claimed and held as the property of a vain and tyrannical ruler, and were treated little better than beasts of burden. They were enslaved in body and in mind, and were not suffered to think or to act but according to the despotic will of their hard-hearted oppressor. Now, if we may measure time by the great events which it brings to pass, the people encamped near the mountain have lived an age. They have seen their cruel persecutors ingulfed in the waters, the grave to which many a new-born Jewish infant, torn from its mother's fond embrace, had been consigned by the sanguinary edicts of the Pharaohs ; they have seen their freedom secured on a firm basis at a time when the danger of a second servitude was imminent, and when all hope appeared to be cut off; they have seen fresh water springs gush forth from the flinty rock to slake their thirst ; they have seen food rained down from heaven day by day for the supply of themselves and their families ; they have known what it is to enjoy true Sabbath rest ; they have experienced the beneficial consequences of a righteous tribunal, where poor and rich, high and low, are patiently heard and equitably judged ; and

they have happily learned that the government which Moses was
charged to establish for them exists for the good and happiness of
all, and not for the private ends of the few. In fine, freedom and
the dawning of civilization have wrought a great change in the condition of the Israelites within the lapse of a few weeks, and we now
behold them assembled with one accord to take counsel of their
Almighty Redeemer, to learn from Him the uses to which they are
to apply their newly acquired liberty, and what course of life they
are to pursue, in order that they may discharge faithfully their office
of a "kingdom of priests," which their leader has just informed
them they are to become.

The verse quoted sets forth the gracious manner in which the Lord
is about to enlighten the minds of His people, to fortify their hearts,
and to confirm their faith, from generation to generation, in the doctrines of divine truth and holiness. " I will appear to thee (Moses)
in the dense cloud, so that the people may hear when I speak with thee,
and so that they may believe in thee and in thy teachings forever."
The Hebrews are enjoined to prepare themselves for this awful communion by abstaining from every sensual indulgence, by abstracting
their minds from all earthly thoughts, and by reflecting maturely on
the mercy and loving kindness which the Lord has shown to them,
since the day when he deputed Moses to the Egyptian court to demand their manumission. At the end of three days devoted to
solemn preparation, the promise recorded in the text is accomplished.
The thunder rolls, the lightning flashes, the earth quakes, and the
solemn peal of the *Shophar* is heard. To speak in the thrilling
words of the Psalmist: "The immensity of space is illumined by
the lightnings of God ; the earth looks on and trembles. The mountains dissolve like wax at the presence of the Lord, at the presence
of the sovereign of all the earth ; and, while the heavens are declaring His righteousness, and all the people are witnessing His
supernal glory," the voice of the Almighty is heard recalling a backsliding world sunk in superstition and sin, and pronouncing before
the assembled nation of witnesses the Decalogue, the ten immortal
principles of the Mosaic or Jewish code, the great repository of duty
to God and man. Such were the manifestations of divine power
and goodness, and such were the means employed by the gracious
Parent of mankind, in order to inspire with faith, and to crown with
salvation, the future generations of the earth.

The chapter from which the text is drawn does not simply record
the important fact of the revelation at Sinai, on which the festival
of the Feast of Weeks is grounded; but it at the same time informs
us in the most precise terms why that revelation was delivered in
so public a manner. The race of Abraham having been redeemed
from bondage, and made to think and to feel like men formed in the
divine image, were now to commence their sacerdotal office, and to

bear the message of truth and light and salvation everlasting unto all the families of the earth. Now, before a man is capable of persuading others, he himself must believe ; before he can be earnest, he must be sincere; before he can be qualified to teach, he must learn and clearly understand.   Hence it was of the first consequence that the faith of the Israelites in the articles of divine revelation should be free from doubt, and from all possible misconception, and that what they were to receive as principles of belief, what they were to do, and what they were to refrain from doing, should be distinctly set before them, and with a clearness that would be demonstrable to their senses.   Equally essential was it that they should be impressed with the conviction that the Sinaic doctrines were fixed and stable, and that God's word, like His divine nature, was in the strictest sense unchangeable.   The Israelites were to be taught that, far different from the enactments of fallible mortals, which can endure for a given time only, and must then give place to the ever-changing circumstances of earthly existence, which the framers of those enactments could not foresee—the laws of God have reference to all times, and anticipate all events in the moral universe; and that while His divine code cannot be thwarted in its operation by anything that is actual or possible, He compels all circumstances and events to bend in submission before the high and infallible authority of His mighty word.   These two important features in Jewish theology; viz.: the public revelation by God at Sinai, which was to carry conviction to the assembled multitude of Hebrews, and the perpetuity and the unchangeableness of this dispensation, are fully embodied in the verse of the text, which may be paraphrased thus : " I will appear to thee, Moses, in the thick cloud, and I will speak to thee in the audience of the congregated mass of thy people, so that they and their descendants may believe in thee, and confide in thy teachings forever." With this clear Scriptural declaration before us, we cannot be said to be true disciples of Moses and faithful followers of our ancestors at Sinai, unless we hold firmly and inviolably that no article of the Sinaic covenant can ever be altered or superseded, and that no dogma which is not there set forth in its plain and obvious sense can ever be entitled to our religious belief.   When the Jew speaks of the divine revelation, he of course understands by that term the whole Mosaic law, as I now shall proceed to show.

We are fully warranted to conclude from the Scripture record that the Almighty would have pronounced every precept found in the Pentateuch in the same audible manner as He spoke the Ten Commandments, if the Israelites had been enabled to support His awful presence.   But when the people fell back to a distance and implored of Moses, " Oh, speak thou with us and we will attend, but let not God speak with us, lest we die, " the Lord was pleased to grant their request.   At a distance of forty years the legislator recalls this circumstance to the minds of his hearers, in the following words, "Now the Lord heard your words when ye spake unto me, and the Lord said, I have heard the words of this people which they spake unto thee: they have spoken well." Moses accordingly receives all future commandments from God, and communicates them to the people; at the same time impressing upon their minds that all these laws are based on the articles of the Decalogue : "for according to the spirit of these words, I have made a covenant with thee and with Israel." We have therefore Scriptural authority for our doctrine, that every ordinance of the Pentateuch is inspired of God, and takes its origin in one of the principles revealed at Sinai ; and hence the passage of our text, "They shall believe in thee forever," applies to the entire Mosaic code. From what has been advanced, it must be evident to the Jew that the road to faith and duty is clear before him. He needs not torture his mind with doubts, whether the revelation vouchsafed to his ancestors at Sinai was to be modified after the breaking up of the political nationality of Israel, or whether it was to be eclipsed by any subsequent dispensations. The words of our text, reproduced in their spirit again and again in other parts of the Scriptures, are absolute and unconditional ; and it may be unhesitatingly asserted, that even the doctrine that God is one and indivisible is not more Scripturally proven, than is the Jewish article embodied in the poem of *Jigdal*, "that God will never alter nor change the Mosaic law for any other." The inspired Psalmist assures us that "the law of the Lord is perfect," and every man's reason will tell him that a code which the voice of inspiration pronounces to be perfect, cannot admit of any change or modification, without its being impaired, and further, that a law which is perfection God will never annul.

Between the laws which God has enjoined, and those which mortal man has framed, it behooves us to draw a broad line of distinction. The laws of man can have but a limited duration, because human affairs are subject to perpetual fluctuations and changes. A mortal legislator may institute laws which are well adapted to his own time ; but he can have no reasonable confidence that they will be suited to the altered circumstances in which mankind may, at some subsequent period, be placed. The law of God, however, is not to be measured by this varying standard. The Omniscient One grasps in His intelligence all time, the future as well as the present, and He knows what *will be* as certainly as He knows what is ; and as it is impossible that God should at any future time be wiser or holier, more benevolent to His children, or more desirous to promote their happiness, than He was on the day when He revealed Himself to our fathers at Sinai, so it is impossible that He should ever change His perfect law for any other.

Let us hold firm to this doctrine, which places Judaism upon an immovable rock—to this doctrine, which is the grand theme of the

holy prophets from Moses to Malachi.   While the inspired Isaiah
reproves his brethren for giving themselves up entirely to ceremonial
observances, and for neglecting the essentials or the moral duties of
Judaism, he emphatically declares that God demands of them and of
all future ages, what he required of the former generations of Israel:
" I, the Lord, the first; and with the last generations, I am the
same."   In the fullness of his inspiration, the same prophet predicts
a period when brute force shall be extinct, and mind shall be triumphant ; when weapons of strife shall be converted into implements
of husbandry ; when creatures in whom the most deeply-rooted an-
tipathies exist shall be brought into concord and harmony, and when
love shall be the one governing principle of the universe. To approximate this golden period, called the age of the Messiah, the good of
all sects and creeds are constantly laboring.   For this the rich man
dispossesses himself of a portion of his wealth; for this the poor man
submits to privation and murmurs not ; for this the school-house
and the pulpit rear their heads.   Among the worthy men who are
exerting themselves to this important end, do you, my Jewish brethren, be ever active ; and remember that the Prophet Isaiah not only
teaches that the practice of the pure Mosaic religion is calculated to
lead man to the highest moral perfection ; but he tells that the blessings of the Messianic age shall be accomplished in the spirit and in
the integrity of the Sinaic covenant.   When the Hebrews shall have
worthily discharged their office as a "kingdom of priests," when
"they shall have filled the earth with the knowledge of the Lord as the
waters cover the seas;" "and when they from the west shall revere the
name of the Lord, and they from the east His glory, a Redeemer
shall come to Zion."   But according to the prophet, the *Goual*
spoken of is not to set aside the covenant with God made with
the Israelites at Sinai, but he is to come in the integrity of the
Mosaic law.   " This is my covenant with them, saith the Lord; my
spirit which is upon thee, and my words which I have put in thy
mouth, shall not depart out of thy mouth, nor out of the mouth of
thy children, nor out of the mouth of thy latest posterity, saith the
Lord, from this time forth forever."   The same Jewish doctrine of
perpetuity of the Mosaic law is taught by Malachi, when he places
the seal on prophecy, in these memorable words: "Remember the
law of Moses, my servant, which I commanded him in Horeb for all
Israel, the statutes and the ordinances."   Having now endeavored to
impress upon you the two important articles of your faith—the public revelation by God at Sinai, and the perpetuity and the unchangeableness of this dispensation, let me remind you of the words spoken
by your fathers at the Mount, " All that the Lord hath spoken we
will perform."   Adopt these words as your own, and continue to
teach, not by your precepts only, but also by your practice, that there
is One God, who must be worshiped in spirit; that He requires of

His children a life of holiness and truth, and that if we bring Him not this inner worship, it will be in vain for us to approach His presence, and to strive to secure His divine favor through the performance of external rites, howsoever important they be. Adopt the words of your fathers, and continue to teach, " O kingdom of priests," that charity and love are the essentials of faith, and that these virtues must be exercised toward all men without distinction. Continue to teach that Judaism respects the religious opinions of others, and never presumes to violate the sanctity of conscience ; and that it accords salvation through the mercy and the lasting kindness of the Universal Father, to all men, of every religious denomination, provided their lives be morally good. Continue to teach that Judaism breathes love to all men, peace to all men, toleration to all men, and that its moral character is well portrayed in the sublime ethical precept, which was born of the Jew, and reared by the Jew, that it might become the common property of future generations: " Thou shalt love thy neighbor as thyself." In your capacity as " a kingdom of priests," it behooves you to make known these doctrines, and to give them vitality by the uniform practice of your own lives, and you have the assurance of your heavenly Father, that if you exert yourselves, earnestly and sincerely, to this end, you will find favor in the sight of God and of man.

This holy festival commemorates the day on which was conferred upon Israel, to the latest generation, the greatest of all treasures; let us remember the day and duly appreciate the gift; let us respect our faith, and the respect of mankind for us and for our religion will not tarry long behind. We live in an age, God be thanked and praised. when the narrow prejudices and the sectarian rancor which were once so universally directed against the Jew are fast disappearing, if they have not altogether died away, and are giving room to the feeling of natural confidence and love, strengthened by the sacred ties of a common country and of equal citizenship. Now, to what cause are we to ascribe this beneficial change ? Are we Hebrews of the present day less Jews than our fathers were in the middle centuries; have we put aside our distinctive religious character ; have we abandoned any of the principles of our hallowed creed; or have we compromised our consciences in any way to win the popular favor? No, we have not sacrificed, and I feel that I am not saying too much when I venture to assert that, as a body, we never shall sacrifice, at the shrine of power, of honors or of immunities, any doctrine of the sacred covenant which the Lord made with our fathers and with us. With all due allowance for the humanizing influence exerted by the spread of education, it is not sufficient to account for the great change which has come over men with regard to their sentiments toward the Jews. I cannot but think that the cause is to be sought for in this: that the Jew is beginning to be better known, and that the practices of his faith are better understood than they formerly were. In bygone ages the persecutions to which the sons of Israel were exposed obliged them to live in retirement, and to perform in secrecy their worship; this secrecy probably gave rise to suspicion, and suspicion to gross misrepresentations. Hence the Jews were accused of the most outrageous and revolting practices, and among the number, that of shedding human blood for the inauguration of the Passover, a calumny which, not many years ago, was seriously believed by a great number of simple-minded persons.

But these things are passed away. We have outgrown the fear of being observed from without; we have laid aside the drapery of mourning and despair with which our synagogues were hung in the iron ages of persecution, and we have brought ourselves more prominently before the public gaze. The consequences have been, that many misconceptions concerning the Jew and his religion, which took their rise in ignorance, are removed. It is now discovered that we may be sincere and zealous Israelites, and at the same time loyal subjects and patriotic and useful citizens; and that, while we are peculiar in our religious belief and in our religious practices, we seek no ascendancy for our creed, nor presume to urge it on the consciences of others, but that we proclaim and practice toleration in its widest sense. If these principles, which are as old as Judaism itself, may not have been made manifest by our ancestors for many centuries after the fall of Jerusalem and the annihilation of our political nationality, the cause must be sought in the galling persecutions to which the Jew was subjected, and which denied him the opportunity of being heard in his own defence against the unfounded prejudices with which he was assailed from every quarter. Yet, in the midst of their sufferings, the Rabbis never failed to impress their disciples with the pure Jewish teaching, "that the pious of all sects and creeds are rewarded by God with salvation everlasting." But it well behooves us, who live in happier times, to give evidence of our faith by our teachings and by our conduct; so shall we call down upon us the benediction of Him who revealed His law at Sinai; and so shall we, by moral means, conquer for ourselves that *equal* position in the land of our birth to which we boldly assert our claims. The time is rapidly drawing near when these claims must be acknowledged, and when the only blot on the code of our beloved country, as far as religious freedom is concerned, will be obliterated.

Let, then, our watchword be "for the law and for the testimony"; let our earnestness indicate the sincerity of our religious belief, and let our conduct toward God and man give ample proof that we are the worthy descendants of the men of Sinai, who promised "to perform all that the Almighty had commanded them."

PROF. D. W. MARKS.

REV. PROF. D. W. MARKS, minister of the West London Synagogue of British Jews. Dean and Professor of Hebrew at University College, London.

SANGUINARY—Cruel; bloody.
SACERDOTAL—Priestly; belonging to the priesthood.
ANTIPATHY—A natural contrariety to any-thing so as to shun it.

FALLIBLE—Liable to error.
TO APPROXIMATE—To approach; to draw near to.
RANCOR—Inveterate malignity.
IMMUNITY—Privilege; exemption; freedom.

PAST, PRESENT AND FUTURE.

THE PAST.

"When I forget thee, O Jerusalem!"
.On distant shores, in happier times,
In sterner days but brighter climes,
The Jew upheld with steady hand
The banner of his Fatherland—
The throne of Judah's princely line—
The Temple on the height divine—
The present home where wife and child
Beneath the hallowed roof-tree smiled.

Oh, lovely land! blithe, bright and blest!
Sweet cedars capped by mountains' crest—
What laughing fields! what stately trees!
What fragrant myrtles kissed the breeze!
The purple grape, the golden grain,
Decked grassy glade and pleasant plain ;
The wealthy harvests crowned the soil,
The towns were gay with sounds of toil;
Rich-laden ships embraced thy coasts,
Thy glens were glad with glittering hosts.
Oh, great in peace and great in war!
Thy name, thy fame, were known afar.
Full oft the fierce invader's stroke
Shivered before our "hearts of oak !"
Full well the Greek and Roman knew
To tremble at the name of Jew.

THE PRESENT.

"We hung our harps on the willows."
Where are thine ancient splendors now?
No circlet sits on Judah's brow;
No Temple rears its halls of state,

No high-born elders throng the gate;
No laughing harvests crown the fields,
No sparkling wine the berry yields,
No ruddy anvils gaily ring,
No flower-wreathed boys nor maidens sing,
No busy cities crowd the plain,
No buxom herds delight the swain,
No trade ships in the harbor dance,
No foeman fears our broken lance,
The raven flies o'er fields unsown,
To brood on Judah's shattered throne !
All, all is lost! Alas, no more
The sounds of life bless Israel's shores;
Our harp is on the willow hung,
All voiceless, tuneless and unstrung"!!

THE FUTURE.

"The Sun of Righteousness shall rise!"
All is not lost! In yonder skies
I see the gleams of hope arise.
Star of the East ! thy glimmering ray
Is brightening "to the perfect day,"
Again shall Judah's flag unfurled,
Wave forth its signals to the world !
Again shall cattle crowd the plain—
Her fields be rich with golden grain—
Her towns with busy voices ring,
Her swains rejoice, her maidens sing!
See in yon East, the glowing gleam !
Faith 'tis not false, nor hope a dream.
Messiah came ! rejoice our eyes;
And lo ! in yonder Eastern skies
The "Sun of Righteousness shall rise,"
And on its healing pinions bear
Love, Peace and Joy—for all the world
to share. MICHAEL HENRY.

MICHAEL HENRY was a native of England, a man of great literary attainments and for-merly editor of the London *Jewish Chronicle.* His untiring exertions in forwarding the cause of education and every interest belonging to Judiasm, and, above all, his kind and amiable disposition, gained him a large circle of friends among all classes alike.

ART AMONG THE ANCIENT HEBREWS.

I.

UNDER art, in an eminent sense, is generally understood the mere representation of the beautiful in its various divisions, so that many activities which require the application of art, and even industry, are conventionally thus excluded therefrom. This custom of language can easily be adhered to in confining myself for the present to the fine arts only; but it cannot be expected that we shall find, in speaking of the Hebrews, the same accomplishment in art as we meet with among the Greeks and a few other modern nations. This art-culture seems to be only possible when a nation, after a long period of intellectual development, meets subsequently with a favorable epoch for fostering art, this creative impulse having no outer barrier to contend with.

But, for the most part, the Hebrews lacked those pre-conditions; their favorable time for the development of art under Solomon and his successors, anticipated by many years their intellectual progress, and as soon as the latter had become matured, we know that art found there but little sunshine. Besides, the fact that the Hebrews spent most of their time in unfortunate political struggles, and that they were depending entirely on agriculture, was naturally another cause which checked the advancement of art. They were aware, too, of their chief mission in fostering and advancing the religious idea, which partly was another hindrance, inasmuch as many of their eminent men were thus led upon other paths. And although by the Greeks, and in later periods still more so by Christians, great triumphs in art were achieved in the service of religion, among the Hebrews the fact that images lead to image-worship prevented the cultivation of many branches of art. However, they found some compensation in those divisions which could appear in the service of religion, such as poetry, music and architecture, and in these they have indeed proved very successful. At the same time it will be necessary to remark that, from Moses until the destruction of the Temple by Titus, a period of almost 1,600 years, only two authorities, the Bible and Josephus, can be resorted to ; and, although these refer largely to Temple architecture, and the poetry which the Bible has preserved for us, they are, nevertheless, in regard to all other branches of art, silent, and thus our whole knowledge becomes mere piecemeal-work as far as we are able to glean from the resources at our disposal. But, as I shall have occasion to refer, now and then, to those periods during which these particular productions of art were brought to light, it will be necessary to make a few observations upon the alternate course of those 1,600 years. Already in Egypt the Hebrews acquired some knowledge of art, which even then flourished in that country to high perfection, and of which, after their departure, they gave sufficient proofs in the building of the Tabernacle. But the forty years of their sojourn in the wilderness, as well as almost the next 400 years under the Judges, were so unsuited for fostering art, that even the skill they had acquired in Egypt seems to have been forgotten. In the following period under King Saul, it was in no wise any better; but, during the reign of David, a more favorable time appeared for poetry and the science of music, which progressed under Solomon, who attempted and practiced many other branches of art as well. The next 390 years, till the last two tribes were led into captivity, were unfavorable for the cultivation of art ; but as a monarchial government is generally known to promote art, it appears, at least, that the Hebrews during this unfortunate period had not retrograded in their acquirements. In the fifty-two years of the Babylonian captivity they became acquainted with the splendid architecture of that country, and its celebrated industry in many branches of art; of which, however, we find no traces among those who, under Cyrus, were permitted to return to their fatherland ; nor can we find any among the exiles who remained in Babylon, with whom, perhaps, these impressions had thriven.

Those who had returned to Judea remained now two hundred years under the government of Persia, and their impoverished state, as well as the almost puritanic nature of the Persians, may account for our meeting but seldom any traces of Jewish art during that period. Alexander the Great followed, and then the Jews were one hundred and sixty years under the Macedonic-Grecian scepter, comprising the era of the art-loving Ptolemies, and afterward of the not less ingenious Seleucidæ, who resided in Antioch. At that time it appears that, in spite of the frivolous Grecian system, the Jews applied themselves again to the cultivation of arts; for we find both in Judea and Alexandria, whither hundreds of thousands had flocked, sufficient proofs of their industry. A reaction now took place, owing to the cruel measures of Antiochus Epiphanes, who brought about the glorious contests of the Maccabeans, which wholly put a stop to Grecian life and manners. After a lapse of one hundred and twenty years, the rule of the Maccabeans declined, and, by way of craftiness, blood, and the courted favors of the Romans, Herod came to the throne. Owing to his fondness for building, he erected many extraordinary monuments of art. But it appears, nevertheless, that art among the Jews did not receive any fresh impetus during his reign, partly on account of the excessive cost of his buildings, which turned the impoverished nation against such fancies, and partly owing to Judea being declared soon after a Roman province, when their bloodthirsty governors, greedy for money, began to deprive them of their peace of mind.

Hereupon the destruction of Jerusalem followed, then another violent struggle for fifty years, and the history of ancient Israel is closed, comprising a period of sixteen hundred years, and representing the field upon which the productions of Jewish art must be sought for. It will here be necessary to remark that art stood in great estimation among the Hebrews, and not only poetic and musical genius was of high repute, but also other works of art, in gold and silver, in stone and wood, in brass and iron, such as we meet with in the building of the Tabernacle, which was erected by the chief surveyor, Bezalel, to whom a divine spirit was attributed, signifying, according to Bible interpretation, the highest art genius. It must be acknowledged that, in the susceptibility of the people for impressions of art, and their high appreciation of art-culture, we perceive a powerful impulse toward its practice; and, therefore, our task is to enumerate the various branches of art attempted by the Hebrews, and also to state how far they succeeded.

I shall commence with architecture, generally divided into sacred and worldly, and of which I shall choose the former for my first subject. Of this we have a notable instance in the tabernacle in the wilderness, which, although only a mere movable temple-tent, cannot be passed over, partly on account of its architectural form, and partly owing to its fundamental designs, being afterward retained by all temples in Jerusalem. A space thirty ells long, ten ells broad, and ten high, was inclosed on three sides by walls of strong Acacian planks, joined by bolted beams, and gilt all over; each plank formed below two tenons deposited in heavy silver supporters. From above the space received four covers placed one upon another, and of which the interior one consisted of a valuable carpet interwoven with cherubim, while the second was made of fine goat's hair, the third of morocco leather, and the uppermost was from the skins of "Tachash"; of this place, the foremost twenty ells were appointed for the sanctuary, and ten ells of the posterior for the Holy of Holies. A curtain, exactly the same as the cherubim tapestry, separated the two; while a similar curtain, but without interwoven cherubim, formed the eastern portion facing the sanctuary. In the latter stood a table for the shew-bread, a small altar for incense, both covered with a thin plate of gold, and also a seven-branch lamp of massive gold, by which this space was lit up; while the Holy of Holies was entirely dark, containing only the Ark of the Covenant and the tablets of the Ten Commandments. In front of the sanctuary stood the sacrificial altar, a wash-vessel of bronze, which women had supplied with their metallic mirrors; and around the whole a fore-court was formed, having a space of one hundred ells in length and fifty ells in width, inclosed by sixty pillars at five ells distance from each other, and between which a Byssus web extended, except that, on the east side, the middle portion appointed for entrance contained another costly broad curtain. It will also be necessary to observe that the Hebrew ell was equal to about eighteen inches of our measure, and that the cherubim on the ark, as well as those on the tapestries of the sanctuary, represented superterrestrial guardians.

Thus we see that the Tabernacle was a simple, yet noble structure, and the religious impression which the appearance of a house of God should produce, was surely not lost sight of in this instance. There were certainly no Gothic spires projecting into the sky; but being placed exactly in the center of the Israelitish camp, within a beautiful circular fore-court for the devotees, a magically illumined place for the higher functions of the priests, and behind that the Holy of Holies, an entire dark sanctuary, the place where other religions put up their idols, containing merely the law tablets concealed by cherub wings, the whole was thus well calculated to awaken sublime ideas among the people.

II.

The next monument of Hebrew art was Solomon's Temple, erected on Mount Moriah at Jerusalem. The surface of this mountain top being insufficient for the intended building, they commenced raising walls of square stones from the foot of the mountain to the incredible height of three to four hundred ells, and the space left between these walls and the summit was filled up with earth. The Temple-house, also of square stones from eight to ten ells in length, was about seventy ells long, thirty broad, and forty high; but behind, a third part thereof, it was ten ells lower, containing within its very thick walls only the sanctuary of colossal dimensions, and immediately behind that the much smaller and lower Holy of Holies, similarly situated as the sanctuaries of the Egyptian temples, which was also lower than the remainder of the building. The former was forty ells long, twenty broad, and thirty high, while the latter was twenty ells long, broad and high. The roof of both was no doubt flat, and the one over the sanctuary was furnished with balustrades of red sandal wood. The inner walls of the sanctuary, and those of the Holy of Holies, were adorned with a covering of cedar boards, carved with cherubim palm trees and flowers, which were gilt, while both rooms were entirely overlaid with gold, even the floors, which were of Cyprus wood. The Holy of Holies was here also quite dark, receiving, besides the ancient Ark of the Covenant, with its two cherubim, two more cherubim much larger, and being on the east side separated from the sanctuary by a cedar wall only, having, the same as the eastern portal, colossal folding-doors with similar gilt carvings; but the sanctuary had again the small altar and the table (according to 2 Chronicles, ten tables), and, instead of one, ten seven-branch lamps, while some extra light was obtained by lattice-windows placed at the upper part of the walls.

Before the sanctuary was a porch (according to Chronicles) one hundred and twenty ells high, in which two high hollow pillars of bronze were placed, being twelve ells in circumference, and with very ornate capitals. The one was called Jachin, and the other Boas, in order to express, probably, that no earthly pillar could bring firmness, but that God alone·is able to make firm (Jachin); in Him there is strength (Bo-as). And it is well known that the first views of Free Masons proceeded in reference to these columns. While thus the porch, which was reached by steps, was facing the building, there was attached to the other three sides a small and much lower additional building, three stories high, containing rooms for the priests, and other apartments used for purposes of the temple. The whole was surrounded by a fore-court, and inclosed by a wall built of square stones, with cedar pallisades on top, and the numerous gates therein were all overbuilt in archlike form. Three sides of this fore-court were not of any wide dimensions, but the east side was the more spacious. There stood, in the first place, the offering-altar of bronze, twenty ells long and broad, and ten ells high, with steps and sidewalks, which, in terrace-shape, became gradually narrower on the top; besides, there were ten larger rinsing-vessels and so-called molten sea, which, like the former, was a valuable piece of art in bronze casting. The molten sea was a vessel filled with water, five ells in height, and ten ells in diameter, and was undoubtedly used for the priestly ablutions, the same being also furnished with other necessary arrangements pointing to a similar purpose.

A second fore-court. still larger, also easterly from the first, but lower situated, was probably added by some of Solomon's successors, who, it is known, made various alterations. King Achas ordered afterward a fresh altar, according to the model of one he had seen at Damascus, which he considered more beautiful; and thus the one already existing had to be somewhat moved aside. There was also a double porch on the eastern border of the Temple-mount, formed by three rows of pillars, and covered with a wainscoting of cedar boards, which, however, is attributed to Solomon. The building of colonnades appears to be a characteristic of Hebrew architecture, which, on account of the hot climate, became necessary in order to secure as much shade as possible. Those who have expressed the opinion that Phœnicians, to a great extent, took part in the building of Solomon's Temple, I have to oppose, on the ground that it was in all respects a mere execution in stone of the Tabernacle; and although some parts may be traced to a Phœnician style, it is, nevertheless, substantiated by the Bible that the Phœnicians who were employed were merely used for hewing down the trees on Mount Lebanon, as well as the cutting of the square stones, together with some assistance they gave in the articles made of bronze and other metals.

We are without any record as regards the temples erected for the worship of idols, which were in existence during the demoralization in Judea; we know, however, of the great Baal's temple which King Ahab had built in Samaria, that it was undoubtedly in Phœnician style. The temple which Ezekiel saw in a vision, and of which he has given a full description, we must also pass over, the same having never been executed, although the sketch shows some value in reference to art. Respecting the one built after the Babylonian captivity, there is also but little known, except what we gather from scattered fragments. We are informed that it was in all respects like Solomon's Temple, but in splendor much inferior, and in extent and architectural design approaching the one erected by Herod, of which we possess a minute description. This pomp-loving king undertook, what was never done before, to pull down the existing Temple and to erect a more splendid one in its stead, without venturing, however, to deviate from the fundamental principles of the old one. The edifice was apparently distinguished by its ascending distinctly in terrace-like form toward the chief sanctuary.

This will become more clear by describing at first the exterior, which consisted this time of a wall running round the front of the mount, being five hundred ells long on each of the four sides, and containing five gates, of which remarkably the top arch of the northern one could already plainly be seen. In the interior double porches ran the whole extent of the two thousand ells of wall, which were thirty ells broad, and constructed of pillars of white marble of twenty-five ells in height, and a roof made of cedar wainscoting. On the south side there was even a triple porch still more beautiful, the middle being higher than the two outside ones, and the floor being entirely overlaid with colored stones. A few steps further toward the interior there was, in circular form, a splendidly finished railing of stone about twenty ells high, being the limit for heathens, who were not admitted any further. In the inner part of this railing fourteen steps on each side led up to a square plain, which steps, like all the rest, were laborious to mount, reminding one of the high stairs of the Pyramids. Upon this square plain, within a vacant border of ten ells broad, a wall forty ells high inclosed the two temple courts. This contained nine large portals, four each on the south and north side, and one easterly, each being fronted by stairs for ascending, and having also folding-doors studded with inlaid gold and silver, while the wings of the eastern gate were of Corinthian bronze, and even more splendid in ornamental design. Each portal had inside a much wider fore-hall, built of two colossal pillars, upon which a tower-like superstructure rested.

By the eastern gate, or by one of the two first side-doors, the fore-court of the women was reached, having that name on account of women being only permitted to enter as far as this, where a loft, a gallery, was erected for them, one hundred and thirty-five ells long and broad, which space was rather diminished owing to the four corners containing large squares, branched off by lower walls, and that right and left a beautiful colonnade proceeded from each of the gates. On the west side of this fore-court a half-round winding staircase of fifteen steps led up to a gigantic portal forty ells broad and fifty ells high, by which access was gained to the inner fore-court, which also contained to the right and left of its seven gates beautiful colonnades. The first eleven ells leading into this fore-court were set apart for the laity, being separated by a bar skillfully cut in stone of only one ell in height, behind which were three steps leading upward and stretching the whole width of the one hundred and thirty-five ells of the fore-court, on which the Levitical singers were placed over one another, and then the very extensive fore-court of the priests.

Here we find the offering-altar, thirty-two ells long and broad, and ten ells high, which intermittingly became narrower at the top, rising in an oblique form on the south side. Then westward from the altar followed the proper sanctuary, constructed of white marble blocks, which were nearly twenty-five ells long; twelve steps, intermittingly arranged, led up to the fore-hall, which was not large, but one hundred ells broad and ninety ells high; above its open portal, of seventy ells in height, the gable wall showed five cornices over one another, inlaid with gold, and getting always broader toward the top. There was also a colossal vine in this hall, to which we shall have to refer afterward. Behind the latter stood the apparently much smaller main building, containing a middle nave thirty-two ells broad, seventy-three long and ninety-six high. In its front wall, covered entirely with gold, we find again a splendid curtain, a large portal with quadripartite folding-doors, and now at first appeared the sanctuary, twenty ells broad, forty ells long and sixty ells high, with table, lamp and altar; and merely separated by another costly curtain from the Holy of Holies, only half as long, but, like the sanctuary, sixty ells high, and entirely empty, except in the flooring; a raised slab only three fingers broad pointed out the place where once the Ark of the Covenant stood. Over both these were some other rooms constructed, which raised the height of the building to ninety-six ells, as previously stated; the flat roof was surrounded by a railing, the points of which were gilt, serving as lightning rods. Except the foremost side, we find here again that this high middle nave had, on three sides, an additional three-story building, sixty ells in height, consisting mostly of rooms for the priests, as well as for other temple requisites. Other numerous buildings for similar purposes could be met with at the eastern part of the priests' court, of which I shall only mention the so-called fire-house, in a northeasterly direction, with a roof in the shape of a dome; also a large basilica, southwesterly from the altar, where the Sanhedrim held their assemblies.

There were also other structures that deserve to be mentioned; the works for supplying the Temple with water, which was rather a difficult task, on account of its being situated on an eminence. The well which Solomon found proving insufficient, he procured for the Temple a supply of water by constructing a wonderful aqueduct, whereby he obtained water from Etam, a small place, three hours from Jerusalem, carrying it through pipes by way of Bethlehem, and also by throwing a bridge over the valley of Gichon, and thence to the mount of the Temple. In this manner, however, the water reached the mount only to a certain height, and it became rather troublesome to raise it to the summit. But they afterward constructed a reservoir under the Temple, which held all the water procured from Etam, and was then by wheel-work lifted to the top of the mount. There was also under the Temple an extensive bath for the priests, and a canal to carry off the unclean water into the brook of Kidron.

Another branch of architecture in connection with the Temple was the construction of bridges. The one already mentioned over the valley of Gichon was noted for its arches, while another, uniting Mount Zion and Mount Moriah, was also a beautiful structure. The bridge which Robinson discovered, and which led from the Temple into the town, cannot exactly be traced at the present day. There was also another which led from the Temple mount over the valley and brook of Kidron, as far as the Mount of Olives, which was a beautifully constructed viaduct of many arches; while also another is spoken of which led from the Temple into the wilderness.

During the last centuries of ancient Judaism, we find also synagogues established in some large cities, and the one in Alexandria is worthy of notice, the same being a basilica of extraordinary dimensions, surrounded by a double row of colonnades, and containing, among others, seventy golden seats for the Sanhedrim. The one in Tiberius was surrounded by a double row of colonnades, while one in Antioch is said to have surpassed all others. But we lack further records of these antiquities, and my observations on sacred architecture are closed for the present.

III.

In considering the art accomplishments of the Hebrews in regard to worldly architecture, I shall have to omit referring to its use in common life, inasmuch as all private dwellings were for the most part artless and insignificant in structure; while public edifices for wordly purposes were also very scarce, owing to assemblies being usually held in open places at the city gates, or in the fore-court of the Temple. I shall, therefore, only mention monuments, which, as already stated, on account of religious objections, never appeared in the form of statues personifying men. Absalom having no son to propagate his name, erected for himself a monument near Jerusalem, in the form of a marble pillar. The one pointed out by modern writers is of late origin, which its Ionic order of architecture sufficiently corroborates.

In later times a monument of the much-praised Queen Helena, consisting of three small pyramids, and also one of King Herod, are spoken of; more is known of a monument erected at Modin by Simon Maccabee, containing the mortal remains of all belonging to this heroic family. It was a broad pedestal, upon which seven small pyramids stood, being surrounded by high pillars and carved in various designs. During the time of the Greeks, we find a gymnasium erected by the Hellenistic High-priest Jason, and afterward Herod also built a large amphitheater for gymnastic exercises. In several towns large water basins could be met with, having steps for descending and being surrounded by a wall. King Solomon made use of one for watering his garden, and Hezekiah also had a similar one combined with an aqueduct to prevent scarcity of water; some of these served for baths, and one was even considered possessing healing properties, being surrounded by porches and named Bethesda (place of mercy). While King David erected a palace with the assistance of Tyrian workman, Solomon constructed one according to his own ideas, which in taste and splendor could vie with the Temple. The middle space containing a hall one hundred ells long, fifty broad and thirty high, was divided lengthwise by four rows of cedar pillars and covered with a wainscoting of cedar boards; above this hall two rows of chambers were situated, each row containing fifteen, one after another, having sideways a bow window each, and a corresponding arch in the middle wall, besides a flat roof with balustrades of sandal-wood. In front was a spacious court, accessible by a portal surrounded with pillars. Behind the above-named hall there was a second one, appropriated by the king as a law court, and containing the famous lion-like ornaments, of which more hereafter. To the right and left of this middle hall other magnificent edifices were situated, one being occupied by King Solomon himself, and another was set aside for the queen, a daughter of Pharaoh. A wall of square stones, with cedar palisades on the top, inclosed the entire building. This palace was called the house of Lebanon's forest, owing to its large hall being supported by cedars imitating a cedar forest in architectural style.

Later we find mentioned several palaces of the kings of Judea and

Israel, but lack further information. Likewise, nothing is known of the pompous buildings of Joiachim, whose extravagance Jeremiah reproached. We also know but little of the tombs of the ancient kings, except that most of them had a sepulcher in common, of beautiful construction. The statement that Hyrkanos, the Maccabee, took 3,000 talents of silver from the tomb of David cannot be credited, although Herod, with similar intention, opened it again, and found therein many golden and valuable trinkets; but, being prevented by the advancing flames to penetrate any further into the sepulcher, he ordered, in expiation of his act, that a marble monument should be erected at its entrance. There is yet a grotto in existence, although not identical with the one just named, which is called "the sepulchers of the kings," containing a fore-court and seven chambers, and well worthy of notice. The family sepulchers of the common people were rather complicated, plain and of indifferent style.

After the exile we know of a palace belonging to the Maccabean kings, but possess no further information; while the buildings erected by Herod are described in all their detail. His residence, in the upper part of the town, has been noted by Josephus as one surpassing in splendor almost all others. Amid beautifully laid out grass lawns, rose several marble buildings of different designs, having admirable roofs and porches of variously constructed colonnades, according to the peculiarity of the building, to which groves of trees were attached, intersected by pleasant walks and surrounded with basins serving as artificial waterworks, all made of bronze castings, and having tower-like pigeon houses resting upon them. The whole was inclosed by a wall thirty ells high, with towers on the top, placed at equal distances from each other. Herod also erected many buildings for military purposes, all in splendid style, and delightful as places of resort. Remarkable was the wall surrounding the upper part of the town, upon which he placed sixty towers at two hundred ells distance from each other, three of which were of white marble, one being called Hippicos, twenty-five ells long and broad, and eighty high, and it was singular that the lower half served as a reservoir, yet carrying two stories more above it; the second was named after his brother, Pharsael, being forty ells long and broad, and ninety high, surrounded at middle-height by a beautiful porch of colonnades, above which the tower continued to lessen, containing splendid dwellings and bath houses, and being in construction similar to the celebrated beacon in Alexandria; the third was named after his consort, Marianne, being fifty-five ells high, but in structure more splendid than the rest. There was also in the upper town the two towers Psephinos and Xystos, the former seventy ells high and of octagonal form, and the latter containing a large open space surrounded by arcades, besides fourteen other towers, constructed upon a second city wall.

In Ascalon Herod built a beautiful bath-house with colonnades, in Ptolomea a gymnasium, in Jericho a castle, and in a southeasterly direction, a few hours' ride from Jerusalem, he erected on an eminence a splendid citadel with towers, being reached from the valley below by two hundred marble steps, and supplying the same with water by means of an aqueduct. He named it after himself, Herodium, in memory of a victory gained by him on that spot. The best part of Samaria he also embellished with many public buildings, establishing a beautiful park, and being ignominious enough to erect therein a splendid temple for Augustus, besides a second one of white marble on the banks of the river Jordan. A small seaport town, Strotonstower, he entirely rebuilt in lavish style, and in honor of the emperor he called it Cæsarea. Here he also built a harbor by sinking into the sea, which is here twenty fathoms deep, large square stones, fifty feet in length. The pier was very broad, and upon the same stood several high towers, while the entrance to the harbor was on the north side, almost in the form of a gateway, accessible by a tower on the left, and two still higher monoliths, connected from above on the right. The border of the entire landing place was covered in by arches, behind which beautiful walks were laid out, amid which, on a hillock, there stood another temple for the emperor, with colossal statues of himself and the Roma, being surrounded by a large semi-circle of houses, built of white marble, the remaining part of the town containing a forum, theater, and amphitheater. Herod, in his extravagance for building, causing thus the disordered state of his nation, received certainly some compensation in the favorable smiles which Augustus thought proper to bestow upon him. There are other buildings ascribed to him, almost too many to be enumerated, and in passing over several palaces of ancient Jerusalem, I shall only further mention here that the new town was also surrounded by a wall containing ninety towers. It is almost impossible to delineate the overpowering aspect which Jerusalem imparted at some distance.

The flat roofs, with their gilt cross-bars, generally served as lightning conductors, of which Arago, the learned French naturalist, gives the following statement: "The Jewish Temple in Jerusalem existed nearly one thousand years; as the first stood nearly four hundred and the last about six hundred years. By its site this Temple was very much exposed to the severe thunder storms, whereby Palestine is so often visited. Nevertheless we find neither in the Bible nor in Josephus, that this building was ever struck by lightning. The reason thereof is very simple, for the wise King Solomon was not unacquainted with the laws of nature, and had made his arrangement purposely, so that the Temple was provided with a lightning conductor, which was very near the same as the one invented by Franklin, and which is in use by us now. The roof of the Temple was covered with heavily gilt cedar wood, and was provided from end to end with long steel bars, whereof the long points were also gilt. The walls were heavily gilt outside, and finally in the court of the Temple cisterns were placed, wherein the water from the roof ran through metal pipes." We find here so many conductors for the electricity that Lichtenberg was right in saying that the constructors in our days are far from arranging an apparatus so useful for its purpose. I can also not omit here some art accomplishments in the productions of landscapes, for which we also possess Humboldt's testimony, who remarks that nowhere in antiquity can we meet with, even not among the Greeks, so much ingenuity for natural productions as in the Bible. The garden which King Solomon found at Jerusalem was noted as a pleasure garden, containing trees of almost every description, beautiful shady walks, extensive lawns, with odoriferous flowers and plants, artificial hills with pleasant summer bowers, ponds, canals, bathing places, and sometimes even mausoleums. Some were extensive, containing also preserves for all kinds of games, and these were called in later times gardens of paradise. Solomon had a similiar one near Etam, and another in the beautiful district of Lebanon, being described in the Canticles as a paradise of pomegranates, and of all other excellent trees, such as the cyprus and narcissus, the crocus and cinnamon, the myrrh and aloes, as well as of every other aromatic plant.

I shall now have to break off this subject in order to make some further statements in regard to the insignificant accomplishments of the Hebrews in plastic and imitative arts, and, at the same time, to represent that after all poetry, eloquence, and music were the only branches of art on which was stamped the true nature of ancient Israel. Now and then, indeed, they practiced also other divisions of art, but all this was accomplished only in an imperfect manner, and even their celebrated temple buildings were but feeble expressions of the Jewish mind. At the outset of their career, it has been stated by Moses, that even an altar of earth may suffice; a fact sealed in the consolation that, after the last Temple in Jeruselam was laid in ashes, the wrath of God averted from wood and stone. At first in lyric poetry, amid the melody of David, Asaph, and others, and in the spirited orations of the prophets, did the Jewish fundamental idea obtain the most perfect, pure and æsthetic expression.

IV.

Every plastic representation of gods, and other objects of adoration, Judaism strictly prohibited ; and, owing to fear lest sculptures might bring about idolatry, this prohibition was extended to the typifying of men. Therefore, only a narrow compass would be left for Hebrew plastic art, had not the law continually been transgressed; yet it clearly proves that it was effective enough to prevent

in the Hebrews all typic representation from becoming important.
Works of sculpture were only made use of for idols in idolatrous times,
and must have been of rough description, inasmuch as it was customary to cast them in precious metal, or to carve them in wood,
and then cover them with gold.

In art productions of metals the Hebrews accomplished much.
The Ark of the Covenant contained two cherubims of gold, which,
with elevated wings, overshaded the same, and inclined toward it
with inward turned faces; their head and arms were of human
shape, but the form of the rest of the body is unknown. These
cherubim must have been of extraordinarily skillful construction,
for they were not cast, but rendered prominent by being elaborated
from the very lid of the ark. Of the same kind was the workman-
ship of the seven-branch gold lamp, each branch being ornamented
with almond-like cups, knolls and blossoms. We also know that
during the absence of Moses a golden calf was fabricated, as well
as that he himself made a brazen serpent. Whether in later times
Solomon made the ten golden lamps of the front part of the sanctuary,
according to this skillful Mosaic design, is a matter of uncertainty.
But the two cherubim under which he placed the ark, each being
ten ells high, and each wing five ells broad, so that the two forms
with extended wings filled up the entire inner width of the Temple;
these cannot have been a valuable production of art, inasmuch as
they were merely carved from olive wood and covered with gold.

Solomon, probably not exactly satisfied with the castings of his
own men, called one from Tyre to assist in those works of metal for
the Temple. The most remarkable were the two pillars before the
sanctuary, with capitals of lily-like shape, over which a network
extended, and each being hung with two hundred pomegranates,
which were in the form of pyramids; then the ten large rinsing-
vessels, each resting upon a frame furnished with wheels, and being
each surrounded by garlands and engraved with lions, bullocks,
cherubim and palms; and also the molten sea. These bronze castings, although executed partly by a Phœnician, were nevertheless
conceptions of Hebrew masters, who also assisted largely in the
execution thereof. The throne of Solomon was a fine specimen of
art. Six very broad steps led to an estrade, which, as well as the
steps, was covered with gold, having in the background a high-
footed chair of ivory, furnished with elbow-supporters. In front
was a footstool attached, and on each side stood a lion, while right
and left of each step a lion also was placed, staring into the face of
those ascending, and all being compounded of gold and ivory.
After the exile, we know that the front hall of the Temple contained
a colossal golden vine, having grapes, according to Josephus, of the
size of a man, and which became gradually almost overloaded by
the many golden leaves berries and grapes continually hung thereon

by way of contributions. The art of engraving and carving was also practiced to some extent, and we know that, already in the time of Moses, the precious stones in the breastplate of the high-priest were engraved with names, which proves a remarkable skill, on account of the extreme hardness of these particular stones. The inner part of the sanctuary and the folding doors Solomon had engraved with orloquints, cherubim, palms and flowers, and also the brazen rinsing-vessels had various glyptic ornaments. According to Ezekiel, the palaces of the nobles generally contained particular rooms set aside for works of sculpture. Hyrkanos had some colossal figures of animals engraved upon the white marble of his castle on the banks of the Jordan; and also in the Herodian Temple the ceiling of the sanctuary, as well as the flooring, were engraved with beautiful designs.

Respecting the art of painting among the ancient Hebrews very little is known, except a few works executed in red ocher upon the walls of palaces, especially on one belonging to Joachim; and another, a representation of Susa, the capital of Persia, on the gable of the eastern portion of the Temple. Weaving and embroidery were also carried on to some extent, being already known in the time of Moses. One of the curtains in the Herodian Temple was a representation of the starry firmament, besides others containing cherubim, lions and eagles, all of which, according to Josephus, were executed by Jews; one being retained for the Temple as chief artist, who, at one time, had as many as eighty-two women and girls employed in this kind of work. The representation of figures, however, became almost extinct in after times; for, owing to the rigor of the Sanhedrim, even the emperor's likeness on the Roman eagles was prohibited in Jerusalem, and there is no doubt that the various works mentioned afterward cannot have been executed by Jewish masters.

The result of this review clearly shows that in the various branches of plastic art many attempts were made, which partly deserve acknowledgment; although, as previously stated, owing to religious objections, their accomplishments were never considerable. The opinion that the Hebrews, like all Semitic nations, possessed no talent for plastic art, is a common opinion, which rests upon ignorance, both of the religious prohibition in the matter and of the renowed plastic accomplishments, not only of the ancient Hebrews, but also of modern Jews, who have indeed never ceased to be genuine Semitic people. A similar assertion, that the Hebrews lacked objectiveness and artificial aptitude for dramatic productions, has no better foundation. For even if it be admitted that with them objectiveness outweighed the lyric element, nevertheless in the accomplishments already enumerated, as well as later in their well-meditated plans and perfected forms of many lyric productions, that objectiveness and aptitude which first-rate dramas require are never missing. The want of actors among the Hebrews is to be accounted for from the fact that owing to their strict morality, it would have been considered a sin to bring women upon the stage, while their natural good taste protected them from having recourse to the insufferable Grecian expedient, to have men acting the part of women. But as the Hebrews had no dramas, for even the tragedies of Ezekiel are something quite different, it is clear that mimic art could not become developed among them. We find, however, that some care and cultivation was bestowed by them on the mimic branch of dancing. This was their favorite pastime, especially on festivals, at marriages and in the time of vintage; but then only women and girls performed, beating a small hand-drum, and at times they also sung to it. With music and dancing the victorious army was welcomed on its return home, and this was also peculiar with the Egyptians, Indians, Greeks and Romans; but by the Hebrews it was only on religious occasions that they made use of the dance. The thanksgiving song on the Red Sea was chanted by women in turns; they also danced around the golden calf, and even David danced before the Ark of the Covenant. This custom must have spread more than we really know, inasmuch as the same Hebrew word *chag* signifies feast, as well as dance; even on the Day of Atonement, the most sacred in the Jewish religion, the girls dance in white dresses in the vineyard, which dresses were all lent to the dancers, in order not to put to shame those who could not procure them. We also know of the Therapeutics in Egypt, a kind of Jewish monks and nuns, that they held, from time to time, nightly devotions, when they also danced and chanted hymns; men and women in separate rows, one opposite the other.

Still more significant was the custom made use of in the women's fore-court of the Temple, during the six nights of the Feast of Tabernacles, when men of almost all classes, even the most venerable, took part in the dance, accompanied by flutes, and carrying torches in their hands, which sometimes were thrown upward and caught again, while, in the intervals, the Levites chanted psalms. That these peculiar customs reveal a religious character becomes evident (Succa 53) by different sayings made use of at the performance. The pious generally chanted: "Blessed are they who have not sinned; and those who have, may He pardon them." The old people sung: "Blessed are our former youthful days, that these do not shame us when we now are growing old." Those who could not conscientiously sing with the latter, usually chanted, "Blessed our age, which now atones for our youthful days."

V.

We have no positive knowledge of the extent to which the art of music was cultivated among the ancient Hebrews, since the most musical expressions in Scripture are very obscure, and compositions of those days had not been preserved. The so-called accents of the Bible form certainly notes—musical figures, as it were—but they are of modern origin, and not exactly adapted for singing, but merely for recitative discourse in synagogue and school. However, some knowledge of music the Hebrews must have early acquired from the conduct of Moses and Miriam on the shores of the Red Sea. In later times the victorious Saul was met by women singing and playing on musical instruments. The strains of the harp under the skillful fingers of a shepherd lad soothed Saul's melancholy, and David's harp, defective though it may have been in many respects, sufficed to sound all the varied aspirations and struggles, the despair and suffering of humanity when David composed his sublime Psalms.

The most perfect form of music attained was that in vogue in the Temple, for while, since Moses, the sacrificial service was accompanied by silver trumpets only, it became more comprehensive during the time of David, and, after the erection of Solomon's Temple, the service was conducted with vocal and instrumental music, which gradually improved. The instruments of the Hebrews were of three kinds—strike instruments, wind instruments and string instruments. According as occasion required, these instruments were made use of at all religious ceremonies, on festivals, coronations, victories, weddings, at harvest time, and later even at funerals.

The school of the prophets embraced singing as well as the acquirements of the tambourine, flute, psaltery and harp, and we find it repeatedly stated that the prophetic disciples marched through the streets with music and song. The instruments of the poets who composed the Psalms were the harp and psaltery ; and it was peculiar with David to compose some of his psalms before the break of day, exclaiming therein : "Rise psaltery and harp! I will awaken Aurora!" and probably this gave rise to the well-known assertion that over his couch an Æolian harp hung, by which he himself was awakened. At morning and vesper prayers the psalms were chanted by at least twelve Levites, of whom nine played the harp, two the psaltery, and one the cymbal, but on Sabbath and festivals, and other solemn occasions, their number was extraordinarily large, and, as already stated, their standing place was a staircase of three steps, stretching the whole 135 ells, the width of the fore-court of the Temple, and there is no doubt that the instruments were proportionate in size with the trumpets of the priests, of which at one time as many as 120 warbled forth their deafening sounds.

The musicians, who had the privilege of being employed for the service of the Temple, amounted once (according to Chronicles) to 4,000, and it is certain that this large number must have produced, now and then, composers of first-rate talent, especially as this was their only vocation. Boys were trained to the service, and the technical expertness, as well as the precision of execution, must have become heightened and improved to a great extent. Altogether, if we reflect upon the varied spirit exhibited in the psalms—here child-like confidence, there complaint, which at times droops almost into whimpering, and then again rises into fresh confidence; in one place calm instruction, in another the profane discourse of scoffers, is introduced; now dejection or anger, then again, a victory or any other deliverance is celebrated; rejoicings, gratitudes, songs of praise in all gradations, sometimes in separate psalms, and sometimes in wondrous swift transitions in one and the same psalm; if we consider all this, how could this ebb and flood have received musical accompaniment, without the latter possessing proper harmony? The practical master-spirit shown in the Psalms warrants the inference of an equal musical talent. One thing, however, appears to be probable in regard to Hebrew music, that, where no complete instrumentalization existed, that it must have been tremulous, too soft, and of a melancholy cast.

In discussing poesy and prophetical oratory, in which the highest development of Hebrew art was achieved, it will scarcely be possible to suggest the fullness of the beautiful which meets us here, much less to delineate it. The Bible is acknowledged to be not only the holiest of all books, but also to include the most beautiful of all literatures; the most eminent of poets have not disdained to pluck from it the choicest flowers. One of the oldest and a well fostered branch of poesy was the almost epic use of the ancient history of the people, and which we also meet with in the book of Judges, as well as in David's youthful career, besides in the sayings of the prophet Elijah, and even later in the books of Esther and Daniel. In the episode from Balaam we find epic prose and lyric intermingled and cleverly represented, while the narrative of the gleaner Ruth, the ancestress of David, approaches the idyl. Of this Goethe has declared that it is the most charming of epic idyls which has ever existed.

Another form of poetry was the mythic, in which the first book of Moses is very rich, comprising the history of creation, Paradise, the creation of woman, the seduction of the serpent, together with the loss of Paradise, Cain's fratricide, and perhaps the deluge, and the rainbow as a token of peace. More recent mythic forms are the visions of Elijah and Nebuchadnezzar's dream, all of which costly pearls, if structures of poetry, are not to be taken literally. As a special branch appears the poetical description of superterrestrial beings and occurences, such as that of the throne of God, depicted by Isaiah simply and sublimely; by Ezekiel, in wondrous alternation of fantasy and pensive symbols; or of the heavenly assemblies in the first book of Kings (chap. xxii.), and the beautiful introduction to the book of Job; or the personification of celestial wisdom, as in the

Proverbs of Solomon and Sirach; besides the visions of Zachariah and Daniel. In later times they enlarged upon the mythic form for the use of legends, and also for more detailed narratives of a religious and moral tendency, such as the writings of Jonah, Tobiah, Judith and Susannah reveal, which, however, are of less significance.

Similar to the mythic form, although of peculiar character, were the parables, such as those of the vineyard (Isaiah v.), in Ezekiel, the exposed child, the eagle which came to Lebanon, the lioness, the two female paramours, the hippopotamus, the cedar and several others; also in Amos, such as the locusts, the plummet, the casket of figs, all beautiful, and still more comprehensive on account of the prophets generally accompanying the application of the parable by a spirited oration. These parables never ceased in later times, of which we possess ample proof in ancient Hebrew writings, and even in the New Testament, while the Midrashim are an inexhaustible mine in themselves. In fables, unfortunately, not more than one has been preserved for us; I mean that interesting fable of the trees (Judges ix.), which seek for a king; nevertheless, even to this division of art much attention must have been paid, inasmuch as the Oriental mind inclines to the practice.

All the divisions of poetry hitherto quoted were in prosaic style, while those I have yet to refer to were in more measured form. The old Hebrew verse knows of no counting of syllables, also of no long and short measure, whereby it certainly loses in external beauty, and yet gains therewith many advantages. It is not limited in regard to the choice and position of the words; and thus for each thought the most striking expressions can be chosen, as well as every word can be assigned to the most suitable place. The Psalms, the Proverbs of Solomon, of Sirach, and many others, are incomparable in this division of poetry; and it is doubtful whether anything in poetry has ever surpassed the beautiful contents and form of the 93d, 104th and 107th Psalms. I must also not forget to mention the best finished of Hebrew didactic poems, which is the half dramatic book of Job, of which Bauer asserts that it is quite as significant as Dante's divine comedy.

VI.

In lyric productions, the old Hebrew literature is very full, which postulates the possession of well-matured perceptive and contemplative powers, sometimes only momentarily inspired, but often conveyed with all the rich fantasy, heartfelt feelings and liveliness of thought which is the peculiar heritage of the Oriental mind. But this inner fluctuation among the ancient Hebrews was instigated by religious views, nay, even penetrated and directed by them. The Psalms are transcendent examples of this feature, but the one hundred and fifty psalms alone do not possess it; we see lyric strains in the words of the mother of Samuel, in Isaiah, Hezekiah and Habbakuk. Others have the form of the psalms without the subject-matter; for instance, the blessing of the dying Jacob, Miriam's song of triumph, the prophecies of Balaam, Moses' farewell song and last words, Deborah's poem of victory, David's lament over Saul and Jonathan; all of which would be more costly pearls were their expression fuller and more adequate. Beautiful, also, though perhaps too lengthy, are Jeremiah's lamentations. Of what form partook the one thousand and five songs (1 Kings v: 12) which it is said Solomon composed, one cannot say, for they have not come down to us. Likewise we possess no further information concerning the two books containing songs, called the "Books of the Wars of God," and the "Book of the Righteous" (4 Mos. xxi: 14; Jos. x: 13; 2 Sam. i: 18). Of poetry of a cheerful character there was no lack, as well as of songs of love, which Ezekiel refers to (xxxiii: 32); and what is known as the Forty-fifth Psalm is rather an epithalamium in honor of the Bible. Herder calls the Canticles the most excellent of all erotic poems in all literatures.   •

As examples of oratory, we find in the Bible excellent speeches of Moses, Joshua and Samuel, as well as the address-like prayer of Solomon at the dedication of the Temple, which has served for centuries as a model whenever synagogues or churches were consecrated. But oratory reached its highest phase in the prophetic times of the kings. For the most part, their orations were delivered to the people, whose errors they upbraided, announcing to them the evil consequences thereof, or comforting them in times of need, and holding out a brighter future to those who repent. Their effusions of wrath against the luxury and violence of the great, as well as against the partiality and corruption of the priests, together with their strictures on the venality of judges, were sometimes addressed to these in person, or they were generally referred to in their orations to the people. Often they penetrated even the palaces of kings, or appeared before them wherever they could meet them, and then reproached them for their cruelty, injustice, debauchery and desertion from God, or for whatever they may had to censure them; and all this they did with a candor which never shrunk from any danger; and after every persecution they suffered, their voice became even louder in uttering their condemnations. A frank religiousness, entirely free from hypocrisy, an absolute confidence in God, a morality perfect and pure, an unshaken conviction of the ruling moral system of the world, and the future victory of all the good in mankind, without, however, losing sight of the fact that the chief mission of the "first-born son" consists in treating as younger brethren all the nations of the earth. Such are the sounds which reach us from all orations of the prophets, and with such inspiration do they ring, that it is no wonder if the reader, overcome by their grandeur and beauty, fails to value their worth as art productions.

The speeches were seldom in prose, but had generally a poetical parallelism, sometimes also a strophic-like plan, and even lyric parts are often detected. The expression is then always carefully chosen and penetrating, and also occasionally sprinkled with antithesis and sarcasm. The representation is uncommonly vivid, and the orator's own feeling bursts through every artificial link; now in a concentrated call of grief, and then, again, like a stream breaking through its embankments. The delineations are strictly Oriental finery, and, where perceptions are to be represented, it is done with such natural truth as if the curtain were drawn from soul and heart. No forbearance is shown, but baseness is unmasked. The language begins to rise, after a few verses, echoing like distant thunder; metaphor follows metaphor, striking like flashes of lightning; and the castigation which every sin deserves is painted in such vivid colors as to almost lead one to believe that he was witnessing the tortures of the day of judgment. But this severity is not innate in the prophet's nature, for often, in the midst of the most cutting or most terrible of words, lively sympathy overpowers him, and but seldom does an admonition end without representing that the announced misery is but an expiation, after which purer and happier times will follow.

In the prophetic orations, we note striking changes of thought. In the first place, we meet with visions of supernatural occurrences, like those already mentioned by Isaiah, Ezekiel and Zachariah; and then the destruction of a universe is delineated, or the subterranean world is uncovered, and the shadows begin to speak, or we behold the blazing of hell and the tyrants of the earth swallowed up in the flames thereof. Here, again, inimical kings, in their full splendor and insolence, are introduced; how they practice, in times of peace, every abomination; or, in a hostile manner, advance against the heights of Judea; and then their end "terminates badly." Again we find delineated the pomp and luxury of Nineveh, of Babylon, or the ancient Tyre, as the queen of the sea, and a picture of the world-wide traffic is placed before us; or the vanity and the childlike worship of idols is scourged with exquisite satire; or events in nature are pictured, such as earthquakes, pestilence and a plague of locusts.

A second change was brought in by the individual form of the prophet's speech. The style of Isaiah is thoroughly grand, noble, vigorous, and always at the crest of the produced idea. Jeremiah is sometimes gloomy, and sometimes also bright, but good-natured amiable and perhaps the most passionate and irritable of all prophets. Ezekiel is less classical in his language, but original; in words and representations, gigantic; and, owing to his exiled position, his writings show an Assyrian coloring. Hosea is ingenious and full of bold leaps in all his ideas, which are of epigrammatical brevity. Joel's language is flourishing, beautiful and rich in style. Amos is entirely classical, although he was only a herdsman. So every one of the rest had his individual aim of thought, his special diction and elegance.

In conclusion, I shall only just refer to the Ptolemies, under whom the Jewish population of Alexandria became exceedingly numerous, and state that in their midst a literature of the Greek language grew up, which can also boast of many valuable productions in poetry. Philo, owing to his splendid style and his sublime thoughts, is often compared to Plato; and the historian Josephus is generally styled the Jewish Livy. Taking now all that has been said in a comprehensive form, it clearly proves that, although Israel's highest mission, the pulsation of his heart, consisted in his religion, nevertheless in productions of art he also took a place of honor, not only in ancient times, as delineated here, but during nearly every period in his history.   L. HERZFELD.

DR. L. HERZFELD, an eminent man of letters; Chief Rabbi of Brunswick; one of the editors of an annual for the advancement of Jewish literature, and author of many other useful publications.

IMPETUS—Violent effort.
HIERARCHY—A sacred government; ecclesiastical establishments.
CAPITAL—The upper part of a pillar.
ABLUTION—The act of cleansing.
QUADRIPARTITE—Having four parts; divided into four parts.
BASILICA—A large hall.
IONIC—Belonging to Ionia, to one of the dialects of the Greek language, to one of the five orders of architecture.
MONOLITH—A pillar consisting of one stone.
MAUSOLEUM—A grand funeral monument.
PLASTIC—Having the power to give form.
LYRIC—Pertaining to a harp; odes or poetry sung to a harp.
TYPIC—Figurative of something else.

GLYPTIC - Pertaining to the art of engraving.
MIMIC—Imitative.
THERAPEUTIC—Curative; endeavoring to cure diseases.
RECITATIVE—A kind of tuneful pronunciation; rather musical.
IDYL—A short poem in the pastoral style.
MYTHIC—Fabulous.
FANTASY—Fancy; imagination; image of the mind.
DIDACTIC—Giving precepts.
EPITHALAMIUM—A nuptial song upon marriage.
EROTIC—Pertaining to love.
EPIGRAM—A short poem terminating in a point.

A VISION OF JERUSALEM.

(While listening to a beautiful organ in one of the Gentile shrines.)

I saw thee, oh, my fatherland, my beautiful, my own!
As if thy God had raised thee from the dust where thou art strewn,
His glory cast around thee, and thy children bound to Him,
In links so brightly woven, no sin their light could dim.

Methought the cymbal's sacred sound came softly on my ear,
The timbrel, and the psaltery, and the harp's full notes were near;

And thousand voices chanted, His glory to upraise,
More heavenly and thrillingly than e'en in David's days.

Methought the sons of Levi were in holy garments there,
Th' anointed one upon his throne, in holiness so fair,
That all who gazed on Him might feel the promise be fulfill'd,
And sin, and all her baleful train, now he had to come, were still'd.

And thousands of my people throng'd
the pure and holy fane,
The curse removed from every brow,
ne'er more to come again;
Th' Almighty hand from each, from
all, had ta'en the scorching brand,
And Israel, forgiven, knelt within our
own bright land!

My country! oh, my country! was my
soul enrapt in thee
One passing moment, that mine eyes
might all thy glory see?
What magic power upheld me there?
Alas! alas! it past,
And darkness o'er my aspiring soul the
heavy present cast.

I stood alone 'mid thronging crowds
who fill'd that stranger shrine,
For there were none who kept the faith
I hold so dearly mine;
An exile felt I, in that house, from
Israel's native sod,
An exile yearning for my *home*—yet
loved still by my God.

No exile from His love! No, no; though
captive I may be,
And I must weep whene'er I think, my
fatherland, on thee!
Jerusalem! my beautiful! my own! I
feel thee still,
Though for our sins thy sainted sod the
Moslem strangers fill.

Oh! that thy children all would feel
what our sins have done,
And by our every action prove such
guilt the exiles shun,
Until they seek their God in prayer. Oh!
will He turn to them,
And raise thee once again in life, my
own Jerusalem!

"If they their own iniquity in humble-
ness confess,
And all their father's trespasses, nor
seek to make them less;
If they my judgments say are right, and
penitently own
They reap the chastisement of sin,
whose seeds long years have sown,

"Then will I all my vows recall, and
from them take my hand,
My covenant remember, and have
mercy on their land."
So spake the Lord in boundless love to
Israel His son;
But can we, dare we say, these things
we do or *we have done?*

Alas! my country, thou must yet de-
serted rest and lone.
Thy glory, loveliness and life, a father's
gifts, are flown!
Oh, that my prayers could raise thee ra-
diant from the sod,
And turn from Judah's exiled sons their
God's avenging rod!

And like an oak thou standest, of
leaves and branches shorn;
And we are like the wither'd leaves by
autumn tempests torn
From parent stem and scattered wide
o'er hill and vale and seas,
And known as Judah's ingrate race
wherever we may be.

Oh! blessed was that vision'd light that
flash'd before mine eye;
But, oh, the quick awakening check'd
my soul's ecstatic sigh!
Yet still, still wilt thou rise again, my
beautiful, my home,
Our God will bring thy children back,
ne'er, ne'er again to roam!
                                    GRACE AGUILAR.

MOSES.

HIS FAREWELL TO ISRAEL—HIS DEATH AND BURIAL.

OF the song of Moses, which preceded his ascent of Mount Nebo,
the learned doctor said: "And Moses gathered all the elders and
officers of the tribes and spoke in their ears that stirring psalm, in
which the shout of thanksgiving and the song of joy alternate with
the roll of terror, which sounds as if the thunders of Sinai were

reverberating anew. For poetic sublimity, for devout piety, for holy expostulation, and for solemn warning, this farewell ode has never been surpassed; and it furnishes an incidental proof of the fact that, unlike most other men, Moses continued to the very end of his life to grow in those qualities of imagination and fiery enthusiasm which are usually regarded as the special characteristics of youth. It has nothing in it of the pensive sadness which forms the undertone of the Ninetieth Psalm, and out of which, like a bird darting up above the mist that fills an Alpine valley, his faith rises only after what seems to be a long and labored effort. Rather is it akin in some of its strains to his song upon the Red Sea shore; while, in its exquisitely beautiful reference to the eagle with her young, as well as in the frequent allusions which it makes to the rock-like majesty, stability and strength of God, it connects itself with his meditations and observations when, as a shepherd, he followed Jethro's flocks in the desert of Midian. There is thus in it a wondrous combination of the strength of manhood with the experience of old age, and of the imaginative force of youth with the wisdom which increasing years supply. Nor is this all; there is in it a marvelous interblending of the various relationships in which Moses stood at once to God and to the people. He praises Jehovah with the fervor of a seraph, and he pleads with the people with the tenderness of a father. He deals with national subjects in the spirit of a statesman, and warns of coming doom with the sternness of a prophet. Now the strains are soft and low, as if they came from the cords of an Æolian harp, stirred by the breeze of a gentle summer's eve; anon, they are loud and stormful, as if some gust of passionate intensity had come sweeping over his spirit. Now they are luminous with the recollections of God's mercies, and again they are lowering as if laden with the electric burden of God's coming wrath. This ode conclusively proves that if Moses had not been the greatest law-giver and statesman of his nation, and even of the world, he might have been one of its noblest poets. It shows, too, that there was in him the exceedingly rare alliance of a mind which was alive to the importance of the minutest details of legislation, with a soul whose wings could soar into the loftiest regions of thought and feeling. With undimmed eye, he looked on more trying light than that of the common sunshine; and with unabated force he ascended, even at the age of six-score years, a more ethereal height than that of Pisgah. So that, if this ode had been found elsewhere than in the Bible, mere literary critics would have risen into ecstacies over its exquisite manifestation of beauty in the lap of terror.

Then Moses blessed the tribes in language far above the blessing pronounced by Jacob on his sons, as the character of Moses transcends that of the "Supplanter;" and, having set his house in order, there is nothing for him to do but to die. And his death was in keeping with the majesty of his life. The Lord told him to ascend Mount Nebo in the land of Moab, over against Jericho, and view the land promised to the children of Israel for an inheritance. Withdrawing from the camp, perhaps, in a quiet and undemonstrative manner, he took his way alone up to the range of Abarim, the Pisgah summit, which travelers have tried to identify with Jebel Neba, that is, "over against Jericho." And who may attempt to describe his feelings as he gazed out upon the land which he was not to be allowed to enter. At his feet, flowing along the edge of the plains of Moab, was the Jordan, hastening to lose itself in the Dead Sea. To the right his eye took in the land of Gilead until it ended far away in the north. To the left the grassy shades of Beersheba shaded off into the brown barrenness of the Egyptian desert, while directly in front of him lay all the land of Judah, with the distant hills of Naphthalion, the northern horizon, and the "utmost sea in the far west." With such a prospect before him, the words fell upon his ears: "This is the land which I swear unto Abraham, unto Isaac and unto Jacob, saying, I will give it to thy seed. I have caused thee to see it with thine eyes." And then, not in sternness, not in anger, but in utmost love, like a mother lifting her boy into her arms, the Lord added: "But thou shalt not go over thither;" and in a moment—in the twinkling of an eye—the soul of Moses had passed within the veil, and was at home with God. But even the dust of his people is precious in the sight of the Lord; and the body of that honored saint must not be left to become the prey of the vulture, nor his bones to lie whitening on the mountain. So God buried him, and, as Thomas Fuller quaintly says, "buried also his grave;" so that "no man knoweth his sepulcher to this day." What a death! What a burial! How peaceful the one; how unostentatious the other! He died "by the word of the Lord," or, more literally, "by the mouth of the Lord," and we do not wonder that the Jewish rabbis understand it to mean "by the kiss of the Lord." As the father kisses his boy when he lifts him to his knee, so death came to Moses as a token of his Lord's affection. And in that lonely burial, whose sublimity touches even the most cursory reader of the narrative, what a rebuke is addressed to those who seek to hide the solemnity of death beneath floral offerings and military processions, or who vainly attempt to perpetuate the memory of an uneventful life by a monumental marble! Thus died this many-sided man, as many another here has died, within sight of that which through life he has been straining after, but without reaching it. Yet, his life was not therefore a failure. On the contrary, he had made it possible for Joshua to succeed; while in his character he achieved the grandest success; so that, take him all in all, he stands before us the noblest of Old Testament worthies, and the peer, if not in some respects even the superior, of all that came after him. As the carpenter in "Adam Bede" says: "He carried a hard business well through," and it may be said that he did so because the Lord carried him. Rev. Dr. Taylor.

To Reverberate—To beat back; to resound.
Expostulation—Debate.
Interblending—Mingling together.

Unostentatious—Not making show.
Cursory—Hasty; quick.

THE BURIAL OF MOSES.

By Nebo's lonely mountain,
  On this side Jordan's wave,
In a vale in the land of Moab,
  There lies a lonely grave,
And no man dug that sepulcher,
  And no man saw it e'er;
For the angels of God upturned the sod,
  And laid the dead man there.

That was the grandest funeral
  That ever passed on earth;
But no man heard the trampling,
  Or saw the train go forth.
Noiselessly as the daylight
  Comes when the night is done,
And the crimson streak on ocean's
    cheek
  Grows into the great sun;

Noiselessly as the spring time
  Her crown of verdure weaves,
And all the trees on all the hills
  Open their thousand leaves,
So, without sound of music
  Or voice of them that wept,
Silently down from the mountain crown
  The great procession swept.

Perchance the bald old eagle
  On gray Bethpeor's height,
Out of his rocky eyrie
  Looked on the wondrous sight.
Perchance the lion stalking,
  Still shuns that hallowed spot,
For beast and bird have seen and heard
  That which man knoweth not.

But when the warrior dieth,
  His comrades in the war,
With arms reversed and muffled drum,
  Follow the funeral car;
They show the banners taken,
  They tell his battles won,
And after him lead his masterless steed,
  While peals the minute gun.

Amid the noblest of the land
  Men lay the sage to rest,
And give the bard an honored place
  With costly marble dressed,
In the great minister transept,
  Where lights like glories fall,
And the sweet choir sings, and the or-
    gan rings
  Along the emblazoned wall.

This was the bravest warrior
  That ever buckled sword;
This the most gifted poet
  That ever breathed a word;
And never earth's philosopher
  Traced with his golden pen,
On the deathless page, truths half so
    sage
  As he wrote down for men.

And had he not high honor?
  The hillside for his pall;
To lie in state while angels wait
  With stars for tapers tall;
And the dark rock pines, like tossing
    plumes,
  Over his bier to wave;
And God's own hand, in that lonely
    land,
  To lay him in the grave.

In that deep grave without a name,
  Whence his uncoffined clay
Shall break again—most wondrous
    thought!
  Before the judgment day,
And stand with glory wrapped around
  On the hills he never trod,
And speak of the strife that won our
    life
  With that blessed law of God.

O lonely tomb in Moab's land,
  O dark Bethpeor's hill,

Speak to these curious hearts of ours, | He hides them deep, like the secret
And teach them to be still.   sleep
God has his mysteries of grace—   Of Moses He loved so well.
Ways that we cannot tell;   ADAPTED.

EYRIE—Where birds of prey build their nests.

MOSES AS A STATESMAN.

IT is doubtful whether a single instance can be found in the history of the human family in which the measure of the highest standard has been completely filled, unless it may have been in the illustrious lawgiver of the Jews. Although many of the most interesting and important facts in his personal history have probably been lost to us in the long waste of ages which have elapsed since they transpired, while others are only revealed to us through the dubious and uncertain medium which tradition crystalized into history centuries subsequent to their occurrence, there is enough in his own brief and unpretending narrative of the great events in which he was the principal actor to satisfy the reflecting mind that he was more richly endowed with all the elements essential to the highest order of statesmanship than any other whose name has illustrated the annals of mankind. What a sublime philanthrophy must have influenced him to resign the pleasures of a voluptuous court, to resist the temptations of wealth, and power, and luxury, and ease, to forego the companionship of the learned, and the society of the great, and to withstand all the bright allurements of personal ambition, for the almost hopeless task of liberating his down-trodden countrymen, and leading them back to the conquest and possession of their ancient heritage! What a singular persistency of purpose; what untiring zeal; what marvelous diplomatic skill he displayed in procuring the royal edict for their manumission ; what wonderful powers of organization he exhibited in transforming a stagnant mass of humanity, enervated by centuries of servitude, into a conquering host; finally into a powerful and prosperous commonwealth! What a strange, resistless influence he must have been able to exercise over the wills of his fellow-men to induce a fickle and effeminate people to follow him through all the vicissitudes of forty years of wandering through a barren wilderness, with famine and disease and danger and death besetting them on every hand ! What ceaseless vigilance, what fertility of invention, what judicious calculation, what unwearying patience, inflexible justice, and invincible courage, were required to control and cultivate and soften and refine a semi-barbarous and seditious multitude of three million souls !

What accurate, yet enlarged and comprehensive, views he must have had of political science in its highest sense, to be able to contrive, in the midst of an inhospitable desert, and harrassed by almost every conceivable difficulty, a system of government centuries in advance of the remote and idolatrous age in which he lived; a government which, though not absolutely perfect in every particular, was perfectly adapted to the genius and circumstances of those for whom it was designed ; with a constitution embracing the fundamental ideas of republican freedom, and a code of laws founded upon a sublime system of morality, which constitutes to-day the substratum of social order and civil jurisprudence in every enlightened community on the globe! Having created a nation which was to exercise the most important influence upon the destinies of the human race through all the cycles of coming time, he harbored no thought of perpetuating the dynasty of his own family; and the same self-abnegation which influenced him to thrust aside the diadem of the proudest kingdom on earth to become the deliverer of his people was as conspicious to the latest moment of his extraordinary career, when he preferred a secluded and unknown sepulcher to the pomp and ceremony of a public funeral. But he needed no gorgeous tomb to enshrine his moldering dust, no sculptured shaft to tell the marvelous story of his life. "The whole earth is his sepulcher," and the history of Christian civilization his epitaph. Where in the entire catalogue of illustrious statesmen shall we find the peer of such a character? When we come to consider them through the calm, clear medium of enlightened reason, we are amazed to find that a large majority of the great political leaders were the mere accidents instead of the architects of circumstances which made their names immortal. When we eliminate from their characters the love of power, the thirst for popular applause, the greed of gain, and other motives of a purely selfish nature by which they were controlled, and especially when we understand precisely how much, or rather how little, the human family is really indebted to them for the progress it has made in social and political improvement, we are mortified at the amount of genuine heartfelt, enthusiastic admiration we have unwittingly wasted upon them.—*From a lecture, " The Model Statesman," delivered at Philadelphia.*

HON. J. PROCTOR KNOTT.

MANUMISSION—The act of giving liberty to slaves.
TO EFFEMINATE—To soften; to melt into weakness; to unman.
VIGILANCE—Watchfulness.

SUBSTRATUM—A foundation; a basis.
CYCLE—A periodical space of time.
ABNEGATION—Denial; renunciation.
ELIMINATE—To thrust out; to expel.

THE SONG OF MOSES.

My song, arise in majesty,
Ascend in peerless brilliancy !
Horse, chariot, host in sea's depths laid
Prove Egypt's gods have brought no
    aid.

My strength and song is *Jah*, the
    Lord,
Salvation gleams through all His word.
My eyes here catch that future sight,
The temple on Moriah's heights.

The Lord made war, defence of right;
His face crowned night with wondrous light.
Bewildered, blinded, Pharaoh's host
Stamp'd no footprint on this dry coast.

The officers of triple crown,
Those numbered *first* in earth's renown,
All perished like some sinking stone,
When parted floods rolled back to one.

Most mighty is that hand, the Lord's!
Its strokes, like this, are sin's rewards.
At God's breath roll the silvered seas,
Or stand in crystal walls and trees.

What lustful eyes, closed in death's sleep,
Have now their graves in that Red deep!
" I'll overtake," the proud foe said,
" I'll capture all, alive or dead."

The breath of God touched glassy walls.
Two floods approached—tremendous falls;

The bottom held an army dead,
As helpless there as sunken lead.

Who is Thy like, most glorious King?
Thy holy name the seraphs sing ;
Thy praise diffuses trembling awe,
Thy hand suspends prime cosmic law.

Suspends, restores ; for nature's law
Restored the floods. Thy people saw
Themselves preserved a holy race,
To build on earth Thy shrine of grace.

This day will be like deadly darts,
Piercing the nations in their hearts.
Edom and Moab lose heart to fight,
Old Canaan swoons ev'n now from fright.

These nations, Lord, will melt away,
And, therefore, fail Thy march to stay;
Thy priests at home will teach Thy will.
Thy tribes rebuild Thy holy hill.

Unchangeably, Thy house shall shine
In holy beauty, grace divine ;
Thy kingdom shall endure for aye,
Nor ages bring one tint's decay.

A. I.

COSMICAL—Relating to the world.

TRUE GREATNESS.

MEN truly great never know how great they are. It does not appear to them that their services rendered to the human family are so very important, so very productive of blessings, that they deserve special recognition. One coin in a bottle, if shaken, makes a noise; a bottle full of coins makes none. The good, to be great, must be done unconsciously. It must be done by an irresistible inner impulse without any care of consequences. This greatness is called meekness. "And the man Moses was very meek " (he had no idea of the greatness of his doings), "and he knew not that his countenance was beaming " (he was not aware of the greatness of his wisdom and holiness).

Look at the story of the Korah rebellion, as recorded in the sixteenth chapter of Numbers. That man Korah with his conspirators rose against Moses, and prefaced their mutiny with the words: " For all the Edah are all saints and God is among them," and Edah means the body of the people's representative. So the demagogue speaks, so the hypocrite and agitator ingratiates himself with the credulous and selfish masses. "We are all saints," said he, as a modern demagogue would say, we are all patriots, all virtuous citizens, all of us statesmen and heroes; why do you rule over us? Or, as a modern preacher would say, we are all so truly good, so eminently pious, so thoroughly learned, so excellently advanced in art and science, so pure in our intentions, so holy in our conduct, why do you moralize with us? It is the language of the demagogue, intended to reach selfish aims and to ruin the unsuspecting masses. "When Moses heard this he fell upon his face;" for he must have understood at once that it was not the language of honest men, and the rogue's intrigues must be discountenanced by honest men; in fact, this is the test of straightforward honesty and candor, that it cannot face the impostor's alluring and deceptive words at once. It bewilders him; he must have time to make up his mind to the fact that there are such rogues and sharks in this world; Moses fell upon his face.

The proposition of Moses was to let the Almighty decide. "And the man whom God will choose, he is the holy one. Believing as he did, that God would not decide in favor of the wicked, and dreading the punishment which he believed would surely overcome them, Moses sent for the main leaders, Dathan and Abiram, hoping to persuade them to do better, and not run themselves into the abyss of destruction. They would not listen, would not come to Moses; and sent him an insulting message, which is again the language of the demagogue. "Thou hast taken us out of a land flowing with milk and honey to kill us in the wilderness," said they, and thus maliciously perverted facts, as demagogues will do. To be redeemed from bondage and slavery, from oppression and misery, they called to be brought away from a land of milk and honey. To receive the law and the commandments, to be organized to a peculiar people, an independent people, a free people, and to be sanctified to a holy people, God's chosen people, they called dying in the wilderness. This is a true picture of lying demagogues in their mean attempts to pervert facts. And then they added an appeal to the sensuality and covetousness of thoughtless masses, to the passions of the dregs of society, exactly as demagogues do. "Thou hast not brought us to a land flowing with milk and honey, hast not given us an inheritance of field and vineyard; wilt thou blind the eyes of these men?"

"And Moses was very wroth." Of course he was. An honest man cannot listen to such language with equanimity. He cannot. It sounds so vilely in his ears; it appears so unnatural to his feelings; it rouses so violently his commiseration for those who are to be deceived, and his sorrow that a man should be able thus to deny and degrade human nature; he must be very wroth. But he can be silent as Moses was, who made no reply to that abusive language. He must not curse because others do; he must not be coarse because others are; he must not come down to the low level of his assailants. A good man can seal up his grief in silence. To God, however, Moses did speak: "Turn not to their offering," said he to God; "I have not taken one ass of them, and I have wronged none of them."

These words sound very peculiar. Does a man deserve particular consideration because he took no ass of anybody and wronged none? It is true, if the ruler of a nation wrongs none in the enjoyment of his rights, and appropriates to himself none of his subjects' property, he might be called a tolerably good ruler, and very little better can be said of the best of rulers; but had Moses to say no more in his favor before God? Of course, he could not say to God, behold I have brought them out of Egypt, led them through the Red Sea, gave them manna, and water from the rock, gave them law, religion, ethics, organization, a tabernacle and covenant, etc., for he was the "servant of God," and claimed nothing of the kind. He knew that God had done it all, and that he was a mere instrument in the hand of providence. The man of destiny knows it, and can claim nothing for himself. He is a messenger, an agent, a servant, an instrument. Moses was too meek to deny or for one moment to forget this. He could say before God nothing of all that. But as a man, a teacher, a character, a mighty leader, had he nothing to say for himself except that he stole no ass and wronged nobody? Nothing, not a word. He could not possibly be conscious of his superior wisdom, goodness and energy; he could not be aware of the great and good things he had done for Israel and the human family and be Moses. He could not boast before the Almighty of his own merits, works and superiority, and be the servant of the Most High. Nothing, not a word had he to say of himself, about himself; although he was very wroth, he was wronged, he was outraged by his own brethren, he had nothing to say of himself or for himself, and that marks the man of true greatness; he knows not how great he is.

What he did say in that state of excitement was simply this: "If I deserve punishment, chastisement, visitation, or mortification, why must you, Dathan and Abiram, do it, when I have not injured you in your property or rights? Who has appointed you to insult me, if I have never insulted you?" Moses could not imagine how a man could do evil to his neighbor who has done him no wrong, and believing they speak what hey think and feel, he said, "They speak of property, of fields and vineyards, they love wealth and earthly possessions, and I have not touched anything which they claimed; they speak of the beauties of Egypt, the charms of slavery; they love slavery, and I have not forced them to follow me, to partake with me of the privations in the desert; I have done them no wrong. Having done them personally no wrong, why do they thus mortify me?" Moses was too good to know that there are bad men, who know of no consideration when they are after selfish purposes; who care for none but themselves, feel with and for none in their wicked ambition; and in his faith in human nature he exclaimed before God, "I have not wronged them," and proved how far superior he was in human greatness to his antagonists.   I. M. W.

DR. ISAAC M. WISE, minister of "Benai Jeshurun" Cincinnati; founder and chief editor of the "American Israelite."

THE SUN OF ISRAEL.

Was it thus, stricken remnant, the glory of God
Burst forth on thy fathers, and show-ered its light
Across the rough path that those weary ones trod,
A cloud-pillar by day, a flame-wit-ness by night?

As it guided the sire, it now gleams o'er the son,
As it shone in the wilderness lonely and drear,

So it bursts to assure thee, oh! desolate one,
That in sorrow and exile His pres-ence is here.

Then say not the day of thy triumph has fled,
Say not that the star of thy glory has set,
While the same holy blessings still rest on thy head,
And the same "fire from heaven" illumines thee yet.

                    REBEKAH HYNEMAN.

WRITTEN on seeing the sun suddenly break forth, and illuminate the Book of the Law, as it was being carried to the Ark.

THE SYNHEDRIONS.

It must be admitted that a knowledge of the law was widespread in Israel, since the twenty-three judges, who were appointed in every place of 120 inhabitants, were bound to indemnify a person whom they should have condemned in error if they had no diploma. Now diplomas were, at least after the destruction of the Temple, very rare, since illustrious doctors like Sumkhus, Simon, son of Nonas, the son of Azai, or Samuel, had none.

We have also other proofs that the judges were all learned men. Nevertheless, despite their learning, they were only allowed to judge matters involving fines, and, of course, still less impose any bodily chastisement, unless they were provided with diplomas. A diploma conferred on the possessor the title of Rabbi, and authority to judge matters involving fines. Three competent persons were required to give a diploma. Such a diploma, moreover, freed a judge from the obligation of indemnifying a person condemned in error. Sometimes temporary diplomas were given, or only for certain countries.

For the rest the Synhedrions were elected by universal suffrage.

The inhabitants of every city nominated, by universal suffrage, both the judges and the Synhedrions of their cities, selecting them from among those who were learned, humble and popular. The Synhedrion of Jerusalem, of seventy-one members, confirmed the authority of the provincial Synhedrions. At Jerusalem itself there were three Synhedrions; the first, consisting of twenty-three members, recruited itself from the several provincial Synhedrions; the second, likewise composed of twenty-three members, recruited itself from the first; lastly, the third, composed of seventy-one members, and which constituted the supreme authority of the nation, recruited itself from the second.

All these judges received no salary either from the city or the litigants; they continued, after their nomination, in their occupations as before, some working in the field as simple laborers, others as shoemakers, blacksmiths, etc. On Mondays and Thursdays the judges were the whole day at court attending to the pleas ; on other days they did not go there except when necessary ; for the two days of the week mentioned, the country people came to town to listen to the reading of the law, and this was turned to an account in the matter of law-suits. If the suitors wished for a judge while he was engaged in field work, he had the right to require them to hire a substitute for the time that he might be engaged with their suit, but he could not ask for more. The functions of judge, therefore, were purely honorary, and they were discharged as religious duties ; for to give judgment was considered as a mitzvah (a meritorious action). There were, moreover, numerous academies directed by illustrious doctors, which, at the same time, constituted as many tribunals. These academy-tribunals enjoyed greater moral authority and inspired more confidence than the other tribunals.

For the rest the Synhedrions of the cities occupied themselves not only with the dispensation of justice, but also with all public and private affairs which came within the province of the magistrates and the police. They inspected the houses of public safety ; they inspected the measures, often causing new ones to be made, and attached their seals to the old ones, that it might be known that they had been verified ; they also occupied themselves with public charities, schools, the fortifications of cities, the re-partition of imposts, etc.

The procedure was very simple. The suitors were heard, and then sent out of the hall in order for the court to deliberate ; they were then recalled and judgment given. But what is to be noticed is, that the judges were bound to state the reasons of their judgment to the suitors.

The Synhedrion of seventy-one at Jerusalem, had, in addition, a political function. It could declare war, and install Synhedrions of cities. A capital sentence could only be passed by a Synhedrion of

388

SCHOOL AND FAMILY READER

twenty-three, but a civil case only required a court of three judges.—
"*Legislation Criminelle Du Talmud.*"   DR. RABBINOWICZ.

DR. RABBINOWICZ, D M, of the University of Breslau, a great literati; an eminent Hebrew scholar; author of a Hebrew grammar, "Life of Maimonides," and a great many other useful works on education and theology.

DIPLOMA—A letter or writing conferring some privilege. | LITIGANT—One engaged in a suit of law.

AFTER RABBI JEHUDAH HA-LEVI.

I.

Thy undefiled dove,
Thy fondling, thy love,
That once had, all blest,
In thy bosom her nest—
Why dost thou forsake her
Alone in the forest?
And standest aloof,
When her need is the sorest?
While everywhere
Threatens snare;
Strangers stand around her,
And strive night and day
To lead her astray,
While in silence she,
In the dead of night,
Looks up to Thee,
Her sole delight.
Dost thou not hear,
Her voice sweet and dear;
Wilt aye thou forsake me?
My darling, my one!
And I know that beside Thee,
Redeemer, there's none!

II.

How long will thy dove
Thus restlessly rove
In the desert so wild,
Mocked and reviled?
And the maid-servant's son
Came furiously on.
Dart after dart,
Pierced through my heart,
Horrid birds of prey
Lie soft in my nest,
While I, without rest,
Roam far, far away.
And still I am waiting
And contemplating;
And counting the days,
And counting the years;

The miracles ceased
No prophet appears;
And wishing to learn
About thy return,
And asking my sages:
Is the end drawing nigh?
They sadly reply:
That day and that hour
But to Him are known.
And I know that beside thee,
Redeemer, there's none!

III.

And my wee, cooing dear ones,
The bright and the clear ones,
Were dragged in their slumbers
By infinite numbers
Of vultures so horrid
To cold climes and torrid,
Far, far away.
And those birds of prey
Try to render them faithless,
And make them give up
Thee, their sole hope!
To turn their affection
From Thee, O Perfection!
Thou friend of the friendless!
Thou beauty endless!
Ah, where art thou?
My darling, my one!
My foes are near,
My friend is gone.
Fainting in sorrow,
I'm here all alone.
And I know that beside Thee,
Redeemer, there's none!

IV.

Oh, hasten, my love,
To thy poor, timid dove!
They trample with their feet me,
They laugh when I mourn;
There's no friend to greet me,

I am all forlorn !
My foes in their passion,
And wild frantic ire,
Employ sword and fire,
And all kinds of tortures,
And know no compassion.
They drive from land to land me ;
There's none to befriend me.
The stars there on high
Hear me silently moan.
  And I know that beside Thee,
  Reedemer, there's none !

V.

Didst thou reject me ?
Dost love me no more ?
Didst thou forget all

Thy promises of yore ?
Oh, rend thy heavens !
Oh, come down again !
My enemies may see
That I, not in vain,
Have trusted in Thee.
As once upon Sinai,
Come down, my sole dear,
In Thy majesty appear !
Hurl down from his throne,
The maid-servant's son !
And strength impart
To my fainting heart.
Ere sadly I wander
To the land unknown.
For I know that beside Thee,
Redeemer, there's none !
    PROF. EMANUEL LOEWENTHAL.

THE TALMUD.
I.

AMONG the nations of antiquity to whom the modern world is indebted for the basis of its civilization, the Hebrew people occupies confessedly a notable position. One book, nothing more, represents the contribution of the Hebrews to the great bequest made by the past to the present; while the inventory of the treasures inherited from Greece and Rome enumerated an infinite variety of the most beautiful productions of human genius. Still, such is the inherent majesty of that book, that, since its introduction, no attempt on a large scale has ever succeeded in weakening the power of its counsels over the hearts of the countless millions to whom it is a trusty guide on their way from the cradle to beyond the grave. To this book of books, the whole of the Hebrew literature, covering, as it does, the large space of time from the close of the Canon to our own period, forms a grand appendix. Science, ethics, history, fiction in prose and verse, every exercise of the mental faculty, bears, if clad in Hebrew, the stamp of its Biblical origin—a circumstance which necessarily imparts to the character of that literature a center of onesidedness, for which, however, the gravity of the diction and the absence of commonplace make no slight compensation. This complex of literary productions constitutes Rabbinical literature, based upon tradition in the widest acceptation of the term.

More strictly speaking, the authoritative tradition is deposited in the Talmudical treatises only, which it was considered illicit to transmit otherwise than orally, until distressful events placed the teachers of the people between the alternatives of either preserving their doctrines in written codices, or of exposing them to neglect, and even to oblivion. In its widest sense, however, the tradition includes all the ancient Hebrew literary monuments, with the sole exception of the Pentateuch, the reproduction of which in writing was looked upon as a highly meritorious act. The Hellenistic writings of Alexandrian Jews, although they were evidently dictated by the patriotic desire to impress the Grecian world with respect to the religion and the ethics of the Jewish people, made hardly any impression on the Hebrew-speaking Palestinians. Even the Alexandrian version of the Scriptures was for a reason looked upon as an irreligious attempt, sure some day to lead to the substitution of dubious imitations for the one original sacred exemplar. As for Flavius Josephus, but for whom there would not be an intelligible past Biblical history of the Jews, his name is sought for in vain among the records of his countrymen; it might be on account of the cringing adulation offered by that historian to the destroyer of the sacred Temple and city, were not an equal disregard the lot of the Alexandrian philosopher, Philo, the ardent defender of the civic rights of his brethren before the throne of the Emperor Caligula. The contents of the Hebrew Bible were accessible, since the second century before the Christian era, to the inquisitive familiar with Greek—that is, to all the educated in the Roman Empire; and especially so when, in the first Christian age, as Augustin states, innumerable Latin versions were published. But the Jewish tradition and its dialectics remained a mystery, of which a select body out of a small population held the key. And thus it has been ever since, with rare exceptions. It would, however, be a great historical error to deny to the traditional school of the Jews a deep effect on the philosophy and the ethics of the world, far beyond the narrow precincts of the synagogue. What more powerful, more lasting, than the effect wrought on the thoughts and feelings of men, generation after generation, by the argumentative writings of the apostle Paul, a most diligent student, according to the strictest system of tradition, under R. Gamaliel the elder, who was the grandson of the illustrious Hillel, at that time president of the Sanhedrim (or Synhedrion) at Jerusalem. The close conformity of the apostle's dialectics to those of the doctors of the tradition is fully brought out in the Rabbinical Commentary on some of the Pauline Epistles, published in Hebrew by a great German Talmudist. Thus, at the commencement of the world's new era, the traditional method of the Jewish schools achieved triumph second to none in the history of the education of mankind; and the astounding revolution produced in the moral, and gradually in the political world, nearly 2,000 years since, by the spread of Pauline Christianity, had its parallel, although on a less extensive area, in the age of the Reformation.

When the Reformation had become an accomplished fact with the overthrow of Spanish political supremacy, the emancipation of the European mind from mediæval tutelage proceeded rapidly. The bonds were loosened which had until then held science attached to doctrinal theology. A new basis was laid for the study of experimental science, and speculative philosophy strove to discover a new and superior method. Eight years after the death of Lord Bacon Benedict Spinoza was born at Amsterdam, in 1632, from whom departed that mighty impulse which has carried the philosophy of Germany to the height attained by it in our days. Now, that man was a paragon of Talmudical learning, the favorite pupil of R. Morteira, of Amsterdam, before ever he commenced the study of Latin grammar under good Dr. Vanende; and it is therefore fair to attribute to the intellectual discipline of the Talmud the largest share in the preparation of his mind for his vast achievements as a philosopher. He was misunderstood; he was ill-treated by his contemporaries, but full amends have been made to his memory by a more enlightened generation. Thus the apostle of the first, and the philosopher of the seventeenth century, however really or apparently antagonistic on dogmatic points, concur in affording strong personal evidence of the effect of the Talmudical system upon the onward movement of mankind. T.

THE VISION OF RABBI HUNA.

The sun had set upon Jerusalem,
And scattered rosy circles round the Mount
Whereon the ruins of the Temple lay
Like faded leaves by autumn winds displaced.

Beneath the shadow of a crumbling wall
Sat Rabbi Huna, and his mind was sad
With anxious thoughts and bitter memories.
Here, on this spot, not many years before,
The gorgeous Temple of his race had stood.
And now, how changed, alas! and desolate
The sacred precincts! Not with litanies,
And vows and prayers, more would they resound.
Gone, like a dream, the glory of the past.
No future promise; only presages
Of want and woe, and still more troublous times.

"Oh, how I love thee, my Jerusalem!"
So sighed the Rabbi as he sunk to rest—

"Oh, how I love thee, tho' upon thy neck
With crushing force the conqueror's foot is pressed.
The last glad strains of the prophetic lyre
I seem to hear across thy sloping hills.
Bright visions of thy glory thrill me yet,
When in thy prophet's words, in bridal dress,
With peerless gems upon thy radiant brow,
Thou wert betrothed unto Israel's God;
And now—" The Rabbi faltered as he thought,
And sighing sunk into a dreamy sleep.

Strange fancies came to Huna as he slept.
He trod once more the Temple's sacred courts,
But there no altar dripped with streaming gore,
No groans of sacrificial sheep were heard;
No priests in sacerdotal splendor dressed;
No swelling chant, no pomp of liturgy;
No incense fragrant to propitiate.
A brighter radiance seemed within to shine

From the eternal light of purity,
Which, shedding far and near its bliss-
ful rays,
Clad every worshiper in holiness.
There was no spoken prayer. no mum-
bling lips,
No smiting of the breast, no postures
vain;
A reverent crowd with every impulse
bent
To worship God thro' sacred brother-
hood.
They had indeed their holy litanies,
Which not in book or roll alone were
writ;
An open hand, a humble heart and
mind,

An overflowing font of love and truth.
And aspirations for the beautiful,
The true, the good, the pure.

The Rabbi wakes.
Dread sounds of tumult rouse him from
his sleep,
A prowling band of Roman soldiery.
With cries of triumph, tracked him to
this spot.
His helpless form their glittering swords
soon pierced,
And with "Shema Yisroel!" Huna
dies.
Upon his face there rests a placid smile,
As if he trod the New Jerusalem.
                                        J. M.

THE TALMUD—Continued.
II.

Ezra reintroduced the law of Moses from Babylon into the Holy Land. Neither the homeward emigration under Zerubbabel, nor that under Ezra, or Nehemiah, disturbed, permanently, the Hebrew settlements in the Persian dominions. The Talmud insists on the fact that the most notable families, while rejoicing in and supporting the political regeneration of their ancestral country, did not abandon their dwelling-places between the Euphrates and Tigris, where they had founded new homesteads for themselves. The Hebrews in Persia lived in compact communities, according to their own customs, and mainly under their own laws, watched over by the Prince of the Captivity. Palestine was looked upon as the center of authority, to which a degree of allegiance was conceded by the whole race, sections of which were already then, and particularly after the era of Alexander, settled in numerous places in Western Asia and North Africa, and afterward, about the time of Augustus, in many a province of Greece proper, and Italy. Alexandria, for some centuries after its Macedonian founder the emporium of the world, and the Athens of the age, contained a large Jewish population, which occupied the Delta and another of the five divisions of the city; these strangers threw themselves with energy into the intellectual movement, encouraged by the Ptolemies; they were famous artisans, and rose to importance through the extent of their commerce—a pursuit scarcely known among them in the Holy Land, but for which they seem to have acquired great skill and an imperishable taste in their rivalry with the Greeks of Alexandria.

The Alexandrian synagogue—a grand building in the form of a basilica, with double colonnade, became, in after times, the theme of many a popular legend, illustrative of its magnitude and splendor.

Egypt possessed, moreover, from about 160 b. ch. e. until 73 a. ch. e. (233 years), a temple, a miniature copy of that at Jerusalem, and the only one that existed beyond the boundaries of the Holy Land. It was built and inaugurated by Onias, the last remnant of the priestly family of Joshua, who was the companion of Zerubbabel. Onias fled into Egypt to escape from the intrigues of Jason and Menelaus, the rival usurpers of the high-priesthood in the beginning of the reign of Antiochus Epiphanes. He was kindly received by Ptolemy Philometor, and, for some political services rendered, the King granted Onias leave to dedicate, on the site of the former heathen altar, a temple to Jehovah, in the district of Heliopolis, some twenty miles from Memphis, within the land of Goshen, to the high gratification of the Egyptian Jews, who saw therein the fulfillment of a prophecy in Isaiah xix: 19. "In that day there shall be an altar to the Lord in the midst of the land of Egypt." In Jerusalem the existence of the temple of Onias was not considered to betoken a schism, inasmuch as the Egyptians themselves conceded to the temple at Zion its metropolitan supremacy, and in every other way maintained friendly intercourse with the brethren at Jerusalem. The Alexandrians did not, however, contribute in an appreciable degree to the development of the study of the law, and there is, indeed, no mention in Jewish literature, either of their schools, or of representative teachers produced by them, until long after the Talmudical epoch.

Babylonia, on the contrary, was studded with schools and synagogues, some of which date from the time of Ezra, and even of Ezekiel, if the local traditions may be trusted. Long before the destruction of the second temple, there were seats of learning in the valley of the Euphrates, at Nehardea, Sura, Pumbadita, and elsewhere, but the history of these academies and their leaders is sadly defective prior to the first century b. ch. e. Learned men, and youths desirous of learning, frequently passed between Babylonia and Palestine, whereby the unity of doctrine was maintained. Thus Hillel in his youth went to Jerusalem to study there, then returned to the country of his birth, till in the year 32 b. ch. e., at the age of forty-three, he was called to occupy the presidential chair in the great Sanhedrim. With him a new era begins. Hillel is the moral hero of the tradition. He exhibited those qualities which form the ideal Hebrew character—great gentleness, deep humility, and perfect equanimity under all trials—the product of the love and fear of God. The deterring austerity of his otherwise estimable colleague, Shammai, is used as a foil to set off Hillel's superior amiability. Numerous sayings of a high moral beauty are attributed to Hillel. He it was that said (Aboth i: 11): "Love peace and pursue it; love all men, and thus bring them nearer to the law of God." To the heathen, who wished to be made acquainted with the whole law in

one lesson, he said (Sabb. 31): "Do not to thy fellow-man what thou
wouldst not that he should do unto thee. This is the whole law;
all the rest is commentary." He also said (Aboth i: 13): " The man
that hunts after fame shall lose his good name ; he that does not
progress in knowledge goes backward; he that does not care for
knowledge commits suicide; but the man that uses learning for self-
glorification derseves to be forgotten." He passed legal reforms, especially in the direction of the transfer of landed property, which
were demanded by the change through which the people had passed,
from an agricultural life to the more varied pursuits introduced and
fostered by a livelier intercourse with foreign countries. But the
memory of Hillel is chiefly revered for his greatness as a teacher
of the law. He collected the numerous oral traditions handed
down from generation to generation by the learned ; he arranged them into six well-defined orders, according to their
subjects; in fact, he prepared the materials which one of his lineal
descendants used some 200 years later for the compilation of the
Mishna.

The Mishna cannot be called a commentary, in the ordinary acceptance of the term, on the Pentateuch, for it does not elucidate
seriatim the chapters and books of the sacred text; it rather professes
to give an account of the manner in which the laws of the Pentateuch
were legally interpreted and historically carried into effect. The
commandments and the prohibitions of the law are distributed under
six heads, named orders, subdivided into treatises, of which there are
63 (some count 62), composed of chapters, 524 altogether, each of
which contains a number of sections called rules, amounting to 3,829
for the whole Mishna. The first order treats of laws relating to
agricultural produce. The second enumerates the festivals and
their regulations. The third contains the laws on marriage and divorce. The fourth details the proceedings in questions of mine and
thine. The fifth relates to the sanctuary and sacrifices. The sixth
defines the notions of pure and impure in ritual matters. From the
arrangement of the contents it is exceedingly difficult to infer the
method followed by the author, as the connection between the subjects discussed in the same chapter is not everywhere logically warranted. But here it must be remembered that the Mishna was not
originally intended for publication in writing, but for oral transmis-
sion, however inconceivable such an operation with 524 chapters,
and their aggregate of 3,829 rules, may appear to a much reading
and little remembering generation. To assist the memory various
mnemonic artifices were employed, among which the association of
ideas has ever been the most approved, and is at this day the most
golden rule on which teachers of the " Art of Memory " chiefly depend. If, therefore, in the Mishna or other compendia of oral traditions, heterogenous subjects are found strung together, seemingly on

no principle whatever, the connecting principle is in reality that of "association of ideas."

The Mishna, in its original form, became the text book at the Palestinian schools, where it took rank before the several epitomes of the tradition, previously known and henceforward described as external Mishnas (Boraitha) and Additamenta (Tosiphta), which were afterward accounted to hold about the same relation to the authoritative Mishna as the Apocrypha did to the canonical books of Scripture. Nearly coeval with the Mishna are three commentaries still extant (Sifra, Sifri, Mechilta) on part of the second and on the third further books of the Pentateuch. In these works, not the discussions and decisions of the doctors, as in the Mishna, but the elucidation of the Biblical word and phrase, is the immediate object of the authors. The Mishna having been communicated by two of R. Judah's immediate disciples to the schools in Babylonia, among which three (at Nehardea, Pumbadita and Sura) acquired the highest reputation, the same system of study in the two countries produced two Talmuds—one of Jerusalem or Palestine, the other of Babylon. Toward the end of the fourth century the political position of the Jews in the Holy Land, under the rule of converted Rome, was deplorable. Fortunately there was a place of refuge for many of them beyond the Euphrates in the Parthian Empire, which the scepter of Rome did not reach. There was then an exodus of teachers to Babylonia. Palestine abdicated its religious hegemony. The patriarch, Hillel II., about 350 published the astronomical rules, by which, joined to some conventional regulations, the annual festivals had been proclaimed from the days of yore by the highest central authority. The schools finally collapsed; the Palestinian Talmud was not finished, but brought to a standstill at Tiberias, some years after the reign of Emperor Julian. The compilation of the Talmud at Babylon originated in the academy of Sura a full century later (in the year 498); its latest date is about the middle of the sixth century, from which time onward the activity of the Rabbis has been concentrated on the sifting of the material deposited in the two Talmuds and their tributaries; a whole library exists of commentaries on the Gemara, which is itself a commentary on the Mishna, as this in its turn is an explanation of the laws contained in the Mosaic code.

T.

GEMS FROM CHARISI.

I.—GRAY HAIRS.

Oh, look! The ravens black
  Which tarried on my head,
Seek a nest within my heart,
  And from above have fled!

II.—TEARS OF LOVE.

Tears, O traitorous tears,
  Why did you reveal
What, deep within my heart,
  I strove so to conceal?

My heart, it needeth not to say
What my gushing tears display.

III.—TO DECEITFUL FRIENDS.

How sweet they talk, these loving
friends,
How their tongues deceive.
So swift to serve, so gracious kind
If I only could believe
Their words of pleasing flattery.
But, soon, too soon, I find the lie.

Not all their trickery can efface
What falsehood's written on the face !

IV.—(FROM TACHKEMONI.)

When all the sages discontinued singing,
Spain's lyre began to 'send forth its
sound;
When Eastern sons no more tunes were
bringing,
Then the singers of the West were
found.   DR. MORITZ LEVIN.

THE TALMUD—CONTINUED.

III.

Both Talmuds are incomplete works. Neither of them extend over
the six orders of the Mishna. Perhaps the non-extant orders were
intentionally disregarded, as treating of subjects then no longer of
national importance ; but this can hardly be the true solution, since
many questions (bearing on the Temple service, wars and conquests),
largely discussed in the Mishna and the Talmud, were at the time
practically obsolete, without being on that account theoretically neglected. Perhaps, and this is historically proved regarding some
sections, the missing portions have been withdrawn from circulation by the destructive hand of time ; or more probably still, the two
Talmuds were discontinued, rather than closed, by the force of external circumstances beyond the control of those interested in the
labor. If *ex ungue leonem* be anything like an arithmetical formula,
the problem may be solved of what the proportions of the Talmud
would have developed into from the fact that the Babylonian Talmud now in our possession, without its companion, is composed, including the marginal gloss, of 5,884 folio pages. The language is
the Aramaic, tinged with provincialisms belonging to the two countries which produced the Talmuds ; all quotations from the Mishna
and the Bible are everywhere in Hebrew. The printed editions,
which, particularly of the Babylonian, are by no means rare, are in a
very unsatisfactory condition, owing to the carelessness or the ignorance of the editors. Those published under the censorship of
Christian ecclesiastical authorities were, moreover, purposely mutilated, or, as it was styled, expurgated—void spaces being left
wherever those learned men fancied to detect allusions disrespectful
to the State religion. But all these passages are found, with their
native semblance on, in editions of the Talmud published in Constantinople, and they are now unceremoniously reproduced in Western
and Central Europe; the conviction having gained ground that the
Christianity of this age has nothing whatever to fear from that

quarter, especially as it is far from probable that in those suspected passages there is any reference to Pauline Christianity at all.

Let me here remark that the history of the rise and the progress of the Church receives no light from the Talmudic traditions. The Mishna, although dating from the end of the second century, betrays no knowledge of the existence of Christianity. How to account for this self-imposed silence is a matter of difficulty. A fear of political consequences cannot have operated, because at that time—200 years after the Christian era commenced—the political status of the Church was fully as depressed as that of the synagogue. The Gemara, the junior of the Mishna by three centuries, does not know the term Christian or Christianity. Several controversies, it is true, are described in the Gemara as having taken place between some doctors of the law and some sectarians called *Minim*, heretics, bearing on the right interpretation of various Mosaic precepts. But the term *min*, heretic, in the then condition of Western Asia and Egypt, covers an immense variety of religious divisions. In the age of the Talmud the countries around the Mediterranean were the arena in which sects that had sprung from Judaism, Christianity, Eastern and Western Paganism, or a mixture of these, fought their spiritual battle. The heretics mentioned in the Talmud were, according to appearance, Jews who, without leaving the pale of Judaism, had adopted some of the dogmas of Christianity; such were, for example, the Ebionites and the Nazarines. Between these and the Pharisees there was still common ground to offer a scope for discussions on matters of the law; but the Pauline Christians, mainly Greeks by birth, on whom the observance of the Mosaic law was not obligatory, were regarded by the Pharisees as Gentiles to all intents and purposes, and accordingly as moving outside of the Jewish world.

There is an essential consideration never to be lost sight of in the appreciation of the spirit of Talmudism. It is that every portion of the Talmud is a compound of two distinct elements, viz.: the Halacha rule and the Hagada saying. The Halacha expresses the legal decision of the Talmud, and it was on this ground binding on the administration of the law as long as and whenever the Jews exercised autonomy, *i. e.*, judging their own causes in conformity with their own principles of jurisdiction.

The Halacha has been extracted from the complicated Talmudical discussions, by a system of canons, the application of which requires many years of study and practice; and the results of the Halacha are to be found duly classified in the various digests of rabbinical laws. The Hagada, on the contrary, is not invested with any legal authority, its conclusions are obligatory on no one, and the interpretation of them is free and open to any one. The Hagada includes all the Talmudical allegories, parables, hyperboles, historical reminiscences, proverbs, popular sayings and maxims; ingenious and touching applications of Scriptural examples—in short, all that tends to point a moral or adorn a tale. The reader of the Talmud, who has no preconceived judgment to uphold, cannot help being unequally affected by the very mixed character of its contents. The defects of the Talmud are at once conspicuous. The Halacha offends by the microscopic attention it bestows upon many questions of ceremonies and observances, which ought never to have occupied the time of grave men clothed with authority over a whole people. No doubt the *tu quoque* argument may be appealed to against many an objector. The Talmudical is not the only religious system in which ceremonies and symbols are raised to an eminence which the uninitiated cannot equally appreciate. The effect, however, remains the same to the prejudice of the Talmud and its minutiæ. The Hagada, on the other hand, cannot be absolved from indulging on too many occasions in undignified, nay gross, exaggerations, never to be explained away by a facile reference to the Oriental fashion of telling entertaining tales, or, still worse, by the supposition of hidden truths underlying the fabulous covering, for that mysterious sublimity is a gratuitous assumption justified by no evidence presentable to common sense. The only apology possible is, that not all the Hagadas are liable to that charge, and that no Hagada whatever is looked upon as an article of faith, but may simply be taken for what it is worth.

Religious tolerance is not exhibited in the Talmud to any greater extent than in any ancient writings, whatever their source. Genuine tolerance—that is, a respect for the religious opinions of those of a different faith—is a production of the most recent period of time, and is only struggling into a more vigorous existence. It has no ancient, it has no modern history; its glories lie in the future before us. While the religions of heathendom are condemned, the largest philanthropy is recommended in the Talmud toward all classes of human beings. "Feed the hungry among the idolators," says the Talmud; "clothe the naked, mourn with the bereaved, and bury the dead, to the end that peace and good-will may prevail among all the families of man." There is a beautiful fiction in the Hagada: "When the Egyptian host lay dead on the sands of the Red Sea, the heavenly choir chanted hymns before the throne of the Almighty; but the Lord forbade them, saying, 'Know ye not that the Egyptians are my children no less than the Israelites?'" The liberality of which the Talmudists were capable manifests itself in the good maxim adopted: "The upright, of whatever creed, shall inherit a portion of the world to come." The scientific knowledge to be met with incidentally in the Talmud is considered by competent judges to have been quite on a par with the acquirements of their Gentile contemporaries. There are Hebrew expressions of terms in astronomy, such as planets, comets, the milky way, the signs of the Zodiac, etc., a fact which may be admitted as a proof that the study of that science was indigenous to, or at least acclimatized in the tradition. The peculiar calendar of the Jews, which was known in the Talmudic times, though published after the close of the Talmud, is admired by Joseph Julius Scaliger, an eminent authority, for the accuracy of its system, which will require no emendation, will suffer no perturbations in thousands of years to come.

It is also believed that the rational study of the Talmudical writings, now coming into cultivation, will add valuable data to the history of medicine, and of the natural sciences in Asia. In fact, if we remember how famous the Jewish physicians became throughout the middle ages, we cannot exclude the belief that a notable share of their knowledge was inherited from the sages of Tiberias and of Sura. The Talmudical standard of ethics is high. Truthfulness, purity, humility, temperance without asceticism; these are the heads under which the numerous attractive sayings may be registered that have secured a celebrity to the Talmud among the learned men of all confessions. The most remarkable treatises of the Talmud are those on jurisprudence. I have no right to express an opinion of my own on a discipline in which I have had no training; but I confide in the judgment of such a man as Prof. Ed. Gans, the great German jurist, who knew the Talmud well. He says that no *corpus* jurist known to him gives evidence of so much critical labor and so much penetration as the Talmudical law on inheritance and succession. The procedure in criminal cases prescribed in the Talmud is marked with the stamp of humanity in almost every particular. As a specimen of the very advanced ideas entertained by some leading teachers of the tradition on the subject of capital punishment, I will quote, in conclusion, from a passage of the Mishna: "A court that passes sentence of death once in a week of years is, indeed, a pernicious tribunal. R. Eleazar added: I hold it to be such, if it does so once in seventy years. R. Tarbon and R. Akiba declared: If we sat in judgment, we should on no account vote for the execution of any criminal. Then R. Simon objected: Well, these men would only increase the shedding of blood in the country." The discussion is short; but it strikes me that nothing of any moment has been added to the argument whenever and wherever this difficult question has been mooted in times nearer our own.

There is in the Talmud many a thing to be rejected, but much more to be respected. The difficult study of the traditions of the Jews carries with it a high intellectual reward; and as to the repository of the tradition, I think that, for its breadth and its depth, for the numerous objects of uncommon formation to be discovered in its recesses, and also for the dangers it presents to those who venture on it without an accurate compass, it has truly been called the Talmudical Ocean. **PROF. T. THEODORES.**

PROF. T. THEODORES, professor at Owen College, Manchester, England; a man of letters and of great research, and as philologist he has gained an eminent name.

DIALECTIC—Logic, the art of reasoning.
MEDIÆVAL—Relating to the middle ages.
PARAGON—A model, a pattern, something excellent.
SERIATIM—In regular order.
MNEMONIC—Assisting the memory.
EPITOME—Abridgement.
APOCRYPHA—Books added to the Scriptures.
COEVAL—Of the same age.

HEGEMONIC—Ruling, principal.
HYPERBOLIC—Exaggerating or extenuating beyond fact.
MINUTIÆ—Trifles, trifling points
ZODIAC—The track of the sun through the twelve signs.
PERTURBATION—Disorder, confusion.
ASCETIC—Employed wholly in devotion, mortification.

JEPHTHAH'S DAUGHTER.

(Judg. xi : 29.)

SHE stood before her father's gorgeous tent,
To listen for his coming.

I have thought
A brother's and a sister's love was much,
I know a brother's is, for I have loved
A trusting sister ; and I know how broke
The heart may be with its own tenderness.
But the affection of a delicate child
For a fond father, gushing as it does
With the sweet springs of life, and living on
Through all earth's changes,
Must be holier !

The wind bore on
The leaden tramp of thousands. Clarion notes
Rung sharply on the air at intervals ;
And the low, mingled din of mighty hosts,
Returning from the battle, poured from far,
Like the deep murmur of a restless sea.

Jephthah led his warriors on
Through Mizpeh's streets. His helm was proudly set,
And his stern lip curled slightly, as if praise
Were for the hero's scorn. His step was firm,
But free as India's leopard ; and his mail,

Whose shekels none in Israel might bear,
Was lighter than a tassel on his frame.
His crest was Judah's kingliest. and the look
Of his dark, lofty eye might quell a lion.

He led on; but thoughts
Seemed gathering round which troubled him. The veins
Upon his forehead were distinctly seen,
And his proud lip was painfully compressed.
He trod less firmly; and his restless eye
Glanced forward frequently, as if some ill
He dared not meet, were there. His home was near,
And men were thronging, with that strange delight
They have in human passions, to observe
The struggle of his feelings with his pride.
He gazed intently forward.

A moment more,
And he had reached his home ; when lo ! there sprang
One with a bounding footstep, and a brow
Like light, to meet him. Oh, how beautiful !
Her dark eye, flashing like a sun-lit gem,
And her luxuriant hair, 'twas like the sweep

Of a swift wing in visions. He stood
still,
As if the sight had withered him. She
threw
Her arms about his neck; he heeded
not.
She called him "Father," but he answered not ;
She stood and gazed upon him. Was
he wroth ?
There was no anger in that blood-shot
eye.
Had sickness seized him? She un-
clasped his helm,
And laid her white hand gently on his
brow.
The touch aroused him. He raised up
his hands,
And spoke the name of God, in agony.

She knew that he was stricken then
and rushed
Again into his arms, and with a flood
Of tears she could not stay, she sobbed
a prayer
That he would tell her of his wretched-
ness.
He told her, and a momentary flush
Shot o'er her countenance ; and then
the soul
Of Jephthah's daughter wakened, and
she stood
Calmly and nobly up, and said : "'Tis
well ;
And I will die !"

And when the sun had set,
Then she was dead—but not by violence. ADAPTED.

PEARLS FROM THE TALMUD.

THE Talmud is the work which embodies the civil and canonical law of the Jewish people; that it consists of the Mishna, or text, and the commentary, or Gemara; that its contents have reference not merely to religion, but also to philosophy, medicine, history, jurisprudence and the various branches of practical duty; that it is, in fact, a law civil and criminal, national and international, human and divine, forming a kind of supplement to the Pentateuch—a supplement such as it took 1,000 years of a nation's life to produce; and that it is not merely a dull treatise, but it appeals to the imagination and the feelings, and to all that is noblest and purest; that between the rugged boulders of the law which bestrew the path of the Talmud there grow the blue flowers of romance and poetry, in the most catholic and Eastern sense—if we say this, what more need be said? Parable, tale, gnome, saga—its elements are taken from heaven and earth; but chiefly and most lovingly from the human heart and from Scripture, for every verse and every word in this latter became, as it were, a golden nail upon which it hung its gorgeous tapestries. But it would be a great mistake to suppose that the poet's cunning had been at work in the Talmud. It was only his heart. The chief feature and charm of its contents lay in their utter naiveté. Taken up, as they appear, at random, and told in their simple, unartistic, unconscious form, they touch the soul. But nothing could be much more distressing than to attempt to take them out of their antique garb and to press them into some kind of modern fashionable dress; or worse still, to systematize and methodize them. It would be as well to attempt to systematize the songs of the bird in the wood, or a mother's parting blessing. He had, however, to endeavor to reproduce a portion of the contents of the Talmud in their own vague sequence and phraseology; and he should confine himself almost to smaller productions, as parables, apophthegms, allegories and the like minute things, which were most characteristic, and required little explanation.

The fundamental law of all human and social economy in the Talmud was the utter and absolute equality of men. It was pointed out that man was created alone—not more than one at different times, lest one should say to another, "I am of the better or earlier stock." And it failed not to mention that man was created on the last day, and that even the gnat was of more ancient lineage than man. In a discussion which arose among the doctors as to which was the most important passage in the whole Bible, one pointed to the verse, "And thou shalt love thy neighbor as thyself." The other contradicted him and pointed to the words, "And these are the generations of man"—not black, not white, not great, not small—but man.

Or, again, they pointed out the words, "And these are the ordinances by which men shall live"—not the priests or the Levites, but men. The law given on Mount Sinai, the masters said, though emphatically addressed to one people, belongs to all humanity. It was not given in any king's land, not in any city or inhabited spot, lest the other nations might say, "We know nothing of it." It was given on God's own highway, in the desert—not in the darkness and stillness of night, but in plain day, amid thunder and lightning. And why was it given on Sinai? Because it is the lowliest and meekest of the mountains—to show that God's spirit rests only upon them that are meek and lowly in their hearts. The Talmud taught that religion was not a thing of creed or dogma, or faith merely, but of active goodness. Scripture said, "Ye shall walk in the words of the Lord." "But the Lord is a consuming fire, how can men walk in His way?" "By being," they answered, "as He is—merciful, loving, long-suffering. Mark how on the first page of the Pentateuch God clothed the naked—Adam; and on the last He buried the dead—Moses. He heals the sick, frees the captives, does good to His enemies, and He is merciful both to the living and to the dead." In close connection with this stood the relationship of men to their neighbors—chiefly to those beyond the pale of creed or nationality, The Talmud distinctly and strongly sets its face against proselytism, pronouncing it to be even dangerous to the commonwealth. There was no occasion, it said, for conversion to Judaism, as long as a man fulfilled the seven fundamental laws. Every man who did so was regarded as a believer to all intents and purposes. It even went so far as to call every righteous man an Israelite. Distinct injunctions were laid down with regard to proselytes. They were to be discouraged and warned off and told that the miseries, privations and persecutions which they wished to take upon themselves were unnecessary, inasmuch as all men were God's children, and might inherit the hereafter; but if they persisted they were to be received, and were to be ever afterward treated tenderly. They illustrated this by a beautiful parable of a deer coming from the forest among a flock of sheep, and being driven off at night, and the gate shut against it, but being after many trials at length received and treated with more tenderness than the sheep. Next stood reverence both for age and youth. They pointed out that not merely the tables of the law which Moses brought down the second time from Sinai, but also those which he broke in his rage, were carefully placed in God's tabernacles, though useless. Reverence old age. But all their most transcendental love was lavished on children. All the verses of Scripture that spoke of flowers and gardens were applied to children and schools. "Do not touch mine anointed ones, and do my prophets no harm." "Mine anointed ones" were school children, and "my prophets" their teachers.

The highest and most exalted title which they bestowed in their poetical flights upon God himself was that of "Pedagogue of Man." There was drought, and the most pious men prayed and wept for rain, but none came. An insignificant looking person at length prayed to Him who caused the wind to blow and the rain to fall, and instantly the heavens covered themselves with clouds and the rain fell. "Who are you," they cried, "whose prayers alone have prevailed?" And he answered, "I am a teacher of little children." When God intended to give the law to the people He asked them whom they would offer as their guarantee that they would keep it holy, and they said Abraham. God said, "Abraham has sinned; Isaac, Jacob, Moses himself—they have all sinned; I cannot accept them." Then they said, "May our children be our witnesses and our guarantees." And God accepted them, even as it is written, "From the mouths of the wee babes has He founded His empire." Indeed, the relationship of man to God they could not express more pregnantly than by the most familiar words which occurred from one end of the Talmud to the other, "Our Father in heaven."

Another simile was that of bride and bridegroom. There was once a man who betrothed himself to a beautiful maiden and then went away, and the maiden waited and waited and he came not. Friends and rivals mocked her and said, "He will never come." She went into her room and took out the letters in which he had promised to be ever faithful. Weeping she read them and was comforted. In time he returned, and inquiring how she had kept her faith so long, she showed him his letters. Israel in misery, in captivity, was mocked by the nations for her hopes of redemption; but Israel went into her schools and synagogues and took out the letters, and was comforted. God would in time redeem her and say, "How could you alone among all the mocking nations be faithful?"

Then Israel would point to the law and answer, "Had I not your promise here?"

Next to women angels were the most frequent bearers of some of the sublimest and most ideal notions of the Talmud. "Underneath the wings of the Seraphim," said the Talmud, "are stretched the arms of divine mercy, ever ready to receive sinners." Every word that emanated from God was transformed into an angel, and every good deed of man became a guardian angel to him. On Friday night, when the Jew left the synagogue, a good angel and a bad angel accompanied him. If, on entering the house, he found the table spread, the lamp lighted, and his wife and children in festive garment, ready to bless the holy day of rest, the good angel said: "May the next Sabbath and the following ones be like unto this; peace unto this dwelling—peace!" and the bad angel, against his will, was compelled to say: "Amen." If, on the contrary, everything was in confusion, the bad angel rejoiced and said: "May all your Sabbaths and week days be like this;" while the good angel wept and said "Amen." According to the Talmud, when God was about to create man, great clamoring arose among the heavenly host. Some said: "Create, O God, a being who shall praise Thee on earth, even as we sing Thy glory in heaven." Others said: "O God, create no more! man will destroy the glorious harmony which Thou hast set on earth, as in heaven." Of a sudden God turned to the contesting host in heaven, and deep silence fell upon them all. Then before the throne of glory there appeared bending the knee the Angel of Mercy, and he prayed: "O Father, create man. He will be Thine own noble image on earth. I will fill his heart with heavenly pity and sympathy toward all creatures; they will praise Thee through him." And there appeared the Angel of Peace and wept: "O God, man will disturb Thine own peace. Blood will flow; he will invent war, confusion, horror. Thy place will be no longer in the midst of all Thy earthly works." The Angel of Justice cried: "You will judge him, God! He shall be subject to my law, and peace shall again find a dwelling-place on earth." The Angel of Truth said: "Father of Truth, cease; with man you create the lie." Out of the deep silence then was heard the divine word: "You shall go with him; you, mine own seal, Truth; but you shall also remain a denizen of heaven; between heaven and earth you shall float, an overlasting link between both."

The question was asked in the Talmud, why children were born with their hands clenched, and men died with their hands wide open; and the answer was that on entering the world man desired to grasp everything, but when he was leaving it all slipped away. Even as a fox which saw a fine vineyard and lusted after its grapes, but was too fat to get in through the only opening there was, until he had fasted three days. He then got in, but having fed he could not get out until he had fasted three days more. "Poor and naked man enters the world; poor and naked does he leave." To women the Talmud ascribed all the blessings of the household. From her emanated everything noble, wise and true. It had not words enough to impress man with the absolute necessity of getting married. Not only was he said to be bereaved of peace, joy, comfort and faith without a wife, but he was not even called a man. "Who is best taught?" it asked; and the answer is, "He who has learned first from his mother."

These few remarks prove as it were but a drop in a vast ocean of Talmud—that strange, wild, weird ocean, with its leviathans, and its wrecks of golden argosies, and with its forlorn bells that send up their dreamy sounds ever and anon, while the fisherman bends upon his oar, and starts and listens, and perchance the tears may come into his eyes.   EMANUEL DEUTSCH.

DR. EMANUEL DEUTSCH, born 1829, and died 1873. A Jewish savant of great renown, formerly Librarian of the British Museum, London, a writer of great note, of which his articles in the "Quarterly Review" gained him a world-wide reputation. He was for fifteen years Librarian, an extensive contributor to "Chambers' Encyclopædia," also to "Smith's Dictionary of the Bible," and to "Kitto's Cyclopædia of Biblical Literature." He was a person of pious and amiable disposition, and endeared by both Jews and Christians.

CIVIL—Relating to the community, political; not foreign.
CANONICAL—Fixed by ecclesiastical laws; spiritual.
CATHOLIC—Universal, used for true in opposition to heretical.
SAGA—Compositions which comprise the history and mythology of the northern European nations.

NAIVETE—Unaffected plainness.
TO METHODIZE—To regulate.
SEQUENCE—Order of succession.
APOPHTHEGM—A remarkable saying.
TRANSCENDENTAL—General, supereminent.
LEVIATHAN—A large water-animal mentioned in the book of Job.
ARGOSY—A large vessel.

A LETTER FROM JUDAH HA-LEVI TO HIS FRIEND ISAAC.

FROM THE GERMAN OF DR. GEIGER.

But yesterday the earth drank like a child
With eager thirst the autumn rain,
Or like a wistful bride who waits the hour
Of love's mysterious bliss and pain.
And now the spring is here with yearning eyes;
'Midst shimmering golden flower beds
On meadows carpeted with varied hues,
In richest raiment clad, she treads.
She weaves a tapestry of bloom o'er all,
And myriad-eyed young plants up-spring,
White, green or red, like lips that to the mouth
Of the beloved one sweetly cling.

Whence come these radiant tints, these blended beams?
Here's such a dazzle, such a blaze,
As though earth stole the splendor of the stars,
Fain to eclipse them with her rays.
Come! go we to the garden with our wine,
Which scatters sparks of hot desire,
Within our hand 'tis cold, but in our veins
It flashes clear, it glows like fire.
It bubbles sunnily in earthen jugs,
We catch it in the crystal glass,
Then wander through cool, shadowy lanes and breathe
The spicy freshness of the grass.
While we with happy hearts our circuit keep,

The gladness of the earth is shown,
She smileth, though the trickling rain-
   drops weep
Silently over her, one by one.
She loves to feel the tears upon her
   cheek,
Like a rich veil, with pearls inwove,
Joyous she listens when the swallows
   chirp,
And warbles to her mate, the dove.
Blithe as a maiden 'midst the young
   green leaves,
A wreath she'll wind, a fragrant
   treasure;
All living things in graceful motion
   leap,
As dancing to some merry measure.
The morning breezes rustle cordially,
   Love's thirst is sated with the balm
      they send,

Sweet breathes the myrtle in the frolic
   wind,
   As though remembering a distant
      friend.
The myrtle branch now proudly lifted
   high,
   Now whispering to itself drops low
      again.
The topmost palm-leaves rapturously
   stir,
   For all at once they hear the bird's
      soft strain.
So stirs, so yearns all nature gayly
   decked,
   To honor Isaac with her best array.
Hear'st thou the word ? She cries—I
   beam with joy,
   Because with Isaac I am wed to-day.

                              EMMA LAZARUS.

THE TALMUD JEW.

I.

IF one asks a student to-day why he studies, at once, in spite of his youth, he will give a very practical answer ; one, too, that is everywhere intelligible —while he mentions the profession for which he is preparing himself, and through which he will obtain a lucrative office, or a comfortable position in life.

It is entirely different with the Jew of the Talmud, or with him who expended his time and powers, his zeal and care, on the study of the Talmud. He wished to derive no benefit and no profit from his studies, not to use them, as a Mishna teacher says,[1] as a spade to dig for treasures, or as a crown to shine before the eyes of his neighbors. Pure love of the law, of its humane statutes and wise principles, which are explained, widened, and deepened in the Talmud ; warm enthusiasm for Judaism, which hundreds upon hundreds of richly talented Talmud sages made the subjects of intellectual labor, and to know which they sacrificed the greatest portion of their lives ; it was this which impelled the Talmud disciples to slake their thirst at the fonts of Palestine and Babylon. "Say not," exclaims the Talmud,[2] "I will study the Scripture and the explanations of its teachers, in order that people may praise me as a Chaham or sage, as a rabbi or master, but study from pure love to God, and to bind thyself closely to him through the knowledge and understanding of His word. Love, not reward, love of truth ; let this be the word of redemption, when thou sittest at the feet of the masters of the law."

What an ideality developed and was fostered in the hearts of the Jewish people !

Day and night did they bury themselves in the study of sections and subjects which had nothing to do with social life, with money and gain ; they became engrossed in the investigation of laws for offerings and purification, although these had long since grown obsolete ; they wished nothing but knowledge, truth, understanding, illumination.

Where is there another people on earth, among whom studies which aimed only at instruction and development of the spiritual life were cultivated, with such pure, devoted and self-sacrificing love as in Israel?

And this incomparable ideality in learning and research produced an ideal devotion for teaching and instruction without money and without price,[1] wholly out of love and enthusiasm for the diffusion of the holy word and religious truth.

Sweet and suggestive sounds the saying of the Talmud, which is despised by the malicious : "See," it says,[4] " there are studies which are ice-cold, without soul-warmth and without love—these are those whose object is not self-ennobling and the instruction of others, but only selfish purposes. Opposed to such are those studies which seek and wish nothing but truth and knowledge, and their diffusion; these are studies of love, love to God and thy neighbor"—the real and genuine studies in the Talmudic sense. Who dares censure the Talmud Jews for covetousness, and accuse them of having susceptibility and understanding only for the tangible material goods of life? Talmud means study, in order to teach pure teaching, unselfish teaching for its own sake, to enrich the intellect, to increase the understanding and to enlarge the world of ideas.

---

1. Pirke Aboth 4, 45.
2. Nedarim 62.

3. Bekhoroth 29.
4. Sukkah 49.

II.

BY WHOM WAS THE TALMUD STUDIED?

Not by a single class or one portion of the people, but by men who were blessed with the greatest wealth, as well as by those who possessed nothing but the desire of knowledge and the ability to work ; by persons who rejoiced in bodily freshness and strength ; by those who were weak and suffering ; by impetuous youth and sober age.[1] All refreshed themselves at the springs which the noblest and best in Israel have dug,[2] and which rejuvenated and strengthened their intellects for centuries.

If we review the long list of masters and disciples of the Talmud, we find among them, in all lands and in every century, the rich and the poor, the noble and the humble, emulating each other in love, zeal, and devotion for those studies which are discussed in the Talmud ; so that there is scarcely a second work in the literature of any people which can boast of so large a number of choice friends and investigators. Let me mention just a few of them.

There is R. Eleasar ben Harsom, who inherited from his father great wealth by land and sea, and who sought everywhere teachers and inquirers of the law, in order to hear them and satisfy his thirst for knowledge.[3]

There is, again, R. Elieser ben Hyrkanos, whose father belonged to the richest men of his time, but whom riches did not satisfy. He secretly left his father's home, to be taught by distinguished teachers, studied with the severest privations, and later became so renowned that he received the name of "Ark of the Covenant," and "the Great." Yes, indeed, such are the genuine great in Israel ; not the men of the sword and the battlefield, but the men of knowledge.

Eleasar ben Asarya, who came of distinguished ancestry, was so wealthy that he paid yearly twelve thousand calves in tithes, and gave rise to the proverb : "He who has seen Eleasar ben Asarya in a dream can expect great riches." He displayed the greatest zeal for the diffusion of Talmudic studies, and encouraged and educated numerous young men, or, as the Talmud says :[1] "On the day when this master began his lectures, it was necessary largely to increase the number of benches in the hall of instruction."

There is R. Judah, the collector of the Mishna, who sifted, arranged, and published the observations and law-principles of his predecessors. He possessed such wealth that it was said of him: "The rabbi's hostler is richer than King Shapur."[5] After his death, the saying spread : "Since the days of Moses, there has been no man in Israel who so united learning and greatness as R. Judah the Holy."[6]

R. Abbahu, of Cæsarea, was a man of dazzling beauty,[7] of high repute in court circles, and so wealthy that he had seats of ivory in his house. Yet he was a diligent student, and promoter of Talmudic lore ; and like Rav Ashi, the codifier of the Mishna, he was distinguished by his wealth and erudition.[8]

Five hundred years later, Samuel Hanagid, a Jewish minister of the Spanish King Habus, not only had charge of foreign affairs and the department of war, but was a Talmud Jew, and gave Talmudic lectures as well, collected disciples around him, and exchanged letters on Halachic themes with scholars and congregations of his time. We possess fragments of an introduction to the Talmud, written by Samuel Hanagid, and many Hebrew poems, among which those are especially to be noted which he composed in his tent before a victory, and wherein he assured God that he kept strictly Sabbaths and festivals as a true adherent of Judaism.

These will suffice as examples of wealthy Talmud Jews. Let us turn to the poverty-stricken ones, of whom Hillel will serve as a specimen. He was so poor that he supported himself by splitting

wood, but became so illustrious a master through his unwearying
patience in learning and teaching, his winning ways, his kindness
toward Jew and heathen, and his love of peace, that the teachers of
his day paled in comparison, and his decisions, with few exceptions,
have been accepted for all time as laws in Israel. And who could
recount the poor youths who in the course of centuries devoted
themselves to Talmudic studies with never-wearying diligence and
the greatest privations? From their midst arose the teachers in
Israel whose names history gloriously preserves. The Talmud
justly observes : " Be careful in the treatment of the poor ; for the
best and most important men of the law, or the most celebrated
Talmud Jews, came from their ranks."[9] This advice, and other
oft-repeated exhortations to value those who cultivated Talmudic
studies, were always cherished in Israel, even to our time, which,
with the neglect of Jewish knowledge, has ceased to revere men of
Jewish knowledge. In every community there were Talmud schools,
Talmud teachers and disciples ; a pious and ideal rivalry arose in
teaching and learning ; the men of Talmudic spirit represented
the nobility in the midst of the people, while the saying was
heard,[10] "The men of intellect are choice and guiding princes,
who by their ideas lead and direct people." The remark, too
was handed down :[11] "Hillel testifies against the poor, Eleasar
ben Harsom against the rich." Say not, I am too poor, must
provide for my living, and cannot mount the ladder of knowledge. Look at Hillel, one of the wisest among the wise, who,
despite his poverty, shines like a sun in the Talmud sky. Say
not with noble mien : I am rich, have the most flattering con-
nections, know the first men of the city, have no room in my
palace for Hebrew books, no time for Hebrew studies. Look
at Eleasar ben Harsom. Numerous cities belonged to him, his
ships in great number sailed the seas, and still he journeyed
without show and escort, to seek out in different places the
masters of the law.

The Talmud, to employ Cicero's words, was not only the "nourishment of youth, the delight of age, ornament in prosperity, comfort and refuge in misfortune," but it developed and preserved a
sense for the ideal, spiritual, and invisible in Israel's midst, unique
in the history of nations. Young and old, rich and poor, land own-
ers and artisans, physicians, astronomers, and philosophers, sons of
wealthy families, and men of the humblest classes, were true, perse-
vering, and inspired students of the Talmud, without expecting or
attaining any profit or earthly advantage. Their highest reward
was the joy of learning, the conflict of truth, the applause of the
sages, the reverence of the people, among whom was the saying,[12]
"Israel is wholly impoverished and abandoned to the bitterest
want among its foes, only when the schools of the law are desolate,"

or when the ideal sentiment, which elevates above need and affliction, has vanished.

The places where the Talmud was studied and taught were schools of temperance, self-control, and self-ennoblement, of joyful and self-sacrificing devotion to an ideal intellectual life, which is entirely neglected in our material age and among our practical youth. A true and genuine Talmud disciple was called a disciple or friend of wisdom; he loves God, loves all his fellow-men, loves truth;[12] his kingdom is the kingdom of peace.

1. Rambam, Hill, T. T., 81.
2. Numb. xxi. 18.
3. Yoma 9, a, 35, b.
4. Berakhoth 28, a.
5. Shab. 113, b.
6. Gittin 59, a.
7. Kethuboth 17.
8. Gittin 59, a.
9. Nedarim 81, a.
10. Shab. 119, b.
11. Yoma 35, b.
12. Mekhilta 81.
13. Perek 46.

III.

" When Moses," so lectured once a Talmud sage,[1] " was about to write down the section, 'let us make man in our image,' he became grave, paused, and asked: 'O Lord, will not these words give cause for misunderstandings and false interpretation? Will not some maintain a plurality of gods on account of the little word "we," and others represent Thee with human traits? Will it not suffice if on the first day of creation I only write, " And God spoke : let man exist ; and he existed ?' "

" ' Write what thou hast received, O Moses," thundered the reply, ' even if some misunderstand it. It is so important that man perceives and feels that he is a heavenly-earthly creation, the noblest in my likeness, adorned with the highest excellence, destined to gaze upward to God alone as ideal and pattern, in order to become ever better and more perfect through development and progress; this is so important that these words should never be suppressed out of regard for the weak and erring.' "

Did Moses really so ask, and did God thus answer him? No ; for no one could listen to such a conversation. It is only a mode of speech popular among the Talmudists, who love to dress weighty truths in the garb of a dialogue, so as to impress more powerfully ; and surely here is a subject of supreme importance. Yes, it is important for the princes of the spirit and the leaders of nations to read and to hear that great, sublime, and civilizing truths should not beweakened or suppressed, and taught only as mysteries to a few disciples, from fear lest hundreds or thousands among millions might misinterpret them and work mischief with them, or in anxious doubt whether the proper time has arrived for their dissemination. God is truth, His zeal is truth, His law is truth, and His chosen spirits are messengers of truth.

In the same way some famous Jews answered the Roman philosophers. They asked, "If your God denounces polytheism and image-worship, why does he not destroy the whole idolatrous world?" "Shall the world go to ruin on account of the fools?" they replied. "The nations deify the sun, moon and stars: shall these therefore cease to give light? No. The beautiful world continues on in its regular course. The sun beams, the moon shines, the stars glitter, and the fools who worship sun and moon will one day be called to account."

And we exclaim to those who wish to sacrifice the Talmud, the work of centuries and numerous gifted men : Shall it be destroyed and disappear on account of the fools who misunderstand and misuse it? No. After the Bible, the Talmud is the most important and comprehensive portion of our old literature ; the archives of our religious history, the record of sagacious law proceedings, the treasure-chamber of golden rules of life and precious sayings of deep wisdom and lofty morality: we wish to preserve, study, investigate, value the Talmud; let the fools continue their work of folly.

Yes, we preserve the Talmud and respect its saying [2] that States go to ruin when hate and enmity are nourished among their people. Hence, we will be Talmud Jews and loyal citizens, holding ourselves far from those who destroy peace and unity in our fatherland, and thereby weaken its strength.

We preserve the Talmud and guide ourselves by its rule of life:[3] Who is reverent or a "Reverend?" Not every one who wears a clerical gown and talks in sanctimonious tones, but he who honors his fellow-men, does not revile, disgrace, ridicule and injure them.

We preserve the Talmud and learn from it[4] that, in days and seasons of need, we shall think of the Jewish as well as non-Jewish poor, and give them, with lavish hand, food, raiment and fuel.

We preserve the Talmud and give heed to its sharp admonition,[5] that he who raises the poisonous tongue of scandal not only against a whole religious society, but even against a single individual, and scatters malicious reports, is an atheist, who denies the God of truth and of knowledge ; the God who demands just scales, not alone for articles of merchandise but for the worth and character of a man or a race. You bewail the decline of faith : who can believe in a God whose servants preach hatred, oppression, persecution, while their slanderous tongues ever agitate against peaceful citizens?[6]

We preserve the Talmud, and comfort ourselves with its declaration[7] that "the evil eye," or envy, cannot injure us if we perform our duty, discharge our obligations to all men, and fulfill the commandments of love. Joseph was exposed to the jealousy of his brothers, and yet he triumphed in the end as a man of peace, of love, and of reconciliation.—*Jewish Messenger.*　　A. ZELLINEK.

1. Beresh Rabba 83.
2. Yoma 9.
3. Pirke Aboth.
4. Gittin 61.

5. Erakbin 16.
6. Ante-Semites.
7. Berakhoth 21.

JAEL.

(JUDG: IV.)

"O BARAK, I came forth to meet thee
　With tidings of joy;
Thou art mighty, O Barak, in battle,
　And strong to destroy,
But he whom thou seekest so hotly
　Was met with a kiss,
Hath escaped from thy strength and thy
　vengeance;
　And I have done this.

"Nay, frown not, and say that I mock
　thee;
And thou by his side,
I know thee, fierce Deborah—curl not
　Thy lips, nor deride
The wit of a woman, thou art one,
　But come to my tent,
I will show how he passed from thy
　vengeance;
'Twas this way he went.

"Yea, enter; now wait till the sunlight
　Hath passed from your eyes;
Till ye see through the gloom of the
　tenting
　Where Sisera lies;
Nay, lay not the hand to the sword-
　hilt—
　He cannot arise.

"I heard the great clamor toward Kis-
　hon,
　When he who lies here
Came wounded and breathless with run-
　ning,
　And cried out in fear:
'They have smitten the armies of Hazor,
　I flee for my life;

I am weary and wounded; oh, woman
　And mother and wife,
As thou lovest thy children, but grant
　me
　For one night to lie
In thy tent, for my mother who watcheth
　Will die if I die.
There is peace between Heber thy hus-
　band
　And Jabin the king;
As thy guest may I enter thy dwelling?
　Wilt thou grant me this thing'?

"Then I knew him, and bade him full
　welcome
　To all that was mine;
'As I am a mother,' I told him,
　'I sorrow for thine.'
Then I bound up his wounds, as I did
　so
　Pretending to weep;
Till comforted, weary and wasted,
　He fell fast asleep.
Then took I the hammer and tent-pin,
　I crept to his side,
And I thought of the mother who watch-
　ed for
　The wheels of her pride,
But the cause was the Lord's and I
　smote him—
　Thus Sisera died.

"Thou art sad; wouldst thou alter, O
　Barak,
　The way that he fell?
But Deborah's smile gives a token—
　It was well."
　　　　　OVERLAND MONTHLY.

THE RELIGION OF ISRAEL.

THE Old Testament, I suppose nobody will deny, is filled with the word and thought of righteousness "In the way of righteousness is life, and in the pathway thereof is no death"; "Righteous ness tendeth to life"; "The wicked man troubleth his own flesh"; "The way of the transgressor is hard." Nobody will deny that these texts may stand for the fundamental and ever-recurring idea of the Old Testament. No people ever felt so strongly as the people of the Old Testament, the Hebrew people, that conduct is three-fourths of our life and its largest concern; no people ever felt so strongly that succeeding, going right, hitting the mark in this great concern, was *the way of peace*, the highest possible satisfaction. "He that keepeth the law, happy is he; its ways are ways of pleasantness, and all its paths are peace; if thou hadst walked in its ways thou shouldst have dwelt in peace forever!" Jeshurun, one of the ideal names of their race, is the *upright*; Israel, the other and greater, is the *wrestler with God*, he who has known the contention and strain it costs to stand upright. That mysterious personage, by whom their history first touches the hill of Zion, is Melchizedek, the *righteous* king; their holy city, Jerusalem, is the foundation or vision or inheritance of that righteousness which was such an object of attention to them that its words were to "be in their heart, and thou shalt teach them diligently unto thy children, and thou shalt talk of them when thou sittest in thy house, and when thou walkest by the way, and when thou liest down, and when thou risest up." To keep them ever in mind, they wore them, went about with them, and made talismans of them. "Bind them upon thy fingers, bind them upon thy neck; write them upon the table of thine heart!" "Take fast hold of her," they said of the doctrine of conduct, or righteousness; "let her not go! Keep her, for *she is thy life!*" ....

Philosophers dispute whether moral ideas, as they call them, the simplest ideas of conduct and righteousness which now seem instinctive, did not all grow, were not once inchoate, embryo, dubious, unformed; that may have been so; the question is an interesting one for science. But the interesting question for conduct is whether those ideas are unformed or formed *now*; they are formed now, and they were formed when the Hebrews named the power, out of themselves, which pressed upon their spirit : *The Eternal.* Probably the life of Abraham, *the friend of God*, however imperfectly the Bible traditions by themselves convey it to us, was a decisive step forward in the development of these ideas of righteousness. Probably this was the moment when such ideas became fixed and solid for the Hebrew people, and marked it permanently off from all others who had not made the same step. But long before the first beginnings of recorded history, long before the oldest word of Bible literature, these ideas must have been at work; we know it by the result, although they may have for a long while been but rudimentary. In Israel's earliest history and earliest literature, under the name of Eloah, Elohim, *The Mighty*, there may have lain and matured, there did lie and mature, ideas of God, more as a moral power, more as a power connected above everything with conduct and righteousness, than were entertained by other races; not only can we judge by the result that this must have been so, but we can see that it was so. Still their name, *The Mighty*, does not in itself involve any true and deep religious ideas, any more than our name, *The Brilliant*. With *The Eternal* it is otherwise. For what did they mean by the Eternal; the Eternal *what?* The Eternal *cause?* Alas! these poor people were not Archbishops of York. They meant the Eternal *righteous*, who loveth *righteousness*. They had dwelt upon the thought of conduct and right and wrong, till the *not ourselves*, which is in us and around us, became to them adorable eminently, and altogether as *a power which makes for righteousness;* which makes for it unchangeably and eternally, and is therefore called *The Eternal.*

There is not a particle of metaphysics in their use of this name any more than in their conception of the *not ourselves* to which they attached it. Both came to them, not from abstruse reasoning, but from experience in the plain region of conduct. Theologians with metaphysical heads render Israel's *Eternal* by *the self-existent,* and Israel's *not ourselves* by *the absolute,* and attribute to Israel their own subtleties. According to them Israel had his head full of the necessity of a first cause, and therefore said *The Eternal;* as, again, they imagine him looking out into the world, noting everywhere the marks of design and adaptation to his wants, and reasoning out and inferring thence the fatherhood of God. All these fancies come from an excessive turn of reasoning, and a neglect of observing men's actual course of thinking and way of using words. Israel, at this stage when *The Eternal* was revealed to him, inferred nothing, reasoned out nothing. He felt and experienced. When he begins to speculate in the schools of Rabbinism, he quickly shows how much less native talent than the Bishops of Winchester and Gloucester he has for this perilous business.

Happily, when *The Eternal* was revealed to him, he had not yet begun to speculate. He personified, indeed, his Eternal, for he was strongly moved, and an orator and poet. *"Man never knows how anthropomorphic he is,"* says Goethe, and so man tends always to represent everything under his own figure. In poetry and eloquence man may and must follow this tendency, but in science it often leads him astray. Israel, however, did not scientifically predicate *personally* of God; he would not even have had a notion what was meant by it. He called him the maker of all things, who gives drink to all out of his pleasures as out of a river; but he was led to this by no theory of a first cause. The grandeur of the spectacle given by the world, the grandeur of the sense of its all being *not ourselves,* being above and beyond ourselves, and immeasurably dwarfing us, a man of imagination instinctively personifies as a single mighty living and productive power, as Goethe tells us that the words which rose naturally to his lips, when he stood on the top of the Brocken, were, "Lord, what is man, that thou mindest him, or the son of man, that thou makest account of him?" But Israel's confessing and extolling of this power came not even from his imaginative feeling, but came first from his gratitude for righteousness. To one who knows what conduct is, it is a joy to be alive: the *not ourselves*, which by revealing to us righteousness makes our happiness, adds to the boon this glorious world to be righteous in.

That is the notion at the bottom of the Hebrew's praises of a Creator; and if we attend,we can see this quite clearly. Wisdom and understanding mean for Israel. "The fear of the Eternal," and the fear of the eternal means for him "to depart from evil," righteousness. Righteousness, order, conduct, is for him the essence of *The Eternal*, and the source of all man's happiness; and it is only as a further and natural working of this essence that he conceives creation. "The fear of the Eternal, *that* is wisdom; and to depart from evil, *that* is understanding! Happy is the man that findeth wisdom, and the man that getteth understanding! She is a tree of life to them that lay hold upon her, and happy is every one that retaineth her. *The Eternal by wisdom hath founded the earth, by understanding hath He established the heavens*"—and so the Bible writer passes into the account of creation. It all comes to him from the idea of righteousness.— *From "Literature and Dogma."*   PROF. ARNOLD.

To INCHOATE—To begin, to commence.
METAPHYSIC—A science ; in Shakespeare it means supernatural or preternatural.

ABSTRUSE—Hidden, difficult.
ANTHROPOMORPHISM--Representing the Deity as having human form or attributes. (Gr.)

THERE IS NO DEATH.

THERE is no death! The stars go down
To rise upon some fairer shore ;
And bright, in heaven's jeweled crown,
They shine forevermore.

There is no death. The dust we tread
Shall change beneath the summer showers ;
The golden grain, or mellow fruit,
Or rainbow-tinted flowers.

The granite rocks disorganize,
And feed the hungry moss they bear ;
The forest leaves drink daily life
From out the viewless air.

There is no death! The leaves may fall,
And flowers may fade and pass away;
They only wait through wint'ry hours
The coming of May-day.

There is no death! An angel form
Walks o'er the earth with silent tread,
And bears our best-loved things away,
And then we call them "dead."

He leaves our hearts all desolate,
He plucks our fairest, sweetest flowers;
Transplanted into bliss, they now
Adorn immortal bowers.

The bird-like voice, whose joyous tones
Made glad these scenes of sin and strife,
Sings now an everlasting song,
Around the tree of life.

Where'er he sees a smile too bright,
Or heart too pure for taint and vice,
He bears it to that world of light,
To dwell in Paradise.

Born unto that undying life,
They leave us but to come again ;
With joy we welcome them, the same,
Except their sin and pain.

And ever near us, though unseen,
The dear immortal spirits tread ;
For all the boundless universe
Is life—there is no dead !

BULWER LYTTON.

Sir Edward George Earle Bulwer Lytton (generally known by his original name of Bulwer), one of the most popular and distinguished writers of England, was born in 1805, and educated at the University of Cambridge. He is the author of a large number of novels, plays, poems and miscellanies.

JUDAISM AND SCIENCE.

My labors in the history of botany necessarily caused me to see the works of Albrecht the Great. His relations to Thomas of Aquino, his dependence upon Aristotle and Arabian writers, brought near to me the question of the interposition of these investigators and of earlier sources. The investigation brought me continually further, and at last caused me to become aware of a circumstance which our great works of history pass over in silence, and yet which is of extraordinary importance to the history of the development of mankind. The following contains a brief view of what I have found.

The Jews are and will remain the most remarkable people, and if we admit the symbol of a providence, one may call them "God's chosen people." They furnish one of the most interesting subjects for earnest and thoughtful historical examination, not only because, despite the severest and bloodiest persecutions by Pagans, Persians, Mohammedans and Christians, they have, for nearly two thousand years and up to the present day, maintained themselves as a people and been true to their original character, but because they continually expand and increase in every climate and under conditions more favorable than those surrounding any other people. They are the oldest people supporting monotheism, and who, because of the purity of the belief in God, have established and adhered to moral laws, whose effect in life is the true demonstration of religious belief. All Europe had its middle age—a period of barbarity, of intellectual and moral degradation; we cannot imagine it to have been worse, only the Jews were excepted therefrom.

Notwithstanding dispersion and oppression, which often robbed them of the simplest human rights—yes, of the right to live—they developed their intellectual life uninterrupted to the end of the middle ages, and preserved and gave to the other people the foundation of morality and spiritual life. They sometimes stumbled, after the manner of spiritually noble minds, when happy moments made life too easy; but reverses and calamities, which barely allowed them to live, had only this result: to ennoble them, and to spur them on to higher intellectual and spiritual exertions.

The devastation of the Jewish State by the Assyrians and Babylonians caused the Jews to comprehend their own spiritual being, and to unite the results of their previous spiritual life into one entirety, which, even at the present time, contains so much that is deemed elevating and holy by Christians. They stamped the boon thus won upon their lives. Unshaken trust in God, and moral conduct, as far as the same was recognized by them as a duty, gave them the power of enthusiasm with which this little nation maintained for centuries the fight with the gigantic Roman empire, whose exertions against them were greater than that exercised toward any nation of similar size. The heroism of the Jews displayed by the Maccabees during the conflict which ended in the destruction of Jerusalem by Titus, at the two years' war under Bar-Kochba, and later, their defence of Naples against Belisarius, and the passes of the Pyrenees against the Franks, place them with the greatest heroes known to history. They succumbed to enormous physical superiority; the nation, as such, was destroyed; the people dispersed all over the globe, from China and India, through Africa and Europe, unto the remotest western regions then discovered.

But the people remained *one people*, continued to maintain an unbroken connection among all its branches, and always recognized, in the progress of moral and spiritual life, a center that bound them together. Wherever the Jew wandered, he found men of the same faith, the same mind, and was sure of receiving practical assistance and a cordial welcome. These circumstances are to be considered, inasmuch as they made easy the diffusion of intellectual activity and its results among the entire people. Thus we find that, during the gloomy, intellectually barren and rotten middle ages, the Jews promoted, the same as in times of yore, agriculture, manufactures, dying, weaving, and other trades and occupations that contributed to the commerce and welfare of the world. We have seen that, with uninterrupted intellectual activity, they cultivated all the sciences, developed them, and then handed them over, at the end of the middle ages, to the nations at last arising from ignorance. They are the founders of the science of philosophy. Opposed to the ignorance and stupidity of the Christian clergy, they were the only ones promoting a thorough and fruitful knowledge of the Oriental and Occidental languages; they were the only nation with whom a free development of intellectual activity in philosophy, and especially religious philosophy, found room, and who built up ethics as no other nation has done. Only with them was to be found a scientific cultivation and development of the medical art; they participated in the progress of astronomy; they established the celebrated schools of Montpelier and Salerno, and materially contributed to the prosperity of the school of Padua. A few years after the invention of printing, they possessed printing houses in many towns. Ribeyra de Santos well says: "We are chiefly indebted to the Jews for the first knowledge of philosophy, botany, medicine, astronomy and cosmography, as well as the elements of grammar and the holy lan-

guage, and for almost all the studies connected with Biblical literature."   PROF. M. J. SCHLEIDEN.

COSMOGRAPHY—The science of a general system of the world.

THE TWENTY-NINTH PSALM.

A PARAPHRASE.

ASCRIBE unto God, O sons of the
  mighty,
  Ascribe unto God His glory and
  might ;
Ascribe unto God His glorious power,
  Sing to Him, worship Him, morning
  and night.

The voice of the Lord resounds in the
  surges,
  Echoes through ocean's most fathom-
  less caves ;
In thunder and storm, in anger we hear
  it,
  While oft'times in zephyrs it ripples
  the waves.

The voice of the Lord rends forests
  asunder,
  The cedars of Lebanon bend to the
  sound ;
While leafless and riven, the monarch
  of ages,
  Crushed by His thunders, lies scattered around.

The mountain is cleft by His mighty
  power,
  The flash of the lightning destroyed
  by His will ;
The wild deer in terror flies deep in the
  forest,
  And Kadesh is shaken from valley to
  hill.

The Lord is enthroned, and ever hath
  been,
  Enthroned at the deluge, and ever
  shall be ;
Dispensing to all His mercy and kindness,
  With infinite wisdom, no human may
  see.

The Lord will give strength to all who
  obey Him,
  And thro' His great mercy shall virtue
  increase ;
Fulfilling the promise given on Zion,
  The Lord will then bless all His
  people with peace.   J. M.

REMARKS ON JUDAISM.

JUDAISM is one of the most ancient religions of the world; it is four
thousand years old. During that period it has naturally came in
contact with the most powerful and intellectual nations both in modern and ancient times; it has come also into collision with some
religious systems and civilizations, which it has contributed its share
toward forming. On some of these religions it has impressed its
stamp, and the Jewish religion was one which was well calculated to
excite the attention of those nations with which it came into contact. It is a religious system which has survived the shocks which
laid low the religious system of nations much more powerful than
the Jews, and possessing advantages superior to theirs. What is
more is that it was the intention of the Jewish lawgiver that it
should arouse the attention of surrounding nations, as can be proved
by numerous texts from the Hebrew Scriptures. In these Scriptures we find all the elements of a missionary people; but I do

not say a "conversionist" people; there is a vast difference between the two. Our mission was not to send out messengers and apostles, but it was to be discharged by deeds and practices of such a nature as to strike the imagination and to impress the mind. The prophets developed it still more.

At a later period we find expositions presented to the Gentile world by the Jews for making them acquainted with the history and principles of the institutions of Moses. They were not composed for Jews, and, therefore, they were not written in Hebrew, but in the languages which were the most widely understood. Philo and Josephus wrote in Greek, and the first translation of the Book of Moses—the Septuagint—was also in Greek. These expositions had their influence, for soon after their appearance we find proselytes to Judaism in the large cities belonging to the Roman and Grecian Empires. We know from Rabbinical writings, and from the Gospels, that proselytes existed at Antioch, at Damascus, at Rome itself, and various other cities; and these proselytes formed the actual nucleus of a subsequent religion. These expositions had a great influence on mankind, and on the current literature of the day. The New Testament itself may be considered as such an exposition, for it was written by Jews, and it was not intended, except by the Apostle Paul, to form a new religion. The writings of the Apostle Paul we place by themselves; of the others I may say that a Jew reading their writings must consider that he is reading from the Talmud—the style is the same, but the aspect of Judaism is quite different.

In tracing the development of Judaism, I have four thousand years to traverse, and I find four convenient epochs in which to divide that time: First, from Moses to Ezra the scribe; second, from Ezra to the destruction of the second temple; third, from the destruction of the second temple to the time of Moses Mendelsohn, which took place in 1786; and fourth, from 1786 to our own period. At the first period we see what I may call the framework of Judaism. The institutions of Judaism did not take root at once in the popular mind. For some time they floated in a religious atmosphere; they waited for a season until the ground should be prepared for them to drop into and strike root. This favorable season, this congenial soil, did not appear until after Ezra. From Moses to Ezra was simply the inception of Judaism. The second period was the period for the consolidation or crystallization of Judaism; it was then that it struck root in the hearts of the people and brought forth fruit. But the moment Judaism was systematized, the moment efforts were made to carry out the institutions, differences of opinion arose, and with them discord. There were three principal sects: the Sadducees, the Pharisees, and the Essenes. The Sadducees were the old Tories of the Jews; they would not admit of the neces-

sity of any change. The Pharisees were those who felt the change
of the times, and were ready to yield to them ; to allow ancient institutions to fall and to establish new ones. The Essenes were the
mystics of Judaism ; they were fond of allegorizing ; they retired
from the world, and withdrew into sacred places. The Sadducees
disappeared under the new regime inaugurated by the Romans ;
they could break but they could not yield. They, however, re-
appeared under the name of the Karaites. The Essenes vanished,
finding a more congenial soil and atmosphere in the new Christian
sect which had risen. The third period was one of martyrdom.
The fourth period was one of regeneration. The Jews woke up as
from a trance, and found they had been isolated from the world
around them. They felt the necessity of harmonizing with those
around them ; they had peculiar notions of their own, and they felt
the necessity of conformity. The efforts they made and the failures
which followed form the religious and intellectual history of modern
Judaism.

There are three features I shall notice in the Jewish character.
First of all, he considered himself part and parcel of the Divine
scheme ; secondly, his courage in distress, as he conceived the idea
that he could not perish, since he was necessary in the world ; and
thirdly, his pride, and this pride arose from the self-consciousness
that he was necessary to the Deity in His providential government
of the world. The first and second features were harmless enough,
but the third led him into trouble, as it provoked antagonism. This
antagonism was shown in ancient literature, which has had its influence even in our own days. One writer had a fling at Josephus ;
Cicero had his fling against the Jews, and Tacitus, the great historian, misrepresented them. Hatred to the Jews arose from this
period. The ancient Sclavonic tribes had no prejudices against the
Jews, but missionaries from the East and South came to them and
planted in their souls the seeds of the new religion (Christianity),
and also the seeds of hatred to the Jews. These seeds remained
latent for a considerable time, but at last they fructified, and the
Jew felt the influences of hatred and prejudice. Hatred to the race
traveled from the East and South, to the West and North. Judaism teaches that God is a spirit, though that dogma in so many
words is not to be found in the Hebrew Bible. Yet there is a nega-
tive proof It is said in Genesis that " the spirit (*Rooach*) of God
moved on the face of the waters," and notwithstanding the critical
school, the etymology of the word *Rooach* gives the idea of a spirit,
and not of a " powerful wind." This conception of God as a spirit
has exerted a great influence on the development of Judaism. The
next idea to which I shall call your attention is holiness ; and in
the Jewish mind, the definition of this word is quite different from
anything it conveys to the mind of others. The next divine attri-

bute is that of goodness; and this attribute sank deeply into the Jewish mind ; it even extended to mercy to animals, and it is curious now to find that the Society for the Prevention of Cruelty to Animals was anticipated by Judaism thousands of years ago. It is the more remarkable since we find no reference in the New Testament to the obligation of human beings to protect dumb animals. In the New Testament, charity is enforced even at the expense of justice (another divine attribute) ; but justice was so impressed on the Hebrew mind that in the Bible judges are called ' gods."

Dr. A. Benisch.

The late Dr. A. Benisch, Editor of the London *Jewish Chronicle*, was well known for his erudition and his untiring interest in all matters concerning the wellfare of the Jewish nation.

CONVERSIONIST –One who prevails upon another man to change his religion.

EXPOSITION—Explanation, interpretation.

CONSOLIDATION—The act of uniting into a solid mass.

To FRUCTIFY—To bear fruit.

THE HEBREW MAID AND SYRIAN CHIEF.

(2 KINGS V : 2.)

Why was she there, mid the Syrian band,
That little Hebrew maid ?
Why was she brought from her own loved land,
Where she in childhood strayed ?

Who took her from her home afar,
Each dear familiar place,
And brought her captive from the war,
To serve a stranger-race ?

Was it the chieftain of the host,
The favorite of the king,
Who counted not the bitter cost
Captivity would bring ?

Perhaps her face was very fair,
Her voice of sweetest tone ;
Perhaps, of Israel's daughters there,
She was the loveliest one,

It might have been that on her brow
There dwelt a holy light
Of truth and innocence, to show
A spirit pure and bright.

We cannot tell—for. to this hour.
We only can be sure
That to her words was given a power
Which wrought a wondrous cure.

The leper by the prophet healed—
Of her, no more is said—
No after history revealed,
Of this young Hebrew maid.

Perhaps her mission then was done.
With that one earnest plea.
" Would God my lord were with that
one great prophet at Samaria ! Soon
He'd cure his leprosy."

Thus was she brought from Israel's land,
A captive and alone ;
Yet led by an Almighty hand.
Unknowing and unknown.

And, though we ne'er have heard her name,
Her memory will endure,
Linked to the fortunes and the fame
Of Naaman and his cure. J. M.

RELIGION AND SCIENCE.

What is faith ? The unconscious permeation of a living truth ; in religion it is natural, immediate presentment of an all-loving Being, on whom we are dependent; and with whom we stand in intimate connection; it is the vital feeling innate in man, to belong to a God who is love, mercy, goodness, grace and wisdom. That coercive power which suggests to the mind of the artist the ideas of the sublime and beautiful, by which he creates those lofty works which excite our admiration; the unconscious power which urges the poet to bring to life the children of the world of sentiment and to represent with irresistible force the eternally beautiful in the symphony of language; the inexpressible enthusiasm which fills the heart of the hero, steels his courage, that drives him to the battle-field to sacrifice his life in behalf of his country and fellow beings; that indistinct something which fans in us the flame of enthusiasm for the beautiful, grand, noble, lofty, eternal and imperishable; the wonderful sentiment of the child which draws it with ardor toward its parents and which enables it to offer any sacrifice for the originator of its life; all this has one and the same unknown foundation, one and the same mysterious root with faith. Faith, the artistic and poetic mind, heroic conduct, enthusiasm and filial love—they all are the fruits of one tree of life; they all emanate from that divine fountain which the all-loving Father has planted in the hearts of His children. Faith is, therefore, fertile and creative; unconsciously, involuntarily, without pondering or meditating, man is prompted to perform deeds grand, noble and lofty, and with a force against which all resistance would be futile. It surges and roars in the heart that is filled with faith; it works and germinates in the mind of the truly faithful; a nameless longing for the service of life, the spring of eternal love takes possession of man and necessitates him to cause faith to come into the world of vision. Faith is *indestructible*, firm and immovable. Because it is innate in the heart of man, it is the divine in the form of the human; it can, therefore, neither perish nor fall a prey to the decay of time. Like a rock upon the stormy sea which remains unshaken amidst the surging waves and billows; like a strong footstep bidding defiance to the obstinate attacks of an enemy, so with faith, to which the words of our *Haphtora*, "thou art my rock and my castle," refer. Faith gives courage in danger, consolation in adversity and comfort in the day of distress. "Though the sorrows of death encompass me about, and the snares of the nether world surround me, then I call upon my Lord in my distress," are the words of the faithful. Dost thou desire, my friend, a picture of faith. Go forth in the open air on a clear and cloudless night. All around thee is lulled into calm stillness; the noise and turmoil of the day have passed over into a deathlike silence; above thee is the blue arch of heaven; myriads of stars are reflecting their bright and refulgent rays upon thy countenance. There is peace within thy breast, a feeling of heavenly joy rushes through thy heart, it is so well, so lovely, so cheerful with thee—thou knowest not how nor why—this is faith.

II.

What is knowledge? The conscious apprehension of an indefinite object; in religion it is the ideas of the divine, as conceived by human reason. Whenever reason, the cold and heartless child of the spirit, directs its innate moulds of thought to the great First Cause, it obtains a knowledge of the same. Just as the cold joins more closely together the loosened particles and forms from them a united whole, so intelligent knowledge acts; it grasps several manifestations, robs them of their vital liquid and then it consolidates them into a close union. The birthplace of knowledge is the external world, because knowledge passes from it into the human mind. The intellect alone and of itself to the very last point of the universe erects a weak and decaying bridge, strides over it, and never penetrates into the depths or root of that which it beholds. The astronomer, who from his circumscribed point of vision, measures the distances and calculates the period of revolution of the heavenly orbs; the general, who draws upon paper the order of battle and the movements of his enemy; the botanist, who arranges the vegetable kingdom into classes and orders; the physician, who dissects the component members of the human frame—they know meditation and study are the implements, *why* and *wherefore* the watchwords of the learned. Knowledge is *clear* and *transparent* because intellect investigates, examines and searches; but it is the *clearness* and *transparency* of the masses of ice which contract the heart and benumb the blood. Knowledge is *a rule* because intellect by means of its two watchwords seeks to penetrate into the very existence and essence of things; the sharpness of a knife, however, separates the fibers and veins from the body, but it cannot imbue it with warmth, vitality and motion. Knowledge is active, since the intellect passes from cause to cause, and from law to law; but it needs the creative element which is the mother of great and noble deeds. Restlessness and the torments of doubt are its companions, which relentlessly pursue it and deprive it of quiet. Dost thou desire a picture of intelligent knowledge, behold the day. The sun sends forth his burning rays; the outlines of everything are clear to the eye; nothing, nothing can escape your notice; the earth is like an open book before you. But there is a bustle and a heaving around about you, you have no rest; myriads of manifestations pass before your view; of all these, however, you can only perceive the external appearance; the bright stars of the night are hidden from your sight and your foot is bound to the earth.

III.

This is faith and knowledge. *To which of them shall we give our adherence?* History and experience can give us the answer. Faith by its proximity, alone and of itself, as a daughter of that which is

doubtful, gloomy and unknown, dwelling near the feelings in the quiet
recesses of the heart, develops itself not unfrequently into *fanaticism*.
Who, my friends, during the middle ages sharpened the sword and
compelled brother to use it against brother? Who brought into existence the pangs of the torture, the most abominable instrument
which ever was conceived in any human brain? Who erected
the stakes, stirred the fires and fed the flames with human blood?
Who have trodden with their feet images of God, drove them forth
into the world without roof or shelter, and hunted them down like
wild beasts? Who have anathemized those of a different creed?
Who else than fanatics? Pestilence, plagues and contagious diseases count not so many offerings as fanaticism. How often has
faith assumed the fury of the beast and has blotted out the feelings
dwelling in one chamber? How much of fanaticism is inscribed on
the pages of *our* history? Knowledge is a mere form which must
conceal the interior; there always remains something external,
since from the exterior it reaches man. Knowledge is cold and
heartless, because it lacks the warmth and intensity of the soul,
since it springs from a calm mind. It is continually subject to
change, and forsakes man in the sorrowful and decisive moments of
life; the closed eyes of your father and the pallid countenance of
your deceased mother crush all your proud knowledge into nothingness, and the pillars of the fire of knowledge are often obscured by
the clouds of misfortune. In fine, knowledge is dependent, then it
requires the support of the material world to keep itself erect; faith,
my friends, is *blind*, knowledge *lame*. Shall we place the lame upon
the blind, according to a well known fable which Rabbi Jehudah
the Pious related to the Emperor Antoninus? The blind would remain always blind, and the lame always lame, even if both were to
move forward. Do the mind and the heart, the spiritual manifestations of faith and knowledge, live apart? Are they not continually
interchanging with one another? Or is the sunny day or the starry
night created for two separate classes of men? Or is there not a
continual changing of one with the other? Indeed, do they not exist
at one and the same time in both hemispheres? *To proceed from
faith, to pass through sensible knowledge and to return to rational faith*,
that is the way men should walk. When the intensity and firmness,
the warmth and mildness of faith, the clearness and insight, the refinement and purification of knowledge intermingle among each
other, and form an inseparable whole, that produces the man complete with head and heart, mind and soul. Those zones are the best
where day and night are in a proper relationship to one another, and
as our sages remark: "The equality of days and nights in Nisin and
Tishri are uniform." An old Talmudical Rabbi has given us a good
illustration of this. Rabbi ben Chana said: "The sea voyagers
told me of a wave which was about to ingulf a ship, and appeared

like white fire. They thereupon struck it with a staff upon which was engraved the name of God, and it became still." Do you know the sea, the voyagers, the ship, the wave and the staff? The sea is the world—"the world is a stormy sea," are the words of the poet Yedaja Penini Bedarshi; the voyagers are the men who sail along in the ship of faith; there rises a foaming wave—empty knowledge with its din and foam—and threatens the vessel with shipwreck; but the name of God, the return to an eternal life which glides over the waters, restores rest, and the travelers sail safely till they anchor in the harbor of eternal rest. But, my friends, even if this is the correct view, it still remains a picture, which really in our age has found no place. On the one hand it is fanaticism and blind faith in an old and a new form, which still hurls its anathemas and joins hands with those who persecuted heretics; and on the other hand science raises its hollow head and looks with contempt upon the tender blossoms of religion. Far greater, however, is the injury and mischief which that hollow and deceitful knowledge produces. If you ask your co-religionist why he has given up all religious forms and betrays by nothing—I will not say that he is an Israelite—but whether he at all has any conception of the existence of a living God, he will answer you with an overbearing mien, expressing to you his regret for your narrow-mindness, that he stands upon the ground of science. Of science? Is it in the valley or in the lowland, so that any one can easily glide into it. Is not *rational* knowledge enthroned upon a high and rugged hill, whose immutable foundation is faith? Examine once the knowledge of your co-religionist and ask him what he has received in exchange for the precious treasures of religion; you will find that instead of days of rest and festivals he has received a continual restlessness which draws his mind from a lofty elevation to a low depth; that, instead of possessing those great boons—sobriety and temperance—which faith teaches us, he is led about by a chain of passions. Ask him about his house of prayer, he will show you his store, wherein you will find a large assortment of his gods, made of gold, silver and silk, lying in cases and drawers, of which he keeps a strict account. And just as he sells his great and little gods, so he will finally barter his God for a sinner's fee, for an appearance of honor. Oh, that mercantile spirit of my people is now beating new and great paths; he *trades* in religion! our national existence has been destroyed, our sanctuaries have been transformed into dust and ashes; we have been driven over every portion of the earth; in the middle ages we were hunted down like wild beasts; and all this, aye, our whole history, would be a mere farce which he could laugh at, and the rivers of blood and floods of tears were only shed in order that we might lavish and squander the inheritance of our fathers. Fools were the six hundred thousand men who left Spain to endure sorrow, grief, hunger and thirst; fools were all those who left their native country on account of their faith; fools were our co-religionists in Sicily to whom God was dearer than country; fools were our northern brethren whose zeal for their faith could not be crushed by tyranny; fools were our brethren in Rome who would not leave their damp and gloomy dwellings for the sake of their religion; fools are all of us who love God and observe His festivals. A new school of wisdom has been opened unto us, thither we must go; there we must sit and hearken to the magic words of the new teachers. Do you know this magic word? Its name is *treachery*, treachery to faith, treachery to religion, treachery to history, treachery to the hundreds and thousands of our persecuted brethren. For in this is contained the wisdom of our age, that wisdom of which Job says: "The wisdom which cometh from nothing." No, we will not act treacherously toward history, we will guard ourselves against both extremes. Neither blind fanaticism shall dazzle our sight, nor shall superficial knowledge deceive us. The knowledge of the Egyptians was an external one and did not impress the heart; but the faith of Israel required a crowning point, knowledge, which was given to it on Sinai. There darkness was made light, the unknown known, and faith became rational. If knowledge and faith then are two poles, then the middle is the point of gravity upon which we should stand in life. May the Lord assist us in this, so that we will be strong in life and not perish in the course of time; may He lead us through history as he led our forefathers, and may He be unto us and our descendants a shield and refuge for evermore.

DR. AD. JELLINEK.

SABBATH THOUGHTS.

I BLESS Thee, Father, for the grace
  Thou me this day hast given ;
Strengthening my soul to seek Thy face,
  And list the theme of heaven.

I bless Thee, that each workday care
  Thy love hath lull'd to rest,
And every thought whose wing was
    prayer
  Thine answering word hath bless'd.

I bless Thee, Father ! Those dark fears
  That linger'd round my heart,
That called for murmurs, doubts and
    fears,
  Thy mercy bade depart.

Oh! Thou alone couldst send them
    hence
  On this bless'd day of peace,
And with Thy spirit's pure incense

Bid workday turmoils cease.

The withering pangs of anxious care
  Were through the week my own,
Eased only in the hour of prayer,
  But never from me flown.

Darkly around me closed the night,
  Though trusting still in Thee ;
And heavily I hail'd the light,
  Fraught with few joys for me.

How came it, then, my Sabbath day
  Is with such bliss replete—
That visions bright around me play,
  Whose smiles my spirit greet ?

Oh ! 'tis as some reviving dew
  Were o'er each sorrow stealing,
Folding in heaven's own azure hue
  Each dark and weary feeling.

As if no sorrow could molest
  My soaring soul again,
Nor find a momentary rest
  For aught of earthly pain.

A Sabbath to my inmost heart,
  Thy day, my God, hath been,
Thy loving kindness to impart,
  E'en to a child of sin.

A verdant spot, a cooling spring,
  On earth's unkindly breast,
Where all who childlike spirits bring
  Shall healing find, and rest.

My God! my Father! 'tis from Thee
  These blessed hours have come ;
I hail them type of joys for me,
  That wait me in Thy home.

Come, then ! if, Lord, 'tis Thy decree,
  My workday thoughts of care,
The day of rest is still for me,
  Thy presence then to share.

And naught shall banish from my
    heart
  Its memories lingering yet,
Their twilight soothing to impart,
  E'en when their sun has set.

Oh ! never let its fleece be dry,
  Thine own day mid the seven,
And wing with prayer, my God, each
    sigh
That yearns for Thee and heaven !

                    GRACE AGUILAR.

HEBREWS AND GREEKS.

LIFE is a battleground of contrasts. These contrasts are of different kinds. In ancient and modern times one nation raised itself above the other, and claimed in opposition to its neighbors to be the chosen people, and the least progressive natives of the Orient, in their religious narrowness, despise all others as unclean. To feel themselves as prominent, in opposition to the rest of mankind, only two nations on earth were entitled—the nation which, in the midst of a world filled by idolatry, possessed the pure perception of God, and the nation which had developed such a rich and peculiar culture that it could proudly look upon other nations as non-Hellenes or barbarians, and despise them.

With both nations, it was a spiritual possession which gave them this proud self-esteem. Both were small, dwindling minorities among the masses that surrounded them. To both, disdain and indifference toward the outside world was a necessary condition, as by the repelling of the foreign elements and the persistence in their own peculiarities, they became self-conscious and strong. Through their exclusiveness, both accomplished what in its intrinsic value reaches far beyond their national existence, both left us an inheritance of such value that, to this day, nations are divided according to the degree that they profited by this inheritance, a treasure for mankind which was cast away, forgotten, uselessly disregarded, then again taken up and ever proved a renovating power of life and bliss.

The two nations were similar in this respect only.

With the one it was an idea that governed its whole life, a point around which everything concentrated, a possession, a diadem, and all forces were devoted to one purpose, namely—to preserve the pure flame of religious service. The property of the other nation consisted in the full development of all human faculties, and in the active diversities of spiritual possessions, whereby it improved upon the perverse indifference of the other nations.

Israel's history commences with a small circle or tribe of nomads in an isolated mountainous region, beginning with the family of an Emir, whose house gradually increased to a nation, led, blessed, chastised by the hand of its God, and always restored again to its peculiar mission.

The Hellenes, on the contrary, were from the beginning left to themselves, as a widely branched human family, in the midst of a world composed of coasts and islands, well adapted to promoting lively national intercourse, and an inborn inclination developed by itself did they learn to feel themselves as a nation in contrast with the non-Hellenes.

Formerly scholars were inclined to accept the notion that the Hellenes, like the people of Israel, were isolated from the beginning, and that their culture arose from their own seed. It has become clearer that the Greeks lived in most ancient times in the country of the Nile, and the Phœnicians in the midst of Hellas. Under these circumstances the Aryan nationality, forming the nucleus, became essentially changed, not only in its exterior culture, but also in its inner life—the pantheistic deities of Asia filling the land of the Hellenes under all kinds of names. Their language remains pure, and therein rested the nucleus of the national feeling that would not admit the incomprehensible languages of the barbarians.

With the worship of Apollo, Hellenistic national feeling came into their manner and religion. Apollo was no native; the way can be pointed out whereby he came from the East—the harbors where his first altars stood. He united both shores of the sea, but not before he arrived on this continent did he gain his true form, and then the tribes of the Hellenes were combined, and their gods were arranged in one family.

In the place of Olympus, where the Hellenistic deities were formed, the Parnassus became the Holy Mount, and Delphi the hearth round about the more nobler tribe formed a selected family circle. Just as the calling of the prophets in Israel to preserve an active recognition of the ideal possession of the people, so the priests and seers of Delphi gave expression to the Hellenic character in religion, art and manner, and from this dated the contrast between Hellenes and barbarians, yet unknown in the Homeric times.

But the Delphic priesthood was neither able nor inclined to surround by strange barriers this ideal nationality. They admired the respect paid to the Delphic Apollo by the tyrants of the other continent. Hence their sympathies for the wealthy King of Phrygia and Lydia, and their supineness when it was attempted to transform Hellas into a Persian tributary. The idea that spiritual possessions can only be guarded by political independence originated with the people, and thereby Delphi ceased to be the guardian of the nationality, the representative of the opposition to the barbarians.   In the place of the sanctuary came the communities; in the place of the priests and prophets, the statesmen of Athens; Athens became the leader in spite of Delphi; and, while fighting, the people first became fully aware what they were fighting for: a small part of Greece surrounded Athens, the Bœotians and Leuchiæ separated, the Peloponnesians withdrew, and, in the end, what could be called in its fullest sense Hellas was really limited to one city.   After the short years of peace under Pericles, the bloody strifes of parties, with all their demoralizing consequences, manifested themselves. The best citizens withdrew from communal affairs, not recognizing therein the character of their nationality, and genuine Hellenism appeared again as an ideal possession not bound to any city or people.   Epaminondas attempted to realize such a general Hellenism not bound to any place, and Isocrates designated it as an honor to the Hellenes that their names express not so much a people as culture and nobility of manners.

With feeling of instability and exhausted in means, Hellas tried again a union with the nations of the earth which it formerly rejected.   But when, among the princes of the north, one appeared willing to join, not, however, as a serviceable confederate, but as an arrogant master, Demosthenes succeeded in again inflaming the hatred against the barbarians, and it was his work that the people again recovered, and that the history of the independent Hellenes closed with a combat of heroes.   During these combats, Aristotle walked under the shady trees of Mieza with the son of the king, demonstrating to him that the Hellenes were called upon to rule over all the nations.   He inspired the fiery soul of his pupil to take up with renewed power the old fight against the barbarians.   After Hellenic science had withdrawn to a narrower circle and at last developed its blossoms in Athens, whence it filled mankind with its odor, the fruit now ripened, and Alexander, like a new Triptolemos, went out to spread the seed over the countries of the Orient, the same countries whence once the first seeds of enlightenment were carried to Europe.

Among the number of nations despised by the Hellenes as barbarians were those whose gifts they did not know—gifts which just replaced the wants of the Hellenes.   They were well aware that a people hastens to its destruction, morally and socially, without religion.   They had preserved from the oldest times the idea of a God, who is no mere natural power, but a father of gods and mankind, who might only be approached by imageless worship.   They had spiritualized all the important deities and raised from the sphere of nature into the spiritual; and their noblest forms,

Minerva and Apollo, point to the closest connection with the original God.

But the purer idea of God was like a colorless remembrance of the paternal house—an empty ideal. Piety was the postulate of ethics deduced from a correct appreciation of the nature of man. They felt that man was created for God; they attempted to approach Him as on the steps of a pyramid, but the apex was wanting, and the acquisition of the few select—an artificial edifice—offered no support to the people, and whenever the stones fell asunder men sunk into the mud of vulgarity, without a hand stretched to redeem them.

So our view is turned to the other of the two nations in question —the only one entitled to stand at the side of the Hellenes with a proud self-esteem—their historial contrast. What was wanting to them forms in Israel the kernel of its nationality, the only reliable and indispensable one. There existed no experimenting, no searching after an unknown God, but a grasping of mankind by the Deity. There were no nebulous surmises, but facts, strong evidences; not merely single rays of lightning which crossed the night like flashes of light without thunder, but a covenant between God and man, starting from simple principles, increasing always to a more complete and complicated connection, with personal reciprocity comprising the total national life.

We have before us such a peculiar state, not to be explained by the process of development of a people left to itself, and the more the range of science increases, the more analogies are offered, but none which might be considered as a sufficient preparation to this state.

Humanity is nothing else than a healthy development of human faculties ; and should the most important, the most human, the faculty of recognizing God, be excluded therefrom? Religion is indispensable and unavoidable to the popular life. Those who would only limit this want to a lower grade of culture I do not consider necessary to refute in this place, where two of the greatest thinkers of the German nation—Fichte and Schleirmacher—evidently proved that religious life forms not only the basis of popular welfare, but the accomplishment of spiritual culture.

Man, belonging to two worlds, is called upon to conquer the matter to which he belongs externally. He conquers it as an artist in spiritualizing the matter, he conquers matter as a student in recognizing in nature, as well as in the affairs of mankind, order and law! for whenever there is order there is the spirit and divine life. But there is also an organ for the direct recognition of divinity, which ought to be cultivated and improved as much as the desire for mental research and the eye of the artist ; for the human heart has implanted the desire to be sure of its God, and there exists a power to adhere to Him. By this power the greatest performances human beings are capable of were accomplished, the most complete submission of the material world, the most willing sacrifice of property and life, the highest triumph of the free human mind.

It is the power by which feeling, cognition and need combine thoroughly—the power of faith. How poor would human history appear if the heroism would be wanting that is based upon that power! Every student follows diligently its traces, art knows no higher task than to represent its deeds, it forms the fountain of the purest poetry, and for our life it should be of no concern; we could be without it, without feeling a want of human culture, a weakness an important incompetence! I cannot believe it, although some try to controvert the matter, and, it very often happens, to speak in a simile, that an eagle, whose pinions were weakened, will convince his companions that the only rational movement is in walking on the ground step by step, instead of springing up too high with intrepid self-confidence. Truth is simple in its nature, and proves itself to the sincere searcher as such. If it could only be gained by a grappling mind, if methodically investigated, it would change its nature or be replaced by something else ; then in reference to the most important question of the commonwealth, a crevice would open destroying its unity and undermining the health and strength of the people. As shown by the example of the Hellenes, as dazzling as individual efforts appeared, the decline of the whole is unavoidable when the thinkers separate from the totality, the vital powers sever, which were destined to work together and to support and complete one another in the organic composition. Thus our entire culture would be endangered, for we cannot think of true art unsupported by a healthy popular feeling.

To secure the continued progress of culture, we must combine extended researches in all branches of nature and history of the Hellenes. with the collection and meditations of the mind, and its resolute devotion to unite them to a central truth, whereto the other of the two nations, the nation of religion, was called upon to carry the intrusted idea like a sanctum through the wild throng of the history of the ancient world, and to lay the basis upon which the entire modern culture is founded. PROFESSOR CURTIUS.

PROF. CURTIUS, an eminent professor of the Berlin University.

NARROWNESS—Want of comprehension.
NOMAD—One who leads a wandering life.
EMIR—A title among the Turks, denoting a prince.
ARIAN—Pertaining to Arius or his doctrines.
OLYMPUS—Greece, games carried on there.
PARNASSUS—A mountain in Greece celebrated in mythology.
DELPHI—Pertaining to the oracle of Apollo.

To POSTULATE—To beg or assume without proof.
APEX—Tip or point.
ANALOGY—Resemblance of things in some manner.
COGNITION—Knowledge, complete conviction.
SANCTUM—A holy place, applied sometimes by individuals to their private rooms.

BY THE OLD SPRING.

A REVERIE.

I LINGERED in the eventide
  Beside the cool moss spring,
And thought of what the past had
    brought,
  The future yet might bring;
The cool breeze fanned my fevered
    cheek,
  Soft as true love's caress,
The lengthening shadows in the wood
  Increased my loneliness,

How hushed! how quiet! not a sound
  Disturbs this still retreat,
Save the soft murmur of the leaves
  That rustle at my feet.
The silver streamlet ripples on,
  Its small wrecks on its breast;
Onward, still on, like wandering souls
  Seeking in vain for rest.

High on yon tree, the mocking bird
  Trills forth his sweet sad song;
Perchance a tale of love, or else
  A tale of fancied wrong.
Far o'er the hill the distant kine
  Go lowing, wending home;
And now the stars are peeping out
  To light the welkin dome.

Alone! no sound of human kind
  Breaks on my solitude;
But specters from the buried past,
  Even here, still dare intrude;
Pale ghosts of youth's bright, mocking
    dreams,
  Roused by the twilight hour,
Like vampires waked by moonbeams
    cold,
  Assert their old-time power.

Alone! the soul can never be —
  Memory walks side by side,
And wakes as if by magic wand
  Ghosts of the hopes that died.
In early youth we see ourselves
  Shadows in a dim glass;
Our glowing hopes, our high resolves,
  Shadows before us pass.

The gathering shades like a black veil
  Shut out day's lingering gleam,
I bid the cool moss spring farewell;
  I wake from my sad dream.
Homeward I wend my weary way,
  Upon my lips a prayer,
That Heaven may draw my drooping
    heart
  To place its treasures there.
                          R. A. LEVY.

WELKIN—The visible regions of the air.

THE END.

BIELICAL AND HISTORICAL MEMORIAL TABLE.

FROM THE CREATION TO THE PRESENT TIME.

The first people were Adam and Eve.
Their sons, Cain, Abel and Seth.
Cain was a husbandman and Abel a shepherd.
Cain killed his brother Abel.
Tubal was the first Cithern-player.
Tubalcain was the first worker in metal.
Methusalem was the oldest man, being 969 years old.
Methusalem's son was Lemech, Lemech's son was Noah.

Noah had three sons : Sem, Ham and Japheth.
Noah built an Ark.
Noah with his wife, his three sons and three daughters-in-law
  entered the Ark. Beginning of the deluge.
After 150 days the ark rests on Mount Ararat.
Noah dispatches a raven, after the water had subsided, and after-
  ward, at three different times, three pigeons.
Noah and his people leave the Ark, and erect the Eternal an Altar.
God blessed Noah and makes a Covenant with him. The Rainbow.
Noah plants a vineyard.
The people begin again to increase upon earth.
Nimrod, a great huntsman and hero, becomes the founder of the
  land of Babel, and builds the town of Nineveh.
The building of the tower of Babel in the valley of Shinar.

Abraham, the son of Therach, born in Ur-Casdim.
His brothers were Nachor and Haran.
Abraham, at the command of God, leaves his home, and went with
  his wife Sarah and his nephew, Lot, Haran's son, to Canaan.
Abraham and Lot separate. Abraham remains in Canaan, and Lot
  departs for Sodom.
Abraham's hand-maid is called Hagar, their son, Ishmael.
Sodom and Gomorrah are destroyed ; Lot is saved.
Isaac is born, being the son of Abraham and Sarah.
Isaac is brought as a sacrifice on Mount Moriah.
Sarah dies, and is buried in the cave of Machpelah.
Eliescr, Abraham's servant, went to Aram Naharajim, in order to
  obtain a wife for Isaac.
Rebecca, daughter of Bethuel, Nachor's son, became Isaac's wife.
Her brother was Laban.

Esau and Jacob, Isaac's and Rebecca's sons.
Jacob flees to Charan to his uncle, Laban.
Jacob's dream.
Leah and Rachel, Laban's daughters.
Jacob meets Rachel at the well.
Jacob is with Laban. He takes Leah, Rachel, Bilah and Silpah for his wives.
Jacob's sons were : Reuben, Simon, Levi, Jehudah, Isashar, Zebulun, Dan, Naphtali, Gad, Asher, Joseph, Benjamin ; his daughter was named Dinah.
Jacob sends messengers to Esau. The brothers become reconciled.
Jacob resides again in Canaan.

Joseph, seventeen years old, is hated by his brothers on account of his dreams.
Joseph seeks for his brothers in Datan, where they were grazing their flock.
The brothers threw him in a pit and then sold him to Ismaelitish merchants, who again sold him to Potiphar, who was one of the king's officials in Egypt.

Joseph in Egypt. He serves his master faithfully, but owing to the treachery of Potiphar's wife is cast into prison.
He interprets the dreams of the Butler and the Baker, servants of King Pharaoh.
Joseph before Pharaoh. He interprets his dream, and is made ruler. He is then thirty years old.
Menasheh and Ephraim are Joseph's sons.
In Canaan, where Jacob dwells, famine prevails, and Jacob's sons go to Egypt to buy corn.
Their first journey to Egypt.
The brothers appear before Joseph.
Second journey to Egypt with Benjamin.
Jehudah's faithfulness toward Jacob and Benjamin.
Joseph makes himself known to his brethren.
Jacob and his family, altogether seventy persons, depart from Canaan and travel to Egypt ; they then live in Egypt in the land of Goshen.
Jacob blessed his sons, and dies at the age of 147 years.
His body is buried in the cave of Machpelah, beside Abraham and Isaac.
The children of Israel augmented largely in Egypt and fall into bondage.
Order of the king to destroy all male children.
Amram and Jochebed, from the tribe of Levi ; Aaron, Moses and Miriam, their children.

Moses saved by the daughter of the king.
Moses kills an Egyptian and escapes to Midian.
Zipora, daughter of the priest Jethro, his wife.
God appears to Moses in the thorn-bush at Mount Choreb.
Moses and Aaron appear before Pharaoh. They announce to him
the divine punishment. The ten plagues.
On the 15th day of the first month (Nissan) the Israelites depart
from Egypt. Feast of Passover.
The Israelites pass through the Red Sea ; the Egyptians pursue and
get drowned. Song of Moses.
The Israelites enter the desert of Shur ; they murmur, because of
the water being bitter.
The Israelites arrive at the desert of Sin ; they murmur, owing to
the want of sufficient food ; Manna.
Amalek attacks the Israelites at Refidim.
Joshua defeats him. Moses, Aaron and Chur on the mount.
Jethro visits his son-in-law in the desert.
In the third month after the departure from Egypt, the Israelites
reach Mount Sinai. Divine Revelation and giving of the Law. The
Ten Commandments.
Moses remains forty days and forty nights on the mount.
Moses comes down from the mount ; the golden calf.
Moses breaks the Law-tablets. He prays God to pardon the people.
New Law-tablets.

The Tabernacle and the Ark of the Covenant.
Bezalel and Aholiab attend to its construction.
The Levites attend to the service in the Tabernacle.
The Camp is divided into four divisions.

The twelve spies are sent to the promised land. After forty days
they return and cause the people to despair.
Joshua and Caleb bring better news.
The whole nation must remain forty years in the desert, till all the
obstinate ones have died.

Rebellion of Korach, Dathan and Abiram.

Miriam dies at Kadesh. The people murmur for scarcity of water.
Moses transgresses.
Aaron dies upon the mount, Hor.
Eleasar, his son, succeeds him as High-priest.
The Israelites conquer Sichon, King of Emori, and Og, King of
Bashan.
Arrival of the Israelites in the valley of Moab.
Balak, king of Moab, sends for Bileam. Bileam's blessing.
Contest with the Midianites.

Moses orders, according to the command of God, that Joshua should become his successor.

The tribes of Reuben and Gad, and half the tribe Menasheh, wish to remain on the east side of the Jordan.

Moses repeats to the Israelites all laws and statutes.

He blesses the people, and dies, 120 years old, on Mount Nebo.

Joshua leads the people across the Jordan into the land of Canaan.

AFTER SANHEDRIM 39 A.

"CANST thou say thy God was honest
　To the man he made of clay,
When a rib from Adam sleeping,
　Scripture saith he stole away"

Rabbi Gamliel would have answered,
　But his daughter craved reply:
"Justice!" cried she, "even justice!"
Let us to the judgment hie!

Thieves into our house have broken,
　And a pitcher rare and old
They have stolen, yet for silver
　Hath been left a cruse of gold!"

"Would that such a great misfortune
　Happened to me every day!"
Said the scorner, but the maiden,
　"See, the theft is cleared away!"

"Mean I not the rib exactly,
　But the way in which 'twas done;
Why could not the man have seen it—
　Gift and miracle in one?"

Then a piece of meat the maiden
　Washed and salted in his sight,
Preparing for a feast to which
　She the quibbler did invite.

"Peace," said he, "I never relish
　What before me is prepared."
Saith the maiden, now triumphant,
　"Thus the ways of God are cleared!"

"That which seeing maketh common
　From our eyes should be concealed;
Her whom Adam most should honor,
　To him perfected, God revealed."
　　　　　　　　　　　TALMUD.

CHRONOLOGY.

THE accuracy of chronology is one of the most difficult points in Biblical history. Already tradition is in doubt as to Egyptian bondage, which lasted, according to Genesis xv : 13, 400 years, or to Exodus xii; 41, 42, 430 years. In the same manner it says in the book of 1 Kings vi : 1, that Solomon built the Temple 430 years after the exodus from Egypt, in contradiction to the previous books of Holy Writ. According to the book of Judges, the time of the Judges alone, without Eli and Samuel, amounts to 400 years, which disagrees with other calculations in regard to the sojourn in the desert, the conquest of the country, Eli's, Samuel's, Saul's, and David's. Also the reckoning in respect to the time of the Kings is unsettled. Further we find much uncertainly as to the time of the Babylonian captivity to the period of the Maccabees, where Alexander the Great serves as guiding point. We have the most diversified account of ancient and modern time before us—tradition Josephus Flavius, Zunz, Jost, Philippson, Herzfeld, and the Christian investigators, Eichhorn, Duncker, Roth, Lepsius, Schlosser, but nowhere we can find agreement. Even the statements in regard to the exact time of Moses differ very much. However, a Chronological table to be a guide for our youth need not enlarge upon all these critical points, and it is only necessary that some fixed plan should be adopted.

ADAM AND EVE

Cain,	Abel	Seth,
Jabal,		Enoch,
Jubal,		Methusalem,
Tubal-Cain,		Lemech,
		Chanoch,
		Noah (deluge) 1656 A M

Shem, Cham, Japheth,
Eber,
Peleg (building tower of Babel, Nimrod)
Tirach.

1948... Abraham, Sarah,   Hagar, Haran,   Nachor (Milka)

2048 .... Isaac (Rebeckah), Ismael, Lot, Milka, Bethuel.

Ammon, Moab, Rebeckah, Laban

2108..Esau, Jacob (Leah, Rachel,   Bilha,   Silpa),   Leah, Rachel.
              Ruben, Joseph*,   Gad,   Dan,
              Simon, Benjamin, Asher, Naphtali.
              Levi,
              Judah,
              Isashar,
              Zebulon,
              Dina.

*Whose sons were Ephraim and Menasseh.

EGYPTIAN BONDAGE.

Amram and Jochebed, from the tribe of Levi.

2588......Moses (Ziporah), Aaron, Miriam,
   Gerson,   Nadab,
   Elieser,   Abihuh,
        Elasar,
        Ithamar.

Deliverance from Egyptain bondage (about 2668 A. M.)
Crossing the Red Sea.
Marah.
Elim.
Sin (Manna, law for the Sabbath).
Rephidim (want of water, invasion Amalek's, Jethro's visit).
Sinai (Revelation).
Golden Calf.
Building of the Tabernacle (Bezalel and Oholiab).
Wandering in the desert.
Graves of lust (70 elders, Eldad and Medad).
Spies.
Korah.
Death of Miriam. - - - - 2708.
Water of Meribah.
Death of Aaron. Elasar becomes High-priest. - 2708.
Conquest on this side of the Jordan (Sichon and Og).
Balak and Bileam.
Combat with the Midianites.
Joshua appointed Moses' successor.
Moses dies, 120 years old. - - - 2709.
Joshua leader of the people.
Conquest of the country (Jericho, Ai, the Gibeonites, the Southern and the Northern Union.

Judges (happening between the twenty-fifth and the twenty-eighth centuries A. M.):

Othniel, Ehud, Deborah, Barak, Gideon, Abimelech,
Yephta. Ruth, Sampson, Eli,   Samuel.
 Kingdom (about thirty centuries A. M.):
Saul,   David, (2948 A. M.),   Solomon.

PARTITION OF THE REALM—3010 A. M.

Kingdom of Israel (dur. 258 yrs.).
Jeroboam (gov. 22 yrs.),

Kingdom of Judah (dur. 391 yrs.)
Rechaboam (gov. 17 yrs.),
Abia (3 yrs.),

Nadab (2 yrs.),
Baasha (24 yrs.),
Ela (2 yrs.),
Simri (7 days),
Omri (12 yrs.),
Achab (22 yrs.), Prophet Elijah.
Achasja (2 yrs.),
Jehoram (12 yrs.),
Jehu (28 yrs.), Prophet Elisha.
Joachas (17 yrs.),
Joas (16 yrs.),
Jeroboam II. (41 yrs.), Prophet
Secharja (6 months),   [Jonah.
Shallum (1 month),
Menachen (10 yrs.),
Pekachja (2 yrs.),
Pekach (20 yrs.),

Assa (41 yrs.),

Joshaphat (25 yrs.),

Jehoram (8 yrs.),
Achasja (1 yr.),
Athalia (6 yrs.),
Joas (40 yrs.),
Amazia (29 yrs.),
Usia-Asaria (52 yrs.),

Jotham (16 yrs.),
Achas (16 yrs.),

Hosea (destruction of the kingdom of Israel through Shal-
manasser, 3268 A. M.

Hiskia (29 yrs) Prophet Isaiah.
Sancherib's invasion,
Menasse (55 yrs.),
Amon (2 yrs.),
Joshea (31 yrs.),
Jehoachas (3 months), Prophet
Jehojakim (11 yrs.), [Jeremia.
Jehojachin (3 months),
Zidkia (11 yrs.), destruction of
the kingdom of Judah through
Nebuchadnezzar, 3402 A. M.

Babylonian captivity (Ezekiel, Daniel, Chananja, Mishael and
Asaria).

Cyrus conquers Babylon (3450 A. M.).   Judah under Persia-
Median rule.

Return to Palestine under Zerubabel's and Jeshua's leadership
(3452 A. M.)   Prophets Chagai and Zachariah.

Rebuilding of the Temple (3472 A. M.).

Esther (Purim).

Esra and Nehemiah (3530–3544).   Rebuilding Jerusalem ; the
Prophet Malachai.

Judeah under rule of Alexander the Great (3656 A. M.)

Judeah partly under the dominion of the Egyptians (Ptolomies), and partly under the Syrians (Seleucides), 3658–3785.

Antiochus Epiphanes (war of liberation, the Maccabees, independence of the kingdom, 3821–3845.)

GENEALOGY OF THE MACCABEES.

Mathathias
|

Jochanan, Simon, Judah, Elasar, Jonathan*.
|

Judah, Mathathias, Johann Hyrkan).
|

Aristobul. Antigonus, Alexander (Jannæus), Absalom?
|

Hyrkan, Aristobul.
|

Alexander, Antigonus.
|

Aristobul, Marianne.

Judea, under Roman rule (63 b. Ch. E.).
Herod, King of the Jews (37 b. Ch. E.) 3951 A. M.
Roman Governors in Judea, the last Gessius Florus (64 a. Ch. E.)
Vespasian invests Jerusalem (67 a. Ch. E.).
Titus conquers and destroys the Holy City (70 a. Ch. E.)

THE JEWS IN THEIR DISPERSION.

Tanaim. R. Judah the Holy, compiler of the Mishna (161–219).
Persecutions under Hadrian (132–134).
Amoraim, closing of the Babylonian Talmud by R. Ashi and R. Abina. 500, and of the Palestinian, 390.
Abolishing the Patriarchate under Theodosius II.
Origin of the Caraites.
Gaonat in Babylon till 1040.
Origin of the Chasareens (Kusarim) King Balan.

*Of Jonathan's descendants only one daughter is known, who was the ancestral mother of the historian, Josephus Flavius.

MIDDLE AGE PERIOD.

Jews in Spain. Samuel Halevi, Rabbi and Minister of State (1027–1055). Solomon Ibn Gabirol, died 1070. Judah Halevi, born 1085. Moses Ibn Esra, died 1138. Abraham Ibn Esra, 1093–1168. Moses Maimonides, 1135–1204.
Disputations.
Cabbala, Moses de Leon, Sohar.
Isaac Abrabanel, Minister of Finance to Ferdinand the Catholic.
Expulsion of the Jews from Spain, 1492; from Portugal, 1496.
Jews in France.—Moses Hadarshan, Gershon ben Jehudah, Rashi, family of Tibbon, family of Kimchi, Levi b. Gerson.
The Crusades.
The black death.
Jews in Italy.—Meshullam b. Kalonimos, Nathan b. Jechiel, Immanuel of Rome.
Jews in Austria.—Hungary.
Expulsion from Steiermark and Salzburg ; Isaac Or Sarua, Meier Halevi ; Israel Isserlein.

MODERN PERIOD.

Jews in Turkey and Palestine.—Joseph Karo, Don Joseph Nassi. Sabbatai Zebi.
Jews in Italy.—Elia Levita, Asaria de Rossi.
Jews in Holland.—Manasse b. Israel, Uriel Acosta, Baruch Spinoza.
Jews in Poland.—Solomon Loria, Moses Isserls.
Jews in Germany.—Persecutions in Brandenburg, Baden, Braunschweig, Frankfurt, Worms. Christian Savants, Johannes Reuchlein, Sebastian Münster, Johann Buxtorf.
Jews in Austria.—Explusion from Kärnten, Crim, Tyrol and Upper Austria.
Expulsion from Lower Austria, 1670.
Return to Vienna, 1675.
Expulsion from Bohemia, 1744.
Return to Prag, 1748.

LATTER PERIOD.

Moses Mendelssohn reforms by Joseph II. Emancipation of the Jews in France and Holland. Amelioration of the condition of the Jews in almost all the European States. Entire Emancipation of the Jews.
Reform movement, progress of Jewish Scholastic institutions, advancement of Jewish science.

ERRATA.

www.ingramcontent.com/pod-product-compliance
Lightning Source LLC
Chambersburg PA
CBHW031057110726
47900CB00003B/969